Orchestral Performance

ORCHESTRAL PERFORMANCE

A Guide for Conductors and Players

Christopher Adey

LONDON · BOSTON

First published in 1998
by Faber and Faber Limited
3 Queen Square London WC1N 3AU

Typeset by RefineCatch Limited, Bungay, Suffolk
Printed in England by Clays Ltd, St Ives plc

A CIP record for this book
is available from the British Library
ISBN 0–571–17724–7

2 4 6 8 10 9 7 5 3 1

to the memory of

ANTHONY FOSTER
(1942–83)

CONTENTS

ACKNOWLEDGEMENTS

It is never possible to acknowledge sufficiently all the people whose ability, enthusiasm and expertise inspire and crystallize into one's personal beliefs. With regard to an undertaking such as this, it is only to those who knowingly contributed, in various ways, that I can publicly give my thanks.

Initially, those who, many years ago, encouraged me by reading the very first drafts and bringing their considerable knowledge to bear upon them – Malcolm Binney, John Dickinson, Richard Smith and Maurice Temple.

Later, those who generously gave of their time to read each chapter and provide their specialist advice and guidance – Julian Baker, Aline Brewer, Colin Courtney, John Glickman, Edwin Roxburgh, Michael Skinner, John Wallace and Denis Wick.

If I have misquoted, misconstrued or, occasionally, chosen to ignore their advice, I take full responsibility.

Beyond these, I should like to express my thanks to my agent, Richard Haigh, for supporting me in this, as in all other ventures, with a friendship and professionalism that saw it through some testing times; and to the staff of Faber and Faber who helped the book through the sometimes painful period of publication – in particular, Belinda Matthews and Justine Willett.

Finally, there are two people without whom the project would never have seen completion. Both painstakingly read every word of all the drafts and manuscripts and were unstinting in their criticism and encouragement. To Carolyn de la Plain, who never let me stop, and Ben Pope, who never let me think I'd finished, my admiration and gratitude is prodigious.

To all these, and many more besides, I extend my grateful thanks.

Acknowledgements for Music Examples

© Boosey & Co Limited: 4.13; 4.16; 10.56; 13.13; 21.4; 22.1.
© Boosey & Hawkes Inc.: 5.4; 5.5; 6.7; 6.8.
© Boosey & Hawkes Limited: 4.11.
© Boosey & Hawkes Music Publishers Ltd: 4.10; 4.20; 5.2; 6.6; 6.11; 6.12; 7.8; 7.9; 7.38; 8.25; 10.4; 10.45; 10.54; 11.2; 11.8; 14.6; 14.9; 15.2; 15.22; 15.23; 16.22; 16.27; 18.3; 18.9; 21.20.
© Bote & Bock, Berlin: 10.24.
© Breitkopf & Härtel, Wiesbaden–Leipzig: 4.9; 4.21; 7.14; 7.25; 7.71; 10.5; 12.1; 15.28; 15.29; 16.2; 16.3.
© J. & W. Chester/Edition Wilhelm Hansen London Ltd and Polskie Wydawnictwo Muzycne, Krakow, Poland: 4.25; 11.37; 11.38; 12.12.
© Chester Music Ltd on behalf of Edition Wilhelm Hansen AS: 5.7; 7.74; 8.24; 9.6; 21.7; 21.19.
© J. Curwen & Sons Limited: 2.7; 3.13; 4.18; 7.77; 17.3.
© David Dorward: 12.16.
© Editions Durand S.A., Paris/United Music Publishers Ltd: 1.4; 2.3; 2.6; 6.1; 6.13; 7.87; 8.32; 9.12; 10.27; 10.28; 10.29; 10.33; 10.37; 11.16; 11.19; 15.6; 18.2; 21.6.
© EMI Mills Music Inc, U.S.A. & Warner Bros. Publications Inc, USA/IMP Ltd: 6.4; 7.21; 7.37; 7.54; 10.25; 13.25; 15.27; 16.5; 16.6; 17.5; 18.7; 18.11.
© Faber Music Limited: 1.7.
© Adolf Fürstner and Hawkes & Son (London) Ltd (a Boosey & Hawkes Company): 6.10.
© Hawkes & Son (London) Ltd: 1.14; 2.2; 4.8; 4.15; 4.17; 4.23; 4.27; 5.8; 6.2; 6.16; 7.2; 7.36; 7.39; 7.43; 7.44; 7.47; 7.61; 7.76; 7.78; 7.79; 8.11; 8.16; 8.28; 9.5; 9.19; 9.22; 10.13; 10.23; 10.43; 10.46; 10.55; 10.57; 11.7; 11.11; 11.13; 11.20; 12.6; 12.7; 12.12; 12.13; 13.14; 13.15; 13.20; 14.4; 14.8; 14.11; 14.13; 14.15; 16.16; 16.19; 16.21; 16.24; 16.25; 17.4; 17.8; 17.9; 17.13; 18.5; 18.8; 18.14; 21.2; 21.17.
© Hawkes & Son (London) Ltd for all countries. Propriété en co-edition Editions A.R.I.M.A. et Editions Boosey & Hawkes: 4.3; 9.16.
© Robert Lienau Musikverlag: 22.7.
© F.E.C. Leuckart Music Publishers, Munich: 10.9; 11.1.
© Editions Max Eschig, Paris/United Music Publishers Limited: 8.29; 11.42; 17.6; 17.7.
© Novello & Company Limited: 6.5; 7.17; 7.22; 10.14; 10.17; 10.18; 10.20; 10.39; 11.25; 11.5; 13.4; 13.6; 13.8; 13.17; 13.22; 21.5; 21.11; 21.15; 21.22.
© Oxford University Press: 7.67; 7.68; 7.90; 8.6; 8.22; 8.23; 9.18; 9.20; 10.1; 10.2; 11.24; 11.34; 11.43; 12.4; 13.2; 14.2; 15.20; 15.21; 15.24; 17.2.
© Paterson's Publications Limited: 4.12; 7.23; 7.24.

© C. F. Peters Leipzig: 1.13; 21.9.
© assigned to C. F. Peters: 10.59; 16.26.
© Casa Ricordi-BMG Ricordi SpA: 12.15.
© G. Schirmer Ltd on behalf of Associated Music Publishers, Inc: 11.17; 21.16.
© B. Schott's Söhne: 7.15; 7.16; 7.28; 7.29; 7.30; 7.31; 7.75; 7.88; 7.89; 8.26; 9.15; 10.19; 10.49; 10.50; 10.51; 10.52; 13.18; 16.10; 16.23.
© B. Schott's, Mainz and Heugel et Cie., Paris: 16.9.
© B. Schott's Söhne and Schott and Co. Ltd: 4.6; 15.25.
© Musikverlag Hans Sikorski and Boosey & Hawkes Music Publishers Ltd: 6.17.
© Stainer & Bell Ltd: 11.15.
© Editio Supraphon, Praha: 12.13.
© United Music Publishers Ltd: 8.31; 12.14.
© Universal Edition (London) Ltd., London: Fig 5.2.
© Universal Edition: 4.24; 5.4; 5.5; 6.7; 6.8.
© Universal Edition A.G. Wien: 4.26; 12.11.
© Universal Edition, A.G., Wien © assigned to Universal Edition (London) Limited: 11.23.
© Warner Bros Music Corp: 10.44; 10.48; 11.44.
© M. Witmark & Sons, Warner/Chappell Music Ltd London & International Music Publications Ltd: 15.5.

INTRODUCTION

'*Much time is needed to find the oceans of music; still more, to learn how to navigate in them.*'

So wrote Berlioz, in the Introduction to his 'Treatise on Instrumentation', and the basic truth of this statement is even more valid today than at the time of its writing in the early years of the nineteenth century. In terms of orchestral music alone, the development that has taken place in the last two hundred years has affected not only the structure of the orchestra, in terms of size and instruments, but the very techniques of performance. Nowadays, orchestral playing is a highly specialized and complicated art, and to 'navigate' it successfully requires the application of many skills from each and every player. The existence of so many superb professional orchestras, coupled with the proliferation of technically advanced recordings, makes it easy to take for granted the staggering diversity of techniques involved. Nowhere is this highlighted more brutally than when faced with inexperienced orchestras, largely possessed of the individual instrumental techniques but, by necessity, devoid of this additional competence. It is therefore with specific regard to the wide-ranging demands made upon such ensembles that I have approached this discussion.

Apart from within the world's specialist music colleges, where orchestral playing has long been part of the instrumental curriculum, the existence of the full-scale symphony orchestra composed entirely of young musicians is a comparatively recent phenomenon. Although it is fairly generally accepted that the first example in the United Kingdom was the orchestra formed by Ernest Read in 1926, it is otherwise hard to predate the founding of the National Youth Orchestra of Wales, which first met in 1946. This, and similar orchestras formed independently on both sides of the Atlantic in the following years, were among the first orchestras of young musicians brought together primarily to *perform* orchestral music and, as such, were marking the first steps on a path that has yet to be fully explored.

Given the enormous emotional and social benefits experienced by the players, it is hardly surprising that the popularity of the youth orchestra increased so rapidly. Yet the vast majority of musicians and public alike still consider it to be a purely educational exercise: an opportunity for young instrumentalists to learn some examples from the great orchestral repertoire from within, and to play under the guidance of experienced professionals. Undoubtedly this is one of the fundamental reasons for their existence, but the widely held belief that this is their sole, or even primary, function must be most fervently questioned. There exists also the possibility to communicate maturing and powerful emotional ideologies through the predetermined structures of the composer, to bring forth an always new and often ignored insight into the works of the orchestral repertoire as seen through the eyes of an emerging generation.

With a typical student orchestra, the task of moulding such divergent instrumental technique and experience into a unit with a performing ability greatly in advance of the average age, without disturbing the wonderful freedom, enthusiasm, direct communication and optimistic colour to be found in the players, is a daunting prospect.

However, contrary to many people's surmise, an orchestra is not necessarily the sum of its parts, inasmuch as its performing standard is not simply the total of the individual playing standards of its members. Much more influential is the sensitivity, support and awareness of balance and ensemble shown by the players one to another. Indeed, one of the earliest and most difficult lessons to be learned by the professional player when auditioning for an orchestral position is that it is not necessarily the most outstanding player who will eventually fill the post, but the one whose sound and approach are most suited to the orchestra in question. This being so, it is possible to produce a coherent and finely honed young orchestra in the most unlikely circumstances. Certainly in the case of stringed instruments, a section composed of players totally aware of their corporate responsibility will always outshine one where individual technical prowess, however advanced, is not successfully combined. Projected unity forms the basis of orchestral sound and is responsible for the 'corporate personality' possessed in some degree by every orchestra once it has achieved any sort of performing identity.

In attempting to examine many of the techniques and requirements that provide the orchestra with its means of musical communication, above and beyond the mere performance of notes, it has not been my intention to provide a work of reference, in which all the possible sounds and techniques available to the instruments of the orchestra are listed, together with a brief résumé of how they might be accomplished. Such information is available in a wide variety of specialized volumes, written by musicians with immense experience of a particular instrument and its capabilities. Neither is it a book of orchestration or any associated craft that may require basic knowledge of orchestral instruments and the limitations imposed upon them. My purpose lies somewhere between the two, being the consideration, in purely practical terms, of how an orchestra may be helped to achieve certain facets of performance and the better understanding of all that orchestral performance involves, be it professional, student or amateur.

The fact that reference has been made to musical examples from the major orchestral repertoire might, at first sight, make it appear that the discussion is relevant to this level of orchestral playing alone. This is most definitely *not* the case: all the works explored here have been performed under my direction by both professional *and* student orchestras. The decision to draw from this repertoire was taken for a number of reasons: firstly, that these works provide the clearest examples of each particular aspect; secondly, that there can be no question of their basic orchestration or construction being at fault; and thirdly, that only by illustration of the ultimate goal is it possible to describe the techniques required to attain it. In themselves, however, such techniques and considerations are as necessary to the small school orchestra playing arrangements or specially written works as they are to the professional symphony orchestra who apply so many of them automatically.

Basic instrumental techniques are not covered here except insofar as they affect collaboration. Similarly, I have not touched upon the history and development of instruments where this took place largely outside the area of repertoire most usually associated with the symphony orchestra – the strings may be taken as a case in point. Furthermore, I have at all times considered the instrumentalists themselves within an orchestral context and attempted to put forward the ideal circumstances in which their individual talents may be most readily integrated. Obviously, when dealing with orchestras of differing age and experience, such an approach must be tempered by the confines of individual circumstances. It is important, for example, not to confuse the responsibilities of individual positions in an orchestral section, as set out in each of the opening chapters, with the notion that these must be the exclusive province of one player. Certainly in the case of horns and trumpets it could be detrimental to the technical development of many younger players if required to sustain the rigours of the 'Principal' position throughout an entire programme. The desire, in this context, has been solely to set out the requirements of the various positions so that the differing technical and musical responsibilities can be more fully appreciated. The job itself remains the same, whether it is performed by one player or any number in turn.

Finally, by far the most important concept to grasp is the *basic* difference between working with professional instrumentalists and with those less experienced. With inexperienced players the processes of refinement – clarification or re-articulation of a phrase, alteration in balance, variation of dynamic, subjugation or supremacy of line – will be attempted on almost every occasion without the professional player's automatic adjustment of technical production that makes it possible. For this reason, the conductor of youth, student or amateur orchestras needs to be able to draw upon a far deeper understanding of the technical solutions to musical problems than would be the case were he or she working solely with professional players (where such explanations would be strongly resented). The fundamental truth of this statement *must* be fully understood, for it is the essential difference between two otherwise identical media and the reason, so rarely comprehended, why some conductors do not easily transfer from one to the other. Young conductors beware!

The complete understanding of these and many related orchestral demands may be considered vital to the performing capabilities of any orchestral ensemble. The status of the youth or student orchestra as a performing medium in its own right is, to my mind, unquestionable, but how often it is recognized as such or attains its potential is dependent upon many things. Each orchestra's varying inherent technical limitations and inexperience can hinder and obscure its eventual musical communication, and it is to the discussion, understanding and even possible eradication of many of these obstacles that the following pages are addressed.

PART I

Fundamental Principles

1 STRINGS

The string section of the symphony orchestra comprises violins (divided into two groups), violas, cellos and double basses, and this quartet of instruments formed the foundation of the symphony orchestra for a considerable period of time before that with which this discussion is specifically concerned. Today's orchestra grew through the addition of various instruments to this basic group, but the strings have always remained predominant, in both size and sound. The term 'orchestra' almost always implies a string section.

The variety of tone and dynamic range available from this most perfectly balanced of orchestral sections is immense, and the range of pitch no less so. The notes to which the open strings of the four instruments are tuned are as follows, with double basses sounding one octave lower than written:

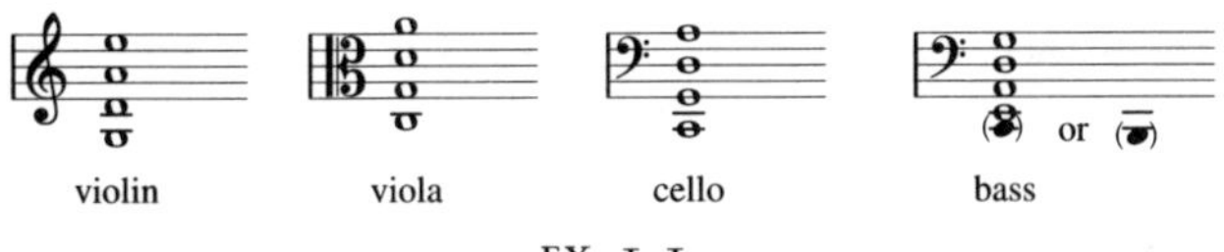

EX. 1.1

For practical purposes the highest notes available to each instrument may safely be taken as two octaves above the upper string but, most particularly in the case of violins, notes above this range are frequently demanded. The lowest C of the double basses, shown in parentheses in the above table, is available only on instruments with five strings (where B is often the lowest string, maintaining the overall tuning in fourths) or those fitted with a special extension mechanism protruding over the peg box. In youth and student orchestras, the number of players with instruments capable of supplying this bottom third of the range is likely to be extremely limited, but the ability has been presumed by composers since the time of Beethoven.

With such range and intensity at their disposal the predominance of the string section becomes understandable. The overall sound of any symphony orchestra rests very largely on the tone, flexibility, precision and focus of the complete string section. Without the ability to accompany orchestral solos sensitively or provide an infinite variety of texture, the strings will produce only a mass of individual lines and the orchestra will never perform any work even tolerably well.

Achieving such techniques of orchestral string playing from a group that is not composed of high-class professional players is immensely difficult and, in its most revelatory form, probably only realizable by a conductor who has a thorough working knowledge of string technique and much experience of using it from within an orchestra. Exceptions are rare, although there have been some outstanding conductors from a non-string playing background who have proved themselves able to help and teach a young section, among them the late Maurice Handford, who openly acknowledged his debt in this regard to Sir John Barbirolli. However, his own remarkable sensitivity to string sounds reveals the extent to which a non-string specialist might evoke sounds of rare beauty from the strings of a young orchestra.

Obviously I am not referring here simply to note lengths, dynamic markings and phrasings, which must be the basic trade of all conductors, but to their more subtle partner, colouring, for which reason the larger string sections evolved.

Although many conductors of student orchestras will put their faith in a group of professional string tutors to elicit the sounds for them, in practice this is simply not possible. Apart from many other considerations, when it comes to the actual concert, only the conductor is there with the orchestra: there are no tutors hiding among the strings to encourage and remind them. The conductor becomes totally responsible for the orchestra's welfare and cannot be expected to provide the ideal framework for their performance without a complete understanding of what the players are trying to do.

There are also issues that even the most persuasive and coherent tutors cannot properly address. Without the relevant instrumentalist, a tutor cannot teach a section to accompany a wind solo, or to adjust to wind intonation. A tutor cannot balance chords across the string group as a whole, or (except in the case of 1st and 2nd violins or cellos and basses working together) find and encourage help in support and sound production from another section. All these things, and many other features of orchestral ensemble, require particular physical techniques and vary so much in degree as to be impossible to teach out of context.

Only the conductor has the opportunity to work on these things and must be able not only to locate what is wrong but also to convey the quickest and most effective way of putting it right – technically. Moreover, he or she must provide the musical design in which such techniques, once mastered, become secondary to their musical necessity and flow easily and logically from the players. Such knowledge and techniques are a basic requirement of the conductor faced with any young orchestra.

It is of no use to attempt to mould performance purely in terms of the final sound required; no young string player will know how to attain it and the most that will be achieved is an uneven, unbalanced and fault-ridden effort that will be as obvious to the discerning listener as it will be detrimental to the precious technical development of the players involved. This delicately shifts the balance of responsibility when working with young instrumentalists as distinct from professional players, who are unlikely to do anything that would damage their own technique. Professionals also know their instruments extremely well, and will probably be the first to discern problems of balance or style which they can rectify almost as quickly as the greatest conductor. Here the task for the conductor becomes largely one of consideration of interpretation and ensemble. Obviously a great deal of sensitivity towards technical difficulty is appreciated and expected but the professional is unlikely to follow an interpretation down a hazardous path. The student orchestra will – the performers in this case being far less likely to see the dangers to either themselves or the works being played.

For string players in particular, orchestral techniques are far removed from those taught in pursuance of day-to-day instrumental development. The method of playing an instrument within a group of ten to eighteen similar instruments playing the same line must necessarily differ in many ways from playing the instrument alone. In many situations, the techniques can be so different as to be perplexing and totally alarming to the inexperienced player, and could well be likened to a learner driver being thrown into a transcontinental rally. If it were possible in such a situation to be swept along by the other vehicles, with no idea of reverse lock cornering or heel and toe control, the panic and bewilderment of the driver would reflect some of the feelings of young string players during their early orchestral experience. Neither is it intrinsically less hazardous, for, although the players are unlikely to be risking life and limb, it is possible to undo many years of patient teaching and put at risk the career of a promising player.

In practical terms, the young orchestral string section presents even the most able conductor with many fascinating and ever-changing problems. But three constant difficulties should be appreciated before a note of music is considered. To begin with, the degree of technical accomplishment of individuals within each section will vary, often to an alarming degree. Secondly, the instruments themselves are not likely to be good and very unlikely to produce anything resembling an even sound, or have enough tonal focus for the individual players to gather more than a general impression of what is actually being produced. Lastly, even after apparently careful consideration, the larger sections will almost certainly be seated wrongly and thus be unable to get help where it is needed.

The first two of these problems are quite impossible to remedy but, happily, very possible to disguise, otherwise this chapter would have no purpose whatsoever! The third point requires a great deal of thought and must inevitably vary from one orchestra to the next, but certain basic guidelines can be suggested and usefully considered.

Forming the Sections

VIOLIN SECTIONS

The biggest difficulty arises in the violins, where the number of players required highlights and widens the diversity of technical skills available. It is of no use drawing up a list of players in order of ability and then placing the sixteen best in the 1st violins and the remainder in the 2nds. This might appear obvious to most musicians, but I have seen it done and even, on one occasion, been expected to work with the result. Amazingly, the exact opposite can also be encountered.

While working with an orchestra in a small town in America I was asked to take a rehearsal of the local community youth orchestra. I arrived to find large gaps in all the string sections but most obviously in the 1st violins, where as many as three seats together were vacant, and the dozen or so players present dispersed over ten desks, so that many appeared only as vague shapes in the distance. Presuming the orchestra to have been struck by an epidemic I suggested that they might like to move up and fill the desks in front of them. However, I was firmly informed by the regular conductor that this was the entire section and the placings deliberate, various players having not yet reached the 'standard' required to fill the vacant chairs in front of them. Dating from around this time has been my recurring dream of arriving at a rehearsal to find all the 1st violins seated on top of one another at the third desk!

Extremes of this kind are fortunately rare but illustrate a prevalent misconception in string seating, where the placing may be solely representative of individual playing standard. Most particularly in a student orchestra this should be avoided and beyond the front desks (the seating of which will be discussed) players of differing standards need to be carefully interwoven.

A small number of players will always be recognizably more accomplished than other members of the section and their placing is crucial to orchestral continuity. Ideally, the best five players should be placed on the first three 1st violins and the first two 2nd violins. The personalities necessary for these positions are distinctive and can be recognized in many young players. An illustration of the seating within the two violin sections can be given in considering a student orchestra able to draw on a reasonable number of talented players – the average 'county' youth orchestra.

1st Violin no. 1 (Leader/Concert Master)

The instrumental abilities required of a Principal 1st violin are well known and need only be reiterated here for the sake of completeness. An able sight-reader, he or she must possess a facility across the range of the instrument, a strong sense of rhythm, clarity and projection of sound and the ability to perform some of the extremely difficult and unrewarding solos that often appear in the repertoire. (No one in their right mind is going to programme Richard Strauss *Ein Heldenleben* or Rimsky-Korsakov *Scheherazade* with a young orchestra except as a vehicle for an exceptionally outstanding player.) There are, however, further considerations which can become deciding factors where there is a choice between two or three players of roughly equal ability.

The unique position of Principal 1st violin in relation to the rest of the orchestra dates from the time when the Leader/Conductor roles were inseparable and this player was responsible for tempi, ensemble, balance and interpretation in rehearsal and performance. Gradually, as works became more complex and more players were involved, it became necessary for the Leader to concentrate entirely on direction rather than playing, and thus the role of conductor evolved as distinct and separate. In the United Kingdom at least, the historic significance of the first player is still recognized through the tradition of separate applause before a concert begins, although nowadays this is often associated with the welcoming of the whole orchestra. However, many chamber ensembles continue to play without a conductor, as well they should, and here the role of Leader/Concert Master fulfils its original duties.

In the professional symphony orchestra, the Leader still retains many responsibilities, in most cases exerting a strong influence upon a range of artistic decisions, from the choice of players to repertoire. Here is the orchestra's spokesperson, representative and diplomat, the link between the orchestra and all its visiting artists, particularly with guest conductors, where the working relationship is so crucial. The position thus entails rather more than simply requesting an A from the first oboe before rehearsals commence.

With the student orchestra, many of these responsibilities do not arise, although the reason for this is more a lack of opportunity, owing to the orchestra's limited appearances, rather than to their being consigned elsewhere. However, the Leader is still likely to be the automatic choice to represent the orchestra at a function after a concert, to participate in any interviews or make presentations on the orchestra's behalf.

These non-musical considerations alone require a well-developed personality and a high degree of self-confidence. It is therefore important that the chosen player be well liked and able to command respect from the orchestra and it is preferable that he or she is at least comparable in age to the oldest member. An error of judgement in selecting the personality for this position can be highly detrimental to both the player and the orchestra, for there is no time in life where personal sensitivity is so acute or pride so easily punctured. It is therefore probably wise, even in the case of an outstanding player, for any doubt to be treated as reason for withholding the appointment until the development of the personality can be more clearly appraised.

Many inexperienced players, even of high technical ability, will mistakenly feel that this position requires them to play louder and more strongly than the rest of the section, shouldering the total responsibility for the section's sound and vainly trying to provide a clearly audible example of every phrase, passage, rhythm and tempo. This is totally self-defeating, in that the player concerned will be quite unable to hear what the section is doing, and also unacceptable musically – the obtrusive individual tone will prevent the section from projecting a corporate sound, or even hearing itself, and irretrievable problems of ensemble will result.

Such an attitude, most frequently the result of apprehension coupled with the desire to succeed, can only be changed through understanding and experience, by gradually making the player aware of the need and his or her own ability to subtly influence the section's sound rather than furnish a soloistic example of it. Having said that, many young players who have been through this situation and then adjusted their approach when they have become aware of what the job *actually* entails, prove to be among the most adept and successful leaders.

1st Violin no. 2 (Sub-Leader/Assistant Concert Master)

The requirements for the no. 2 1st violin are totally different, so much so that the position will probably be filled by a player not under consideration for the first chair. Again a good sight-reader with an obvious command of the instrument is needed, but not necessarily such a strong personality, as the position demands an even temperament, unflappable and utterly reliable in personality and rhythm. The responsibilities of this position are largely those of support and positive assistance, especially in concert circumstances where the degree of influence that this player may have over the Leader's well-being is critical. A really suitable candidate is not likely to be natural Leader material, nor to become so within the usual membership time of a student orchestra, and so the position is possibly best given to a player in his or her final year.

1st Violin no. 3

If judgement is borne out, no. 3 is the most likely candidate for the next vacancy in the 'hot seat', as again one is looking for an accomplished player with a well-developed, flexible technique and strong personality. The second desk is where much of the efficiency and character of the 1st violin section is determined. Bowings and markings from the front, problems and questions from the section can so easily stop here and never see the light of day again. The no. 3 1st violin takes a lot of responsibility for the 'general note-to-note running' of the 1st violin section. Even at school-age student level, one comes across players who quite instinctively concern themselves with the entire section from this position and they are truly worth their weight in gold.

There are thus strong arguments, and many professional precedents, for this being the seat of the Co-Leader/2nd Concert Master, although the designation of such a position is probably unnecessary in the student orchestra. However, should the Leader be indisposed at any time it will cause the section far less disturbance if all the outside players move up – most *divisi* remain unaffected and the players on the edge of the orchestra remain so. It is all too easy to underestimate the difference in playing outside or inside on the exposed line of 1st violins.

2nd Violin no. 1 (Principal)

The third 'Leader-potential' player should be at Principal 2nd violin, in the youth orchestra a position from which he or she can gather the necessary experience to move to Leader when the time arises (or, more likely, to no. 3 1st violin, where similar qualities are needed). However, guard against the obvious choice, for there are more qualities needed here than meet the eye.

The pitfall is one of unavoidable terminology, the term '2nd' being readily translated as 'inferior' or 'easier'. Of all things it might be, it is certainly neither of these. Even a cursory glance at any orchestral score will show the different techniques and specialities required from the two sections. The 2nd violins will encounter a lot of low string playing with its inevitable string crossing, themes and melodic accompaniments in the middle, and less easily projected, part of the instrument, and rhythmic figures that require perfectly controlled bow-arm technique and flexibility: in short, a number of techniques that occur infrequently in the solo repertoire and are therefore rarely taught in detail at this stage in a player's development. Add to these the fact that, at very best, only average quality instruments are likely to be used and one begins to understand the additional problems this whole section is continually expected to surmount.

It follows therefore that the position of Principal 2nd violin must be filled by a player of quality and, as mentioned above, many people will see this position as an opportunity to groom a younger player of leadership potential, but he or she must possess considerable strength of sound in the middle of the instrument. Progression to front-desk 1st violin must not be taken as automatic. Many circumstances, including the development of the player's personality, may prevent it and all cases must be taken on merit and adjustments made at a time when the orchestra and players concerned are least likely to be upset or damaged.

2nd Violin no. 2

Next to the Principal 2nd is needed another reliable and accomplished player. Generally, it should be one of the top five or six players in order to keep the sound across these front desks even and, above all, sensitive. If this hierarchy is not adhered to, one loses not only the strength of players to direct the sections but also, and far more important, the sensitivity of the front. Sensitivity is a relative term but it requires a great deal of skill to convey it in even small degree from an instrument. The example to the violin sections must start from here, however limited the eventual success.

Other Positions

Throughout the rest of the two sections ability and experience should be spread as evenly as possible, avoiding even one pairing of weaker players at a desk. The influence of one player on another at a string stand is immense and has to be experienced to be truly understood, but it affects confidence, sound, attitude and enjoyment.

A number of stronger players are needed in the middle of the 2nd violin section and to achieve this can require considerable diplomacy and persuasion on the part of the string tutor, orchestral manager or conductor, as it will often involve players who consider themselves to be rightfully placed among the 1st violins, not only on account of their playing ability but also their age. Almost inevitably the average age of the 2nd violins will be younger than that of the 1sts. Except in music colleges or national youth orchestras it is unlikely that younger players will be found with either the technique or confidence to overcome the difficulties of playing high-lying passages and many younger players will, of necessity, spend their early years in the 2nd violins. This is an impossible situation to resolve successfully because conductors find themselves not only bound by fact but also, because of it, perpetuating the myth of the seniority of 1st violin playing!

It is possible at least to weaken this prevailing attitude by paying sufficient attention to the 2nd violins in rehearsal, placing heavy musical demands on them and, wherever possible, entreating them to support, and be responsible for, the 1st violin sound. Apart from being essential to any musical result, this will tend to heighten the 2nd violin involvement and make the whole orchestra aware of the aural necessity for equality of sound across these two sections.

Some strength of sound is needed on the last desks of both violin sections where a degree of anticipation is needed because of the distance from the aural centre of the orchestra: the larger the sections, the more difficult this becomes. The rhythmic accuracy of the back desks is essential for clarity and precise movement and, as will be discussed in some detail later, the spread of string sound is very important. One of the most overlooked reasons for the accidental dominance of horns and brass is that they are so often playing directly across the weaker part of the string sections.

In the 1st violins one other crucial placing must be mentioned: that of the player on the outside of the fourth or fifth desk, where the 'break' occurs between the outside and inside line of desks in most rehearsal and concert halls. This last outside position is extremely difficult because it is one of the only two 'corners' in an orchestra's seating (the other being the corresponding placing in the cellos) and, as such, displays idiosyncrasies of aural perception. To any player, whether professional, amateur or student, this position nearly always gives the feeling of playing alone in the middle of a desert but (and this is where it is most dangerous for the unwary) this usually only becomes apparent at the moment the bow touches the string. During bars of rests the orchestra can sound clear and warm and then suddenly, as the individual sound is added, it seems that all other sound disappears and only the personal contribution remains audible, giving the player no idea whether it is with the rest of the section, whether it balances or blends, or is too loud or soft. It takes a strong nerve to contend with this and it can cause distress to the unprepared. For the sake of the player, allocate this position with care and never extend the line of outside desks beyond the orchestra's normal rehearsal seating. The most that can be tolerated is to cut it down by one desk but, and this can hardly be stressed too heavily, under no circumstances extend it, especially at a pre-concert rehearsal in a new acoustic. At best the newly positioned player will be unable to adapt quickly enough to be of any real use; at worst it can damage the player's nerve and confidence. If the regular player is indisposed without warning then it is better that the inside player moves across or the one immediately in front moves back, for these two will at least have been playing under similar conditions.

In many student orchestras such numbers of experienced violinists as have been considered here will not always be available and it is then that the character and personality of the individual players in the various positions becomes particularly important if the two sections are to project the required strength and freedom of sound.

VIOLA SECTION

The viola section, not subject to the violins' division into 1sts and 2nds, is easier to seat, in that a more standard relationship of ability to position can be maintained. It is, of course, still important to keep an even distribution of good players but the numbers required tend to make the possible permutations more limited.

In many student orchestras there still remains the difficulty of the comparative newness of many players to the instrument. Although teaching habits have changed a great deal over the past few years and more students are learning the instrument from an earlier age with specialist viola teachers, instances of up to 50 per cent of a youth orchestra section still struggling with the alto clef are by no means unknown, particularly where the orchestra has an upper age limit of 18, and it is difficult to overcome. In a section of ten players, for example, it is possible that only three or four will be really proficient and their ideal placing becomes a taxing problem. Putting two of these players on the front desk and spreading the others out will throw the entire burden of sound forward. If, on the other hand, these players are grouped together on the first two desks there is likely to be little depth of sound from the section as a whole, and the weaker players will be 'reading' notes rather than hearing them – a state of affairs which always causes players to close up their sound and drag rhythmically. A pragmatic approach is essential, and it can sometimes be better to risk a slightly weaker no. 2 and place the four more advanced players on the outside of each of the first four desks. Meanwhile, one must trust that the marked improvement of student viola playing will continue, making more evenly balanced sections a real possibility for all young orchestras.

One advantage experienced by this section is the need to position players in a compressed grouping, as a result of their close proximity to the front row of woodwind and also the amount of space required by the cello section. This spatial restriction will often result in the desks being placed much closer together than in other string sections and automatically affords the players greater opportunity to hear and influence one another.

In passing, it is worth noting that, in student orchestras, a viola section that does not mix freely with the rest of the strings on a social basis can be symptomatic of a sense of inferiority of orchestral contribution (the exact opposite of the same behaviour in 1st violinists or cellists!). This section's awareness of its corporate responsibility to the strings as a whole, and its importance within the overall string sound, are vital to its morale.

Viola no. 1 & no. 2 (Principal & Sub-Principal)

The Principal of this section can be, and usually is, the best available player, as personality is not so important here, provided that there is a general rapport with the section and that some positive help and encouragement are given. The ability to project a rich sound, however, is probably more vital than obvious agility around the instrument because the orchestral solos for this player will often be of a soft, *legato* nature and yet set within broad sonorities of accompaniment.

Once more, in order to ensure reliable support for the Principal, the Sub-Principal viola needs to be of a similar personality to his or her counterparts in the two violin sections.

CELLO SECTION

It often happens that the cellos are the most proficient and, in terms of sound, quickest responding section of a young orchestra's string group, and the fusion of this section can sometimes become apparent deceptively early. This *relative* ease in blending may be attributed to an amalgamation of many factors.

The balance of the instrument with regard to the relationship of its size to its tonal range is advantageous, the middle register in itself being naturally more efficient in fusing the corporate sounds of a group of players by virtue of the increased overtones apparent. This aspect is enhanced by the freedom of sound the instrument displays due to its having minimum contact with the player's body and direct contact with the floor, factors which complement its resonance. It is noticeably more difficult for a cello section to attain even blending on tiled, concrete or carpeted flooring.

An even more fundamental reason for the section's discernible superiority in many young orchestras, however, is that the instrument requires considerable left hand pressure in order to produce a clear note. Young cellists develop a strong and positive finger action very early in life and this produces clarity and depth of sound: a weak left hand will produce virtually nothing on the cello, rather than the vaguely acceptable sound under the ear that deceives many a young violinist. There is no real place of safety on the cello, the wide finger spacing of the lower positions making them equally as dangerous for intonation as the upper. Also the necessary position of the left arm makes the awful habit of flattening the hand along the neck of the instrument (as seen in some young violinists) quite impossible.

Added to this, cellists are not so prone to using the neck of the instrument as a means of support, the regular use of the thumb as the lowest digit in higher positions causing the hand to be freed from the neck entirely. In orchestral playing, this technique of using the thumb should be extended to the lower positions as well, many orchestral passage benefiting from this 'five digit' availability in order to avoid awkward and unnecessary string crossing, as here, in a passage from Tchaikovsky *Symphony no. 6*.

EX. 1.2

Of all the regular orchestral instruments (that is, excluding piano, harp and tuned percussion) the cello is the one instrument that sounds at all similar both to the player and the listener, and where the player is far enough removed from the source to listen properly to the sound. With the upper string sections one is continually persuading them to project sound and produce it over a distance from the instrument because, with the ear so close and the contact of the facial bone structure so immediate, they are misled into thinking that a sound is being produced that is actually not evident. The playing position of the cello and its immense sound box, coupled with the necessity for powerful finger action and positive contact, give the section a head start.

The intention is not to give the impression that difficulties of sound production do not exist for this section – far from it – but rather to point out that any improvement is more quickly and easily perceived by the players themselves.

Cello no. 1 (Principal)

In recent years, it has not been unusual to find players of outstanding ability in this section, and although, of course, technical standards can still vary widely, this rarely causes such acute problems of coherent sound as it might elsewhere. For this reason it is again possible to seat the section in a more standard order of ability and the Principal, as in the case of the violas, is usually the best available player. However, the orchestral solos that appear for this player are very often of a poignant and gentle nature and require a subtlety of phrasing and touch that can tax the most experienced professional. (Liszt *Piano Concerto in A*; two bars, twice, in *Ronde des Princesses* from Stravinsky *The Firebird*; and, probably the most wonderful use of the solo cello in the whole orchestral repertoire, the two sublime bars towards the end of Mahler *Symphony no. 9* come immediately to mind.) No brash, sensation-seeking technician will survive for very long in this seat.

Other Positions

Other positions within the section are essentially similar to those already discussed with regard to violins and violas, but, once again, the particular position of no. 3 needs to be highlighted. The essential flexibility of this player and the second desk in general cannot be over-emphasized, and the larger the section the more vital this position becomes. Many difficulties of ensemble may be directly related to this desk, and careful consideration of the personality required in these seats will be amply rewarded.

One last word of warning with regard to the positioning of cellists: if at all possible, try to avoid placing very young and inexperienced players immediately in front of the double basses. The intonation of any bass section at this level can be suspect and, even in the best circumstances, it is difficult for cellists to hear clearly when the sound of the basses is very close. A weak or insecure player in this position will only get weaker, without really knowing why.

DOUBLE BASS SECTION

Since most student orchestras have difficulty in finding sufficient numbers of double bass players to complement their cello section, problems of placement rarely arise. Also, the opportunity in most halls and rehearsal rooms for placing them up to six in line overcomes many of the inherent problems often encountered in the other strings. Owing to their most regular placement at the extreme outer edge of the orchestra, the basses can maximize the advantage of having equally reflected sound throughout the section, and the only problem (rarely encountered in student orchestras) becomes one of isolation should the line be allowed to extend too far.

Eight players doubled four and four is a very close-knit group and ten can usually be accommodated in a block. With eight or more, however, a little more care must be given to the even spacing of the good players but, in terms of individual personalities, it is easier to achieve here. Firstly, the status of 1st desk is not so apparent to an audience and therefore not of such importance to the players. Secondly, since the technique and character of the instrument are so unlike anything else, the individuals tend to mould more quickly as a section and are thus less concerned with the positions in which they are actually placed. Furthermore, the historic perception of the instrument as one tending towards ensemble rather than solo performance encourages a generosity of attitude from its players at the outset.

Nonetheless, the Principal still needs to be a strong player and, in view of the section's relative physical isolation, one who will concern him or herself with the production and quality of their sound, be aware of possible technical difficulties, and able to give the help and encouragement needed.

OTHER CONSIDERATIONS

Repertoire that includes long or technically demanding solos for the Principals of these last three mentioned sections should be programmed only when a talented player is available and, preferably, has been the incumbent of the position for some time. Such works include Mahler *Symphony no. 1* (bass solo), Richard Strauss *Don Quixote* (cello solo) and Elgar overture *In the South* (viola solo).

There are many circumstances in which conductors are unable to involve themselves in the actual positioning of the musicians, especially to the degree discussed above. However, the principles must be thoroughly understood and, if necessary, adjusted in relation to the conductor's own influence on the sound, so that difficulties can be recognized and ways found to overcome them.

Seating

The position of the sections in relation to one another is an emotive and much discussed subject. Many orchestras in the late nineteenth and early twentieth centuries sat with the 2nd violins immediately opposite the 1sts, on the conductor's right, as in *Fig. 1.1*.

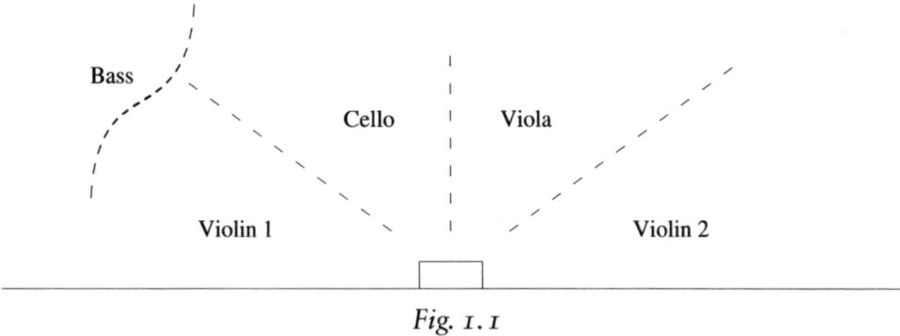

Fig. 1.1

Much of the music of the late Romantic era was obviously orchestrated with this positioning in mind, and a number of pieces only convey their true antiphonal instrumentation if performed in this way (the symphonies of Mahler and Elgar are examples).

This arrangement, shown here in its most traditional form, incorporates the awkward positioning of the basses on the opposite side of the orchestra from their woodwind and brass counterparts (bassoons, trombones and tuba). Therefore, as pointed out by Norman Del Mar in his exhaustive study of the orchestra,[1] the important variation shown in *Fig. 1.2* is more often employed when this antiphonal seating is contemplated.

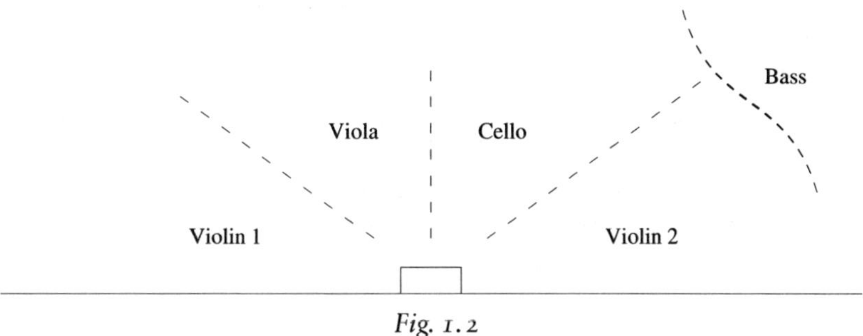

Fig. 1.2

Nonetheless, unless the string sound is to be sacrificed, to seat anything but a fully professional orchestra in this manner is to court disaster. In student orchestra circumstances, the support given to the 1st violins by the 2nds is of paramount importance and can truthfully be said to make the difference between a good and a mediocre 1st violin sound. There is hardly a piece of

1 *Anatomy of the Orchestra*, Faber and Faber, London, 1981.

music in existence where 2nd violins do not support the 1sts one octave below at some point and this support is critical for projection of sound and intonation. In any octave doubling, the lower line must be stronger than the upper – sometimes considerably so – and when it is in the same instrument it has to be immediately adjacent for the true benefit of sound to be realized.

In practical terms, too, few student orchestras will have strong enough players in the 2nd violins to be able to make a combined and sonorous noise with the instruments facing away from the audience. For them to get any real sound they would tend to force, thereby losing all quality and projection, and the string section would therefore have no balanced middle to the harmony and no possible chance of achieving unification.

In professional circumstances the situation is slightly different, although I know from playing experience that orchestras unused to this layout find it extremely difficult. However, these musicians know exactly what they are doing and it is also rarely more than a few hours since they last played together. They have the technique, the ability and the knowledge to compensate for change in ambient acoustic qualities and, in the last resort, sheer experience will go a long way toward ensuring their balance and ensemble.

Personally I am not completely convinced that this positioning really works in any circumstances, as I feel that something of the overall sound quality has to be sacrificed, if only in particular passages. However it does make a lot of sense of certain antiphonal writing and I have to admit to my own insistent use of it in one lone example – Mahler *Symphony no. 9* – where the 2nd violin part is quite exceptional in its individuality and rarely even complements the 1sts. Nonetheless, the programming of this piece can only be contemplated with a student orchestra of such high standard that the difficulties outlined above are possible to overcome. For the other Mahler symphonies, the two Elgars and the many other examples that could be cited, I consider it preferable to retain the seating nowadays most commonly found throughout the world, for the reasons of support and texture already mentioned.

This familiar layout is shown in *Fig. 1.3* and, as can be seen, in placing the

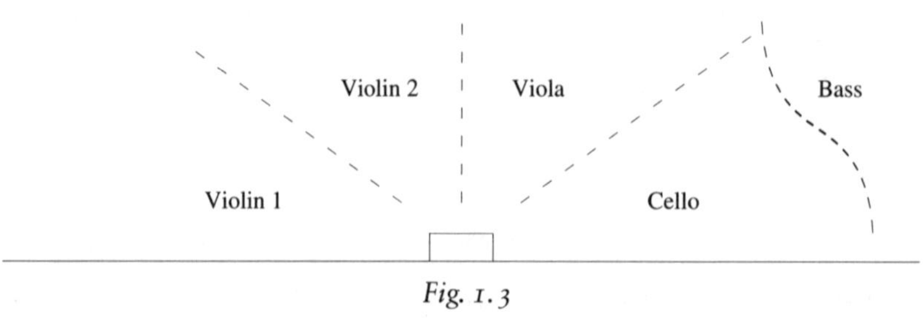

Fig. 1.3

2nd violins in partnership with the 1sts, the cellos have now been turned side on to the audience. The disadvantages of this position have often been given as a subsidiary, although important, reason for the retention of the layout shown in *Fig. 1.2* but if this is the prime factor, there is another solution, as shown in *Fig. 1.4*, with the violas on the outside.

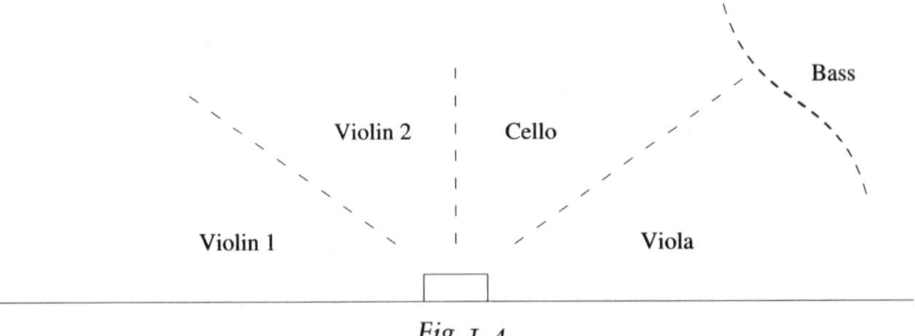

Fig. 1.4

For sheer quality of sound and ensemble, this is probably preferable to the traditional set-up but again unfortunately it poses possibly insurmountable problems for the student orchestra. The viola section is unlikely to be advanced or numerous enough to cope with this arrangement without compromising their tonal quality. Lack of experience will tend to make them respond to problems of too little sound projection by forcing, and nothing will be gained.

A physical problem affecting the cellos in this layout should also be considered. Even with them on the outside, the 'wing-span' of a desk of cellos is always underestimated; it really is at *least* two metres overall and that sort of space is not always to be found inside an orchestra. In *Fig. 1.3* a proportion of this distance is accounted for by non-orchestral space and the room need only be found to the right of the inside players. Comfort is essential to any orchestra's performance and the sometimes necessary squashing of desks cannot easily be applied to a cello section. The few concert hall stages that will not accommodate cellos within the playing area provide sufficient reason to discount the arrangement. It is one thing for a big professional orchestra to play a desk or two short – the musicians are quite glad of a night off – but no student orchestra should ever make redundant players who have rehearsed the programme.

The positioning of the basses also causes something of a dilemma in this arrangement. If left in their usual position, the depth of their sound will have less effect on the intonation of the back desks of violas than on the cellos, but the first desk, being on the outside, will be divorced from the cello section altogether. This is undesirable for any orchestra but with students it makes the blending of the harmonic bass line very difficult indeed. Simply swapping the two affected desks around is not only unnatural for the players but risks a less confident and experienced player on the exposed edge. To put the basses in a line behind the woodwind – however dramatic the visual effect – is musically indefensible and sheer suicide.

Thus the generally accepted seating plan of *Fig. 1.3* seems most advantageous for the student orchestra in terms of promoting satisfactory ensemble, balance and clarity. Actually achieving all or any one of these is another matter.

Divided Strings

There are many occasions in the orchestral repertoire where the string parts divide into two or more separate lines, both within the sections themselves and across the string orchestra as a whole. Such *divisi* can range from division into two equal parts to quite complicated arrangements involving separation of desks, solo lines and many strands of *tutti*.

In the simplest instances the outside players of each desk always take the upper line and the inside players the lower. This is musically preferable for almost all *divisi a 2*, from Barber *Adagio for Strings*, where the sections remain divided throughout, to the occasional bars in the Brahms symphonies. However, passages of apparently simple two-part division exist where such a system is not necessarily musically or technically the most beneficial. The *fugato* section in the last movement of Bartók *Concerto for Orchestra* (bars 265–333) is a case in point, where all the string voices are divided between the subject and its *pizzicato* accompaniment. It is certainly preferable here that the front three or four desks of each section play the upper line and the remaining desks the lower and it would be normal in a section consisting of an odd number of desks to put the extra one on top: that is, a division of 5 to 4, or 4 to 3. With regard to the 2nd violins, who start this theme, it is quite feasible that this half-section *divisi* should begin at bar 265 directly, and not influence the division of even the previous six bars; similarly, 1st violins can revert to normal *divisi* directly at bar 325 if required.

This same variation of two-part division frequently occurs in the cello section, where the lower line can often be a direct octave doubling of the basses, and physical closeness of these two lines is desirable. Examples of this type abound and, especially when preparing a score for a student orchestra (where the rehearsal time is usually sufficient to clarify quick changes of division for the players), it should always be considered, even if later discarded for reasons of practicality or balance.

In more complicated division into three or four parts it is preferable to keep the lines close together wherever possible by extending the principle of the normal division into two. Thus the players divide 'at the desk' – each consecutive player taking the next lowest line; rather than 'by the desk' – first desk playing the top line, second desk the next, and so on. Even where a composer specifies an alternative method, this can still prove to be advantageous. Both Debussy and Ravel, for example, consign players to particular notes when writing for a small group of the same string instruments, consistently designating the higher line to the front players and the lower line correspondingly further back. The simple three-part *divisi* of six violins, shown in *Ex. 1.3* from Debussy *La Mer*, places the lower C♯ on the third desk, some considerable distance from the octave above and therefore unable to give any support of sound or intonation.

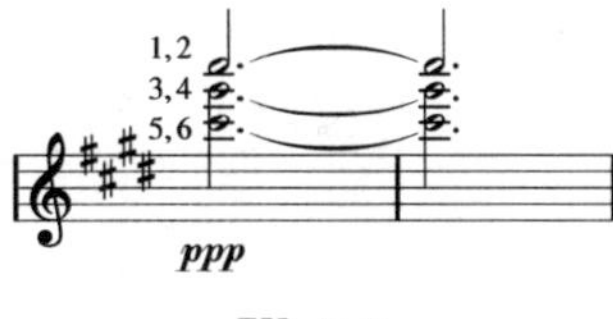

EX. 1.3

Similarly, in his *Piano Concerto in G*, Ravel specifies the following division of eight players, in this case the total 1st violin strength for the work.

EX. 1.4

However, the priority here seems to be less of physical placing than of ensuring the required number of players on each note, the lowest note in this case being played by the fourth desk. Such *divisi* need not be the automatic choice of orchestra or conductor and, in both these cases, presuppose considerable intuitive skill from those playing the lower line in regard to balance, since they would be unable to hear the notes above them. Undoubtedly in the student orchestra, a better division, for balance and intonation, would be that shown in *Ex. 1.5* (a) and (b).

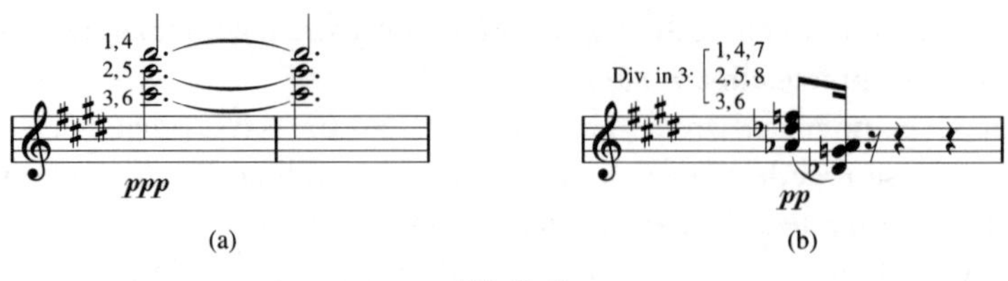

(a) (b)

EX. 1.5

Another, rather extreme example, again from *La Mer*, is that of the famous passage for sixteen(!) cellos, shown in *Ex. 1.6*. Difficulties of balance and intonation are regularly encountered when the four lines are spread across the section in the way suggested by the composer, but become considerably more manageable in the harmonically orientated division of alternate players. A further complication in this example is the almost inevitable re-distribution of parts caused by the rare availability, in even the most ideal circumstances, of a section of sixteen cellists, in which case any even distribution by desk becomes

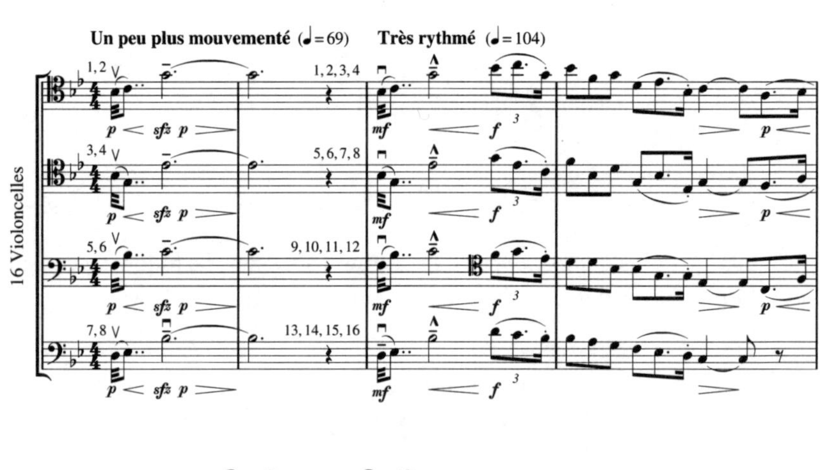

EX. 1.6

impossible. It is interesting to note in passing that, just after the quoted example, Debussy gives a hint of the overall string size he envisages for this work by writing in the violin part 'à 8', followed by 'à 16', followed by 'tous' but at no other point in the work does he intimate the quite colossal string strength needed to obey these directions exactly.

In many cases of specified division, the absence of markings that might point to variations in sound leads to the assumption that the emphasis is on numbers to a part rather than the distance between them. It is thus better in all instances of normal division to keep the chord close together and for each consecutive player to take the next lowest line. As mentioned above, in simple two-part division this system is routinely adopted by most orchestras.

Some exceptions to this pattern arise because of the nature of the printed material. String parts exist where long sections of three- or four-part division are printed on separate staves, with the laudable intention of making them easier to read. If a page turn is required, division by separate players is impossible, the second and fourth lines being non-existent while this task is being accomplished. In these circumstances division by desk becomes unavoidable, often with inherent difficulties of balance and ensemble. Generally speaking, however, the luxury of keeping decisions to reasons of musical priority alone can be indulged.

A notable exception to the divisions already discussed occurs in the third movement of Shostakovich *Symphony no. 5*, where three distinct sections of violins are intended. This can only be achieved by total division of the 1st and 2nd violins. In an orchestra with 16 1sts and 14 2nds, for example, by far the best arrangement is for the first five desks of 1sts to play Violin 1, the first five of 2nds Violin 2, and the remaining three desks of 1sts and two of 2nds Violin 3, thus keeping the three sections separate from each other but in naturally close groupings. Occasionally, as the opening statement of the movement is entrusted to 3rd violins, conductors will be found who prefer that the arrangement given here with regard to the 2nd and 3rd violins be reversed, so that the opening sounds are nearer the front and 'safer'. Such lack of confidence in the back of the sections has never, in my experience, been justified.

It is probably true to say that such a clear division of forces is no longer *divisi* as such but a reconstitution of the string section in whole or part. The Shostakovitch example is a rare instance of its employment in an otherwise standard orchestral layout. In the majority of cases the format will persist throughout the work and necessitate a complete reseating – as, for example, in the numerous works for double string orchestra.

Here the mirror-image placing of two opposing, equal and complete string sections is implied and is often arranged as shown in *Fig. 1.5*.

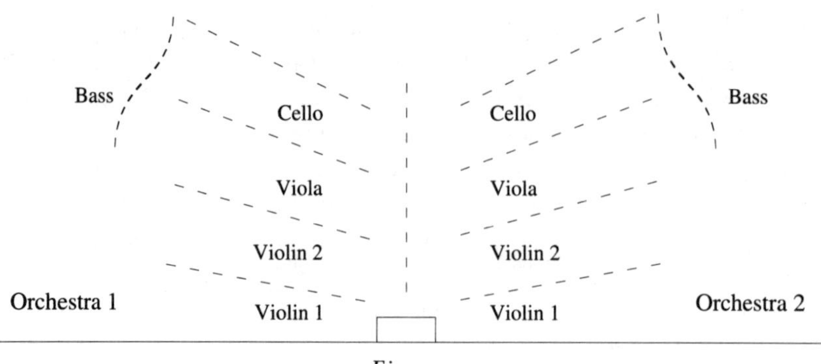

Fig. 1.5

However, the clear aural perception of separation implicit in the employment of two distinct orchestras can become blurred in this arrangement by virtue of the two cello sections being immediately adjacent and their sound combining before it has left the stage. It is thus preferable that both the highest and lowest lines be quite separate, and for this reason the alternative distribution shown in *Fig. 1.6* can prove beneficial.

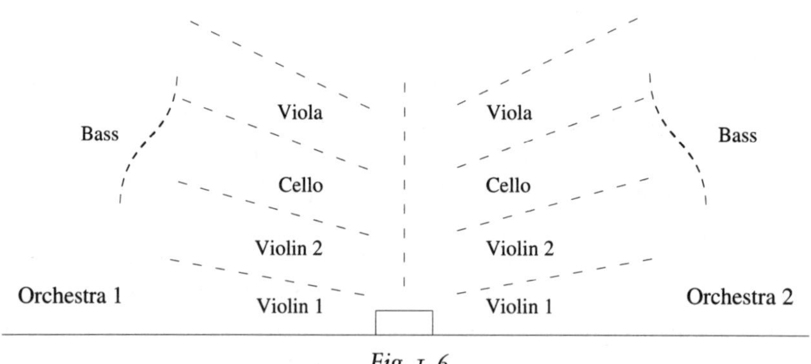

Fig. 1.6

As can be seen, both these examples require considerable depth of staging, and a more practical layout may be considered, provided that the sections are not too large (see *Fig. 1.7*).

This has the added advantages both of placing the basses nearer their respective cello sections and of totally separating the two orchestral bass lines, thereby highlighting the movement and division of sound between the two ensembles. In any platform arrangement of works for two orchestras, difficulties are always encountered whenever the writing requires a section from each orchestra to play the same line together, especially if this involves basses or cellos, as, for example, in many passages in the Tippett *Concerto for Double*

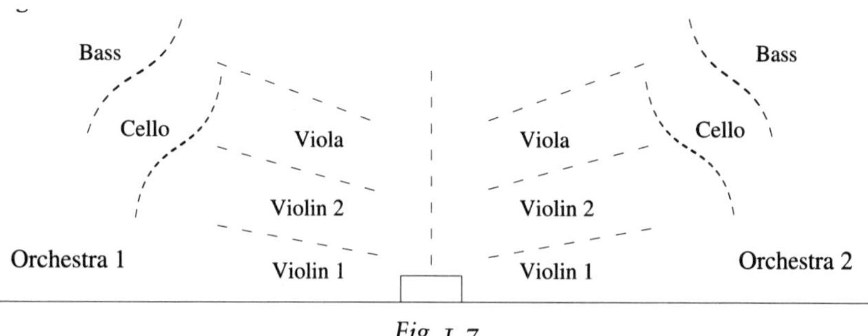

Fig. 1.7

String Orchestra. There are, unfortunately, no easy solutions to eradicate such awkward problems of ensemble, whatever the configuration.

Rare examples exist where division into two string orchestras will require unequal forces, as in the case of Vaughan Williams *Fantasia on a Theme of Thomas Tallis* (*Ex. 1.7*). Here the second orchestra (a double string quartet plus bass) is to be placed at a considerable distance from the main body of strings, which also includes solos for each of the Principal players, who thus form a third, string quartet, grouping.

At first sight the initial page of this score is most confusing (see *Ex. 1.7*).

The quartet appears to be separate from both the other orchestras, a circumstance emphatically contradicted by the composer's note on seating and clarified to some extent on the second page of the score. This opening page must also be unique in showing four solo lines, each commencing with the remarkable direction *divisi*! Furthermore, in a preface to the score, Vaughan Williams intimates (somewhat benevolently) that the work may be performed without separating the orchestras at all. Thus he suggests that the second orchestra be made up of players from the third desk of each group, whereas in practice it is invariably the second desks which take this line. However, we do see an example of the *divisi* cellos mentioned earlier, the lower line being an octave doubling of the basses and here clearly marked by the composer to be taken by the players nearest to them (the last desk).

A study of the part writing in this magnificent work provides a deep insight into the many different aspects of balance, blend and sound variation achieved by masterly use of division within string groups of differing size. Unfortunately, even such a perfect model as this cannot help anyone sort out the tangled web of division that exists at the beginning of Wagner Prelude to Act 1 of *Lohengrin*. Any solutions deduced from the score (hopelessly unclear in itself) are quickly dashed on the rocks of the printed parts where the lines have been almost casually interspersed between 1sts and 2nds. All attempts at solving this particular maze require some degree of re-writing, and what

Largo sostenuto ♩=56 (♪=112) (♪=♪)
Vl solo I
Vl solo II
Vla solo
Vc solo
Orchestra I
Vl I
Vl II
Vla
Vc (tutti)
Vc (last desk)
DB
Orchestra II
Vl I (1 desk)
Vl II (1 desk)
Vla (1 desk)
Vc (1 desk)
DB (1 player)
div.
unis.
pizz.
arco
pp molto sostenuto
pp
p molto pesante

EX. 1.7

Wagner could possibly have had in mind remains a mystery. Such total confusion is fortunately rare, but the matter of string division should never be taken lightly; even Brahms, in the third movement of his *Symphony no. 2*, seems to presume his viola players capable of double stops on one string, by marking his *divisi* five bars after it becomes essential!

One further example where variations in string division might usefully be introduced comes in the following well-known passage at the end of the slow movement of Dvořák *Symphony no. 9 'From the New World'*.

EX. 1.8

The *divisi* shown decreases from four players, to two players, to one player per part. The use of the second- and third-desk players in the first of these sections means that the two players in the following section do not have to change their sound from one of integral accompaniment, under the cor anglais solo, to one of *soli*. In addition, the accompanying string sound for the cor anglais becomes more distant and less tangible in quality. Of course, if the mutes have been removed by all strings in the previous *fortissimo* section then this principle has to be followed in order to allow the first desk to replace the mutes as marked. But since no score prints *senza sordini* at any point in this movement, the direction for the two solo instruments can be read as a reiteration, rather than a new direction. It is in no way inconceivable that Dvořák intended a *fortissimo* passage to be played by muted strings and, if this is followed, many subtle nuances emerge from the use of different players in these two subsequent *soli* sections.

Passages scored for a small number of string players occur throughout the symphonic repertoire. The first four players of violin, viola and cello and the first two basses will often be called upon to play in some form of small combination, either across the entire strings or confined to one section alone.

The 'double string quintet' required by Dvořák from the fifth bar of *Ex. 1.8* is very effective, but the sound will always be more centred and soloistic than those *pianissimi* that comprise the full section. This is partly because of the acoustic qualities of the instruments themselves, but equally because of the natural change in production that will occur when string players find themselves in any sort of solo capacity. The relatively unaccustomed clarity of each individual sound will inevitably cause an automatic response in production technique, honing the sound towards the fiercely independent personalities of each player's tone and musicianship.

Such a change in approach will most often be obvious in passages of interweaving solo lines where, particularly in the case of inexperienced players, the individual production can become so soloistic that the resultant phrasing and style may be at odds with the often intended simplicity.

Little can, or indeed should, be done about it. But it must be remembered that a passage like that quoted above, however much it might look like a continuous diminution of sound, will actually produce only a progressive change of timbre, especially when it finally reaches just three solo instruments.

Ex. 1.9 from the second part, *Gretchen*, of Liszt *A Faust Symphony*, is typical in this respect, the gentle statement of the theme with its flowing decoration sometimes erring towards an impassioned episode from a concerto for four violins.

EX. 1.9

It can take a lot of patient work to implant the simplicity of the passage without destroying the confidence of individual sound production.

One final aspect of string *soli* needs to be addressed, that of two identical instruments performing a single line in unison without support. This is the worst possible combination of instruments in terms of sound, quality, projection and, especially, intonation. It can only work if one player subdues the sound to an unnatural extent and it is generally shunned by players and interpreters alike. Thus, *Ex. 1.10*, a passage for two cellos from Tchaikovsky *Piano*

Concerto no. 1, is always performed by one instrumentalist unless the soloist absolutely insists otherwise.

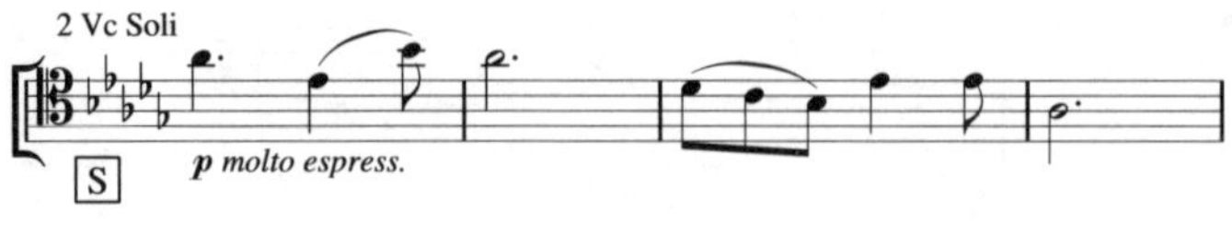

EX. 1.10

Transposition

As has already been mentioned, parts for double basses are always written one octave higher than sounding in order to avoid use of a large number of ledger lines below the bass clef. Conversely, some high cello parts of the Romantic symphonic era retain the historical custom of transposing down an octave when written in the treble clef, though this convention was neither obligatory nor general, and some confusion can result. Dvořák and Smetana in particular are prone to using both systems, sometimes changing from one to another without warning. Careful reading of the parts will usually make the required octave clear, even if both systems are used within the same work.

In *Ex. 1.11* from the third movement of Bruckner *Symphony no. 7*, the appearance of the cello counter-subject apparently pitched a fourth above the 1st violins is evidence enough.

Any attempt to hear this passage at the written octave will quickly dispel any lingering doubts!

Other than these examples for cello and bass, no transposition exists for string instruments unless one or more of the strings is to be specifically

EX. 1.11

EX. 1.11 (contd.)

retuned (*scordatura*, as opposed to the accepted *accordatura*). Under these circumstances it is usual, though not universal, to write for the instrument as if the strings were tuned normally, in order to maintain the automatic connection between the eye and fingers, as is the case with the famous violin solo in the second movement of Mahler *Symphony no. 4* (*Ex. 1.12*).

Strings of Solo Violin to be tuned, one tone sharp, i.e.:

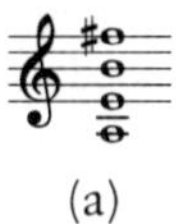

(a)

Written:

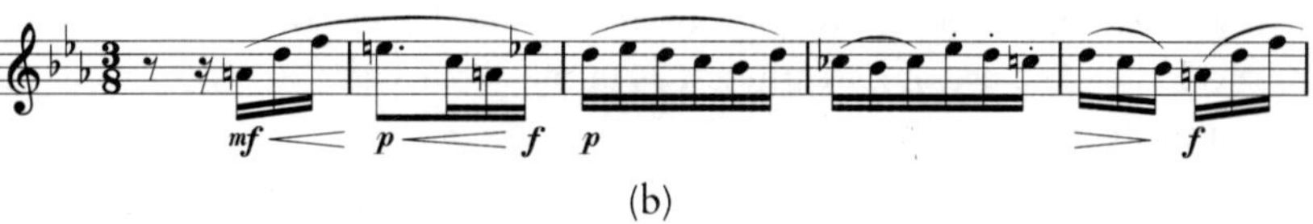

(b)

Sounding:

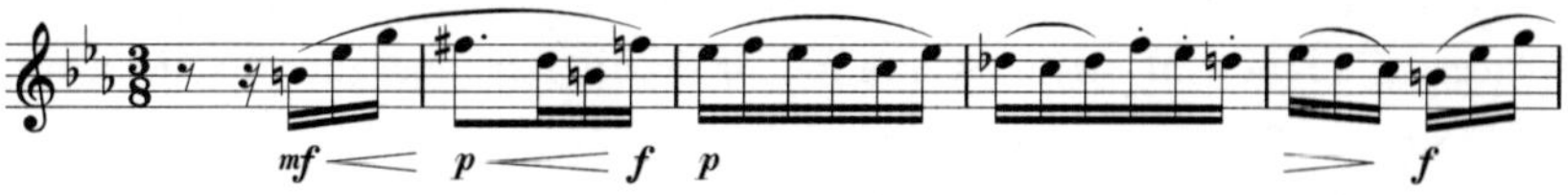

(c)

EX. 1.12

However, writing at pitch will also be found, most usually when only the lowest string has been retuned. *Ex. 1.13*, the well-known 'Sancho Panza' viola solo from Richard Strauss *Don Quixote*, is written in this way, the C string needing to be tuned down to B.

EX. 1.13

Even though the use of the retuned C string is brief in this and the immediately following solo fragments, it is still awkward to read, so automatic is the habit of seeing notes as fingerings.

One small area of occasional confusion with regard to notes written below the normal range of string instruments is when they appear in the parts purely in order to provide an unbroken phrase and are not intended to be played. Perhaps the clearest example of their use is here in Richard Strauss *Metamorphosen*.

EX. 1.14

The impossibility of excluding the F♯ from the Violin line in a phrase such as this is self-evident, even though no attempt can be made to play it. As in many other cases, the substitution of a rest would elicit an entirely different musical line. The use of parentheses, as in the above example, is common but not obligatory.

The Marking of Orchestral Parts

This chapter ends with a brief examination of the one remaining indirect aspect of orchestral string technique of particular relevance to the youth orchestra.

The pencilled addition, alteration and removal of bowings, phrasings, slurs and similar markings made by the players during rehearsal can use up much valuable time. Even the simplest adjustment of a dynamic mark can bring things to a halt while players go through the laborious ritual of deciding which desk partner shall mark it, exactly how and where and, far too often, whose pencil to borrow in order to do it. It is the least considered rehearsal technique and, paradoxically, the most regularly performed. No bowing, fingering, passage or style will be repeated as often as this one ill-considered technique and it is essential in determining speed and accuracy in rehearsal, as well as confidence and success in concert. But it does, like so much else, have to be thought out.

It was once remarked that of the three essential objects any musician must carry, only one could possibly be omitted – the instrument! The other two (pencil and eraser) are far too important to the performance. Undeniably preferable is that all three are remembered and kept together at all times (every instrument case has some small space where they can be housed) and it is unfortunate that the design of so many music stands overlooks the provision of a secondary shelf for the retention of these items when not in use.

To the second player on each desk (the inside player if the orchestra sits with all Principals on the side nearest the audience) falls the task of marking the part and turning the pages, the others having responsibility only to play. With the exception of the Principals themselves, who are ultimately responsible for the uniformity of each section's performance, this is true of all the desks in each of the sections. Much help can and, indeed, must be forthcoming from their 'outside' partners with regard to the exact change of bow needed, other passages to which it might apply, isolated notes that remain unclear, etc. Even when the rehearsal has to stop for a major change of bowing it is better that one player marks the part while the other checks it, or quietly demonstrates the necessary changes, it being far easier to remember a bowing physically than visually.

In all circumstances the old bowing should be erased first and not just contradicted by heavier and more insistent marking, and then replaced clearly in soft pencil that will not leave an indelible impression on the page. To arrive at a passage in concert and find two opposite bowings over every note is confusing and can be fatally distracting. It is not necessary to mark every note, only the changes that are not immediately apparent and those where the automatic reaction would be one of opposite direction – up-bow accents for example. Over-marked parts are worse than those with no marks at all and detract from more important symbols of dynamic and style.

2 WOODWIND

The difficulty in defining which instruments are commonly referred to as 'woodwind' was highlighted on one occasion when I was working with a youth orchestra and the normal section was extended to include a trio of saxophones. At the first individual sectional rehearsals, the three young players involved were unsure whether they were expected to attend with the woodwind, the brass or a completely separate tutoring for them alone. Although more experienced players would automatically have considered themselves part of the woodwind groups the necessity to explain the somewhat tenuous family connection to these particular instrumentalists underlined the unquestioning ease with which we accept the term. Woodwind instruments are not all made of wood, neither is their sound produced in all cases by the use of reeds. Perhaps the negative definition put forward by Walter Piston[1] is the most accurate: '*Rather than attempt to justify a nomenclature accepted by custom let us distinguish the brass as being those whose tones are produced by vibration of the lips held against a cup-shaped mouthpiece. Other orchestral wind instruments are woodwinds.*'

The normal basic requirement for a complete section is two each of flutes, oboes, clarinets and bassoons, although the regular inclusion of piccolo, cor anglais, bass clarinet and contrabassoon in repertoire of the late nineteenth century onwards makes the arrangement of the 'triple wind' section an almost obligatory consideration for youth and student orchestras.

Seating

In the symphony orchestra it is now universally accepted that the traditional seating for the woodwind, in a group placed centrally and immediately behind the strings, is the most successful. Major variations on this are very rare, although most have been tried at one time or another. The players' overall ability to project, blend, balance and hear one another is best served when they are placed in two rows with flutes and oboes in the front, slightly raised above the level of the strings, and clarinets and bassoons preferably raised still

1 *Orchestration*, Gollancz, London, 1973, p. 114.

further behind them. The addition of the extra related instruments to each section is made on the outside of the lines so that the quartet of 1st players remain as close as possible to one another, with their respective 2nd players always immediately next to them. As will be seen, it is vitally important that this close positioning of the sections of similar instruments is maintained under all circumstances, in order that their balance is most easily accomplished.

A triple wind section will, therefore, be seated in the following manner.

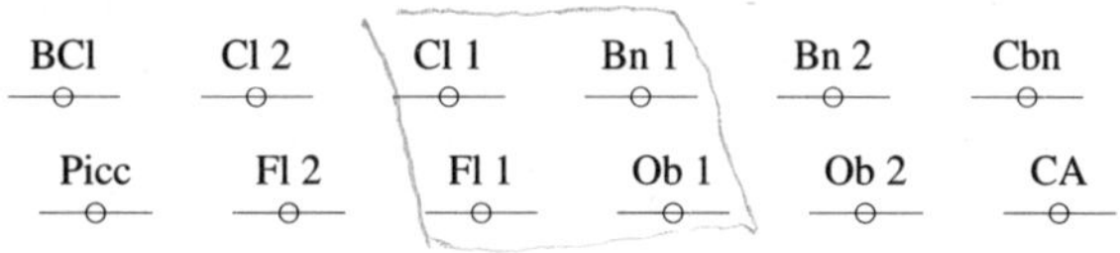

BCl	Cl 2	Cl 1	Bn 1	Bn 2	Cbn
Picc	Fl 2	Fl 1	Ob 1	Ob 2	CA

Fig. 2.1

A slight off-set of the back row is necessary for a clear view of the conductor, but the one shown here has a far more important reason: it brings 2nd bassoon – the base of the harmony and tonal anchor of the woodwind section – as near as possible to 1st flute, most often the top, and also allows 1st bassoon to be heard equally clearly by 1st oboe and 1st flute. Much octave doubling between some or all of the four 1st instruments will be found in most scores, and the lowest pitch (bassoon) must be absolutely clear to the other players for accuracy of intonation. As can be seen from *Fig. 2.1*, were the back row to off-set in the opposite direction, moving 1st bassoon to the other side of 1st oboe, then 1st flute would find itself basing octave intonation on 1st clarinet or 1st oboe; in either case one stage removed from its source.

The off-set of the back row in *Fig. 2.1* shows an even amount of space between each player for clarity of the diagram; in practice both the 2nd bassoon and 2nd clarinet may be nearer their respective 1st players, producing a still tighter block. True alternate seating will involve too great a distance between the players to be tolerated.

It is, unfortunately, impossible to continue any consideration of woodwind sections with regard to youth and student orchestras without addressing the thorny problem of augmentation. In ideal circumstances this would not arise. However, since the concept of more than one player to a part is widespread within many young orchestras and, outside of the specialist conservatoires, shows no immediate tendency to decline, it is necessary to discuss the situation here, especially in view of its effect on balance and intonation.

Reasons for its existence need to be examined before any further discussion of individual players may be undertaken or basic concepts of orchestral woodwind playing understood. It is not to be confused with the importation of extra players for musical reasons, sometimes practised by professional orchestras at the insistence of some conductors for particular repertoire. The problem peculiar to the young orchestra is the deliberate invitation of more players than necessary, resulting in what might more truthfully be termed 'duplication'.

DUPLICATION

Without doubt, limiting numbers in the woodwind section to two or three players of each instrument causes considerable difficulties to those responsible for the allocation of positions and the choosing of personnel for youth and student orchestras. Next to the strings, the woodwind include some of the most popular instruments, and there have always been many more applicants than opportunities, a situation that would seem unlikely to change in the immediate future. However, it must be stated at the outset that there exists in this section no musical reason whatsoever for the provision of players superfluous to those requested by a composer for a particular work. The use of an extra player to take some of the weight of playing from the Principals, a practice often adopted in the horn and brass sections, is unheard of in the woodwind section, and where extra players are available they will never be used for this purpose. And yet it seems that the availability of two or even three players to a part is a regular feature of many youth orchestras and is fast becoming something of a tradition.

The arguments for and against involving a larger number of students than would normally be possible are intense and personal, those in favour ranging from essential experience for younger players to emergency cover in case of illness. All contain certain logical criteria on paper (although why they should be levelled at this section alone is something of a mystery) but none confronts the problem of what to do with the players once they are there. Obviously they cannot be allowed to play every note. The doubling of solo wind lines is not even worth considering in relation to present performing standards. It is possible in a large area of the Romantic and later repertoire to double some of the playing in the louder *tutti* sections, but only in carefully chosen passages, giving only limited scope to these extra instrumentalists. It cannot be contemplated in anything approaching Classical repertoire, or in any concerto, where the balance and ensemble are too critical to the soloist to put at risk, even in the *tutti* passages.

The only available alternative is to change the personnel of the section for various pieces within the programme, which almost certainly means performing the major work of the concert with some players not even on stage. For young players this is very disappointing and dispiriting and should be avoided if at all possible. In any case, while one section might have enough quality players to consider alternating the Principal, another may not, and it is invidious to make one section change round while another performs the entire programme. The whole wretched business tends to leave the conductor (or, more likely, the section tutor) the distasteful task of choosing the people to be left out – the very job the organizer so carefully avoided at the auditions!

Clearly, from the point of view of both the music and orchestral morale, neither alternative has a lot to recommend it and the least damaging answer would seem to be a mixture of the two. It is reasonable to assume that the scoring of the major (and therefore probably last) piece of the programme will accommodate some careful doubling, in which case the full quota of players may be used. Elsewhere a cautious exchange of players may be considered, though it is difficult enough to mould one balanced wind section, let alone two or even three within the same rehearsal time. The whole situation is fraught with problems.

It is very unlikely that a group of players will be automatically interchangeable, and it is inadvisable to display a noticeably weaker section in the same concert as a stronger one. It is also dangerous to include one or two Principals who cannot hold their own against the others, especially if there is someone sitting by who can. Furthermore, the apparently more modest demands on particular wind players in some of the smaller-scale repertoire can actually be far higher than those of the symphony or major work of the programme. A miscalculation here can lead to untold strain upon the player concerned and to the possibility of having to rearrange the section after rehearsals have begun – an unnecessarily disheartening experience for young players.

It is not intended to give the impression that the problems of doubling cannot be resolved: they can, and sometimes quite successfully. But if the matter has not been addressed at the auditions, and duplicate players specifically chosen, then it falls to the wind tutors to assess quickly and accurately the standard and potential of each instrumentalist and how the interests of the individual as well as the group might best be served.

The duplicated section is not without inherent difficulties both for the players and the conductor. It can only be considered with regard to the main instruments – flute, oboe, clarinet and bassoon. No doubling of cor anglais, bass clarinet or E♭ clarinet should be contemplated, nor even that of the less soloistic parts sometimes found for piccolo. The contrabassoon, probably the least familiar of all the extra wind (very few players have anything like regular access to an instrument), can sometimes be doubled discreetly by a third bassoon at the octave above, but the balance of chording is likely to be upset unless this is handled very carefully. It takes a lot of skill to play quietly enough not to be obvious, yet firmly enough to be of some help.

The seating of an enlarged section must ensure that no player comes between the instruments of the main section, however large it may be, or impedes their ability to hear one another clearly at all times. For this reason the extra players have to be placed outside the main group, with copies and music stands of their own. *Fig 2.2* shows a triple wind section set out in this way, but the same rule applies whatever number of instruments of each family the work requires.

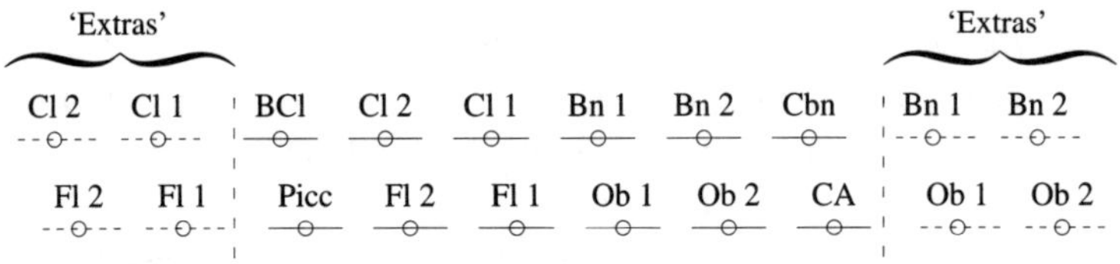

'Extras' 'Extras'

Cl 2 Cl 1 | BCl Cl 2 Cl 1 Bn 1 Bn 2 Cbn | Bn 1 Bn 2

Fl 2 Fl 1 | Picc Fl 2 Fl 1 Ob 1 Ob 2 CA | Ob 1 Ob 2

Fig. 2.2

No alternative seating will give the section the required control of balance, ensemble and intonation. The fact that it makes life slightly more difficult for the extra players has to be accepted, but it does have the advantage of increasing their self-reliance and technique of working in pairs. An awkward situation arises if the additional players comprise an uneven number (or, worse still, if it is just one lone player of a particular instrument), as they will then tend to feel isolated and dissociated from their colleagues, quite apart from the fact that the doubling of a single line is undesirable. In this circumstance it is usually better for everyone if doubling is avoided altogether.

The conductor must address the problem of how to contact, encourage and help the extra players, as their involvement is almost certainly limited to sections of the work where the woodwind are not predominant. It is all too easy to cover a whole series of rehearsals without having made a single comment specifically relevant to any one of them, and a contrived opportunity will certainly be recognized for what it is. While this may not be considered a major drawback to their inclusion, it is important that all members of an orchestra feel their own contribution to be musically necessary.

The most noticeable effect of the duplicated section on the players themselves can be seen immediately following rehearsals where, in my experience, it is much more rare to find players checking intonation or phrasing of their own volition than in sections of one player per part. Such an intimation of attitude will usually divulge far more than can be gleaned by other means.

The question of superfluous woodwind players is most successfully resolved in the national youth orchestras, where many players of a comparable standard are available and (probably the most important aspect) are all aware of the situation long in advance of the first rehearsal. The indefensible practice of rehearsing oversize sections and then cutting them down on, or immediately prior to, the day of the concert having long since vanished.

Reference to the woodwind section from here on may be taken to mean one composed of single players to a part, unless clearly stated otherwise.

Forming the Section

Although a wide choice of players is not always available, some general consideration of the attributes necessary for the main woodwind seats might prove helpful.

FLUTE

In the flutes it is not uncommon to be spoilt for choice as far as dexterity and instrumental facility are concerned, but less often for control, sound and projection. While agility and brilliance are obviously essential, these last three are the determining factors for a 1st flute, the long phrased, *legato* solo occurring frequently, as in this famous example from the second movement of Tchaikovsky *Piano Concerto no. 1 op. 23.*[1]

EX. 2.1

This first statement of the main theme, accompanied by muted *pizzicato* strings alone, requires superb control of breath, sound and projection. In common with many apparently simple passages which exploit the lucid tranquillity so natural to this instrument, this phrase conceals a multitude of pitfalls for the inexpert performer.

1 The third note (F♮) of this phrase differs in all scores from that of the answering statement by the solo piano, where it appears as B♭. Some soloists will request that it be changed to correspond.

Nonetheless, the most common deficiency to be found in the young or inexperienced flute player will always remain that of powerful articulation. The sheer energy that should characterize every note of *Ex. 2.2*, the opening of Stravinsky *Petrouchka*, is fundamental to its performance.

EX. 2.2

Over and above such instrumental skills the frequent scoring of the instrument on the top of the harmonic line requires a very sensitive ear for intonation and balance, and an ability to listen past the more immediate centre of the chording to the fundamental must be cultivated. It is easy to become accustomed to playing on top of the full woodwind line and expect everyone else to adjust accordingly. Equally, it is very important that the player should be able to produce (and project) a big sound in the lower regions of the instrument, an area much exploited by the late-Romantic composers.

For the 2nd flute, sensitivity to close partnership and, as in all 2nd players, strength and flexibility of supporting sound (especially in the first octave of the instrument) may be added to a solid technique. The creative qualities of soloistic playing are not so necessary here but the ability to recognize them

EX. 2.3

and enhance their quality is vital. This short, often-quoted phrase from Ravel *Ma mère l'oye* (*Ex.* 2.3) clearly illustrates this and many other aspects of 2nd flute playing.

The calm simplicity apparent in this phrase when played really well is easily ruined by insensitive movement, balance, phrasing or breathing on the part of the 2nd player. All the confidence of free production that 1st flute requires may be determined here by the ability of the 2nd.

OBOE

Of all orchestral instruments, the oboe is the least able to cover deficiencies in production or to disguise immaturity in sound. Its presence within the texture is always noticeable and the poignancy inherent in much of its solo work is only available through the skilful colouring and control of pure tone. This takes a long time to acquire, and thus variations in type of sound and development between different players can be extremely wide, and the youth orchestra cannot be relied upon to produce with regularity a player of mature and outstanding technique in this respect. Although there have always been some remarkably talented young players, their number will remain severely limited.

Solos such as that which opens the slow movement of Brahms *Violin Concerto op. 77* are quite impossible to contemplate with anything but a mature and musically sensitive instrumentalist capable of extreme control and fluency (a talent essential to every other woodwind player in this particular circumstance). However, in less demanding situations, much can be achieved in a short space of time when the personality and approach of the players permit it and it is incumbent on the conductor and tutors to foster the confidence and soloistic conception of the sound at all times. If there is one player who has the most influence upon the concentration and attitude of the woodwind from within the section, it is the 1st oboe, and the quiet strength of a musically confident personality is of great benefit here. Much of the dynamic control and ensemble of the corporate section centres around the other players' awareness of, and sensitivity to, this line and even young players can exercise a considerable degree of control.

Quite apart from musical considerations, the two oboes must be of positive help to one another, the idiosyncrasies of their instrument being unlike any other. Reeds dry or suddenly feel uncomfortable; notes can mis-produce or fail altogether at the most inopportune moments; and if the two players are not supportive and sensitive to one another, or the 2nd harbours desires of usurping the 1st position, disaster looms. The 2nd oboe needs fully to appreciate the difficulties of the 1st part, and where musical support is sought and needed. Again, obvious qualities of soloistic potential are not as necessary as secure control and sensitivity.

The 2nd oboe part often incorporates difficulties which, especially on a modern instrument, can severely test a young player. The Czech repertoire in particular not only frequently requires the instrument to play very softly in a low register but also demands more often than not that it enter unobtrusively at this same pitch. Examples abound but the opening of the second movement of Dvořák *Symphony no. 7* is notorious.

EX. 2.4

The lower register of the oboe, unlike the flute, displays a natural increase in sound, and is extremely difficult to control in soft playing, especially where the level and attack are determined by an instrument as flexible as the clarinet. The layout of the chord, almost a full octave below the solo, and the immediate placing of the oboe on the exposed fifth add extra problems soon to be compounded by the *pianissimo* of the third bar. A superb professional section will immediately focus the listening ear to the clarinet before the fact of its being the solo line is made obvious by the theme, and this will be contrived by the balance, level and quality of the other three instruments. This passage demonstrates one instance of why this particular symphony may not be considered ideal repertoire for the average youth orchestra.

CLARINET

The 1st clarinet will often be among the most extrovert personalities of the woodwind section, the versatility of the instrument and its suitability for many differing styles of music having influenced its initial choice in many cases. Its wide dynamic range throughout all registers and its unique ability to blend in the most unlikely combinations have inspired a rich and varied chamber music repertoire. This, coupled with the availability of the E♭ clarinet, bass clarinet and all the saxophones with little extra tuition, provides clarinettists with a plethora of musical opportunities, and can account for their somewhat soloistically orientated approach to much of their playing.

Most young players pass through a phase of feeling that it is incumbent upon them to 'do something musical' with almost every phrase. This tendency usually coincides with the period of their membership of a youth or student orchestra and can be quite disconcerting as it is most often confined to the elongation of long notes, rushing of *arpeggios*, and a noticeable reluctance to leave the velvet tones of the lower register. (If there were to be a Valhalla for these young players it would surely consist of playing the opening bars of Rossini overture to *William Tell* transcribed for five clarinets.) But it is the control of inherent *rubato* that is most often required of the young clarinettist, and this natural tendency, properly applied, is sometimes capable of providing the most illustrative and subtle phrasing of the entire woodwind section.

For both players, the comprehensive dynamic range of the instrument makes sensitivity to changes in balance vital. Much of the time the basic level of the wind group is out of their hands, being dependent upon the positioning of other instruments within the chord and the dynamic limitations these impose. The ability to relate the printed dynamic to the relevant orchestration is essential, and inexperienced clarinettists will find themselves under-playing or over-playing with disturbing regularity, often within the same passage. The situation is made no easier by the frequency with which many composers require the 1st clarinet to change roles, from melodic solo to thematic accompaniment to chordal texture and back again, often in the space of one short phrase. A player equipped solely with a brash technique will be of no use to this position.

A natural 2nd clarinet is even more difficult to find, for much of the 1st player's earthbound practicality must be influenced from here, and the 2nd player must also be able to move in perfect harmony through the solo duets that exist for the two instruments. This famous example from Mendelssohn *Hebrides*, where in order to balance successfully, the 2nd player usually finds it necessary to produce a little *more* sound than the 1st, is never easy:

EX. 2.5

Many 2nd clarinet parts demand dexterity and tone production equal to that of the 1st player, frequently repeating the same agile phrase or accompanying it with an awkward and fast-moving figuration. There can be no noticeable difference between the two in the clarinet variation from Britten *Young Person's Guide to the Orchestra*, for example. No two woodwind instruments are required to be so interchangeable in one aspect and so diverse in another.

BASSOON

The low pitch and relatively limited dynamic range of the bassoon have conspired to divide its orchestral use into two separate and distinct tasks. For much of the time it may be found either providing or doubling the lower line of harmony, or adding inner voices to low strings or horns, blending equally, in chameleon-like fashion, with both. Then it is required to take on almost the entire burden of characterization in pieces where the scenario is set around its unique tonal qualities. Nor is this confined to the comic character so easily associated with the instruments; even the magically empowered broomstick in Dukas *L'Apprenti-Sorcier* has a malevolent demeanour as it comes back to life. Both the pomposity and the pitiful search for self-respect in Elgar *Falstaff* and the incredible quality of primeval desolation in the famous opening of Stravinsky *The Rite of Spring* are hardly available to any other instrument.

That Tchaikovsky first realized the potential of the dark side of the instrument is evident in his elevation of it as his prime weapon of emotional despair. It is entrusted with the opening paragraph of both the tormented *Manfred Symphony* and the more sinister *Sixth*, the first statement of the restless theme of the *Fifth*, and it appears immediately to temper the confident fanfare at the beginning of the apparently optimistic *Fourth*.

Using the bassoon in this way, whether alone or in pairs, tends to make the solos long and taxing, and even to exaggerate their importance because of their intrinsic relevance to the mood of the piece. Less immediately noticeable is the dexterous playing required of the instrument when complementing the bass line, most particularly in music of the Classical era. Here the speed of tonguing and inordinate length of phrases, with scant opportunity to breathe, can pass almost unnoticed, but is a common aspect of writing in this style. Both players need to have developed a sound overall technique and a solid sense of rhythm to cope with either of these extremes. Of all the wind instruments, the demands made upon the bassoons can be most easily underestimated.

Fast solos also exist for one or both bassoons in more recent repertoire, especially that of the twentieth century, where it is often exposed and characteristic of the lighter style of the instrument. Nonetheless, few players would expect to come across a passage so unforgivingly awkward as the famous example from Ravel *Piano Concerto in G* more often than rarely.

EX. 2.6

The position of 2nd bassoon is one of the most responsible in the orchestra, for however unsuited to the role the instrument might be, it provides the basis of intonation for the woodwind section. There is no possibility of the top of the chord being in tune if its base is not and the vagaries of intonation in certain registers of the higher instruments make life extremely difficult for this player. Bassoons, especially in the low register, tend to be pitched a fraction sharp to aid brightness and penetration, but to allow this to influence the bass of the harmony will give disastrous results. Much of the time the bass note must be held down in pitch so that the top of the chord, three or even four octaves above, may sound in tune. A clear and reliable sound on which the other instruments may set their intonation and balance is a prerequisite.

In common with the other 2nd players, musical and personal rapport with the Principal is important, but more crucially, he or she must assume responsibility for the confidence and security of the whole woodwind section.

It has become clear that all the woodwind Principals are finally dependent on the sensitivity and support of their 2nd players. The phrasing and line of solo passages can be implanted effectively in an intelligent instrumentalist, but the less tangible qualities of support and accompaniment are much more difficult to influence. Often the ideal 2nd player would not necessarily make an ideal 1st, and may even be unsuited to the spotlight of sustained solo playing. The young instrumentalist sometimes finds it hard to grasp this fact of orchestral life, the lure of the 1st seat being all important, but an underlying principle must be understood and kept in mind at all times: there is not just a number of examples of each instrument in a woodwind section; there is a specified number of separate and uniquely demanding parts for each instrument.

THE TRIPLE WIND SECTION

In the scores of many twentieth-century composers in particular, the triple wind section might well consist simply of three examples of each of the instruments mentioned above. However, more usually it will comprise two of each standard instrument plus one closely associated relative, and it is these instruments which must now be considered. Although the complete section of twelve instrumentalists does not appear regularly before the latter portion of the nineteenth century, many examples exist of one or more related instruments being added to the Classical section.

The piccolo and contrabassoon appear in isolated instances as early as Mozart. Beethoven uses both in the *Fifth* and *Ninth Symphonies* and instances of their use thereafter increase, until the former becomes almost indispensable. In the Classical writing of the German symphonic tradition both instruments are used mainly as extensions to the range of the woodwind in *tutti* scoring or wide orchestration of woodwind and brass. The penetration, agility and brilliance of the piccolo, however, quickly took it to a more soloistic and specialist role. The famous solo in the *Scherzo* of Tchaikovsky *Symphony no. 4* for example never fails to get a shuffle of approval from colleagues in the orchestra, as does the far less virtuosic but horrendously difficult sustained solo at the end of the first movement of Shostakovich *Symphony no. 10*.

Such examples have tended to make the instrument the province of a single designated player, even though most flautists will own a piccolo and be perfectly capable of playing it. Many composers will take its availability for granted, and think nothing of using it as an instrument of convenience, assigning it to whichever player has the most time to take it out of his pocket. Two isolated bars exist in the third movement of Dvořák *Symphony no. 7* for example, apparently just to cover a top C, without the instrument being listed or more than three seconds allowed for its preparation.

Although the cor anglais (or English horn) is a direct descendant of instruments used by composers of the Baroque period and even earlier, its addition to the symphony orchestra wind section may be taken from the late 1820s, where it appears as a solo instrument in works such as Rossini *William Tell* and Berlioz *Symphonie Fantastique*, where it was not incorporated into the textures of the wind section as a whole. On both these occasions it appears as a doubling instrument for 2nd oboe, but this practice is no longer general and nowadays the official cor anglais is usually the third member of the section, a player who will specialize in all the major solos for the instrument. It was only much later in the century that the position of the cor anglais as an integral part of the oboe section began to be realized and its subtle addition of colour to the woodwind texture fully exploited.

As for the bass clarinet, it is as an infinitely versatile bass to the whole wind section that it comes into its own with its dark, velvet sound and extraordinary dynamic range, coupled with agility throughout the compass. It can perform all the various tasks assigned to it with equal success, from exposed solos to supporting the sound of a large orchestra almost single-handed, though its appearance is probably less frequent than the other three extra woodwinds.

All four of these instruments tend now ideally to be the province of a specialized player. Although the general layout and fingerings are very closely related across the 'family' of instruments, the embouchures required, especially with regard to cor anglais and bass clarinet, are quite different, as is the feel of the instrument in terms of its response and fluency in particular registers. Much of the reason for avoiding doubling is so that the lip tension need not be upset. It also allows opportunity to keep the instrument warmed and prepared during periods where it is not actually playing.

In student orchestras the first difficulty caused by the addition of these instruments, with the exception of piccolo, is that of availability, since very few young players have an instrument of their own and are therefore unfamiliar with the idiosyncrasies of the particular example they may be required to use. It is difficult enough to play the cor anglais solo in Berlioz *Le Carnaval Romain* without having to attempt it on a sub-standard instrument that has passed through the hands of countless other students and has probably only been available for a few days' practice. Such circumstances place an undesirable burden upon players least able to cope with it. In the case of the cor anglais, bass clarinet and contrabassoon, the instrument should be lent to the player as far in advance of a concert as possible.

Solos apart, the addition both of cor anglais and bass clarinet to the young woodwind section can be helpful to the aural perception of balance and integration for all the players. The most immediate and perceptible change in texture will often be that of a more homogeneous orchestration which provides a compact harmonic layout. This more even distribution of the notes within the harmony can make balance and intonation easier to feel and also less dependent upon the relative timbre of different instruments spaced at wide intervals.

Franck *Symphony in D minor*, which adds these two instruments alone to a standard double wind section, is instructive in helping a student section to appreciate the need to listen to one another for blend and balance and to become aware of the requirements of the other players around them. Apart from being a very good work in itself, the many examples of inspired woodwind scoring it contains allow the section to hear varied aspects of balance and ensemble in circumstances which they can understand and which are immediately apparent.

In recent years this symphony has received criticism from many quarters for being too overtly chromatic and over-scored. The first opinion is a matter of personal taste – although one that the performing musician should never use as an excuse for neglect – but the second is a thoughtless observation. The confusion of 'doubling' with 'combining different sounds' is one that is made all too frequently. For this symphony to sound thick and heavy is both unnecessary and indicative of a faulty reading of the score, where the multiple variations of wind writing and the careful blend of instrumentation are quite apparent.

Infrequent Additions to the Woodwind

Many composers will require the addition of one or more less familiar instruments to the woodwind section in order to extend the range or provide particular orchestral colour. In the youth orchestra, the problem of availability usually outweighs that of finding a capable player as, in most cases, the performance techniques are very similar to the related instruments and the fingering almost always the same. Provided that the designated player has access to the instrument for long enough to become familiar with its particular idiosyncrasies, such rarities need not involve the services of a specialist performer.

FLUTE FAMILY: ALTO FLUTE

In the flute family, the gorgeous alto flute (sometimes referred to as the bass flute or flute in G) will occasionally be added, one most notable example being in the second suite of Ravel *Daphnis et Chloé*. This instrument sounds a fourth lower than the normal flute and, in common with all additional instruments to the woodwind section, is usually placed on the end of the line (there exists little opportunity for any variation in seating in this case as the instrument itself takes up so much lateral space).

The above instance confines the instrument exclusively to one player but many other composers treat it as a doubling instrument. Britten, in the *Sinfonia da Requiem* for example, requires 3rd flute to double both alto flute and piccolo. In the student orchestra this is neither necessary nor desirable as it provides opportunity for an extra player.

Although the term 'bass flute' will generally be found misappropriated to the 'alto flute in G', there does also exist a true bass flute in C, sounding one octave below the normal concert instrument, for which both Puccini and Mascagni wrote parts. It would have been helpful if the term had been reserved for this instrument alone, but instances where the name has been mistakenly applied should be obvious by the necessary transposition of the part – even if 'in G' has been omitted from the instrumental listing.

OBOE FAMILY: OBOE D'AMORE, BASS OBOE AND HECKELPHONE

Once again it is in the scoring of Ravel that the youth orchestra is most likely to encounter one of the rarest of all visitors – the oboe d'amore. The short passage in *Boléro* for this 'alto oboe', where it also appears in harmony with its two relations, the oboe and cor anglais, is scored as a doubling instrument for the 2nd player and, in this instance, must be so. Not only is the part too small for a separate player to be worthwhile but the harmonic relationship of the part – placed between oboe and cor anglais – makes it impossible for the player to be seated anywhere else. Though this instrument was regularly used in music of the Baroque period, occasions of its re-employment in the symphony orchestra are limited but it is sufficiently similar to the oboe (being pitched only a minor third lower) to be, at least mechanically, of little problem to the player. However, doubling on the instrument cannot be treated casually, as it is notorious for problems of intonation and, as with all related instruments of any group, belies its apparent similarity by virtue of a noticeably different feel and response.

A wonderful part exists for the instrument in Richard Strauss *Symphonia Domestica*, where inspired variations in the scoring of the accompaniment allow it to sound at its most mellow.

The bass oboe is a development of the heckelphone (see below) and it sounds one octave lower than the standard oboe. The magnetic attraction for British youth orchestras of Holst *The Planets* makes the instrument more of a familiar figure than would otherwise be the case. In this score it appears as a doubling instrument for 3rd oboe, but it should certainly be considered as an extra part and the player seated on the outside edge of the row. In passages such as *Ex.* 2.7 this positioning would make more sense of the harmonic context.

EX. 2.7

The fingering is the same as for the oboe so, once more, it is the slightly changed embouchure and feel of the instrument that pose the main difficulties for doubling. Perhaps also, especially in youth orchestras, availability of the instrument becomes a further consideration in the limitation of its use.

The heckelphone was invented by Wilhelm Heckel in 1904 and was first used orchestrally a year later, by Richard Strauss, in *Salome* and subsequently in *Elektra*. It is actually the bass instrument of what was originally conceived as a new family of woodwind instruments but the others, as far as one can determine, were never written for. It is a cross between bass oboe and bassoon, having a vast bore and using a very similar reed to the bassoon. Many parts exist for the instrument – Copland *Symphony no. 2* (*'Short Symphony'*) and the Henze opera *The English Cat* both contain notable examples – and nowadays the correct instrument is always used. The heckelphone and the bass oboe are not interchangeable, even though it may appear that the former was a German and the latter an English promotion of roughly corresponding timbres.

CLARINET FAMILY: E♭ CLARINET, C CLARINET, BASSET HORN, CONTRABASS CLARINET AND SAXOPHONES

The clarinet family is unique in that two instruments are in general use, the B♭ and the A, and are freely interchanged by the player. The complete list of clarinets runs to twelve, or possibly even more, and comprises: 3 sopraninos in A♭, E♭, and D; 4 sopranos in C, B, B♭ and A; 1 alto in E♭; 1 tenor (the basset horn) in F; 2 bass in B♭ and A, and one contrabass in B♭. Many of these instruments are now virtually obsolete but the list is included here in order to facilitate understanding of the relationship of pitches and the appearance of so many transpositions in orchestral scores (consideration of this will be made at the end of this section).

Of the sopranino instruments, the E♭ has now almost universally replaced the other two and plays all the parts originally required of them. Indeed, so regular is its inclusion in the modern symphony orchestra that, in normal circumstances, it need no longer be considered an infrequent visitor. However, the instrument requires a little more familiarity and specialization than many family relations. The very cramped finger position of such a small instrument needs practice, as does the change in embouchure occasioned by the small reed and mouthpiece.

Most orchestral uses of the E♭ clarinet exploit the very high register, putting considerable strain upon the player's embouchure (and temperament) for this is the area of the instrument most likely to break and squeak. An equable, even fatalistic personality is required for this position, because misfortune is forever at hand. Unless the part is extremely small, use of the E♭ as a doubling instrument is to be avoided for the reasons mentioned above; far more considerate to the section is the use of a separate player wherever possible.

Nowadays, the genuine C clarinet is making a welcome return to the orchestra, especially for use in the parts written for it by Rossini, Schubert and Richard Strauss. Modern examples of the instrument are considerably more reliable than their predecessors in terms of intonation, and the slightly 'thinner' sound of the instrument is much more appropriate in the orchestration of these works. (It was never scored by accident!) If offered, its availability should be seized upon.

The basset horn (or basset clarinet) is the orchestral version of the alto clarinet and is sometimes referred to as 'alto clarinet in F'. Its orchestral appearances are rare but, accepting the range of repertoire now encountered by the student orchestra, Mozart's use of it in his *Requiem*, the opera *The Magic Flute* and other works makes its consideration necessary. It mostly appears as a doubling instrument for 1st or 2nd clarinet, depending on the number required, but can also be found as a totally separate part, most notably in Richard Strauss first *Sonatina for Wind Instruments* where it is referred to by the Italian title 'corno di bassetto'. Again, performance on the instrument may be undertaken by any competent clarinettist but high quality instruments are rare.

The vision of a contrabass clarinet (pedal clarinet) was at one time restricted almost entirely to performances of Schoenberg *Five Orchestral Pieces* but has lately appeared in sufficient new scores to warrant inclusion here. Pitched one octave below the bass clarinet, its sound is surprisingly rich and sonorous, and it makes a natural addition to the low woodwind line. It is not difficult for anyone who has had experience of the bass clarinet and instruments can be found, making avoidance of performing works that might include it quite unwarranted.

Strictly speaking, saxophones should be included in a family of their own, so individual is their sound and so distinctive the materials used in their manufacture. However, the use of a single reed suffices to classify them as woodwind instruments, and the similarity of the mouthpiece ensures that many clarinettists will play them. Nonetheless, the situation is not as straightforward as with the genuinely related instruments. In addition to a considerable change of embouchure the saxophone employs a different fingering system from the clarinet, its 'octave key' raising the pitch of fingered notes by one octave, rather than the universal twelfth of the clarinet family.

There are four main instruments of the group: the soprano in B♭, alto in E♭, tenor in B♭ and baritone in E♭, although Ravel (once more in *Boléro*) writes for sopranino in F. This particular part, however, is perfectly possible, and usually performed, on the soprano B♭.

Most orchestral use of the instrument involves the inclusion of just one player, often for a clearly featured solo, as is the case for E♭ alto in Ravel's orchestration of Mussorgsky *Pictures from an Exhibition*, or B♭ tenor in Prokofiev *Lieutenant Kijé*, but a trio comprising alto, tenor and baritone is required in Gershwin *An American in Paris*, and a most unusual quartet of soprano, alto, baritone and bass in C by Richard Strauss in *Symphonia Domestica*.

In the context of the youth orchestra it would be heartening to think that such repertoire could give valuable opportunity to a group of instrumentalists who might otherwise never experience playing in an orchestra but in reality this can rarely be done, the young saxophonist who has known no other instrument being usually too inexperienced in even the most basic rigours of ensemble playing. Much more likely is the clarinettist who also plays sax, or someone who considers the two instruments as a joint main study.

Their positioning, either singly or as a group, is to the right of the clarinets, immediately adjoining bass clarinet or whichever instrument is last in line. In the case of more than one, this extreme extension of the line can lead to difficulties of sight-line, most regularly through to the horns, in which case the saxophones may be slightly separated or even lowered in relation to the clarinets with no adverse effect upon their sound. Intonation is always suspect, mainly because of the way the instrument is generally played and the type of *vibrato* associated with it, but it is rarely used in a situation of direct doubling or chordal support. The last chord of *Young Juliet* from Prokofiev *Romeo and Juliet* (*Suite no.* 2) places it in exactly this position however, and precise intonation between the solo saxophone and one of each clarinet and flute proves extremely difficult to achieve.

There are no members of the bassoon family beyond bassoon and contrabassoon and any orchestral parts designated for the sarrusophone are now universally performed on contra.

Transposition

Based upon personal experience of student conductors and instrumentalists, it would seem unwise to complete any consideration of orchestral woodwind without some reference to the traditional horrors associated with transposition. That it can prove very awkward is undeniable, but the difficulties and misunderstandings it seems to foster in the minds of so many people seem quite disproportionate. It should be appreciated that, for the most part, complications of transposition are confined to the orchestral full score and that the musicians themselves, unless playing the part on the wrong instrument, are not involved.

The instance of clarinets will provide a useful working example. The original clarinet was the one pitched in C, but the increased size and bore of the B♭ and A instruments were found to have such a beneficial effect upon the more mellow quality of the instrument that these became generally preferred by both players and composers. As in the case of natural horns and trumpets, where the basic techniques of sound production were common to various sizes of instrument, the note pertaining to the basic pitch of the instrument was always written as C. Thus the same relative harmonic or fingering could be selected and the length of tube would make the necessary alteration in pitch. Without this method of 'transposition' a new fingering system or new lip positions would have to be learnt from scratch, requiring a specialist player for each closely related instrument. The primary consideration for performance on any melodic instrument is the fingering system, without which variations of pitch cannot be produced. This technique becomes second nature, the sight of a particular sign giving rise to a corresponding movement of the fingers. In all the clarinets given above, the fingering system is identical and a player who has learnt one may play any of the others. Thus, if the mental linkage of the sign, for example middle C, to the associated finger movement remains constant, the one player may perform a part on any of the clarinets listed, with the instrument transposing the actual sounds in relation to its size. The score (with some modern exceptions) reproduces the signs that each player has in front of them, a fairly logical state of affairs.

Only when a part is attempted on the wrong instrument does mental transposition become necessary. If a clarinettist chooses to perform a part for clarinet in A on the clarinet in B♭ then actual transposition will have to be employed in order to make the required notes sound – exactly the same process that the score reader encounters when playing a part for clarinet in A (or any other transposing instrument) on the piano in C.

A certain amount of actual transposition for many instrumentalists is unavoidable, some instruments having become obsolete. Thus the E♭ clarinet will have to transpose when playing from parts intended for the D instrument; and the bass clarinet, nowadays always the version pitched in B♭, make similar adjustment for those written for the obsolete A. However, so general have these two transpositions become that many publishers furnish parts both in original notation and in transposition for the instrument most likely to perform them.

Most parts for the bass clarinet are written in the treble clef (sounding a ninth below written pitch). The bass clef (sounding a tone below) is a little less familiar and parts in this clef that were originally intended for the instrument in A can cause great difficulty. The provision of B♭ parts is something of a priority in such cases – Rachmaninov *Symphony no. 2* is a notable example.

Apart from clarinets and saxophones, other instruments of the woodwind section written at transposed pitch are:

Flute family:

piccolo, sounding one octave above written pitch

alto flute (in G) sounding a fourth below
bass flute, sounding one octave below written pitch

Oboe family:
oboe d'amore (in A) sounding a minor third below written pitch
cor anglais (in F) sounding a fifth below
bass oboe and heckelphone, both sounding one octave below written pitch

Bassoon family:
contrabassoon, sounding one octave below written pitch

In Conclusion

Many further matters relating to the woodwind, and some consideration of the exploratory demands made upon them in recent years, will be found in the following chapters. The capacity of woodwind, imaginatively used, to provide ever-changing colours of orchestration and varying degrees of dramatic and emotional response is endless. But, for anyone working with them, the overall vulnerability of these solo instrumentalists to any form of musical mishandling becomes a responsibility that must never be forgotten. Especially in student orchestras, where belief in the direction may sometimes be taken to extremes, the conductor's ability to persuade and support from within an accompanying role is crucial.

3 HORNS

Separating horns from the rest of the brass for purposes of reference is common practice and indeed perfectly correct, for the varying requirements of their involvement is without parallel in the orchestra. To any woodwind instrumentalist the horns are an indispensable part of the woodwind section, while a brass player would fervently dispute this and consider the horns to be, unquestionably, part of the brass section. The horn players themselves, however, would brook neither argument – to them their position is irrefutable. Individual, absolute and uncompromising, they are the horn section and their contribution is as multifarious as it is unique.

Along with oboes, the addition of a pair of horns to the basic string orchestra became a regular feature of early symphonic orchestral scoring, and the instrument's ability to hold long, sustained lines of harmony unobtrusively was exploited from the first.

Fundamental Principles

After the initial use of hunting horns (*Cors de Chasse*) by Baroque composers (mainly as *obbligato* instruments), the first horns used orchestrally were also 'natural' horns, with rather larger bells than their predecessors, but whose range was still confined to the harmonic series. Notes, most especially those of the middle and upper register, could be adjusted to varying degrees only by sometimes virtuosic flexibility of the player's lips.

For completeness, the notes theoretically available to an instrument pitched in 12-foot F (i.e. 12 feet long) are given here at written pitch – sounding a perfect fifth below.[1]

EX. 3.1

1 Classical instruments were considered to be most effective in F or similar tube-lengths (E or E♭). The modern 'double' instrument is pitched in F and B♭ – the latter to facilitate easier use of the higher register.

The overall length of tubing could be altered by the insertion of 'crooks' of various sizes, which changed the fundamental pitch of the instrument and the 'open' notes available to it. Thus, theoretically, there existed a wide range of pitch within a single sound colour, produced by making, in effect, a whole family of instruments available to each and every horn player. However, in practice this somewhat cumbersome adjustment took time, and a considerable period of rest had to be allowed for such a change of pitch to be negotiated, a basic drawback that very often caused the instruments to be unavailable for passages of harmonic transition or restatement in a different key (this situation applied equally to the use of trumpets).

It is generally accepted that no real advancement towards filling the chromatic gaps in the instrument took place until 1754, when a Dresden horn player, Anton Joseph Hampel, while searching for a way of muting the sound of the instrument, quite accidentally discovered a method of altering the pitch of individual notes by inserting the hand in the bell (although it seems unlikely that some experimentation along similar lines had not taken place previously). This improvement was only possible by virtue of a refinement to the method of inserting crooks into the instrument which had also been developed by the same player. The addition of differently coiled crooks into the main body of the instrument meant that the relative position of mouthpiece to bell remained constant. It was therefore possible to lower the playing position of the instrument from the more upright hunting horn position to one more similar to that used by present-day players, where the right hand may be inserted into the bell and 'hand-stopping' becomes feasible.

Even with the obvious chromatic advancement of the 'hand' horns, the situation remained somewhat unsatisfactory when compared to the total chromatic flexibility available to the orchestral woodwind for example, because it relied on an individual player's ability to alter notes accurately and with minimum change of sound quality. Until pistons or valves, which could be used to open or close various lengths of tubing, were permanently incorporated in the instrument, the practice of pitching the horn in fundamental keys which would facilitate the use of the maximum number of 'open' notes remained common, and great demands upon hand technique are not generally found until the famous passages of Beethoven some fifty years later.

However, frustrated composers began to employ an altogether more simple method of increasing the availability of horn sound by adding two more players with instruments crooked in a different key. This could alleviate much of the problem of horns being unavailable for certain passages, and the careful choice of new crooks by the composer, for substitution by the resting players, would extend the availability still further.

Thus, by the late Classical and early Romantic era, we find an increasing number of works requiring four horn players considered as two plus two. In his glorious G minor *Symphony no. 39* Haydn uses two pairs of horns pitched in different keys throughout the three movements in which they play. Mozart's early symphony in the same key (*no. 25*) composed some five years later, also uses the same device, cunningly arranging the parts to suit his needs while still retaining shape for individual players. A remarkable instance is this complete appearance of the main theme in the last movement.

EX. 3.2

A further example may illustrate the technique even more clearly. In the last movement of his later G minor symphony (*no. 40*), Mozart scores for just two horns, one of which is pitched in B♭ alto and one in G. *Ex. 3.3* shows the horn parts together with the woodwind line to which they correspond and provide support.

EX. 3.3

Written out with both horn parts in actual pitch we perceive the following:

EX. 3.4

which nowadays, when the work is performed on modern instruments, could easily be divided thus, since valve instruments have all notes available.

EX. 3.5

Comparison of *Exx. 3.3, 3.4* and *3.5* amply demonstrates Mozart's versatile orchestration technique as well as the problems faced by the Classical composer wishing to add horns to even as simple a figure as that played by the woodwind in *Ex. 3.3*. However, here the solution lies in the woodwind orchestration, which persuades the ear to hear the original distribution of the horn lines as if they were written as in *Ex. 3.5* anyway.

The use of two pairs of horns was continued by Beethoven, especially in the overtures, where they appear both for purposes of utilizing different pitches (as in *Egmont, The Ruins of Athens, King Stephen, Leonora nos 1 and 2)* and purely for increase of texture (as in *Fidelio, Namensfeier, Consecration of the House*) when all four are pitched in the same key.

In the overture *Leonora no. 3* both considerations exist side by side, the second pair of horns commencing the work pitched in E, a factor largely dictated by their requirement in two isolated passages of harmony in the introduction and the following solo passage in the main *Allegro*.

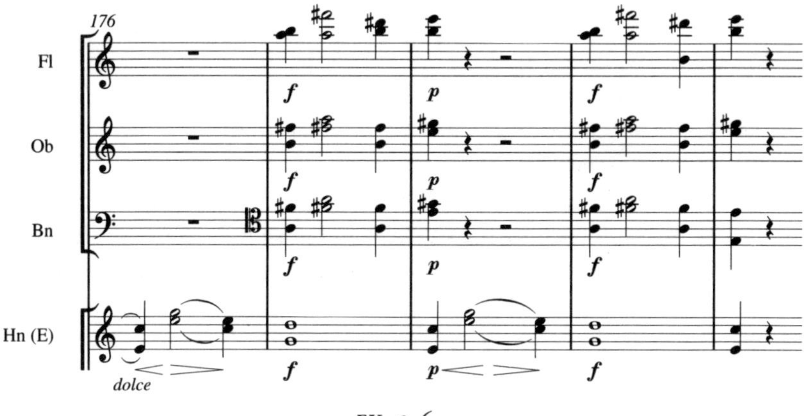

EX. 3.6

For the last half of the work they join the first pair (in C) whom they double throughout the entire final *Presto*. It is interesting to note that Beethoven gives them one hundred and ninety bars to facilitate the necessary change of crook!

The technique of 'hand-stopping', which had undoubtedly become more versatile and reliable by the early nineteenth century, requires considerable skill in combination of hand and embouchure control, so that the quality of sound remains as consistent as possible and the aural difference between the 'stopped' and the 'open' note is minimal. As well as enriching the harmony by doubling the number of players (which retained the limitations of the natural horn), Beethoven's wish to exploit the horn sound melodically led to ever more demanding examples of technical difficulty, from the first movement of the *Third Symphony*, to the *Trio* of the *Eighth* to the almost unbelievable 4th horn solo in the slow movement of the *Ninth*.

A clear aural perception of the difficulties involved will be gained by looking at the first phrase of Schubert '*Great*' *C major Symphony*, where the most accomplished technique of the hand horn is required from the outset. Very few players in Schubert's time would have been able to execute this passage with anything approaching an even sound.

EX. 3.7

Reference to *Ex. 3.1* will show that the first two notes of the second bar (A and B) as well as the first note of the third bar (F) lie outside the range of the open series for a horn in C. These notes could only be obtained by degrees of closure of the bell by the hand and some flexibility of the lip within the mouthpiece. The A, for example, could be obtained by half stopping from the 'open' B♭ a semitone above, and the B similarly obtained from the C, albeit using a little more hand.

This partial stopping of the tube will have the effect of lowering the note produced, the intonation being variable and dependent upon degree – most easily referred to as ¼, ½ or ¾, but never quite as accurate as such fractions might imply. Full-stopping, however, will raise the chosen fundamental by approximately half a tone (a result which needs to be remembered whenever hand-stopping is required for colouristic effect).

The example above is remarkable. Two years earlier Weber had opened his opera *Oberon* with a similar rising pattern of three notes scored for one solo horn, but never before had the instrument been required to state a long, totally exposed melodic passage at the outset of so major an orchestral work – and this not for one horn, but two in unison!

There was never a necessity for composers to indicate hand-stopped notes in their scores (such technical niceties being left to the player) but by the later nineteenth century some composers who retained at least the nominal use of hand horns marked certain notes for purposes of purely colouristic effect and tonal variation. There is an interesting and rare example of *gestopft* being marked for horns in E at the beginning of the second movement of Brahms *Symphony no. 1*, to obtain a slight 'closing' of the sound in order to complement the *pianissimo* in the strings (see *Ex. 3.8*).

Professional horn players give different and often conflicting reasons for the origin of this marking, some maintaining that it was intended for when the part was played on a valve horn (an increasingly common practice in Brahms'

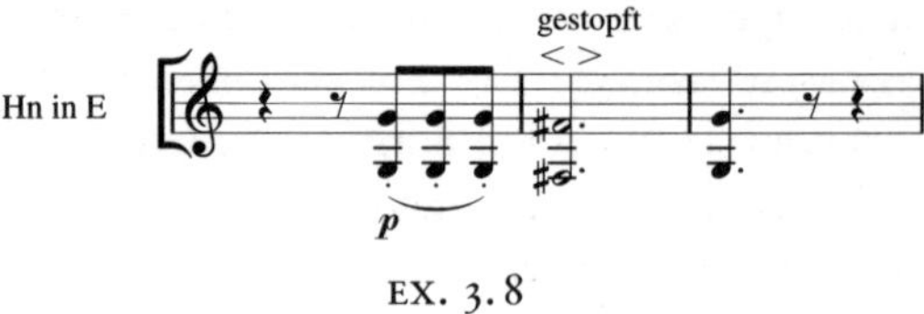

EX. 3.8

time) and thus does not specifically refer to the horn in E. However, most modern players, including 2nd players with the low octave, will observe it, hand-stopping the written F♯ from the G and then closing it a little further to produce a stopped sound.

Seating

The increasing regularity with which such influential composers as Berlioz, Brahms and Tchaikovsky orchestrated for four horns had, by the late nineteenth century, established this as standard symphonic practice, which persists to this day. However, the traditional consideration of two plus two, whether or not pitched in the same key, has also remained, and one still finds the majority of horn scoring placed in descending order of 1st, 3rd, 2nd, 4th – the second pair interlocking with the first pair. This unusual situation may be said to amount to two Principal players within a single instrumental section.

The horn is the only instrument whose true sound is perceived not directly but by reflection, the instrument being designed to be played with the bell facing away from the listener. It is therefore important that the sound be allowed to escape freely, neither impeded by the body of another player nor distorted by the proximity of a reflective surface.

Because of these unique facets of development and projection, the placing of the horns, both relative to one another and to the rest of the orchestra, must be carefully considered. In the United Kingdom, the universally accepted position for the horn section is to the left of the woodwind when viewed by the audience or conductor, as shown in *Fig. 3.1*.

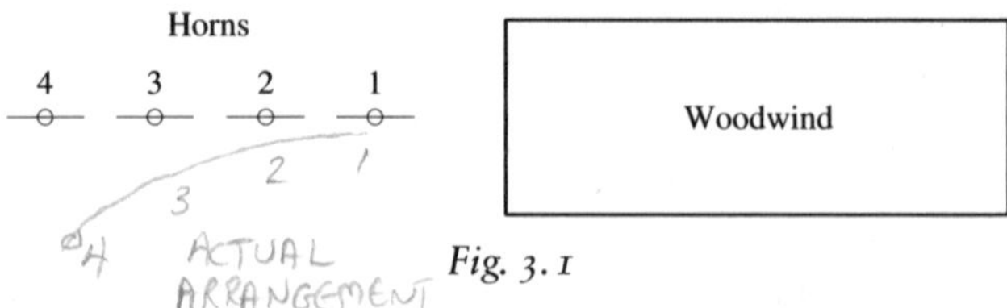

Fig. 3.1

Rather than the straight line shown here, a slight arcing is preferable, making the players equidistant from the conductor and resulting in 4th being placed somewhat nearer the front of the orchestra than 1st. Apart from the obvious improvement in the sight-line, this arrangement allows a little more room for the sound to escape from the instrument unobstructed. Placing 1st on the right hand end of the line brings that player into closest possible contact with the centre of the orchestra and the woodwind Principals, but gives 2nd horn the disadvantage of hearing only the immediate sound of the Principal and not the 'true' reflected sound. For this reason, some Principals used to insist upon an exact transposition of the line (i.e. with 1st player on the far left) but the practice has long since lapsed.

It is also possible, especially if space is limited, to arrange the section in a block with horns 3 and 4 behind.

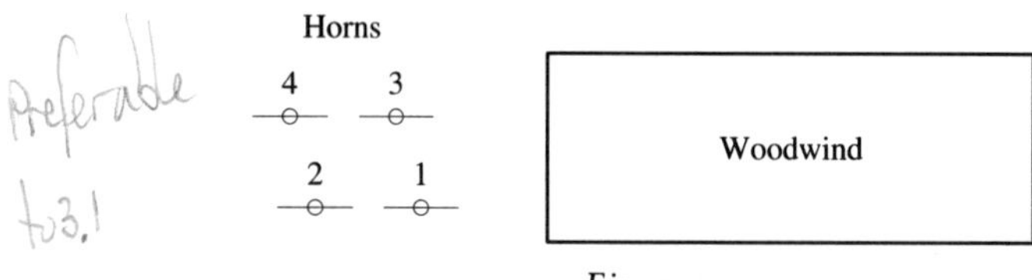

Fig. 3.2

This arrangement is preferred by some sections as it adheres more closely to the traditional 'two plus two' layout of the parts, and has the added advantage that 3rd horn can clearly hear 1st, and 2nd 4th, thus facilitating the improvement of ensemble and intonation.

With a section of four players, the advantages of transportation to the other side of the woodwind are dubious, although this is often encountered, especially in European orchestras outside the United Kingdom. For student orchestras the disadvantages seem too numerous to be successfully overcome. Firstly, it is impossible to play without directing the instrument's bell towards the bodies of other players. Secondly, the presence of trumpets, trombones and tuba means that the only available position is much too far forward to achieve balance with the woodwind. And thirdly, and probably most importantly, the woodwind receive a totally false impression of the horn sound, as they are engulfed by the extraordinary timbre emanating directly from the bell. It must also be mentioned that, as soon as six or eight horns are required, one usually finds the whole section transported across to the unfamiliar territory of the other side of the orchestra simply because of lack of space! The resultant replacing of the timpani and percussion, who will have got used to filling the wide open spaces next to the flutes and clarinets, totally disrupts the orchestra's habitual balance and causes untold problems of adjustment.

As far as is humanly possible the seating of every section of the orchestra should take into account the largest instrumentation that is likely to be required of it, however rare such an occurrence might be, so that the players' ability to maintain balance is only ever minimally disturbed. It is worth mentioning here that the seating of the entire orchestra should be considered as one compact unit and not as a sprawling conglomeration of players making use of every inch of available space. The smallest practical performance area should ideally be the regular set-up for every orchestra, regardless of how much extra space might sometimes present itself. It must never be forgotten that there are delicately scored passages within even the most lavish orchestral scores.

The final possibility to consider is placing the horns in a line immediately behind the woodwind, as shown in *Fig. 3.3*.

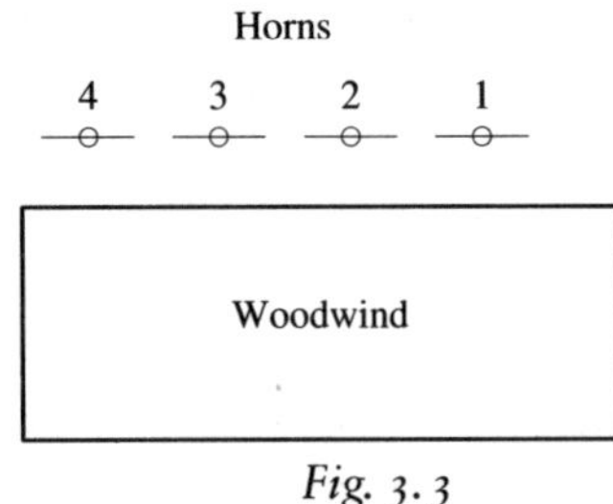

Fig. 3.3

Unless there are limitations of space (for instance, when large string and percussion sections have to be accommodated in concert halls with a small stage area or fixed risers), it is best avoided wherever possible as the horns can cause problems of intonation in the lower woodwind instruments seated immediately in front of them. In the case of inexperienced orchestras, the players are unlikely to overcome this problem unless sufficient space is allowed between the horns and the woodwind. In such a situation the advantage to 1st horn is that of being closer to the brass and woodwind Principals, but it is often impractical in the smaller concert halls. It also places the horns too far away from the main body of strings and separates the tonal centre of the orchestral sound.

Thus it becomes clear that to place the horns on the clarinet side of the woodwind causes fewest problems and, for student orchestras, this position, whether in a single line or the two pair blocking shown in *Fig. 3.2*, is undoubtedly preferable.

If the line of clarinets is particularly long, it is just possible to move the horns back a row, as shown in *Fig. 3.4*, but the overlap should be kept to a minimum.

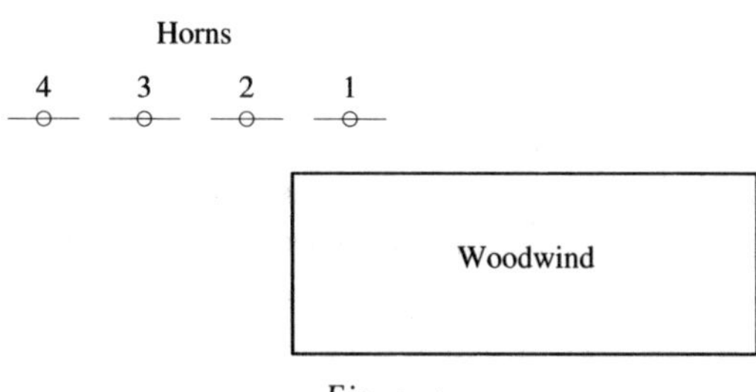

Fig. 3.4

DUPLICATION

Although, as with the woodwind, the unnecessary duplication of instruments should be avoided, nowadays the professional horn section is almost always increased by the addition of at least one player. The duties of this extra instrumentalist, who will be placed next to the 1st horn on the side away from the rest of the section, are to relieve the 1st horn of some of the *tutti* playing, especially before an important solo, so that the Principal is sufficiently fresh and rested. In the United Kingdom and some other European countries this player is referred to as the 'bumper', whereas in Canada and the United States he or she often rejoices in the somewhat dubious title of 'Bull horn'. In Germany however, two Principals quite commonly appear together. The only practical difference in this subtle refinement is that the work load, both solos and *tutti*, is shared equally by both players, which is not the case where one finds a bumper. In professional sections, where and when the bumper plays is determined solely by the Principal, though the conductor may ask the extra player to 'double' a line of *tutti* where the Principal is already playing. In student orchestras however, it is more likely that the experienced section tutor will have decided the passages to be taken.

In these circumstances it is not uncommon to find a bumper provided for 3rd horn as well, especially in the main piece of the programme, but this usually has more to do with providing playing opportunities for a less experienced player than with musical or physical necessity. However, the age and experience of the available players will sometimes cause a specialist horn tutor to request that six players be provided, especially if all the works on the programme involve four parts. The amount of playing required from each performer can be heavy even in the most innocent-looking programme, and to be able to change players from one work to another, even if keeping to no more than four at a time, is often essential.

It is difficult to determine the real weight of playing required unless a great deal of experience has been gained within a section. Quite apart from the obvious 'horn pieces' of Richard Strauss, Mahler and other exponents of the *Grosse Orchester*, there exist many works where the general layout of the parts makes them extremely demanding and may well put them beyond the reach of a young or very inexperienced section. The degree of involvement of this section requires particular thought when compiling programmes and every conductor must heed the advice of the specialist tutor. It is not within the nature of horn-writing to present many opportunities for a section to fudge their way through and it is the least possible of all sections to rebalance or disguise with other textures.

The exact positions of these one or two extra players, relative to their Principals, is here incorporated into the two primary seating positions considered earlier.

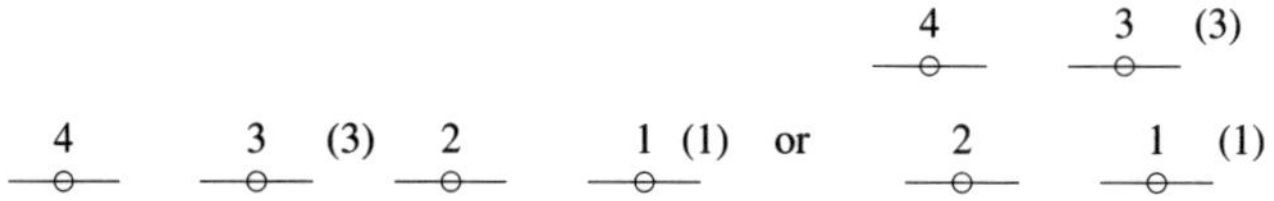

4 3 (3) 2 1 (1) or 4 3 (3) / 2 1 (1)

Fig. 3.5

As can be seen, the addition of a bumper for 3rd horn reinforces the consideration of the section as two plus two. A separate stand is never required for these extra players.

Forming the Section

Notwithstanding the ever-increasing similarity of all horn parts in terms of range and exposure and the lack of differentiation made by many composers in recent years, the majority of orchestral horn parts lie in a higher register for 1st and 3rd players than they do for 2nd and 4th. The major part of the late Classical and Romantic repertoire conforms quite rigidly to this rule and therefore, with regard to youth and student orchestras, it is the more experienced and fluent players who will usually be given the odd-numbered seats. Not that this should be taken to imply that playing for 2nd or 4th is easier; indeed many contradictory examples could be quoted, but the 1st and 3rd parts will, generally, be more likely to contain exposed solos and sustain longer periods of high playing.

1ST HORN (PRINCIPAL)

Of all the orchestral Principals the 1st horn needs to be blessed with a clear head and an equable temperament, for the horn is a perilous instrument in the higher registers, the harmonics being so close together that the pitching of notes becomes a very exact science. Obviously the player requires a fluent technique across the range of the instrument, but this must include the ability to play softly without loss of tone or projection. The greater portion of orchestral horn playing is spent in support of other lines or textures and at a dynamic of *mezzo forte* or below, so the 1st player must not only be able to control the section's level of sound with his or her own but also provide the prime example. In an instrument so easily associated with dramatic character and glowing solos, such apparently mundane playing can be easily overlooked, but it is very much the section's basic responsibility and without it the orchestra stands little chance of blending within itself.

A subtlety of approach is a prerequisite in a 1st horn, but this must be complemented, rather than subjugated, by boldness and confidence. The roundness of tone associated with the great horn solos of the orchestral repertoire is the hallmark of the truly distinguished player, but to achieve this the overall mental approach to the instrument and the personal appraisal of its character are paramount. With an instrument whose sound emanates directly from the player's lips with no intervening reed, this assessment will largely determine the players' limitations or otherwise. Thus a player who favours and nurtures the louder, more forceful, side of the instrument exclusively would be unable to provide in *Ex. 3.9*, the most famous of all horn solos from Tchaikovsky *Symphony no. 5*, the necessary serenity in the *sound*, even if the

EX. 3.9

phrasing, dynamic variation, line and endless other factors were to be fully understood.

Undoubtedly this would be true of other instruments, but the unique qualities of sound production on the horn, coupled with the changes of timbre that exist across its large dynamic range, make the basic quality of tone production that much more persistent.

When choosing a Principal, any tendency to sacrifice purity of tone for other technical aspects of playing should be noted at the audition stage (few experienced professionals would miss it) for it will be magnified once the player is surrounded by orchestral sound. Though the ability to project a well-centred and cleanly articulated sound is important, the musical sensitivity of the player must be the prime qualification, a fact which many 'managers' of young orchestras seem unable to appreciate (although, in their defence, the available choice is unlikely to be vast and seniority of tenure becomes an almost inescapable factor).

Beyond the performance of exposed solos, the 1st horn has a responsibility to his or her section similar to that of the string Principals. The player must foster care in intonation and awareness of ensemble and articulation, especially with regard to the ending of notes and their length, undertake to contact the brass and woodwind Principals to establish the finer points of phrasing and balance, and be continually aware, without causing antagonism, of what the other members of the section are doing and how they are playing. In short, it is a position of immense responsibility and pressure – heading a section which is second only to the strings in its ability to mould and vary an orchestra's personality and sound.

3RD HORN (PRINCIPAL)

The 3rd horn probably occupies the most rewarding seat in the section. The player is not only involved with the centre of the harmony but also has the opportunity to play many solos. In the repertoire of the late nineteenth and early twentieth centuries, the position covers much the same range as the 1st horn, and receives almost as many solos. Moreover, during the mid-nineteenth century, when valved instruments were beginning to be used in the orchestra, composers such as Mendelssohn and Saint-Saëns wrote for 1st and 2nd horns using natural instruments and 3rd and 4th horns using valved (both composers' third symphonies, for example), a practice that meant 3rd horn parts were sometimes more chromatic and exposed than those of 1st or 2nd, and often more important. Similarly, some 3rd horn parts of Brahms are higher than those written for the 1st player. Consequently the player must have all-round ability and musical sensitivity, and be able to produce the most refined sound while remaining aware of the surrounding harmonic structure.

In the rare instances of a three-horn section, the role of the 3rd horn varies. In Beethoven *Symphony no. 3* (the first and still the most famous example) the position remains much the same as it would be in the larger group, the first movement using 3rd as an alternate Principal while 1st is allowed time to change crooks – 41 bars to change to F and 89 bars to change back to E♭. The subtle changes in scoring and rhythm for horns and trumpets in the middle of the recapitulation (bars 472 to 490) are worthy of note. These are unlikely to have been solely because of the 1st horn's unavailability, as Beethoven could certainly have used the player again by this point, 51 bars after the part in F finishes.

The three-horn group of the Dvořák *Cello Concerto* uses 3rd both as an independent solo voice and – for nearly all of its comparatively rare appearances in the third movement – as an integrated line in three-part chording. All the solos occur when pitched in a different crook from the other two, and the use of 3rd, in this respect, was a matter of convenience. In practical terms it would be interesting to discover at what stage of the work's inception Dvořák decided that the texture precluded the use of a 4th; it is all too easy to accept him writing 'Concerto for Violoncello' on the top of a blank piece of manuscript paper and then 'Three Horns' halfway down the page!

Prokofiev, however, probably did just that when he came to score *Peter and the Wolf*. Here the three horns only appear together (as the Wolf) and always in three-part chording or unison. However, in line with classical practice, 3rd is always placed between 1st and 2nd.

In respect of student orchestras such varying orchestrations become quite important considerations for, in the last example, a less 'soloistically orientated' player could play 3rd, whereas this is not the case in the other two works.

2ND HORN

Life for the 2nd horn player is similarly divided, albeit mostly within a lower register and largely bereft of melodic solos. The use of only two horns in the orchestra is surprisingly commonplace, since many of the apparently larger works do not require four. Beethoven *Symphonies nos 5* and *7*, Schubert *Symphony no. 9*, Schumann *Symphony no. 2*, Vaughan Williams *Symphonies nos 5* and *8* are prime examples. In such cases, the role of 2nd is very similar to that of the woodwind sub-Principals and requires the player to provide octave support and careful balancing of sound and intonation, often in the most exposed and difficult circumstances – who, for instance, would envy either horn the sustained B♭ that links the second and third movements of Beethoven *Piano Concerto no. 5*?

However, in twentieth-century works for smaller orchestra (a desperately important repertoire for conservatoire and university orchestras) the 2nd horn has to undertake a very different role. Works such as Stravinsky *Dumbarton Oaks* and Schoenberg *Second Chamber Symphony* are uncompromising for the 2nd player, while Nicholas Maw in his wonderful *Sinfonia* makes virtually no distinction between the two parts.

In the four-horn repertoire the part for 2nd tends to lie between that of 3rd and 4th, most closely allied to that of the Principal (1st) but often doubling a line with 4th. In common with all 2nd players, this instrumentalist is often allotted a solo line in an awkward and less easily projected register immediately before the 1st player reiterates it in a more flattering one. This short passage, from Chausson *Poème* for violin and orchestra, is by no means easy for the players to combine successfully.

EX. 3.10

Here 2nd appears from within the texture of a brass chord and actually starts the phrase pitched below all three trombones. To make the phrase sound as *legato* and inevitable as the one that immediately follows requires very fine playing indeed.

This one example demonstrates that the 2nd horn position is no place to hide and that its role is extremely specialized and demanding. It is common, for example, for the sound of an inexperienced 2nd horn to swamp that of 1st, even if only pitched a fourth or fifth below, owing to the relatively fuller quality of sound compared to that of the higher register.

In student orchestras, where a wide choice of players is not always available, the demands of any programme should be carefully considered before automatically consigning a less experienced player to this seat. The part will require a technique as versatile and confident as that of the 1st horn and comparable stamina.

4TH HORN

Much that has been said with regard to 2nd horn applies here also, though the parts will frequently be even lower-lying. In student orchestras a difficulty arises for the low players in all instruments. The register required of them in the orchestral repertoire is not likely to be so regularly encountered in the works they will play elsewhere.Therefore, one is dealing with unpractised players as much as anything else and this one fact lies at the root of many problems of orchestral balance and intonation.

For the 4th horn in particular, propping up the entire section in terms of tonality is a daunting task. In this register a young player is unlikely to possess either the roundness of sound necessary to match the other three, or the means of projecting it fluently. Clear projection of the bass notes is as crucial in this section as elsewhere, and the distortion of harmonic balance frequently encountered in inexperienced horn sections is not always the fault of an over-enthusiastic 1st.

The 4th horn is best-placed to perceive and comment on the balance, intonation and quality of the section as a whole, and thus needs to be a musician of sensitivity and diplomacy. Such a role is not normally required from the 4th horn of a student orchestra but, nonetheless, this additional responsibility should be taught and nurtured.

Solos do come the 4th horn's way and the player must be equipped to deal with them. They are generally of the short, unrewarding variety, which makes them all the more difficult in performance, as in the unaccompanied example with which Franck actually opens his symphonic poem *Le Chasseur Maudit*.

EX. 3.11

At least Franck sets this solo in a reasonably comfortable, resonant part of the instrument and not, as is so often the case, pitched somewhere below the player's boot straps! In fact it would be hard to accuse the composer of being unreasonable in this instance for, just eight bars further on, he repeats the passage (with triplets replacing the single crotchets of *Ex. 3.11*) for 2nd and

1st – perhaps the ultimate example of even distribution among the horn section.

Solos of a more melodic nature do exist, however, of which the most famous is undoubtedly that from the 3rd movement of Beethoven *Symphony no. 9* mentioned earlier. (The apparent missing ligature between the seventh and eighth bars of *Ex. 3.12* – the low G's – corresponds to a page turn in the autograph. It is usually included in performance.)

EX. 3.12

Whatever the historical reasons for its original scoring might have been (on which subject much has been written), it is now an unquestionable part of the 4th horn repertoire and should not be routinely re-allocated to any other player, even though 3rd horn at least (whose part for this movement starts with 119 bars rest) is tantalizingly redundant. It need hardly be remarked that this work is monumentally difficult for all concerned – not least the conductor – and can only be performed by an orchestra of quite outstanding technical ability.

Other occasions where fluency across the full range of the instrument will be required from 4th horn are often encountered when the section is increased in size.

The Enlarged Section

The addition of extra players to the standard section of four horns occurs increasingly in orchestral music from the beginning of the twentieth century and much of the repertoire essential to music college and conservatoire orchestras requires six players or even more. In most circumstances the section will be increased by pairs and the standard format of 'high' and 'low' adhered to in principle at least. However, in a six-horn section, a combination of three + three is by no means rare and both combinations may be found within the same works, for example in Holst *The Planets.*

Throughout *Mars*, the first movement of this work, the configuration is of two groups of three, and 4th is placed in the somewhat unaccustomed position of leading the second group while 3rd maintains the lowest line of the other three. In *Venus* Holst returns to the more frequent grouping of three pairs, 5th horn now taking an upper part, along with 1st and 3rd, while 4th reverts to a more accustomed role. Apart from *Mercury* and *Neptune*, where only four horns are used, this division is continued. The exceptional amount of six-horn unison encountered in *Jupiter* (and to a lesser extent in *Uranus*) underlines the remarkable originality of this score and the versatility required from all six players. Perhaps one last example of the meticulous care in orchestration that this work demonstrates is worthy of quotation.

EX. 3.13

Here in *Saturn* a passage which is obviously three + three is divided by pairs in order to conform to the layout of the rest of the movement, but, of all the possible alternatives, Holst chooses the one that keeps the standard four-horn group in their most natural division.

The use of six horns allows no alternative seating to one straight line, neither two rows of three nor a grouping of four and two catering for all the variations of their ensemble. Many further examples of six-horn orchestration will be found, most notably in works by Mahler, Richard Strauss, Stravinsky, Schoenberg and Berg. Even Webern, that most concise of all composers, uses six in the original version of the *Six Pieces for Orchestra* (1909) but dispenses with two of them in the later, somewhat less effective, reduced orchestration of the same work (1928).

Eight players, the complete doubled section, occurs less often but is by no means rare. Mahler demands it in three of the symphonies (*nos 3, 6* and *8*) as do Richard Strauss (*Ein Heldenleben*), Prokofiev (*Scythian Suite*) and Wagner (*The Ring*). Many of the idiosyncrasies of horn balance and blend can be gleaned from close scrutiny of these scores and comparison with those for a smaller section by the same composers, but the prime example of apparent effortless use of eight players must surely come from Stravinsky in *The Rite of Spring*. In overall concept the scoring is for four pairs of instrumentalists, although much dramatic use is made of the interplay of four against four. However, the careful division of the parts and the sheer inevitability of every line are wrought with deceptive ease. One of the most remarkable things about this work is the feeling of indispensable involvement it engenders for every single player in the orchestra – the ultimate example of chamber music expanded to massive numbers.

Larger forces than eight horns will only be found in isolated instances for special effect. The ten players required for Mahler *Symphony no. 2* are in two separate sections (six + four) with the smaller group, who only play in the last movement, off stage until they join the main group to reinforce the climax. Such clearly defined separation is also true of the even greater numbers sometimes required by Richard Strauss and Wagner.

The rare instances of the horn section comprising an odd number of players have been referred to above with regard to the three-horn sections of Beethoven, Dvořák and Prokofiev. For larger odd-numbered sections one must turn to Mahler who provides examples of both five horns (the *Scherzo* of *Symphony no. 5*) and seven (throughout *Symphony no. 1*).

In the case of the *Scherzo* of the *Fifth Symphony*, the six-horn section required for the rest of the work is reduced by one player, and Mahler makes his intentions very clear by demanding a normal section of four players plus an *obbligato* horn whose part remains quite separate throughout the movement – a fascinating concept and one that works superbly well. However, the well-meaning attentions of various editors have meant that the printed orchestral material provides a slight discrepancy worthy of consideration. As might be considered logical, the *corno obbligato* part has been assigned to 1st. The original 3rd horn, Principal of the second 'pair', therefore takes over the 1st part of the four-horn group, and 5th (the Principal of the third 'pair'), the 3rd. So far, so good. But now a small, thoughtless piece of over-simplification provides an unnecessary problem of balance. In the printed orchestral parts, 2nd and 4th retain their line and it is 6th horn who becomes redundant, which immediately sets the lower player of each pair on the wrong side of his or her corresponding Principals, as in *Fig. 3.6* (a).

(6)	(5)	(4)	(3)	(2)	(1)
[6]	3	4	1	2	obbligato

(a)

(6)	(5)	(4)	(3)	(2)	(1)
4	3	2	1	[2]	obbligato

(b)

Fig. 3.6

If, however, player 4 takes the 2nd horn part and player 6 the 4th, then the far superior positioning of *Fig. 3.6* (b) results, with the added bonus of distancing the *obbligato* horn from the quite separate quartet. Such a situation may be achieved simply by passing the copies along the line, but it would be preferable either to provide extra 2nd and 4th parts or, even better, to redistribute the parts in the original material.

The seven-horn section scored throughout the *First Symphony* requires the extra player to add weight to the lower parts, doubling 2nd or 4th as the occasion arises or, more rarely, supplying the lowest line of the group.

Transposition

Because of the inventive methods of pitching horns mentioned in the first part of this chapter, horn parts may be found in every conceivable key, notwithstanding the fact that some may be encountered very rarely. In all cases (except performance on period instruments) these will nowadays be performed on the orchestral single horn in F, or, more frequently, the double horn in F and B♭, requiring the player to transpose many of the parts at sight. The player will automatically transpose them directly into F and not into concert pitch first (this also applies to passages played on the B♭ side of the double instrument). For this reason it is best for the conductor always to refer to notes in written pitch. Surprising confusion, particularly with regard to chromatic passages, can otherwise result.

In the treble clef all horn parts, in whatever key, transpose downwards, the only exception being the rarely encountered 'horn in C alto' which is notated at pitch. In the bass clef, however, two opposing systems are to be found –

which can lead to complications, especially when both are to be found in the same work (Elgar '*Enigma*' *Variations*, for example).

Originally, bass clef notation reversed the procedure by writing at the lower octave, requiring transposition upwards. Thus, for horn in F, both the following notations would provide the same sounding note.

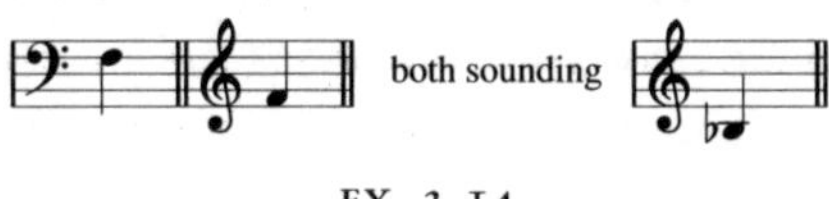

EX. 3.14

This is sometimes referred to as 'old notation', the later variation being to retain the downward transposition applicable to the treble clef, known as 'new notation'. In this case, the two written notes shown above would sound an octave apart, as their written pitch implies.

On most occasions the intended pitch will be clear from the score but, except in the case of very low notes, it will not always be so from the parts, and some questions might arise.

Infrequent Additions

WAGNER TUBA

The sudden mention of tubas in a chapter dealing solely with horns might appear confusing but these particular instruments are the province of horn players for many reasons. It is the name that is somewhat misleading for these are not really tubas at all but considerably modified horns.

Wagner's intentions and experiments in this area are well documented but, in brief, the original desire was to provide a new sound colour in the orchestra which would be strong enough to complement trombones and trumpets but close enough to the horns in timbre to bridge the gap between them and the brass. What evolved were what he called the 'tenor tuba' in B♭ and the 'bass tuba' in F (not to be confused with the real tubas of the same name), each of slightly larger bore than the horn but corresponding exactly in length of tube to their similarly pitched cousins, and retaining the conical bore and an identical mouthpiece. In outward appearance they are considerably different; the bells point upward and the coiling of the tube is elliptical rather than circular. There are four valves, three directly corresponding to those of the horn and the fourth making available an extra downward interval of a perfect fourth. This valve may also be used to adjust intonation, especially in the lower register.

Much has been written about the unfortunate misunderstandings that these instruments have caused, through their misleading name and their inventor's regrettable decision to change the method of notation in mid stream. For student orchestras, who are unlikely to perform *The Ring*, it is probably sufficient to say that these *are* the instruments required by Bruckner (in the *Symphonies nos 7, 8* and *9*), Stravinsky (*The Rite of Spring*) and Bartók (*The Miraculous Mandarin*); but are *not* the instrument required by Holst (*The Planets*), Janáček (*Sinfonietta*) or Richard Strauss (*Don Quixote*), where the real tenor tuba must be used.

A full account of the problems relating to these intruments appear in Norman Del Mar's *Anatomy of the Orchestra* and elsewhere, but they should also be mentioned here. Some inexplicable variations in notation were unfortunately perpetuated by Bruckner in the late symphonies (where the student orchestra most frequently encounters these instruments). Although he retained B♭ and F as the transposing notation, he became very confused by the octave. In the *Seventh Symphony*, at the beginning of the *Adagio*, the tenor tubas in B♭ sound a major ninth below written pitch and the bass tubas in F one octave and a fifth below.

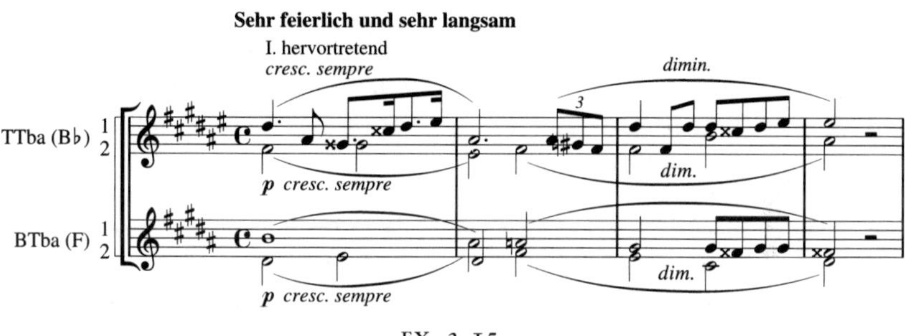

EX. 3.15

In the *Eighth Symphony* the B♭ tubas continue in the same written pitch but always with the addition of *8vo basso* in the score. The F tubas are now, much more logically, assigned to the bass clef, but sound a perfect fourth above.

This method of notation for F tubas is retained in the *Ninth Symphony*. However, the B♭ tubas are here written at the lower octave (sounding a major second below) until a horrendous mistake occurs in the score (see *Ex. 3.16*).

Here, at rehearsal letter Q, Bruckner has suddenly reverted to habit and, in the score, the B♭ tubas are written one octave too high. As far as I know, this is not followed in any set of orchestral parts, where the right octave is always maintained. However, if nothing else, this example illustrates the dangers of blindly believing any printed score.

EX. 3.16

Seating

Since Wagner tubas most often appear as doubling instruments for horn players, their position becomes enforced rather than ideal. When just two are required they will be played by the last two players of the section (horns 5 and 6 or 7 and 8) but a quartet is more common, played by horns 5–8. Only in works where no doubling is required (for example, Bruckner *Symphony no. 7*) is it possible to consider a position close to the orchestral tuba, with whom their ensemble is regularly linked. In this rare instance it is feasible to consider placing them immediately behind trombones, or in a block (two + two) to the left of the tuba player, although few platform areas will allow it. A further possibility in this circumstance, which works well if the orchestral tuba can be persuaded to move to the 'wrong' side of the trombone section, is to extend the line across the back of the orchestra, between woodwind and timpani.

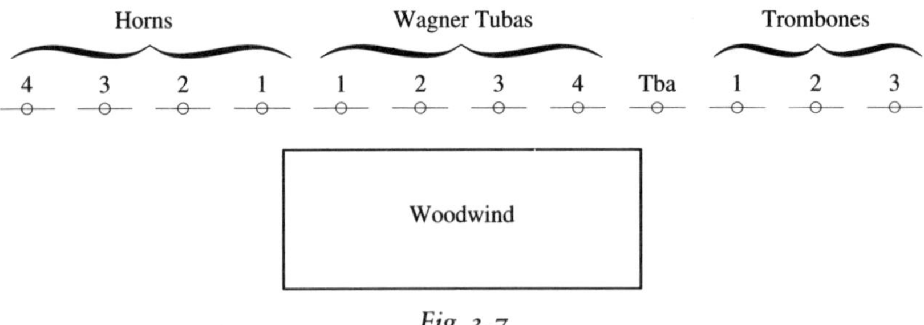

Fig. 3.7

In this arrangement, trumpets will be placed in front of trombones and horns will move a little nearer the centre of the orchestra, so that none of the sections are too far apart.

Elsewhere, when doubling is essential and the horn section must remain in the normal position, an arrangement of two banks of four rather than eight in a line will, again if space permits, improve matters slightly. These two variations are shown as (a) and (b) in *Fig. 3.8*.

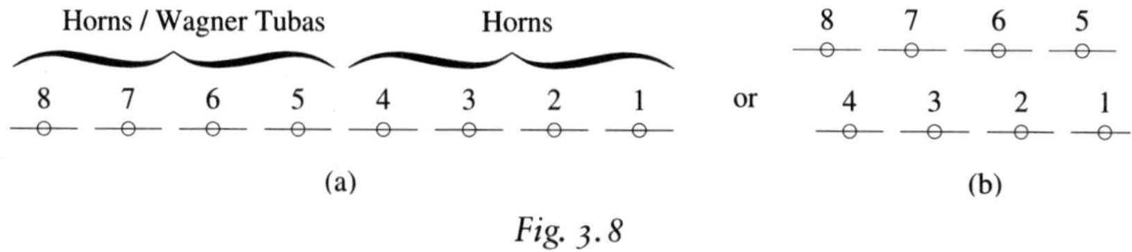

Fig. 3.8

The various arrangements outlined above, each with its own problems of ensemble and collaboration, illustrate one of the salient differences between live performance and recording. In the studio re-seating can be effected every bar if desired, and the manufactured results stitched together later.

4 BRASS

Trumpets, trombones and tuba are the foundation of the orchestral brass section. Although the trumpets in particular will tend to vary in numbers, the most frequent and standard combination of the symphonic brass group may nowadays be taken as three trumpets, three trombones and one tuba.

Trumpets were the first of these brass instruments to appear in orchestras, although their use in music for wind and brass ensembles and within the Baroque string band was already well established. In the orchestral repertoire, the addition of a pair of trumpets to the basic orchestra of strings, woodwind and horns (often in direct partnership with timpani) occurs with increasing regularity from around the middle of the eighteenth century.

Fundamental Principles

TRUMPETS

The situation facing composers writing for the trumpet before the development of valves resembles that already described in relation to horns, for trumpets were also originally confined to the notes of the harmonic series. Crooks to extend or shorten the tube length and thereby alter the basic pitch of the instrument were available, though never in the profusion of keys associated with the horn.

Few symphonic composers working in the first decades of the nineteenth century were moved to take up the challenge offered by contemporary modifications of the instrument. The slide trumpet, for example, which provided a number of notes outside the harmonic series as well as some adjustment of intonation, was available and in use from as early as the mid-1790s. This may have been partly because the musical convention, established in the Classical era, of trumpet and drums confined to the prevailing keys of the work proved sufficient for their needs (although it still caused considerable, and doubtless frustrating, juggling of melodic lines and attention to their resulting harmonic implication). Only the most progressive composers such as Berlioz and Wagner showed real interest in advancing the orchestral scope of this family of instruments, although Schumann experimented with hand-stopping trumpets of cruciform design. Orchestral trumpet parts were thus largely confined to the 'open' harmonics for a considerably longer period of musical history than horns, in fact mainly throughout the first half of the nineteenth century. Furthermore, doubling the section from two players to four in order to obtain extra notes by use of different crooks was rarely attempted by composers other than Berlioz and Wagner.

If one considers an eighteenth-century trumpet in C, the range of harmonics theoretically available is exactly the same as for the horn (*see* Chapter 3), the instrument having a tube length of eight feet (twice that of the modern C trumpet). The very high trumpet parts sometimes found in music of the seventeenth and early eighteenth centuries were occasioned by players developing the extreme harmonics at the very top of the range. This technique of *clarino* playing was to disappear very quickly as composers embraced a more symphonic style, and seems to have been a skill in decline by the middle of the eighteenth century.

It is of great importance, especially when considering orchestral works of the late eighteenth and early nineteenth centuries, to bear in mind this fact, and to appreciate the gradual shortening of the tube length that has taken place over the last two centuries in order to facilitate the higher range of the instrument. Although even eighteenth-century parts for trumpet in C were most probably played on a D or E♭ instrument crooked down for the purpose, by the time Mozart was at his prime the most common instrument was that pitched in F (a tube length of about six feet). Indeed, it was this instrument that first appeared with valves in the middle of the nineteenth century, the three valves extending its length by nearly two and a half feet and giving it a usable chromatic range of about two and a half octaves.

One of the most frequently used modern orchestral trumpets, that pitched in B♭, measures fractionally over four and a half feet excluding the valves, half the length of its Classical counterpart. The modern player will therefore obtain the upper part of the range (from C to G for example) from the 4th to the 6th harmonic, whereas, to obtain the same notes, his classical forebear would have used the 8th to the 12th harmonic of the larger instrument. The inherent insecurity of such high playing accounts for the harmonic nature of many Classical trumpet parts, since composers were often unwilling to carry thematic material into the higher range of the instrument. Beethoven provides this famous example, among many others, in the *Eroica* symphony. Security is the sole factor in the decision to drop the 1st trumpet down to the supporting octave (see *Ex. 4.1*).

It is of passing interest to note that the striking difference in sound between the two sizes of instrument when producing the same note was one of the

EX. 4.1

original factors in the comparatively recent quest for 'replica instrumentation' in the performance of pre-Classical (and, later, Classical) repertoire.

TROMBONES

The only member of the brass family to have originated as a chromatic instrument, the slide trombone has existed in almost unchanged basic form since before the fifteenth century and has, therefore, never been limited in its chromatic range. Trombones have formed part of brass groups and wind ensembles for hundreds of years, but were not regularly included in the symphony orchestra until well into the nineteenth century, when they generally appeared as a compact group of three – one alto, one tenor and bass. The invention of the valve trumpet gradually reduced the necessity of writing for trombone in the highest register and the alto instrument fell into disuse, with two tenors and a bass being required or, as was usual in France, just three tenors.

The standard instrument, if such a thing there be, is the tenor trombone pitched in nine-foot B♭ – that is, producing B♭ as the fundamental harmonic with the slide in the closed or least extended position. In this position the instrument has a tube length identical to that of the B♭ alto horn, though its bore and mouthpiece are designed for production of the lower harmonics. Thereafter the length of the tube may be increased by extending the slide through a further six positions, each of which lowers the note produced by one half tone. Reference to *Ex. 4.2*, which shows the seven positions and the first four notes of the harmonic series obtainable from each, demonstrates how the gap of a perfect fifth, between the second and third notes of the series, is successfully bridged.

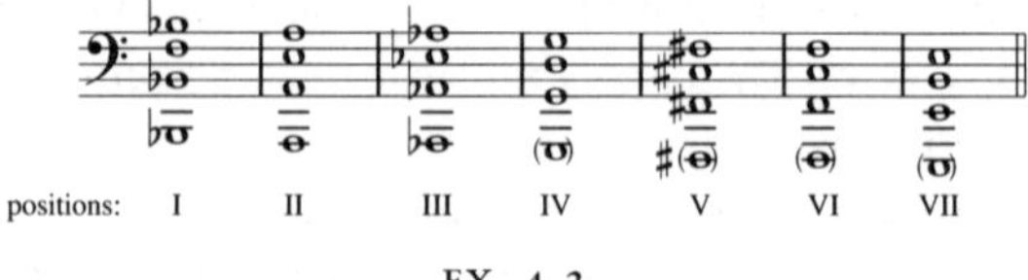

EX. 4.2

The bracketed fundamentals are, for all practical purposes, unobtainable.

It will, however, be noted that there is still a gap of a diminished fifth between the fundamental harmonic in 1st position B♭ and the lowest second harmonic in 7th position (E). This has now been overcome by the modern instrument of slightly wider bore and fitted with a thumb-operated valve. This instrument is basically the B♭ tenor with an extra length of tubing controlled by a rotary valve which, when engaged, pitches it in F – a device identical to that found on the double-horn. Not only does this increase the number of notes available on a single instrument, it also provides alternative slide positions for notes across a large area of the range. The engagement of the extra tubing for the F side of the instrument does, however, increase resistance of the air-flow and alter the relative positions of the slide, because the greater tube length requires a similarly greater distance between the fundamentals. This means that only six basic positions are available on the F side, because the system employs *additional* tubing fitted to an instrument which retains the B♭ tenor slide length. Thus, the lowest B natural is impossible to obtain on the F side of the instrument.

The modern bass trombone is a very similar instrument. It has an extra large bore and an earlier expansion of the tube to a wider bell, and many instruments will be fitted with a second valve on the F valve tubing, extending the lower end of the range to E or E♭. A large mouthpiece should always be used in order to provide a rich sound in the lower register. This instrument is slightly less familiar to the student orchestra, where most players will own the modern tenor – a magnificent beast in its own right.

While it is possible to play the majority of bass trombone parts on the smaller instrument, young players of conservatoire standard are usually expected to begin to specialize, often at an even earlier stage of their development than is the case with horn players, and one must be wary of forcing a tenor-orientated player into the depths of bass playing, and vice versa.

The alto trombone has made a spectacular return in the last twenty years or so and is now once again used for the sustained high playing of the Classical symphonic repertoire. This instrument is pitched in E♭, a perfect fourth above the tenor, and facilitates easier control of the high register. It also carries less inherent weight of sound than its modern counterpart and is considered better suited to the more open orchestration of the Classical era. If the alto trombone is used, it is perfectly acceptable for 2nd to retain the modern tenor, which is eminently capable of producing the same qualities as the older version. (It is the visual aspect that proves alarming to the purist, the size of the modern instrument giving an entirely false impression of its capabilities.)

The alto trombone is a specialist instrument and has to be learnt as such. Quite apart from particular difficulties of intonation caused by the shorter slide, the slide positions are different from those of the tenor. The trombone is not a transposing instrument and a player needs some time for the process of relating note to slide position to become familiar. Nowadays one could expect a few high-class young players intending to play professionally to have learnt the instrument, and some even to possess one of their own.

Some discussion on its relevance and advisability will be undertaken in Chapter 10.

TUBA

There is probably no word in music that covers a wider range of misnomers and misunderstandings than 'tuba'. Through the years composers have written for instruments that no longer exist, or never did exist, or that they thought were something else entirely. Confusion is absolute and its resolution is most often the personal preference of the player concerned. A description of most of the variants to be encountered may be obtained by recourse to *Orchestration* by Walter Piston (Gollancz, 1973), supplemented (historically) by Cecil Forsyth's book of the same name (Macmillan/Stainer and Bell, 1944) and (for modern usage) *Anatomy of the Orchestra* by Norman Del Mar (Faber and Faber, 1981). Such a comprehensive catalogue of instruments need not be repeated here.

As far as student orchestras in the UK are concerned, the most likely candidate is the so-called orchestral tuba pitched in E♭ – often referred to as the 'double E♭'. This is the four- or sometimes five-valved instrument most generally recommended to the serious student as it is equipped to deal most adequately with the majority of orchestral tuba parts. Occasionally one might still come across the slightly smaller example pitched in 12-foot F, and some professional players are now favouring an instrument pitched in 16-foot C.

However, one is not always working with young musicians who have reached such a stage of refinement or, indeed, who can afford to purchase an instrument of their own. Quite often, as with all instruments, one may well be faced with the slightly battered example, found abandoned in the loft, that first fired their interest.

Notoriously high, solo or idiosyncratic parts traditionally performed by the tuba player should only be programmed if it is known that an adequate instrument is available and the player concerned can cope.

Seating

The positioning and individual seating of the full brass group will depend upon the available space in a particular hall. Ideally, a single line to the right of the conductor and one row behind the woodwind will best allow them to hear, balance and blend with the orchestra as a whole, but such depth and lateral space as this requires will usually only be found in a purpose-built concert hall. Where such positioning can be considered, the individual seating needs to be as follows:

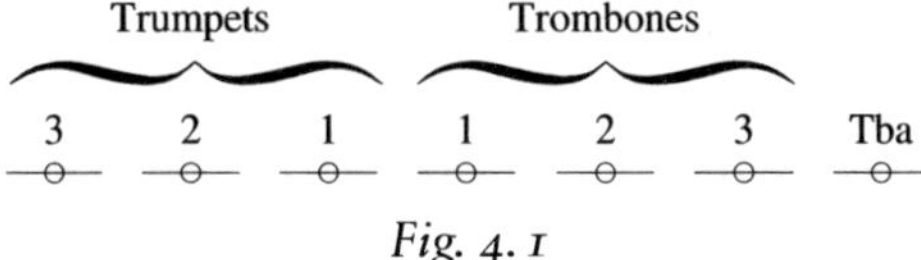

Fig. 4.1

The alternative is to place the trumpets immediately in front of the trombones, a position that is sometimes less highly regarded by the players, especially in heavily orchestrated music, because the trombones will be blowing directly into the necks of the trumpet section. However, many great players who have persevered with this seating will insist that it is superior to any other once the section has become accustomed to it, particularly if the trombones are raised above them and the seating slightly staggered. It is certainly true that, from the front, the overall balance of the brass section is more easily assimilated and controlled in this position. In any event there are many occasions where no other positioning is possible, whereupon the individual seating should be:

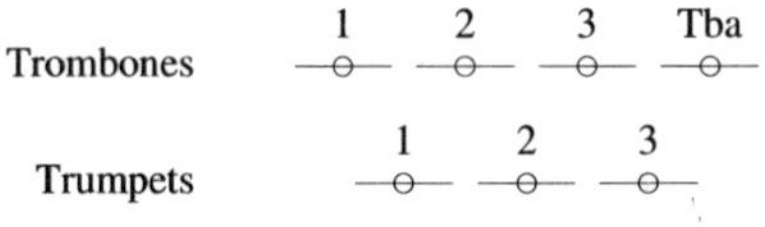

Trombones 1 2 3 Tba

Trumpets 1 2 3

Fig. 4.2

It will be noticed from the preceding examples that the trumpet line needs to be reversed in the two seating arrangements to keep the 1st player as close as possible to 1st trombone. The player most affected by this change is 2nd trumpet, who will have the 1st player to the left in the single line and to the right in the double. Although this is not crucial it is inadvisable to change the arrangement suddenly. In student orchestras it is probable that one layout will have been adopted for all the rehearsals, and the change will coincide with the general rehearsal at the concert venue, just as the players are having to cope with a new acoustic and the conductor is least understanding regarding accidents and mis-performance. This is not the time for even one member of the orchestra to be uncomfortable or confused if it can be avoided. Where possible, especially with very inexperienced players, the seating should be kept constant, even if this necessitates using a less preferred alternative throughout the rehearsals.

With the brass in this arrangement a further important consideration is slide room for the trombones, who need enough space for the slide to be fully extended without coming into contact with the chair or body in front of them. Sufficient *clear space* must be found. It is not enough to make room simply by off-setting chairs and expecting the players to aim their slides between them. This is a hazardous practice guaranteed to create havoc in concert. At least two feet of unencumbered space beyond the music stand is essential.

DUPLICATION

The provision of an extra player for 1st trumpet is becoming more general in repertoire that places heavy demands on the instrument in terms of range and endurance. With young players this practice has much to recommend it, since it keeps more players fully occupied and avoids strain on an immature embouchure. The player will have much the same responsibilities as the bumper horn (*see* Chapter 3) and should not merely double the part except in rare circumstances, and then only for short, confined passages. No further duplication of trumpet parts is either necessary or desirable.

Duplication of trombone and tuba parts should not be considered unless specifically requested in the score.

Forming the Section

As mentioned previously, the following comments on individual responsibilities within the brass section refer to those incumbent on each position, and should not imply that players, especially those of limited experience, cannot be interchanged. Indeed, in the trumpet section some spreading of the work load by alternation between 1st and 3rd, 2nd and 4th can prove beneficial.

1ST TRUMPET (PRINCIPAL)

As with all other orchestral Principals, the technical facility of the 1st trumpet must be excellent across the range of the instrument. The musical demands placed upon this instrumentalist require a superb standard of agility, articulation and dynamic variation. But even beyond these, the position demands a control of sound that is not always quite so obvious. Perhaps beyond all other orchestral instruments, passages abound for trumpet that, whilst they can be quite adequately achieved within the most recognizable aspect of the instrument's character, actually require a far greater consideration of timbre and colour than might be immediately apparent.

This is particularly true of passages appearing at or near the start of a work, where the orchestral texture has had no time to influence the player's approach, and can cause problems for student instrumentalists (although it is not altogether unknown in other circumstances!).

Among the most well known orchestral solos for the trumpet is that shown *Ex. 4.3* which, in Ravel's orchestration, opens the tour depicted by Mussorgsky *Pictures from an Exhibition*.

EX. 4.3

The essence of this short introductory phrase has nothing to do with the heroism or drama often implied by the trumpet sound but is simply the undisturbed statement that a journey is underway. The key to such aural inference does not lie in the dynamic level or the delineation of movement, but solely in the control of sound.

Similarly, *Ex. 4.4* from Mahler *Symphony no. 5*, probably the most famous of all trumpet openings, relies on the technical and musical ability to control the substance and nature of the sound produced as much as on articulation, range and confidence.

Even in young players, the foundations of such abilities must be evident, for there is no instrument in the orchestra so beguiling to a young player in its capacity for dramatic inflection. Nor is there one which provides its Principal with less cover. Because of the dominant timbre of the instrument and the way composers write for it, there is hardly a single note played by the 1st trumpet that isn't heard. This fact influences both the mould and approach of the player concerned, and it is hardly surprising that trumpet players often display

EX. 4.4

an attitude towards playing not always fully understood by the profession at large. Sensitivity, however, is equally important, and even short, fragmented solos, such as *Ex. 4.5* from Debussy *La Mer* will soon expose any lack of musicianship or feeling for the phrase.

EX. 4.5

All extremes of dynamic level are required of 1st trumpet. As always, soft playing is the most technically demanding, especially across the top of the range, as is the case with the upper notes of *Ex. 4.6* from Stravinsky *Symphony in C.*

Although not ideally situated to appraise the balance and ensemble of the brass group, the 1st trumpet must nonetheless possess a focused sound that can be felt across the entire section at any dynamic.

In student orchestras this player should be encouraged to accept responsibility and provide the example for the whole brass section, not only in terms of playing but in attitude and punctuality as well. Even in such relatively inexperienced orchestras 1st trumpet will almost certainly be the unelected spokesperson for the brass group, and this role cannot be undertaken without the personality and playing confidence that will influence much of the

EX. 4.6

section's performance. This aspect of the 1st trumpet position must be understood and respected by all those who have any dealings with the orchestra.

One final word of warning. Often in student orchestras a larger number of players is available to the trumpet section than may be required in any one work of the programme and some discretion is necessary when deciding who plays in which piece. In my experience, especially with rather more advanced orchestras, the senior player sometimes 'divides the spoils' and works out the section's playing in advance of any advice or tutoring, usually by appropriating the more obviously interesting works, thereby leaving those which are often more exposed and difficult in the hands of less experienced, weaker players. Such a situation must be quickly noted and rectified, preferably by the tutor, because it is often too late to change it when the conductor comes to rehearse the piece where the weakness will be apparent. The overall good of the orchestra must take precedence over an individual's desire to play a particular part in a particular piece. Any good player will understand this premise – if a little grudgingly at first!

2ND TRUMPET

Musically, the position of 2nd trumpet is no less exposed or vital than that of the 1st. By far the most frequent use of trumpets is in combinations of two or three and, in either circumstance, this player's ability to provide tonal support, automatic balance and variation in colour is crucial.

One of the most notorious trumpet entries in the entire repertoire – that in the seventh bar of Tchaikovsky *Symphony no. 4* – relies almost entirely on 2nd trumpet's projection, intonation, articulation, and the degree of confidence thus engendered in the 1st player.

EX. 4.7

Nor is the seat less technically demanding, for most of the passage-work assigned to 1st trumpet comes the way of 2nd sooner rather than later – and often in a lower, more awkward part of the instrument. Hardly a score can be opened where the trumpets are not found to be in octaves, thirds or sixths, declaiming the same intricate rhythms devised to sound as one instrument. It is doubtful whether any other 2nd player has so much exposure to playing in a 'solo' capacity.

Unlike 2nd or 4th horn, 2nd trumpet parts will not generally lie in the low or middle register of the instrument, since traditional scoring for trumpets tends to place the part in closer harmonic proximity to the Principal. Furthermore, the predilection for trumpet doubling of the upper line requires of 2nd the same range as 1st. Many examples may be found, but *Ex. 4.8*, from the final movement of Bartók *Concerto for Orchestra,* is probably as notorious as any, coming so near the end of an extraordinarily demanding work.

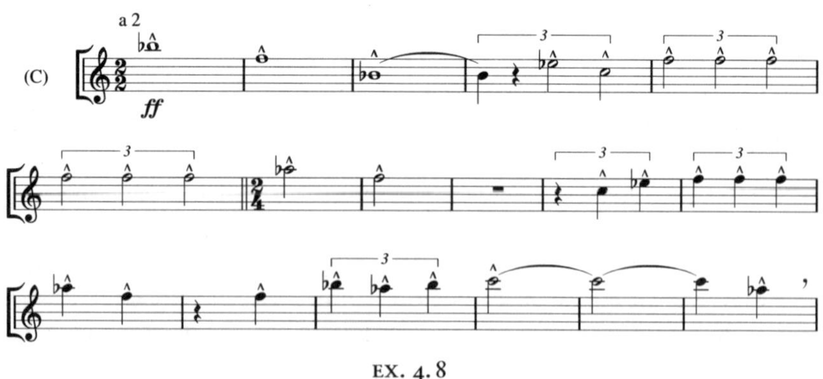

EX. 4.8

As with all wind instruments, the requisites of articulation, range and projection are apt to obscure the vital aspect of breath control until this is brought to the attention by a passage of inordinate length, where extra breathing is impossible. A further example of the cruel nature of much trumpet writing can be seen in the totally exposed 2nd trumpet note that occurs in the second movement of the tragically neglected '*Asrael*' *Symphony* by Josef Suk.

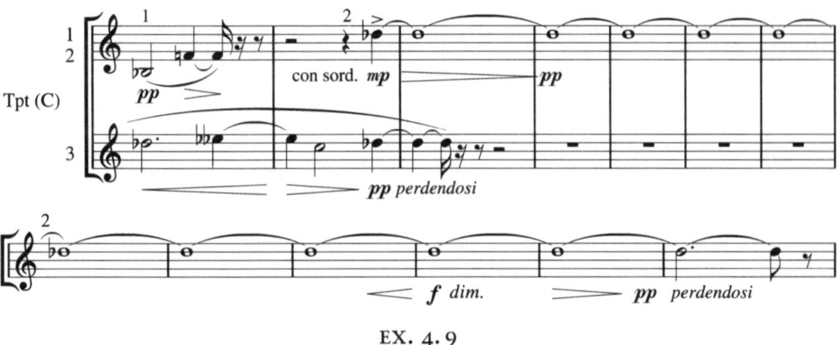

EX. 4.9

In this *Andante* each of the three trumpets in turn sustains the D♭ for all but 36 bars of the movement, but neither 1st nor 3rd has a passage of quite such unbelievable length. With consummate skill it is just possible for one of the other trumpets to take over from 2nd somewhere less than half way through these quoted bars, but to do so unobtrusively is almost as difficult as 2nd's holding it.

3RD TRUMPET (PRINCIPAL)

The position of 3rd trumpet is extraordinary in the range of duties it entails. Rarely required in the more Classically orientated symphonic repertoire, it becomes an increasingly essential addition to the section from the latter part of the nineteenth century.

Its use varies dramatically, many composers employing a similar approach to that of the Baroque section, where a third part remained largely independent of the other two. As a integral member of a three-trumpet section, the part will tend to lie below the other two, taking sole responsibility for the low octave or, more often, supplying the foundation of triadic movement, as seen in the famous march-like theme of the 1st movement of Shostakovich *Symphony no. 5 (Ex. 4.10)*.

Elsewhere the part may be quite separate and almost totally soloistic. Such is the situation throughout Rachmaninov *Symphony no. 3*, where the part is intended for the 'tromba contralta in F' (probably the F valve trumpet,

EX. 4.10

renamed because of its inherent weakness in the upper register) which frequently appears in Russian scores, though none later than this (1936), as far as I am aware. The part, like the whole work, is written with meticulous care but it always seems to lose something when played by a 3rd B♭ trumpet (although this might be an illusion brought about by the enhanced individuality of the part on the printed page).

In Britten *Four Sea Interludes* from *Peter Grimes* the 3rd trumpet part is pitched in D (the other two being in C) and spends much of its time playing above them as well as taking on all the virtuoso passage-work. The wonderfully inventive writing with which this and all Britten's orchestral work abounds is illustrated by *Ex. 4.11*, a passage for two trumpets, divided between three players. The 3rd trumpet alone is given the entire theme, although it is debatable whether the rigours of the sustained passage or continual re-entry are more demanding.

It is nowadays common practice for all three players to use the D trumpet for this passage and further re-arrangement of the parts to be contemplated (the original almost certainly owes much of its idiosyncratic division to the influence of a well-known player of the time).

The choice of player for 3rd trumpet in student orchestras requires considerable care, and the ability of this player will often influence the choice of programme. Once three trumpets are required the 3rd part is rarely less demanding than the other two, and often more so. A player of excellent overall technical ability is needed, probably a very close competitor for 1st, and certainly one equipped to take over the position in the foreseeable future.

A further responsibility for this player arises with the inclusion of cornet parts in the brass group, and this will be discussed below.

(Allegro spiritoso 𝅗𝅥 = 80)
Solo
(C) 1 2
Tpt
Solo
(D) 3
ff
Solo ff
più f
cresc.
fff tr

EX. 4.11

1ST TROMBONE (PRINCIPAL)

As with all first players, the position of 1st trombone brings with it a degree of responsibility for the section and a necessary ability to lead by example. The sheer volume of sound available to players of this instrument makes control and sensitivity vital ingredients in the personality of all the players, but particularly the 1st. Orchestral trombone playing is an art requiring, in addition to instrumental ability, much patience, self-discipline, aural concentration and tact. One ill-considered entry, one over-demonstrative dynamic, and the work of eighty people can be destroyed in an instant.

It must also be remembered that this is the first orchestral section under discussion that generally spends more time waiting to play than actually playing, and the ability to cope with this has to be learned. A 1st player who fully understands the implications of this is of inestimable value to the section and can have a lasting influence on those less experienced players to whom the unforeseen rigours of waiting to play can prove something of a shock.

This can be as true 'off the stand' as within the orchestra for, even though the conductor can inform them of approximately when they will be required, they are still, especially on a residential youth orchestra course, not free in the true sense of the word. Instruments will probably be out of the case and ready, and the clock a determining factor in what the players can do with their time.

The difficulties of such an extraordinary performing life-style must not be lightly dismissed, because they have a great bearing on each individual's playing. Perhaps the most essential ingredient for an orchestral trombone player is a well-developed sense of humour!

As to performance requirements, the 1st player must have an excellent overall facility on the instrument, immense control of tone and projection and a very keen ear for balance. Most of the playing will occur either in close partnership with 2nd or with all three trombones together. Chording tends often to include tuba, which can make life trying in terms of balance and intonation, especially for young players. With regard to the latter, however, the trombones are the only instruments to have totally adjustable intonation, apart from the strings, by virtue of the slide (even 1st position on many modern instruments sets back on to a spring system, allowing it to be pulled a little sharp if necessary). Less blame may therefore be placed upon the vagaries of the instrument than is the case elsewhere.

Regrettably, the soft, pensive side of the instrument is rarely exploited in the symphony orchestra, except by the full section. Rarities such as the long, immensely difficult, solo in Ravel *Boléro* only serve to increase the frustration that the instrument is so little used in this vein. Elsewhere, fragmented solos appear, but those of any substance tend to be virtuosic and display the more forceful side of the instrument's character, as in that from Malcolm Arnold *Tam O'Shanter*.

EX. 4.12

Both these solos are *tours de force* for the 1st trombone and neither piece should be programmed for a youth orchestra that does not possess an exceptional, mature and experienced player, preferably of post-graduate conservatoire standard.

A facility across the full range of the instrument is essential for 1st trombone. Many twentieth-century composers are not averse to using the lower part of the instrument, and Elgar in this example from his concert overture *Cockaigne* has no qualms about taking the solo 1st trombone into the unaccustomed regions at the bottom of the bass clef.

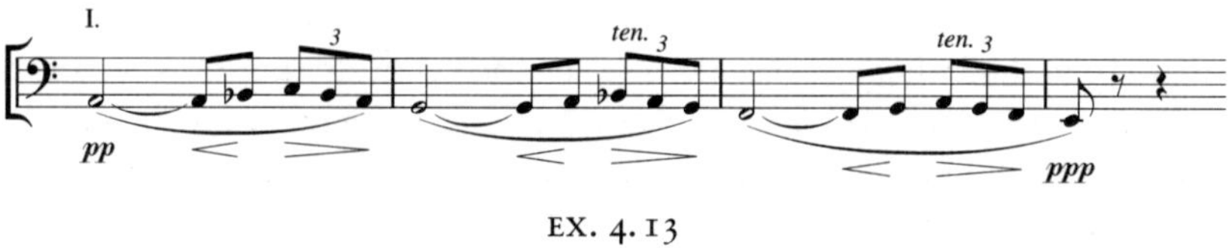

EX. 4.13

Such scoring, in a part that incorporates the C two and a half octaves above, may be considered somewhat unusual but not unique.

2ND TROMBONE (SUB-PRINCIPAL)

As with 2nd trumpet, this position is unlikely to be less demanding than 1st, although it is less often pitched in the uppermost range of the instrument. In passages involving three trombones, or three plus tuba, the balance of this second part is critical, and the player must be capable of a mature, projected sound. The balancing down of 1st and (more especially) 3rd, beyond certain limits, will often prove impossible.

Many solos exist for the 2nd player, usually pitched towards the middle register of the instrument because the Classical section comprised alto, tenor, and bass. The following *ad libitum* solo from early in the second movement of Rimsky-Korsakov *Scheherazade* is for 2nd trombone on both occasions

EX. 4.14

while the long solo, in partnership with 1st, from Kodály *Variations on an Hungarian Folk Song – The Flight of the Peacock* demonstrates how essential it is to have two players of commensurate sound and technique (see *Ex. 4.15*).

A further difficulty of this particular passage lies in projecting a controlled and rounded sound through the fully orchestrated *legato* subject that surrounds it.

In discussing the attributes required of trombonists, it is worth remembering that there are many ebullient and carefree passages that make all the waiting worthwhile. A magnificent passage, again from Elgar *Cockaigne*, shows 2nd trombone in a higher register than in the previous examples (see *Ex. 4.16*).

Here 2nd trombone is in unison with 1st and two cornets. In a footnote at the beginning of the score, Elgar sanctioned the addition of two further trombones to the line if available. Elgar's unique and uninhibited writing for trombones will be discussed further in Chapter 10.

3RD/BASS TROMBONE

The roles of a true bass trombone and that of a third tenor instrument have become inextricably bound together. Many composers use the player in both

(Adagio)

EX. 4.15

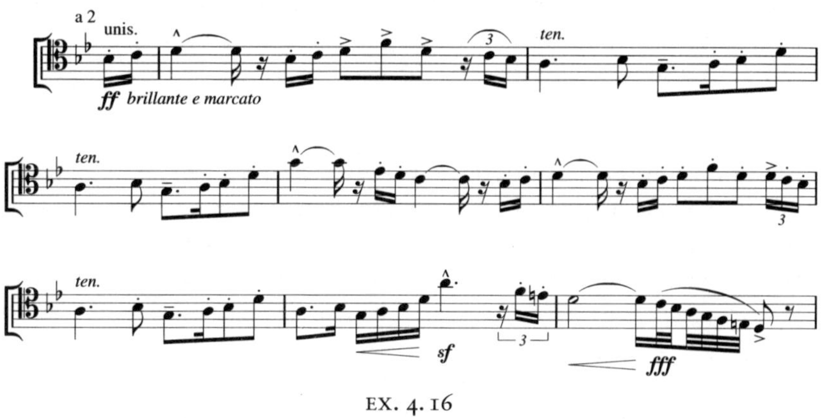

EX. 4.16

roles within the same work, which explains the almost universal acceptance of the modern instrument. For a young player, life in this seat can be extremely difficult, and very tiring in a work that demands sustained low playing.

For much of the time the 3rd player will be in direct partnership with the tuba, occasionally in unison but more frequently at the octave. This accepted coupling is at best an unhappy relationship, the two instruments being devoid of similar characteristics with the exception of range. Indeed much of the writing for the two instruments together seems blatantly to use 3rd trombone as an agent for clarifying the articulation of the tuba – a resort that becomes quite unnecessary when the latter instrument is used for its own sake and not just as bass reinforcement. However, the situation is now firmly entrenched and both instrumentalists have to deal with it as best they can.

The 3rd player (be it bass or tenor) in three-trombone writing will support the lowest line of the harmony and be responsible not only for intonation but also, in many cases, for clarity of movement. Even in an accompanying passage such as *Ex. 4.17*, again from Kodály '*Peacock Variations*', the slightest tendency on the part of the 3rd player to lengthen the notes will 'bind' the sounds of the instruments above, in this case trumpets as well as the other two trombones, however 'short' they might play.

EX. 4.17

It is very difficult, especially for a young player, to give the notes clear and precise *staccato* articulation at this low register. A player without good control of the diaphragm will tend to blow into the notes, thereby losing clarity and almost certainly producing the notes late into the bargain. Such a fault in production, while always apparent to some degree, tends to be more noticeable in notes pitched particularly low, the greater volume of air and looser embouchure required to make the notes speak inducing, except in advanced and disciplined players, a less supported and controlled production. Although all students will have covered this register of the instrument, it is here that a specialist player will stand apart.

Most of the problems of balance and ensemble that apply specifically to 3rd trombone emanate from these, or closely associated, technical considerations, and a player in this position who has yet to master them will be floundering, often without knowing why.

Passage-work occurs as frequently for 3rd as for the other two but often again sits firmly in the low, awkward register. The following little tongue-twister comes from *Jupiter*, the fourth movement of Holst *The Planets*. This work contains a true bass trombone part throughout.

EX. 4.18

Real solo playing is rare but it does exist, though often in fragmented form. However, the lone trombone parts of the two Chopin piano concerti are both for this player, as are those single parts that appear (or should appear) in a number of Rossini overtures. In these works the player may be seated next to the bassoons or even alongside the cello group, but should not be left to languish alone in the exalted heights of the back row – such an oversight looking almost as ridiculous as it sounds.

Consideration of the previously-mentioned difficulties which can arise when 3rd trombone is orchestrated in combination with the tuba will be found in Chapter 10, as this is more relevant within the context of the whole section than in a discussion of the requirements from individual players.

TUBA (PRINCIPAL)

The tuba is unique among the wind group in forming a section of one. As such, the player's own choice of instrument, both for general playing and specific repertoire, is only constrained by suitability to blend and balance with the prevailing orchestration. The younger player however is unlikely to have a choice of instrument and is likely to have to cope with a less than ideal example.

From the point of view of sound production, it will also sometimes appear that this player is technically in advance of the trombone section, especially in the middle and lower register, largely because of the instrument's increased resonance over the smaller bore trombones and its natural tendency to complement sounds once a reasonable technique of production has been achieved.

However, it is in the total control of soft playing that the real tuba player emerges.

Orchestrally the role is varied, sometimes solo, sometimes taking full responsibility for the orchestral bass, sometimes complementary to the string basses, but most often to the lower brass. In all circumstances a sensitivity to balance, a restraint of dynamic level and a subtle regulation of tone are vital. In its typical association with trombones, a passage from Tchaikovsky *Symphony no. 6* vividly displays the necessity of all three.

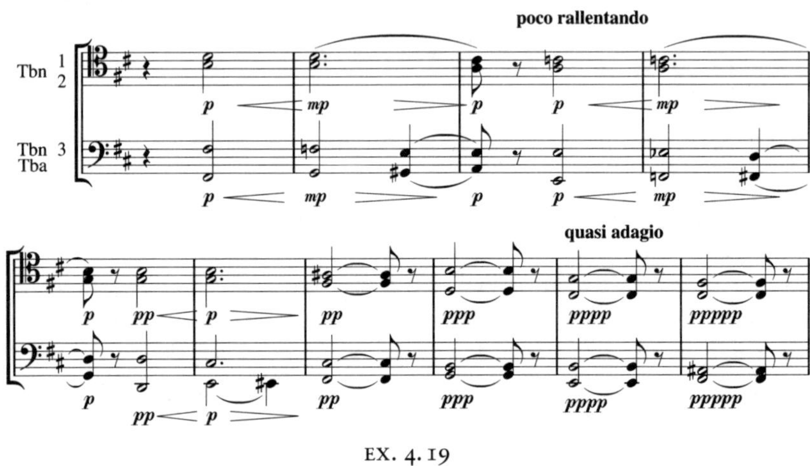

EX. 4.19

Here a further technical demand becomes apparent, which afflicts all instruments but is most magnified by the weight and timbre of the tuba: the need to end notes with immense care. Often, as in the case of this example, the final note will be heard to 'bump' on to its resolution because the player tongues too hard, neglects to control the air-flow and breathes too quickly. Of all instruments it is the tuba that must be played 'through the rest', keeping it alive by the quality of the previous note and finding time within the phrase to breathe. The sheer volume of air required by the instrument, in *piano* as much as *forte* playing, must not be allowed to induce panicked or shallow breathing, or a preponderance of accents and curtailed phrases will result. This built-in adversary of the *legato* phrase lives with the tuba player all the time, which is probably why, paradoxically, the great players can fool us all into believing the opposite.

This aspect of tuba technique highlights a major requirement for all the brass: the necessity to sustain sound, over and above the need to play loudly.

Surprisingly, despite its size, the tuba is capable of great agility. Apart from the need to replenish the lungs regularly, the tuba player can compete on equal terms with the most accomplished trombonist and rapid passage-work is not unusual. *Ex. 4.20*, quoted from Shostakovich *Symphony no. 7*, is perhaps longer than most, but by no means uniquely demanding.

EX. 4.20

Long solos tend to be in the high range of the instrument, and it is here that the umbrella term 'tuba', referred to earlier in the chapter, leads to most confusion. The famous solo from Ravel's orchestration of Mussorgsky *Pictures from an Exhibition*, although playable on the smaller F tuba, is unlikely to be within the capabilities of a young player, and advice should be sought as to whether a more suitable instrument may be found for this particular section of the work. In any case, this is a further example of a work that should only be programmed when a sufficiently proficient player is available. Similarly, the lone 'tuba' of Mendelssohn overture *A Midsummer Night's Dream* was written for the now obsolete ophicleide (a key-operated brass instrument with an appearance similar to the bassoon) and its performance on a modern tuba needs a careful choice of instrument.

Short solos in the more standard, lower register of the instrument are frequently found, the instrument being well able to project in this area at relatively soft dynamic levels. *Ex. 4.21*, once more from Suk *'Asrael' Symphony*, provides a wonderful moment of orchestration, the dark tuba sound being discovered more than three octaves below its shimmering accompaniment (see page 102).

EX. 4.21

The Enlarged Section

TRUMPETS

The increase of the trumpet section beyond three trumpets (for a moment discounting the addition of cornets) is comparatively rare in the symphonic repertoire. Many works which demand additional woodwind and horns make no increase in this section, and even Richard Strauss, in his gargantuan *Alpine Symphony*, finds four trumpets enough to counter-balance twenty horns, four Wagner tubas, four trombones and two bass tubas.

A section of four trumpets first appears with Berlioz, the overture *Benvenuto Cellini* requiring four instruments (in addition to two cornets) pitched in three different keys in order to state the main theme of the *Adagio* introduction in full orchestration at the end. Even so, the 4th trumpet has a pretty thin time of it, with its grand total of fifteen notes! The scoring seems not to have been repeated until Wagner in *Rienzi*, after which it appears intermittently, most notably in scores by Schoenberg (*Pelleas und Melisande*), Holst (*The Planets*), Berg (*Three Orchestral Pieces*), Bartók (*Four Orchestral Pieces*), Richard Strauss (*Also sprach Zarathustra*, *Symphonia Domestica*, *Alpine Symphony*), Lutosławski (*Concerto for Orchestra*) and Mahler (*Symphonies nos 3* and *5*). Of the French school, where the use of cornets is most prolific, both Debussy (*Gigues* from *Images*, and *Jeux*) and Roussel (*Bacchus et Ariane, Symphonies nos 3* and *4*) occasionally prefer four trumpets alone.

A striking use of four trumpets appears in Panufnik *Sinfonia Sacra* where the composer asks that 'The four Trumpets should be widely separated at the four compass points of the orchestra throughout the whole performance of the Symphony'. While it must be admitted that their use throughout the work is very soloistic, the parts would still be undertaken by the orchestral trumpeters.

Above four trumpets, the increase is usually made by the addition of one or more related instruments (the D trumpet or the bass trumpet) as considered below. The six trumpets of Shostakovich *Symphony no. 7* and the nine required for Janáček *Sinfonietta* are two extraordinary exceptions.

CORNETS

By far the most frequent visitors to the trumpet section are the cornets, usually appearing as a pair with two trumpets but very occasionally alone. The 1st cornet part is always the province of the 3rd trumpet player, even if more than two trumpets are also required – as in the Berlioz overture mentioned above. In the student orchestra, such a hierarchy need not be adhered to so strictly but the usual two plus two format will predetermine it much of the time.

The cornet is *not* an optional instrument, and the modern tendency in some sections to play the parts on trumpet is regrettable, to say the least. The often-heard excuse that nowadays the two instruments are so similar as to be virtually indistinguishable is, in the hands of many players, unfortunately all too true. The orchestral cornet has developed – or perhaps it might be better simply to say changed – from the short, rotund instrument still to be seen in brass bands, to a more sleek, elongated instrument, very much along trumpet lines. It is played, in many circumstances, by players with no real determination to exploit such different tonal characteristics as remain, often using a trumpet mouthpiece. One can only watch in horror as the classic 'Catch-22' situation develops – it is not worth insisting on cornets because they sound like trumpets, so one cannot find cornets because nobody asks for them!

But it *is* worth asking for them and insisting on instruments that retain much of the roundness of sound associated with the older instruments. It is also worth persuading people to specialize in their performance, albeit in a trumpet-orientated style with firm rooting in the orchestral tradition (no one expects orchestras to keep two players for cornet alone). The instruments blend much more easily than trumpets and, because of the inherent warmth of their sound, they can accomplish fast, agile passage-work without the dazzling brightness of the trumpet.

The cornet originated in France, and nowhere are its intrinsic qualities more clearly demonstrated than in the scores of French composers, where the instruments are frequently used in a completely different way from trumpets and for an entirely different effect and purpose. To confuse the two instruments and their functions is to lose an essential link in the brass section and an equally essential ambivalent quality to much harmonic orchestration.

Even when the orchestration seems to make no obvious use of their most audible characteristics, further inspection proves their presence to be essential. Franck, in his *Symphony in D minor*, provides his two cornets with no thematic material at all, confining them to the outer movements and using them solely to unify the sound of the trumpets and the horns or, in the two small chorale-like episodes of the third movement, the trumpets and the lower brass. There is hardly a bar where two trumpets could fulfil the same purpose.

Outside the French repertoire, cornets are used most frequently, and to best effect, by those composers influenced by French culture or musical language – Russian composers of the late nineteenth and early twentieth centuries – or those to whom the instrument had historic associations. In England, however, the cornet was regularly used for trumpet parts up to the time of the First World War, the facility of the instrument taking precedence over the requested sound! (This may be one reason why the British orchestral player tends to view the instrument in a more trumpet-orientated light, although such an attitude is not confined to these islands.)

Tchaikovsky, whose ear for orchestration was second to none, uses the darkening qualities of two *piano* cornets to great effect in the opening bars of *Francesca da Rimini*, edging their sound with two interlocked trumpets.

EX. 4.22

This extract must be one of the most ominous and atmospheric pieces of writing in all music, a stroke from the hand of a genius if ever there was one.

In an entirely different style, more akin to the general appraisal of the cornet, Stravinsky imbues the entrance of the Ballerina in *Petrouchka* with a certain sense of foreboding and unease by scoring so lively a theme for one solo cornet.

EX. 4.23

Compared with the mellow sound of the cornet, this solo can sound altogether too bright and optimistic when performed on trumpet, as requested in the later, reduced orchestration version of the score.

Parts for trumpet *doubling* cornet are rare but Bartók, in his *Four Orchestral Pieces op. 12*, requires all four trumpets to play cornet in the final movement.

Although cornets most usually are required to 'hunt in pairs', the addition of just one is requested by some composers, Prokofiev (*Romeo and Juliet*) and Berlioz (*Rob Roy*, and *Beatrice et Benedict* overtures) providing perhaps the best-known examples.

Finally it must be said that many Principals still insist on their section using cornets where designated, as do many conductors, but the practice is in danger of lapsing.

TROMBONES

Any increase in numbers beyond three trombones is very infrequent. In fact a reduction to just two players, rare in itself, will probably be encountered as often.

When the extra player is not used simply as a written-in doubling instrument for the major climax, the section of four trombones most often divides two + two. In Janáček *Sinfonietta* use of the extra player allows a four-part division of harmony within the one timbre.

EX. 4.24

It also gives the opportunity for two-part writing to be doubled, not to add extra volume but rather to increase the potency of the sound. This device is also used by Lutosławski in the *Concerto for Orchestra* (see *Ex.* 4.25).

A total doubling of the section may be found in Shostakovich *Symphony*

a 2
1
2
Tbn
3
4
ff
a 2
ff
sff
sff

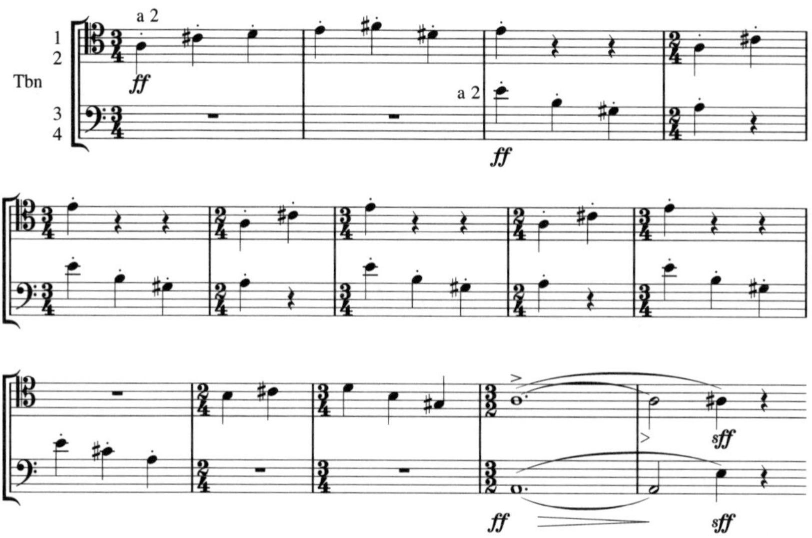

EX. 4.25

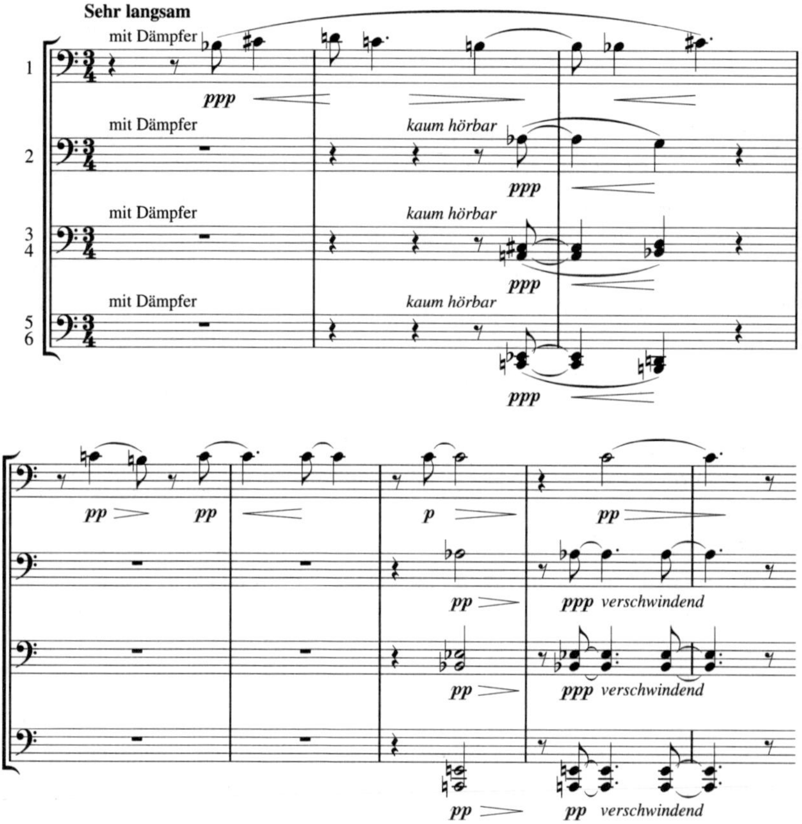

Sehr langsam
mit Dämpfer
1
ppp
mit Dämpfer
kaum hörbar
2
ppp
mit Dämpfer
kaum hörbar
3
4
ppp
mit Dämpfer
kaum hörbar
5
6
ppp
pp
pp
p
pp
pp
ppp verschwindend
pp
ppp verschwindend
pp
pp verschwindend

EX. 4.26

no. 7, the players remaining in two distinct groups of three. Webern, in the original orchestration of the *Six Pieces for Orchestra*, uses six muted trombones for just eight bars of the fifth movement, producing a unique combination of sound (see *Ex. 4.26*).

A request to double a single line of trombone writing is extremely rare but Elgar asks this in the overture *Cockaigne* (remarking in a footnote that two tenor trombones 'may' be added in designated places). The relevant passages are marked by drawings of a left or right hand with index finger extended, pointing accusingly at the start and finish of the passages. Unfortunately they are not positioned with total accuracy, the left hand (which denotes the end of the doubling) being omitted on more than one occasion.

Transposition

All members of the trumpet family are transposing instruments except, of course, trumpet in C (although this, in places where the B♭ instrument is standard, becomes a transposing instrument as far as the player is concerned). The most frequent transpositions of B♭, A and F will nowadays mainly be played on the B♭ instrument, as will the less often encountered parts for E, B♮, A♭ and G. Parts for D trumpet will nowadays most usually be performed on the specified instrument. The treble clef is normal for trumpets although the bass clef is not unknown, most notably in Mozart *Don Giovanni* where the 'old notation' (in this case up an octave and a tone) is to be inferred.

Neither trombones nor tuba transpose, both being written at sounding pitch, and such designations as 'B♭ trombone' or 'tuba in F' refer only to the species of instrument required and never to the key of the written part. The tenor tuba is sometimes written as a transposing instrument in B♭. Parts for 1st and 2nd trombone will often be found written in the alto or tenor clefs but 3rd, whether a true bass part or not, tends to remain in the bass clef, which is used for all orchestral tuba parts.

One word of warning however: the tradition of writing brass band tenor trombone parts in the *treble clef* can, in youth orchestras, make for a situation where some players are unused to reading alto, tenor or even bass clef. Some interesting harmonic variations can result (and persevere for some considerable time).

Infrequent Additions

Variations of instrument may appear in the trumpet section depending on which instrument individual players feel can most comfortably achieve particular timbres. The smaller trumpets in D or E♭ will often be used for sustained high parts even when the instrument itself is not specified. The choice of available instruments must be left to the discretion of the players themselves or, in the case of inexperienced orchestras, the tutor or individual teacher.

FLUGELHORN

An even more mellow member of the cornet family, the flugelhorn is an essential member of all brass bands and, as such, a more familiar instrument to the brass fraternity than one might expect. Most young players will certainly know where to find one, and might well manage to borrow one if necessary – actually playing it might well be a different matter! Its use in the symphony orchestra is, in the general repertoire, limited to two works – Mahler *Symphony no. 3* and Vaughan Williams *Symphony no. 9* – although in recent years its use and popularity have been growing. Both the above mentioned parts are largely soloistic and should be approached with caution. Indeed, unless an older, experienced player is available, these works should be avoided.

BASS TRUMPET

Appearing with surprising frequency, the bass trumpet is usually played by a trombone player, its deep mouthpiece being more familiar to players of this instrument. It is remarkable in retaining the true trumpet quality at very low pitch, and is probably best known for its appearance in Stravinsky *The Rite of Spring* where it supports two C trumpets.

EX. 4.27

In my experience, student orchestras have no difficulty in finding either the instrument or a competent exponent to perform the parts.

ALTO TROMBONE

This instrument has already been mentioned as an alternative instrument for 1st trombone, but it is actually requested by Schoenberg, in addition to four standard instruments, in *Pelleas und Melisande*. Although Alban Berg is also known to have requested the instrument as the uppermost of his four trombones in the *Three Orchestral Pieces* and other works, it is not separately identified in the instrumentation of scores I have seen. Use of the instrument in works of the Classical and early Romantic eras is dealt with elsewhere.

CONTRABASS TROMBONE

Conceived by Wagner for *The Ring* and required by Havergal Brian (among others) in at least three of the symphonies, this instrument is not completely obsolete, although the modern bass trombone is capable of performing parts for which it was originally necessary. Some professional players have started to use it again because of its 'dreadnought' weight and darkness of sound, and at least one double-slide example exists within the London conservatoires. However, its use by student players is not to be recommended.

The parts of bass and contrabass trombone cannot be amalgamated, and where separate parts exist (bass *plus* contrabass) two players will always be required, even though they will generally be using identical instruments.

TUBA

A totally different situation exists for tuba, where almost every instrument may be regarded as an 'infrequent addition', in that one never seems to meet with identical instruments from one orchestra to the next. I read only recently of the existence of a thesis dealing solely with the 150 variations of the E♭ tuba contained within the walls of just one American University museum! It is worth reiterating that the choice of instrument for everyday orchestral purposes is a matter for the player alone and, unless obviously unsatisfactory, is not within the conductor's jurisdiction.

Having earlier explained that most orchestral players generally use some variation of the orchestral E♭ tuba, and having included the misnamed Wagner tubas in the previous chapter, it only remains to mention one further instrument under this heading (the great contrabass B♭ being virtually restricted to Wagner operas and, therefore, outside the scope of this discussion).

EUPHONIUM (TENOR TUBA)

The smallest of the true orchestral tubas, pitched in nine foot B♭, this instrument is again a familiar member of the brass band. Referred to orchestrally as the tenor tuba this instrument (especially in the student orchestra) will often play the famous solo from Ravel/Mussorgsky *Pictures from an Exhibition*. It is also the instrument required by Holst for *The Planets*, where it is correctly designated as tenor tuba in B♭. Again, there is rarely any difficulty in supplying instrument or player.

SAXHORN

Saxhorns are a family of brass instruments with a conical bore somewhat narrower than that of flugelhorns. It is almost at this point that confusion begins, for no two sources entirely agree upon number, size or shape, and the wide variations that exist in nomenclature from one country to another compound the situation even further.

Generally, seven instruments are listed (although there is strong evidence of there being at least one more than this): four 'half-bore' instruments of the upper range, with forward-facing bell (similar in design to a cornet or keyed bugle), and three 'whole-bore' of the lower range with upward-facing bell (true tubas). The lowest of the upper range instruments almost certainly also appeared with an upward-facing bell and this is quite probably true of some or all the others. Indeed an advertisement of Henry Distin & Co., Cornet and Sax-horn Manufactory, London (c.1849, reproduced in Baines *Brass Instruments: Their History and Development*) shows all the upper-range instruments in both horizontal and upright versions. Baines describes the entire range illustrated, which includes cornets, trombones, euphoniums and ophecleides (*sic*), as being 'almost entirely French imports, most of them designs by Sax'.

Be that as it may, for all practical purposes the instruments no longer exist in recognizable form. Confusion thus becomes acute when deciding which instruments most resemble or could best replace them (especially when saxhorns themselves occur as a replacement for something else). Apart from one or two instances in works outside the range of this discussion, the most famous example of their specified use is that encountered in the first movement of Mahler *Symphony no. 7*, when one B♭ tenor instrument is demanded

(*Tenorhorn in B♭*). Other than this, especially for student orchestras, their immediate association will be with two works in whose scores they do not even appear.

In both *The Pines of Rome* and *Feste Romane*, Respighi scores for *buccine* (six in the first work and three in the second). These were instruments of the Imperial armies of ancient Rome, but little specific information exists about them and Respighi, having implied the aural and dramatic association, suggests that the parts be played on *flicorni*, a series of Italian instruments closely corresponding to members of the saxhorn and flugelhorn families, but no longer available. If they still exist at all, it is only in small, amateur Italian town bands. A colleague recalls seeing a band in the streets of Rome, all of whom were using rotary valve upright instruments from soprano to bass. Were these descendants of the real *flicorni?* Even so they would be of little use to the symphony orchestra, since they would require specialist players to hold anything even resembling concert intonation.

Thus the *flicorni* are traditionally considered in terms of their related saxhorn and this, in turn, translated into the modern equivalent (often, it has to be said, somewhat arbitrarily). The initial part of the process can be summarized as follows.

The *flicorno soprano in Si♭* corresponds to the B♭ soprano saxhorn (sometimes referred to as 'contralto saxhorn', although this can cause confusion with the true alto instrument in E♭). The *flicorno tenoro in Si♭* is the B♭ tenor saxhorn (also known as the baritone saxhorn, sounding a ninth below written pitch) and the *flicorno basso* is the B♭ bass saxhorn (also known as the baritone tuba). Of these, the first two are from the half-bore upper group of instruments, and the third is the uppermost of the whole-bore lower group.

Now comes the real problem, although the student orchestra might find itself at an advantage, having both more time for experimentation and being able to use players without being inhibited by professional responsibilities. For all practical purposes, the three saxhorns will correspond with:

(1) the B♭ cornet or (more closely) the flugelhorn in B♭; (2) the narrow-bore B♭ baritone, as used in brass bands and pitched like the trombone; and (3) the euphonium.

In professional circles the B♭ baritone is unlikely to be considered. It is a very awkward instrument for intonation and requires too much time to be spent with any individual example. This part would more likely be played on horns. Student orchestras, however, may either import young baritone players or explore the possibility of using specialist baritone players from the local brass band. These instruments, coupled with flugelhorns and euphoniums, would probably be as near as one could come to the right sound without employing some rare and wonderful instrument gleefully kept hidden by some local brass *aficionado*. If such an unforeseen opportunity should occur, remember one thing: *Pines of Rome* requires *two* of each instrument – and they must match!

5 TIMPANI AND PERCUSSION

In a chapter that attempts to deal with such a vast range of instrumentation some logical confinement is necessary, since it would be impossible even to list, let alone consider, all the instruments that may be placed under this general heading. The intention therefore is to limit discussion to those instruments most frequently encountered, plus those that might have a particular bearing upon some aspect of performance or positioning.

Timpani have long been essential to the symphony orchestra, first in direct collaboration with trumpets but later exploited in their own right. Percussion instruments, apart from those pertaining to nationalistic dances, only begin to appear with any regularity in the nineteenth century, when the search for colour and effect became more widespread.

Fundamental Principles

TIMPANI

Timpani are the only drums capable of producing notes of definite and variable pitch, the exact tension of the playing head of each drum always governed by some means of mechanical adjustment that will allow distinct and precise alterations to be made within a particular compass.

This definition remains essentially true, even allowing for the recent addition and increasingly frequent appearance of 'rototoms' – a family of drums closely related to tom-toms but without an enclosed body shell, that can produce similar variations in pitch across a wide compass. However, their clear resonance makes their sound unlike that of the timpani and they tend to be used as a distinct and individual addition to the more soloistically orientated percussion armoury, rather than as part of an integrated orchestral texture.

The timpani are a family of horizontal drums whose playing head is fixed upon a bowl-shaped resonating body supported clear of the floor. The original instruments stood on either a metallic tripod stand or three adjustable metal legs which were withdrawn into the body of the instrument for storage or transit, but modern instruments are encased in a supporting framework with wheels to facilitate manoeuvrability and transportation. In the case of high standard, professional instruments, the body will be constructed of copper, machine-formed or hand-beaten to very exacting standards. Student instruments, no less precise in manufacture but lacking the very highest quality of tonal production, are also available with bodies of fibre-glass or a metallic mixture.

The framework which cradles the modern timpani also encloses the mechanics and linkage which allow the tension of the head to be controlled by a single foot-operated pedal, the increase or slackening of the tension of the playing surface thus producing different, clearly definable notes. Such a system of tuning is a comparatively recent innovation, before which the pitch was altered by means of screw taps placed at intervals around the perimeter of the head. Although these fulfilled the same purpose, their action was confined to a small area of the head and the attainment of an even tension was, therefore, a considerable art in itself, apart from making the retuning of any particular drum a slow and time-consuming business. Various improvements, of which the successful application of a single 'master key', connected to and controlling the movement of all the others, was the most important, were attempted throughout the latter part of the nineteenth century. This led directly to the invention of the pedal mechanism, which freed the player's hands and provided an almost instantly attainable chromatic range.

The perfection of the pedal mechanism for the timpani was, like the earlier addition of valves to the horn and trumpet, to release a fundamentally harmonic instrument into uncharted realms of melodic opportunity. There is probably no single fact more responsible for the phenomenal rise in percussion usage and technique. Even ignoring the specific effects of which only the modern pedal timpani are capable, most timpani parts written since the 1940s would be unplayable on the hand-tuned instruments.

The head itself is today most often made of plastic although a few individual players prefer the traditional calfskin. The relevance and suitability of the distinctly different timbres produced by these two surfaces will be considered in a later chapter. For now it need only be pointed out that traditional heads have much against them in purely practical terms, being more vulnerable to changes in temperature, prone to damage (both accidental and that incurred during normal playing), of much shorter life-span and considerably more expensive to replace.

The timpani originally appeared orchestrally as a pair, limited to the tonic and dominant notes of the prevailing harmony, and it was well into the nineteenth century before composers required the addition of a third drum. Even the 16 drums of Berlioz *Requiem* are still arranged as eight pairs.

Nowadays, the sight of a symphonic player surrounded by fewer than four drums is rare, many scores requiring five or even more. They are arranged to form a semicircle around the player in order of size, the largest (lowest in pitch) drum almost universally placed to the player's left in the UK and USA, but just as regularly reversed in the rest of Europe and elsewhere. Regardless of number, all drums are placed equidistant from the player and at exactly even height, so that total control of touch may be guaranteed.

The player will be equipped with any number of different pairs of drum sticks in order to elicit a comprehensive range of sounds and quality. Each stick has a carefully balanced handle of wood or metal, but the head will vary in material, size, consistency and shape, from the softest sponge to the hardest wood, and every possible nuance in between.

'Sticking' – the order in which the hands are used to strike the drum head – can become very complex in scores that require a large number of drums or frequent re-tuning of one or more. However in more simple rhythms confined to one or two drums the hands usually alternate.

When not in use the playing heads of each instrument will be protected by a plywood disc of exactly matching diameter and the whole instrument then covered with a tailor-made padded 'jacket'.

PERCUSSION

The instruments of the percussion section may be classified in two distinct groups:

(a) instruments of indefinite pitch
 and
(b) instruments capable of definite and recognizable pitch – the tuned percussion.

(A certain relaxation of such definitive boundaries may be noticed in professional parlance however, where only instruments of chromatic capability, with notes arranged in keyboard fashion, will be termed tuned percussion; single bells, bell plates and similar items are excluded in this context.)

The number of instruments within the former group particularly is quite colossal and increasing all the time as new sounds are being invented or discovered. For the most part many such instruments are limited to very few appearances, often confined to just one work or composer. Any attempt to produce a comprehensive list would be out of date even before it was commenced and is, anyway, quite outside the scope of this discussion. There are, however, a large number of instruments that appear with considerable regularity and are very familiar to every concert-goer as necessary members of the orchestral section. It is only with some of these that we shall concern ourselves at present.

Percussion Instruments of Indefinite Pitch

BASS DRUM The largest orchestral drum, producing a very low sound of no definite or discernible pitch, the bass drum can vary considerably in size, although the small, portable variety, associated with marching bands, is far too small for orchestral use and should not be contemplated.

Nowadays most instruments are of the double-sided variety, usually attached to a purpose-built metal framework by leather straps or a pair of adjustable restraining bolts which allow the playing head to be tilted to any position that may be desired, usually no more than 10°–15° off vertical. Smaller instruments may be found supported upright (the playing surfaces vertical) on a low, collapsible frame of wood or metal. The single-headed instrument, professionally referred to as a 'gong drum', tends often to be of even larger diameter than its double-headed counterpart, but its orchestral use is becoming increasingly uncommon and fewer examples are being manufactured.

The bass drum is generally associated with the sound quality induced by the use of fairly soft, large-headed sticks, which increase the resonance and apparent depth of sound natural to the large, comparatively loose-tensioned head. However, a variety of sticks, ranging from these to hard wood, should be available for use in the many differing orchestral textures in which the instrument will be found. A number of these will be discussed in later chapters.

The bass drum is often found in direct collaboration with cymbals.

CYMBALS A pair of slightly convex metal plates very carefully machined to *identical* thickness and diameter, the cymbals are each held in the hand by a leather strap attached to the plate through a hole drilled at the exact centre. Sizes may vary from about 16″ diameter up to 20″ depending upon the passage for which they are required and the individual player's preference. Smaller plates can be found, but these are only of use to small school bands and percussion groups. In addition to variations in diameter, different specifications of thickness may also be obtained, making available a range of sound qualities. Indeed, manufacturers tend even to identify varieties of thickness by terms characterizing their most appropriate orchestral texture, such as French or Germanic.

At their most impressive the cymbals are clashed one against the other with a passing movement of the player's hands – never directly! – and may then be held aloft where they will continue to ring for a considerable time. In addition, short sounds may be made by immediate damping against the player's body; trills or rolls by vibrating the two plates together; and effective elongation of the sound by brushing one against the other, either in passing or starting with the plates together. All these effects may be achieved at a wide variety of dynamic levels.

When at rest the cymbals should be supported on a specially constructed stand comprising a central support, on either side of which hang two U-shaped leather straps. Each plate is safely retained in its sling until required, and is thus unable to fall accidentally or vibrate in sympathy with other sounds. They should most definitely not be left face down on a table or chair. Good cymbals are extremely expensive and can be damaged very easily!

SUSPENDED CYMBAL This is a single-plate cymbal attached at the centre to a stand which is adjustable for height. In this position the cymbal is played with a stick, usually a vibraphone mallet, but soft-headed sticks are sometimes requested, as are those of wood and rubber. In rare cases other implements, such as triangle beaters, are required. Again the instrument may be left to ring, or it may be damped by clamping between the fingers and thumb. A roll, performed by use of two sticks striking opposite edges of the suspended plate, is extremely effective and may be attained from the softest *pianissimo* to the most ear-splitting *forte*. A roll of this type, within a long *crescendo*, is often used to approach a moment of major climax.

SNARE DRUM Probably the most widely known percussion instrument, the snare drum is the smallest of the orchestral drums, usually of 14″ diameter and between 4″ to 6½″ deep. The easily identifiable sound is made by the vibration of cords of metal wire or gut against the lower skin when the upper head is struck. These 'snares' may be taken out of contact with the drum by use of a sprung lever situated on the lower edge. In this condition the drum takes on an almost definable pitch but remains high in relation to all other drums. The sticks are of wood with a small, pear-shaped bulb at the end.

The instrument described is the most standard snare drum and that which will generally be expected in performance of scores requesting *Caisse claire, Kleine Trommel, Tamburo* or *Tamburo piccolo*. However, other sizes of snare drums exist, and terms such as *Tambour militaire, Militärtrommel, Tamburo militare* and even *Tamburo* can sometimes also refer to a drum of similar diameter but around 10″ deep rather than to the unsnared 'Tenor' or 'Military' drum. Considerable confusion exists with regard to terminology for this instrument which will often only be resolved by careful analysis of the individual writing, and even then not always definitively.

In English-speaking countries the standard snare drum was generally referred to as the 'side drum', a name taken from its military counterpart that was slung slightly to one side of the marching soldier. In student orchestras it will often be found to be the most sought-after percussion instrument, as its orchestral parts tend to be longer and more interesting than others, though few students are really capable of playing the instrument.

The snare drum requires a unique stick technique, which makes it something of a specialist instrument even though all percussion players will have learnt it. Mastery of this technique is a long, arduous business and even apparently simple parts should not be undertaken by a player who has not had considerable specific training.

TRIANGLE As its name implies, the triangle is a single metal rod bent into triangular shape, its two ends not touching but almost forming the apex of one corner. It is usually struck with a short metal beater, although one of wood may be used for special effect. The triangle comes in a variety of sizes but only in direct comparison of the small and large will the pitch differences be apparent, the size being more influential on volume and 'tone'. Really large triangles (those with sides measuring 9″ or more) have a definite bell-like quality however, and lose the delicacy of sound associated with the smaller instruments. The triangle is suspended by a thin gut loop, either from a right-angled frame or from a small steel clip by which it can be held in one hand or attached to a music stand or similar support.

Metal beaters are manufactured to differing standards of thickness to facilitate variations of tone and dynamic level. Even young players should be equipped with light, medium and heavy examples at the very least. Some variation in timbre is also possible depending upon where precisely the instrument is struck, but major alteration will only be possible by careful choice of beater.

The triangle's most effective attribute is the trill, which may be performed either with a single beater, striking rapidly across the inside edges of one corner, or, in the case of a freely-suspended instrument, with two beaters on the outside of the angled sides.

TAMBOURINE The tambourine is a small, hand-held drum with a single calfskin head. Arranged in slots around the supporting edge are a number of pairs of thin brass plates supported on wire, which will freely sound when the instrument is struck or shaken.

The tambourine may be played in many different ways and is capable of numerous delicate and subtle effects. Complicated rhythmic patterns may be obtained at most dynamic levels, the softest being obtained by supporting the lower rim of the instrument on the knee and gently tapping the edge of its head. It can also be played by using the knee as a striking object and bouncing the instrument between it and the knuckles of the free hand. By contrast, the 'jingle roll', performed by shaking the instrument in the air, can be a stunning effect.

The short trill, a tricky technique to master, is induced by passing the thumb around the perimeter of the head with such pressure as to make the contact uneven, thereby causing a rapid series of strokes to the head which also set the jingles in motion. In the hands of an expert quite an extended 'shake' may be obtained by this method, but the duration is limited by the fact that it is not possible on the side of the head nearest to the supporting hand. At this point either a change in direction or a complete re-start becomes inevitable.

TAM-TAM The last percussion instrument of indefinite pitch to be considered briefly here is the tam-tam, sometimes confusingly referred to as a gong. Although no precise distinction between the two terms exists, 'gongs' are generally considered to be those instruments having a raised centre, thereby emitting a rather clearer and more definite note than the dark, ominous sound associated with the tam-tam.

The tam-tam is a large circular plate of beaten bronze, the edges being turned to allow only the centre to vibrate, thereby producing a low hollow tone. The largest orchestral tam-tams may be up to 40″ in diameter but many smaller ones exist and some composers specify the size that they require, if only approximately. The instrument is freely suspended from a large metal frame.

It is usually played with a large, soft-headed beater and a good instrument will tend to swell the sound momentarily after it has been struck. The full tonal quality is best achieved by slight 'warming' of the instrument, gently and inaudibly setting it in motion with the stick immediately before it is played. Struck very hard, the tam-tam provides an enormous sound with an exceptionally long period of decay, but such force must be applied with care as the sound will 'break' if the face is struck wrongly.

The above are seven of the most frequently encountered instruments of a group that stretches to hundreds. No one can be familiar with all of them, not even professional percussion players, and it is no disgrace to have to seek advice, even on variations of the most common instruments. Many books exist that provide exhaustive lists of the instruments used in various orchestrations up to the present day, explain variations in usage, and make some attempt to disentangle the often confusing (and sometimes interchangeable) names by which they can also be known. As indicated in the brief résumé above, no two examples of any one instrument are identical, and it is important to be as familiar with the actual instrument to be used as with its general type, since it is this that will determine the possible sounds to be obtained.

Percussion Instruments of Definite Pitch (Tuned Percussion)

Tuned percussion will be found to vary less between various examples of the same instrument. Although the available compass will often differ, orchestral parts will tend to utilize the most common range of the instruments. However, octave transposition of certain notes or complete passages is by no means unknown, instruments with the required range being either of restricted availability or a complete figment of the composer's imagination.

XYLOPHONE The xylophone is a chromatically tuned instrument comprising horizontal rosewood bars strung on a large, tubular steel or wooden frame. Each bar lies over a vertical resonator and the whole instrument stands on wheels at playing height. Two main sizes of instrument exist, the largest with a span of four octaves, a sounding range from middle C to four octaves above. Instruments of three-a-half-octave span lose the bottom of the range, starting most usually F or G. Three-octave instruments also exist and individual variations may be found within these as well as the two instruments mentioned above, not all examples necessarily covering the full range. The sticks, referred to as mallets in the context of tuned percussion, have thin wooden handles and small round heads of very hard rubber or wood.

The xylophone is the clearest of all the tuned percussion as far as articulation is concerned, the period of decay of each note being extremely rapid. Very fast passage-work will be crystal clear and will sound through quite heavy orchestration. Many players specialize on this instrument and there are some outstanding virtuosi, but many of the exploratory techniques they employ are unnecessary within an orchestral context.

GLOCKENSPIEL The glockenspiel is constructed on similar principles to the xylophone but the tuned bars are of steel. Orchestral instruments are small and are contained within a flat carrying case, which may either be laid open on a table or supported on a specially constructed stand for performance. The chromatic range is two and a half octaves, and the mallets are small, light and round-headed. An even greater variety of textures is available in these mallets than is the case with the xylophone, the heads being made of wood, rubber, plastic or sometimes – only to be used with the greatest care – metal.

Because of the clarity of the initial impact, the instrument is capable of rapid articulation, though this will tend to blur because of the uncontrollable ring to each note. Most good glockenspiel parts will contain regular moments for the sound to clear, for example, by interspersing a continuous running passage with rests or notes of longer value.

True glockenspiels of just under three octaves exist, as does the metallophone which takes the instrument down in written range to middle C (as opposed to the F above). This instrument resembles a xylophone in appearance in that it incorporates resonating tubes beneath each of the bars but they are fitted with a pedal damper so that they may be taken out of use if so desired. In this condition the instrument performs exactly as a glockenspiel.

VIBRAPHONE For the last half-century, this instrument has been featured in scores with sufficient regularity for it to be considered an essential member of the tuned percussion group. Like the glockenspiel, the vibraphone uses tuned steel bars, but it also incorporates part of the xylophone's specification by the addition of vertical, steel resonating tubes under each bar, and takes this a step further by including an electric motor to revolve small discs fitted in the open top end of each tube. The result is a unique sound, the revolving discs increasing the length of resonance and adding a very noticeable *vibrato*.

The standard instrument spans three octaves, upwards from F below middle C, and is contained in a tubular steel frame which also incorporates a full-length, foot-operated bar for the purposes of damping. Larger, four-octave instruments, obtainable from percussion hire companies, take the range down to the C below middle C.

Mallets are similar in construction to those used for the xylophone but usually have heads of wound yarn (the initial impact of the note not necessarily being the most important feature). Wooden sticks may, very rarely, be requested by a composer but no form of metal head must *ever* be contemplated. The instrument can also be used with the motor switched off, which transforms it into a type of deep, glowing, steel xylophone. The availability of such a variety of timbres probably accounts for the ever-increasing frequency of its appearance.

As with all tuned percussion instruments, the layout of the resonating bars is identical to the piano keyboard.

Seating

The seating position of the timpani and that of the percussion must be discussed separately since, although they are traditionally placed close together, their individual requirements are quite different.

TIMPANI

The amount of space required for even three timpani is considerable, two metres square being the minimum comfortable working area. This allows for almost no space in front of the instruments (in other words, between them and the backs of the nearest wind players) and this must also be provided, especially if timpani and wind instruments are on the same level.

As far as actual positioning is concerned, a central placing at the back of the orchestra is traditionally most favoured, but a position to either side may often be necessary. The three basic positions are shown in *Fig. 5.1* and will be discussed in order.

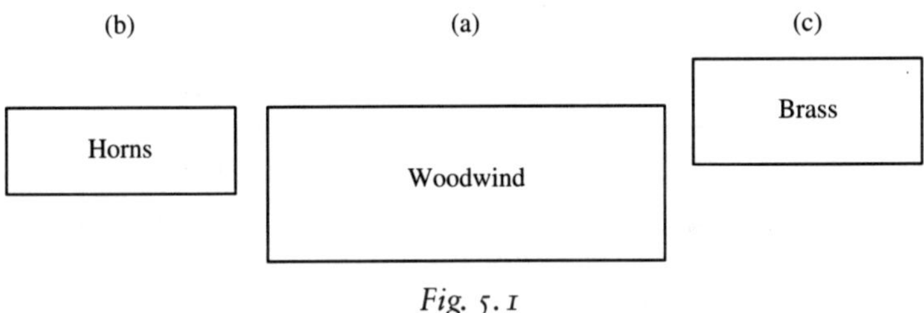

Fig. 5.1

From position (a) the timpanist can assess the balance of the orchestra as a whole, and judge personal contribution accordingly. Even in an acoustic which will not allow the strings to be clearly heard, there is still a width of orchestration in immediate proximity and no preponderance of bass or treble.

In anything approaching a purpose-built concert hall, the most likely reason for this position's being unavailable is the presence of a fixed organ console, which may severely restrict the usable depth of staging. An alternative position must then be considered.

Position (b) is probably the more frequently adopted, simply because there is often more space to be found on the 'violin and horn' side than 'cello, bass and brass' side, but there are drawbacks to be borne in mind. With the orchestra in the arrangement shown, a certain amount of free space behind the horns is vital and the timpani must not be placed too close. Norman Del Mar discusses this problem, from personal experience as a horn player, remarking also on the extraordinary phenomenon of vibration travelling up to the horn player's lips by reason of the backward-facing bell (*Anatomy of the Orchestra*, p. 340). It is important to remember that student players will not have the experience or expertise to overcome such unforeseen acoustic tricks in the way that might be expected of professionals.

This problem aside, position (b) distances the timpani from the lower pitched instruments, making a controlled harmonic foundation that much more difficult to achieve. However, on the opposite side of the coin, timpani writing of a more soloistic nature, especially that which involves antiphonal playing against the lower part of the orchestra, can be very effective from here.

Position (c), although ideal for the 'trumpet and timpani' orchestrations of the Classical era, is adopted less often in larger orchestral ensembles, mainly because of limitation of space once the brass, cellos and string basses are adequately accommodated. One must also consider the resulting close proximity to trombones and tuba, especially with regard to dramatic and colourful orchestrations, where the lower brass are rarely free from the added weight of timpani. For the sound to be continually coming from immediately behind them is both wearing and, to a large extent, counter-productive. It will noticeably affect intonation, balance and sound production and – equally true from the point of view of both sections – it will often cause an inexperienced player to overplay as if in direct competition with the surrounding sounds.

An increase in height (no more than 9″ to 12″) can alleviate the problems considered for both (b) and (c), but it may have a yet more detrimental effect, depending on the qualities of the stage itself. In purpose-built concert halls the risers will usually be built into the stage, either in fixed sections or adjustable by hand or electrically operated lifts. Either way, the orchestra will be evenly raked from front to back and the stage will be open, with no tabs, flyers, curtains or proscenium arch. Most significantly, the area behind the orchestra will be designed to reflect the sound evenly. This situation will allow the sound of raised timpani to project over and above the immediately adjacent instruments, retaining textural clarity and allowing a more exact appraisal of individual requirements.

In a theatre or multi-purpose hall, however, the use of portable box risers is most likely. These are a mixed blessing for timpani, the wooden-sided examples often acting as a great resonating box, exaggerating the booming qualities of any low sound. In such circumstances a hall that actually exhibits a dry, unyielding acoustic to the audience might well produce something near the opposite effect in the immediate area of this one instrument. The characteristics of such a hall can be quite misleading from the front of the orchestra, where one might only be aware of the lack of sound escaping beyond the proscenium arch and not of the all-enveloping low resonances caught at the back.

Such idiosyncrasies are of vital importance when considering the placing of timpani but cannot always be easily rectified, because of limitations of available space. Wherever possible, a layout should be adopted that avoids the worst of them.

Speaking entirely from the viewpoint of a conductor, if a central position is unavailable, I would favour movement towards the brass and lower strings as, despite its inherent problems, it does keep the interdependent lower sounds of the orchestra together.

PERCUSSION

It is not possible to list the multiple variations of layout and position that might be required of the percussion section, but a few basic priorities are worthy of consideration.

In the first place it must be said that *all* percussion instruments require more space than is generally allowed, and certainly more than just the minimum dimensions of the instrument plus one under-nourished mortal! Unfortunately, the necessary space for percussion can often be the last consideration when setting out an orchestra, and there are many occasions when one finds oneself saying 'I'm sorry, but the percussion will just have to find a way of fitting into there'. This is a sad fact of life on stages with limited playing area and it is just as true for professional sections as for those of student orchestras. However, there *is* a difference between accepting there is insufficient available space and ignorantly leaving too little.

Most percussion instruments require some free space around them, both for reasons of sound and practicalities of playing. A prime example, regularly overlooked, is the snare drum. This instrument's qualities of clarity and 'tightness' are severely lessened by the absorbing effect of nearby human bodies, a situation which will regularly cause an inexperienced player to over-compensate by attempting to play louder, often thus obtaining a completely different result from the desired increased projection of the original sound. Additionally, the placing of the snare drum too close to other instruments can cause the snares to vibrate sympathetically and produce a continuous rattle – it is not practical to remove them for every few bars' rest. More importantly, the instrument, in common with many others, provides nowhere to leave sticks safely when not in use, a fact of little consequence until the player is required to use some other instrument quickly, whereupon all sorts of embarrassments may occur. Few youth orchestras have the luxury of one player per part at all times. Provision of room for percussion 'trap trays', where sticks may be safely left when not in use, creates a further demand on available space.

The layout of the percussion must be considered in relation to the requirements of each particular programme; only very rarely is it possible to set the instruments in the most space-efficient manner. When one or more tuned percussion are called for, room for manoeuvre will always be required behind the instruments in order to have access to each, and get from one to another. In many cases this can be further complicated when an instrument is shared by more than one player. The placing of the common equipment in such cases is vital and, unfortunately, will regularly leave few options as to the placing of some awkwardly large instrument. Even in a sizeable concert hall, thoughtless arrangement of the main body of the orchestra can lead to cramped and unsuitable conditions for these players to give of their best.

The actual placing of the instruments, once the general space has been found and allocated, *must* be done by the players themselves. It is simply not possible for anyone else to interfere, beyond ensuring that the practical boundaries are not disturbed. As for the position of percussion relative to the rest of the orchestra, the priority is more one of sufficient playing space than of necessary association with any other instrument or section. However, the natural alliance with timpani should ideally be preserved and the two sections kept in close proximity.

In circumstances where the timpani have to be placed off-centre (as is the case in (b) and (c) of *Fig. 5.1* above) it is preferable to keep the percussion on the same side. If such an arrangement proves impossible it is feasible to move the entire percussion section to the opposite side from the timpani, but complications of ensemble may well have to be overcome. The division of the percussion section itself, to any noticeable degree, should be avoided.

The placing of instruments on different levels within the same block is perfectly acceptable, provided that access and availability are not impaired, in which case the main rhythmic instruments (for example, bass drum, snare drum, cymbals, suspended cymbal) are best kept together on the same level as the timpani, and the others placed up or down as necessary.

As a final qualification it may be said that it is unreasonable to expect percussion players to remain standing through long periods of enforced non-participation and that chairs or stools should always be provided, a factor that increases the required area still further.

Duplication

There are virtually no circumstances where the duplication of any percussion instrument should be contemplated except where specifically requested by the composer. The use of surplus players to double parts where instruments are available (side drum is an horrific example of this) is unnecessary and, generally, unmusical.

Forming the Sections

TIMPANI

In orchestral terms the timpanist is quite separate from the percussion group. Indeed, in professional circumstances this player would never play any other instrument as the position is one of total specialization. The instruments, usually the player's own, will be carefully matched and meticulously maintained, the player taking responsibility for overseeing their removal, transportation and storage.

In student orchestras none of the foregoing, except perhaps the very last, is likely to be true, and one often finds the situation where this player, sometimes the most inexperienced and least technically proficient among the Principals of the orchestra, is additionally faced with substandard and poorly maintained instruments.

This is a sad but somewhat self-perpetuating situation, brought about by many non-musical circumstances which are hard to rectify but rather too often fostered by a general lack of expectation on the part of people who should know better. It is for example so often the case that the 'very talented timpanist' boasted by many young orchestras turns out to be nothing more than someone with a moderate sense of rhythm and the ability not to get lost more than once in each rehearsal. Such attributes, essential as they are, have little to do with actually playing the timpani – or any other percussion instrument for that matter – and even less with being a timpanist.

Probably more than any other orchestral instrumentalist, the timpanist has to be totally aware of personal involvement at all times, and fully understand the concept that the sound is all-important rather than simply the ability to put it in the right place. It becomes almost essential for this player to be totally conversant with the score, for a highly developed awareness of any work's orchestral textures is of paramount importance, since much orchestral balance has to be 'felt' rather than heard.

It does, of course, take a great deal of slowly amassed experience before a timpanist can fully appreciate the effect of his or her contribution within the projected orchestral sound, but once a player has reached the required standard for even an average youth orchestra, the emphasis must begin to be concentrated in this direction and not simply on the basic aspects of placement and rhythm.

A timpanist must also have an unerring sense of pitch, despite the difficulties that the instruments impose. As has been remarked in previous chapters, it is an acquired art for any instrumentalist to assimilate the difference between the pitch of an instrument at its source and that projected a distance away. For the wind or string player, both of whom are involved in the production of a sound throughout its length, instantaneous adjustment becomes possible. Unnoticeable compensations are made in one area of the technique to allow for some required alteration in another – increased bow pressure, for example, or soft wind playing, both of which require adjustment of intonation. For the timpanist, this contact with, and control of, the sound throughout its duration is not possible except in the case of trills and extended rolls. Most often, after the initial impact, the quality and intonation of the sound are beyond recall, duration being the only remaining factor that may be varied, and this only by shortening the natural period of decay by damping.

Such a method of producing sound focuses a great percentage of the playing technique into the precise moment when the sound is forged – intonation, duration, quality, dynamic and balance all being dependent on the initial impact alone. But another pressing problem remains. Of all instruments, the uneven wave patterns of the timpani sound cause the greatest variation to be apparent at different distances from the source. No more stunning example of this phenomenon may be observed than that affecting intonation, where the projected note may be of considerably different pitch from that heard by the player.

This can be true at all dynamic levels but it is certainly within the softer spectrum that it is at its most noticeable. The long *ostinato* accompaniment that underpins the strings and woodwind as they make the gradual return to *tempo primo* just after the second subject in the first movement of Tchaikovsky *Symphony no. 4* is notorious, especially the low F♯ (see *Ex. 5.1*).

The same is true in the recapitulation, where the passage reappears transposed up a diminished fifth, but this time the high drum (F natural) tends to cause most problem. In both these passages considerable skill is required to balance the two notes evenly and to project the span of a continuous phrase, the high F being prone to sound very dry and the low F♯ of the quoted example equally likely to 'boom'.

EX. 5.1

While it is quite possible for problems of intonation in very loud playing to be caused by the same phenomenon, they are more usually the result of over-enthusiasm on the part of the timpanist or the unequal resonances of less than superb instruments.

The situation becomes acute in circumstances where the same passage occurs at widely varying dynamic levels. The following passage, from the fourth movement of Shostakovich *Symphony no. 1*, involves a meticulous adjustment of pitch for the *pianissimo* statement of the third bar.

EX. 5.2

The choice of drum will also be a strongly contributory factor in both the pitch and timbre of the note projected. In passages of solo playing or prominent orchestral texture the note should always be performed, as far as possible, on a drum whose skin is relatively tight.

The young timpanist must evolve a complete understanding of these and all associated aspects of the instrument, including the vagaries of each individual playing head within a certain compass, and be able to judge the acoustic liabilities of certain halls, and of positions around the orchestra. No other player is likely to have to cope with such drastic variations of placing or immediately adjacent sounds.

When these isolated aspects of the technique are viewed in this somewhat surgical light, the joke about the four D naturals which open Beethoven *Violin Concerto* (flat – sharp – too loud – inaudible) comes uncomfortably close to the truth.

PERCUSSION

In the full-time professional orchestras it is most usual to retain three percussion players on contract. The Principal will then be responsible for the personnel employed on a freelance basis for the augmented section, which may total up to seven or more players, depending on the requirements of the work performed. These players will, as far as possible, always be from the same regular pool and will be well known both to each other and to the orchestra as a whole. The distribution of work will be the overall responsibility of the Principal but most of the players will specialize in certain areas of playing and therefore most often be seen to perform the same instrument or group of instruments.

In student orchestras, although some hierarchy will doubtless have become apparent, the position of Principal is neither so obvious nor necessary, since the allocation of parts and the positioning of instruments is more usually arranged by the tutor. However, when an orchestra is performing a number of concerts at different venues or undertaking a foreign tour, it will be necessary for the Principal to shoulder responsibilities such as the overseeing of storage and transportation, the checking of the layout on the stage, even the redistribution of playing in the event of illness. It is therefore better to designate the oldest or most experienced player to the position as a matter of course, rather than waiting for these circumstances to arise.

As for the playing requirements demanded of the members of this section, many basic principles must be embraced, for more time will be spent waiting to play than actually playing. For professional players this aspect of musical life becomes part of the job, but it is undeniably frustrating and, for young players, one of the most trying features of percussion playing to assimilate.

The situation is even worse than that considered in the previous chapter in relation to the lower brass because, with a few exceptions, the instruments themselves are not easily portable, which means that they are not available for private practice if needed for any part of a full orchestral rehearsal. Even instruments such as triangle, cymbals, tambourine and snare drum, which may be carried fairly easily, need to be taken far from the rehearsal venue if they are to be played without disturbing the working orchestra, and there follows the worse problem of replacing them without wasting time.

Additionally, the parts tend to be briefer and more sparsely distributed than those for any wind or string instrument, a player's total contribution to a thirty-minute piece often amounting to less than twenty seconds, even if the part looks quite busy from the score. Furthermore, although all pieces will use the whole section at some point (usually the end), percussion parts are rarely of uniform involvement, a large section often making use of one or two of the players to a greater extent than the others.

In the student orchestra it must also be appreciated that the instruments are not likely to be of the highest quality, nor in immaculate condition, nor are they likely to belong to the players concerned. In such circumstances inexperienced players cannot be expected to be totally familiar with the guaranteed idiosyncrasies of the instrument they may need to use, a situation which, in full orchestra rehearsals, can lead to confusion and loss of confidence.

There is no way that all these problems can be overcome for the young percussion player and, to a large extent, they must be accepted and dealt with as painlessly as possible. It is, however, possible to minimize the difficulties by insisting that all percussion players accepted into a youth or student orchestra are serious-minded enough to start collecting some equipment of their own. It is not unreasonable to expect a student joining the section of even the most elementary orchestra to own a practice pad and a pair of side drum sticks, to which may be gradually added further items – a pair of timpani sticks, a pair of xylophone beaters, triangle beaters, a trap tray and various small and relatively inexpensive instruments. The collection will quickly grow, and if a player has recourse to even one item of his or her own in performance the playing confidence and a sense of identity with the instrument will be enhanced.

Finally, to round off this opening summary of the negative forces at work in the percussion section, attention must be drawn to one more important consideration.

It is very possible that one player's involvement during an entire concert might amount to a single cymbal clash – a quite unremarkable technical feat, unless, of course, it is missed, whereupon it becomes a lifelong embarrassment. The tension caused by the ever-present possibility of disaster is an easily overlooked feature of all instrumental playing, but it probably weighs most heavily on the inexperienced percussion player, and it cannot be lightly dismissed. The fear of missing an entry, or ruining some aspect of it, lives with players of every instrument, but the associated tension may often be dissipated by their overall involvement and the amount of playing required. Tension of this sort will generally have no direct bearing on the technical or musical difficulty of the passage in question. It is solely dependent on the degree of exposure, and will manifest itself in inverse proportion to the number of similar passages to be played. For the percussion player, as in the example mentioned above, there is often no further passage where redemption may be sought. Awareness of this frailty, present in even the most brash personality, is an important aspect of the conductor's approach to percussion involvement. An emphasis of the *musical* aspect of their contribution is as vital to these instrumentalists as to any others. Although this might seem obvious it is by no means apparent in some conductors' approach to the inexperienced section.

Nowadays the percussion players of most youth orchestras will have received some sort of specialist training, since the days of spare woodwind or string players being co-opted into the section at the last minute are fast disappearing. Nonetheless, many of the players are of very elementary standard and not capable of dealing with some of the more awkward passages of the repertoire. While it may be possible to procure a serviceable cymbal stroke from someone who has never before played them, a passage like the following, from the last movement of Tchaikovsky *Symphony no. 2*, is a totally different matter.

(Allegro vivo)

Cymbal

p

EX. 5.3

Here the cymbals must be played at an even, soft dynamic and damped against the body after every touch, an extremely difficult technique at this speed. It should, perhaps, be pointed out that the use of suspended cymbal for this passage neither provides the correct sound nor, in fact, makes it noticeably any easier!

The substitution is, however, often used for the equally difficult 'two-plate' roll, as in *Ex. 5.4*, from Bartók *Dance Suite*.

Again the sound is unlikely to be that which Bartók intended but, with careful use of triangle beaters, it can be made to sound much closer to the

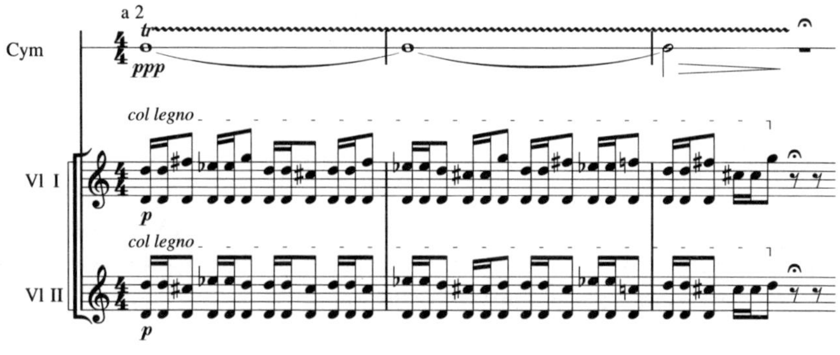

EX. 5.4

original than would be possible in the previous case. Basically, however, such substitution is wrong and should only be contemplated, even in this instance, when no player of sufficient prowess is available. Similar moments requiring advanced technique may be found for nearly all the untuned percussion and it is only in relation to this one instrument that any opportunity for rescoring presents itself.

Although many works may be found that require only simple rhythmic patterns from the percussion section, adequately performable by players of modest attainment, parts for the snare drum will always incorporate some of the patterns that form the foundation technique of the instrument, and cannot be attempted without specialist training. A really good snare drum player, apart from being an exceedingly rare animal, is one of the most influential instrumentalists of the section, whose influence on the rhythm and ensemble of the whole group is remarkable. Nothing less than a proficient player is acceptable on this instrument, its characteristic usage being far too soloistic and the qualities of dynamic control and subtlety demanded of it far too advanced.

One may be forgiven for citing subtlety as the one most frequently missing ingredient of the young percussion player and perhaps the lack of expectation, mentioned in respect of timpani at the beginning of this portion of the chapter, applies here also. One does not have to look far to find as many soft examples of percussion playing as loud, and the subtlety with which these instruments are used to colour the surrounding texture is often amazing – the cymbal and bass drum parts of Vaughan Williams *'London' Symphony* are a good example. Such writing requires very firm direction in terms of balance and control if the percussion tail is not to wag the orchestral dog, and yet, so often, one finds this aspect of the young section's playing almost ignored, or referred to only in terms of dynamic. It is the subtlety of timbre that is so important, the total awareness of the sound that is being coloured and the gradations of shade and hue available. Simple *forte/piano* variations have little to do with it.

Tuned Percussion

Like snare drum players, those playing tuned percussion instruments need specialist training, it being quite impossible to approach orchestral xylophone parts, for example, without mastery of the requisite stick technique and total familiarity with the instrument.

The one possible exception to this is the occasional single note, bell-like parts which may be found written exclusively for the glockenspiel. Even the following example, once more from Bartók *Dance Suite* and requiring two sticks for the E and F♯ may be successfully managed by a non-specialist player.

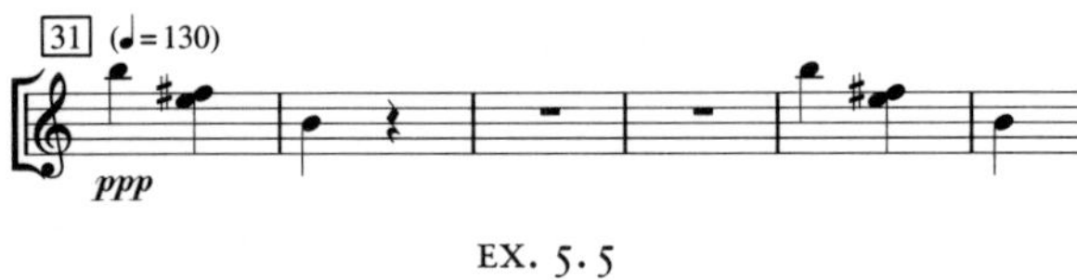

EX. 5.5

Other than these rare exceptions, all tuned percussion parts tend to be soloistic and require a fluency born only of practice.

By definition, percussion parts are rarely subdued beneath the texture of the orchestra and allow no opportunity for indecisive or uncontrolled performance. Essentially, the players must be capable, rhythmically secure, musically sensitive and confident, after which every opportunity for nuance and variation should be instilled.

Although some consideration of repertoire will be undertaken in a later chapter, it is worth stating here that considerable attention must be paid to the demands of percussion writing when choosing works to be performed by any non-professional orchestra, and the fears and concerns of the percussion tutor always seriously heeded. Many works, apparently suitable for the orchestra as a whole, contain examples of very advanced technique for this section.

The Enlarged Section

As far as timpani are concerned the criterion for this heading is not the number of drums required but those few works which include extra players.

Probably still the largest section demanded in the standard repertoire comprises the four players needed for the passage depicting rolling thunder clouds in the slow movement of Berlioz *Symphonie Fantastique*. Each player is confined to one instrument and the passage is built on the culminating effect of their separate entries.

EX. 5.6

As can be seen, although the drums for players II, III and IV are only a tone apart, the choice of the upper F for player I, and its use, in the first three passages, in direct confrontation with the lowest drum, creates an illusion of wide intervals. The drums for this movement and the two following are arranged in two separate sets, but should be kept together as one timpani unit.

A completely different, more flamboyant use of the double section may be found in the last part of Nielsen *Symphony no. 4 (Inextinguishable)*, and a short excerpt from one of the many solo passages for these two players is reproduced in *Ex. 5.7*.

EX. 5.7

Here the two players should maintain their position at the back of the orchestra but be placed far apart, as near as possible to the extreme edges. The instruments required for this symphony are pedal timpani, the quoted passage ending with a two-bar *glissando* for each player across an interval of a sixth, virtually the maximum range of each head! As with all timpani passages the various sizes of drum should be equally matched and of identical specification and design.

Further examples of the use of more than one player for the timpani may be found but these tend to be isolated passages within a work essentially scored for one player, as is the case in *Ex. 5.8* taken from the third movement (*Elegia*) of Bartók *Concerto for Orchestra*.

In such circumstances a specialist 2nd timpanist will not generally be required, one of the percussion section taking responsibility for performance of the lower part.

For the percussion the term 'enlarged section' should not apply, for the section has no specific or most normal maximum number. However, we may be allowed to use the heading to explore briefly a required grouping of percussion that occurs in twentieth-century scores with increasing frequency. The

EX. 5.8

designation of a certain number of players, each with responsibility for a specified selection of instruments, may be found in many works with large percussion involvement. This method not only often increases the soloistic nature of their contribution but prevents the slightly haphazard setting of the instruments that might otherwise result.

A fairly compact example, using a limited number of instruments, may be taken from Lutosławski *Livre pour Orchestre*, which also incorporates the rare requirement of timpanist doubling percussion; however, this is most often performed with recourse to an extra percussion player, thereby dividing 'Percussion 1' still further. The listing given here is as set out in the score:

Percussion 1	timpani, 1st xylophone, 5 tom-toms
Percussion 2	vibraphone without motor, 2nd xylophone, side drum, gong, tam-tam
Percussion 3	bells, glockenspiel, tenor drum, 2 suspended cymbals, bass drum

The interesting reference in Percussion 2 to both 'gong' and 'tam-tam' is an example of the differentiation considered earlier.

These days, once a composer has embraced this method of division, it is usual to find even more groups (anything up to seven) and a considerably larger range of instruments for each, often accompanied by the most detailed description of size and tonal quality. The example below (*Fig. 5.2*), by no means unique, is from Birtwistle *The Triumph of Time*.

(see notes) →

COLUMN	A	B	C	D
player 1	Xylophone		Bass Drum	Glock
2	Vibraphone	1 Timp	Bass Drum	
3	Xylophone	1 Timp	Bass Drum	Crotales
4	Vibraphone	1 Timp		
5	Xylophone			Glock

notes:

COLUMN A Vibraphones with amplification.

COLUMN C The Bass Drums should sound three different pitches, all as low as possible. No. 1 very big.

COLUMN D Crotales – one (or two) chromatic octave(s).

COLUMN E 4 Tenor Drums as large as possible and identical.

COLUMN F 6 Suspended Cymbals – all must be of different pitches as low as possible. 6 Drums without snares, all of different pitches, the lowest must be a fairly large vertical Bass-drum higher in pitch than Bass-drum 3 of percussion player 3.

COLUMN G 4 Bongos, all of different pitches. The lowest must be higher than the highest Timbale. 4 Timbales, all of different pitches. The lowest must be higher than Drum No. 6 of player 5. Conga Drum, also different pitches. Ratchet – small metal or wooden one with tongue set under very low tension. If unavailable use very small one inside a felt-lined wooden box.

Fig. 5.2

E	F	G	H
Tenor Drum	8 Cow Bells	4 Bongos	
Tenor Drum	8 Temple Blocks	4 Timbales	
			3 Tam-Tams
Tenor Drum	6 Suspended Cymbals	2 Conga Drums	3 Tam-Tams
Tenor Drum	6 Drums without Snares	Ratchet	3 Tam-Tams

COLUMN H 9 Tam-Tams – seven pitches as low as possible, arranged as below:

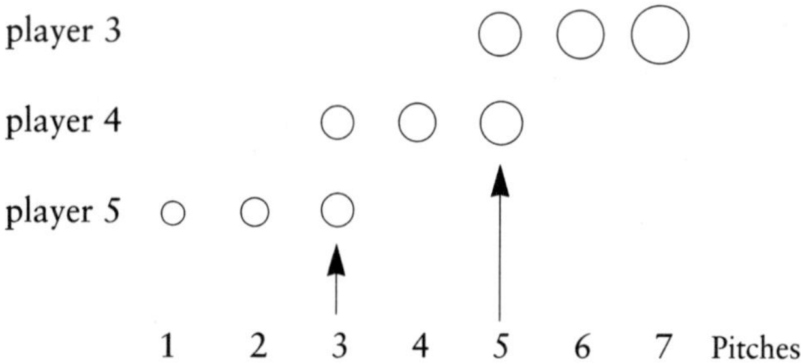

(Pitches 3 and 5 roughly equal)

Fig. 5.2 (continued)

In the original the composer has made use of columns in order to relate these copious notes more clearly to specific instruments. The appearance of timpani among the percussion section here (one each for players 2, 3 and 4) is subtly different from that shown in the previous example. In this case no timpanist is required, as the instruments are used as single drums of definite pitch.

Quite apart from showing the responsibilities of a large percussion section, this example has been chosen because it demonstrates, within a work scored for full symphony orchestra, the much more precise approach to percussion instrumentation that has been apparent in music of recent times.

Transposition

Strictly speaking, the timpani are not transposing instruments, since their parts are written in the bass clef at sounding pitch. However, the Classical tradition of using only two timpani tuned to the tonic and dominant of the prevailing key led to the rare occurrence of the part being notated by use of the notes C and G while the actual notes required were printed at the head of the page. Thus, for example, the very opening of Schubert *Symphony no. 2* is written in the following manner.

EX. 5.9

The same notation is used throughout the work, although the pitch of the drums is altered to C and G for the third movement and returns to B♭ and F in the fourth.

In the case of tuned percussion two instruments are regularly notated at a transposed pitch:

– The xylophone, unless otherwise stated by the composer, is written one octave below sounding (hence some notes are found written in the bass clef, as, for example, in *Gnomus* from Mussorgsky *Pictures from an Exhibition*.

– The glockenspiel (with the same proviso) is written two octaves below.

Infrequent Additions

As has already been remarked, the enormous variety of percussion instruments available to composers is far too great to contemplate description here.

A few of the less-frequent (but nonetheless standard) instruments might, however, benefit from inclusion.

BELLS

It is impossible to produce bells of the very low pitches demanded by many composers, and transposition upwards of an octave or more is not unusual. No sort of church bell can be considered: the weight and size of anything sounding much below middle C would require a hall to be specially built and strengthened.

Instead, one finds in the orchestra a rack of chromatically tuned tubular bells whose pitch often starts at 'middle C' or just below and extends upwards for about an octave and a half. Many parts are written with these in mind. They are played with rawhide mallets and struck at the top to give a clear, resonant sound, and it is important that the size of the mallet used should be directly related to the size of bell, very long, low bells requiring a considerably larger mallet than those of higher pitch. Plastic mallets are also manufactured, which have recently proved to be of a more durable design.

The overtones present are multiple and many instances of bells sounding the wrong octave, or even a completely different note, have been recorded. The search for something to approximate to the low bell tolls required by Berlioz *Symphonie Fantastique* or some of the Mahler symphonies is endless, and the use of 'bell plates' – rectangular plates of cast steel (the quality of which has been improved dramatically in recent years) – often proves preferable.

I well remember a youth orchestra hiring bells of the 'right pitch' for this passage in Mahler *Symphony no.9*.

EX. 5.10

The first I saw of them was during an early full rehearsal in a college hall where the orchestra was set out on the floor in front of the stage. A few bars before the entry the stage curtains slowly opened to reveal a frame containing three colossal tubular bells, next to which was a tall pair of wooden step ladders. A young percussion player appeared from the wings, dressed in a hooded cloak with a cushion jammed high on his back to form an unsightly hump. He limped across the stage in 'Laughton-esque' fashion and slowly mounted the steps. Needless to say the rehearsal had long since come to a faltering halt. However, he persisted in his task, eventually gaining the top-most rung and making his strike for immortality.The bell produced the wrong note an octave too high!

TENOR DRUM

Similar to the snare drum but most often of lower pitch and greater physical depth (10″ – 14″ or more), the tenor drum generally has no snares though snared examples do exist and are sometimes specifically called for. All types of tenor drums tend to be played with snare drum sticks, although occasionally soft sticks are requested or found to be preferable in certain passages. It is often only when composers give such specific instructions that one can be certain of the sound they intended, since the term 'tenor drum' can be found applying to everything from a high-pitched drum resembling a small tom-tom to very large and low-pitched instruments.

ANTIQUE CYMBALS

These are machined small brass discs, which are held hanging freely, one in each hand, while the rims are struck together and allowed to ring. The two discs of each pair are manufactured at very slightly different pitches, and are available in a chromatic range, starting at a written pitch of G above middle C (sounding two octaves higher) and extending upwards for about an octave and a half.

If many specific pitches are required in one work a chromatic set, with single discs attached to a metal frame, may be obtained. In this case they are played with very hard plastic or metal glockenspiel mallets. A heavy triangle beater may also be considered for particular effect. The written range is normally from middle C to two octaves above, although variations in the upper limit may be found.

The sounds of the two designs are quite distinct from one another, the pairs of discs providing a unique timbre unavailable to the rack-mounted version. Thus many percussion sections will insist on two players for a passage such as *Ex. 5.11*, from Debussy *L'après-midi d'un faune*, in order to obtain such a delicate effect.

EX. 5.11

CASTANETS

Orchestral castanets need not be played in the same way as those used by Spanish dancers, where a pair is held in each hand and clicked together. Although this is by far the best method for sound, clarity and performance of intricate rhythms, it is not always either practical or possible in the orchestra (technical mastery of this method of performance takes years of practice and is a very specialized art).

Various orchestral techniques may be found but the present day professional will tend to use a pair of real castanets set into a wooden handle and played by tapping against the knee. The student orchestra might well find it easier to execute intricate rhythms by using a 'castanet block' (two single castanets fixed on top of a wooden resonating box and played with the fingers) or 'paddle castanets', where a pair are hinged on a handle with one or both designed to hit a similar shaped piece of hollowed hardwood set between them. Basic rhythmic patterns may be accomplished and shakes are very effective.

It should also be mentioned that it is possible to play real castanets, with a pair looped over a finger, by methods slightly easier to master than the traditional Flamenco technique.

WHIP

Two distinct designs exist. The first can be played using only one hand and comprises a single strip of wood with a handle, on which is hinged a second strip, the surfaces slapping against each other when the instrument is flicked with the wrist. This is more generally known as the slapstick.

The second, and preferable in sound and dramatic effect, consists of two strips of wood hinged at one end. Grip handles are provided on the outer surfaces of each and two hands are used to slap them together.

MARIMBA

The marimba is a close relative of the xylophone, its resonating tubes being set one octave lower.

Although orchestral parts for the instrument are at present limited, the instrument has been included in this list by virtue of the prime position which it holds in present day teaching of tuned percussion. It is the basic instrument of instruction in the art of two-mallet, four-mallet and independent four-mallet playing and figures with increasing prominence in modern writing for solo percussion and percussion groups. The existence of many established virtuosi players throughout the world has ensured its firm acceptance within a very short time and virtually guaranteed its increasing appearance in orchestral orchestration.

Most modern instruments have a range of four octaves and a third, extending down to the A one octave and a third below middle C, but both four-and-a-half and five-octave instruments are available, the range again being extended downwards. The tone is dark and mellow.

Selecting the Section

The frequency with which student orchestras are forced to select percussion sections from players of very limited instrumental experience necessitates some consideration as to the method of selection, since it is not always possible to audition in the normal way and adjudicate primarily on proven ability.

Even more than the calibre of instruments and general performance, it is the attitude towards percussion playing that has altered so substantially in recent years. The days when student percussion sections were considered an optional extra, their necessary attendance reluctantly accepted and their contribution indifferently patronized, have vanished for ever, along with the sight of sections peopled by conducting students, members of the keyboard faculty or other 'spare parts'. The present situation demands a very serious approach from the outset, such that, even when considering the inclusion of a player with limited, or no, experience, the selection process must involve some long-term judgement as to attitude, motivation, musical sensitivity and future capability, as well as physical aptitude towards the requisite skills.

To be able to recognize suitable material requires much expertise and insight, and appraisal by a specialist is absolutely essential. Only someone with a thorough working knowledge of percussion technique, and who is conversant with the demands of the repertoire, can safely determine the suitability of each individual with regard to percussion playing in general and the specific needs of the orchestra at any one time.

The format of the audition will need to be agreed in consultation with a professional specialist, but it should involve some kind of basic ear test (both rhythmic and tonal) as well as an assessment of dexterity and rhythmic co-ordination. While it is true that a student with a good ear can probably develop into a very passable timpanist and a player with some keyboard facility will intuitively cope with many of the elementary problems of tuned percussion, the intricate rhythmical demands of the untuned percussion instruments, most especially snare drum, require immense co-ordination of the hands, commensurate dexterity and muscular parity. The foundations of these diverse talents are not always apparent in one person and considerable experience is required to ascertain the area of playing in which a student might be most beneficially guided in the early stages.

6 HARP AND KEYBOARD

The addition of the special tonal qualities of the harp and keyboard instruments to the orchestral palette came relatively late in the day when one considers the frequency with which such instruments appeared in a solo capacity. Indeed, the sudden demise of a keyboard continuo from the Classical orchestra seems to have encompassed a total rejection of any related instrument as an independent part. Whether the reasons lay in the over-powering association of such an instrument with its former use, or the increasing tendency of ensembles to be directed by a conductor, is probably impossible to determine with certainty. The most likely explanation would seem to be a combination of reasons, as their disuse corresponds exactly with the search of late eighteenth-century composers for a more homogeneous and 'symphonic' orchestration (a fact which suggests the former reason), together with the burgeoning number of performers required and the consequent need for a non-playing director.

Be that as it may, the first dual-staved instrument capable of performing multiple notation to appear in its own right in the symphony orchestra was the harp. It was first embraced in its present form by Berlioz (who else?) in the *Symphonie Fantastique* (1830) and then with increasing frequency by composers of the Romantic period. By the early years of the twentieth century, the instrument had established itself so firmly that no large-scale orchestra of the present day can afford to be without a player on staff.

Having taken care to qualify Berlioz' use of the instrument as 'in its present form' it is probably worth mentioning at least one famous example that pre-dates it and could possibly fall within the natural repertoire of the student orchestra – that in Beethoven ballet music *The Creatures of Prometheus* (no. 5 in Act Two). However, although this part is nowadays always performed on the modern instrument, it was intended for its predecessor, and was written some nine years before the invention of the totally chromatic double-action mechanism. Isolated earlier examples may be encountered in works by composers writing in the eighteenth century (most notably Handel and Gluck), but such repertoire is beyond the scope of this volume.

The appearance of keyboard instruments is less widespread, although the piano, long established as the most versatile and easily balanced concerto partner, appears with increasing regularity as a purely orchestral sound throughout the twentieth century.

Fundamental Principles

HARP

The harp has 47 strings tuned to the diatonic scale of B major which, as each string is capable of being raised in pitch up to a full tone from its fundamental, is conveniently referred to as C♭, whereby all open strings are flats and their progressive altering of pitch moves through 'naturals' to 'sharps'. With seven strings to the octave its open range comprises the C♭ two octaves and a semitone below middle C to the G♭ three octaves and a tritone above.

Seven pedals are provided to alter the pitch of the notes and each pedal affects every string of the same note name. The pedals are located in a notched frame around the base of the harp in such a way that each may be retained in its desired position indefinitely, a spring action returning it to the uppermost (open) position when it is released from its retaining notch.

Rather in the manner of adjusting the pitch of piano strings, the tuning of each open harp string is accomplished with a special key, which is fitted over the requisite peg situated in the neck of the instrument. Immediately below every peg are two small discs, each of which is fitted with two projecting pins at the diameter. When a string is in the 'open' (flat) position these will be on either side of the string and make no contact with it. When a pedal is depressed to the first position the uppermost disc will rotate about an eighth of a turn, bringing the pins into firm contact with the string and thereby reducing the length of the vibrating string and raising its fundamental pitch by one half tone (from 'flat' to 'natural'). When a pedal is depressed to its fullest extent the lower disc accomplishes the same task, thus raising the pitch of the string by a further half tone, making a whole tone in all. The position of the pedals may quickly be altered during the performance of any passage providing it is at a moment when the strings they control are not in use.

This double-action mechanism was the invention of Sébastian Erard in or around 1810, and superseded the single-action mechanisms of the previous century. It also managed to withstand the appearance of a chromatic instrument (with one string for every semitone, introduced in Paris by Messrs Pleyel in 1897) and has never seemed likely to be displaced by it.

The three types of instrument mentioned above represent the only fundamental refinements to the harp in over four thousand years although many variations of shape and range have existed at various times.

Sound is produced by setting the strings in motion with a plucking action, using the tips of the first three fingers and the edge of the thumb of either, or both, hands (the little finger is not used). This allows up to eight notes to be sounded simultaneously, although by far the most commonly used method of performance involves a slight spread of the chord from bottom to top.

The direct action of the fingers upon the strings permits great sensitivity of touch and provides the player with endless degrees of subtle variation in tone colour. More extreme contrasts may be obtained by varying the point on the string at which they are set in motion. The direction *près de la table* is found in many scores and requires the harpist to pluck the strings at a lower point than normal, nearer the sound board, thus imparting a tighter, less vibrant tone quality.

Although the natural production of the harp will allow the strings to ring, control over the period of decay must be exercised for obvious musical reasons and this is achieved by damping the strings with the open hand or even, if very short notes are required, with an instant return of the finger that set the string in motion. Normally the string will be damped at the end of the required duration of the printed note but, if a longer and more indefinite period of decay is required, most composers will append the term *laisser vibrer* (allow to ring) or *sans étouffez* (without damping). The word *vibrato* may also occasionally be found in the same context.

Harmonics, sounding one octave above the open string, are regularly required of the harp and are of best effect in the middle register of the instrument. They are achieved by placing part of the hand against the half-way point of the string and plucking just above it. Because of the slightly different playing position of each hand the techniques vary, the left hand using the ball of the thumb to stop the harmonic and the side of the same digit to produce it, the right hand using the knuckle joint of the closed second finger to stop the string but again plucking with the thumb.

Harmonics are designated by surmounting the note with a small 'o', as in *Ex. 6.1* from Dukas *L'Apprenti-Sorcier*, sometimes with reference to the string required (as here, sounding one octave higher) but, equally often, designating the actual pitch (*see* Chapter 12).

The confinement of harmonics to only the middle register of the instrument is clearly seen in this example, open strings being used for all notes above the stave in the treble clef.

EX. 6.1

The harp is very rarely played with any sort of plectrum although the following example occurs for 2nd harp in the 1st movement of Bartók *Concerto for Orchestra*.

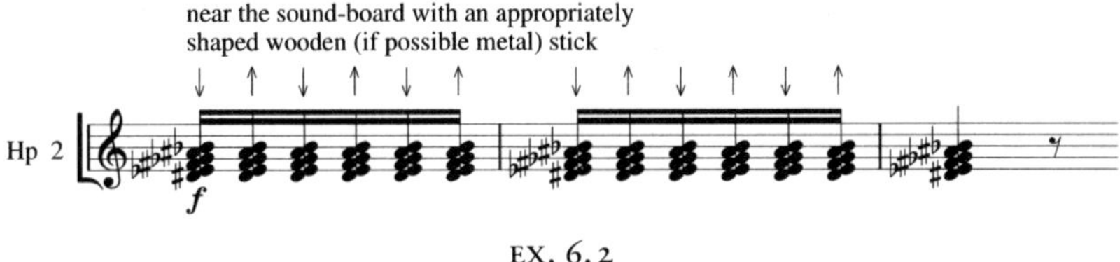

EX. 6.2

Techniques for the performance of this passage include the use of triangle beaters or the slightly curved ends of the handles of two teaspoons, the arrows showing the direction of alternate hands.

The nails of the fingers or thumbs are quite often used in *glissandi* effects to produce a more metallic and cutting edge to the sound.

PIANO

It is safe to assume that the piano is the most familiar of all instruments and that there is no need to describe its mechanism or playing technique in detail here. Nevertheless, for the sake of completeness, a general outline of the principles of performance will be reiterated.

The normal range of the grand piano is seven and a quarter octaves, from the A three and a quarter octaves below middle C to the C four octaves above it. Some instruments extend the range to a limited degree in one or both directions but, in orchestral circumstances, such extremes are unlikely to be demanded. All grand pianos, for the majority of the range and certainly down to the C below middle C, are triple strung – the hammer striking three strings fine-tuned to produce a single note when struck alone but to sound 'in tune' when struck in combination with any other note or combination of notes, whether this results in a consonant or dissonant interval. All the strings in this area of the range are made of single-strand wire. For the bottom two octaves or so the strings are of wound copper, the first ten to fifteen notes being double strung and the very bass notes single.

All grand pianos are provided with at least two pedals, the right of which lifts the dampers away from the strings, allowing all strings to remain vibrating up to their maximum period of decay. The left moves the entire hammer action to the right of the player so that each hammer contacts only two of the three possible strings (or one of the two) for each note, thereby noticeably altering the volume and, more importantly, the timbre of the instrument. Such action does not affect the single strings of the lowest notes.

Many pianos will be fitted with a third, centrally located, pedal which serves to hold the dampers away from notes only after they have been struck, as opposed to raising the entire damper action. This device allows individual notes to be retained without the key being held, and was invented by Messrs Steinway in 1874. Some confusion can arise however when a third pedal is encountered which serves an entirely different purpose, simply softening the action of the instrument for practice purposes. Such a fitment has no musical use whatever.

The degree of volume emanating from the instrument may be further controlled by the position of the lid – closed, raised on the short stick, raised on the full stick or completely removed. The instrument is very rarely played with the forward-folding hinged section down, although this is possible even if music is required, the music desk being removed and stood (carefully!) on top.

As already mentioned, the piano as an orchestral instrument arrived late on the scene. Bartók and Stravinsky were the first to incorporate it in their scores with any regularity although, almost inevitably, its first appearance as an integral orchestral texture may be found in Berlioz, whose *Lélio* (1832) uses two pianos to great effect in the finale.

EX. 6.3

(Although many scores list this work as requiring one piano, four hands, which is perfectly possible, Berlioz – in his *Treatise on Instrumentation* – clearly refers to two separate instruments.)

As will become apparent, orchestral use of the instrument varies considerably, from simple doubling of instrumental lines to quite independent and virtuosic passage-work. Indeed, there are many instances where it is hard to distinguish between the solo piano and the orchestral, since many examples lie somewhere between the two. D'Indy *Symphony on a French Mountain Song* uses the instrument in both capacities and probably works best with the instrument placed within the orchestra, yet is unquestionably conceived as a work for solo pianist. In contrast, Stravinsky *Petrouchka* contains a horrifyingly difficult piano part, and yet this is not the province of a solo pianist, but rather a virtuoso orchestral part.

What may be stated with certainty however is that, except where specifically requested otherwise, the intended instrument is the nine-foot 'concert grand', as this is the only piano able to hold its own in orchestral circumstances. However often one may be forced into using smaller instruments by considerations of space or availability, it is important to remember that this is a considerable compromise and that balance, at the very least, will be substantially affected. The upright piano is a total non-starter (although we have all had to use it at some time or another), because only the large iron-framed versions even approach the right sound and such an instrument is far too tall to allow the player to see anything beyond the music. Orchestrally speaking, there can be little doubt that our forebears had the right idea about this instrument when they confined its use almost solely to the support of framed photographs and ornaments!

One instance of the upright instrument being specifically requested by the composer occurs in Rachmaninov *The Bells*, where the instrument is listed in the orchestral score as *pianino*.

The same composer's footnote in the original editions of his *Symphony no. 3* stating: 'If no second harp is available a small upright piano may be substituted' is extraordinary. Apart from this note, no mention is made of a second harp, either in the list of instrumentation or the title page of any movement, and it surely cannot have been his intention to double the part all the way through the piece; much of the second movement writing in particular would be quite unsuitable for this practice. Elsewhere, any piano doubling of the line at the same octave could not possibly produce more sound (the only feasible intention) as the very different methods of sound production would tend to cancel each other out. I find it amazing that Rachmaninov – a superb orchestrator and one of the greatest pianists of all time – should sanction such a substitution, and I can only think that he must, for once, have fallen prey to the English school, typified by Vaughan Williams, of somewhat self-deprecating *ad libitum* orchestration.

Demands on platform space (discussed below) often make the inclusion of a work requiring orchestral piano a carefully considered decision. In this respect one further important point should be mentioned. If the piano is to be used orchestrally the same instrument cannot, under any circumstances, be used as a concerto instrument in the same programme. The concerto piano is for the exclusive use of the soloist and, apart from professional tuning, must not be used for any other purpose or played by any other person on the day of a concert. If a piano concerto is programmed in a concert that also involves a work with orchestral piano then two instruments *must* be provided. This is more than a simple courtesy to the soloist, it is a plain unavoidable fact.

CELESTA

The outward appearance of the celesta resembles that of a very small upright piano but its sound is produced by hammers striking steel plates, each of which rests on an individual wooden resonating box. Dampers, which rise free of the plates when a key is struck, automatically fall back into place when the key is released, allowing for very clear articulation. On most instruments a damper pedal is provided which raises all the dampers clear of the plates, and works in much the same way as the 'sustaining' pedal on the piano by allowing all sounds their maximum period of decay. The rather unfortunate name of this pedal has been known to cause some confusion but this is easily rectified if one remembers that it refers to the mechanism controlled by the pedal and not to its musical function.

The tone of the celesta is gentle and rounded, but the instrument is afflicted with a severely restricted maximum level of dynamic, although, surprisingly, it may be heard through quite dense orchestration, especially if the texture is carefully designed. In this respect, some instruments will prove far superior to others, with much of the variation being found to lay in the design of the case itself. Those simply provided with a rear panel of cloth or perforated wood are far less able to project their sound successfully than more modern instruments equipped with meshed wire panels at the back, top and lower front.

The instrument is not the province of the percussion group (even though sometimes erroneously placed there in the score), but of a separate keyboard player. Parts for the instrument are rarely technically demanding, so in student orchestras a fairly competent pianist will usually suffice. However, the celesta does need a much more percussive finger action than the piano, a pianistic *legato* touch being of little use if the instrument is to be heard. Indeed I have often requested a young player to strike the keys in a hammer-like fashion and avoid pianistic fingerings altogether, even, in some cases, when performing a simple scale passage. This technique will provide a much clearer sound, especially in the case of a poor-quality instrument, and will not affect the apparent dynamic or sense of *legato* in the same way as it would if used on a piano.

A superb use of the instrument which may help to make this point clear is found in the duet with harp in the second movement of Rachmaninov *Symphony no. 3*.

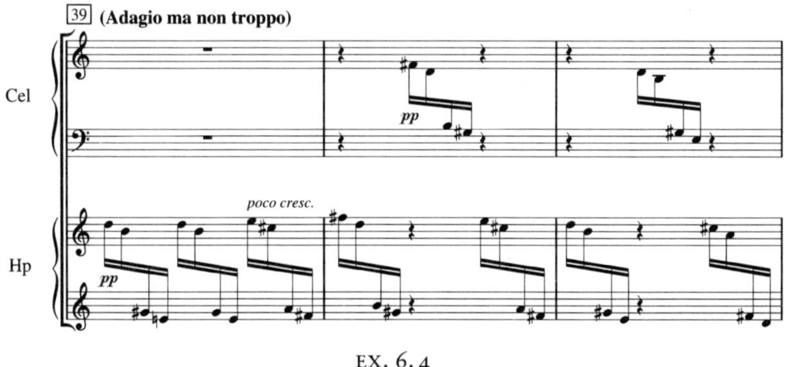

EX. 6.4

Not only must the balance between the two instruments be meticulously maintained, but the articulation must appear as similar as possible. A pianistic *legato* technique is likely to produce neither result. The fact that this, in common with all celesta parts, is written on two staves only serves to enhance the player's misconception of required technique.

One further disturbing aspect lies in wait for the unsuspecting pianist playing celesta. In many cases the sound emanates from an unexpected part of the instrument. The resonating boxes take up a lot of space, especially those of the lower notes, and are consequently double, or even triple, banked inside the instrument case. Often those of the lowest register are placed to the player's right while those of the higher notes are to the left, a most disconcerting reversal of the expected position.

HARPSICHORD

The remarkable difference in tone between the harpsichord and other keyboard instruments arises from the fact that its strings are plucked rather than struck with any form of hammer. When a key is depressed, a small pillar fitted with a plectrum comes into passing contact with the chosen string, causing it to vibrate. As the pillar falls back to its place of rest no contact is made, thereby ensuring only one sound is made each time a key is activated. Individual dampers, raised when a note is selected, automatically fall back when the key is released.

On modern instruments the pillar and plectrum tend to be made of high-quality plastic, but older instruments will contain pillars of wood with quill or leather plectra attached. Such instruments will contain a complicated escapement mechanism designed to avoid contact by the plectra on their return, an unnecessary refinement when using moulded plastic. In all cases repetition of a single note, although not capable of anything like the speed obtained from a high-class piano, may be achieved at a surprisingly fast rate.

A varying number of pedals may be provided, situated in a notched face board so that they may be retained in a selected position, in much the same way as those of the harp. These enable the performer to alter aspects of the tone of the instrument as well as, on the larger instruments, providing low octave, upper octave or unison doubling of all individual keys.

In twentieth-century orchestral scores which include harpsichord writing these larger, often two-manual, instruments are most desirable, since they can produce far more sound than their smaller counterparts.

ORGAN

The fixed nature of church, cathedral and concert hall organs, coupled with the specific knowledge of each instrument that is required to make best use of them, makes discussion of their few common characteristics unnecessary in this context as one is never likely to have a choice either of instrument or position. Suffice it to say that every instrument is unique in many aspects, not least in matters of tonal variation, immediacy of response, clarity and range. It is unfortunate from the point of view of combining with an orchestra that, in all but rare cases, intonation can be added to the foregoing list!

In most circumstances the organ will be found in orchestral scores already requiring augmented instrumentation, and is most often included to give weight and nobility to a major climax or underpin the harmonic progression of the bass line. That a really fine instrument can fulfil this task with consummate ease, adding a tremendous physical presence to even the most heavily orchestrated *tutti*, will be immediately apparent to anyone who has ever heard one of the numerous performances of Tchaikovsky overture *1812* in London's Royal Albert Hall. However, the particular capabilities of the instrument need not be used solely for its great reserves of power and the delicate side of its personality can be employed to telling effect. Perhaps no better example exists than one masterful appearance, quoted as *Ex. 6.5*, from Elgar *The Dream of Gerontius*.

EX. 6.5

The organ is alone among instruments in being able to provide the utter tranquillity and sense of timelessness required by this moment, but only a composer of rare imagination and technical mastery could handle it, especially at the focal point of so dramatic a work.

The organist has recourse to a wide range of tone-colours which can be selected at will by careful choice of individual 'stops' ranged at the sides, and often along the front, of the keyboard console. In most cases each of these controls an entirely separate set of pipes, making it possible to use a great many of them in combination, and extending the available range of sound still further. It should perhaps be mentioned that the sound, however variable, remains intrinsically that of the organ, and it is not possible, as some would have us believe, to imitate truly the sound of human performance on an orchestral instrument, whatever the names on the stops might suggest to the contrary.

Whilst it is possible for other keyboard instruments to provide automatic octave and unison doubling, the organ goes a considerable step further. Uniquely, it is able to combine 'real' sounds of the natural fundamental overtones (the fifth, third and seventh) in carefully balanced conjunction via the 'mixture' stops. Though all stops are primarily intended for additional colour in solo use, the enormous variation available to some instruments can, in the right hands, make it possible for the organ to blend with, or stand apart from, the most subtle orchestral textures.

On large instruments there may be as many as five keyboards, each of which provides contrasting tone-colours through the player's selection of appropriate stops. Foot pedals – or, more accurately, a foot-operated keyboard – make it possible to add a further individual melodic line or to reinforce widely placed and impressive harmony.

HARMONIUM

The harmonium is a small reed organ with stops, pedals and, most usually, two keyboards, but many variations of the instrument exist. Its tone is quite distinct from that of the large pipe organ, in that it is more nasal in quality and far less imposing. While it can be freely moved it is by no means portable in the strict sense of the word and, once positioned within an orchestra, its relocation would cause considerable upheaval. It should not be confused with the portable consoles of some pipe organs occasionally found in concert halls – not that these are any easier to move, being limited by their attachment to the pipes.

Although it is sometimes unavoidable, the harmonium cannot adequately be used as a substitute for the organ, since it lacks the capacity to underpin widely orchestrated harmonies or provide audible *ostinato* accompaniment. It is, however, specified in a number of scores for its own distinctive tonal qualities – for example, in Shostakovitch ballet suite *The Golden Age* and Mahler *Symphony no. 8* (where a separate part for organ is *also* required).

Use of the instrument in opera scores, where it is intentionally scored as a substitution for the organ, is rather more frequent, but such appearances are beyond the context of this discussion.

ELECTRONIC KEYBOARD

Not to be confused with the harmonium or its electronic organ derivatives (such as the theatre and cinema organs) this section refers to the 'synthesizers' of multitudinous design which provide sounds of purely electronic origin.

Chief among these from an orchestral point of view is the Ondes Martenot, by virtue of the important parts that exist for the instrument within mainstream repertoire, such as Messiaen *Turangalîla-Symphonie*.

The instrument was first exhibited by its inventor Maurice Martenot in

1928, taking part in a performance of *Poème symphonique pour solo d'ondes musicales et orchestre* by Dimitri Levidas. The excitement caused by its appearance may be judged by the spate of works to include it. One source quotes some thirty composers of international repute who had written for the instrument within ten years of its invention, a quite astonishing number in such a short time.

The design is of a single line, melodic instrument, capable of being performed in two distinct ways; either as a keyboard producing separate notes of distinct and unwavering pitch or as an instrument of totally variable pitch including such effects as *glissandi, vibrato* and quarter-tone intonation. In both cases the instrument is 'played' with the right hand, the left maintaining control of dynamic level and tonal alteration by means of electronic regulators. The Ondes and all related electronic instruments require a specialist performer familiar with their individual functions and capabilities.

A further development of electronic performance, regularly encountered by orchestras of the major conservatoires and probably inescapable from the point of view of any adventurous student orchestra, is the introduction of electronic participation in live performance in terms of amplification, reverberation, tape delay, ring modulation etc. Inasmuch as the operator will be situated at some sort of control panel, such equipment bears remarkable similarity to all the instruments listed above. However, the range of options open to both composer and performer is huge and, as each piece of equipment is a separate item in itself, the 'instrument' will pertain only to the score for which it has been assembled. The knowledge and expertise demanded of the performer/operator/technician is such that few students (even of electronic instrumentation) would be capable of producing a satisfactory outcome unless under direct and highly experienced supervision.

Seating

As each section dealt with in this chapter consists of only one (or at the most two) performers and none requires additional instruments to complete the section, the seating for these players tends to be more variable in extreme circumstances and more prone to the demands of available space than rigorously implemented planning. There are obviously preferred solutions, but the vastly different stage areas in which the same orchestra will be forced to work will mean that pragmatic choices need to be made.

Often, however, more than one type of these instruments will be required in the orchestration, and ways must be found of keeping them in touch with one another. Such problems, as is the case with all orchestral seating, cannot be conclusively solved in theory alone, but certain guidelines need to be considered. With that in mind this section of the discussion is best divided into two parts: firstly, the seating of the instruments individually, and secondly, the seating when two or more different instruments are employed.

INDIVIDUAL SEATING

Harp

As far as harps are concerned I do not intend to consider positions of simple visual effect which have no musical relevance or thought for the performer. Those who wish to isolate the harp on the topmost riser may continue to do so for as long as players can be persuaded to appear like the decoration on a Christmas tree.

For all musical reasons the harps need to be situated within the orchestra wherever possible, as near to those instruments they are most likely to accompany as is practical. Partly because much of the writing in full orchestral instrumentation is complementary to the upper string group, harps are most frequently placed near the violins. However, a further reason is that they often accompany woodwind and horn solos. Should the horns be on the conductor's right then the placement of harps on the 1st violin side becomes, in many pieces, less desirable.

A setting for single harp on the violin side is shown in *Fig. 6.1*. If two harps are used in this position they should sit as close together as possible, to maintain the minimum break at the back of the adjoining string sections.

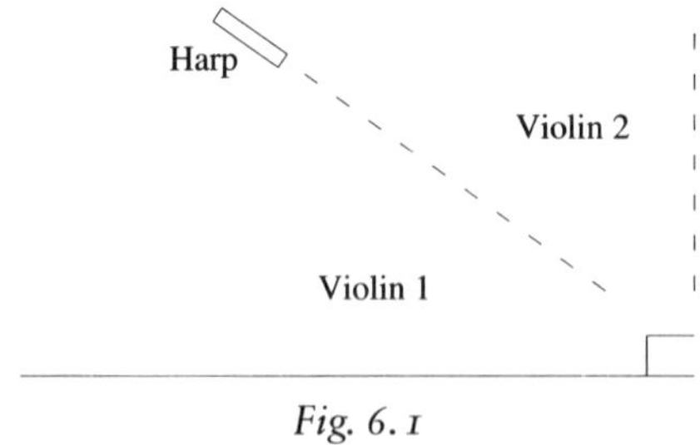

Fig. 6.1

In the case of a particularly large string section (or small orchestral space) the harp(s) may well be forced to sit behind the violin sections rather than within them. In this circumstance they should be moved round towards the centre of the orchestra as far as the height of their instruments will allow, neither affecting the sight-line of any instrumentalist behind them nor causing a section to split up in order to see the conductor.

The placing of one or two harps on the opposite side of the orchestra can be problematic in that they are far less often scored in direct association with lower strings and are almost never found accompanying solos of the trumpets or brass. Even though an apparent advantage may seem to be that the players no longer have to sit at an obtuse angle in order to see the conductor around the frame of the instrument, the musical disadvantages tend to militate against it. One exception that comes to mind is that of Mahler *Symphony no. 1*, where the writing is closely allied to the lower strings. In this case my personal preference is to place the harp on the cello side, but care must be taken not to interfere with the sight-lines of the basses.

Positions in the centre of the orchestra can generally be ruled out, as the height of the harp will drastically affect the sight-lines of the woodwind. On the majority of stages even slightly off-centre positions will be found to cause similar difficulties to the horns or brass.

Piano

The size of a concert grand poses many problems on platforms that have not been purpose built – and many that have. Wherever it is placed within the orchestra, careful rearrangement is necessary, and awkward positioning is certain to ensue for at least some string players. Stages with wide, low-level risers might overcome the worst difficulties but even a superb orchestral space of this sort will not rule out some disturbance of the other players' normal seating.

Musically the instrument is best considered in one of three specific places, dependent largely on the role it has to play. In most circumstances it will be placed on the violin side in much the same position as that shown for the harp in *Fig. 6.1*. The instrument appears so regularly in this position that one is sometimes forced to question whether any serious thought has been given to its involvement in the work to be performed. However, if it is felt, for reasons of balance, that the piano must be kept in roughly the same position in relation to the orchestra across a range of concert venues, then this, with the piano lid on short stick, is probably preferable, since it causes minimum disruption and is appropriately placed for much of the repertoire in which it appears.

Be that as it may, many instances occur when this positioning seems far from ideal. Shostakovich *Symphony no. 5* is an example where the piano's most telling orchestration is that of its first entry, a famous doubling of the cello and bass line (see *Ex. 6.6*).

EX. 6.6

Here the instrument would be better on the other side of the orchestra, an exact mirror image of the position shown in *Fig. 6.1*, and among the violas and cellos. Later passages in the work are not adversely affected but the quoted passage gains immeasurably.

For those soloistic orchestral piano parts such as Stravinsky *Petrouchka*, mentioned earlier in this chapter, a central position, dividing the violins from violas and cellos, is highly desirable. The instrument is placed as in *Fig. 6.2*, the player directly facing the conductor and the length of the instrument virtually bisecting the full string section.

For a work of this sort, with the piano in this position, the lid of the instrument should be removed completely. It must be stressed, however, that the total removal of the piano lid is a dangerous practice in orchestral circumstances and should only be contemplated in works where the piano has a very soloistic role. Even with the dampers down, many short orchestral chords can be ruined by the ensuing sympathetic vibrations of the piano strings.

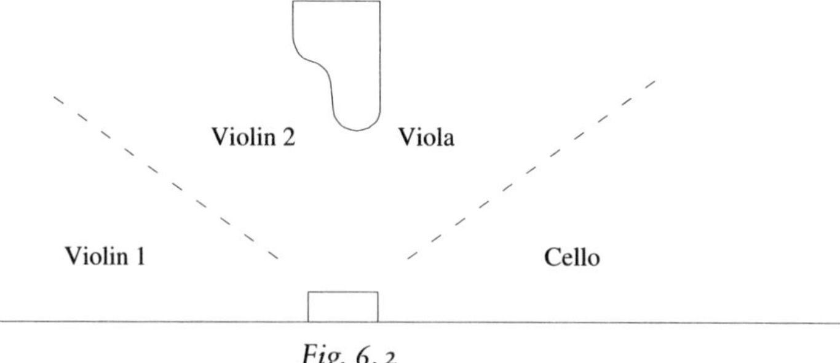

Fig. 6.2

Many works of more general piano orchestration will also be found to benefit from the central positioning of the instrument. Bartók *Dance Suite*, for example, includes passages where the piano is coupled both with the lower strings (*Ex. 6.7*)

EX. 6.7

and the upper strings (see *Ex. 6.8*).

However, in such instances, where the piano is not treated as a solo instrument, the lid should be placed on the short stick. (The long stick is reserved *solely* for concerto performance and used in no other orchestral circumstance.)

Many conductors always prefer this central position and there is much reason in this argument. It is true that the *concertante* parts of composers such as Martinů (a prominent orchestral piano part being scored in five of the

EX. 6.8

symphonies) sound most unified from here, but it can become more difficult to balance the string section as a whole. In many cases, it is possible to lose more than is gained.

The rare orchestrations that require piano duet (two players on one instrument), such as Debussy symphonic suite *Printemps*, make no extra demands on space except, of course, that the instrument must be at such an angle that *both* pianists have visual contact with the conductor.

Celesta

The priority in positioning a lone celesta in the orchestra is solely that of helping the instrument to be clearly audible. As such, almost any position becomes viable provided that the player can see the conductor when necessary and is not isolated from the surrounding sounds.

As is the case with harps and piano this instrument appears most often in a position within or behind the violins, but with far less reason. Unless it is raised above them, preferably by 12″ or more, it is unlikely to be clearly heard and will prove extremely difficult to balance successfully with the lower strings, simply because they will hear nothing more than a vague, distant tinkling.

In a solo passage, such as *Ex. 6.9*, from Tchaikovsky *Dance of the Sugar Plum Fairy* from *The Nutcracker* (a very early use of the instrument and yet to be surpassed), the importance of this aspect of balance becomes clear.

EX. 6.9

The sort of 'celesta priority' balance frequently associated with commercial recordings is a total impossibility in the concert hall and in concert performance of the suite this dance will often prove extremely difficult to balance. In this instance the whole ensemble will benefit if the celesta is placed immediately in front of the conductor, with the player directly facing the audience. This need involve only minimal disturbance to the semicircle formed by the front desks of the strings, the celesta being positioned close to the conductor's rostrum (in this instance the player needs to hear, rather than see).

As is the case for the piano, orchestration for celesta duet (a rare occurrence, but Stravinsky *Petrouchka* provides a famous example) makes no extra demand on space.

Organ

Obviously the position of the organ cannot be adjusted, a fact that can present monstrous difficulties to both player and conductor. The performer is almost never in a position from which the conductor can be seen directly and is dependent on carefully angled rear-view mirrors, electronic relay of the orchestra's sound, or even a 2nd conductor in order to gauge the exact moment at which to play.

Any aural conception of the orchestra that the organist may have during performance is likely to be extremely limited and almost certainly dangerously distorted, the tricks of acoustic in churches and cathedrals in particular being notorious. The problems of just keeping together with the orchestra do, on some occasions, seem insurmountable, especially given the further complication of delay between the keyboard being activated and the instrument actually sounding.

Such difficulties can only be addressed through the patience and understanding of the conductor (coupled with a fluency of technique which can, if sufficiently adept, be used to keep the orchestra playing slightly later than the beat that the organist sees) and the technique and ability of the organist.

Solutions to problems of balance can only be solved by the player's ability to control the instrument being used. This fact explains why so many composers leave the finer points of registration to the judgement of the individual performer.

Harmonium

The limitations on mobility that apply to this instrument have already been stated. Its position will have to be decided according to the space available but the player is usually able to see directly over the instrument. This will allow it to be positioned on any point of the periphery of the orchestra directly facing the conductor.

Electronic Keyboard

The inclusion of instruments using electronic keyboard creates fewer problems as the actual sound will emerge from an amplification system that need not be placed particularly close to the player. In such circumstances the player may be sited in a convenient position (near to an electric power point) and the amplification system some distance away. However, normal considerations apply with regard to the performer being reasonably close to any associated instrument.

If a long length of electric cable is needed, it is imperative that this be fixed down at regular short intervals along its length and not left to trail through the chairs and stands of other players, however easily visible it might appear to be.

Such an oversight would be dangerous and extremely discourteous to other members of the orchestra.

For the placing of the control desk and equipment for what was referred to earlier as electronic participation, special arrangements will have to be made pertaining to the individual work and the hall in which it is to be performed. Very often the performer can be placed at a great distance from the orchestra, perhaps utilizing a purpose-built control room at the back or side of the hall, or being placed at the very back of the auditorium or even just off-stage. The possibilities can only be generalized, as every situation and score requires a different solution.

By and large, scores including electronic participation will require varied orchestral layouts, as they rarely demand a 'standard' symphony orchestra without any omissions or additional players.

COMBINED INSTRUMENTATION

Harp(s) with Keyboard

Close proximity of more than one harp and piano is very difficult to achieve, since the sheer physical space required for the instruments, while maintaining sight-lines for the players concerned, is prohibitive for most playing areas. While every attempt should be made to keep them on the same side of the orchestra, the harps – being the more freely manoeuvred of the two instruments – will frequently end up behind the pianist or even on a different level.

A single harp, however, may often be placed next to the right-hand end of the keyboard. At the left side of the piano, although preferable for the harpist's contact with horns and woodwind, some difficulty in sight-line may be experienced and balance can prove problematical when both instruments are playing. Positioning the harp in the 'crook' of the piano, an area which at first would seem tailor-made, is unwise. No actual contact is possible between the players themselves and the harp strings will pick up the vibrations and overtones of the piano, sometimes with highly undesirable results.

Scores that involve a single harp with piano do not generally demand any direct combination of timbre and the somewhat natural desire for physical proximity is based more on similarities in design than on actual performance necessity. This is less true of harp and celesta, where certain characteristics of the instruments are often inextricably bound into one combined sound.

A passage such as *Ex. 6.10*, from Richard Strauss *Rosenkavalier Suite* requires that the two harps and celesta be placed very close together.

EX. 6.10

In addition all three instruments must be situated on the left-hand side of the orchestra (from the viewpoint of the conductor) in order to be as near as possible to the three solo violins, flutes and piccolo. As in all passages of combination between these two instruments it is preferable that the celesta be placed nearest to the audience so that its sound has the least possible distance to travel.

An even more critical example, this time for just one harp and celesta, may be taken from the end of the third movement of Shostakovich *Symphony no. 5*.

EX. 6.11

This wonderful piece of scoring requires the two instruments to be in very close visual as well as aural contact, the placing of every note needing to be 'felt' together. Here we begin to get a clear idea of the practical decisions that have to be faced by the interpreter of every orchestral score. In this work the writing for celesta and piano is patently intended as a doubling part, since neither instrument plays at the same time as the other and the extent of both parts is limited. Earlier in this chapter we contemplated the advantage of transferring the piano to the cello and bass side of the orchestra, with the celesta if it were to be played by the pianist. Were this to be the case, the harp must obviously also be on the same side but, earlier in the same movement, comes this (*Ex. 6.12*).

Although it is not impossible to execute this passage with the harp greatly separated from the two flutes, such positioning is not ideal. If two keyboard players are available then all well and good. The piano can join the cellos and

EX. 6.12

bass while the harp and celesta remain together on the other side. But few professional orchestras would be prepared to pay for two keyboard players for a performance of this work and, in student orchestras, although two players could doubtless be found, the amount of playing for each would be hardly overwhelming. So what is to be done? As in so many cases, no simple answer is possible and a decision has to be taken long before the work gets into rehearsal as to musical priorities, adopting whichever layout is personally considered to affect the interpretation least in terms of sound and practical performance.

It is worth mentioning that at least one recording of this work places the piano with cello and bass for the first movement and with the violins for the rest, and moves the harp next to the flutes for just the few bars quoted above. Never, never trust a recording in terms of balance or apparent ease of ensemble!

Keyboards

As has been discussed, the most frequent coupling of keyboard instruments, that of piano and celesta, may involve a single player or two separate performers. When using two players, the instruments need not be placed together unless the musical demands of their parts require it.

In the case of one performer doubling, the two instruments must obviously be in close proximity, preferably so that the performer can successfully reach both keyboards with no more movement than to twist the body to one side, as shown in *Fig 6. 3* (a) and (b):

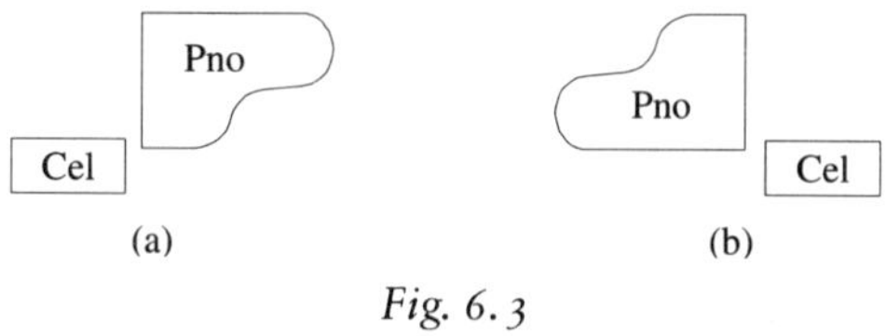

Fig. 6.3

Not having to cope with delicate pedalling as for the piano, the player need only sit on the side edge of the piano stool in order to play the celesta. As can be seen, this configuration will work equally well on either side of the orchestra, the celesta always being placed on the 'outside' of the piano, for reasons of sound and so that the player need not face the back of the orchestra. The only constraint to (b) is the possible lack of available space on the cello and bass side of the orchestra.

The linking will not work so well with the piano in the centre of the orchestra however, for here, whichever side of the piano the celesta is placed, the performer will be facing one side of the orchestra and side-on to the conductor. This is possible where the celesta part is very simple, but it will always feel uncomfortable at the very least. If the piano is to be centrally placed and a doubling celesta part exists, then it is better that the latter instrument be positioned so that the performer directly faces the audience at both instruments, as shown in *Fig. 6.4*.

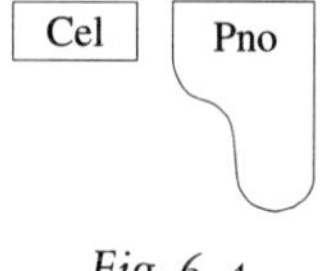

Fig. 6.4

Albeit no great distance, the player now has to move surreptitiously between instruments as required and probably transfer the part each time as well. In this situation two stools *must* be provided.

It is neither possible nor desirable to attempt to cover seating arrangements for all possible combinations of keyboard instruments considered in this chapter, but the outlines given above should give a broad indication of the problems to be faced and some methods of overcoming them. In many cases it will be found that a combination not specifically dealt with here requires only the substitution of instrument names to become applicable but the playing area available and the conductor's own priorities of balance will have a great bearing on each individual situation.

Duplication

Except in the case of harps, duplication is unnecessary and, for obvious reasons, largely impossible. Single harp parts will often be doubled if two players are available and many composers are adamant that this should be so. However, great care should be taken if a part is doubled in a work where no such request or sanction is evident.

Forming the Section

1ST HARP

The technical and musical demands incumbent upon an orchestral harpist are no less stringent than those on any other player. A highly developed technical facility across the range of the instrument and a natural ability to blend, accompany and project are all essential, together with an exemplary sense of rhythm.

While many harp parts do not extend the technical ability of a good harpist, some certainly do (the parts of Debussy and Ravel for example), and all possess, at the very least, difficulties in relation to ensemble that call for a high degree of sensitivity and concentration.

Among the greatest initial problems faced by the young, inexperienced harpist is the lack of immediacy apparent from the ambient orchestral sound, especially at low dynamic levels. To place correctly the sound of an instrument which is considerably more instantaneous in its production than most others in the orchestra is an immensely difficult art. Even in an apparently simple line like *Ex. 6.13*, from the opening of Dukas *L'Apprenti-Sorcier* (reproduced above in relation to harmonics but shown here in its full orchestration) it is by no means easy for the harpist to 'feel' the moment of sound production of each note.

Such a feeling for orchestral ambience takes time to acquire and every young harpist will need help and consideration in this direction.

Every conductor needs to maintain an attentive and watchful attitude

Assez lent ♪ = 90 à 105
Picc 1
Fl 1 2
Ob 1 2
Cl 1 2
Hp
Vl I
Vl II
Vla
Vc
DB
pizz.
arco
pp léger
pp
p
1° Solo
p espress.
dim.
3 Soli
Harmoniques
sous ordinaires
Tous pizz.
8va
(score in C)

EX. 6.13

towards an inexperienced harpist as many initial problems faced by this player are not directly connected to playing the instrument. In this respect it must also be remembered that the young harpist is less likely to feel socially part of the orchestra in that they will not enjoy the same immediate contact with other players of their own instrument. The particular nature of the problems faced by this instrumentalist – and indeed all keyboard players – only heightens the difficulties of overcoming them. In this instance there is something to be said for employing two harps whenever players of limited experience are used.

The harpist must be able to tune the instrument successfully, a complicated and time-consuming business. All good teachers will lay much emphasis on this important facet of technique but not all young players will remember to allow themselves sufficient time, especially on arrival at a first full rehearsal. A gentle reminder might save that terrible initiation for the young harpist of proudly sitting behind a gleaming instrument only to find, on the first entry, that it is totally unplayable.

Finally, as has been the case for all other instrumentalists, no work involving extended virtuoso solos should be included for the harp without first ascertaining that the player can handle it with confidence. The extended *cadenza* which forms the introduction to the *Pas de Deux* from *Swan Lake* by Tchaikovsky (no. 4 in the usual suite) is a prime example, although this is usually quite rightly avoided by youth orchestras because of the enormous demands made of the solo violin.

2ND HARP

The position of 2nd harp is unlike any other in the orchestra, in that it is a straightforward duplication of the instrument and provides no musical support for the 1st harp in the orchestrally accepted sense. Very often it is an exact doubling of the only harp part, and even the printed material will make no distinction between the two, simply providing two identical copies marked 'harp'. When two individual parts do exist it is rare to find one less difficult than the other or confined to a particular register or harmonic role.

In this circumstance the use of a second harp will not only give the composer a means of providing chromaticism without recourse to rapid and complicated pedal changes, but it will also allow an orchestral texture involving the harp to remain undisturbed if the instrument is also required in a solo capacity. In such a situation it is just as likely for 1st to undertake the accompanying role as 2nd, as may be seen in *Ex. 6.14* from Debussy *La Mer*.

EX. 6.14

This work is extremely challenging for both harpists and, like much of the French repertoire, is easily underestimated. However, a close study of this score will reveal almost every conceivable use of two harps, including the most wonderful examples of division of simple rhythmic figurations.

ORCHESTRAL PIANO

The requirements of an orchestral pianist are primarily a fluent technique, musical sensitivity and, above all, an unerring sense of rhythm. As with the harp, the main pitfall for the inexperienced player lies in judging the moment at which to play when combined with instruments employing such varied methods of sound production.

The technical range of orchestral piano parts is extensive and the variations in sound and tone quality required of the instrument may be very subtle, necessitating a player of advanced technique and musicianship. It takes a musician to play the opening phrase of Debussy *Printemps*, not just someone who can play the notes in the right order.

EX. 6.15

Probably because the piano is so familiar as a solo instrument, its orchestral use is frequently limited to its more percussive qualities, adding initial impact to the sound of another instrument. This is certainly the case in *Ex. 6.6* from Shostakovich *Symphony no. 5* (p. 160), and holds true for all its appearances in that work. However, the full effect of this function can be deceptively difficult to achieve, and demonstrates how, of all instrumental parts, the demands of orchestral piano writing should not be appraised merely by the apparent technical difficulties since the decisive rhythmic requirements of such a part frequently prove to be the undoing of an otherwise proficient player.

This fact is nowhere more apparent than in the totally integrated orchestral piano writing of composers such as Martinů where a passage such as *Ex. 6.16* from the *Symphony no. 5* (and just one of a dozen similar passages in this piece) is unlikely to have been encountered by the pianist under any other circumstances.

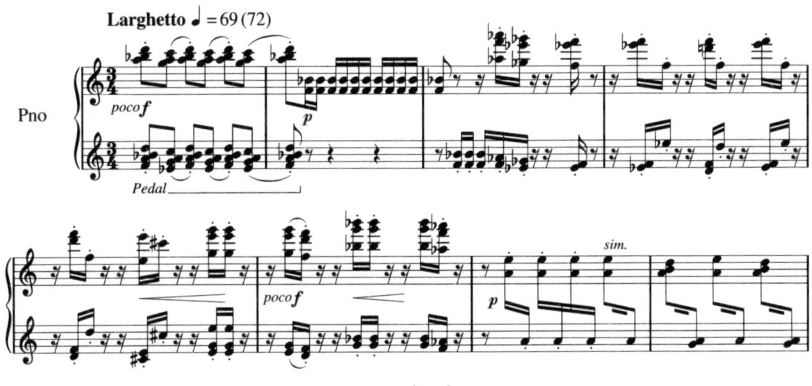

EX. 6.16

The rhythmic difficulties of the passage, especially for an inexperienced player, are self-evident, but added complications arise because of the pianist's need to fit with instruments whose sound production is less immediate, and which may be some distance from the piano. While the player of the piano as an orchestral instrument draws on much the same techniques as for solo playing, the role can be quite disorientating, since many accepted priorities of solo performance may be fundamentally disturbed. It is therefore essential to assign such parts to a flexible and technically advanced student, especially as, in my experience, no orchestral tutor will be assigned to this instrument, and there may be no one with direct experience of the position available to give advice.

CELESTA

Much of the above, in relation both to the player's ability and the problems faced, applies to all orchestral keyboard instruments. The celesta's needs have been discussed in the context of the instrument itself and need not be reiterated. As also mentioned, orchestral parts for the celesta will often be found playable by a pianist of no more than average ability. Thus it is possible to entrust the part to a capable pianist from within the orchestra (always provided that the section will not be affected by the loss). This can prove beneficial, for the player will appreciate many of the problems associated with orchestral playing. However, the use of a less than outstanding player is limited to the celesta alone among keyboard instruments and does not hold true in the case of piano or organ.

HARPSICHORD

The true art of the harpsichord player is demonstrated in the realization of *continuo* parts of the pre-Classical orchestral repertoire, an area that is not of direct concern to this discussion. Should works requiring harpsichord *continuo* be programmed, it is strongly recommended that a professional player be engaged, for the realization of the part will depend very much on the standard and technique of the orchestra it supports and less on preconceived ideas of style. Such flexibility can only be achieved by a player of considerable experience.

In twentieth-century orchestral literature, however, some works use the harpsichord purely for its distinctive qualities of sound and production. A magnificent example, using simple repeated chords, may be found towards the end of the Schnittke *Viola Concerto*.

EX. 6.17

Although at this point doubled by piano and celesta and emerging from a very powerful *tutti*, the unmistakable timbre of the instrument is surprisingly evident, and becomes increasingly pronounced as the work gradually subsides. Such writing may often be successfully performed by a good keyboard player who has limited familiarity with the instrument itself, although some depth of knowledge of the available registration is necessary.

ORGAN/HARMONIUM/ELECTRONIC KEYBOARD

In the case of each of these instruments a specialist player, with detailed knowledge of the specific instrument being used, is absolutely vital. The likelihood of such experience being found within the age-range of the student orchestra is remote, making the question of choice irrelevant in this context.

The Enlarged Section

An increase in number of any of the instruments contained within this section is rare.

In the case of harps, most additional numbers involve doubling, though Stravinsky requires three harps both in the full ballet version and the 1911 suite of *The Firebird*. The four harps in Richard Strauss *Alpine Symphony* are two parts doubled (but if you can mount a piece requiring twenty horns, what problem is a couple of extra harps?), and the twelve in Berlioz *Te Deum* play a single part – magnified out of all proportion with great glee, burning enthusiasm and some sound musical reasoning.

Two pianos are required in Stravinsky *Symphony of Psalms* and four in *Les Noces*, although both works make use of a reduced orchestra, the former containing no violins or violas and the latter only percussion. In the rare cases of two pianos being required within a normal size symphony orchestra (for instance, in Orff *Carmina Burana* and Berlioz *Lélio*), positioning will have to be determined by available space, the only limitation being that they be placed side by side.

The piano duet (one instrument, two players) required in Debussy *Printemps* and Bartók *Dance Suite* has already been mentioned, but the harpsichord duet part in Respighi *Ancient Airs and Dances* suite no. 2 is also of interest.

Transposition

The only true transposing instrument in this section is the celesta, whose part is normally written an octave lower than sounding (*see Ex. 6.4* above, from Rachmaninov *Symphony no. 3*). This curious fact seems to have arisen from a desire to co-ordinate the player's eye and hands to the centre of the instrument in much the same way as on the piano – so-called middle C being about central on both instruments but of course the C of the celesta sounds one octave higher. Be that as it may, not all composers follow this practice, and great care should be taken in determining whether octave transposition is intended or not.

Beyond those instruments capable of coupling various octaves or additional intervals to the played note, the only other transposition will be found in the general writing of harp harmonics.

Infrequent Additions

There are no infrequent additions beyond the 'prepared' piano which may be found in some modern scores. On all occasions the 'preparation' will be detailed in the score and the multitudinous variations need not be detailed here. Suffice it to say that great care must be taken with the treatment of a hired instrument and that most 'preparations' can only be accomplished on a privately owned piano especially reserved for the purpose. I have been involved in a number of performances that never materialized because the owners of the orchestral piano quite rightly refused permission for lamp bulbs to be dropped on the strings or the lid to be tapped with side drum sticks.

PART II

Performance Techniques

7 STRINGS

For all string players, bowing is the most fundamental and personal technique and, especially in countries where a rigorous training in one school of technique is not current, many different styles can appear within any one section. This can cause problems of unanimity of approach in many areas of the orchestral repertoire, but it can also provide a flexibility of opportunity not often encountered where more 'nationalistic' uniformity prevails. The conductor of student orchestras in the UK, for example, can be faced with a situation where all things are possible, for the simple reason that no single style is dominant. It is therefore of paramount importance that the conductor should fully understand the requirements of any bowing in terms of its relationship to the choice of tempi and desired sound, as well as the way his or her direction of phrasing and line may influence and affect its application.

Before considering the basic types of bowing in detail, it is worth mentioning at the outset that the direction of bowing need not necessarily have as much effect on the result as would seem to be generally thought. Many effects are equally possible in either direction, and an exaggeration of dynamic or accent does not automatically require a change in the bowing. It is, therefore, always preferable to request any specific emphasis first in musical terms and then to *listen* to the result, rather than watch it. If a change of bowing is really necessary it will very quickly be apparent. As in professional orchestras, some student sections will achieve a sound by one means and others the self-same sound by another. Although many bowings work as a matter of course, they must still be related to the individual orchestra's need and accomplishment, and great care should be taken not to impose a bowing for its own sake, especially on an orchestra with which the instigator (whether conductor, leader, tutor or composer) is not familiar.

With student orchestras, the size of the string sections (relative both to each other and to the orchestra as a whole) may well affect any decision of bowing, especially when a sonorous *legato* sound is required. It is not always easy to achieve an evenly balanced string section, and any discrepancies will often need to be adjusted by the use of more, or fewer, changes of bow direction than might at first seem necessary for any given phrase. For example, the bowing for many passages in any Bruckner symphony for an undersize section of 12 to 14 1st violins will probably differ in many respects from that used by the more ideal section of 18 to 20, and one must consider the added complication that even the larger section is unlikely to include a sufficient number of quality players to make balanced orchestral sound a foregone conclusion.

Equally, the string sections in relation to one another will often display an imbalance, again not simply in terms of numbers but, more often, in their ability to produce a compatible sound. Situations will frequently be encountered where a small 1st violin section is playing to a cello section of large proportions. While it will never eradicate the problem completely, some adjustment to the individual bowing of the sections involved will often be of help.

Clearly, therefore, the primary considerations when deciding on bowing style and direction must always be those of sound and musical communication. To these ends, the direction in which the bows of a string section travel is nowhere near as important as the *position* within the bow. Therein lies the key to achieving uniformity of sonority and style.

Having said this, it must be admitted that some uniformity of bowing marked into the parts before the first rehearsal can greatly benefit the orchestra and save considerable time. In student orchestras such preliminary decisions of bow direction may be made by the specialist string tutors, although some consensus of opinion across the sections will be necessary as to details of phrasing, style and accents. However, any markings made before rehearsals begin should be regarded as a working basis that may need to be adjusted according to the sound and facility of the string section using it.

It is therefore not without some reservation that I embark on any discussion of specific bowings, lest they be imposed on some young orchestra for which they happen to be unsuitable. That all the following techniques are usable and facilitate certain sounds or phrasings has been proved. That situations exist in which they may not be the most pertinent for the orchestra or performance in question is equally true.

Legato

This apparently simple technique, where the bow never leaves the string and the tone is even and continuous, involves considerable skill in production, especially at either end of the bow, where the smoothness of the turn is vital. At the point of the bow a noticeable loss of sound can occur if the lack of weight is not compensated for correctly, and at the heel gaps in sound will be apparent if the turn is accomplished rigidly or hastily. Exercises in *legato* sound production are (or should be) the staple diet of all young string players and the accomplished teacher will find endless opportunities to reaffirm the necessity for constant attention to this all too elusive technique. Orchestrally, additional complications exist that can together make players less attentive to their own production, not the least of these being a decreased awareness of individual sound. Furthermore, any lack of synchronization in the bow change will tend to cover deficiencies of bow control, most noticeably at the heel, by the general continuation of sound. Precision in the movement of a *legato* phrase is essential, for only when the turn of the bows is exactly synchronized will the conductor have any control over the sound at the moment of turning. It is this one moment in *legato* bowing where the sonority of the phrase is won or lost, where the conductor's sensitivity in sound control, facility and timing of gesture, and knowledge of orchestral technique are most exposed.

A consideration of the wider implications of string sound, with much emphasis on *legato*, will be found in Part III. At this point, one needs only to examine some instances of *legato* bowing with regard to where the changes in direction might take place.

In all circumstances the essential criteria are to reproduce the phrase as nearly as possible in accordance with the composer's wishes, and to ensure that any bow changes within a phrase are unavoidable and will not disturb the line or inevitability of the musical sentence.

Thus the combined statement of the theme, by 1st violins and cellos, at the reprise in the last movement of Brahms *Symphony no. 1* (*Ex. 7.1*) can be bowed exactly as phrased, with the one addition of a 'linked' up-bow at the separate crotchet in bar 4.

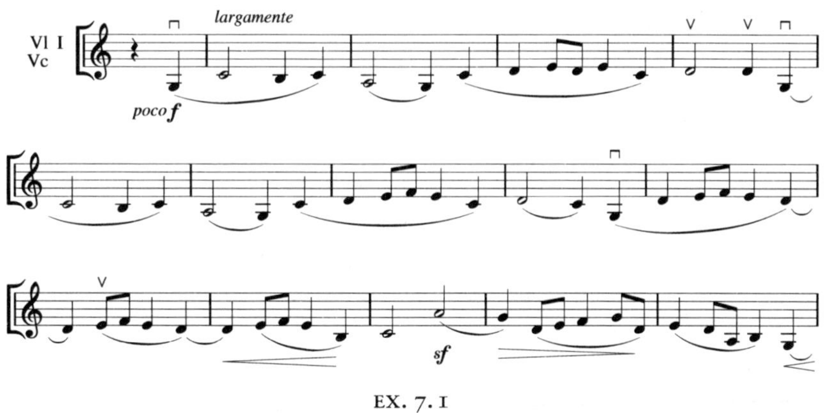

EX. 7.1

Unfortunately the opening statement (bars 62–77) given by 1st violins alone is a little more complicated, owing to the slight alteration in phrasing between the 12th and 13th bars. Although it is not unknown for this to be amended to correspond with later statements of the theme, such a decision must be taken by each interpreter alone. However, until this point the virtual 'bow to a bar' phrasing still applies.

Any sign of tightness in the sound will be caused by an attempt to play too loudly, thereby forcing the sound (the marking is *poco forte*). As will be discussed later, the very apparent 'size' of this sound cannot be achieved by loudness alone.

In another famous example – the opening theme of Rachmaninov *Piano Concerto no. 2* – the same relationship of slurs to bowing can be used.

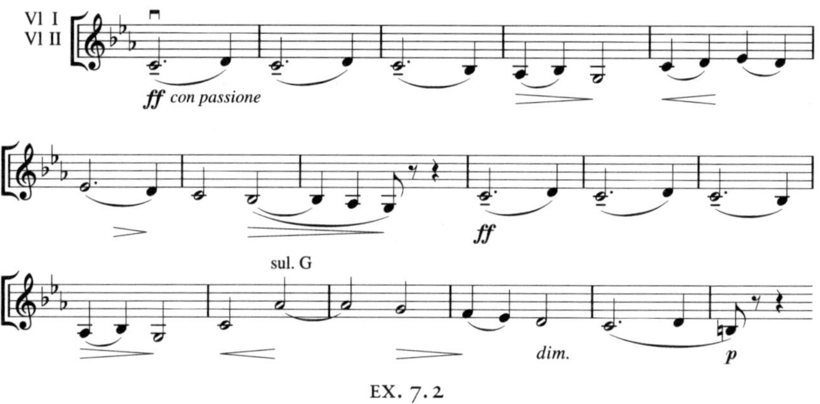

EX. 7.2

Here, however, a yet more subtle degree of control is required of the players, in that the bars containing two bows necessitate an adjustment in both speed of bow and pressure, in order that the dynamic markings are observed.

The danger inherent in both these examples – and, indeed, all *legato* bowing – is that the bow may be used too quickly at the beginning of the down stroke with not enough left for the end of the bar, resulting in unwanted accents and false *diminuendi* every other bar. With young orchestras in particular, it is important that, quite apart from making the players aware of what is happening, the conductor should have sufficient technique of gesture to impose the required bow-arm control of these and similar passages on the section in both rehearsal and performance.

The two examples cited above require a warm, cultured sound, and lie very conveniently for them to be bowed much as phrased. With many examples of similar sonority, however, we are not so fortunate, and one of the most notorious can be found at the very opening of the same Brahms symphony.

EX. 7.3

Here, the overall dynamic marking is *forte* (only) and Brahms is careful to be explicit about the sound he hears – *espressivo e legato*. In other words, much the same substance of sound as the previous examples, but, of course, within a totally different texture. It is immediately obvious that the slurs demonstrate the expanse of the phrase and cannot possibly be attempted as bowings. So, where in this wonderful long phrase may we change the bow direction, as we certainly must? The most regularly performed bowing is to turn on every change of note, slurring the semiquavers, to give a roughly even bow speed of three quavers per bow after the first bar. Ignoring the different considerations apparent in bar 7, this bowing allows the freedom required by all three string sections to produce a rich sound, especially with the 1st violins being so high. But there are drawbacks. The difficulty of avoiding accents at the bow change is compounded in this case by the deliberate movement of the wind and middle strings in asserting the main rhythmic structure and the additional emphasis of every quaver in the bass. The first two pages of the score in full are shown in *Ex. 7.4*.

In performance it is very difficult for the orchestral string player to feel other than that the orchestra is positively divided in its movement, and that the syncopation requires as much emphasis as the main beat. The action of turning the bow on each and every one of these 'up-beats' removes even the opportunity of physical help in avoiding this pitfall. However, bowing of broader span is not without problems. The conductor will need to be acutely aware of the limitations it places on decisions of tempo and dynamic level, not only in original conception but also in performance which, especially with the student orchestra, can bring a radically altered approach to the production of sound.

Un poco sostenuto
Fl
Ob
Cl
Bn
CBn
Hn
Tpt (C)
Timp (C, G)
Vl I
Vl II
Vla
Vc
DB
f legato
f
f espr. e legato
f pesante
(score in C)

EX. 7.4

EX. 7.4 (continued)

If the string sections are sufficiently advanced, the dynamic level of *forte* is not exceeded by any instrument (including timpani!), and the tempo is that of a *sostenuto* opening rather than a Mahlerian climax, then a bowing shown in *Ex. 7.5* may be considered.

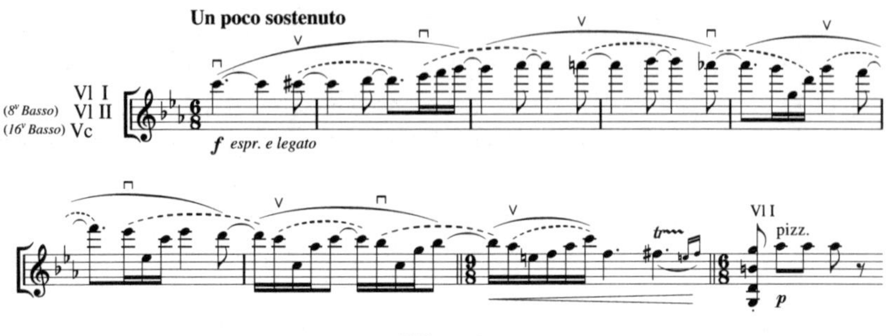

EX. 7.5

False accents are now difficult to achieve because the bow is moving so slowly that none of it dare be wasted. But the necessary clear articulation of slow note changes is an advanced skill when entrusted to the left hand alone. The first two bars will, in all probability, work well, but bars 3 and 4 are a different matter, particularly for cellos and 1st violins. At this pitch, the sound can easily become tight and thin, especially if instruments of poor or only average quality are being used. However, this bowing does have a musical advantage that becomes very apparent only a few bars further on.

EX. 7.6

Here, at bar 25, Brahms marks his first *fortissimo* and, even more significantly, by removing the phrasing slurs, openly suggests the very emphasis of syncopation that we have been at such pains to avoid. Using the first considered bowing, this change in phrasing can either pass unnoticed or be endowed with such extra emphasis of accent that the following oboe solo becomes an anti-climax. In passing, it is worth mentioning that this solo is the signpost to the basic tempo of the introduction – just try singing this phrase (*ten* bars, not three) at anything even approaching *adagio*.

Be that as it may, we are still left with two bowings, each of which displays obvious benefits, and neither of which is ideal in itself. The possibility of combining the two (outside players changing at different times from inside) is not really suitable in this example, such a technique being more adept at defining a rhythmic figure within a *legato* phrase than, as necessary here, disguising one that is naturally apparent (this will be discussed in greater depth in a later chapter). However, if carefully handled, combining aspects within one unified bowing can often be the answer. The freedom of sound production inherent in the more usual bowing, infused with some use of the broader phrase span will not only project the desired effect, but also increase the players' awareness of both aspects of this unique line. The third quoted example of bowing this same phrase shows one way of achieving this.

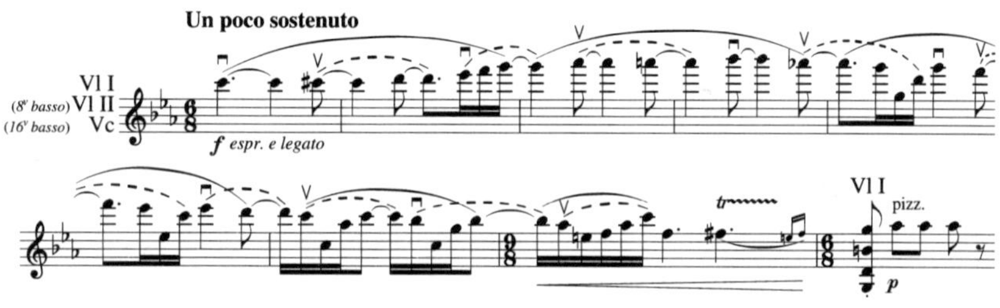

EX. 7.7

The use of the slow sustained bowing across the two bars for which it is most suitable, ensures the dynamic level and *legato* quality at the outset, but the extra speed of bow that can now be given both to the highest note and the one most awkward for intonation (A♭) dispels the risk of noticeable thinness. The restrained power of this passage can now be physically felt by the players, without fear of tightening on the high exposed line, and thus conveyed to the listener more easily and convincingly.

With regard to the last bars of the passage, it will be noticed that *Ex. 7.7* shows a separation in the last two notes of bar 5 and that, in order to facilitate arrival at the final chord on a down-bow, this has not been repeated in the following bar. It is, of course, perfectly possible to replace the slur and play these few bars the other way round, finishing with an up-bow chord, which has the advantage of leaving the 1st violins set for the *pizzicato* that follows. The wider spread of the final chord is the main disadvantage to this bowing rather than, as might be immediately suspected, any difficulty in obtaining a *crescendo* on the down-bow.

However problematic the bowing of this type of passage may be, it is certainly in the softer sounds that the difficulties of *legato* are most susceptible to miscalculation. In these circumstances the bowing required by the combined sounds of a string section is often quite different from that used by a solo player. Thus any attempt at bowing the principal subject of Shostakovich *Symphony no. 5* (*Ex. 7.8*) as phrased in the first three bars is courting disaster, since it is unlikely that even a superb section will be able successfully to project the sound over any distance.

EX. 7.8

The desire to obtain such an ethereal sound quality by slow bow movement can be overwhelming, but it is essential that such sounds are not locked into the instrument and do in fact maintain considerable qualities of projection. The strength imparted by the left hand has a lot to do with this but, most important, the bow must not restrict the vibration of the string or an introvert, tense sound will result.

Without at this stage even considering the vast range of sound control techniques required from orchestral strings in accompaniment, the variations of sound necessitated by passages simply marked *piano* are staggering. (Elgar, in just the first movement of his *Symphony no. 1*, covers a range of tonal variation at this dynamic that is bewildering in its complexity and has yet to be fully exploited.)

Nor does the situation end there, for variety of control is frequently required within one passage to elicit regularity of tone colour. A little later in Shostakovich *Symphony no. 5* we find the following theme for 1st violins, later repeated by violas.

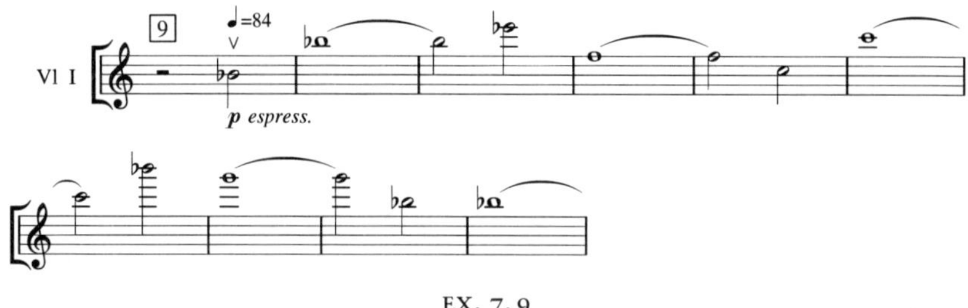

EX. 7.9

The bow speed here must be modified every other bar, the up-bow recovery being three times as fast as the down-bow, and yet no alteration in quality can be perceptible. The adjustment in arm weight needed to achieve this is considerable. There exists an alternative: bowing two bars to one bow and just delineating the minim by a slight halting of the bow. Here, however, the security of intonation of the rather awkward intervals is likely to be impaired for the student orchestra by the lack of bow movement available at the moment of left-hand shift.

Such marking of rhythm within the *legato* bow is a common occurrence nonetheless (*Ex. 7.4* requires it of the basses) and many slow movements of Mozart and Haydn display it in its most obvious form. It can quite easily be extended to include rests, in rhythms such as those in *Ex. 7.10*.

EX. 7.10

Here, no recovery of the bow is required, the note after the rest continuing from the position where the previous note finished. Any extension of the rests themselves can be accommodated until a situation is reached where, regardless of the direction of the following bow, it always continues from the place at which it arrived, being quite static in any period of silence. Such a technique is imperative to both the players' understanding and communication of the phrase line in a deliberately distorted passage, such as the opening of Berlioz *Symphonie Fantastique* (*Ex. 7.11*).

The difference between the second half of bar 7 and the corresponding passages at bars 11 and 13 is worth noting. Essentially these two bowings can be made to sound identical, but the actual difference between them is that the up-bow version will emphasize the 'lift' of the separated note and the down-bow the continuity. The phrasings in *Ex. 7.11* are as printed, to my knowledge, in all scores and the tiny variation in the seventh bar assumed to

EX. 7.11

be Berlioz' own. The opportunity to accentuate this subtlety is thus provided, without being obligatory. The linked bowing of bar 5 (third bar of the theme) is a direct analogy with *Ex. 7.10*.

The multiple variations available when bowing just these few quoted bars are too numerous to be discussed in depth here, but their effect on interpretation must be thoroughly understood. Minor phrase lines, comparative dynamic levels and relative emphasis all need consideration in terms of aural, physical *and* visual requirement – there is little so distracting to the pensive quality of this opening as the bows of sixteen violinists moving about in the rests!

Legato Entries

When it comes to the entry note of *legato* phrases then the natural weight distribution of the bow becomes a little more restrictive. For ease of reference, *Fig. 7.1* shows the five basic divisions.

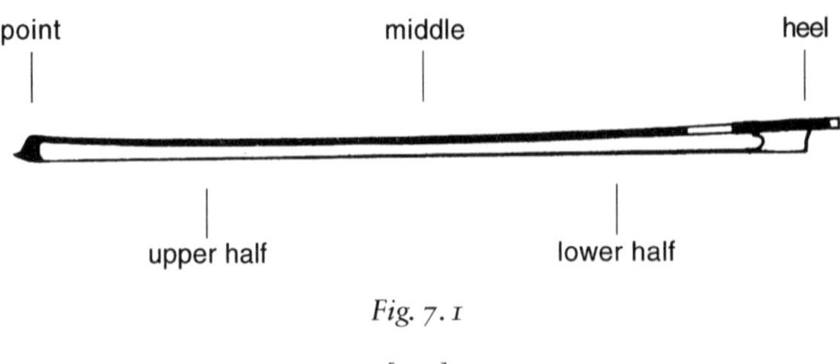

Fig. 7.1

As can be seen, point, middle and heel are terms of general position, while 'upper half' and 'lower half' are terms of area. In order to accommodate the tension screw mechanism, the stick at the heel is considerably thicker than at the point and tapers uniformly along its length, the point of balance being nearer the heel than the middle. Thus the bow is considerably heavier towards the heel, even without considering the extra weight that can be brought to bear by the player's arm and hand. In starting a phrase at either extremity of the bow, the truth inherent in the very basic concept of 'up-bow = soft, down-bow = loud' becomes apparent. This can even be taken further, for the degree of control imparted by the hand at the moment of contact tends to decrease, the greater the distance from the heel. The direction of the bow and its proximity to the string can easily be controlled 'under the hand' at the heel, but this becomes considerably more difficult as one progresses to the point. The resultant technique of beginning a phrase with the bow already moving can thus be achieved in the lower half by control of the moment of contact, whereas in the upper half only gradual addition of weight to the already contacted bow will achieve a similar effect.

When determining the initial direction it is therefore necessary to consider not only the sound required but also the length of bow needed to be used after the change. In a phrase such as *Ex. 7.12* a greater proportion of bow is obviously required for the sustained note than for the crotchet.

EX. 7.12

If a warm, flowing sound is required, whether *forte* or *piano*, it is better for the bow already to be in motion as the first note is played. To achieve this in the lower half and still leave enough bow for the sustained note, one must start on an up-bow.

If a more intangible, distant quality were required, then the lack of weight inherent in the upper half would be preferable. Again, the consideration of the bow needed for the long note is paramount in determining a down-bow start near the point.

Were the second note to be short, then the first could be achieved in either direction in the lower half, and the second note similarly, in the upper, the determining factor in this case being only the degree of emphasis, lift or smoothness required on the second note. It follows, therefore, that as these directions of entry are brought nearer to the middle of the bow, so their characteristics become more similar.

'Off the String' Bowing

All bowing 'off the string' that does not make use of the natural spring of the bow is simply rapid performance of the 'entry' techniques described above. The continuous quaver movement so beloved of Haydn and Mozart in thematic accompaniment, for example, is performed by alternate bows just below the middle – usually close to the balance point – in order to maintain essential control of length, rhythm and dynamic level. In all normal passages of notes of equal length, this bowing requires a down-bow on the first available beat of the entry and continues alternately from there on. The insertion of a rest causes very little difficulty in the execution of this bowing, but (especially for the student) the appearance of a longer note within such a passage can cause problems of rhythm and ensemble. The extra distance travelled by the bow on the longer note, coupled with the apparent absence of anywhere to recover it, present a major technical obstacle to the successful performance of such a regularly encountered figure as that shown here.

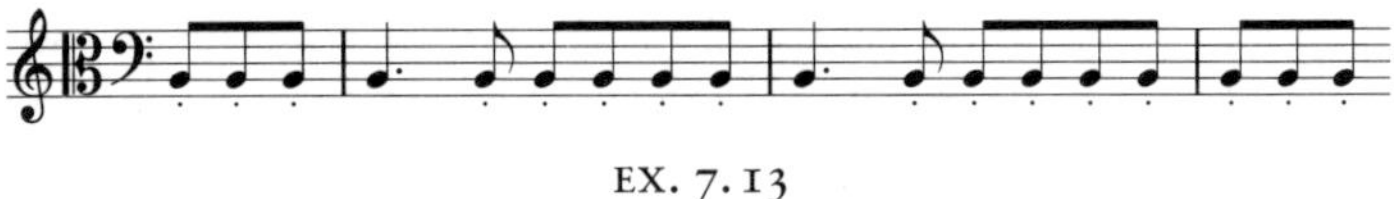

EX. 7.13

The length of bow required for each dotted crotchet note, if not recovered at all, will obviously cause loss of position for the lifted quavers. If recovery is attempted on the quaver immediately following, this note will be uneven in length and probably heavily accented. As was apparent in the similar slow, *legato* example of *Ex. 7.9*, the advanced technique necessary to achieve continuous lines of separated, uneven note lengths calls for immense control of bow-arm weight and speed, since all the recovery here must take place *between* the long note and its following quaver in the very short time that the bow is not touching the string.

In practice, it is often stylistically more appropriate in passages similar to *Ex. 7.13* to shorten the long note slightly as well, which allows more time for the bow recovery to be effected. However, the essential technique remains a deliberate slowing of the bow speed so that only the minimum distance need be recovered. A conductor's misreading of this type of passage – easily done, especially if it is based on a pianistic appraisal of string technique – can lead a string section into very embarrassing situations. In all orchestral string writing there is no more difficult technique than this and none that is generally performed so unsuccessfully. The 'life' imparted to bars of continuous repeated notes by the great chamber orchestras of the world is almost impossible to emulate with inexperienced players.

In faster passage-work (continuous semiquaver movement at speeds above 'crotchet = 120') the wrist movement necessary for the natural *spiccato* of the bow will be used and the resilience of the bow stick brought into play. This technique, available only in the middle of the bow, requires the stick to be tilted so that it is vertically above the hair (rather than the usual position, with the stick slightly towards the finger-board) in order that its maximum natural spring may be utilized. In rapid tempo the hair does not actually leave the string, the springing action of the stick clearly creating the necessary articulation. The most frequently encountered problem is that players work too hard to control the movement instead of letting the bow work by itself.

At this point there is a need to clarify the terminology. The precise word for describing the technique referred to above is *sautillé*, *spiccato* more properly applying to techniques such as those considered earlier, where slower tempi require more individual control of each bow stroke. However, in general usage (certainly in the UK) *spiccato* has come to be associated, rightly or wrongly, with the natural spring action of the bow, and most British orchestral string players consider the technique at slower tempi simply as 'off the string'. Misunderstandings can arise when a composer or conductor uses the term in reference to a passage where this natural action cannot be attempted, as is the case for the cellos in *Ex. 7.14* from the slow movement of Sibelius *Symphony no. 2*.

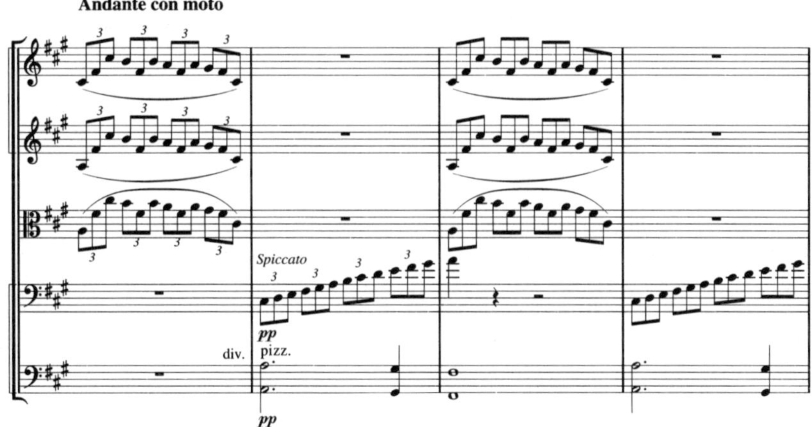

EX. 7.14

This is one of many occasions where a composer is theoretically correct in the request for *spiccato*, as the passage is patently too slow for any involuntary spring of the bow to succeed. But more dangerous is an example where the tempo is just fast enough to lure the unwary player into persisting in an attempt to bounce the bow, as in Stravinsky *Jeu de cartes*.

EX. 7.15

Here the tempo and the dynamic marking conspire to make the passage only possible lower down the bow than any natural spring of the stick can occur. Regardless of whether Stravinsky's use of the term is accurate, confusion may result, causing many inexperienced players to splash about in the middle of the bow. It is interesting to note that a similar passage from *The Firebird*, printed with pointed dots rather than any written direction, will rarely cause a player to make the same initial miscalculation (see *Ex. 7.16*).

A further limitation that might have become apparent from these last two examples is that *sautillé* can less easily be played *forte*. The most frequent use of the technique, therefore, is in passages of running semiquavers, as shown in the following example from the *Scherzo* of Elgar *Symphony no. 1* (see *Ex. 7.17*).

As has been described, no obvious effort of the bow arm is necessary to perform this passage, the natural spring of the stick providing the necessary articulation. But beware: the prerequisite of this bowing is a tempo and rhythmic structure in which it can work. As such, this *Scherzo*, and many other exmples that could be quoted, are probably far more of a test for the conductor than for the orchestra!

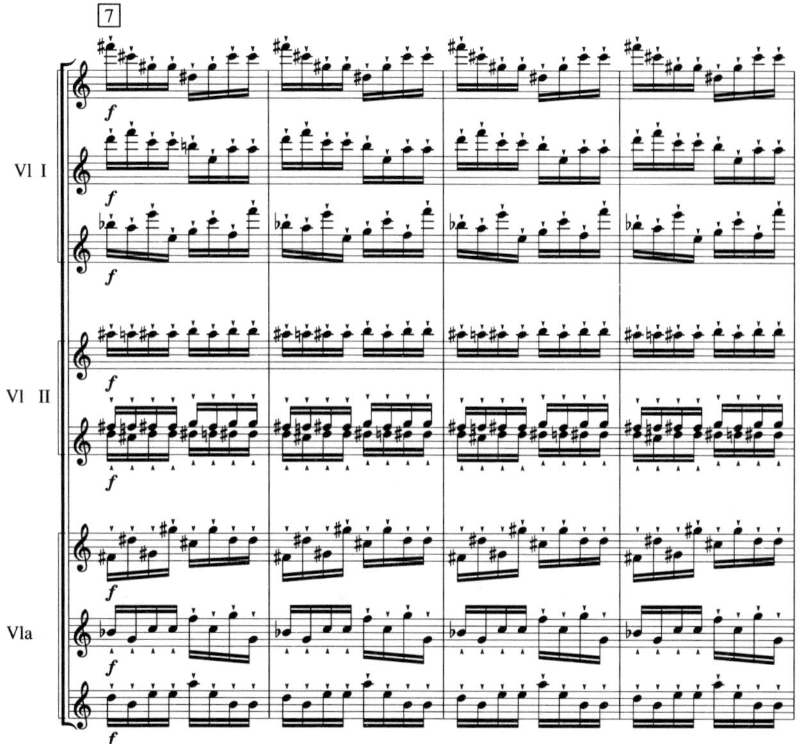

EX. 7.16

EX. 7.17

'On the String' Separation

The most frequently used technique of bowing, with the possible exception of *legato*, is one of the forms of *détaché*, where a slight accent is applied to each bow change by increased pressure at the commencement of the bow stroke. Its purpose is to provide delineation of the turn of the bow without pause or rest, and it can be performed in whole bows (the so-called *grand détaché*), half bows (middle to point) and small bows, depending upon the tempo, style and dynamic level of the passage. The accent produced can vary from a hard *sforzando* to a most delicate touch, and it is the string player's prime weapon of articulation. Although it is frequently used to point the turn of slurred patterns it is most readily associated with separate notes, as in *Ex. 7.18* from Tchaikovsky *Symphony no. 5* in which all three bow-lengths are discernible.

EX. 7.18

A close relation, in a much more strident style, is the *martelé* stroke, which is used in circumstances where a gap may be perceived between the notes (see *Ex. 7.19*).

In this next example, from Beethoven *Symphony no. 4*, pressure is applied between the notes and released at the instant of movement, using as fast a stroke as possible in order to secure a brilliance of sound. This technique is always performed in the upper half of the bow, but the effect can also be

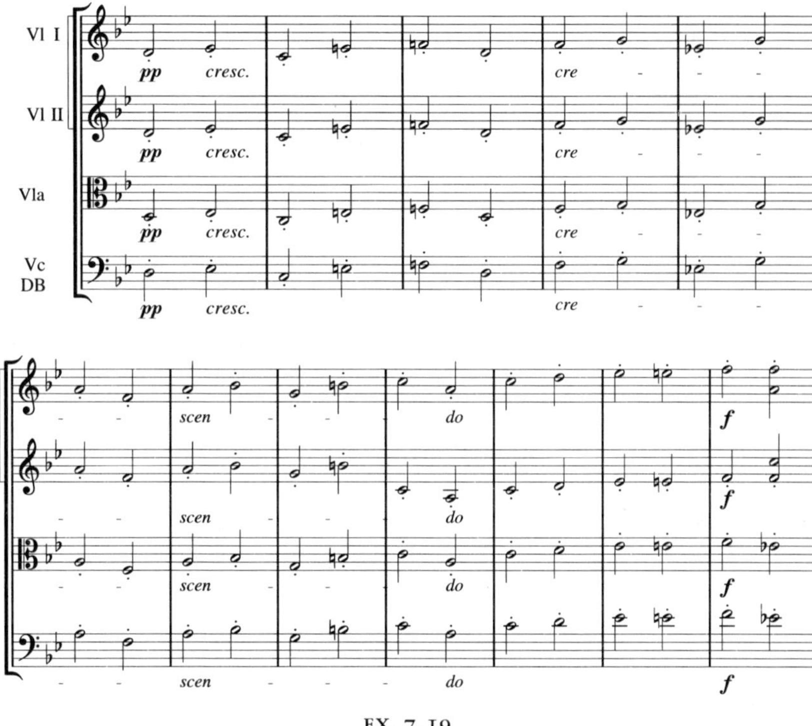

EX. 7.19

achieved lower down, usually in circumstances where rests are implied rather than printed, and in this form it is known as *marcato*.

The clear distinction between these three similar types of bowing is essential to the performance of the numerous virtuosic string concerti written in the nineteenth century by Vieuxtemps, Wieniawski, Paganini and others, but the fact that these techniques were taken as read by players and composers of the period is often overlooked. Thus this passage in Brahms *Symphony no. 2* (*Ex. 7.20*), so often subjected to variations in dynamic level so that the main subject remains dominant, would cause fewer problems of balance if the subtle changes of bowing technique, clearly indicated by the addition of dots, accents and written instructions, were fully understood and adhered to.

An awareness of the probable technical variations implied by many composers' note markings, especially those schooled in the great string traditions of the Classical and Romantic eras, is of paramount importance when preparing a score for performance. There can be no doubt that composers such as Beethoven and Brahms were well aware of the stylistic implications of their

EX. 7.20

markings. However, much remains ambiguous, especially with regard to the music of the later Romantics and beyond. Differences in techniques from one country to another, the use of indications or written instructions in combination (for example, the infamous line + dot), the idiosyncratic use of many different symbols to represent accents or types of *tenuto*, all leave considerable

EX. 7.20 (continued)

scope for individual interpretation. But they must each be considered with reference to the composer in question and the prevailing style of the day if any useful artistic judgement is to be reached.

Variations in Bowing Styles

The bowing techniques discussed so far are all taught as aspects of solo performance, although their use in orchestral circumstances can bring many added problems. There are, however, many difficult and perplexing techniques that relate only to orchestral playing, and these, unfortunately, are rarely specifically taught.

Before considering any of these bowings in greater detail, it is worth examining why certain aspects of string playing change so drastically when the single instrument becomes a member of a larger ensemble. Such differences are largely confined to techniques of the bow arm, the method of fingering remaining constant in all circumstances, although subtle variations in control of *vibrato* and pressure will certainly enhance the blending of a section's overall sound. Essentially, however, any major alteration in approach and technique relates to immediate sound production, the available increase in tonal colouring, and the associated decrease in personalized sound projection. As such, this becomes as much a matter of the individual player's psychological approach as of defined changes in craft. In any ensemble, limitations and responsibilities that do not exist in a solo capacity fall on the instrumentalist, and this process is intensified when a group of similar instruments combines to play one line.

Collaboration requires a degree of uniformity that imposes restraints on the individual instrument but also opens horizons that it would be unable to contemplate alone. In the basic string ensemble of the quartet, the four players retain considerable control of their own sound production, dynamic intensity and individual *rubato*. Their tone, temperament and musical ideas are matched at the outset and they work together as four instruments in combination. But phrasing still has to be accommodated by accompaniment, sonorities must be related one to another, and the moment two or more instruments play the same phrase the production of one or all must be radically altered in order to project the combined line. Something more than just the germ of orchestral technique is present here. As the combination increases through sextet to octet so the personal limitations become more acute for each player, but the overall possibilities of texture, harmonic contrast and melodic emphasis become greater. For these to be fully explored, many techniques have evolved that could not be considered if one instrument were responsible for the presentation of the work in all its aspects.

Orchestral string playing amounts to the combined techniques of the string quartet, magnified by the greater number of players involved (and the resultant increase in available texture) and diminished by the consequent lessening of each instrument's sound as an individual entity. Thus the many methods of production peculiar to orchestral strings seem alien only if a particular instrument is considered in total isolation (rarely the case except in private practice) and become quite natural when considered in the broader context of combined sound.

Unquestionably most troublesome is the frequent necessity to change the position of the bow in relation to the bridge and finger-board in order to elicit sounds of varying substance from the section. In solo circumstances most instruments have an optimum point – approximately midway between the two – where the tone is at its most focused, and players will have spent many of their formative years practising to control the bow in this position. Even a slight change will break the sound very noticeably. Towards the bridge it becomes hard and shrill, towards the finger-board vague and uncentred. Players will only move from this point with great reluctance, and yet flexibility in this area is probably the most useful aid to balance in the string sections' repertoire. With a large number of players the specific unevenness displayed by the single instrument is dissipated and these variations in playing position may be discerned as changes in sound rather than quality. Especially in music of a slow, quiet nature, the production of sound with the bow nearer the fingerboard lends a distance and simplicity that is impossible to achieve in any other way. Also, the definition of small phrases or specific figures can be made clearer by movement of the bow back towards the bridge, thereby focusing certain lines rather than increasing their volume. Some professional orchestras use this technique instinctively but, unfortunately, it is by no means generally adopted.

Sul Tasto

The instruction 'On the finger-board' will be found in many scores (French: *sur la touche*; German: *am Griffbrett*), often in relation to slow passages of rather ethereal quality. As has been remarked, this effect has a scope far wider than is generally accepted and can be used to achieve a variety of subtle differences in sound, from that produced just over the edge of the finger-board to the extremely soft, flute-like quality some two or more inches further from the bridge. Sadly it is rarely explored to its full potential but, with the extra time available to the student orchestra, no excuse can be made for any half-hearted attempt.

One of the most remarkable and beautiful examples of its requested use occurs in the last movement of Rachmaninov *Symphony no. 3* (*Ex. 7.21*). When performed exactly as marked, its appearance in this context defies description.

(score in concert pitch)

EX. 7.21

Sul Ponticello

The exact opposite of the above, the instruction 'On the bridge' (French: *sur le chevalet*; German: *am Steg*) exhorts the player to move the bow as close as possible to the bridge in order to obtain a tight and rather unpleasant effect. Obviously the direction cannot be taken literally as the string has no room to vibrate where it crosses the bridge and thus no sound will result. As with *sul tasto* the possibilities are greater than generally realized.

It is most usually associated with soft, slow-moving *tremolo* passages, where the harshness of its sound may be controlled and the tight 'edge' be made most apparent, as in the magnificent example, for solo and *tutti* strings, in Elgar *Introduction and Allegro*.

EX. 7.22

At this dynamic level the effect will produce a transparency through which instrumental solos will easily penetrate.

A little more pressure will give the eerie quality, sustained under massive outbursts by wind and percussion, required by Malcolm Arnold in his

EX. 7.23

overture *Tam O'Shanter*. In this case the *tremolo* is measured and the bow needs to be very firmly in contact with the string.

Contrary to some opinions, a considerable degree of *fortissimo* can be achieved in *tremolo sul ponticello* without lessening the effect or making it so shrill as to lose all sense of tonality. A few bars later in the same overture one can find *Ex. 7.24*, whose wild *crescendi* are perfectly feasible when performed in the middle of the bow.

EX. 7.24

However, in the rare examples of the use *of sul ponticello* in *legato* passages the increased ease of its production by the lower strings (violas and cellos) becomes apparent, as in the famous example beginning at bar 482 in the last movement of Bartók *Concerto for Orchestra* (rather too long to be quoted here). Here the 1st violins are placed for much of the time on the E string, and reach repeated high Gs in bars 519 – 521. The tightness of this string will make it difficult to play *sul ponticello* at the best of times, but in *legato* it becomes almost impossible to maintain such a small area of bow contact. The longer strings of the lower instruments, however, have a far greater response to this technique in high registers.

Saltato and *Jeté*

Strictly speaking *saltato* is the technique of playing continuous fast *spiccato* notes, usually across three or four strings, by controlling the bounce of the bow to contain at least two notes in each direction. Rarely used orchestrally, the technique is extremely difficult for a large section to control, and it is thus better suited to the solo repertoire. Perhaps the most obvious example of its use is by the soloist at the end of the *cadenza* in the first movement of the Mendelssohn *Violin Concerto*. It does occasionally appear in orchestral scores, as in Sibelius *En Saga*, where, if performed at a true *pianissimo*, it produces a wondrous effect.

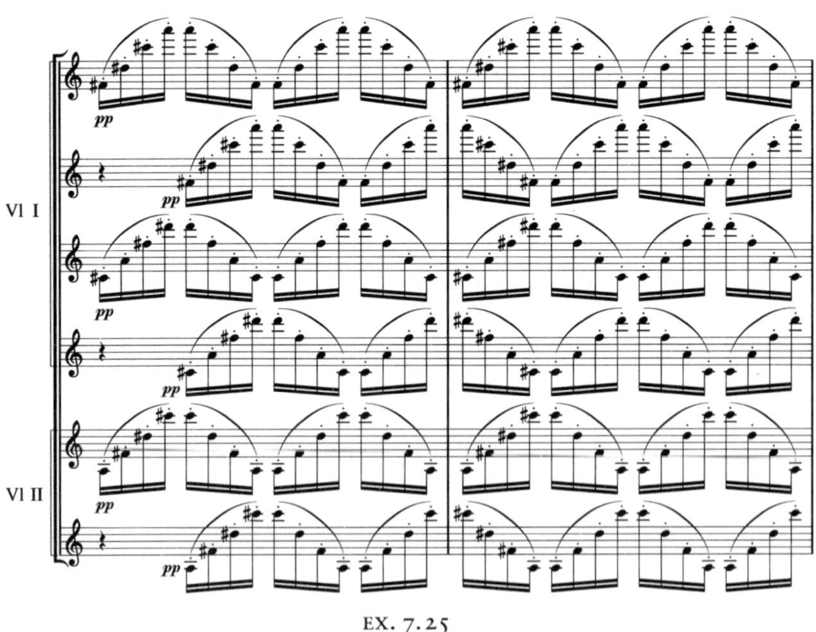

EX. 7.25

Its appearance in Borodin *Polovtsian Dances* (*Ex. 7.26*) however, is rather more akin to *jeté* by virtue of the rests.

EX. 7.26

Jeté requires the bow to be dropped (not thrown!) onto the string in a down-bow motion allowing it to bounce of its own accord. As it can only be used really successfully in this direction it cannot be applied in passages of continuous notes, but it can clearly articulate six, or even eight, notes in one stroke. Regularly found in both the solo and orchestral repertoire it is a standard bowing style and, as such, is taught from quite an early age. However, in solo playing, this technique usually allows some rhythmic freedom, and for this reason it is taught slightly further up the bow than the more rigid requirements of ensemble playing will allow. Thus its frequent use in the last section of Rossini overture *William Tell*, for example, will require the technique to be employed well towards the middle of the bow if the semiquaver figures are to be clearly defined by five entire sections, a circumstance not always fully appreciated by younger players.

EX. 7.27

Where the space between the notes needs accurate rhythmic control, *jeté* will only be accomplished at a considerable distance from the bow tip, whereas isolated passages of brilliant effect can be played successfully higher up the bow. In these cases, as with *spiccato*, the bow needs to be turned in the hand so that the maximum spring of the upper half may be utilized. Such a use can be quoted from Stravinsky *The Firebird*, a score that abounds with *jeté* in all its forms.

EX. 7.28

A slightly more awkward use of the technique may be found in the same work, during the *Danse Infernale*

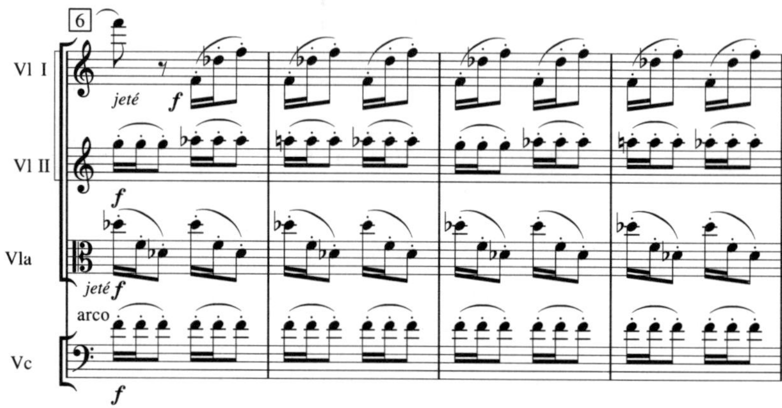

EX. 7.29

where it is intended to be played with alternate bows, rather in the manner of *saltato*, and can work well for the 2nd violins and cellos, although the printed dynamic level is not easy. For violas and 1st violins, however, it is much more problematic, especially for less experienced players. It will be remembered that the *saltato* example (*Ex. 7.25*) allowed a rocking motion of the bow arm, in that the last note of each group was the same first note of the next. In *Ex. 7.29* this is not so, and a recovery across the strings has to be effected for each succeeding figure, an extremely awkward technique when it involves up-bow *jeté*. The somewhat coarse, *forte* style apparent here makes it just possible, but if any rhythmic difficulty or thickening of sound are experienced it is better that this passage be performed by splitting the bowing, two together and one separate, in the following manner.

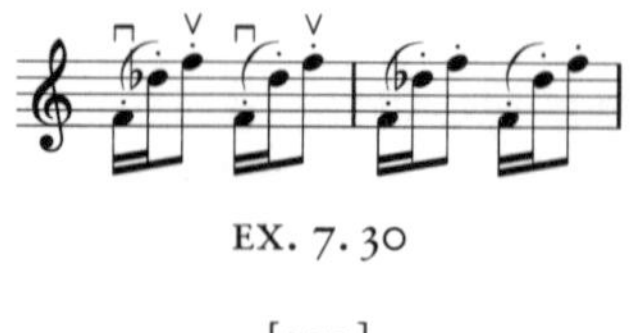

EX. 7.30

On the whole, *jeté* is a bowing that needs to be treated with considerable discretion by the conductor, particularly with regard to the manner of its acheivement by the individual player or section. It is better that a section be allowed to play it in the manner familiar to them, rather than insisting on the letter of the score. One final example from the 1st violin part of *The Firebird* might help to make this clear.

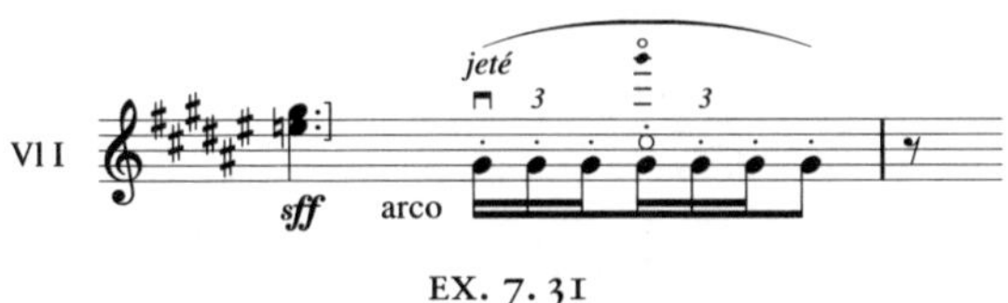

EX. 7.31

As far as I can recollect I have never, either as player or conductor, seen this figure bowed exactly as printed. The insertion of a harmonic in the midst of a single *jeté* stroke is somewhat optimistic to say the least when required from a full section, and the last note is unlikely to appear in the same place from fourteen or more players. This note, if no other, must be separated. It is not unusual for only the first triplet to be 'dropped' and the remaining notes (from the harmonic on) separated, in order to get enough contact on the harmonic for it to speak. Most often the entire figure is discreetly bowed out, using a very vertical *spiccato* stroke, the orchestration and correct separation of the other strings making it unnoticeable in this context. The addition of a *crescendo* and *diminuendo* to the second appearance of the figure (four bars later), printed even more precisely in the 1945 edition, simply adds the final nail to the *jeté* coffin!

Jeté and *saltato* will often be referred to by the descriptive term *ricochet* although, as far as I am aware, this constitutes no particular style of its own. However, so general is the use of the term among players that most conductors have embraced it to avoid any misunderstanding.

It has been my deliberate intention to allocate an apparently disproportionate amount of space to these relatively unimportant effects for, particularly in the youth orchestra, these small figures, requiring unfamiliar techniques, can be perplexing and the cause of much concern. No section can be expected to make a beautiful sound in a *legato* phrase if its players have previously lost control of the bow by virtue of muddling through a passage they cannot understand.

Col Legno

Strictly speaking, this technique should not be considered as a bowing in that it makes use of a part of the bow that was not originally intended for sound production. It is, however, quite closely related to the previous bowings, in that its normal use requires such vertical movement as to make bounce unavoidable. *Col legno*, the use of the bow stick alone for production of a percussive sound, does require control from the bow arm and, for that reason, may be legitimately considered in this context.

It is readily associated with such well-known passages as *Ex. 7.32* from Berlioz *Symphonie Fantastique*.

EX. 7.32

Rhythmically (even with normal bowing) this is not an easy passage to play in fast tempo, but the unfortunate habit of many players of twisting the hair of the bow *away* from them when attempting to play *col legno*, thereby rigidly flattening the fingers of the bow hand, makes it impossible. No control can be imparted to the stick by this method. Indeed one is fortunate to stop the bow bouncing out of the orchestra altogether. The removal of the hair from contact with the string *must* be made in the opposite direction, with the hand turned forward in an exaggerated version of the usual bow hold. In such a position all the intricate rhythms of normal *spiccato* bowing are available and control of the bounce is assured. Only on cello and bass is it possible to reverse this procedure and retain a degree of real control.

Because of the length of string and the depth of pitch, these two instruments are also alone in producing a true fundamental note in *col legno*, adding impact to the effect. Hence its use for these two instruments alone in the last movement of Mozart *Violin Concerto in* A K219 where it is somewhat confusingly requested by the direction *coll'arco al reverscio*.

Rare examples of its use in *legato* passages may be found, the most famous being that in the third movement of Mahler *Symphony no. 1* (*Ex. 7.33*).

EX. 7.33

It must be admitted that although this produces virtually no sound from the standpoint of the individual player, its corporate effect is extremely valid.

Professionally the whole technique is unpopular as, performed without extreme care, it can easily cause damage to the bow, an item of considerable value. With the student orchestra it is as well that the conductor bears this point in mind for the effect can be approached with such enthusiasm that parental bankruptcy is well nigh certain.

Chord Playing

The increased difficulties of fingering in the performance of three- or four-note chords can, in orchestral circumstances, often lead to the relegation of more subtle considerations of bowing or performing style. The erroneous belief that two or more notes sounded together automatically require a great length of bow, coupled with the string player's habit of somewhat arbitrarily spreading widely spaced chords, will cause much of the brilliance and vigour intrinsic to this technique to be lost. It is perfectly possible, when necessary, to play the notes of a three-note chord simultaneously on all orchestral stringed instruments, and chords in four parts can be performed so that the spread is almost imperceptible. Perhaps the opportunity that exists for the players in any large ensemble to divide chords among themselves makes them more inclined to perform those that remain *non divisi* in *arpeggiando* fashion. However, much the same approach can be found in the solo repertoire and one is much more likely to hear a large chord performed like this:

(a)

than like this:

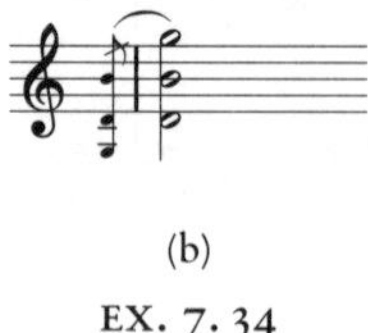

(b)

EX. 7.34

Certainly in *staccato* chords any spreading is unnecessary and usually quite inappropriate. Where is the size of the two great pillars upon which Beethoven '*Eroica*' *Symphony* stands if the 1st violins play *appoggiatura* up-beats to the wind and lower strings? Not only are the weight and purpose of the chords themselves affected, but also two entirely different methods of production become apparent within the string group as a whole, for it is impossible to approach the single notes for cellos and bass with a bowing style similar to that used for a spread chord.

Obviously, many passages exist where the very quick spread of a chord is desirable, especially in works of the Classical repertoire where much of the life and forward momentum of the style would be lost by a more vertical production. This is probably nowhere more true than at the beginning of a phrase, such as the opening bars of Mozart *Violin Concerto in G K216* (*Ex. 7.35*).

The technique of positively contacting all the notes of the chord before the bow is moved and then releasing the strings with a short movement of the bow arm can be used successfully at all dynamic levels, provided the initial pressure has not been so great as to cause distortion on its release. It is unnecessary to produce the hard accent so often associated with a bow movement of this

EX. 7.35

EX. 7.35 (continued)

type. With practice, the tone at the moment of release can be infinitely graded. Much of the quality of shorter string chords is determined by the strength of the left hand in maintaining the stop on the vibrating strings *after* the bow has set them in motion. As with so many orchestral bowings, this exaggerated technique of production is designed for use within a corporate sound. In this instance a short, sharply defined stroke from a number of players is effective because it is less susceptible to a loss of substance than would be the case if the same approach were adopted by a solo instrumentalist.

In the violin variation from Britten *The Young Person's Guide to the Orchestra* such a method of production is imperative for the three-note chords if the precise figuration of the brass accompaniment is not to be obscured.

EX. 7.36

EX. 7.36 (continued)

EX. 7.37

Essential to the 'nationalistic' style of the Polonaise, these chords will lose brilliance if played in any other way, with potentially dire consequences for the rhythm of the variation.

The progression of chords near the beginning of Rachmaninov *Symphonic Dances* (*Ex.* 7.37) will be performed in the same way, although here it is easier to accomplish, as the chords contain only two notes for each player.

This style of bowing may also be used to great effect in passages of single, isolated notes. The dramatic impetus imparted to much of the 2nd movement of Shostakovich *Symphony no. 10* for example, especially this quoted figuration, is quite stunning (*Ex.* 7.38) as is the violent execution of the same technique by the cellos on the main beat chords of *Ex.* 7.39 from the fugue in the *Scherzo* of Rachmaninov *Symphony no. 2*.

Even where a more sustained chord is indicated, the concept of spreading it, whether before the main beat or on it, is most often undesirable. At the beginning of Brahms *Piano Concerto no. 1* the great B♭ chord, set menacingly low in the orchestra, offers no opportunity for the 1st violins to treat the bottom octave as a grace note, especially as the soloist is unlikely to attempt to emulate them when the piano explodes onto the same sustained D with a chord of E major at the recapitulation (*Ex.* 7.40).

The thunderous outburst of this incredible opening, engineered with remarkably small forces, is totally lost if the sound of the combined chord is forestalled in any way.

Many composers will be at pains to emphasize the necessity for a chord to be sounded simultaneously by the use of the somewhat dualistic term *non divisi*. Thus Stravinsky, at the opening of the *Symphony in Three Movements*, marks *non divisi* before a succession of rather awkward chords, thereby (quite correctly) implying division to be the only alternative way of playing them in the correct manner (*Ex.* 7.41).

There are many such occasions in the orchestral repertoire where use of the direction *non divisi* will more truthfully imply *non arpeggiando*.

Elgar, whose score markings (along with those of Mahler and Richard Strauss) show a keen understanding of orchestral 'habit', will tend to differentiate clearly between his desire for chords to be spread or otherwise. An examination of his *Introduction and Allegro* makes this apparent within the first two bars, however often performers might ignore the different chord productions implied by alternative layouts at later points in the score.

EX. 7.38

EX. 7.39

EX. 7.39 (continued)

EX. 7.40

Chord Division

As has been seen, the division of chords by separate players so that the notes may be sounded simultaneously is common orchestral practice and far superior to any approach of *arpeggiando* production in all but specifically requested circumstances. All the chords of more than two notes discussed in the previous section may be performed in this way with no perceptible alteration in their projected sound, the only proviso being that the initial attack from the bow remains the same. Two-note chords are liable to be produced with a more static initial position of the bow than those of three or more, where a production from the air with an already moving bow is necessary in order to strike the strings simultaneously.

The division of four-note chords will be accomplished by the inside players taking the lower two notes, and the outside players the upper two. When dividing three-note chords it is preferable that no player should take only one note, and therefore the middle note of the chord is most usually doubled, inside players taking the lower and middle, and outside the middle and upper. Sometimes (as may be the case in the example from the Stravinsky *Symphony* at *Ex. 7.40*), it may be better for outside players to take the octave (the lower and upper notes), although inside players should still take the lower and middle to maintain the low octave support.

A further possibility when players are faced with layouts similar to *Ex. 7.41* is for the chord to be divided between the sections, 1st violins taking the upper *divisi* and 2nd violins the lower. A slight change in weighting will be the only discernible difference which, in these circumstances, could well be preferable (see *Ex. 7.41*).

The division of chords is obviously only possible when all the notes are of equal duration.

Tremolo

This method of producing an indeterminate number of notes by very rapid movement of the bow was mentioned during the discussion of *sul ponticello*. It can be performed anywhere from just below the middle to the point of the bow and at virtually any dynamic level. Continuous use of the effect was much-loved by Bruckner and all his symphonies contain extended passages of *tremolo* harmony or measured repetition in melodic line (a closely related technique). In such passages it is essential, while maintaining the required sound, to perform the *tremolo* as effortlessly as possible, for the arm will quickly become tired if any tension is apparent over a long period. Basically the bow must be made to do most of the work and the weight of the bow at the middle, or the lightness of the point, judiciously used to provide the necessary variations of dynamic and tone. This particular use of the technique, virtually confined to the works of Bruckner, requires a *tremolo* that is not particularly fast and, especially in passages of melodic content, one that utilizes intentionally different speeds of bow movement from the players within the section.

In less prolonged passages the technique can be used very softly to provide

EX. 7.41

an underlying tension in passages such as *Ex. 7.42* from the slow movement of Chopin *F minor Piano Concerto*

EX. 7.42

often with the addition of quick *crescendi* and sharp accents as in *Ex. 7.43* from the flute variation of Britten *The Young Person's Guide to the Orchestra*.

As a dramatic effect *tremolo* needs to be played very fast so that no rhythmic configuration of notes is detectable. For this reason Sir John Barbirolli would vehemently insist on every player's using the extreme tip of the bow in *pianissimo tremolo*, so that the bow arm would be almost locked straight and the immense speed produced by a 'nervous reaction' of the wrist. However, the

EX. 7.43

same is necessary in the middle of the bow in order to achieve *fortissimo*, and the shattering brilliance of the *tremolo* B natural with which the strings end Stravinsky *The Firebird* needs an exemplary control of speed and contact.

Probably the most frequently encountered difficulty with *tremolo* is determining when to use it. Composers are rarely so exact with their markings as to add the direction *trem.* as in *Ex. 7.43*. More often an arbitrary number of strokes through the tail of the note will be the only hint of its possible use, and decisions will have to be made on the basis of tempo, content and style. It is fairly safe to assume that two strokes or fewer refer to a measured number of notes but this is by no means universal, and the extension of such an assumption (that three strokes or more automatically means *tremolo*), is equally dangerous. To add to the confusion there are grey areas where a definite instruction to use either technique will cause certain passages to lose much of their inherent vagueness. Thus one prays never to be asked whether *tremolo* or measured notes are required at the wonderful moment of orchestral vaporization at the last bar of the introduction of Rachmaninov *Symphony no. 2*.

EX. 7.44

Of the two possible answers neither is true if it can be clearly distinguished, the movement of the bow needing to be so subtle as to provide only intangible substance to the chromatic harmony.

However, on many occasions the tempo of a passage is such that very little difference in execution will be apparent. In *Ex. 7.45* from Tchaikovsky *Francesca da Rimini* the performance of double notes is so near the speed of *tremolo* as to make any real technical difference irrelevant.

In such a passage it is the energy that is focused *into* the string that will provide the sound, *not* the quantity of bow used.

Tremolo that requires the repetition of two notes, rather than one, is rare but its use in the Schumann *Cello Concerto* makes its consideration necessary

EX. 7.45

EX. 7.45 (continued)

(*Ex. 7.46*). With young, inexperienced players it can exhibit a horrible tendency to slow down in order to facilitate synchronization between the fingers and bow, a situation not helped by the constant change of interval.

EX. 7.46

The desired effect can only truly be accomplished by rejecting the normally desirable synchrony of the two hands, and instead exercising an independent control so that each hand is moving at roughly the same speed – a virtual negation of everything the young string player has striven to master. What must be avoided is the increase in effort and dynamic level that is inevitable in a situation of stress or concern. However unnatural or technically difficult this passage might be, it is inappropriate to force the sound or ferociously attack it in the manner of some dangerous adversary. A conscious lessening of the bow's contact with the string and a relaxed movement of the fingers will be far more helpful.

The more regularly encountered *legato tremolo* is a simple extension of the trill to an interval wider than a major second. In the lower positions, unless based on an open string, the interval is limited to the maximum extended compass possible between the first and fourth fingers: for all practical purposes a perfect fifth on the violin, an augmented fourth on the viola and a major third on the cello. On the double bass, *legato tremolo* in higher positions is most usual, since the sound of the low register makes quick, continuous repetition of two notes very indistinct and is limited in compass to a major second – a normal trill. On or above sixth position (a major seventh above the open string) wider intervals become possible and *legato tremolo* can sound very effective. Wider intervals are more easily fingered in the higher positions of the other instruments too, but most *legato tremolo* makes use of the lower positions on the violin, viola and cello, as in *Ex. 7.47*, again from Britten *The Young Person's Guide to the Orchestra*, but this time accompanying the harp variation.

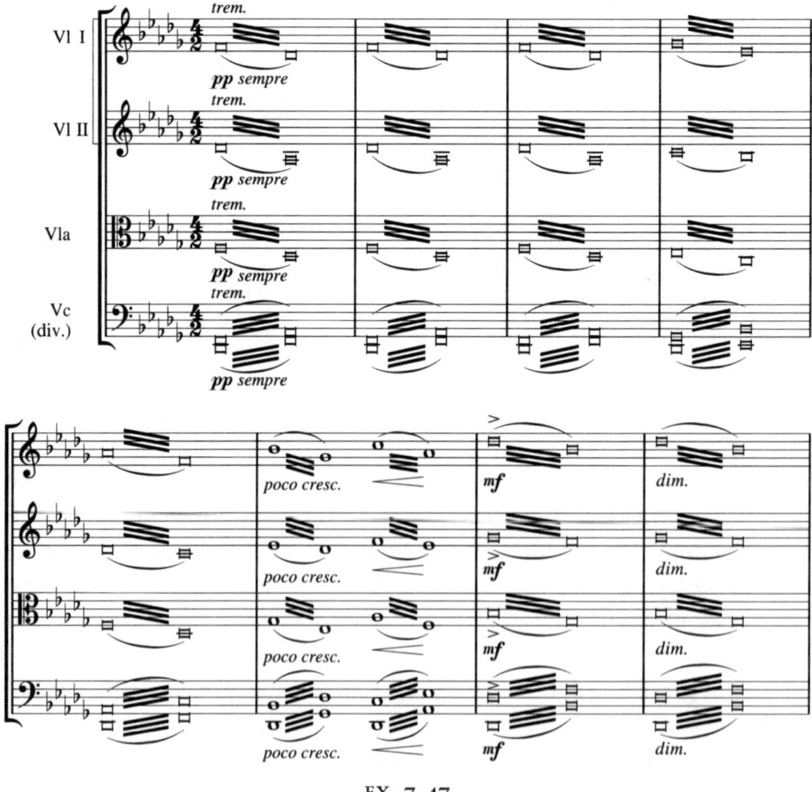

EX. 7.47

In this example the 2nd cello part begins with a wide extension of first to fourth fingers (D♭ to F) and then, after one bar's relaxation, proceeds to place the upper note progressively higher. Unless the player has a very big hand the whole passage will need to have been started in thumb position, that is with the thumb, rather than the first finger, stopping the low D♭, in order to make the D♭ to G♭ possible in the sixth bar. Once the note of the next open string is reached, the passage may be played with an undulating movement of the bow across two strings.

This method of producing *legato tremolo* is more usually applied to passages of determined rhythmic structure (as in *Ex. 7.48*, from Brahms *Symphony no. 1*) than to indeterminate repetition, as its usable speed is limited by the loss of clear articulation by the fingers and the increased movement of the bow.

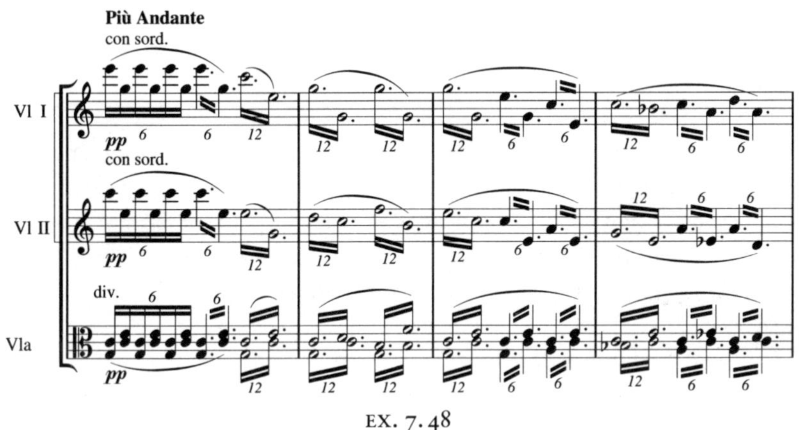

EX. 7.48

Apart from this, the main difference between these two styles is that in fingered *tremolo* the two notes should be played, as far as possible, on one string, even when this involves awkward extensions of the fingers. When the undulating movement of the bow is required however, the notes need to be fingered across two strings wherever possible. Thus the 2nd violins in *Ex. 7.48* should finger the first group in the second bar by using a first finger D on the A string and a fourth finger C on the D string, maintaining what is, in effect, the use of spread double-stops.

The concept of double-stopping is most usefully applied to this technique, in that the bow should only just avoid sounding the two notes together and make the absolute minimum movement necessary to prevent touching both strings at once. Obviously, as the bow hand gets further away from the point of contact so the amount of movement of the hand increases. For this reason, regardless of dynamic, this bowing is best accomplished across the middle of the bow, the lowest point at which advantage may be taken of both even balance and minimum movement. What is sometimes referred to as the 'village pump act' – when the bow arm makes exaggerated movements up and down – is both disastrous to the result and distracting to watch.

Linked Bowings

As has been seen, all these bowings, from *legato* to *saltato* to *tremolo*, require highly developed techniques of the bow arm and use different parts of the bow, according to the demands of tempo, dynamic level and blend. Unfortunately only the most idiosyncratic of them will appear in isolation. For the most part their use will be spread unevenly through any page of a string part, up to three or more occurring in a single phrase, demanding rapid changes from one to another.

It is in such circumstances that changes of bow direction are crucial, and the most subtle and (to the non-string player) perplexing separation and linking will be needed to ensure that a passage is reached in the right place in the bow. Often the bowing of the phrase itself is less important than that needed to approach it and many conductors are taken by surprise when a simple request for change causes complicated adjustment of bowing two or three lines back.

It would be futile to attempt to give any sort of complete guide to the bowings used for simple convenience. Bowing is a proudly creative art and there are too many permutations. However, it is possible to look at some of the 'linked' bowings in more general use in order to offer some insight into their application in this role. (It is worth stressing here, once again, that every single bowing can produce many different results, and that *all* maintain a dual purpose – that of stylistic interpretation and that of convenience.)

The linking of bowings in *legato* phrases, both continuous and across rests or pauses, has been discussed earlier. Linked bowings can also be used to control the position of the bow (most often in passage-work but also in isolation) in order to facilitate the execution of a subsequent phrase or style.

The most frequent example of this use is the line of semiquavers, phrased two slurred and two separate, bowed 'two and two' (see *Ex. 7.49*).

At dynamic levels up to about *mezzo forte* this is performed in the middle of the bow, progressing towards the heel as more sound is required and reaching the extreme position under the hand only when intense weight or violence

EX. 7.49

is demanded. Because it is basically a lifted bowing it will not work in its characteristic style in the upper half or at the point, but it can be made to sound so similar to the 'on the string' separate bow variety that it may be used in this context to bring the bow from the upper half to the middle without pause or apparent change in articulation. Exactly the same applies to its frequent use in sextuplets and uneven phrasings such as in *Ex. 7.50* (a) and (b) below.

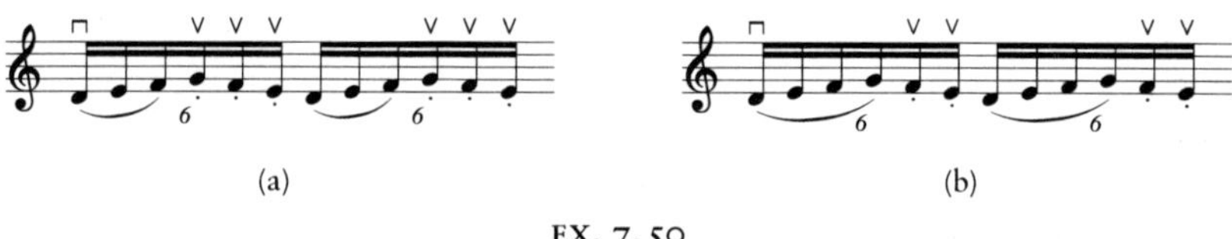

(a) (b)

EX. 7.50

The main advantage of this bowing in passages of recurring figuration is that it retains the bow in one position while providing uniform phrasing for every figure, alleviating the problems of subtle adjustment to bow weight and length that would result if the passage were to be bowed out. It is almost obligatory in passages of syncopated phrasing, as in this example from Beethoven *Symphony no. 6*

EX. 7.51

and may be extended to incorporate more than two notes if considerable emphasis or length has been applied to the down-bow, as in *Ex. 7.52* from Berlioz *Symphonie Fantastique*.

Its use in triplet figures, although similar, is of more limited value in this respect. Here, any linking of bowing will obviously produce an uneven distribution and therefore only if repeated emphasis is required will triplets generally be bowed with two notes linked. Much more likely is the necessary linking of all three notes in order to return the bow to the required position. *Ex. 7.53* from Smetana *Šárka* (the third of the *Má Vlast* cycle of symphonic poems),

EX. 7.52

demonstrates such a bowing at the beginning of each bar in order to make up for the unavoidable use of length on the preceding half bar slurs.

EX. 7.53

There need be no perceptible difference in the two bowings, even when immediately adjacent or, as here, demanding a rather 'nationalistic' style lower down the bow than normal. The only alternative would be to separate the quaver at the end of the bar, breaking the slur.

At risk of stating the obvious I must emphasize that there is no bowing that will reproduce a slur, except a slur! Separate notes may be performed in countless ways with negligible difference in effect, but once the bow is turned, however smoothly, a slur is lost.

Unfortunately, the same inexact symbol of the curved line is used for slurs of bowing, phrasing and ties, a fact that allows some leeway in deciding which is the predominant meaning, but if the *legato* slur is intended there is only one way to reproduce it.

Lighter, *staccato* use of continuous triplet figures can most easily be bowed in simple alternate fashion, but insertion of a single note rest may sometimes make adjustment necessary, especially if the figures require identical emphasis, as in this example from Rachmaninov *Symphony no. 3*.

EX. 7.54

The most awkward triplet rhythm for decision of bowing style is that beginning with a lengthened first note such as occurs throughout the first movement of Beethoven *Symphony no. 7*. In this case at least two separate styles of bowing are required as the rhythm is written in three different ways, both with and without a rest and with the addition of *staccato* dots, as at (a), (b) and (c) below.

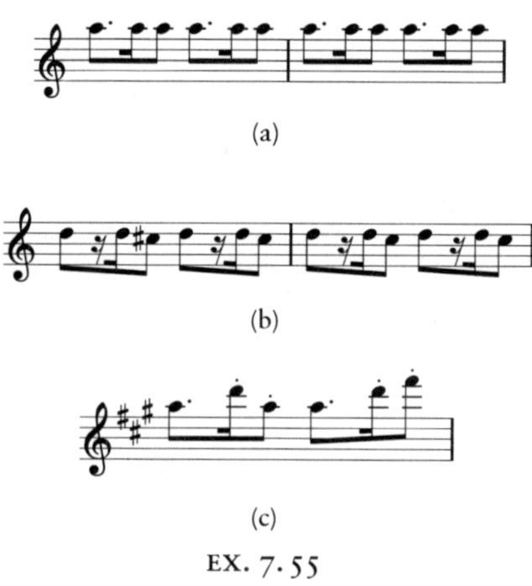

(a)

(b)

(c)

EX. 7.55

Setting aside any interpretative decisions as to the degree of differentiation required, the only bowing that will give an exact performance of (a) is simple alternation, or 'as it comes', whereas both (b) and (c) will be produced by the use of linked down-bows on the first two notes, as shown in a very rhythmically orientated passage from the coda of the same work (see *Ex. 7.56*).

In the last movement of Schumann *Symphony no. 4* this down-bow linkage becomes even more vital in duplet rhythm because of the continual recurrence of the dotted quaver after an even number of notes. Other than making recovery on the last quaver of each figure there is no way to stop the passage proceeding higher and higher up the bow (see *Ex. 7.57*).

EX. 7.56

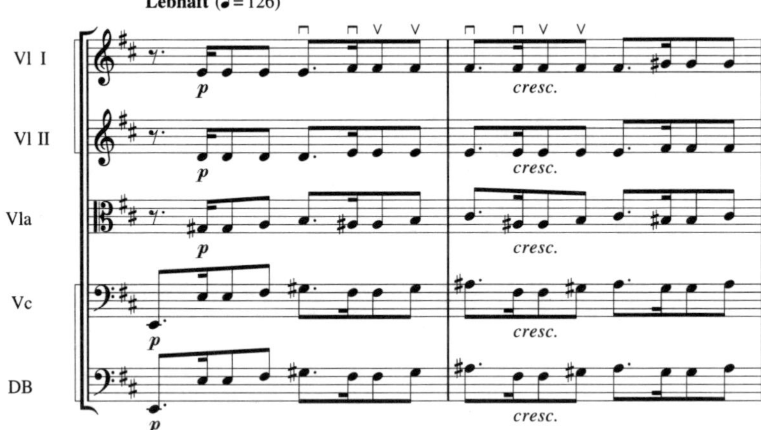

EX. 7.57

Many continuous dotted rhythms, for instance *Ex. 7.58* from Schubert *Symphony no. 9*, will be bowed in the same way.

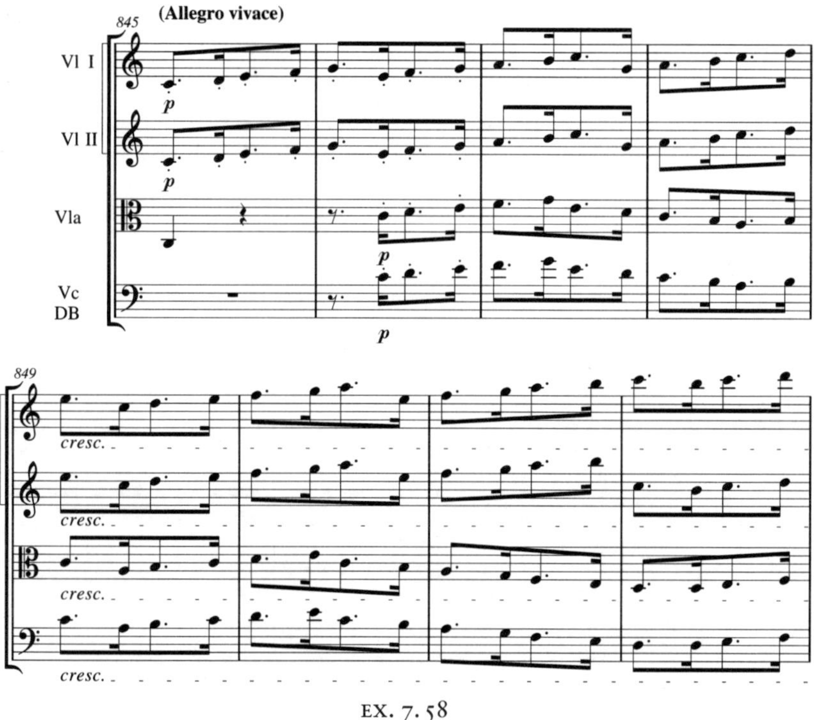

EX. 7.58

An alternative bowing for this passage, and one that can make it much clearer in performance, is to use alternate bows in the upper half but with the *down*-bow on each semiquaver, like this:

EX. 7.59

In practice this would be performed almost entirely by use of the wrist, and produce two short notes of roughly equal length – not necessarily the articulation that Schubert might have had in mind for this passage but nonetheless providing a very exciting clarity and forward drive. When performed low in the bow, virtually under the hand, this approach is most suitable for loud passages that require obvious panache in execution. The somewhat exaggerated movement of the wrist makes it a very visual effect, which is perhaps why, in this context, it is referred to by orchestral players as the 'shoeshine bowing'. Regularly used for dotted rhythms at dynamic levels of *forte* and above, it may be used for passages such as *Ex. 7.60* from the last movement of Beethoven *Symphony no. 7*.

EX. 7.60

Almost the same wrist action in a more circular motion will be used to achieve continuous, or re-taken, down-bows, often specified by composers in order to add weight and emphasis. It will usually be found in a deliberate reiteration of closely orchestrated chords such as in *Ex. 7.61*, from Prokofiev *Peter and the Wolf*, where it vividly describes the fury of the captive animal as it desperately tries to break free from the choking rope.

In this instance no other bowing could give the same effect, but its use in more expansive passages can be questionable. *Ex. 7.62* reproduces the string parts of a full orchestral unison passage from the last movement of Bruckner *Symphony no. 4*. Consecutive down-bows are requested for the last ten notes of the phrase (but not, interestingly enough, on the first three, where their use is far more desirable).

The implication is one of exaggerated weight and equal emphasis but, given the triplet figuration in bars 4 and 6, this bowing is unlikely to provide an articulation commensurate to that of the brass and woodwind. In

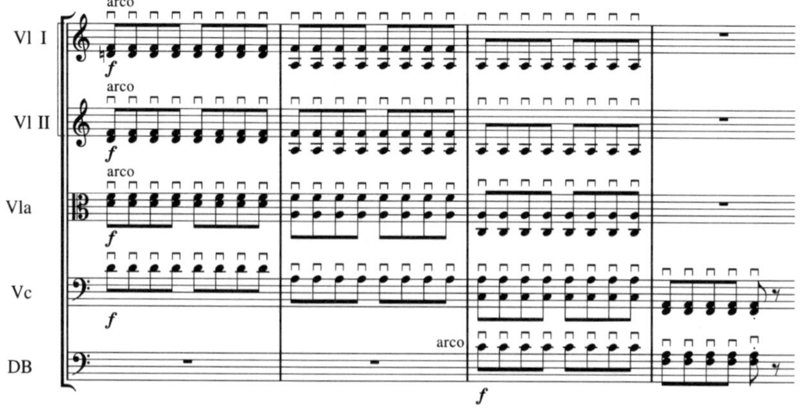

EX. 7.61

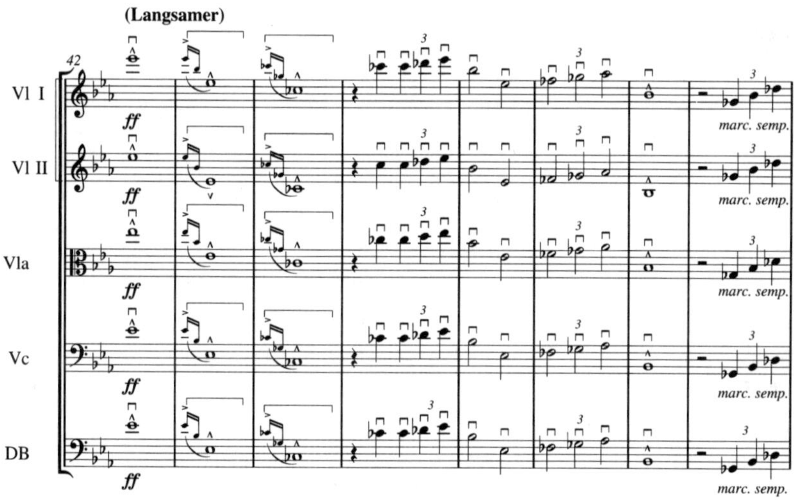

EX. 7.62

addition, from the players' point of view, this bowing is very awkward in this passage, the varying note lengths placing undue emphasis on the problem of simple rhythmic ensemble, and thus almost negating the purpose of the down-bows. The fear that any interpolated up-bow motion will lose power is unfounded, and unlikely to have been otherwise in the 1880s. Two up-bows on the second and third notes of each of the triplets, with even bar 5 bowed out as well, can easily produce as substantial a sound, without upsetting ensemble or continuity. As an alternative, the last minim triplet could be bowed out and the final note arrived upon as an up-bow.

The request for successive down-bows can be equally unproductive in passages bereft of brass or woodwind support. Later in the same movement the strings parts are again similarly notated, in a passage that responds to two immediately previous statements by horns and brass alone.

EX. 7.63

To provide the expanse of sound required using this bowing is almost impossible and, I suspect, Bruckner employed it as much to indicate his desired note length and degree of emphasis as for any other reason.

The use of repeated down-bows in fast tempi is rare but by no means impossible. It can be a stunning effect in the hands of a virtuoso section, and will sometimes be used in this passage from the *March to the Scaffold* in Berlioz *Symphonie Fantastique* (see *Ex.* 7.64).

Not to be confused with the re-taken down-bows, the *linking* together of two down-strokes has a use in circumstances far less obvious. It is consciously employed by many orchestras to avoid the 'full stop' accent that can be given to many of the three-note cadences of the Classical repertoire. Thus throughout Mozart we find opportunity for the bowing illustrated by *Ex.* 7.65 (taken from the first movement of the *Clarinet Concerto*) in order to help the performance of a lightened cadence point by reaching the last note on an up-bow in the upper half. (As with all composers of the Classical era, the inherent style is much more one of carefully placing a precious object on to a shelf than firmly planting it on the table.)

Reliable markings to differentiate positively between slurs, re-takes and

EX. 7.64

EX. 7.65

linking (except in places where their use is obvious) do not exist, although the square bracket designating a bow link, as used in *Ex. 7.65*, is understood by many players.

All the variations of style, degree and direction of bowing that have been examined briefly here form the basis of orchestral bowing technique, and the flexibility, interaction and modification of their multiple uses is enough for the conductor to form broadly-based judgements of the practicality of an interpretation and its possible translation into sound. A bowing should not dictate any aspect of interpretation, but rather the boundaries of its use should be clearly understood so that the process of music-making may be conceived as one inseparable whole.

The majority of examples quoted above have been related to violins and violas and, so far, little mention has been made of bowings peculiar to the lower strings. This has been an intentional omission for two reasons. Firstly, all the bowings included apply to all strings equally. Secondly, the vast majority of orchestral bowings will be dictated by, or emanate from, passages involving the upper strings – in particular the 1st violins.

The cello bow is slightly shorter than that of the violin and viola and considerably more sturdy in design. In contact with the string it is slightly tilted away from the bridge of the instrument but, because of the upright position, the stick is thus towards the player.

There are two distinct designs of bow for the double bass which correspond to the player's chosen technique, referred to as French or German, the difference lying in the shape of the frog, which will accommodate one of two quite separate methods of bow-hold. Both bow types are a little shorter than that of the cello, and noticeably thicker in both the stick and the width of hair. In other respects the French bow is similar in design to a cello bow and held in much the same way, though individual variations in the thumb position are sometimes seen. The frog of the German bow is very different. It is almost twice the depth of its counterpart and shaped so that the hand may hold the back end of it. The thumb is placed on top of the stick, so that it is this, rather than the forefinger of other bow holds, that exerts pressure onto the string. Each bow requires a specific technique of production and they are *not* interchangeable.

Such individual bowings as exist in the orchestral repertoire for cello and bass apply mainly to the length of *legato* phrases, the shorter bow combined with longer and thicker strings often requiring a faster movement if a controlled and even sound is to be produced, especially in the case of the bass. It is also easier to take rapid string crossing in the opposite direction from violins and violas by reason of the upright position of the instrument and the corresponding reversal in position of the lowest string. Such considerations will be almost automatically incorporated into the technique of these instrumentalists, and the slight variations that may be necessary will be of little consequence to the overall concept of string bowing.

Certainly in student orchestras, bowings for the double bass need to apply directly to the size, strength and ability of the section and need not correspond to those used by the rest of the strings except in relation to the start of phrases or particular effects. The bass support of the cello section is vital and the *sound* produced becomes the over-riding factor, regardless of the direction or number of bows required to produce it. Apart from perhaps marking the part with a skeleton guide as to how the cellos are approaching certain phrases, the position of bow changes within a sustained passage is best dealt with by the section or tutor, and specifically related to the amount of support required. More than any other section a certain degree of 'free' or unco-ordinated change may be utilized by the basses in *legato* phrases without distortion of the line.

The small variations that might be of benefit to the cello section, usually with regard to the approach and performance of a passage involving string crossing, should also be accommodated without the all-pervading consider-ation of trying to make things 'fit'. It is perfectly feasible for the cellos to take a small isolated passage in an entirely different way from the upper strings, provided that it does not effect any variation in the musical result. If it does, it is usually a matter of technique and rarely anything so simple as bow direction!

None of the variations that may be applied will constitute any new bowing technique in themselves, and all will be examples of those already discussed. Although there is often a noticeable reluctance on the part of cello sections to incorporate bowings that constantly utilize the upper half of the bow (an aversion that should be firmly resisted), for the vast majority of interpretative bowings the whole string section is equipped to reproduce them in identical fashion.

Accents

The number of available variations in accent exceeds even the innumerable different symbols invented to request them. Ultimately, the specific type of accent must be determined within the context of the work and the orchestra performing it but, for the strings, there are four main techniques of production from the bow-arm:

A increase in pressure of the bow;
B increase in speed of the bow;
C sudden release of exaggerated bow contact to the string;
D exaggerated weight in attack from above the string – only possible on an entry and therefore necessarily preceded by a rest or, at least, some sort of lift.

It is usual for all of these to be accompanied by a similar emphasis in the left hand, usually attained by an increase in speed of *vibrato*; indeed, such a parallel physical reaction is very difficult to avoid.

The inclusion of B in the above list is somewhat dubious because it is almost never used as a technique of accentuation in its own right. All it will give is a 'bulge' to the sound without defined start or finish. However, it will always be found, to greater or lesser degree, in combination with the other methods mentioned and regularly becomes the determining factor in the variation of their strength. For this reason it must be included but it will not be discussed in isolation.

The momentary increase of bow pressure will most often be used in passages of *legato* quality where a uniform speed of bow is desirable. This type of accent will always include some degree of *vibrato* emphasis from the left hand and is, in fact, most easily understood by players as a 'left-hand accent', its general method of accomplishment being one of 'leaning into the instrument'. Although it can successfully be used in circumstances requiring isolated emphasis it is more natural when a *crescendo* to the accent is in evidence. Thus, early in the last movement of Dvořák *Symphony no. 8*, all the *arco* strings use this technique in order to keep the overall sonority under total control.

EX. 7.66

As can be seen, it is practicable in a separated bowing (in the cello theme of this example) or slurred (as in the violins and violas). In common with all accents, it is perfectly possible to perform with the bow travelling in either direction.

Although it is always easiest to effect an accent in the down-bow – with the arm travelling away from the body and, in the case of violins and violas, using the natural pull of gravity – it is not necessary to determine a bowing by this criterion alone and make awkward and fussy changes simply to arrive upon every accent in this one direction. Not only can up-bow accents be made to sound exactly the same as those performed in the opposite direction, but also the rather more subtle accent natural to this bow direction will often prove to be the most suitable.

The sudden release of strong or exaggerated contact with the string will give an altogether sharper accent and is most easily associated with *forte-*

piano (*fp*). The momentary static contact with the string will give a very sharp bite to the note on its release and may be graduated at will by control of the amount of pressure exerted in the first place. Such pressure may be applied very quickly and the technique does not necessarily require any loss of *legato* on the bow change, although the most explosive examples will require a moment to 'set'. The colossal *fortissimo-piano* entries for the full strings in Walton *Symphony no. 1* require instant release of extremely powerful contact.

EX. 7.67

In orchestral circumstances such a dramatic effect will be enhanced by stopping the movement of the bow immediately *after* the initial attack, thereby creating a moment of almost no sound at all. The bowing is less often considered within a slur, being naturally more suitable at the beginning of a stroke, but it is perfectly possible and often very effective.

A similar method will be used even if the continuation of the note is *tremolo*. Earlier in the same symphony the strings have this passage.

EX. 7.68

Started from the lower half of the bow (in this case, where the strings will have arrived) the sudden contact is instantly released and the bow kept travelling at tremendous speed to the point, the whole technique performed in one action quicker than the eye can follow. A stunning effect is produced which may virtually be repeated four bars later by subtly working the intervening *tremolo* back down the bow. This particular effect was much beloved of Sir John Barbirolli's Hallé Orchestra, but it should be mentioned that it is not without its dangers. I well remember performing it in over-enthusiastic fashion on one occasion and sheepishly having to retrieve my bow from the front row of the audience!

The exaggeration of weight in attack from above the string is the most natural accent when required at the commencement of any passage. Here the emphasis is simply produced by speed through the air as the bow is brought down on to the strings, and the variation available is infinite. Such an accent will be used at the opening *tutti* of Brahms *Piano Concerto no. 1*, the moving bow giving weight and size to the sound.

EX. 7.69

In certain circumstances this technique may also be accomplished in the up-bow, much more of a 'slap' being apparent in the initial contact. Once again, however, it would be wise to consider the dangers that any violent approach to an instrument may harbour. A very well-known player in another orchestra of which I happened to be a member misjudged an immense up-bow accent and drove the bow into the body of the instrument, surrounding himself with delicate splinters of inestimable value!

When working with inexperienced players it is vital that any request for such abnormal techniques is accompanied by a *complete* understanding of how to accomplish them.

*

In final reference to the performance of accents it needs to be mentioned that their most difficult aspect is avoiding distortion of the note immediately before or after. Especially when a line of equal length notes is in evidence, a noticeable lengthening of those with accents can only be avoided with extreme care. *Ex. 7.70* from Schubert *Symphony no. 9* will regularly be performed with every alternate note inordinately long.

EX. 7.70

This is partly because of the added strength of the down-bow but mostly because the accent is produced by length of bow instead of weight. Individually quite a small amount of energy is required, the corporate response of the sections being enough to make the accents perfectly clear.

Divided Bowing

The duplication of numbers within any one string section allows non-co-ordinated changes in the direction of the bow to be actively considered. Such a technique of 'free change' may be used in respect of long sustained notes, both to release the sound by use of greater bow length and as a means of convenience demanded by some following passage. The only difficulty for the players is often that of *not* coordinating the bow change, and yet maintaining an even note without bulge or accent.

For very long notes, where a change of bow direction becomes absolute necessity, a true *divisi* bowing style can be adopted, as may be seen in *Ex. 7.71* from the slow movement of Sibelius *Symphony no. 1*, where the composer marks exact division of double bass bowing across the full 33 bars of their held E♭.

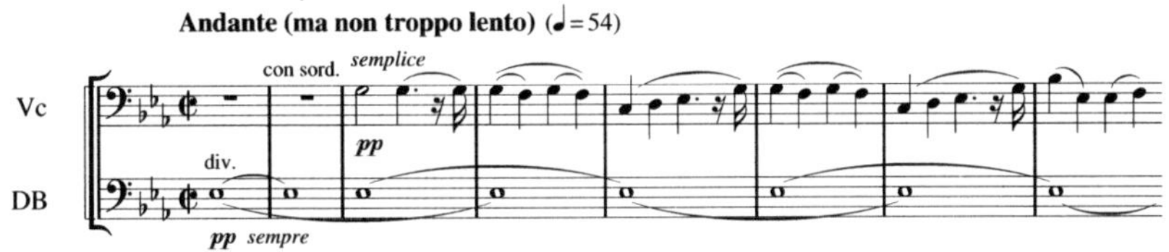

EX. 7.71

While this is the most common use of any divided bowing, the technique can also be used to define some aspect of a *legato* phrase that would otherwise remain unclear. In Beethoven overture *Egmont*, for example, the two quavers at the end of each bar are often indistinct, both because of their downward movement and because they are difficult to articulate within one bow.

EX. 7.72

In this circumstance it is perfectly possible to divide the bowing so that inside players use a separate up-bow in the performance of the two quavers, while outside change bar by bar with the printed phrasing.

Such a division can only be contemplated in passages where it does not disturb the projected line. The alternative bowing must always remain less dominant, providing increased articulation but *not* phrasing. Quite obviously, this technique should never be used for more than two conflicting bowings at the same time.

Pizzicato

The only production of musical sound from the string orchestra that does not require use of the bow, *pizzicato* is capable of the most varied and sublime effects which are all too rarely heard. Somewhere in the teaching of this technique the similarity of the words *pizzicato* and 'plucking' became confused and some evil-minded person devised the system of firmly planting the thumb on the edge of the finger-board and hooking the first finger behind the string. I am still convinced that this method was invented solely to provide the keyboard specialist examiner with some tangible evidence of practice on which to base his marking. I have yet to be convinced of any musical justification for its use outside the examination room, and why it should persist as the basic technique for a most beautiful method of sound production I fail to understand. Most *pizzicato* requires a vibrancy and refinement of touch that the tip of the finger will not provide, and only the most 'dry' and explosive examples need to be played as high on the string as this hand position dictates.

When *pizzicato* is produced *pianissimo* by a group of string players, the string needs only to be touched, placing the finger a considerable distance over the finger-board and just lifting it away, allowing the release of slight pressure and the natural adhesion of the ball of the finger to instigate the smallest motion of the string. Hardly any sound will be produced by the individual player but, especially in passages involving all the string sections, the resultant effect can be magical. Because of the small amount of movement involved, this technique is usable at great speed without losing delicacy and, partnered by a strong left hand, has surprising projection. The use of this technique in the *Scherzo* of Tchaikovsky *Symphony no. 4*, where the bow is not required at all and may be temporarily discarded, facilitates an extremely wide range of dynamics without the need to force or produce hard, uncultured sounds, and the increased use of the hand in this method of production, rather than just the finger, allows a more natural control of rhythm. In melodic *pizzicato* of this nature it is important that as much flesh of the finger as possible is used, the 'plectrum' effect of the bony tip or nail being reserved for very special purposes. In such a way, even the *forte* chords of this movement can be made to 'ring', matching those of the wind in resonance as well as dynamic.

Although by no means the primary purpose, the use of the hand and arm that becomes apparent once the thumb is released from the finger-board relates the rhythmic control of *pizzicato* to bow movements of similar style, making the whole technique of fingered production more familiar and fluent.

The sound of *pizzicato* will be altered by the position of finger contact along the string, well over the finger-board producing a mellow effect, while movement towards the bridge will make the sound increasingly centred and hard until positioning just below the normal bow position will result in a very short, tight sound. It is neither desirable nor necessary to play much nearer the bridge than this, as no advantage in sound will be gained and grease from the finger on that part of the string most regularly used by the bow will cause the hair to lose contact.

For all this, it is the strength and intensity of the left hand that will finally determine the projection of quality in *pizzicato*. If the string is not stopped firmly and the *vibrato* is allowed to lapse then the sound will travel no distance at all and the subtle techniques of the right hand will be lost.

In the frequently encountered passages where *pizzicato* strings accompany

EX. 7.73

woodwind, a considerable substance of sound is required in order that *pizzicato* chords provide tangible support for the solo instrument and not just a dull emphasis of the main beats of the bar.

In *Ex. 7.73*, taken from Tchaikovsky *Francesca da Rimini*, the balance of these chords is as important as if they were *arco*, especially as the scoring here tends to place them across the upper two strings in all instruments except 2nd violins. The relative response to *pizzicato* will obviously change as the basic tension of the string is increased. On the violin it becomes more difficult to sustain a sound as one progresses upwards from the G string to the D, A and E. A lot of care, left-hand intensity, and sensitivity of the finger are required if these higher notes are not to sound 'dry'. Where there is time to prepare each one (as in *Ex. 7.73*), an added movement of the hand away from the player, along the string, will lose much of the instantaneous production that causes vibration to deteriorate so quickly. Perhaps it may be described as requesting the sound from the instrument rather than demanding it.

All variations of *pizzicato* are available with the bow still in the hand. Regardless of whether there is time for it to be drawn up into the palm, one can use the ball of the finger and control the position of its contact with the string. Cellists will often use the thumb to produce a real *legato* resonance, and this technique can be applied to the other instruments as well, although the suggestion, when put to violinists, will often be met with a grimace of incredulity. The pad of the thumb provides more area of contact than any of the fingers, and a *pizzicato* on the lower strings of the violin may resonate for up to two seconds if this method is employed. Again, the bow being in the hand need not be a hindrance, as it can be drawn up into the fingers and turned almost parallel to the finger-board, allowing the thumb to lie along the side of the string.

The demand for *pizzicato* playing in immediate proximity to *arco* can be the cause of great difficulty and will often lead to a distortion of the phrase. Such juxtaposition is rarely required within a *legato* phrase without sufficient time being allowed for readjustment of the hand, but *Ex. 7.74*, from the slow movement of Sibelius *Symphony no. 5*, insists on allowing no such luxury.

The preceding *arco* phrase must be taken with an up-bow starting a little above the middle of the bow so that the last note ends right at the heel 'under the hand'. As the index finger of the bow hand passes the string it can be straightened off the stick so that it has contact with the string almost before the last *arco* note is completed. In this way, no gap between the two techniques will be apparent and the end of the *legato* phrase will not be distorted. The only alternative in such situations is 'left-hand *pizzicato*', but *Ex. 7.74* cannot be attempted in this way, for obvious musical reasons.

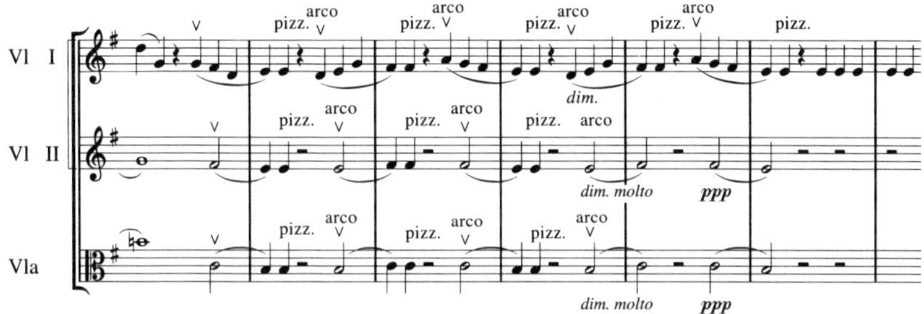

EX. 7.74

Pizzicato with the left hand produces a hard and short-lived result due both to the closeness of the action to the finger stopping the note, and to the fact that simultaneous *vibrato* cannot be accomplished. It is most often used for *pizzicato* interspersed within fast passage-work, and is at its most successful when used on open strings. In many circumstances proficient use of the technique can rescue an otherwise extremely awkward passage as in the case of the last note before the *arco* in *Ex. 7.75* from Stravinsky *The Firebird*.

EX. 7.75

Pizzicato Chords and Other Effects

Chords may be played at all dynamic levels by striking the string with one finger, both very fast, to give an almost simultaneous production, and more slowly, to make individual notes clear. It will also sometimes be found beneficial to use a separate finger for each string. All four fingers may be used at one time (although this method is most usual for two- and three-note chords) and, in this case, the bow will be held between the palm of the hand and the thumb. A somewhat short-lived simultaneous chord is obtained, with little or no following vibration, especially if all four fingers are used, and it takes a moment longer to 'set' the hand for it, making it impractical for use in quick succession.

Chords may also be played by alternating direction of the hand, as requested by Bartók in the *Concerto for Orchestra*.

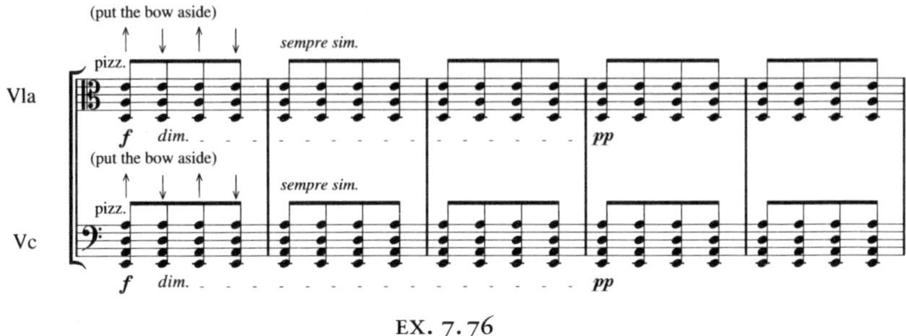

EX. 7.76

In this case the particular direction of the hand is indicated by the use of arrows. This method is also requested by the term *quasi guitara* (or *alla chittarra*), sometimes with the addition of bowing marks to indicate direction. Also possible in violins and violas is the positioning of the instrument on the lap, in the manner of a guitar. This is common in many orchestras (although not requested by the composer) for much of the opening section of Ravel *Boléro*. Its use there, however, is as much for visual effect as aural.

According to contemporary sources Elgar insisted on the *alla chittarra* position from the upper strings for the wonderfully effective *pizzicato* that accompanies the solo violin *cadenza* in the third movement of his *Violin Concerto*. Here the composer adds a footnote for those playing *pizzicato* (half of each string section), requesting that 'the pizz. tremolando should be "thrummed" with the soft part of three or four fingers across the strings'. Such an effect across the three- and four-note chords that are written is certainly most easily accomplished with violins and violas in the 'lap' position.

Very fast *pizzicato* in precise, unrelieved semiquaver rhythm for 21 bars is required of violas and cellos in the fourth movement (*Jupiter*) of Holst *The Planets* (see *Ex. 7.77*).

On both instruments the first two fingers of the bow hand are used alternately on the open G string, ensuring the minimum physical effort for aural result. Here, the bow must be retained in the hand, there being no time allowed to pick it up before the next *arco* marking.

Bartók frequently requests that a single note of *pizzicato* be allowed to 'crack' back onto the finger-board (a demand for which he invented the sign '⏁'), an effect that requires the string to be pulled upwards by the thumb and

EX. 7.77

first finger and then released against the wood, in much the same way as one might 'ping' an elastic band. He uses the technique at various dynamic levels, the softest needing to be performed a long way down the string, very close to the left hand, where the string is nearer to the finger-board. Such a position is clearly essential in *Ex. 7.78* from his *Violin Concerto no. 2* where, while quite audible, the crack of the *pizzicati* must remain within a subdued and accompanying dynamic.

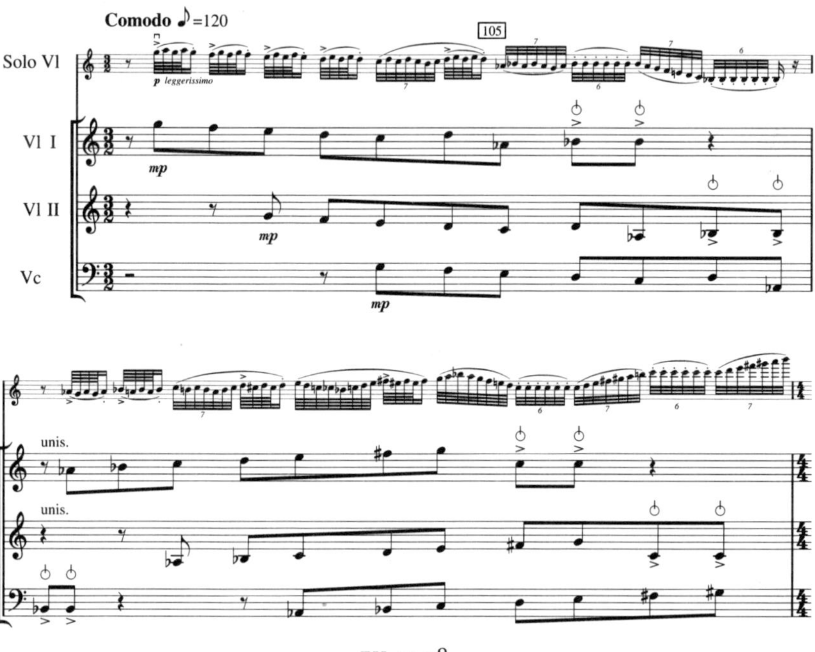

EX. 7.78

The appearance of two notes phrased together in *pizzicato* is rare but, once again, Bartók makes use of it, on this occasion in the *Concerto for Orchestra* where it is required of four solo cellists.

EX. 7.79

The effect is equally possible for all strings, and Rimsky-Korsakov requires it of 1st and 2nd violins in a very short phrase from *Skazka op. 29*, adding the marking *legato* above the two notes in question.

EX. 7.80

In these and similar examples of upward motion the *pizzicato* is actually produced on the first note of the slur, a firm left-hand finger placing producing the second note quite clearly before all vibration is gone from the string. In intervals as small as a semitone, the positive lifting of the finger to produce downward motion is sufficient. Above a tone, both movements are unsuccessful, the intervals being too great for the string to retain vibration across such a dramatic change of length. However, it is possible to produce *glissandi* effects at much larger intervals by sliding the finger along the string, though upward (shortening the string length) is somewhat less limited than downward.

Mutes

The use of mutes in *pizzicato* will have been noted in *Ex. 7.73*, though it rarely occurs, because the sound required is usually soft and the limitation of vibration caused by the mute somewhat self-defeating. Sounds of hardly noticeable difference can be produced without the mute, and the marking would seem mostly to relate to a closely following bowed passage rather than the *pizzicato* itself, as, I suspect, in *Ex. 7.73*, where no other convenient moment exists for their application. In bowed passages, of course, no such alternative applies, and the peculiar quality the mute elicits can be produced in no other way.

It must be remembered that muting *changes* the sound and that the prevalent misconception that they are used only in passages of soft playing is entirely wrong. Once again in *Skazka*, Rimsky-Korsakov requires violas to mute a violent *fortissimo* two-bar outburst in combination with *bouché* horns and upper woodwind.

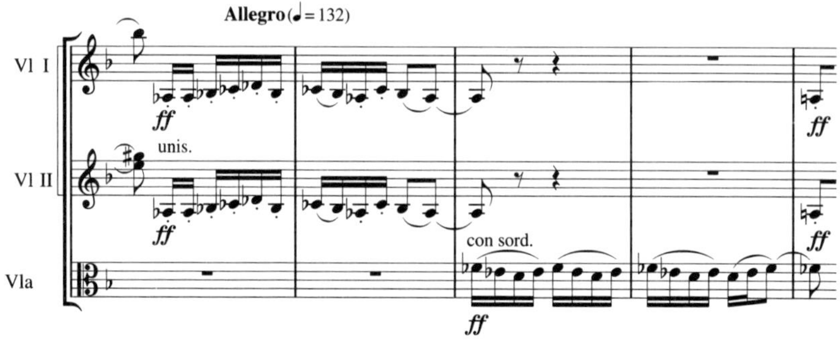

EX. 7.81

Nowadays, various versions of the sliding mute, fixed in permanent readiness between the middle two strings below the bridge, have been almost universally adopted, the older accident-prone and easily mislaid separate variety being virtually obsolete within the orchestra. Soloists, however, still continue to use versions of it, insisting (with some justification) that retention on the strings affects the tone of the instrument. The much more frequent positioning and removal of mutes required of orchestral string players tends to make considerations of convenience outweigh this very minimal loss of individual quality.

What has proved to be unquestionably true, however, is that this type of mute is less effective on the larger bridges of the cello and bass. Certainly, with respect to the double bass, there is a musical argument for the retention of the separate type that grips the bridge more firmly. The noticeable reluctance of more and more bass players to use the mute at all – on the basis that it makes little difference in so low a register – may be construed as evidence of the ineffectiveness of the modern design.

Harmonics

The amount of confusion over string harmonics, and the sometimes irrational and contradictory methods used in their notation, make it essential to look at them in some detail here.

The only occasion when firm pressure of the left hand is consciously released is in the production of natural harmonics. In this case the exact position of the harmonic needs to be touched very lightly in order to free the vibration of the string, since too much pressure results in a 'breaking' of the sound. Harmonics are available at all dynamic levels and should not be automatically associated with a fast bow movement, although in their most idiosyncratic use this may be desirable.

The first and most obvious harmonics available from any given open string are those of the octave, double octave and fifth as shown in *Ex. 7.82* (where, for convenience, the G string of the violin has been used, though a similar situation exists for every string on all instruments of the string section).

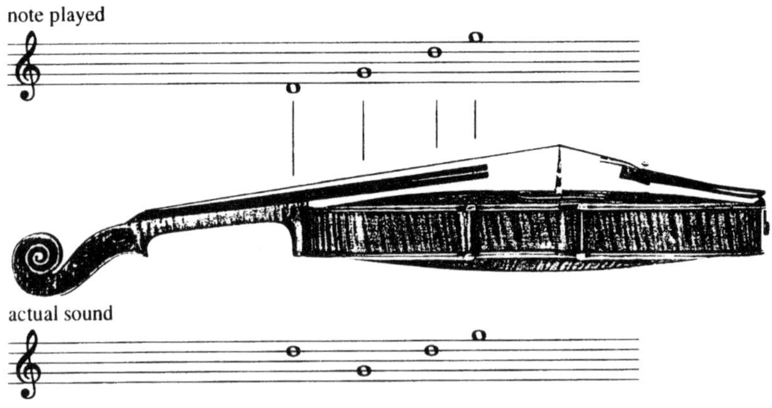

EX. 7.82

In addition to these basic harmonics there are a number of others, chief among which, because of a versatility that will become apparent, is that at the fourth, sounding two octaves above its base note, as shown in *Ex. 7.83*.

For all instruments except the double bass, this harmonic falls within the natural span of the hand and it thus becomes possible to 'stop' a new fundamental and still reach this harmonic above it. String players refer to these as 'false harmonics' because their fundamental is no longer the open string but a note stopped with the finger. They are notated by marking both the stopped

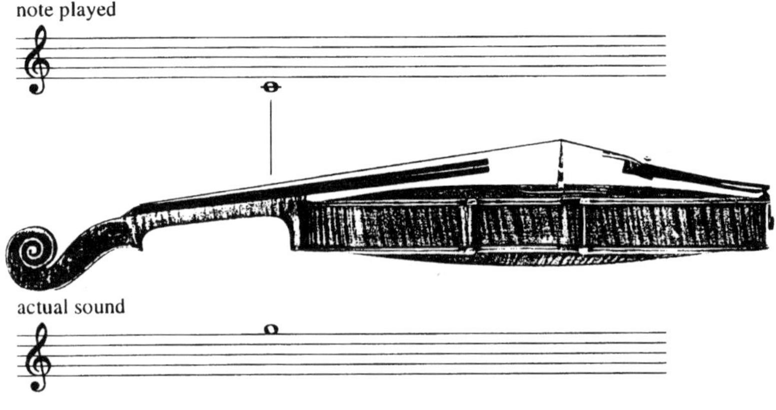

EX. 7.83

note *and* the harmonic itself (usually as an open diamond). A succession of these is shown in *Ex. 7.84*, with the actual sound appended in brackets.

Note: Only the fundamental (stopped note) is provided with accidentals, the perfect 4th above is *always* understood.

EX. 7.84

On the violin and (less easily) the viola, with a slightly extended stretch, the same process can be applied with regard to the harmonic at the fifth (the first of those shown in *Ex. 7.82*). This makes available a large range of notes that may be performed as harmonics, many of which may be obtained by more than one of these methods of production.

Further reference to *Ex. 7.82* will show that, since the lowest actual sounding note available from any harmonic is one octave above the open string, the bottom 'harmonic' for each instrument is that sounding an octave above their lowest string: there then exists a gap of a fifth, above which, for the upper strings particularly, all notes are available.

The 'false harmonics' are not available on the double bass because the longer strings cause them to occur beyond the span of a normal hand. The same is generally true for the cello with regard to the 'false harmonic' at the fifth. (However, for both instruments, this method of producing harmonics does become available in high positions where the distance between notes becomes considerably shortened.) But these larger instruments will be able to produce a number of other 'open' harmonics which, while available to violin and viola, are by no means so safe and are generally avoided. Simply for continuity and ease of comparison these are best shown still in relation to the violin G string.

EX. 7.85

Within the above examples we now have the complete range of open harmonics available to any one string. If there were to be a universally accepted method of notation the above would constitute the total information required by an interpreter, any decisions of alternative technical production resting solely upon practicalities afforded to the player with regard to any particular passage. But, unfortunately, this is not the case, and it is here that the problems really begin.

There are two common ways of indicating that a harmonic is required:

1 by use of the sign 'o' surmounting the note in question, and

2 by writing the note with a diamond-shaped head.

Equally, there are two basic ways of notating the pitch of the note required:

1 by writing the sounding note, and

2 by writing a note which, when played as a harmonic, will produce the required note (in other words, showing the technical method of production).

Regrettably, these last two are somewhat interchangeable, as may be seen from the following examples, where the violin harmonic E (one octave above the open E string) is shown.

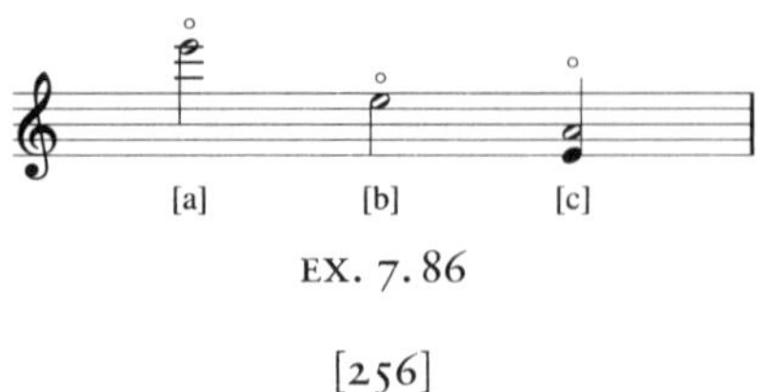

EX. 7.86

All three harmonics provide exactly the same note, but [a] indicates not only the note required but also the means of producing it (the harmonic at the octave from the open E string), whereas both [b] and [c] refer only to the method of production: [b] as the harmonic at the fifth from the open A string and [c] as the harmonic at the fourth from the stopped E on the D string.

Two possible confusions immediately present themselves, both concerning [b] in the above. Firstly, it is possible that the 'o' refers not to a harmonic but simply to an open string (identical notation exists for both). While this ambiguity is limited to the notes of the three upper strings on each instrument it does appear surprisingly often and it can only be resolved by use of the diamond-shaped head. Secondly, it could refer to the *sounding* note, available in this case by stopping A on the G string and touching the fifth above.

Although the habit of writing all 'open' harmonics without reference to their fundamental is general and perfectly logical, a further refinement, all too rarely used, would be to add the required note in all circumstances, either in brackets or as a small additional note head (this would, for example, remove any anomaly regarding note [b] in *Ex. 7. 86* above). Otherwise numerous decisions, especially of required octave, can only be deduced from the context.

Complicated as this might appear, it is insignificant in comparison to the confusion and misinterpretation surrounding low harmonics for the double bass where, apart from the use of some of the least frequently encountered examples (the minor and major third, the major sixth), yet further intricacies exist.

Perhaps these may be best explained with reference to one particular work, *Pavane de la belle au bois dormant* from *Ma mère l'oye* by Ravel, a composer notorious for his misguided confidence in the musician's total grasp of physics (see *Ex. 7.87*).

In nearly all cases a process of deduction will prove necessary. In this example the double bass harmonic is given as G natural, so we know that it is likely to apply to the lowest string because it appears below the normal written pitch of the next highest (A). Although E is normally considered to be the lowest string of the double bass when no specific request for additional range is evident, many composers write down to C as a matter of course. Thus, the written G could be the minor third harmonic on the E string (sounding B two octaves and a fifth above the open string) or the perfect fifth harmonic on the C string (sounding G one octave and a fifth above). As no harmonic exists on the minor sixth, we can, fortunately, discount the large number of *five string* basses that have the lowest note as B. Nonetheless, there still remains a third possibility. Many composers, when writing harmonics for the bass, write at

EX. 7.87

pitch, ignoring the normal octave transposition. The G might therefore be the perfect fourth harmonic on the D string (sounding D two octaves above the open string).

To be certain about this one it will be necessary to examine further aspects of the work. In the fifth bar of the quoted example the bass harmonic changes to written D, and from this bar and, even more conclusively, its repetition at the end of the movement, it is clear that a sounding A must be intended. This is indeed the case, as the printed note is the perfect fourth harmonic above the A string, sounding A two octaves above. From this we may deduce that octave transposition has not been abandoned and that the third possibility outlined above can be discounted.

We are now left with only two alternatives – those of sounding B or G – and one must be considered against the other. Harmonically it could conceivably be either, but the B, one octave and a fifth above the sustained E of cellos, seems the more likely. Could Ravel have been writing for basses with a low C?

In this instance the answer comes later in the work where the basses are specifically requested to tune down. Therefore, this harmonic is definitely based on the low E and is intended to be the sounding B.

This process, while perhaps appearing somewhat pedantic and even tortuous in this context, *must* be undertaken in any circumstance where an element of doubt could be present, and applies to all instruments. Just as many examples of confusion, ambiguity and downright error exist in parts for cello, viola and violin as double bass. The correct result will not be immediately obvious – even in professional circumstances – for the requirement is often even *less* obvious in the part than in the score.

Accidental error by players is also possible, a regular example being demonstrated in *Ex. 7.88* from Hans Werner Henze *Symphony no. 5* (1962).

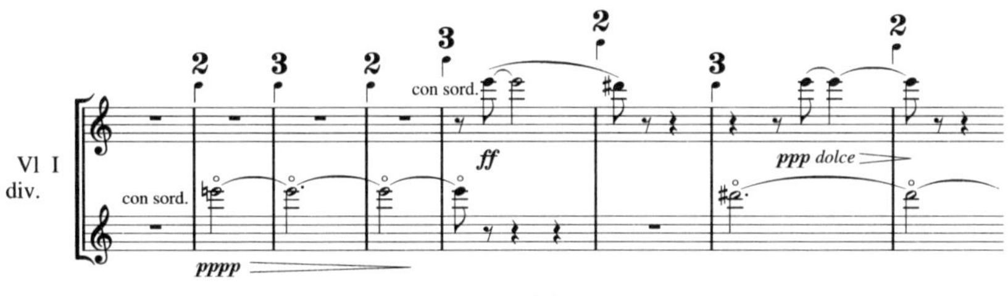

EX. 7.88

In the first four quoted bars, the second line of 1st violins have a harmonic E, identical with that shown in *Ex. 7.86* and likely to be performed (and intended) as the octave above the open string. This then changes to a D♯ only available as the 'false' harmonic of the perfect fourth from the fingered fundamental. An almost automatic response will be to play this with the fingered note one octave below that which is written – the D♯ on the A string – without immediately realizing that this will produce a harmonic one octave too high. The fingered D♯ needed to obtain this octave is the one low on the D string, but the tremendous difference between the visual perception of a note high above the stave and the physical action of producing it two octaves lower will frequently cause it to be mistaken.

The ability to produce many harmonics in more than one way does, however, sometimes have its advantages. With reference once more to the E harmonic shown in *Ex. 7.86*, the following extract (*Ex. 7.89*) is taken from Stravinsky *The Firebird*.

The availability of this harmonic as the perfect fifth above the A string ([b] in *Ex. 7.86*) avoids the constant shifting to and from fourth position on the E string, and allows the phrase to be played truly *legato*.

EX. 7.89

Similarly, the first four bars of the violin solo towards the end of *Les entretiens de la belle et de la bête*, once more from Ravel *Ma mère l'oye*, is printed as harmonics of the stopped fifth on the E string, whereas, because of the previously mentioned unreliability of this harmonic, it is usually played by using harmonics of the stopped fourth, pitched a fourth below the first written B♭.

Related Techniques

A large number of effects and alternative methods of performance may be required of all strings, particularly in music of the latter half of the twentieth century. *Ex. 7.90* from Roberto Gerhard *Concerto for Orchestra* displays a number of them within a very few bars of music.

Pizzicato below the bridge – the string is to be plucked in the area between the bridge and the tail-piece ('behind the bridge' might be a better description). Indeterminate notes at this printed pitch will refer to plucking of the E string and it is best accomplished in a downward direction from the side of the string – the more normal horizontal or upward *pizzicato* movements producing considerably less sound.

Harmonic arpeggio – a quick up-bow movement across all four strings while 'fingering' the four harmonics (fifth, fifth, major third and fourth). Surprisingly effective, but not easy to achieve.

Col legno and *pizzicato* are the normal techniques.

Col legno on the tail-piece – tapping of the tail-piece with the bow, producing a sound of very clear resonance. This technique must be performed with care or damage to the bow might easily result. A very gentle level is all that is required when performed by a number of players.

Col legno, strike the chin rest – self-explanatory variation of the above involving similar care.

With finger-tip, striking the table – this is dangerous! There should be positively no occasion where the body of the instrument is struck except, perhaps, for softly tapping with the knuckle joint of one finger. Some alternative method of producing a very similar sound *must* be used, for any striking of the body, even with the softest part of the finger, will entail damage to the

EX. 7.90

varnish or to the instrument itself. Such hazardous misuse of the most precious and expensive item most musicians possess is an anathema to the professional. Many alternative methods of providing the same sounds are available. For student orchestras such demands, however 'musical' their intention, should be strenuously denied.

Beyond the techniques requested above there is that of bowing the strings behind the bridge, producing a very high-pitched 'squeak' but with a noticeable difference in pitch across the four strings.

Considerations of the left hand will be discussed in conjunction with wider concepts of string sound in Chapter 13.

8 WOODWIND

For the orchestral woodwind section the greatest difficulty to be encountered is that of intonation, both within the section itself and in relation to the rest of the orchestra. Although woodwind instruments have a degree of control over intonation, it is by no means as easy to achieve as on stringed instruments and requires considerable skill and technical ability. It is also, as with so many other orchestral problems, inextricably linked to balance and ensemble.

These days, the dangers of taking for granted the apparently effortless standards of excellence frequently perceived in recorded sound are nowhere more apparent than in considerations of woodwind intonation. Even the world's finest orchestras will frequently have to record a passage many times before a successful 'take' is achieved, sometimes adopting esoteric mechanical adjustment of instruments or even re-seating of the section. Such instrumental juggling is rarely possible in concert performance, and, if attempted with anything except the most superb players, will probably be the cause of untold problems. In many ways woodwind intonation is probably best approached from entirely the opposite viewpoint – that to expect a number of completely different methods of sound production to produce any form of consistent corporate intonation is so ridiculous that it is amazing that it happens at all.

For the orchestra, of course, all things have to be possible and most are expected. Instruments made to differing standards, by companies in Europe, America and Asia, must be brought together and all the inherent vagaries of pitch, quality and resonance overcome by the players in order that an acceptable degree of woodwind intonation can be achieved. Such a situation is inevitable within orchestral music-making. Compensating for the known variations and instantly adjusting to the unknown is a large part of the wind player's art. Professional players are not only among the few most technically proficient exponents of each instrument; they can also anticipate the circumstances in which problems will appear and, for the most part, they know each other's playing very well. In student orchestras none of these things are likely to apply and the section must be helped to understand the difficulties of intonation within each piece of a programme and be given time to approach the problem from the point of view of simple harmonic note relationships, in order to take the first steps on a long, never-ending road.

It must be said that it is a total waste of everyone's time to attempt anything but the most rudimentary work on intonation with an over-staffed wind section. As has already been remarked, one player to a part is essential for many reasons, but intonation above all.

Intonation

Adjustment of tuning in concert performance is an instantaneous thing. The maximum time that dubious intonation in a sustained chord can escape general detection is about a quarter of a second, and there can be no guarantee that isolating it for careful work in rehearsal will achieve success in context. The approach must always be to heighten the players' awareness of potential difficulties and then to create the circumstances in performance where good intonation is possible – allowing players time to breathe, phrase intelligently and control levels of balance. Without such consideration to the section there can be no hope of even the greatest players achieving anything.

Actual rehearsal of intonation is extremely difficult, one experienced conductor being heard to remark that it was rather like stripping down a car engine – once it is reassembled there is always a piece left over that doesn't belong anywhere!

There are two basic concerns. Firstly, all tuning must take into account the difficulties inherent within one particular chord layout, and should therefore be concerned with the adjustment of individual notes, and not necessarily any retuning of the instrument itself. Secondly, the chord must be rebuilt in a way that enables the players to appreciate their place within it. Many problems of intonation are resolved as soon as the players understand the structure of the chord in question; for this reason, as well as the more obvious one related to ease of hearing, it is important to reduce a chord to its most simple component parts, using basic triads and intervals as the foundation and adding any 'false relations' after this basic chord is in tune.

For the conductor who is essentially a keyboard player, the understanding of intonation as practised by instruments with variable pitch control can be difficult to grasp, the tempered tuning of the piano, for example, automatically compensating for any microtonal alterations that harmony may require. Essentially, the difference lies in the heightened relationship of one note to another and the intervallic tensions that cause notes to be pulled in certain directions, both in single chords and, often more obviously, in cadential or chromatic passages, where the pull of notes towards their tonal centre is most pronounced. The C in an A minor chord is *not* the same note as the C in A♭ major, even though the same key will be struck on the piano, the same symbol used in the manuscript and, often, the same fingering performed on an orchestral instrument. If any doubt exists as to the aural validity of this statement, a group of untempered instruments will very quickly dispel it. If the C is tuned to the minor chord and then holds exactly the same note while the root and fifth drop by a semitone, it will be horribly flat in the resulting major one. Such vagaries and inequalities of intonation, arising from the relationship of notes to each other and the interaction of overtones and harmonics, must be accepted and understood before attempting the difficult task of combining different sounds and methods of production. It is also very rare to find any scoring of woodwind chords where the problem of intonation is that of notes alone and does not also include considerations of blending different instruments, and the balancing of one particular timbre against another. Making all these closely interrelated aspects clear to the players must be done at one and the same time.

The root position C major chord, shown in *Ex. 8.1*, is scored for a classical woodwind section comprising two of each instrument, and may be used to illustrate both the basic relationship of the notes and the balance of the instruments involved.

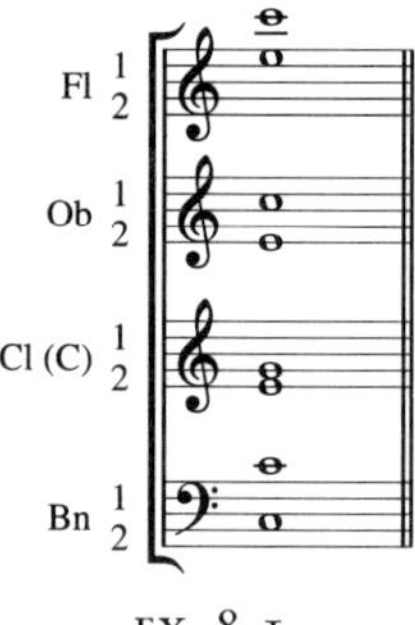

EX. 8.1

Such a heavily biased scoring of the tonic note at both extremes of the chord will occasionally be found in isolation, either as a final cadence approached by another section of the orchestra or as a definitive statement of tonality.

Here the chord rests firmly on 2nd bassoon, the lowest scoring of the C and that on which the three octaves above must be based. This note must be correct before anything else can be achieved. The octaves of 1st bassoon, 1st oboe and 1st flute may be added to it singly or together, but it must be heard by them at all times as the basis of their intonation, and cannot be altered or ignored for their convenience. The balance will also be naturally weighted towards the lowest octave. In this example the flute provides the range of the chord, and the 1st oboe and 1st bassoon hold the centre. Some adjustment of intonation will be necessary, especially by the 1st flute at such a range from the bass – a prime example of the necessity for flute 1 and bassoon 2 to be seated as close together as possible. The lone appearance of the fifth, in 1st clarinet, is not uncommon in Classical scoring, the note being so heavily apparent in the overtones of the tonic. This is always the next note to tune, again totally relative to the tonic octaves and added to them. In this example, with the C so close and obvious, it will not be difficult to hear or balance. The third (2nd clarinet, 2nd oboe and 2nd flute in octave), the note responsible for the major or minor tonality and thereby prone to the greatest tensions of intervallic relationship, will be added last, the intonation being clear even before it is played.

The addition of notes to the common chord will drastically alter its layout, not only because there are extra notes to be played but also because of the necessary resolution that is likely to exist in the same instrumental parts and the restrictions therefore determined by the position of the following chord. At the very opening of Beethoven *Symphony no. 1* a dominant seventh chord resolves on to its F major tonic.

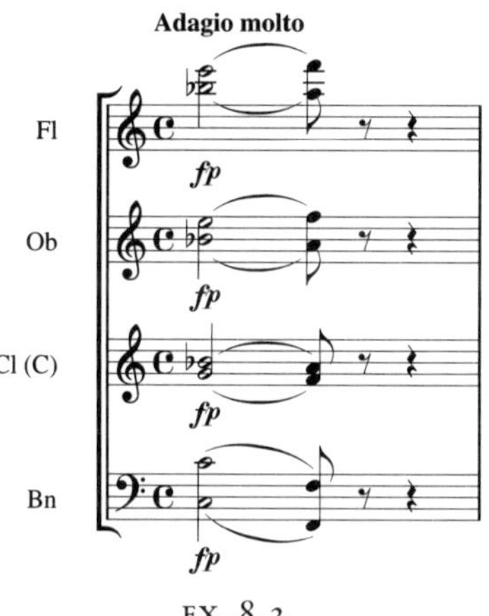

EX. 8.2

Gone is the four-times orchestrated tonic of the C-based chord in *Ex. 8.1*; only two bassoons hold this fundamental. The fifth remains the sole responsibility of one instrument – 2nd clarinet – but the third, although still doubled at the octave (1st flute and 1st oboe), now appears at the top so that it can resolve on to the upper tonic of the root position chord of F major. The seventh is placed for its natural and powerful resolution on to the third of the following chord.

The tuning of this chord in isolation will be built up in exactly the same way as before, root followed by fifth followed by third, and the seventh added last because its tuning depends on the major triad's being correct. Once again the intonation will be clear to the players before it is added but this time, owing to the tonal strength of this type of seventh chord, the following resolution will also be heard, and it is unlikely that a similar process will need to be repeated for this F major chord.

Two aspects of Beethoven's scoring for woodwind are apparent in this example and are worth noting as they typify the somewhat stark nature of his sound which characterizes his entire orchestral output. The lack of any overlap, apart from the unison between 1st clarinet and 2nd oboe, is immediately noticeable and the scoring of the instruments, paired in ascending order of their most frequently used range, is typical. In the second chord, the absence of the fifth allows the woodwind almost total responsibility for the potent third. It is, in fact, quite difficult to find any major or minor common chord where Beethoven scores the fifth anywhere in the woodwind voices except in passages of a solo nature.

The much more integrated and even distribution of notes favoured by composers of more Romantic persuasion can often cause the problems of balance to be even more acute than in the widely spaced examples quoted above. The balance of eight woodwind players, divided three, three and two can be critical, especially if a soft chord is intended. *Ex. 8.3* shows the final chord of the second movement of Tchaikovsky *Symphony no. 1*.

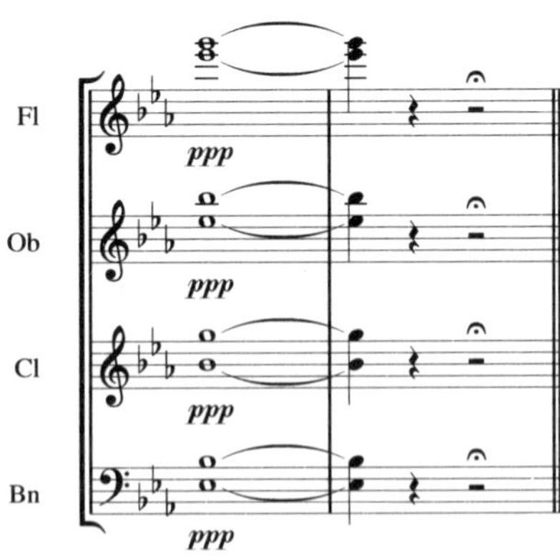

EX. 8.3

Both oboes and bassoons hold the bare interval of the perfect fifth and each of these notes is doubled once more – the E♭ by 2nd flute and the B♭ by 2nd clarinet – so that they exist in three separate octaves. In this case, an over-balancing of the fifth can very easily result, making the major third tend to sound out of tune even though it might not be so, by lessening its apparent relationship to the fundamental. Such an aural misconception is not infrequent in closely orchestrated chords involving doubling of the fifth, and examples of this type can be found throughout the repertoire from the middle of the nineteenth century onwards. Tuning of these will include a very strong emphasis on balance, even allowing for the fact that it might well be helpful initially to rehearse intonation of soft chords at a louder dynamic than that prescribed for performance.

The system of tuning chords on octaves, fifth and thirds is useful because these intervals are closely related and can be clearly heard by a player who is producing a note at the same time as listening – a totally different perspective from that of someone who can concentrate solely on listening. It must not be assumed that players are unable to hear augmented or diminished intervals, fourths, ninths, or anything else; it is simply that the intervals of the major or minor triad will complement each other when in tune and can therefore be 'felt' to some extent as well as heard.

Although this method of tuning can obviously be used in isolating chords of a much more complex nature than root position triads and dominant sevenths, it is certainly in the often smaller scoring of linear harmony that most intonation problems are likely to be found. A passage such as *Ex. 8.4* from Beethoven overture *Egmont* will very possibly cause trouble to an inexperienced section, for a number of reasons.

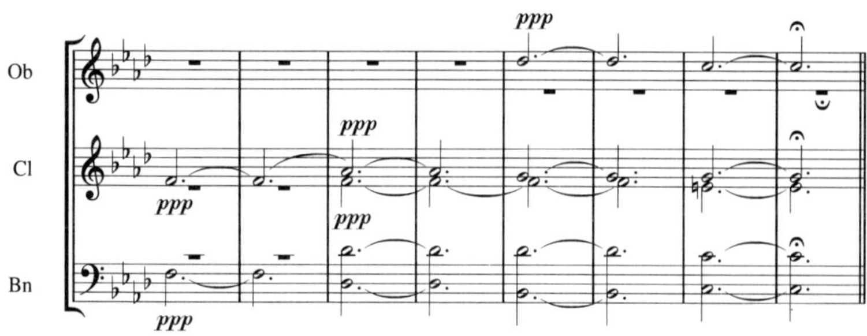

EX. 8.4

The conductor has the initial problem because the entry is preceded by a pause, and the up-beat must provide time to set the sound and produce a soft but safe note. Presuming this very difficult gesture is within the conductor's technical ability, then the F, like all octaves, must be based on the lowest note, both in balance and intonation. Here again, it is for the 2nd bassoon to take the weight of balance, intonation and dynamic level throughout the whole eight bars of this passage, especially in the support of sound for the oboe entry at bar 5. If absolutely necessary even this difficult secondary seventh chord may be built in fifths and thirds by reason of its inversion (B♭ – F = the fifth, D♭ as the minor third and G added as the non-related sixth), but it is most appropriate for all parts to hear the resolution on to C major. It is fortunate, and no accident, that the sustained F does not remain in the same instrument across the first four bars but moves from 1st to 2nd clarinet, since its position in the D♭ chord will need a slight change of balance from the previous octave and even fractional adjustment of pitch. The final C major is a more concise scoring of *Ex. 8.1*, just one fifth against three tonics placed over two octaves.

Anyone with access to a full score may care to note a very interesting piece of scoring in the bar immediately following the quoted example, which highlights a fascinating use of bassoons in this work. The *pianissimo* entry of the strings is accompanied by the same C major chord in the same position, but the low octave is now taken by horns instead of bassoons. Throughout the overture the bassoons very rarely play *piano* or softer at times when the string basses are playing, a practice which would not seem to be general in Beethoven's orchestration.

All rehearsal of woodwind intonation is designed to help the section perfect the habit of listening to one another and to be increasingly aware of each other's sound and dynamic levels but it cannot be expected to guarantee success in the same way that the rehearsal of a rhythmic figure or particular musical phrase might – only time will do that. It will, however, substantially increase the chances of good intonation and nurture a corporate and fluent sound from the section. Even if for no other reason, this should be a strong incentive for keeping a section together long enough for them to learn at least the broad outlines of the basic trade of woodwind playing.

Balance

The balance between the instruments of a woodwind section is integral to every aspect of their playing and as vital in considerations of projection, sound and colour as it is to intonation. Only very gradually do young players realize the degree of responsibility they carry for each other's performance, especially in matters of integration and support. Each woodwind instrument has techniques that are natural to it as well as some that are more alien. In low register, for example, a clarinet can easily play very softly, whereas this is an extremely difficult technique on the oboe. On the other hand, an oboe at this register can pierce almost any texture with consummate ease, an ability that neither clarinet nor flute can match. Awareness of such differing qualities as these lies at the very heart of woodwind balance and affects the way that any professional player will approach a passage.

The gradual improvement in instruments and playing standards throughout the nineteenth and twentieth centuries enabled composers to exploit them more widely, and to change and even disregard many accepted practices of orchestration. Mention has been made of Beethoven's general use of the woodwind in blocks of instrumentation that do not overlap, a scoring long used by Mozart and Haydn even before the introduction of clarinets to their repertoire. Thematic and melodic writing for the instruments followed the same pattern, and there are only isolated instances where a solo line is placed on a woodwind instrument of lower overall pitch than those that accompany it. Melodic use of clarinets, for example, is most often to be found with only bassoons in support, the oboes taking over the solo role on their entry, as do the flutes on theirs. Although careful balance is still vital, it is much easier to achieve with the solo line on top of the instrumentation.

Perhaps one of the earliest examples to explore the new sounds available to a 'transposed' orchestration is to be found in the second movement of Beethoven *Symphony no. 6 (Pastoral)* (see *Ex. 8.5*).

Here 1st clarinet and 1st bassoon take the solo line with flutes and oboes in an accompanying role – a none too common experience for them but a device that is much used in this movement, the melodic line being contained within very firm boundaries of pitch. This movement also provides examples (for instance, in bar 103) of a chord interlocked between oboes and clarinets (from bottom to top: clarinet 2, oboe 2, clarinet 1, oboe 1) – a rare occurrence in a Classical woodwind section. These, and similar details of orchestration, are largely responsible for the feeling of tranquillity that this movement imparts, and were to have a great influence on later composers of more Romantic persuasion.

Subtle changes of layout and use of instruments can be traced as an evolutionary process that continued through the music of Mendelssohn, Berlioz, Schumann, Liszt and Wagner right to the present day. Each composer adopted an individual and searching approach to the use of woodwind that extended and developed both instruments and players. It almost never occurred as an intentional revolution but rather, one that was naturally linked to style and

EX. 8.5

means of expression. Brahms's use of flowing groups of thirds and sixths, often doubled throughout the woodwind, places the emphasis of support on to the 2nd players and creates a homogeneous sound, with the instruments harmonically bound together. It is but a short road to the totally interdependent scoring of the larger sections found in composers as diverse in their musical language as Mahler, Richard Strauss and Debussy. Tchaikovsky's use of closely meshed chording has already been illustrated, but his development of long exposed solos and the emotional characteristics of particular textures and individual tone qualities was to prove an irresistible influence on many later composers.

Each variation of scoring and use brought with it a change in individual and collective responsibility for the players, a process that often involved new and demanding techniques of collaboration and sound production. Sometimes these were to spawn refinements of the instruments themselves, ranging from the subtle individual modification of reeds or embouchure to the most major reappraisal of key action and fingering. Neither has the process shown any signs of slowing. The possibilities of exploration open to the present-day composer remain seemingly as limitless as ever.

Such changing demands on instrumentalists, especially when they instigate subsequent modifications to instruments, can involve a related opposite reaction, an improvement in one area of the instrument often being the cause of some difficulty in another. The fact, for example, that the modern bassoon is built a little sharp in the bottom fifth of the instrument in order to aid brightness in this register makes control of intonation of the bottom E at the beginning of Tchaikovsky *Symphony no. 6* extremely difficult, especially when it is so reliant on the intonation of the string basses in the first place. The diversity of technique and production required by all modern woodwind instrumentalists applies no less to the student performer than to the professional, the range of repertoire encountered within one programme being equally challenging on many occasions. However, the frequency with which the student will encounter particular orchestral problems and the number of opportunities available to gather and build on the experience of overcoming them are very different. No style of orchestration is likely to be performed often enough for even the majority of the woodwind section to be instantly aware of its peculiarities of balance and changing responsibilities of ensemble. Positive help and understanding must be forthcoming from the conductor during full orchestral rehearsals if the section is to mature and develop along with the rest of the orchestra.

It is not, of course, always easy to detect the more subtle difficulties of balance when preparing a score for rehearsal, since many become apparent only when differing methods of sound production or individual limitations of nuance happen to be combined. Every section will display different qualities of integration by virtue of the combination of personalities within it, and one might very well falter upon a passage that another performs with ease. However, it is always as well to be prepared for some possible misjudgement of balance in the performance of soft or delicate passages.

Ex. 8.6 shows a passage from the third movement (*Romanza*) of Vaughan Williams *Symphony no. 5*, which is a woodwind scoring of the string chorale to be considered in Chapter 13 and a similar aura of undisturbed calm is required.

In this instance two horns are added to the middle octave of the woodwind group in order to bind the sound by their close doubling of the two extreme

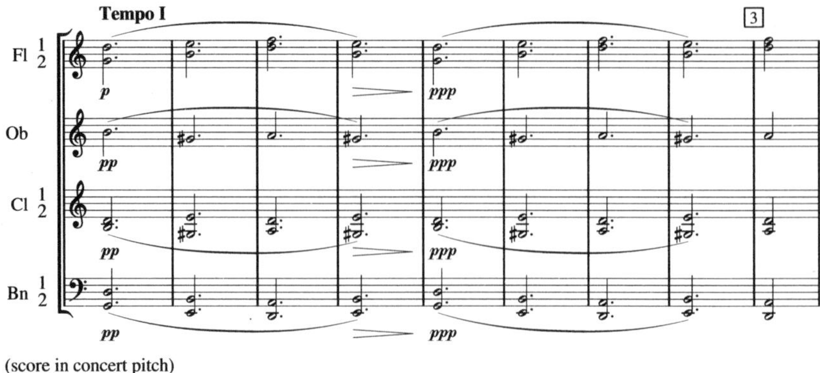

EX. 8.6

voices, but the overall balance may still be considered in relation to woodwind alone. The determining factor is the possible dynamic level of the fifth bar. If this were to be flutes and clarinets alone then the most extreme example of *ppp* could be obtained, no more than a whisper of sound being audible. But such a dynamic level is of no use to the oboe or bassoons; they cannot possibly match it, especially with 2nd bassoon holding the base of the chords at such a low pitch and with intonation being so vital. The softest level must almost be determined by this player alone, but certainly it has to be based on the *pianissimo* ability of all three instruments, the flutes and clarinets apparently balancing to them.

But now we encounter a difficulty that brings the techniques of orchestral woodwind playing into sharp focus. The flutes cannot actually balance to what they hear of the oboe, for if they did so the oboe line would be the most prominent, and this must obviously not be allowed. They must, in fact, play to the lowest level at which they *know* that the oboe can safely balance to them – a very different situation and one that calls for considerable sensitivity, understanding and control throughout the section.

The dynamic level of the first four-bar phrase is now confined by its relationship to the softer sound of the second in such a way that its production is critical if both the stillness of the sound and the *diminuendo* are to be accomplished. In this particular case the composer provides a subtle and calculated means of achieving this in the marking of both flutes – *piano* rather than *pianissimo*. Not only will careful use of this dynamic make the theme of the first phrase clear, but the somewhat greater drop in level that it provides for the flutes will also provide the illusion of *ppp* with only a minimal *diminuendo* from the other instruments. Thus the level of *pianissimo* may be set by oboe and bassoons with some certainty, and their following *diminuendo* will not be so extreme as to make the second phrase dangerous.

This changing responsibility for different aspects of the same passage and the need to know the exact degree to which each player may be limited in different registers of the instrument is unique to the woodwind, since no other section combines such a disparity of sound or technique. Examples may be found throughout the repertoire, but become noticeably more frequent in music of the late nineteenth century and after, where the search for new tone colours causes the instruments to be merged in a variety of ways.

UNISON AND OCTAVE BALANCE

As mentioned in relation to both strings and woodwind, all octaves need to be balanced to the lowest pitch for reasons of blend, projection and intonation, but many awkward situations arise whenever more than two instruments are involved and, most especially, when one or more notes are doubled. The famous sustained B♭ that opens Beethoven *Symphony no. 4* is always difficult to tune, a fact that can cause the equal problem of balance to be overlooked. It is very easy to over-weight the bassoons and horns at the bottom of the range and eclipse the centre sound of the unison clarinets altogether.

Another example, this time involving only four players, occurs near the beginning of the first movement of Tchaikovsky *Symphony no. 4*, where the two clarinets and two bassoons play *Ex. 8.7* one octave apart.

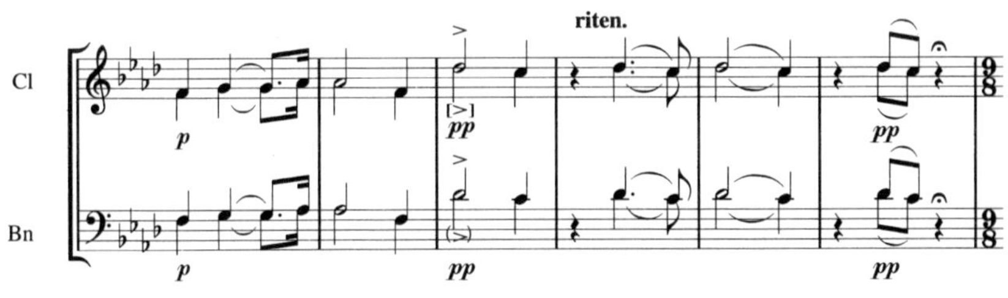

EX. 8.7

The doubling of both notes of the octave makes intonation awkward because the two bassoons must be in absolute unison before the clarinets can begin to base their octave upon them. Again the dynamic level of the lower octave can very easily be too loud, not only by reason of the two instruments playing together but because their concentration must be on the safety of their intonation as much as balance, the three notes F-G-A♭ having been already subject to dangerous changes of instrumentation. The sudden appearance of *pianissimo*, at both the highest note of the phrase and a most unexpected change of tonality, is typical of this magnificent score, but adds yet another difficulty. In practice this is very often taken by just the two 1st players, the 2nds stopping after the completion of the first two bars and allowing the removal of their sound to help the change in dynamic level. Such a course of action can obviously only be considered across an even distribution of identical instruments, and opportunities of similar relief to the wind section are rare indeed.

A more common example of octave doubling may be quoted from the second movement of Brahms *Symphony no. 3*.

(score in concert pitch)

EX. 8.8

Here the required sound is elicited from just two solo instruments, bassoon and clarinet. While in no respect easy to accomplish, the melodic line of the phrase and its obvious soloistic quality increase the likelihood of two players approaching it in similar fashion from the outset.

In doubling that involves a wider range of instrumentation the lower octave will, in most cases, be taken by more instruments than the upper, a situation that tends to enforce a natural balance of sound but does not make intonation easy for the lowest instruments, unless the dynamic level is relatively strong. The reverse scoring, with the majority of instruments playing the top octave, is usually only to be found in passages of orchestral *tutti*, where it still manages to make an orchestration sound unnaturally heavy. Dvořák is prone to use it on rare occasions, as in the first of the *Ten Legends*, where two flutes and one oboe in unison hold the top octave against a single bassoon below. The result, even with the other oboe and bassoon scored in the middle octave, can be rather ungainly unless handled carefully.

A single bass instrument will work very well, however, if the sound is low enough and only the middle octaves are doubled. The placing of a lone contrabassoon on the lowest line in this passage of colossal range from Hindemith *Symphonic Metamorphosis* is quite sufficient.

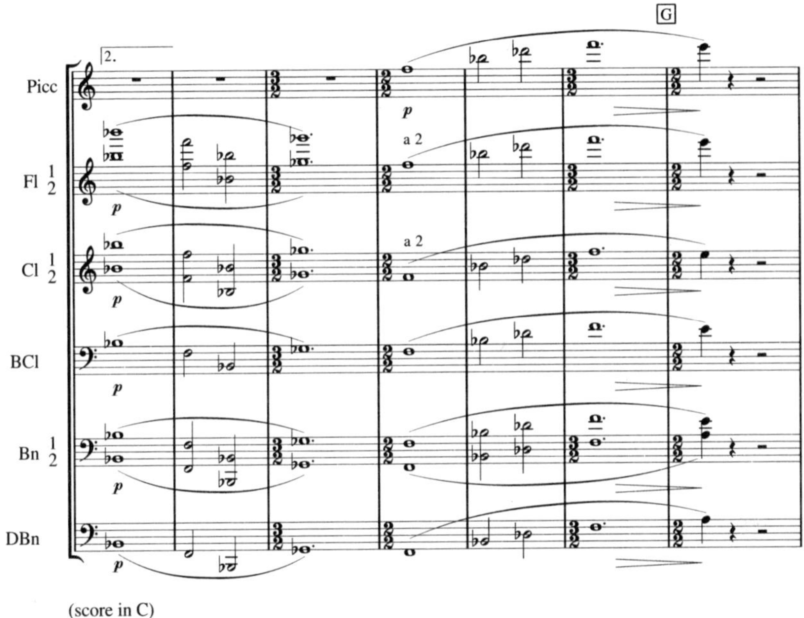

EX. 8.9

(The stark octave scoring that is such a feature of Sibelius' woodwind orchestration however, and rarely requires any sort of adjustment, is an object lesson in the craft of combining instrumental sound.)

Once instruments appear in unison the required predominance of timbre has to be assessed, together with the particular quality of the sound and its relative position within each instrument. In the case of two instruments only, this may well be self-evident, since combination is often used either to enhance the focus of a bright, optimistic sound, as here in the *Scherzo* of Dvořák *Symphony no. 8 in G*

EX. 8.10

or to darken and diffuse the edge of a more sombre tone-colour, as in *Ex. 8.11*, from the second movement of Rachmaninov *Piano Concerto no. 3*.

EX. 8.11

In both cases a blend of sound is required, with neither instrument predominant.

The use of more than two instruments in unison requires careful consideration, especially at a soft dynamic level. Mahler was very fond of combining the sound of three woodwind instruments at the same pitch in *piano* or *pianissimo* and in a way that requires careful control of balance. *Ex. 8.12* from the first movement (*Funeral March*) of his *Symphony no. 5*, is one of many.

Here, the changes of timbre that each instrument will produce because of the wide range of the melodic line provide a further obstacle, and one that is made no easier by the number of times a professional wind section may appear to overcome it with consummate ease. At different points in the phrase, each instrument finds itself within an area where it naturally projects a more distinctive quality of sound and where its own tone may be more or less sharply defined in comparison with the other two. Yet such vagaries of

EX. 8.12

instrumental design and construction must not be allowed to affect the overall balance of the passage, and a considerable amount of individual adjustment is required if the blend of these three players is to remain constant.

In a further example, from Verdi overture *The Force of Destiny*, the same three instruments are combined in an even more blatantly soloistic scoring. In the overture, the entire statement of the *Andantino* is entrusted to flute, oboe and clarinet in unison, accompanied only by string *pizzicato* and punctuated by fragmented statements of the 'theme of destiny'.

EX. 8.13

This is an extremely difficult passage to accomplish successfully, from the point of view of both balance and intonation. For the inexperienced section it is essential that the point of aural concentration is the 1st oboe and that the other two instrumentalists achieve parity by reference to this sound alone.

The addition of the closely related subsidiary instruments brings the size of the woodwind section from eight players to twelve (three of each group) but does not necessarily result in a proportionate increase in difficulty from the point of view of balance. On the contrary, the general augmentation of texture throughout the whole orchestra, and the ability to place three-note harmonies within the timbre of each instrument, often makes life easier. The complete triple-wind section does not appear with any regularity until the turn of the twentieth century, but the frequent addition of single examples for more than a hundred years before has dictated that the full symphony orchestra should always have this number available.

Specific Techniques

All the above must be borne in mind before the woodwind section can begin to function as a whole, and neglect of any or all of them will result in a complementary lack of unity, projection and finesse. They may be said to constitute the broad outlines of the fundamental courtesies that must be afforded to the section in order for it to achieve anything near its potential. Over and above such knowledge of the needs of the section as a whole, a conductor must possess a clear understanding of the tasks facing individual instrumentalists, and possible ways in which they may be helped to accomplish them.

There is not the opportunity for disguise, diffusion or corporate alteration that exists in the strings, or even to an extent in the brass, because there are so few of each instrument and their methods of performance and timbre are so different and distinctly individual. Any remarks or suggestions that the conductor may make with regard to a particular instrument will, by necessity, be directed at one, and only one, performer, and must take into account the sound, production and technical ability of the individual to a far greater degree than if it were to be the concern of a large section. The ability to influence the perceived sound of the single line by degrees of technical adjustment by a number of players is no longer directly possible. Suddenly the conductor is dealing with the technique of a single player, and the boundaries of change become severely limited.

BREATHING

The entire foundation of the wind player's art is contained in the skill of absorbing, controlling and expending the air that provides the means of making sound. No other technique has anything like equal relevance to the final outcome and nothing, on any instrument, is quite so personal or deeply bound to the physical. By comparison fingering, tonguing, dexterity, sight-reading and other attributes fade into insignificance, for if the air column cannot be controlled all is lost.

Many volumes of discussion have been devoted to this, the most profound basis of wind playing. Here, I shall simply consider the technique to heighten awareness of its importance, and to highlight some of the more obvious pitfalls. If a more thorough appraisal of the technical aspects is required, there are specialist publications readily available.

First of all it must always be borne in mind that, although the terminology is the same, breathing to produce sound has little in common with that most fundamental of human actions necessary to sustain life, in that the taking in of air is only an integral part of the battle. Breathing for any form of sound-production involves the added control of diaphragm, stomach muscles and lungs while the air is being used. Above all the air must be supported at all times and no sudden untutored snatch of breath allowed to disturb it. Among student instrumentalists, this last aspect is most easily forgotten and most frequently affected by outside influences and mistimed preparation, especially when considerable concentration is deflected towards the challenges of playing together.

Solely because of their familiarity and consequent ease of aural perception I make no apology for quoting the very famous (and horrendously difficult) opening bars of Mendelssohn overture *A Midsummer Night's Dream* as a working example, even though very few student orchestras should attempt to perform it.

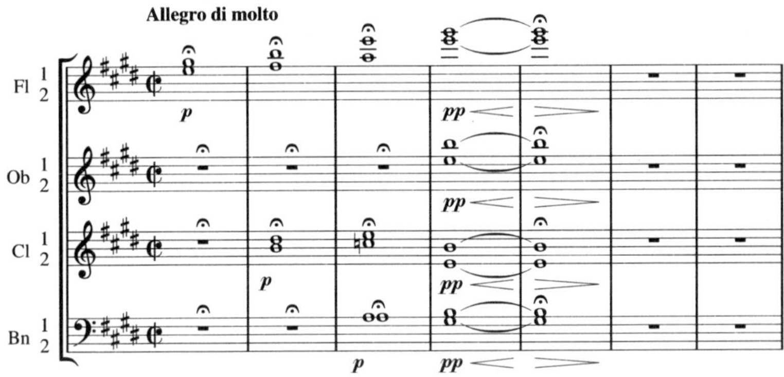

EX. 8.14

In effect each bar is a re-start because of its additional instrumentation, and each chord harbours subtle changes of balance and intonation as well as the problem of co-ordinating the entry. The successful overcoming of all these obstacles is governed entirely by breath control. For there to be any possibility of the chords being in tune the air must be perfectly supported by the diaphragm so that the pitch of each note is under total control at all times but especially at the moment each chord is being phrased off. Such an example of critical tuning also requires the players to perfect the technique of 'hearing' the note just before they actually produce it. Then, too, the balance will suffer if the tone is not constant and clear, regardless of the soft dynamic: this in itself is a monumental task at a real *piano* level. Lastly, the entries cannot possibly be together unless they are prepared together.

The four quoted chords are prime examples of the absolute necessity for a conductor to breathe with the wind section and have the moment of immediate preparation so safely governed that the placing of the entry is inevitable. This is not to say that the instrumentalists should be encouraged to make their entire intake of breath coincide with the conductor's up-beat, for in most circumstances (including the above) this will cause it to be too shallow. However, the final 'top-up' of air, taken after the reservoir has been filled and supported, is a natural process of entry, especially in a situation where no accent or explosive attack to the sound is required.

The technique of breathing with the wind section should become, as far as possible, a general rule of the conductor, and should certainly apply to the accompaniment of all woodwind solos, since there is no other way to ensure the time and space within the phrase or to appreciate the extent to which possible sub-phrases may be necessary.

As far as long *legato* passages are concerned, high-class woodwind players will tend to regard the marking of slurs as primary considerations of phrase length, and be loath to take a breath within them unless forced to do so – quite unlike the strings who may well change the direction of the bow quite frequently within a single *legato* slur. With student orchestras such diligence among the woodwind may not always be so apparent, since the players may not be so adept at determining the amount of breath they are going to need, or so practised in the art of proportioning it. Moreover, certainly in the early stages of rehearsal, few will have looked far enough ahead to see where even the printed phrase might end, and will be relying on the often forlorn hope that a rest must surely appear before they actually dry up! In the majority of cases such short-sighted preparation will be largely eradicated by the players themselves once the musical span of individual phrases has become apparent, but the ability to recognize and execute a meaningful phrase length at sight must be fostered at all times.

Sometimes one comes across a slur that is too long to be attempted in one breath or simply cannot be managed by the players concerned without loss of tone and projection. In this circumstance a breath must be inserted at the moment most appropriate (or least harmful) to the musical sentence, the great difficulty being to allow the necessary time without disturbing the natural flow of the line. In this respect the note immediately prior to the breath is crucial, for it will suffer if any attempt is made to snatch air. Both in order to disguise the break and to render it most natural and useful, the previous note must be given its full value as far as is humanly possible, and the sub-phrase completed with no sign of unnatural abbreviation.

Even when not covered by a single slur many woodwind lines make little or no concession to the necessity of replenishing the air supply, and opportunities must be engineered even if, in concert, a longer span is found to be possible. Such opportunities are dependent on a number of considerations and are often best determined by identifying the most important places where a gap *cannot* be tolerated. This will, of course, vary from one interpretation to the next, but an example of the general principle may well prove useful.

In the second appearance of the well-known 'love theme' from Tchaikovsky fantasy overture *Romeo and Juliet* (quoted in full as *Ex. 8.15*), the line for flutes and oboes extends to thirty-two bars without pause. Given no recourse to the highly specialized (and by no means general) technique of rotary breathing – that is, continuing the flow of air through the instrument by controlled pressure of the cheeks on air retained in the mouth while, simultaneously, inhaling air into the lungs – frequent opportunities for breath must be found. In *Ex. 8.15*, the inserted breath marks adhere to strict musical and practical criteria: firstly, that the emotional and architectural importance of the rising sixths, fifths and fourths should always be attained without a break, and that the most wonderfully poignant *diminuendo* into the curtailed restatement (bars 233 and 234) should be performed in similar fashion; secondly, that the spans should be of roughly equal length and not so long as to risk deterioration of quality.

Obviously, in a passage where the composer has been so specific in his marking as here, no breath can be considered within the slurs, especially between bars 219 and 220 where a quite indefensible re-phrasing may sometimes be perceived. All but one of the breathing places occur after a long note, the exception being in bar 232 in order to attain the *legato diminuendo* already mentioned. This is by far the most dangerous moment, since it is very difficult to avoid drastically shortening the first E♭ of the bar, but close examination will reveal few alternatives in this section. The identical problem applies if the breath were to be allowed at the end of the *diminuendo*, and to take it through to after the first crotchet of bar 235 would cause the phrase of the main theme to be broken in a different place from either of its previous appearances.

All techniques of performance must be subservient to the projected result, and no noticeable holes must ever be allowed to disturb the flow of a musical sentence. However, even with young players, this wonderful phrase can be refined to the point where, on first hearing, it would be hard to determine the exact points of breathing. No solution will ever serve to make a passage easy to play since the mere fact of having to break a sustained line adds difficulties of its own, but some solid foundation and premeditated reasoning is essential to any workable result.

EX. 8.15

NON-*LEGATO* PHRASES

The evenness of breath control that is demanded by long *legato* lines may often be overlooked when equally protracted paragraphs are apparently broken up by rests or *staccato* notes. For student instrumentalists the desire to breathe at every possible opportunity will always be the cause of added difficulties of rhythm and ensemble, as indeed is the case when professional sections fail to avoid the same trap. The passage of repeated figures from Martinů *Fantaisies Symphoniques (Symphony no. 6)* actually allows the oboes, clarinets and bassoons very little more scope for breathing than did the expansive theme from Tchaikovsky.

EX. 8.16

Breathing between each of the repeated figures will make them unrhythmic, too loud and accented, quite apart from losing the inherent movement of the line. This, and many passages like it, must be considered in terms of the complete phrase and performed with as few breaths as possible.

In the notoriously awkward passage that approaches the final *Presto* in the last movement of Beethoven *Symphony no. 5* it is even more vital to employ the same technique. A breath taken during almost any of the rests in these bars is a recipe for total disaster, the final eight bars, at least, having to be achieved as one continuous span.

EX. 8.17

EX. 8. 17 (continued)

Just as essential, and probably even more difficult, is the control of breath in a phrase that involves both *legato* and *staccato* movement. The four bars of *Ex. 8.18* are from the first movement of Schumann *Cello Concerto*.

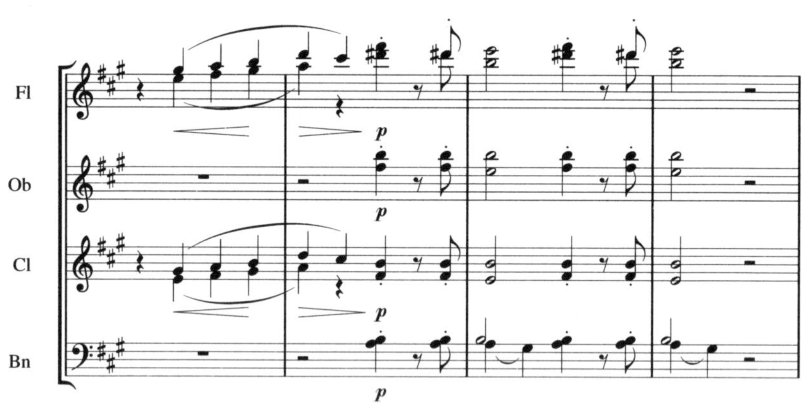

EX. 8.18

Here 1st flute and 1st clarinet approach the *staccato* by means of a short *legato* phrase that should allow no room whatever for the quite unnecessary breath often heard to distort it. Not only is the single breath required to make sense of the passage, but the small 'hairpin' dynamic marking is quite impossible to achieve without it. Even when no breath is taken, it is difficult to finish the *legato* portion of the phrase without shortening the last note, while still achieving distinct articulation of the *staccato*.

TONGUING

As with bowing in the case of strings, the wind player's essential aid to articulation is the use of the tongue to delineate note lengths and phrasing. The tongue is used to stop air passing into the instrument until the moment that it is required to produce a sound, and then released exactly in the way one would pronounce the syllable 'te'. The sound will be stopped by use of the diaphragm except in fast passages, where the return of the tongue to articulate the next note will serve both purposes. This technique can, with practice, be repeated at considerable speed to produce any number of short notes in succession but it will be most easily illustrated by use of a passage in moderate tempo such as *Ex. 8.19*, the famous phrase from the 2nd movement of Haydn *Symphony no. 94 in G.*

EX. 8.19

This technique of definition will be used throughout the woodwind and brass as a matter of course and with equal ease. However, owing to the vastly different techniques of sound production required by the various woodwind instruments, the student orchestra will often highlight a noticeable alteration in the degree of articulation between them. Thus, because of the pressure of air required to make the double-reed oboe speak clearly, a more accomplished action of the tongue will almost automatically be employed. Conversely, the comparative ease with which one can elicit a sound from the reedless flute allows a more flaccid tongue action to be perpetuated with some degree of success, particularly among young players. Indeed it is not uncommon to find elementary flute players hardly using the tongue at all, but rather blowing each separate sound – a technique often referred to by other wind players as being 'all wind and no whistle', and one that usually results in entries sounding late. The effect on the clarity and ensemble of the wind section is disastrous. The clean, precise control of the tongue is essential to the projected articulation of woodwind sounds, and the degree to which this action has to be emphasized in ensemble playing is regularly underestimated, even among players of quite high standard.

In *staccato* notation however, especially in respect to short *sforzando* chords, the most neglected aspect of this technique has to do with the ending of the note. The situation frequently arises where a wind section will produce a sound exactly together, only to ruin all their hard work by allowing imprecision and thoughtlessness to blur the end of it. Even in fast repetition a truly projected quality of tight *staccato*, at whatever dynamic level, will only be achieved if the end of the note is – by perfect control of the tongue and diaphragm – as clearly defined as the start.

In these circumstances the tongue will be used in conjunction with the diaphragm to stop the note, constant pressure being maintained during the momentary silences, so that there is an immediate response when the tongue is released. In a passage of sharply defined chords, like those that appear at the beginning of the second movement of Beethoven *Symphony no. 8,* articulation is transformed by what might simply be described as the difference between repeating the syllable 'te' and one more akin to 'tet'.

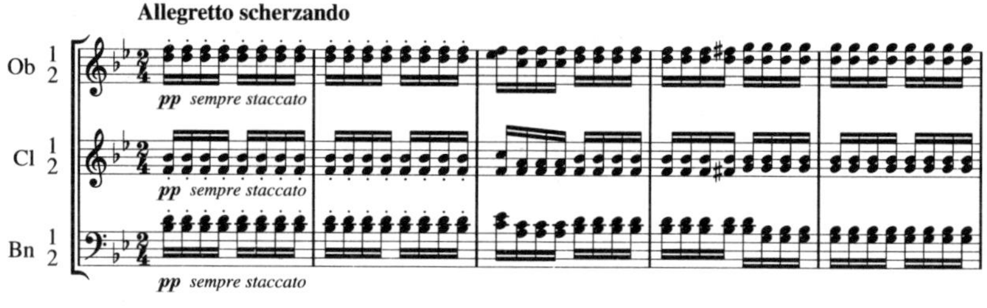

EX. 8.20

If the passage of air is not stopped abruptly, a certain tailing off of sound must be apparent. If continual support of the diaphragm is lacking, an indistinct or soggy attack will result. In either case the strength and purpose of these chords will be lost.

However, an intentional rounding-off of the sound, cutting the air supply to the instrument gradually, is essential in obtaining any form of *legato* phrasing and will be needed to define the phrasing of notes in pairs that occurs later in this same movement (see *Ex. 8.21*).

Nonetheless, it is most often the deliberation of the tonguing that is most at fault. Certainly in the case of defining and projecting small notes, the action of the tongue must be much quicker than many players will automatically perform. Thus in a passage like *Ex. 8.22* from Walton *Symphony no. 1*

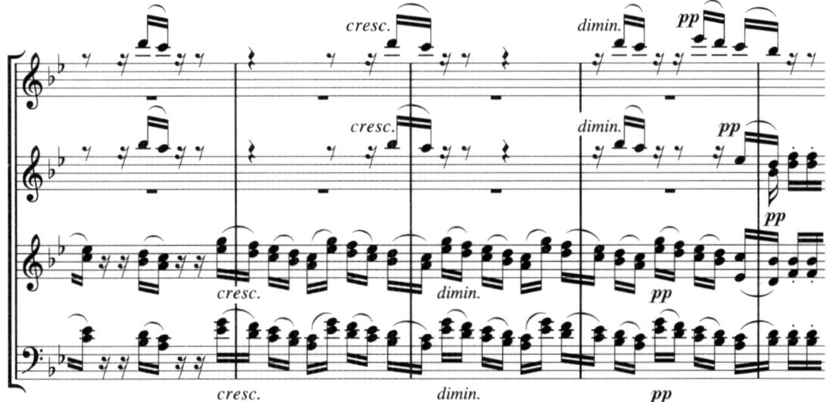

(score in concert pitch)

EX. 8.21

(score in concert pitch)

EX. 8.22

or *Ex. 8.23*, from the same work

EX. 8.23

the semiquavers must be tongued as positively as the notes with printed accents if they are to be clearly articulated.

Such extreme definition is not easy to achieve, especially when, as in *Ex 8.22*, the printed accents appear over notes which are so obviously the resolutions of each short phrase. In this example there is not even a change of pitch to help the rhythm through the texture; everything must be achieved by the players' clarity of articulation. The only course of action is to remind the section of their responsibility to make the short notes tight and powerful, and to urge the players virtually to spit out the figures that are most likely to be obscured. This is especially important in respect of clarinets and flutes, who do not have to overcome the inertia of the reed in the same way as oboes and bassoons, and are therefore less likely to employ the same energy of attack. In common with many similar passages of full woodwind scoring, it is probably fair to say that the clarity of tonguing employed by flutes and clarinets in *Exx. 8.22* and *8.23* is the key to its successful execution.

The soft approach to a phrase is considerably more difficult to execute than firmly tongued production which, as we have seen, is much more likely to be missing through default than for reasons of real technical inability. Especially with regard to the double-reed instruments, the skill of introducing a gentle phrase with a controlled tone but no obvious start to the sound is one that may be within the grasp of only the truly high-class professional. However, disregarding examples of quite superb technical artistry, some help can be afforded to student instrumentalists if the moment of production is approached correctly by all concerned.

In simplified terms the basic problem is twofold: a fear that the instrument will not speak, coupled with an attempt to provide the sound on the instant. Inevitably, if one feels that the appearance of a sound is to be determined by a 'millisecond' response, then the desire to attack the note will be almost overwhelming. Both the actual production of the sound and its preparation will be restricted by confines of time that will inhibit the composure and confidence of the performer. A psychological impression of latitude with regard to the moment of entry is imperative, even if such an indulgence cannot be allowed to show. In actual terms of production the player must be allowed to feel that the sound may be placed a fraction *earlier* than intended and then settled in place rather than committed to it.

In *Ex. 8.24*, from Nielsen *Symphony no. 4*, the contrabassoon makes its

EX. 8.24

only appearance in the entire work at a moment of high dramatic tension and expectancy.

Not only is the entry technically difficult in terms of intonation and balance, but the instrument is also cold and unfamiliar to the player who has spent the previous thirty minutes or so playing 3rd bassoon. Beyond even these considerations, the note is the resolution of a delayed cadence, a fact that heightens both the tension and the prominence of its eventual exposure. Given its inclination to a multitude of accidents, the entry will only work successfully if the player feels a measure of autonomy as to the precise moment it appears, and that it may be introduced from *within* the previous texture, as opposed to marking the commencement of a new section.

Similar examples abound for all the instruments of the woodwind section and the method of approach holds true for the great majority, whether in ensemble, solo, theme or accompaniment.

LEGATO TONGUING

All variations in degree of tonguing may be employed where necessary, the very soft touch – closest to the syllable 'de' – being used to point the phrasing within a sustained line or to effect definition of soft *legato* movement.

Legato tonguing will be used to clarify the phrasing slurs that may appear at places where breathing is neither necessary nor desirable. It may be performed with an almost infinite variety of strength, ranging from the smoothness with which a good string player will turn the bow, to a firm and accented deliberation. The degree to which the tongue is actually used is obviously determined by the overall method of sound production of each instrument – since those with double reeds, for example, are unable to employ the almost stroked action that can be used on the flute – but a large variety of definition is available to all.

The soft action that is associated with *legato* tonguing need not be confined solely to passages of true *legato* but may also be used to define notes that require a greater degree of separation. In this case it is most likely that the note immediately preceding the gap will be phrased off by using the diaphragm to control the passage of air through the instrument. For the wind section the difficulty lies once again in judging the length of the last note and finishing together. There is no corporate sound to chamfer the edge, as would be true of a string section, but only the combined sound of individually discernible players. This basic difference between the two sections leads to a situation where the ends of sounds take on an importance altogether more vital for wind players than for strings, a circumstance that is overlooked surprisingly often.

An even bigger difference between string and woodwind sections is the method of articulation employed. Bowing will very often automatically affect two aspects of the note – its start and its duration – simply by the physical necessity of reversing direction or lifting the arm to repeat the same movement. Simple articulation of the tongue need involve no similar constraints on the length of note produced and professional players place great emphasis on their use of peripheral vision in order to end phrases together. This technique of controlling the corporate articulation from within is very important and should be implanted in a young section very early.

However, it in no way reduces the responsibility of the conductor in terms of the organization of interpretation. In many cases considerable thought is given to the bowing of the strings in order to attain uniformity of phrasing, but the wind are simply expected either to reason the lengths for themselves or automatically to emulate a bowing style. With an inexperienced woodwind section, even were they to be attempting such finesse of orchestral technique, such an arbitrary approach is very unlikely to succeed, if only because of the extent to which the aural appraisal of phrasing differs from the various techniques needed to reproduce it. It is imperative that the exact expression of this section's sound should receive proper consideration, and that some priority be given to the shaping of the end of phrases.

DOUBLE-TONGUING

The technique of double-tonguing – using the syllables 'te-ke te-ke te-ke' in repetition – can be developed to overcome the problem of high speed articulation, although it is not ideal on either oboe or clarinet and should really be avoided, as the speed of single-tonguing can be developed to compensate. Bassoons use it by virtue of a more relaxed embouchure and because less reed is taken into the mouth, and for the flutes it is a standard technique. Its appearance is usually confined to the execution of short, rhythmic figures, although extended passages exist of which *Ex. 8.25* from the 2nd movement of Shostakovich *Symphony no. 7* (only a small section of which is reproduced here) is one of the most original.

This rhythmic accompaniment to the bass clarinet solo actually extends uninterrupted and in the same sparse scoring for thirty bars.

In student orchestras, however, it is quite common to come across players who simply cannot double-tongue successfully, and this constitutes something of a problem if the speed of their single-tonguing has not been sufficiently

EX. 8.25

developed. With an otherwise advanced player who may just not have encountered the technique before, it is sometimes possible to teach it quickly, especially if the line of the phrase is enhanced and false accents are totally eradicated; but care must be taken that it is not being executed wrongly as this could have dire consequences for the development of the player involved.

TRIPLE-TONGUING

Triple-tonguing – the repetition of 'te-de-ke' or 'te-ke-te' only appears of necessity for the flute or piccolo where, as with double-tonguing, its execution is perfectly possible at remarkably fast tempi. It is demanded quite frequently but the most famous instance will probably always be this from Stravinsky *The Firebird* (*Ex. 8.26*).

The idea that it must be used for all passages of triplet rhythm is erroneous, and *Ex. 8.27*, from Wagner Prelude to Act III of *Lohengrin*, for example, is quite possible to execute with fast single-tonguing.

EX. 8.26

EX. 8.27

As with any fast passage-work it is important that there are no false accents and that the continuity of the phrase is clearly understood. Nothing makes a passage more difficult than losing the point of reference and the natural flow of the line.

FLUTTER-TONGUING

The technique of flutter-tonguing is achieved by performing a rolled 'r' through the duration of the note, giving a form of articulation that corresponds to the strings' *tremolo*. It is most effective on the flute or piccolo because of the absence of a reed and, although perfectly possible, it is less often required of the other woodwind instruments. However, many examples of its use may be found for all instruments and *Ex. 8.28*, the *Dies Irae* from Britten *Sinfonia da Requiem*, is a rare example of the technique being required of the entire section including cor anglais and alto saxophone.

There are alternative methods of producing a similar effect, the most common of which is to raise the tongue away from the reed and use the back of the tongue and the uvula in combination. In the case of oboe and bassoon

(score in C)

EX. 8.28

the technique may sometimes be replaced altogether by one of reducing the pressure of air until a coarse, uneven sound is obtained. In such a tumultuous piece of orchestration as this the marking is more to ensure the absence of any pure sound than an insistence on how it is produced. Being a colouristic effect, the technique is most regularly performed at a distinctly exaggerated dynamic level, a consideration that adds greatly to the fatigue involved in its use for extended periods.

Flutter-tonguing is most often requested by the placing of two or more strokes through the tail of the note, a method identical to that employed for string *tremolo*, but with the addition of some word of direction. The actual term used varies considerably and can sometimes be so imprecise as to cause confusion. In most instances, as in the English 'flutter-tongue' the direct terminology of technical performance will be used: *Flatterzunge* in German; *Tremolo dental* in French and *Frulato* in Italian. However, the rather odd direction *vibrato* is sometimes used by Ravel, and Britten, in its first appearance in the above-mentioned work, uses the abbreviation *trem.*, with the addition of an explanatory footnote.

In conclusion, reference must be made to the fairly frequent request for flutter-tonguing in somewhat contradictory circumstances, albeit rarely as blatant as the direction *tremolo non frulato*(!) unearthed by Norman Del Mar in the flute part of a score by a Romanian composer (*Anatomy of the Orchestra* p.195). A number of examples exist where the marking pertains to a passage in which it is difficult to understand the exact intentions of the composer. *Ex. 8.29* from Szymanowski *Violin Concerto no. 2* occurs at a tempo far too slow for *frulato* to be attempted.

EX. 8.29

MUTING

There are no types of manufactured mute available for any of the woodwind instruments and on the very rare occasions it is requested of oboe and bassoon (for instance, in Liadov *The Enchanted Lake*), it is fulfilled by inserting a soft cloth into the bell of the instrument.

VARYING THE PITCH

Of all orchestral instruments the general pitch of the woodwind is most affected by temperature and there is simply no benefit in trying to get the section to sound in tune with itself, or anyone else, in a cold hall. Although a professional section, faced with a school concert at 9 o'clock in the morning in an unheated cinema, can go some way towards achieving reasonable agreement in pitch, the necessary technical gymnastics would be of little use in the case of a rehearsal for some future performance. To provide any worthwhile and lasting results the student wind section must work in a reasonable temperature.

Once some degree of control of the overall pitch of the instruments can be relied on, the tuning of individual notes during performance can be adjusted in a number of ways – in the case of some notes slightly more than a quarter-tone. Such microtonal variations are generally achieved by control of the embouchure, the pressure being strengthened or relaxed depending upon the direction of adjustment. On the flute a similar result can also be obtained by slightly altering the angle of the mouthpiece in relation to the lips, but, as is the case with all wind instruments, the possibilities of adjustment are severely limited. However, control of this sort is essential in attaining the minute and instant adjustment of intonation required for woodwind chords and must be the sole method used when intonation is rehearsed in the manner discussed earlier in this chapter.

Use of the diaphragm, or varying the actual pressure of air, will also cause the note to change pitch, but such practice is most usually confined to a more premeditated adjustment of a note that is known to be sharp or flat, either in itself or in conjunction with other instruments. These techniques are used when players automatically adjust the pitch of a note when they are called on to produce particularly loud or soft dynamic levels. With all woodwind instruments except the clarinet, blowing hard will sharpen the note and soft playing will tend to flatten it. Because they, uniquely, reproduce the acoustic behaviour of a stopped cylindrical pipe, instruments of the clarinet family produce exactly the opposite result.

Alternative fingerings will also produce slight variations of pitch and timbre, and may be used by players to make allowance for known idiosyncrasies of the instrument, harmony or ensemble. However, the number and reliability of these vary from one instrument to another and from note to note. Although reference may be found to the oboe having recourse to more than ninety different fingerings that will produce B above middle C (Bruno Bartolozzi, *New Sounds for Woodwind*, OUP, 1967), many of these are somewhat contrived. In normal orchestral circumstances the even tone of a passage is so important that very few alternatives can be considered.

Of the many problems of pitch that affect woodwind players, perhaps that which catches most student players by surprise is when the instrument goes cold, and consequently flat, in a long rest. Too often, a young player will complete the most sensitive rendition of a slow movement solo, diligently count seventy or eighty bars' rest and then re-enter on a low *piano* note, only to stop and stare at the instrument in disbelief. The crisis is one peculiar to orchestral playing, for at no other time will the inexperienced instrumentalist be lulled into ignoring the instrument for so long, and awareness of the danger is certainly the prime remedy. Whether it is overcome by occasional blowing through the instrument to keep it warm, or by adjusting the reed, crook or head joint to cover the entry and the notes immediately following, depends on the length and nature of the passage about to be negotiated.

In addition to such general variations in pitch, other adjustments may be made by woodwind instrumentalists in order to cope with particular circumstances. For the most part these can only be learnt through experience and experimentation, as they usually apply solely to the individual example of the instrument being used and are therefore not normally within the scope of the conductor to suggest. Nonetheless, it is essential that an atmosphere be nurtured where such positive experimentation is known to be tolerated and a true understanding of the problems facing the wind section is apparent.

Related Techniques

EMBOUCHURE

Strictly speaking, considerations of embouchure are beyond the limits of this discussion, since it is a basic technique that must not be tampered with in orchestral circumstances. Mention has already been made of the flexibility of embouchure necessary to obtain adjustment of intonation, and to this must be added the equal relevance of the embouchure in projecting sound and eliciting pure tone.

For the conductor of student orchestras some basic knowledge of the requisite embouchure for each of the four main woodwind instruments is helpful, if for no other reason than that its visual aspect, combined with the sound produced, will sometimes help to ascertain the limits to which a section or individual may be pushed. If the conductor has no experience of playing a woodwind instrument, such specific information must be gleaned from one of the many teaching manuals or, preferably, in conversation with a professional player, but beware of jumping to conclusions of inability based on the sight of an unusual embouchure alone. I well remember the student conductor who, after dramatically imploring the woodwind for more sound, added in a stage whisper to the front desk strings the knowledgeable comment that, with such an extraordinary embouchure, the 2nd clarinet stood no chance. To his eternal credit the relevant instrumentalist, who – among his other attributes – was not deaf, subsequently proceeded to produce the level of sound that only an irate clarinettist can!

VIBRATO

The ability to produce and control a *vibrato* that enhances the sound of any instrument is a technique acquired at various stages of development and therefore, once again, is outside the conductor's realm of interference. However, certain aspects apparent in its use must be considered.

A good, controlled *vibrato* will be performed by use of the diaphragm in conjunction with the embouchure, the former producing the pulse of the sound and the latter the slight variations in pitch. Such a technique, when fully developed, is totally within the player's control and may be modified at will. The wrong technique is one originating from the lip, a method which tends to creep in by default rather than considered practice. Unfortunately examples of this in young players are by no means rare and the resultant lack of regulation will cause many difficulties.

In some situations *vibrato* can easily make a chord sound out of tune when it is not, and can interfere with the clarity and balance of various lines. This usually happens when it is used in an ill-considered way, taking no account of the timbres around it, and is a problem most relevant to the inexperienced section. The conductor must be aware of the interaction of various players' *vibrato*, and should be prepared to exert some degree of regulation in its use. If some control of *vibrato* is in evidence, the player will normally at least be able stop it, even if the many subtle variations that lie between the two extremes cannot be attained.

Strangely, the opposite effect on intonation can also be true and, particularly with regard to the pure tones of the flute, the addition of *vibrato* can be all that is needed to set a chord in tune. Such apparently conflicting phenomena are caused by the fluctuation of overtones experienced when *vibrato* is used and the fact that their presence in the timbre of each of the various woodwind instruments is so different. Once the sounds of two or more instruments are combined, the use of *vibrato* can give rise to 'beats', causing certain notes to be highlighted or altered in pitch, although this may also be caused by the simple interaction of different timbres. Occasionally so-called 'ghost notes' – notes that are not being played at all – become audible, confusing the unwary section and conductor alike. (These are the differential of the vibrations per second of any two notes sounded together. Thus, with A = 440, if one plays the C a twelfth above (1056) and the E♭ above that (1267.2) and tunes them perfectly, the A♭ (211.2) two octaves and a third below will clearly be heard. Played on the relatively pure tones of two flutes, these two notes, at this pitch, are often used to demonstrate the phenomenon to advanced students.)

The total removal of *vibrato* in soloistic passages should be used sparingly. Except in the hands of a highly skilled player the resultant sound may be very 'dead' and lose too much of its quality of projection. However, it may sometimes be considered where a direct contrast to the richer tones normally employed is required; for example, in the case of a recurring motif that undergoes changes of dramatic emphasis, or the rare places where the pure sound's natural qualities of unearthly distance and immobility may be utilized. Certainly, opportunities exist in some works of a programmatic nature, an early example being the famous demoniac wails of the gathering witches from the final movement of Berlioz *Symphonie Fantastique*.

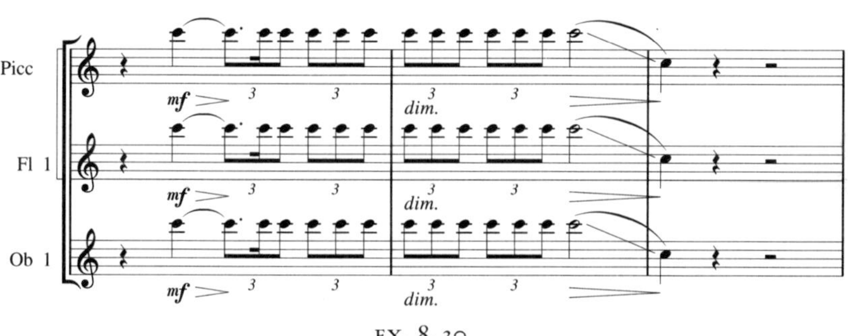

EX. 8.30

Here, the use of a totally static sound will also increase the effect of the malevolent disintegration of pitch.

The downward *glissando* effect is produced by an exaggeration of the technique of varying the pitch – 'lipping' the note down – but many younger players find this very hard to achieve, a vague flattening of the note being all that is discernible, which often sounds as if the players have been unaccountably struck by a momentary disability. Once some degree of control has been achieved (by constant private practice) it is sometimes possible to increase the perceived effect by fingering the semitone below and 'lipping' the first note *up*, thereby extending the controlled drop by passing through the fingered note.

REEDS

The making, care and maintenance of woodwind reeds is a highly specialized study and will be taught to young players as an integral part of their instrumental development. The choice of a particular reed is an individual decision and allows no interference whatever from the conductor, however knowledgeable or well meaning. The reed is the lifeline between a player's technique and its ultimate realization and, as such, its selection must be made, however misguidedly, by the player alone, or in private consultation with a regularly performing professional if such guidance is sought. In student orchestras this aspect of the role of the wind tutor demands a deeply respected instrumental ability combined with considerable tact.

In personal experience I have never come across the occasion where a player will perform noticeably better on a suggested alternative reed unless the choice has been entirely mutual. For the conductor the fact that the fluent and liquid sounds of yesterday might well be transformed into stuttering gibberish today must be accepted and sympathetically handled – no one will be more aware of it than the player!

MULTIPHONICS

As was the case regarding stringed instruments, many scores of the late twentieth century will require a number of secondary techniques from the woodwind. Chief among these is the production of multiphonics.

This phenomenon of producing 'chords' is possible on all woodwind instruments but is not to be confused with the type of production employed by stringed instruments. The woodwind cannot produce chords composed entirely of fundamentals but rather, groups of notes generated by a number of frequency vibrations within the single column of air. These scientifically complex groups of sounds, referred to as sound amalgams rather than chords, will comprise partials of differing quality, and the ear will pick up the loudest of them, translating them into understandable tones and intervals in much the same way as it does when 'hearing' a single note.

Many of these amalgams can be produced without any change of fingering from that used for a single note, although the clarinet is unique in being able to produce them from all fingerings. In all cases a slight change of embouchure and an increase or decrease of air pressure is required, and this will vary not only from one example of an instrument to the next but also from player to player. The only constant is a considerably fluent technique with regard to breath control and sensitivity of the lips.

A further method of production is the use of fingerings that will *only* provide a group of sounds, and necessitate no change of lip position or air pressure. A number of these exist on all woodwind instruments.

Where multiphonic production is required, the necessary fingering will always be appended but any attendant change of embouchure or pressure will tend to be left to the player for the reasons stated above. *Ex. 8.31* for flute, oboe and clarinet, from Edwin Roxburgh *Saturn* demonstrates this method of notation.

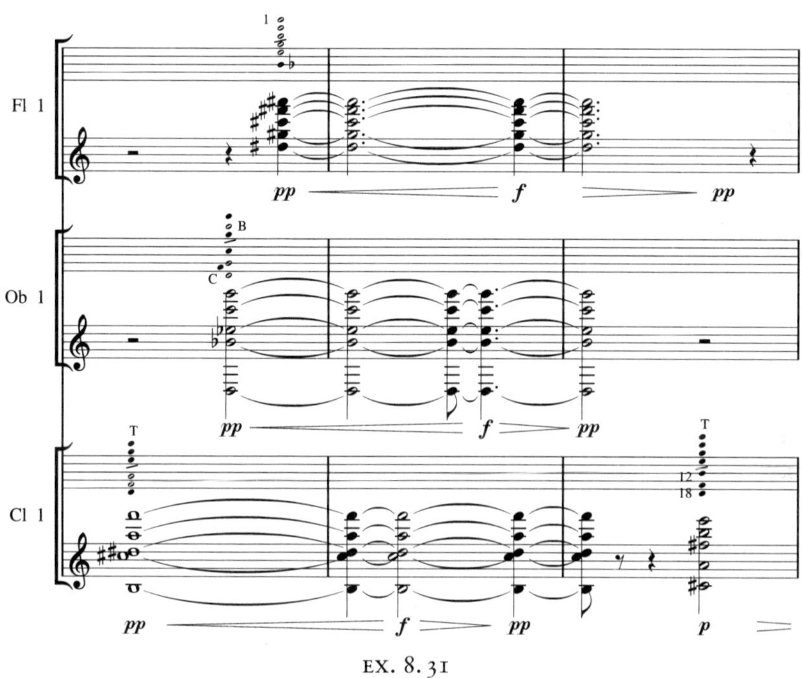

EX. 8.31

A considerable degree of experimentation from each player will always be required but, once the technique is mastered and some fundamental multiphonic fingerings learnt, such sounds may be produced at will and are quite reliable.

HARMONICS

Prevalent in music from the beginning of the twentieth century, harmonics will be found requested of flute and, less often, oboe. They are available through a standard range of harmonic fingering and produce a very different tone quality, considerably less resonant and somewhat 'pure' in sound. For this reason they are most usually found orchestrated within soft and soloistic instrumentation, as *Ex. 8.32* from the first part of Ravel *Daphnis et Chloé*, where they are also requested of alto flute.

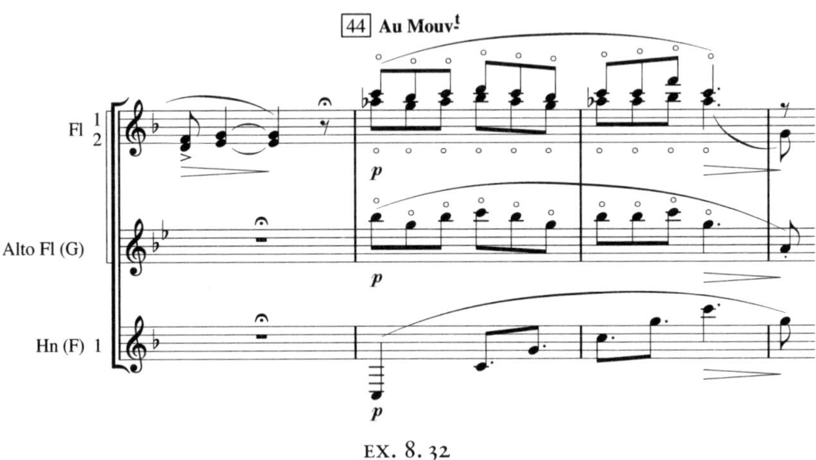

EX. 8.32

MISCELLANEOUS SOUNDS

Beyond these last two actual techniques of playing, a number of percussive or indeterminate sounds will be demanded of the section. Most of these will be self-explanatory (blowing double reeds detached from the instrument, blowing air through the instrument without producing notes, etc.) and will only require the sort of disposition and understanding that is, fortunately, becoming more widespread among student instrumentalists. But the relatively frequent request for rattling the keys of the instrument needs to be approached with care. Over-enthusiastic or careless compliance with this demand can have a sudden and very detrimental effect on the keys, pads or linkage of any woodwind instrument. A fairly safe area of the instrument needs to be located and aggression kept under severe control.

9 HORNS

Character and Influence

The character most readily associated with horns is the 'hunting call', firmly based in the instrument's history and an inseparable part of its nature. Numerous instances of horn writing may be traced directly to the influence that the original instrument still maintains in the mind of all composers. Even examples as varied in style as the first notes of Weber *Oberon*, Tchaikovsky *Symphony no. 4* and Britten *Dies Irae* from his *War Requiem* all stem from the same source.

From its earliest appearances in orchestral music to the present day, through countless refinements of design and technique, the horn has preserved a resolute link with its origins; perhaps only the trumpet can compete with it for so clear an aural perception of one particular facet of sound and character as is grafted in the mind of layman and musician alike.

Within the context of student orchestras, the uses that appear so regularly in symphonic writing of the eighteenth century need not be of direct concern (although the famous calls that appear throughout the 1st movement of Haydn *Symphony no. 31 (The Horn Signal)* show two pairs of horns, harmonically interlocked (1–3–2–4), even at this early date – c. 1765). The earliest example that need be quoted is that of the *Trio* in the third movement of Beethoven *Symphony no. 3*, where the rare combination of three horns dominates proceedings (see *Ex. 9.1*).

Once again the writing may be seen to be interlocked, with 3rd never rising above 1st or falling below 2nd as they traverse three octaves of E♭ major. While any direct allusion to hunting is very unlikely to have been intended by this passage, the historic character of the instruments is unmistakable, even to the embellishment of the downward figure in 2nd horn at the end of each phrase. (In passing, may I perhaps note that the tempo of this entire movement must surely rest as much on the 2nd horn's ability to articulate bar six of the above as it does on the four quavers that appear in the ninth bar of the *Scherzo*. I have never managed to understand the reasoning behind performances that suggest Beethoven was unable to differentiate between *prestissimo* and *allegro vivace*.)

Similar historic associations may be discerned in the more *legato* duet

EX. 9.1

that comprises the *Trio* of the same composer's *Symphony no. 8* (*Ex. 9.2*), although the enforced limitation of notes and pervading rhythm are really all that provide the connection in this instance, where Beethoven has extended the more melodic side of the instrument.

EX. 9.2

In both these examples Beethoven was writing for an instrument that differed little in essentials from its original, except that the playing position had been altered to exploit the variation of tone and pitch made possible by inserting the right hand into the bell.

The melodic qualities of the instrument had, of course, long been recognized, not least by Haydn and Mozart, but it took the invention of valves to release the instrument's true potential to the point where we accept mellow *legato* melodies to be as much part of the horns' natural character as the harmonically restricted 'signals'. In music composed since the 1850s, the horn section's orchestral responsibility has become more varied than any other section apart from the strings.

Intonation and Balance

As a group, the section of four horns regularly employed by composers since the early part of the nineteenth century has the inbuilt advantage of being the only harmonically complete section of truly similar instruments in the entire orchestra. It is therefore possible to balance and control intonation at all levels without the added consideration of the type of production necessary to combine different timbres. This can prove to be an invaluable asset as far as coherence of the section as a whole is concerned, not least because it provides the opportunity to balance *down* to the supporting voice with much greater ease than would be possible were the instruments to be of different character – flutes or clarinets supported by bassoons, for example.

Within the orchestra, however, their ever-changing responsibility to woodwind and brass (mentioned at the begining of Chapter 3 and considered more deeply in Chapter 15) can create some problems, but the two inseparable considerations of intonation and balance, when applied to this section in isolation, may be more easily discussed under one heading than is the case elsewhere.

The intonation of all notes on the horn may be adjusted by small variations in the position of the hand within the bell and, to a lesser extent, by slight adjustment of the lips. Combination of both methods allows most notes to be varied sufficiently to produce accurately tuned chords whether they be scored for horns alone or blended with other instruments, but the extreme top and bottom register prove more restrictive.

The use of the modern double horn in F and B♭ also allows for alternative fingerings across much of the range, and thereby extends the means of adjusting intonation still further. As with all problems of intonation, however, the difficulty, especially for the young player, arises not so much in physically adjusting the note as in hearing that which is required.

Much should be done to make the horn section aware of their internal balance and intonation during sectional rehearsal, and any good tutor will be aware of this as one of the prime objectives. However, as always, much of the careful work done in sectional rehearsals may be lost once the orchestra comes together. The richness of texture, coupled with the sheer emotional power of orchestral sound, encourages over-playing in many areas of the orchestra but most especially from horns, brass and 1st violins. As with all cases of orchestral balance, it is the *quality* of the sound that will provide penetration and not simply loudness. The forcing of any sound through a texture tends to diminish its projection and clarity, quite apart from imprisoning the player concerned in a situation of physical exertion that precludes attention to phrasing or intonation.

This should be avoided at all costs, especially in a section whose overall orchestral responsibility is, so often, one of support and integration. Even if it means balancing the rest of the orchestra down to them, the horns must be encouraged to maintain a controlled and balanced output at all times.

In practical terms this is nowhere near as easy to achieve in student orchestras as it might at first seem, since the section itself is often unbalanced simply in terms of playing ability. The gap of experience and technical facility between 1st and 4th, for example, may often prove to be very wide indeed, and the subsequent difference in maturity of the two sounds will cause severe difficulties in itself. In truth, such a situation cannot be rectified – in the solo sounds of all orchestral wind instruments the better player will always be noticeable at some point, however evenly balanced and supportive the rest of the sections might have learnt to become. It can, however, be disguised to the point of being virtually unnoticeable at times where the sections are involved in producing corporate sounds. (It should be said that the term 'disguised' must not be taken to imply any sort of falsification, for what one is trying to achieve is possibly best described as an even balance based on such strengths as may be found in the less mature players, rather than the more easily comprehensible integration of evenly matched performers.)

Attempts to increase the contribution of a weaker 2nd or 4th player will be more successful if the stronger voices first balance down to them and then, over a period of rehearsals, the entire section is gradually brought up to a more natural level as a single entity. It will then often be found that the required increase in sound happens largely by itself, as the less experienced players become accustomed to the sound of a balanced section and begin to understand the overall level required. Such a patient approach to the improvement of the balance will prove far superior, even in the short term, to begging for a simple increase in sound from players who do not fully appreciate the importance of their role and whose only recourse is to blow harder into the instrument – an act as likely to destroy all hope of integration as it is certain to impair their ability to hear it.

In a most simple and frequently encountered form of instrumentation a group of four horns will be harmonically interlocked, the notes being distributed, from bottom to top, 4–2–3–1 as can be seen in *Ex. 9.3*, taken from the final section of the Prelude to *Hansel and Gretel* by Humperdinck.

EX. 9.3

From this point the horns proceed in similar close harmony virtually uninterrupted until the end, and the layout remains essentially the same, varying only in the very occasional transposition of 2nd and 3rd where considerations of line demand it. The last few bars of the work give illustration of this where, in the third and fourth bars of *Ex. 9.4*, the relative harmonic positions of 2nd and 3rd are interchanged in order to avoid holding the same note throughout each bar.

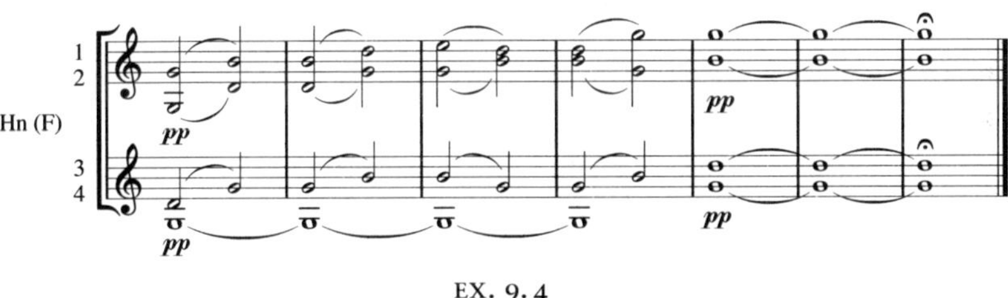

EX. 9.4

The layout of the final C major chord is typical horn distribution and perfectly easy to hear and balance within the section, even if, as on this occasion, it lies unusually high.

In chording of a more chromatic nature, where less doubling at the octave is to be considered, a distribution more closely allied to the Classical 2 + 2 arrangement of the four-horn group will often be encountered.

In *Ex. 9.5*, taken from the horn variation from Britten *A Young Person's Guide to the Orchestra*, the four horns are obviously paired, but responsibility for the two extremes of the range is still maintained by 1st and 4th.

EX. 9.5

In either allocation, intonation and balance may be readily discerned and rectified by the players themselves. Typically, the chords lie close and movement is restricted to notes in near proximity. Should the need arise, intonation may be rehearsed in the same way as for woodwind – by adding individual notes with clearly audible intervallic or harmonic relationships – but without the added problems of adjusting balance between instruments with totally dissimilar tone qualities.

In passages of a more linear nature, where the separate instruments may take on a more melodic and individual role, the situation for the horns becomes rather more difficult. In *Ex. 9.6*, from the very opening of Sibelius *Symphony no. 5*, in addition to the overall harmonic importance of the horn writing, there is also a noticeable degree of individual melodic movement, especially for 2nd and 4th. The layout, however, clearly maintains the Classical interlocking of the four lines as shown in *Ex. 9.4*.

Although, at first sight, this passage might well seem no more than an original, if exposed, use of horn sound, it repays a little patient dissection to reveal difficulties of intonation, control, production and balance that – especially in these days of familiarity through recorded performance – are all too easily taken for granted.

In the very first bar the concert G of 4th horn is awkward for intonation simply because it is the bass note of a minor sixth but here it is made more so by the entry of the B♭ above, which firmly identifies it as the third of E♭ major. In this particular case some of the problem could be alleviated by an exceptionally good timpanist, the opening B♭ completing the chord at the outset, but no youth orchestra is likely to come across a player of such standard

EX. 9.6

or, indeed, possess instruments of the required quality. To all intents and purposes the horns are 'on their own' and the difficulties are theirs to encounter and overcome.

The 1st inversion always proves to be the most difficult of common chords for wind players to tune because the third lies so far below the tonic note and tends to be approached as the basis of the chord rather than the third within it. Wherever it is placed, the qualities of the minor or major third remain dependent on the tonic note and any attempt to alter their relationship will cause disaster. Thus, in this example, the added difficulty for 4th lies in clearly 'hearing' E♭ major before a note has been played and holding a G that he or she knows will cause the chord to sound in tune when it appears.

Still within the first bar, the entry for 1st and 2nd, coming just after the second main beat, is difficult to negotiate without any sign of accent and at a level which grows from that already determined by 3rd and 4th. An entry on the beat would be far more simple in this respect. Perfect balance of the chord, if only momentary, must be accomplished here so that the tension of the delayed imperfect cadence is heightened by the gradual prominence of 1st and 2nd and not through any disturbance of the intentionally uneven rhythmic structure. (Any accidental accent or change in balance can be avoided by 1st and 2nd entering very softly, and feeling that their entry is *on* the second beat, to which they simply supply the sound a quaver late.) 2nd must maintain support towards the rising phrase of 1st, especially when it reaches the octave B♭ and not to the notes of 3rd and 4th who must themselves avoid the temptation of joining the *crescendo* (the *diminuendo* hairpin for 3rd is to ensure that the note finishes inaudibly – as in bars 5 and 7 – and is therefore not the same as that marked for 1st).

By the fourth bar, 2nd and 4th begin their repeated answer to the melodic movement of the bassoons in third. This is not altogether an easy task for young players, especially when separated by the sustained note of 3rd, but Sibelius requires it in order to effect a smooth approach to the standard interlocking of the diminished chord at bar eleven.

In fulfilling all that is required of them in these few opening bars, the horn players are entirely dependent on one another and on each player's ability to predetermine the balance necessary both to the immediate sound and in relation to the voices that follow – an interdependence which may appear relatively simple when one is equipped with the full score but far less so when confronting only a single-line part.

In this respect it is fortunate that, nowadays, many young horn players are also proficient keyboard performers, often having initially embraced the horn as a second instrument. The sense of harmonic integration consequently engendered is invaluable to their understanding and performance in this pivotal position of orchestral wind playing, and many of the finest professional horn players are exceptionally complete musicians, with a very thorough and wide-ranging background of musical education.

However, the would-be conductor might begin to appreciate just how vital clarity of gesture is to the players, both in determining the precise moment of entry and in *not* adversely affecting any technical aspect of it. Whoever invented the myth that a conductor's mistakes don't show?

OCTAVE AND UNISON BALANCE

Octave doubling occurs much more frequently in this section than any other and usually, for reasons already stated, with fewer resultant problems of intonation. Nonetheless, successful balance is not always easy to achieve, especially at soft dynamic levels in low register. The following tense, but highly effective moment from the final movement of Tchaikovsky *Symphony no. 6 (Pathétique) (Ex. 9.7)* will often display rather too much of the upper octave.

It is an infamous passage for 2nd horn, made more difficult because the

EX. 9.7

player will have approached the note via a solo line in the two previous bars (often at a stronger dynamic than Tchaikovsky would have approved) and it must now be reiterated, *pianissimo*, in support of 1st. Responsibility for a great deal of the resigned desolation inherent in the following string entry also stems from here.

The difference in sound quality of the horn when pitched below the top two octaves of its range is decidedly more noticeable with young players, and this causes many of the difficulties of balance and intonation that may be experienced once the low octave lies within this area.

Higher pitched octaves at a stronger level tend to be less difficult to negotiate and are capable of penetrating the most powerful orchestration. From the first movement of the same Tchaikovsky symphony comes *Ex. 9.8* where it is much more likely that young string players will be incapable of sustaining the climax than horns.

EX. 9.8

EX. 9.8 (continued)

Perhaps the most famous example of the potency of a horn section in octave layout may also be found in Tchaikovsky's orchestration, in the opening bars of the *Symphony no. 4*. Here, however, although all the above holds true, a maze of additional problems faces the whole brass section and this formidable introduction will be dealt with in some detail in Chapter 16.

The interlocking of parts as considered earlier will, of course, regularly produce octave writing between the extremes of the chord, but may expose more blatant examples, usually between 1st and 2nd. To return to the first movement of Tchaikovsky *Pathétique* once more, the initial appearance of the second subject provides the spacing seen in *Ex. 9.9* in both pairs of horns.

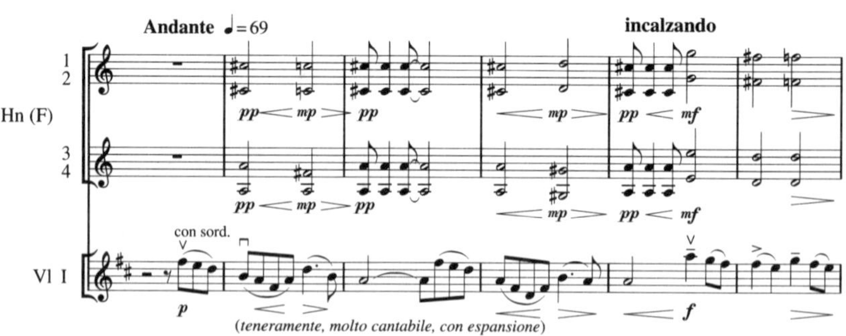

EX. 9.9

The breadth of this orchestration, engineered by setting the chords so wide and *not* providing the full harmony within the horns, is miraculous.

One final little devil of octave orchestration is worthy of remark before we leave this symphony. In the second movement comes this

EX. 9.10

which, from inexperienced players, often sounds like an embarrassing accident. The octave leaps are quite tricky to accomplish cleanly, but the desire to move off the first note sooner than will allow the sound to be placed is overwhelming. The clear articulation, by every player, of the first note of each group is vital, in order to make the passage both logical and inevitable in performance.

In many of the above examples, doubling of both the upper and lower line is apparent, and the unison playing that ensues is, again, a common facet of horn writing. The difficulties frequently associated with this type of orchestration for other instruments are generally far less apparent in this section for two reasons: firstly, the regularity with which simultaneous doubling of the low octave occurs within the same instrument; and, secondly, the more resonant quality of the horn in its most utilized range. While care will always be required, it is only in particularly high or low writing that the partnership of two instruments becomes specifically dangerous.

Obviously, the internal balance of the horn section falls prey to the same vagaries of perceived sound already considered in relation to the woodwinds, and which occur throughout every section of the orchestra. The difficulties of external balance, however, are an altogether different question. No section of the orchestra is required to switch its support from one group to another so often, or to blend intricately and balance with such a diverse range of instrumentation. The vital role of the horns in this respect will be considered in a later chapter.

Specific Techniques

BREATHING

While the general considerations of breathing discussed earlier with regard to woodwind instruments apply equally to horns and brass, the regular use of horns in extended solo passages and sustained lines of harmony makes some consideration of their breathing in specific circumstances essential. Whether by dint of their apparently effortless sound or because of the cumulative effect of so much poor writing in the form of 'blanket' harmonic background, the horns often seem to be given insufficient orchestral space in which to breathe. Such opportunities require little or no noticeable distortion of tempo but simply an awareness of the instrument's character and a corresponding fluency in accompaniment.

Perhaps the easiest way to illustrate this is by considering a passage which, in itself, presents no real difficulty in accommodating the breath, but displays the necessary continuation of line to preclude unsightly gaps or thoughtless shortening of notes. *Ex. 9.11*, from near the end of the first movement of Brahms *Symphony no. 2*, is ideal.

EX. 9.11

As in *Ex. 8.15*, from Tchaikovsky *Romeo and Juliet*, discussed in the context of woodwind instruments, some opportunity to breathe needs to be found within the long span of Brahms' slowly climbing phrase. In this case the first sub-phrase is of convenient length and, more importantly, is provided with a *diminuendo* (*Ex. 9.11*, bar 7) which allows the horn to take the sound back towards the supporting strings. The natural resonance of the instrument will allow a breath to be taken almost imperceptibly, before the written F in bar 8. At first glance this would seem to be the extent of the problem, for the four crotchet rests of bars 12–15 seem to provide ample opportunity for any further replenishment. Musically, however, the rests form the most potent part of the phrase and cannot be considered as any sort of relaxation of the overall line. Either the breath must be taken right through, to some point past the top A♭, or two shorter spans must be considered, the first covering just four bars up to the initial crotchet rest, once more making use of the required *diminuendo*. To use more than the first of the rests as a place to breathe will certainly cause a younger player to break the forward movement of the line by losing the musical sense of the unbroken phrase (this is similar to *Ex. 8.16*, the passage of recurring rests discussed in the previous chapter).

It is just possible, with superb control, to take the entire remaining phrase in one breath, but this requires an outstanding player and, even then, is only possible if the *ritardando* is quite subtle and only takes the phrase back to tempo rather than beyond. In practice such a long expanse is dangerous and rarely attempted, even if it is totally successful in rehearsal, for when it comes to the live concert the passage will certainly take a fraction longer to accomplish and the *ritardando* will tend to broaden. Just the feeling of extra time being taken can be enough to induce uncertainty here. Much more usual is for a breath to be taken after the tied written F in bar 19 of the example, even though it breaks Brahms's slur. Consideration of all other possible places will prove them to be fatally damaging to the phrase.

It will be noticed that, once again, the breath has been taken at a point of natural *diminuendo*, the subsiding phrase being used to disguise the gap and deceive the ear into accepting a sustained line. Such a technique is probably more successful on the horn than any other wind instrument, as the resonance of the sound lasts a little longer – a fact that causes the most common memory of horn sound to be one of 'roundness'. However, all wind players will ideally use a point near to the natural easing of the musical sentence as the place to replenish their air.

In the above example no adjustment is required from the strings to accommodate the breathing places. Indeed, as will be discussed later, the inevitable movement of the phrase in these instruments does much to help the solo player give an illusion of unbroken line. Obviously, as in all instrumental techniques, it finally comes down to a question of *how well* something is accomplished and not simply *when*. Tone and dynamic control, timing, sensitivity and musical understanding are equally important elements. The situation concerning passages which involve the full section, or any number of its members, is clearly identical to that pertaining to the solo instrument.

One particularly demanding aspect in the control of a *legato* phrase that occurs more frequently for horns than any other orchestral instrument is the extended cadence performed at a soft dynamic level. Of the many instances it is possible to quote, *Ex. 9.12* from the end of Suite 1 (Act 1) of the ballet *Bacchus et Ariane* by Roussel is one of the most difficult.

EX. 9.12

Except for the doubling of the lower line (4th horn) by *divisi* cellos, the four muted horns are solely responsible for the harmonic support of the first four bars *and* the formidable rising cadence in *diminuendo*. Every aspect of the players' control of breath – duration, sound, support, balance and intonation – is laid bare by this passage. It is extremely slow and, in performance at least, the final approach to the E♭ major chord will probably be extended further. The opportunities for breathing are minimal. One place exists for 1st (after the written C in bar three), and there is a possible place for 3rd and 4th in the middle of bar two (but this is so near to the beginning that it is of little help), but nothing immediately presents itself for 2nd. Obviously some relief must be found for a section comprising mere mortals, but this is likely to extend another aspect of their expertise, namely the extremely subtle ability to break a phrase without letting it show. 2nd *could* breathe with 1st (provided that 3rd and 4th don't) and 3rd and 4th might use the bar-line at bar 4, but both cases depend entirely on the support and control exhibited by the players around them.

A rising cadence within a *diminuendo* is always difficult, even if it is restricted to the leading voice alone, but this one demands it of all three upper lines in parallel movement. Such chromatic movement rarely allows either room to separate the cadence from its approach, or width to settle on the final chord. It is not only in the student orchestra that this passage, along with many similar, will demand a considerable degree of thought, practice and experimentation from the section as a group.

NON-*LEGATO* PHRASES

Generally, the remarks made concerning the woodwind in this respect apply equally to the horns, it being no less vital to sustain a line through passages that include short silences in these instruments as any other. The frequent appearance of repeated rhythmic patterns broken by rests of short duration is always awkward to negotiate without addition of false accents or distortion of line. The last few bars of an extended example of such writing, from Stravinsky *Symphony in Three Movements*, provide a useful illustration, the irregularity of the rests in this case increasing the difficulties of articulation by deflecting the players' concentration towards the (apparently) more pressing concerns of accuracy.

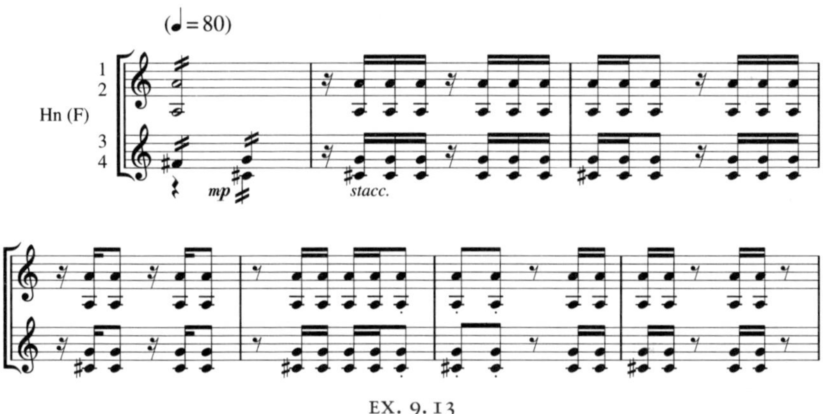

EX. 9.13

The composer's direction *staccato* ensures that all notes are of equal length, a fact that increases the desire and opportunity to breathe between the fragments by seemingly enhancing the apparent time available. In practice the very opposite will be the case, since a hurried and uncontrolled quick breath will cause the entry to be *earlier* than required. In music of such a vertical nature it is all too easy to allow the understandable obsession with rhythmic accuracy to obscure the real reasons for its absence. In the quoted passage, breath spans of the first three and last four bars are all that should be contemplated.

It is very unlikely that any member of the wind or brass would make a similar miscalculation as to the availability of breathing spaces in *Ex. 9.14* from near the end of Tchaikovsky *Capriccio Italien*.

In truth there is no less time here than in much of the previous quotation, but the forward drive of the passage becomes overwhelming.

EX. 9.14

In these, and similar passages, all clarity of delineation will be provided by use of the tongue and diaphragm in combination as the sole means of controlling the duration of air passing through the instrument.

TONGUING

The physical techniques necessary in the use of the tongue to articulate rhythms of various speeds and complexity are detailed in Chapter 8 and need not be repeated here, as the method of production remains essentially similar throughout the wind, horns and brass. The clear enunciation of every line will require this combined use of tongue and diaphragm, whether it be to achieve an explosive *forte* entry or gently to imply the most subtle phrasing.

Techniques of tonguing, especially those of soft and *legato* production, are a fundamental skill of all wind players. In the most positive application of the technique, essential to the performance of continuous short notes or particular rhythmic passages, all forms of tonguing considered in relation to woodwind are available to the horn, but the natural 'roundness' and 'weight' of the sound, determined by the length of the tube and widely flared bell, preclude the razor sharp edge to articulation that may be attained by trumpets or the double-reeded woodwind. In orchestral terms, this may be considered more of an advantage than a disability because it extends the versatility of combined instrumentation and allows for a wide range of colours. Thus, the single-tongued rhythm of *Ex. 9.15*, from Stravinsky *Jeu de cartes*, complements a similar articulation in the strings, and provides a combined weight that is available from no other orchestration.

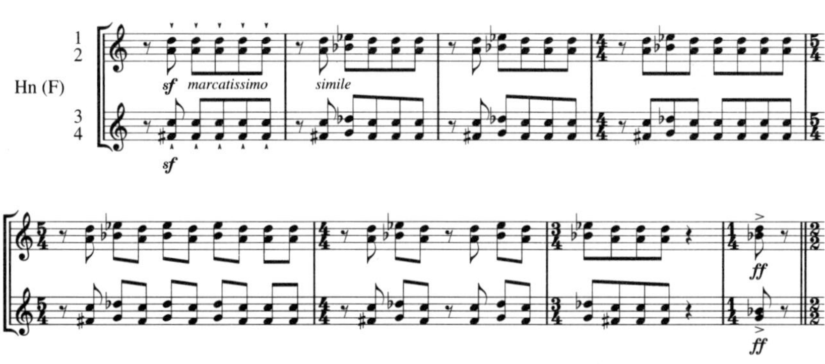

EX. 9.15

DOUBLE-TONGUING

Double-tonguing (described in Chapter 8) in passages of extended length is very tiring to produce and rather less effective in solo circumstances than is the case with instruments of brighter quality. Again however, in writing for full orchestra, it will add a weight and power to the centre of the scoring that few instruments can match. The following often-quoted example is from the Ravel's orchestration of Mussorgsky *Pictures from an Exhibition* and occurs at the end of *Limoges – Le marché*.

EX. 9.16

EX. 9.16 (continued)

The passage remains very difficult and, with young players, can show an audible deterioration in power if they are unable to sustain the breath and technical control. It is a fact of any orchestral *tutti* that the sudden loss of an integral sound will be very noticeable, and it therefore becomes vital that the initial level of all instruments is totally conditioned by their ability to preserve it.

In this example a loss of strength may sometimes be attributed to an over-enthusiastic approach to the first bar, which requires only moderate self-discipline on the part of the players to correct. It is equally likely, however, that because their overall technique is not fully developed, they will simply lack the necessary endurance – a situation that is considerably more difficult to overcome.

If, as is the case in many youth orchestras, six players are available (providing bumpers for both 1st and 3rd) then the passage may easily be divided between them, Principals taking the first bar, the first two beats of the third bar and the final chromatic scale, with the extra players taking the remaining alternate sections. With a little care, a similar system may be employed with only one bumper, by maintaining the use of just two of the available three players at any one time. Although it is more complicated to arrange, the use of overlapping responsibility can engineer sufficient rest for the individual players to make the passage successful. Any attempt at rearrangement that might include 2nd and 4th horns, however, is not to be recommended, as the passage lies dangerously high for these players – which is why Ravel left them out in the first place.

TRIPLE-TONGUING

Triple-tonguing can be very effective, especially in passages of rhythmic accompaniment as in *Ex. 9.17*, from the third movement of Rimsky-Korsakov *Scheherazade*.

The register and quality of the horn sound ensure that none of the warmth of orchestration is lost (as might be the case were the figures to be scored for upper woodwind) and that the compelling rhythmic impetus remains entirely

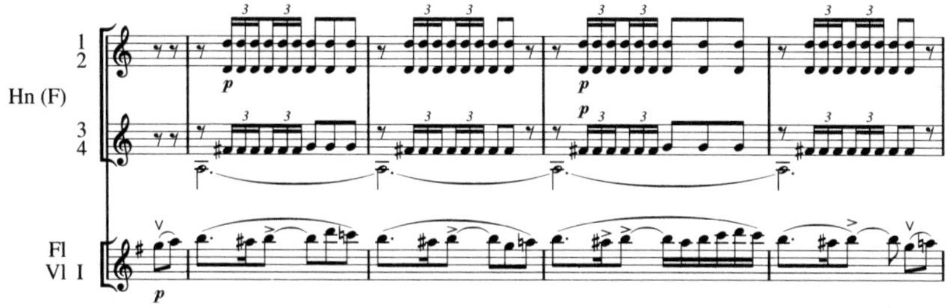

EX. 9.17

clear. Short phrases of this sort are comparatively easy to execute but, as is true of all tonguing, require a very positive articulation which becomes increasingly vital the greater the number of players involved. (Nowadays, mainly in order to clarify the second note of a fast triplet, many players will enunciate *te-te-ke* rather than the *te-ke-te* described in the previous chapter.)

FLUTTER-TONGUING

A technique reserved for very particular dramatic effect, flutter-tonguing is theoretically available across the full range of the horn but is rarely requested of extreme high notes and almost never of those at the bass of the instrument.

In the middle to upper range of the horn it is both effective and penetrating when orchestrated carefully, but the amount of air required in its production limits any ability to sustain it beyond a few seconds. *Ex. 9.18* from Walton *Symphony no.* 2 illustrates the maximum practical duration, especially considering the inclusion of an accented entry and violent *crescendo,* and is pitched, particularly for 2nd and 4th, in the ideal range.

EX. 9.18

EX. 9.18 (continued)

In this example, as is most frequently the case with horns, the demand for flutter-tonguing is combined with that of hand-stopping, which produces an even tighter and more rasping quality.

MUTING AND HAND-STOPPING

The use of purpose-built metal or fibre mutes is common practice in horn-playing and these will normally be kept close at hand on the floor beside each player. If very little time has been allowed between an 'open' and 'muted' passage, it is possible to hold the mute between the knees for a short time or even to play with it retained in the right hand, making an extremely quick change possible. A very similar, although by no means identical, sound can be obtained by placing the hand firmly into the bell and hand-stopping the tone.

With the hand forced firmly into the bell the pitch is raised a half-tone making transposition necessary for the player. The more muffled, closed sound performed at a softer dynamic and without accent or extreme force requires the hand to be inserted less firmly and will cause a lowering of the pitch by one half-tone, which will involve transposition upwards. Such niceties are often overlooked by young players with results that need not be catalogued here.

Markings which refer to the use of a separate mute always include the word in the direction – *muted, con sordino, avec sourdine, mit Dämpfer* – and are cancelled in similar fashion – *without mute* (very occasionally, *open*), *senza sordino, sans sourdine, ohne Dämpfer.*

References to hand-stopping are made by use of the terms *stopped, chiuso, bouché, gestopft*, and cancelled by *open, aperto, ouvert* and *nicht gestopft* or *offen*, although Lutosławski, in the *Concerto for Orchestra*, adds to this list by choosing to use *coperti* (muffled), a direction usually reserved for timpani and percussion drums. On frequent occasions written instruction will be totally absent and replaced by the symbol '+' for stopped and 'o' for open.

Apart from the different tone quality obtained by hand-stopping, the technique considerably curtails the duration of the horn sounds and its use in short, *sforzando* chording will add noticeable bite to even the fullest orchestration. However, the bell has to be stopped completely, and this can prove difficult for young players with small hands. Particularly for passages in the lower register, the use of a 'sizzle mute' replacing the hand reproduces the sound effectively, but the relevant notes will still need to be transposed.

The aural similarity of the two methods of 'closing' the horn sound, especially at dynamic levels below *forte*, has led to many muted passages being performed simply by hand-stopping, to avoid the somewhat cumbersome insertion and removal of a separate mute altogether. Indeed, a number of passages involving rapid changes from open sound to muted and back again can only be successfully negotiated by this method. Any attempt to follow Bartók's directions in *Ex. 9.19*, from the *Eligia* of his *Concerto for Orchestra*, although theoretically just possible (a mute does not have to be completely removed to become ineffective), would certainly lead a young player to disaster.

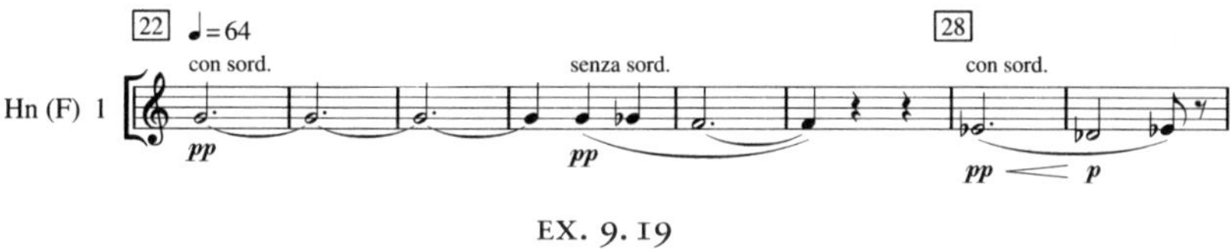

EX. 9.19

A practical solution is for the three 'open' notes to be taken by 2nd horn.

The normally meticulous Bartók is notorious in his requirement for the 'closing' of horn sound, intermixing the direction *con sord.* and 'hand-stopped' (indicated by use of the sign '+') with apparent disregard for practicality or even, on some occasions, sound. A little later in this same movement (bar 54) he appears to mark both at once. Unless this is the result of an oversight or simple forgetfulness, the only possible reading is that the '+' is here intended to denote a 'forced and brassy' accent (*cuivré*) to be performed in addition to use of the mute, a perfectly normal request but one that is here negated because there is insufficient time for the mute to be inserted.

The general situation is further complicated by the frequent occasions on which present-day composers, or those working within living memory, are reported as having changed their minds from the use of one method of production to another. One example, worth quoting as it cannot have been occasioned by reasons of convenience or expediency, is shown in *Ex. 9.20*, from the very opening of the second movement of Vaughan Williams *Symphony no. 4*.

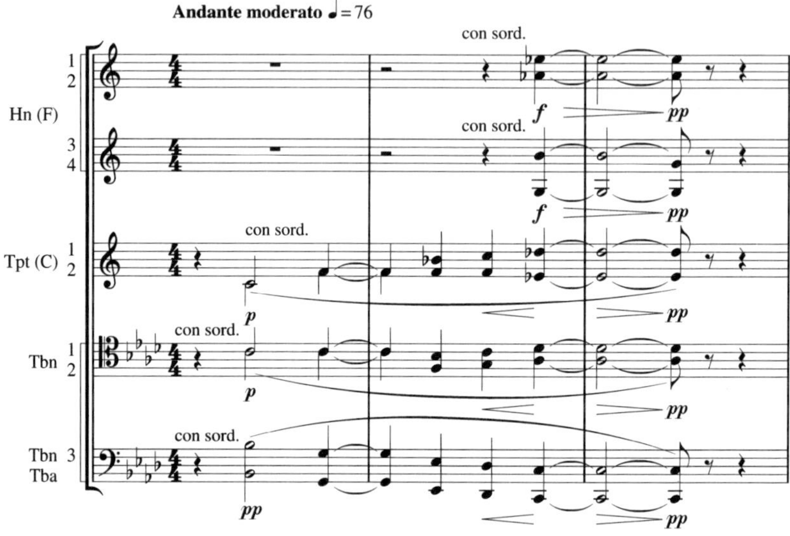

EX. 9.20

During rehearsals with the BBC Symphony Orchestra, the composer, who was conducting the performance, asked the horns to ignore the *con sord.* marking and hand-stop. Since Vaughan Williams had noticeably increased and dramatized the small *crescendo* in the 2nd bar, the reasoning behind this change might well have been psychological, in that the players were more likely to 'crown' the progression hand-stopped than if they were faced with the naturally more reticent marking of 'muted'.

Nonetheless, an attitude emerges that, in some quarters, becomes reminiscent of that already mentioned in respect of the muting of string basses: namely, that hand-stopping and muting are so similar as to be generally indistinguishable and therefore the use of a separate mute becomes unnecessary. In the majority of cases, and certainly in the Classical and Romantic repertoire, this is patently untrue and must not be sanctioned – any alternative method of production for Beethoven's only use of muted horn for example (the last page of the *Symphony no. 6*) would be a total misapprehension of his use of the instrument.

The French term *cuivré* (German: *schmetternd*) mentioned above requires a noticeably brassy effect which is obtained by causing exaggerated vibration of the metal through a combination of lip tension and over-blowing. It is regularly employed in combination with hand-stopping where the marking will be *bouché-cuivré* or *gestopft-stark anblasen*. However, it is equally possible muted, open and at all dynamic levels above about *mezzo forte*.

TRILLS

Nowadays trills are available throughout the range by virtue of the valves, but in former times they were only available in the higher portion of the range where the harmonics lie close together, so that oscillation between the harmony note and the tone or semitone above could be achieved by the lips alone. Such a method of 'lip-trilling' is still an essential part of horn technique and will regularly be used by the professional player in the Classical repertoire in preference to the valve trill, where the latter's comparative ease of accomplishment often loses some of the quality of ornamentation. Neither method produces a particularly fast trill when compared to those of woodwind or strings, simply because of the considerable length of tubing in use throughout the register, but trills can be used to considerable effect in the middle of the range when a certain ponderous quality is desirable. Their use at all pitches almost throughout the 'Ländler' sections in the 2nd movement of Mahler *Symphony no. 9* provides an excellent example, typical of the composer's inventive and masterly instrumentation. *Ex. 9.21* from Dvořák *Symphony no. 4*, is equally idiomatic.

EX. 9.21

With regard to the appearance of trills in horn parts of the Classical era, especially in works of composers before Beethoven, it should perhaps be mentioned that, contrary to the understanding promoted by many printed scores, it is by no means certain that horn trills would automatically have complemented those in other instruments, even where the range made them possible. In many circumstances it seems far more likely that they would have been reserved for the leading voice alone. Duplication of trills through a number of combined instruments is most often counter-productive and is unlikely to have been embraced as a general rule by Classical performers.

GLISSANDI

A rapid slur upwards through the harmonics produces the illusion of *glissando* and can be achieved across any given harmonic range. The effect can be very dramatic and is always used at a fairly powerful dynamic level, as in *Ex. 9.-12;22* from Stravinsky *The Rite of Spring* where it appears for each of the leading horns in turn.

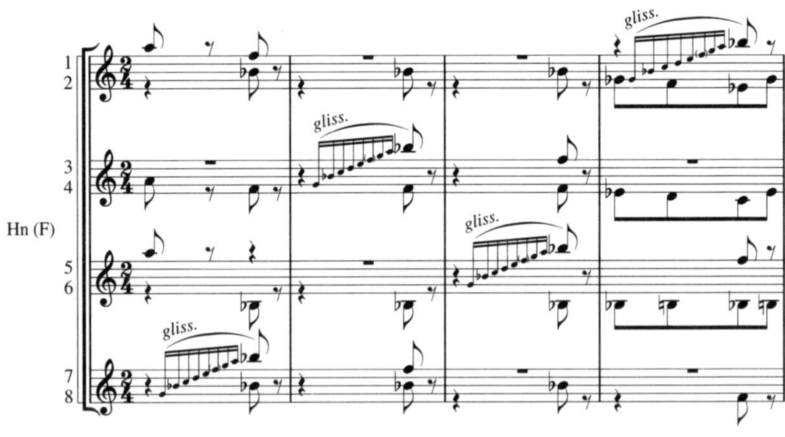

EX. 9.22

It is often accompanied by a *crescendo* marking, with the addition of an accent on the last (highest) note (which is invariably short). Because it *is* an illusion and cannot successfully be accomplished slowly or softly, the technique is never used as a *portamento* within a *legato* passage as is often the case with string instruments.

BELLS IN THE AIR

The exhortation to raise the bell of the horn to a horizontal playing position (*pavillon en l'air, Schalltrichter auf, campana in aria*) combines a number of different effects, not the least of which (but, regrettably, the most regularly ignored) is the alteration in the position of the right hand in the bell, and consequently, the removal of its control over intonation and tone. This, coupled with the fact that the sound emanates from a less restricted position and provides the performer with a totally different feeling, gives the sound a forceful and vital quality.

Generally, the technique is disliked because of the adjustment to the embouchure necessitated by the unnatural position and the loss of some control in the regulation of the mouthpiece on the lips, but it is a perfectly viable technique and need be in no way damaging if correctly executed. It is not enough to lean back in the chair and half-heartedly raise the instrument's normal playing position by a few inches – it is not designed as an aid to aural perception (horns don't need that) but as a sound in its own right. The instrument must be raised to a position where the tube is horizontal and the player must adjust the position of his or her head, so that the angle of the mouthpiece on the lips remains constant, and the hand can remain as accurately positioned as possible.

Beyond musical considerations, of course, the pure visual effect is incredible and, when the whole section is involved, care should be taken to synchronize the lift to an identical position.

The horn is the only instrument where raising the bell produces such a startling difference to the sound. Mahler's similar direction to clarinets, oboes, trumpets and trombones serves only to pierce the surrounding texture or tighten the quality. He does, however, take the visual aspect one stage further at the end of the *Symphony no. 1* by requiring his seven horn players to stand, a situation which, again, requires a certain amount of precise stage management, particularly as to the exact moment at which they sit down again after the final chord. They cannot be left standing like a line of coconuts at a fair, however quickly the rest of the orchestra may be brought to its feet.

PITCH VARIATIONS

Although the ambient temperature of a concert hall or rehearsal room will have a little less direct effect on the intonation of horns than on woodwind instruments, many of the comments under this heading in the previous chapter hold true in this context as well. The marginally greater variety of pitch adjustments available to the horn player (and discussed earlier in this chapter) is of little use in making short-term compromises with a cold instrument, especially to the young and inexperienced player, where the long-term concepts of chordal and tonal modification need to be learnt. In any event, faced with a situation in which the woodwind are unable to cope, the relative ease with which another section may adapt becomes totally immaterial. A working temperature at which all instruments may be relied on to display no more than their normal vagaries of production (quite enough for anyone to deal with) is essential and by no means difficult to achieve – the cost of heating a hall in cold weather is inseparable from that of running an orchestra.

More importantly for the horns, extremes of temperature will affect the amount of condensation that forms within the tubing, causing considerable variation in reliability and occasioning constant removal of slides and tubes in order to keep the instrument free of water. This very essential practice is no less disturbing to the players' concentration the more it is performed and it should be kept to the minimum. There are many young players who need little enough excuse to festoon their hand with gleaming lengths of brass tubing.

Related Techniques

EMBOUCHURE

For all brass players the embouchure *is* the sound, since the vibration of the lips against the mouthpiece is the only mechanics of production. Once again, this most fundamental of all techniques is beyond the jurisdiction of the conductor and lies with the player and the current teacher alone. The relative position of the mouthpiece on the lips and the apparent formation of the embouchure can be of no concern to the conductor, even in circumstances where obvious discomfort, limitation or other faults may be discerned.

VIBRATO

In the United Kingdom and much of North America the use of *vibrato* in horn playing varies from minimal to non-existent but the same cannot be said for many other places, most notably elsewhere in Europe where some schools of playing incorporate the use of very wide-bore instruments and a wider *vibrato* to match. For those brought up in a 'pure tone' tradition, extreme examples of *vibrato* prove very difficult to accept but, for the most part, such techniques extend to other instruments as well and tend to be nationally orientated, so that the whole orchestral sound is coloured by it, rather than just one aspect. In such circumstances the unaccustomed variation in sound becomes synonymous with an overall style and can be accepted very quickly.

Only if a mixture of playing styles is present within one orchestra (or worse, one section) does it become anything of a problem to handle, and then the effect on intonation, balance and ensemble can be considerable. Mercifully such a predicament is rare and, in terms of the student orchestra, will only be encountered on international 'summer camps' where care has not been taken to match the playing customs of the performers in advance.

Wagner Tubas

All of the foregoing applies equally to these instruments but their unfamiliarity to young horn players necessitates some scrutiny of their performing idiosyncrasies. Although Wagner tubas are required in only a handful of works the popularity of at least two of the Bruckner symphonies (*nos 7 and 9*) and Stravinsky *The Rite of Spring* makes them more frequent orchestral visitors than would normally be the case.

Over and above comparable challenges presented by the horn, the Wagner tubas confront the player with certain additional problems. As well as being extremely awkward to hold comfortably, they are difficult instruments on which to produce reliable intonation (a fact which is compounded by the inability to make adjustments by means of the hand in the bell) and, most obviously in soft playing, the initial release of the note is extremely tricky to control. Such characteristics present more of a problem because the repertoire is so limited and therefore players will not specialize in the performance of the instrument.

In the type of writing that appears for Wagner tubas in *The Rite of Spring* neither intonation nor soft playing present insoluble problems by virtue of the surrounding texture and the general dynamic level. However, their use in the Bruckner symphonies is an altogether different matter. In the wonderful opening bars of the second movement of Bruckner *Symphony no. 7* these instruments are entrusted with the first statement of the soft and slow-moving main theme (*Ex. 9.23*). Doubled by lower strings, it is one of the most memorable uses of the Wagner tuba and, once heard, it can never be forgotten.

This entry, which would be by no means easy at the best of times, is also the very first time in the entire work that these instruments play. To some extent the unison doubling of all parts in the lower strings helps to cushion the entry itself, but there can be no doubt that the tubas are, and must be, the

EX. 9.23

aural centre of this statement. The production of the initial sound, both in terms of balance and ensemble, is extremely difficult and cannot be attempted too softly; the marking is only *piano* and it is the *quality* of sound that will provide the feeling of this phrase, not the mere softness.

For 1st tuba the awkward intervals within the melodic line are immediately apparent but the considerable support that must be maintained by tubas 2, 3 and 4 to provide maximum control of intonation is less obvious. As is always the case, this becomes critical with regard to the final note of the phrase or any note that immediately precedes a breath. The phrase is also longer than it might appear from the printed page – these four bars constitute more than half a minute's music in most performances – and so, even allowing for the respite afforded by the sub-phrase in bar two, breath control becomes an important factor, and also has an inseparable effect on intonation.

Bruckner's writing for Wagner tubas is dominated by such 'chorale' passages, which require utmost control of all aspects of technique from the players and may sometimes seem to take little account of any necessity to breathe. Quite apart from having to sustain the third and fifth of the chord, in octaves, throughout the last eight bars of this same movement, the instruments earlier have to negotiate *Ex. 9.24*, which requires extreme proportioning of air from all four players, along with a very advanced ability to disguise those places where it must be replenished.

In both *Exx. 9. 23* and *9. 24*, the addition of 'contrabass tuba' to the quartet under immediate discussion will have been noted. The difficulties relating to the very general association of these two instruments will be discussed later.

One further point can be made here. It is quite often that one hears

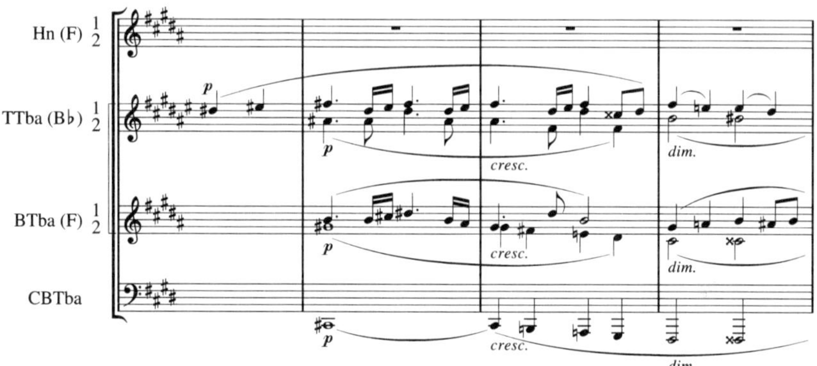

EX. 9.24

comment dismissive of Bruckner's orchestration and part-writing because of his propensity for heavily weighted sound and chordal doubling. *Ex. 9.23* bears close scrutiny in relation to this accusation, particularly the movement of line in tubas 2, 3, 4 and *divisi* cellos. Such writing can only have been based on clear aural perception and a deep understanding of the most felicitous scoring for each instrument. Note especially the overlapping of tubas in bar two and, in the preceding bar, the absence in the lower strings of 2nd tuba's sustained 'concert' F double sharp.

10 BRASS

Character and Influence

The 'heavy' brass – trumpets, trombones and tuba – show noticeably less sign of escaping from their historic roles within the orchestra than has proved to be the case with most other instruments. The fact that they are all so regularly employed in roles of climactic support or dramatic insinuation makes it crucial that the orchestral interpreter is fully aware of the exact nature of their sound and the unavoidable aural connotations of their use.

In any discussion concentrating on orchestral practicality it becomes unavoidable that some very basic generalizations need to be considered before one admits to the obvious half-truths that such statements must entail – especially in relation to an accomplished player. Of all the sections in the orchestra this approach is, perhaps, most necessary when considering the brass, and most particularly, the trumpets.

With regard to both timbre and range, the natural ability of this instrument to attract aural attention can be both dangerous and divisive to the overall ensemble. More than any other instrument, the effect of the trumpet sound, both intended and accidental, must be carefully considered in the broadest sense before its orchestration in any particular work may be examined from the point of view of interpretation and everything that entails.

For this reason it is necessary to start with a somewhat naive and primitive appraisal of the natural quality of the trumpet, for it is vital to understand and accept the often inescapable identity of the sound if true integration of the instrument is to be effected. In student orchestras it is not enough to leave subtleties of ensemble and the consequent variations of quality and timbre to the players alone. Left to their own devices most young instrumentalists will simply play the trumpet like a trumpet all the time – with potentially devastating results!

This very positive and regularly encountered threat to orchestral sonority makes it doubly important to appreciate the ever-present potency of the trumpet sound. Especially in the early stages of a player's development, the undeniable *bravura* qualities associated with the *sound* of the instrument will tempt the player, as much as the listener, to make an analogy with potent drama – after all, this very quality was probably what engendered the original desire to learn the instrument.

TRUMPET

As with the 'hunting' calls of the horn, it is the 'fanfare' style of the trumpet that may generally be recognized as the most characteristic sound. Once again its origins are to be found deep in the instrument's history, which stretches back to biblical times, and they have proved to be of lasting influence. But here there is a deeper significance, inasmuch as the familiar and distinctive timbre of the trumpet will almost always tend to waken associations with its historical use. The natural brightness and penetrating quality of the sound immediately flavours its appearance with a degree of undaunted optimism and assurance.

Although this inescapable impression might often be very short-lived, it is related to the trumpet's 'open' sound, in stark contrast to the richer timbre of the horn which requires the help of tonality and mode to become similarly evocative. The sound of the trumpet has for so long been associated with the summoning of spirited courage that its regal and authoritative voice will still induce the stirring of deep-seated emotions.

In a highly dramatized example from Walton *Belshazzar's Feast*, the flourish of three trumpets precedes the first words of the heretic king: 'Praise ye the god of gold' (*Ex. 10. 1*).

While we might be sceptical about such a directive in the light of our knowledge of later events, we are nonetheless forced to accept its inherent audacity *per se*. The same cannot be said of the beginning of the work, where a somewhat similar device, but this time on three trombones, heralds the prophecy of Isaiah (*Ex. 10. 2*).

EX. 10. 1

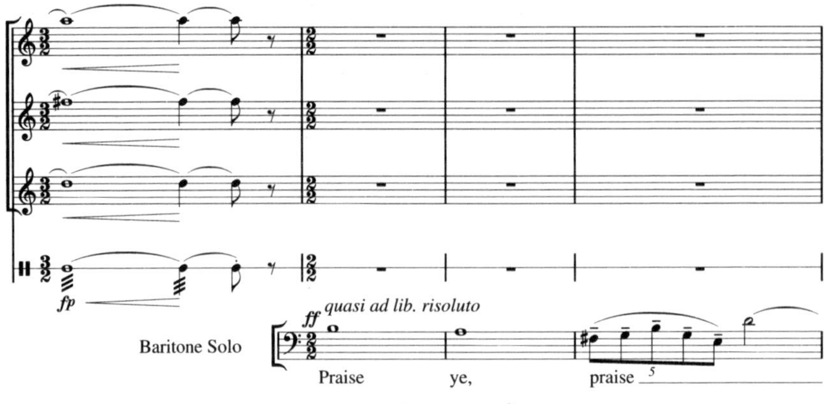

EX. 10.1 (continued)

EX. 10.2

In this second example it is not the relative pitch which alters our perspective, nor any lack of vitality or resolve, but rather the 'heavier', more ambiguous, nature of the trombone *sound*, which centres the attention on a dramatic statement that we are to embrace at face value, without adding 'scenery' to the narrative, as was inevitably the case in the previous example.

It is well worth mentally re-scoring this passage in order to be fully aware of the startling difference that the appearance of trumpets makes to our perception of the scene. With the trombones simply replaced by trumpets, the prophecy takes on an air of such immediacy that one feels it should be declaimed by Isaiah himself rather than the ageless, less personal sounds of the historians that chronicle Walton's parable. The scoring of trombones and trumpets together will be found to give a dramatic influence that diminishes the pain and menace of the original. The inclusion of horns, alone or in combination with the other brass, would subtly alter our perception of the meaning and could even be used to diffuse much of the power of the statement and add an almost benevolent aspect.

Any difficulty that may be experienced in imagining these changes of timbre might perhaps be helped by reference to a more famous, and clearly audible instance that can be found in the last movement of Dvořák *Symphony no. 8*.

EX. 10.3

Here, at the reappearance of the opening fanfare, Dvořák uses the sound of trombones and horns in order to 'turn' the extended phrase-ending from the trumpet-dominated fanfare towards the restatement of the main string theme. Compare this with the spacious feeling of anticipation achieved at the beginning of the movement by the more unexpected sound qualities of clarinet and timpani. Again, it is the potency of suggestion inherent in the trumpet sound which makes the changes of timbre so formidable.

With less literal insinuation than in *Belshazzar's Feast*, but no less evocatively, Panufnik uses four trumpets at the opening of his *Sinfonia Sacra*.

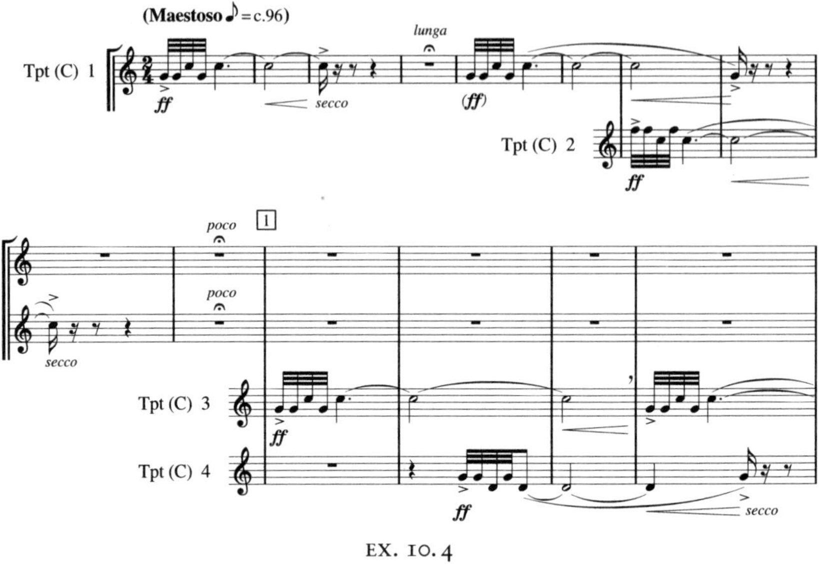

EX. 10.4

This work, which retains the soloistic use of the four trumpets throughout, highlights a further characteristic of the instrument. As already mentioned in Chapter 4, the players in this case are required to be separated, standing at the four 'compass points' of the orchestral semicircle (from the conductor's point of view: trumpet 1 on the extreme left, behind the 1st violins; trumpet 4 on the extreme right, directly opposite; trumpet 3 mid-way between the left edge and back centre; trumpet 2 in a corresponding position at the right side). While this positioning singularly enhances the symbolic nature of their use, it must be remembered that it affects neither their natural ability to be heard above the orchestra in some of the later *tutti* passages, nor the perception of their sound, except in relation to its source. In the context of the immediate discussion, and with such a distinctive example, this point is of great importance. The same treatment of most other orchestral instruments would result in a palpable difference in the actual sound heard from the four players, if only because of the variation of the relative angle of the sound source. While the sound of the trombone and, to some extent, the tuba allow them similar penetrative qualities, the higher range of the trumpet makes it unique in its ability to remain largely unaffected by orchestration or position. Thus the orchestral use of the instrument, from long before Haydn to the present day, remains noticeably circumspect, much of the time reserved only for reinforcement of climaxes, and a considerable amount of the remainder acting as an orchestral *agent provocateur*.

Even when exploiting the instrument in less familiar guise it is impossible to negate all sense of dramatic association. When used in its lowest range or at a subdued dynamic, the trumpet's sound evokes feelings of loss and despair more quickly than is the case with any other instrument. The physical sensibility of this passage from the 2nd movement of Suk '*Asrael*' *Symphony* is unquestionable, even when shorn of its processional *pizzicato* accompaniment.

EX. 10.5

This intentional dislocation of one's instinctive reaction to the sound is as emotive as the sound itself. That is why, especially in dramatic circumstances, muting of the trumpet becomes so effective, for there is nothing so disturbing as the subversion of dependability. The muted trumpet will often become more of a sensation than a mere sound.

It is only when the connotations of the trumpet sound are fully understood that it becomes possible to appreciate the subtle insinuations of feeling implied by the fact that, for example, theirs is *not* the first brass sound to be heard in Tchaikovsky *Symphony no.* 4, but it *is* in Richard Strauss *Also sprach Zarathustra*. Neither of these is a mere accident of orchestration.

Thus it becomes possible to see a little deeper into the genius of Mahler's famous opening phrase of his *Symphony no. 5*.

EX. 10.6

It is as much the *space* created by the instrument's sound as any harmonic or rhythmic aspect of the writing that demands a work of such scope. Once more, a mental replacement by any other instrument will suffice to prove the point.

It is not my intention to represent the trumpet as an instrument solely capable of triumphant fanfares and emotional drama. Such a ridiculous standpoint would not only ignore all other characteristics of the instrument but also denigrate its undoubted versatility and varied orchestral responsibility. Nonetheless, in order fully to appreciate its orchestral use, this unavoidable facet of its character and the awakening of our primitive reaction to it need to be borne firmly in mind at all times.

TROMBONE

Once more, because of the specific range of this discussion, it is necessary to diverge a little from the traditional approach to trombone orchestral history, which traces its logical development through opera, and devote some space to its appearance in symphonic music alone. This, after all, is the confine within which most young players will approach the instrument and it has considerable bearing on their appraisal of it.

The principles of the slide trombone date back at least as far as the early fourteenth century and quite possibly earlier than that. 'Sackbuts' (essentially the same instrument) were frequently used to support the plainsong of ecclesiastical services, and players were listed among the members of ceremonial bands throughout fifteenth-century Europe. Two hundred years later a normal set of sackbuts comprised three instruments, corresponding to the alto, tenor and bass trombone.

Throughout the seventeenth and eighteenth centuries, use of the instrument in choral music becomes frequent, and it appears in accompanying ensembles of varying size, from groups consisting of wind instruments alone to orchestras of strings, wind and drums. Both J.S. Bach and Handel use the trombone in choral music, though with apparent circumspection and never in a solo capacity. There is some indication, however, that existing trombone parts only contain music where the line differs from that of the chorus, and that elsewhere it was played from the chorus parts. Thus trombones might well have been involved in performances of some choral works where their instrumentation is not listed.

Whatever may be the relevance of such a hypothesis, the very close and natural association of the instrument with vocal music up until the turn of the nineteenth century remains clear. Understandably, perhaps, this heritage was largely maintained, and for the next fifty years the most widespread use of trombones was within the confines of the opera orchestra, whose repertoire is rather peripheral to this discussion. Only spasmodically did they begin to appear as an integral part of orchestral sound in the concert repertoire. Nonetheless, considering the ingenuity and discernible impatience with which composers developed all practical facets of every other orchestral timbre, the largely self-imposed restrictions which seem to govern their use of this noble instrument in the symphonic repertoire at this time remain hard to explain. It was, after all, the only chromatic brass instrument available until at least the middle of the nineteenth century and certainly, by virtue of the minimal winding involved in its design, likely to be the most pure and even in sound across its range.

While Beethoven was the first composer to introduce the instrument into the symphonic repertoire, his use of the trombone remains fundamentally within the confines outlined above. Trombones appear in none of the overtures except those directly associated with opera *(Fidelio, Leonora 2* and *3)* or choral writing (the 37 bar *Maestoso* introduction to the overture *Consecration of the House)*. As is to be expected, they are scored in the opera *Fidelio*, the great *Missa Solemnis*, the cantata *Der glorreiche Augenblick*, *The Mount of Olives*, the incidental music *King Stephen* (six chorus numbers) and, of course, the last movement of the *'Choral' Symphony*.

This is not to imply that trombones automatically featured in the orchestration of works that included chorus. Beethoven was far too aware of his mode of expression for that and they do not appear, for example, in the *'Fantasie' for piano, chorus and orchestra*, the *Mass in C* or at least three other cantatas, but the continuing overall association cannot be ignored.

It is remarkable that Beethoven should have left only five further examples of trombone orchestration: namely, the incidental music *The Ruins of Athens*, *Wellington's Victory*, the last movement of the *Fifth Symphony*, the fourth and fifth movements of the *Sixth* and the second movement of the abovementioned *Ninth*.

Wellington's Victory (originally composed for Maelzel's 'mechanical orchestra') is unique in the composer's output both for the size of its scoring in the orchestral version (which includes four trumpets and percussion) and for its unremitting programmatic content. It cannot be said to be in any way representative and, although Beethoven seemed to have retained some affection for it, it remains something of a curiosity. To consider it in direct reference or comparison to any other of Beethoven's works, or any particular facet of his style or technique, would be to risk conclusions both erroneous and desultory. For this reason it is best left to itself.

For the other four works, a considerable degree of choral association may be discerned in at least two. *The Ruins of Athens* music was written in the same three-week period as *King Stephen* and, furthermore, the March became a chorus when transferred to *Consecration of the House*. Despite the more progressive style of writing for trombones in the *Trio* of the second movement of the *Ninth Symphony* (they appear quite independently and at both *piano* and *pianissimo* dynamic), their appearance in a work containing chorus cannot be conveniently separated from this initial instigation.

The final movement of the *Fifth Symphony* is interesting beyond the fact that it is the first appearance of trombones in any symphony. *Ex. 10.7* shows the first few bars of the clarinet, bassoon and trombone parts with just the outline of the theme.

EX. 10.7

With the trombone parts thus highlighted and the movement of the thematic line less dominant as a result, the fundamental structure of the passage becomes more obvious. This triumphal principal subject is only a short step away from Beethoven's recognizable style of choral writing – so short a step, in fact, that it could well be thought that only the chorus is missing! All aspects of choral structure are present in the melodic range, harmonic unity and rhythmic scan of the passage, and it remains singular among the composer's symphonic subjects, both in the character of its sustained triumph and the emotional transcendence of its style. Perhaps if this implied chorus was actually present, Spohr and his earthbound contemporaries would have been less inclined to consider this finale as 'an orgy of vulgar noise'.

It is in the comparatively few notes for the two trombones (alto and tenor) in the fourth and fifth movements of the *Sixth Symphony* that we find the instrument first used as an integral part of symphonic sound, with no possible historic or emotional connotation. Although the writing might at first glance appear straightforward to the point of simplicity, few works before or since have embraced the trombone sound into the overall orchestral fabric so completely and successfully.

A totally different economy of use is apparent in this symphony compared to almost any other example of trombone writing to be found in the next fifty years. Although the instrument still only appears at a dynamic of *forte* or above, it is as if it is an organic part of the music rather than an effect that has been held in reserve for dramatic influence or colour. It is simply an increased *breadth* of harmonic expression that Beethoven exposes with casual mastery, especially in the final movement.

Until the year of Beethoven's death, other examples of trombone orchestration beyond the opera house or works involving chorus are severely limited. For all practical purposes they can be confined to Weber's occasional use of one instrument and the three in Schubert *Symphony no. 8* (1822). Although famously incomplete, this is the first example of trombone orchestration in a symphonic first movement, and would probably have been continued throughout the work – an intention that was to come to fruition in the *'Great' C Major Symphony* of 1828. In both these symphonies, but in the latter work particularly, Schubert's treatment of the instrument as an integral part of the texture, albeit within a very Classical concept, both extended the range of the orchestral brass to equal that of the other sections and displayed the immense subtlety of which the trombone is capable in purely musical terms. The delayed first performances – 43 years for the *'Unfinished'* and 11 years for the *'Great' C Major* – may well have proved to be two of the most unfortunate protractions in musical history, for 1827/8 also saw first performances from a composer whose work was to revolutionize the manner of orchestral expression and indelibly affect attitudes towards brass writing for the rest of the century and beyond.

The so-called Romantic period in music, which elevated the significance of direct emotional reaction and deep-seated literary association, began with Berlioz. It is a measure of the man as much as the ideology that, as far as the symphony orchestra is concerned, this new philosophy burst forth at an almost precise moment – the 20th bar of the *Grande Ouverture: Les Francs Juges* (*Ex. 10. 8*).

Even including Rossini's virtuosic scoring of trumpets and trombones in his operas (*William Tell* in particular), nothing could ever have been heard before to compare with the horrific intent of this octave statement. This was a work designed for the concert hall, albeit gleaned from an unfinished opera, and it registers a flagstaff so remarkable as to be almost alone in artistic history. The equally sudden addition of two ophicleides to the lower brass, a position destined quickly to be usurped by tubas, marks the birth of a further long-lasting association, bonding a weight to the trombones that few composers chose to weaken.

To say that trombone writing never recovered would be to over-state the case and, indeed, to deny some of the most sensitive writing for the instrument that regularly appears in the works of Berlioz himself. However, almost from this point on, the instrument shows signs of being shunned to some extent by the more Classically-minded composers of the period, an omission that tends to reinforce the instrument's association with just one aspect of its character and even qualify the appreciation of its use in other guises.

Even as late as Brahms such an approach is still discernible, as their use is stoically confined in both the First and Fourth Symphonies to limited passages in each of the final movements. To the almost audible chorus proclaiming the genius of Brahms in withholding the instruments, particularly in the *First Symphony*, until the sublime chorale, one can only incline the head in agreement, but perhaps venture to ask whether the glorious horn solo in the 1st movement of the *Second Symphony* is any less effective because we have heard the instrument continuously throughout the movement? Or, for the same reason, the oboe solos in the 2nd movements of the *First Symphony* and the *Violin Concerto*? Personally, I think not, and, without belittling Brahms' supreme understanding and use of the instrument, I will always feel a tinge of regret that a composer of such rare genius chose not to develop it in a wider orchestral context but rather to leave it almost defenceless against the indelible impression of high drama to be forged by the fire-eating Romantics.

Once again, especially within student orchestras, it is just as important that

Adagio sostenuto ♩= 72
Tpt (E) 1 2
Cornet (E♭)
3 Tbn
(C)
Ophicleide
(B♭)
ff
a 2
p

EX. 10.8

the appraisal of trombones and the attitude towards them is correct, as it is to have players of sound technical ability. Because trombones are so often reserved for dramatic effect and vital climax, young orchestral players (and also many of those who direct them) can tend to regard them as instruments solely capable of providing vivid power and dazzling colour. While this aspect of their character cannot be denied, it is by no means the limit of their expressive range. Of all wind instruments, with the possible exception of the clarinet, the trombone is the most versatile in timbre, dynamic range, colouring and intonation – especially in circumstances where it is free of the restrictions imposed by its unnatural orchestral partner, the bass tuba.

TUBA

The most recent addition to the 'standard' symphony orchestra, the bass tuba has yet to be fully exploited as a solo instrument and its role remains very much one of support and ensemble, although in this capacity much independent movement may be found. In recent years a more soloistic approach to the tuba is discernible, doubtless because of the appearance of some virtuoso players, but generally, orchestral solos are comparatively few.

The deeper mouthpiece and width of bore gives the tuba what might be described as a rounder, more ponderous sound than either trumpet or trombone. In this respect it is closer to the horns and the similarity becomes quite striking once the smaller Wagner tubas are used as an 'aural bridge'. However, as Piston remarks (*Orchestration* p. 287) it is probably owing to its great weight of sound that the instrument remains mainly associated with the brass.

In itself the tuba confronts the player with many challenges. It is a very difficult instrument on which to make any immediate adjustment of intonation, since it does not have any form of quickly adjustable tuning slide, although most orchestral players are adept at swiftly pulling tuning slides, sometimes in mid-phrase, to accommodate exceptionally out-of-tune notes. In some areas of the range, the fourth valve may be used to correct pitch, as may the fifth or even a sixth valve if fitted, but these are always provided as extensions to the range, and any pitch adjustment they might provide is certainly secondary and by no means universal. Furthermore, the design and playing position of the instrument cause difficulties of their own. The upright position of the tuba bell tends to shield the player from the sound and make judgement of dynamic very problematic.

Once more, it has to be said that the bass tuba is not the ideal instrument to partner the trombones, although use of the E♭ tuba probably provides the most adequate blend, and this unfortunate but perpetuated marriage has had a lot to do with the relatively slow orchestral exploration of both instruments. Particularly in the youth orchestra, where the niceties of playing in this combination are likely neither to be fully understood nor sufficiently well practised by the players of both instruments, the enforced coupling can cause a number of difficulties in balance and ensemble.

Many professional orchestral tuba players will have 'adapted' their technique in order to blend and balance more easily with the trombones, particularly in the critical area of *piano* chording. The total difference in quality and projection between the two instruments when played softly makes the problems of balance, intonation and blend extremely hard to resolve for all but the most accomplished players. These are partially alleviated by the fact that the tuba will almost always take the lowest note of the chord, a position where some predominance of sound is acceptable, but this regular role as a 'fourth trombone' in the orchestration of so many composers necessitates a subjugation of the characteristic quality of the instrument which is both difficult to achieve and harmful to its identity.

Unfortunately, this has always been the case, and its appearance in the symphony orchestra almost as last resort for this purpose alone is underlined by the fact that it remains the sole example of a section of one – the 'plus ones' (alto flute, cor anglais, bass clarinet, contrabassoon) of the woodwind section are far more closely allied to their partners in all aspects of design and technique.

It is only when the tuba is used in a solo capacity, or when the section is increased to include one or more directly related instruments, that the unique character of the sound comes into its own. A passage like *Ex. 10.9* from Richard Strauss *Ein Heldenleben*, where bass tuba is partnered by B♭ tenor, conveys a temperament that could be expressed by no other instrument.

EX. 10.9

Very rarely the tuba may be found in an orchestration which does not include trombones at all. Prokofiev *Violin Concerto no. 1* is an example. This particular work still employs four horns and two trumpets but resists the temptation to add the weight of the lower brass, exploiting only the more sinister side of the tuba's lower register.

However, there remains a great area of repertoire in which the instrument is most frequently to be found supporting the chording of three trombones or simply doubling the line of bass as in the case of the famous progression of chords that frames the slow movement of Dvořák *'New World' Symphony*. This somewhat problematic use of the instrument is so inextricably bound to the balance and intonation of the whole brass section that it most naturally leads to the next heading of this discussion, for which reason consideration of the instruments will be undertaken in reverse order.

Intonation and Balance

TUBA/TROMBONES

It must not be inferred that the association of tuba with trombones causes difficulty for the tuba player alone – far from it. The third, or bass, trombone is often considerably restricted in its approach to balance and regularly torn between combining with the related sound on one side or the totally dissimilar sound on the other. While it might well be argued that this is something that woodwind players, indeed, all wind players, have to deal with regularly, for trombone and tuba there often remains an essential difference in compositional intent. In terms of symphonic orchestration it is unlikely that the combination of any other two instruments is so fraught with the dangers of impulsive and automatic cohabitation.

The fusion of other orchestral timbres, while often just as expedient, will rarely expose the individual differences in sound production to such an extent, largely because the presence of at least two of each instrument allows for an interlocking of the parts which immediately diffuses the most vibrant characteristics of each. Neither is any instrument so likely to be added in terms of simple support of power or, in the case of 3rd trombone, articulation. Very frequently tuba will be added to a passage that is far more idiomatic of the trombone in quality and inference, or 3rd trombone will double one that is patently more suited to the tuba. This is further compounded by the comparative infrequency with which the heavy brass is used and the considerable 'dramatic' intention often implied when it is. Thus we arrive at a situation for both instruments where their inclusion in a passage of orchestration may well be demanded for reasons of dynamic, clarity or extended harmony rather than individual colour.

An extremely hazardous extension of this supporting role appears far more often than good sense would seem to dictate. There are numerous examples of passages where the tuba is required to add support to an already apparent chord of matched instruments, for example in the often-quoted last five bars from the 1st movement of Tchaikovsky *Symphony no 6*.

EX. 10.10

This is a very awkward role for any instrument to undertake, especially in so exposed a situation, but this example is notorious both because of the close proximity in pitch and the rhythmically uncompromising point of entry. There is also the problem of dramatic intent – what is really required is a mere 'sensation' of the tonic note but the tuba is not pitched low enough to comply, and is forced to take the role of the missing fourth trombone, attempting both to support the chord and to match with the sound of the trombones.

These last five bars must have placed the composer in something of a dilemma for he would have had no wish to discard the bleak significance of the second inversion chord, but the eight-times repeated scale of B major in the strings insists on a final chord with the tonic note in the bass. The scoring of tuba becomes almost unavoidable and its pitch predetermined.

That Tchaikovsky was aware of the hazardous nature of this delayed entry in practical terms may be surmised by his addition of timpani, an instrumentation which proves to be the saviour of this particular passage, especially when performed by a really first-rate player. It is an interesting piece of timpani orchestration, simply because it is not essential either to the musical or dramatic disposition of the work and is most likely to have been considered initially for the above reason alone. Cellos and basses could perform the last three bars with equal success and no apparent change in character. Neither are the timpani necessary in order to reinforce the tonic note in bar 3 – that is the sole purpose of the beleaguered tuba.

Where the combination of tuba with trombones works so much more successfully is when the tuba is entrusted with a leading voice, as in *Ex. 10. 11* already quoted with regard to tuba, from the last movement of the same work.

EX. 10. 11

Although this passage is by no means easy, the demands are mainly musical – control of ensemble, sound and intonation – as it is *relatively* easy to judge the balance from within the section because of the harmonic supremacy of the lowest line. Additional problems can be experienced in the eighth and tenth bars where the tuba approaches to within a major third of the lowest trombone. This layout of root position chords forces 3rd trombone to take the third of the chord (previously scored some distance above the bass note) immediately adjacent to the tuba, which causes the chord to 'close' and become very difficult to hear from within the section. These two chords have to be played with reference only to the levels of those preceding them as they are exceedingly difficult for the section to balance in isolation. (It should also be mentioned that the tam-tam has a role to play in this particular passage, certainly with regard to the initial balance of the section, and this will be discussed in due course.)

The famous quintuple *piano* is a wonderful moment if it really does lead to a resolution considerably louder than the approach. The *piano* dynamic at the *Andante giusto* is the key to this extraordinary marking and explains why *più pianissimo* or *molto diminuendo* could not have sufficed in the previous bars. The temptation to make this B minor resolution the softest point of the phrase can be overwhelming, but this can make it difficult to comply with the composer's instruction of *Andante giusto*.

The interval between tuba and 3rd trombone of a perfect fifth, as seen in *Ex. 10.10* and much of *Ex. 10.11*, is the closest that tuba may approach with any real degree of safety, and wider intervals prove increasingly preferable. These allow 3rd trombone to judge balance with reference to related instruments, and leave the tuba to provide support rather than direction to the overall symmetry. It remains, however, a deflection of the problem rather than any real solution.

At intervals wider than one octave, increasing separation of the two distinct types of sound becomes apparent until, unless the top of the chord is equally far removed, a situation of '1 plus 3' becomes not only obvious but also unavoidable. In itself this is no bad thing and will often prove advantageous to both the balance and integration of the tuba sound. Many of the most successful orchestrations of trombone and tuba chords will exploit the wide interval for this very reason.

The unique problem of this particular orchestral liaison, briefly considered above, only arises when the tuba is scored in close rhythmic and harmonic association with a section of three trombones. Once the tuba achieves even a small degree of independence, the situation for both instruments, as has been seen, becomes considerably easier. This is also true in orchestrations where the trombone section is decreased, or even increased in number. Bartók, for example, uses tuba with four trombones in both the *Scherzo* and *Marcia Funèbre* of the *Four Orchestral Pieces op. 12*, thereby allowing himself the freedom to use the instrument for its own sake, rather than being forced to include it to extend the harmony or provide dynamic support. All four of these pieces are worthy of close study in respect of where, and under what circumstances, the tuba is combined with a varying number of trombones. In the two movements mentioned it is noticeable how the tuba is withheld from almost any role in full cadential harmony or powerful rhythmic movement, and its infrequent direct association is essentially confined to octave support.

The comparatively rare orchestrations of tuba with only two trombones tend to separate the three instruments into two distinct sections. Although the tuba will still frequently be found orchestrated in harmonic combination with the trombones, the absence of 3rd trombone allows for both a wider interval between the two dissimilar instruments and an apparently closer association of the two trombones. This is partly an aural illusion – created because the enforced three-part harmony is less inclined to expose the different tone qualities owing to the natural predominance of the bass note and the non-existence of a complete triad above it – but it does allow the tuba to produce its natural characteristic sound with less need for 'disguise' in ill-matched ensemble. Effective use of this instrumentation can be found in Bartók *Dance Suite,* where a close association between the three instruments is maintained almost throughout, with a noticeable lack of ponderous weight. This simply achieved equality is characteristic of the instrumentation and explains why examples of its use are most often found in the concerto repertoire – Bartók *Violin Concerto no. 1, op. posth.* (the first movement of which is identical with the first of the *Two Portraits op. 5)* and, within the confines of an overall smaller brass section (two horns, two trumpets) Prokofiev *Piano Concerti nos* 2 and 5. However, the Korngold *Cello Concerto* might be cited as an example of how successful this smaller combination can be in an otherwise heavily scored and overtly dramatic orchestration.

The orchestration of tuba with just one trombone necessitates a much more soloistic approach to the individual sounds of each, even if this is not always apparent from the content of the parts – Prokofiev suite *Winter Bonfire op. 122 (*for narrator, boys' chorus and orchestra) and Poulenc *Concert Champêtre* (harpsichord and orchestra) are perhaps two of the most often-encountered examples in which the two solo instruments both appear in the context of an otherwise full brass section (four horns and two trumpets). Perhaps mention should be made once more of Bartók, who also uses this instrumentation in the *Two Rhapsodies* for violin and orchestra, if only to underline this composer's adroit manipulation of these instruments.

As has become apparent, all considerations of balance and ensemble concerning the tuba involve its combination with unrelated instruments. For this reason the combination of tuba with instruments other than trombones, as well as other aspects of its orchestral role, will be considered in the wider concepts of Part III.

TROMBONES

The situation for a section of trombones alone is, as might be expected, altogether more straightforward. Extreme problems of balance are encountered more infrequently and intonation, providing that there is a reliable and accomplished 3rd player, can be adjusted more readily than is the case with any other orchestral section. It would be a mistake, however, to consider that the absence of one particular difficulty makes the task in any way 'easy' since the same problems of aural assimilation and technical control apply to the trombones as to all other orchestral sections.

Without the addition of tuba, the role of the section most frequently undergoes a subtle but distinct change. Scores generally place noticeably less responsibility of a blatantly dramatic kind on the section, but instead, deploy it in a more exposed and refined manner. There also tends to be a less pronounced association with trumpets as a chordal brass group, especially in galvanizing *tutti* passages. This is not to say that the undoubted power of the instrument is altogether shunned – far from it – but other aspects of the section's combined character are exploited.

As has already been implied, the great majority of symphonic orchestrations involving trombones without tuba occur on the perimeters of the Romantic movement, in the works of those nineteenth-century composers who chose to continue writing within the formal outlines of the Classical style and those of the twentieth century who re-embraced aspects of it.

In many cases this orchestration, especially in the latter half of the nineteenth century, will admit a decided emphasis of two plus one, whether 3rd be actually designated as bass or not. Brahms' use of the instruments from the entry of the famous 'chorale' in the 4th movement of the *Symphony no. 1* is firmly in this mould. The 3rd trombone line is quite independent of the other two from the sixth bar on (complementing the string basses) and identical with that of the contrabassoon for the preceding five.

EX. 10.12

The wondrous effect of this passage has much to do with the way in which the trombone overtones are exploited and emphasized by the very particular placing of bassoons, horns and contrabassoon in the chord. But, once again it is worth noticing how three-part orchestration allows for exceptional width in the chording – over an octave and a half – without causing distinctive separation in the three instruments' sound. This clear example of the extraordinary cohesion apparent in three-part writing highlights the problems experienced once the fundamental role of the bass trombone is taken by the unrelated tuba.

From the point of view of balance the passage is not exceptionally difficult – although the lower E♭ and C of the bass trombone need careful control of sound and dynamic level – as the section can hear each other and thus intonation benefits. Perhaps the worst aspect of the passage is that it presents itself after some thirty minutes' inactivity with only five *pianissimo* bars of preparation.

In student orchestras, it is essential that this last aspect is thoroughly understood and prepared for, as it cannot be rehearsed. The difficulty of sitting still, in full view of an audience, for three long movements and then playing an exposed entry can only be appreciated by those who have done it, and inexperienced players *must* be given guidance in how to accomplish it. Mental attitude and physical control are as important to this passage as technical efficiency.

In the central, more sombre, range of the section, the passage of close-position chords from Kodály *'Peacock Variations'* shown in *Ex. 10.13*, works equally well, but the expanse of the passage and its identically repeated rhythm can make decisions of co-ordinated breathing a problem.

EX. 10.13

Even given the interpretative credibility of slight separation before each of the short notes, it is not desirable to breathe at every bar-line and a division of three bars, two bars and three bars is probably most preferable, even though this appears to break the phrase at the point of climax. However, in expert hands, the exact position of breath would be almost unnoticeable as it would automatically be incorporated in the overall technical approach to the phrase.

Such craftsmanship and control are not likely to be forthcoming from younger players and decisions must be based on the capability of the weakest player, for on no account can the section breathe apart. In this respect, choice of tempo has a considerable influence, especially in performance, where it becomes imperative that no interpretative impulse causes the variation suddenly to become very slow. This is where a conductor can seriously undermine any passage that requires extreme control of breath and cause many avoidable imperfections in performance. There is a golden rule for wind and brass: if you want it slow, rehearse it slow! Perhaps even more important than the actual speed there should be a sense of inexorable movement in the first two bars, before ever the trombones have entered, which will not only provide the musical sense of the phrase but also ensure a degree of safety by predetermining the position of each bar.

In this passage there exist further complications, one of which lies in the wide intervals that occasionally appear for first trombone in conjunction with the repetition of a single note for the other two. This can induce different articulation within the section and destroy both ensemble and balance. The alteration of notes by use of the slide rather than keys or valves and the extra fraction of a second that this can entail makes such a problem especially relevant to trombones and requires a sensitive response from the other players to avoid any discernible variation in articulation, dynamic or rhythm within the section.

In harmony as close as in *Ex. 10. 13*, intonation becomes a crucial factor for all three players (most especially 2nd – the C major to D minor chords of just the second bar), as does balance. Once again 2nd will probably have to make most adjustment and will often be too soft in non-professional sections. The role of the 2nd player in a section of three always proves very exacting in terms of balance. It is difficult to get an exact impression of the projected sound from a position sandwiched between two similar sonorities.

Exx. 10. 12 and *10. 13* both show the trombone section within a soft dynamic but considerable control is also necessary when playing loudly. The use of trombones in unison at *fortissimo* level is widespread and the need for the players to regulate breathing, balance, intonation and (especially) sound is no less important. The tendency to force the sound at any dynamic above *forte* is a dangerous by-product of both the enthusiasm of younger players and the technical limitations of the inexperienced. In passages where the breath span causes little difficulty, the necessary control of other aspects of performance tends to diminish in equal proportion. A fragment such as the opening of Walton *Belshazzar's Feast* (*Ex. 10. 2*), illustrates the point since, whatever potency this entry might command, it certainly does not license harsh and uncontrolled delivery.

Such a miscalculation is less likely to occur in passages that exhibit obvious technical difficulty, the concentration involved in one area of production helping to foster a similar attention in others. However, this is not always the case and, to quote another dramatic opening phrase – Holst ballet music from *The Perfect Fool* – both care and neglect can easily be displayed within the same phrase.

EX. 10.14

Any attempt to force the sound is unlikely to occur over the first two bars, where concentration on rhythm, intonation, entry and subsequent ensemble are paramount. But the 'pause' bar is an altogether different matter. A new breath, four 'easy' notes, an established pulse, and all attention to quality of sound can evaporate in a moment. To make matters potentially even more precarious, Holst adds 3rd trombone at this vital moment.

It is all too easy for such finer points to be neglected by young orchestral trombonists, especially when the often apparent need for volume can easily outweigh all other considerations. There are no circumstances where sheer loudness will gain advantage over controlled production, especially at a distance of more than a few feet from the source. But this is a very difficult lesson to learn, and very few young players, on any instrument, have any real control over where they are putting the sound in terms of true projection. Yet, almost regardless of power, energy, number of players or layout, one controlled sound will cut through blatant volume like a knife – and the greater the distance from the source, the more obvious it will be.

This need for positive control of projection is as essential in soft playing and is very much the difference between the section providing non-committal background of three related notes rather than a harmonic line that actually has relevance and influence. Passages similar to *Ex. 10.15* from the 1st movement of Bruckner *Symphony no. 7*, where three *pianissimo* trombones are entirely responsible for the harmonic direction, occur quite frequently, especially within this composer's works.

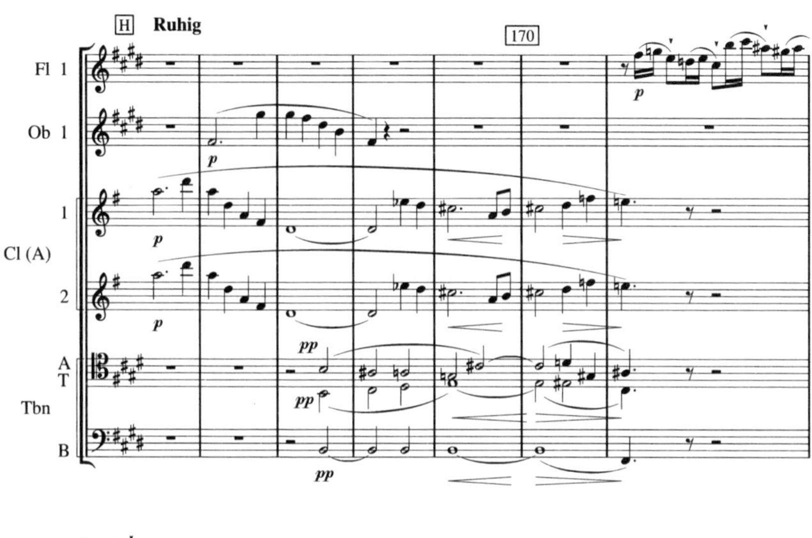

EX. 10.15

Although secondary to the melodic lines of the woodwind, both these phrases are undoubtedly soloistic in character and carry the greater responsibility for the extended modulation which continues beyond the quoted bars. Balance, in relation both to the trombones themselves and to the oboe and clarinets, must be perfectly achieved, and the insinuation of direction, support and harmonic significance subtly implied. All these things depend on total control of the sound, not just its dynamic level.

In professional circumstances this is a passage where the 1st trombone often leads the section in with a small, but noticeable, movement of the instrument at the point of entry, a gesture of unification that extends far beyond mere ensemble. This is a very important technique for the Principal player, for it procures an integration and control of combined sound that is unavailable by any other means, and some perception of its immense influence should be encouraged in even the most inexperienced sections.

In the hands of technically proficient and musically sensitive trombone players, passages such as the two shown in *Ex. 10.15* can benefit from the trombones playing a little softer than marked and slightly raising the bells of the instruments, in order to provide a 'layer' of sound upon which the solo instruments may work.

In any consideration of writing for three trombones, however brief, mention must be made of Schubert *'Great' C Major* and *'Unfinished'* symphonies, not only because of their historical significance but also, and far more importantly, because of their quality. Although the *C Major Symphony* might be considered ahead of the other in respect of the amount of playing, both works have few parallels in orchestral writing for the trombone – or for most other instruments, for that matter.

Passages such as *Ex. 10.16* from the last movement of the *C Major Symphony* stand almost alone in the symphonic repertoire in terms of the *legato* melodic line afforded to all three instruments.

EX. 10.16

Such melodic integration would previously only have been seen in woodwind writing, and it is here that Schubert's approach to the instruments is perhaps the most remarkable. The treatment of trombones in direct association with woodwind, premonitions of which appear in the *'Unfinished'*, is a characteristic sonority of this work and occasions many of its technical and interpretative demands. This specific and quite rare combination will be considered later; for the moment attention can remain focused on the section in isolation.

In the first place both these symphonies are often performed with 1st trombone using the alto instrument, a decision which is largely personal and not absolutely necessary by virtue of the closely integrated writing and generally soft dynamic at which the instrument is required to play in the upper register. (The main aural benefit of the alto in Classical repertoire comes at a stronger dynamic in the upper range, where it does not possess the weight of tone exhibited by the tenor.)

Here we begin to touch on a most likely area of limitation for the non-professional orchestra, for the technical ability and musical maturity required to produce a sound specific and relevant to a particular composition is rare among players of any age. In this case, the use of the smaller-bore alto might help the mental approach of the player concerned, but it is still not simply a matter of changing the instrument. It is the attitude of the player that must be correct, and this will often involve considerable adjustment of approach towards the instrument compared with the more common use of trombones in the general repertoire.

In addition, such highly integrated orchestral texture demands extreme concentration and control of articulation. One isolated example of this is clearly demonstrated in *Ex. 10.16*, where vertical alignment is just as important as line and the trombones must move with the same precision as would be apparent from instruments with a key mechanism. But an extraordinary variety of phrasing, accent and note-lengths is woven into the fabric of this piece, each example demanding similar care and accuracy. Given that the section is continuously involved in a piece lasting almost one hour, the degree of musical awareness and multiple responsibility they have to maintain is quite exceptional.

Thus one must be very wary of an interpretation that puts undue emphasis on the trombone sound. While this may offer a facile solution to a lot of awkward problems (by disregarding them), the work must not be approached as a trombone *tour de force*. They are simply another section of the orchestra.

One of the few composers of symphonic repertoire to embrace a similar level of sustained involvement coupled with such a wide variety of orchestral responsibility was Elgar, who seemed, quite rightly, to have no qualms whatever in his use of the instrument but maintained a keen understanding of instrumental custom. At the opening of the last movement of the *Symphony no. 2* (*Ex. 10. 17*), he adds trombones to the second statement of a long *legato* phrase in horns, lower wind and string basses, but addresses the direction *legatissimo* to them alone.

With 1st and 2nd using unmodified tenor instruments (as would have been the case at the time of composition and still is in some orchestras) this is not an altogether easy passage. While most of the wide intervals lie at fairly adjacent slide positions, one or two – including the C to F in the first bar – involve considerable distance and are quite awkward. Players of the modern tenor

EX. 10.17

instrument have a slightly easier time of it but this is largely offset by the extra care required in control of dynamic (*ppp*, once more for this section alone) and balance. These two aspects of the phrase are desperately important, especially in the student orchestra, as it is obviously not possible to play this passage truly *legatissimo* and, of course, only the lower strings can perform it without breath. If the trombone sound becomes in any way dominant the totally smooth quality of the phrase is lost. On the other hand it must remain an essential colour and cannot afford to be subjugated to the point of inaudibility. It is one of those frustrating passages where one should only be aware of an instrument's involvement by default. Played correctly it is quite unremarkable: played incorrectly or withdrawn altogether it becomes startlingly obvious.

As is so often the case it can be the most easily overlooked and innocuous passage, or even entire work, that conceals some of the most demanding playing, and Elgar's conspicuously virtuosic style of writing for trombones is no exception. This, for example, from the slow movement of the *Violin Concerto* is never easy.

EX. 10.18

The ingenious interweaving of the 1st and 2nd parts helps both the harmonic emphasis and the balance of this phrase and *should not be edited* under any circumstances: to do so would ruin the logical progression of both lines. Particularly at rehearsal number 50, the voice rising from A♭ to B♭ ensures balance and ensemble of the quaver in a way that would not be possible if it were to commence with the upper note.

It is probably with regard to trombones that the rare temptation to realign the parts is at its most acute, but it is generally wise to resist it, especially when approaching scores by composers writing in the first half of the twentieth century, who were generally eminently literate in matters of orchestration.

One example, sometimes changed in order to ease the problems of intonation for both players, occurs at the beginning of Stravinsky *The Firebird* shown in *Ex. 10. 19(a)* in the more clearly printed 1945 version, now complete with the previously implicit semiquaver rests.

EX. 10. 19 (a)

EX. 10. 19 (b)

(b) can be made to sound identical to (a) *provided that both players are fully aware of how much the articulation is dependent on the original scoring.* Even here it is not entirely justified because elsewhere the structural interval of an augmented fourth remains in the same voice throughout.

In terms of difficulty, however, there remain many passages where the eye is not deceived so easily. Few composers would risk *Ex. 10. 20* from the Elgar symphonic study *Falstaff.* This one is as difficult as it looks!

For practical purposes, given a student orchestra good enough even to attempt the work, this passage can be carefully and surreptitiously divided across the section, both to allow some space to breathe and to increase the rhythmic control. Such respite can only be minimal; no player can afford to stop for more than three notes at most (playing up to and including a main beat of the bar and rejoining at the next), and at least two players must be involved

EX. 10.20

at all times. In addition, all three players must start and finish the passage. This last proviso is essential for both the balance and rhythm of the initial entry and the climax of the *crescendo* – in other words the first two bars and last two and a half bars *must* be *tutti*. Although such carefully planned division of responsibility can ease the situation for each individual player, new problems will be encountered for the section as a whole. There must be no discernible false accents or sudden variations in dynamic level, and the passage must sound continuous, uninterrupted and, above all, fluent.

Writing for larger or smaller sections of trombones has already been discussed. There remains only the question of choice of instrument in the more Classically orientated repertoire for 1st (and possibly 2nd) trombone, as has been referred to above.

Nowadays, for reasons of both sound and balance, many examples of the Classical repertoire are performed with 1st trombone using the alto instrument, and many professional players will extend its use to include the symphonies of Schubert, Schumann, Brahms and Berlioz, among others. In these circumstances there might at first appear very good reason for 2nd to use the smaller-bore tenor (the old standard instrument without the B♭/F valve) but, as previously mentioned, this need not be an automatic choice.

It is crucial for the player to be familiar with the technical requirements and idiosyncrasies of the alto instrument. It must be emphasized that, especially for the young player, the alto trombone is not a standard alternative instrument, as is the case when clarinets swap from the B♭ to the A, but one that needs to be learnt. Most students undertaking full-time specialist training on tenor trombone (as distinct from specialization on bass) should possess one, or at least have an instrument available for fairly regular practice. This tends not to be the case for the average student, however, and, unless a player of high standard is available and considerable notice is given, a satisfactory performance on alto trombone cannot be achieved.

The small-bore tenor instrument, which might be considered as an alternative for 2nd, is fairly easy to obtain but its relevance is not as obvious as might be thought. The alto trombone is (as it was always conceived to be) simply an extension of the upper range of the tenor and a means of making high notes safer because they appear lower in the instrument's harmonic series. Many modern examples now retain a much more recognizable trombone sound than their predecessors, even those built a few years ago, and it is this which should determine the choice of instrument to partner it. If an instrument produces the thinner, 'trumpet-like' quality associated with some of the older altos, then the small-bore tenor is probably preferable for 2nd. If a high-quality modern instrument is used, especially in the hands of a really good player, it is often better to balance it with the wider-bore modern trombone. Fundamentally, balance and quality of sound are paramount, and must be the overriding criteria in any choice of instrument.

The common misapprehension that the alto trombone is a softer instrument than the tenor should also be laid to rest. Of all the qualities perhaps its extreme *fortissimo* is the most surprising, and it has always been capable of holding its own in even the most powerful orchestration.

No consideration of the instrument's use can be complete without some reference to the widespread interest in 'authentic instrumentation', even though such extremes of technical adjustment and instrumental availability lie outside the boundaries of this discussion. Mainly because of their size, but also because of their most frequent dramatic orchestration, modern trombones are among the first instruments to face accusations of being too big, too round and too potent to play anything before Richard Strauss. This, of course, is fundamentally untrue, and only in the hands of an insensitive player need they exhibit any tendency towards inappropriate sound. An accomplished player will, in fact, find it easier to play softer and more subtly on these instruments than on their predecessors.

Thus the choice of alto trombone in the modern symphony orchestra for performance of works by Brahms, for example, is basically at the discretion of the player and will depend on his or her preference for the instrument with regard to particular range or sounds. Some professional players find *Ex. 10.21* from the last movement of Brahms *Symphony no. 2* more fluent and penetrative on the alto.

EX. 10.21

It is also perfectly possible on the modern tenor and many players would prefer it. However, once chosen, the same instrument will be used throughout the work, and *Ex. 10.22* (from the 1st movement) is intensely difficult from the point of view of intonation on alto.

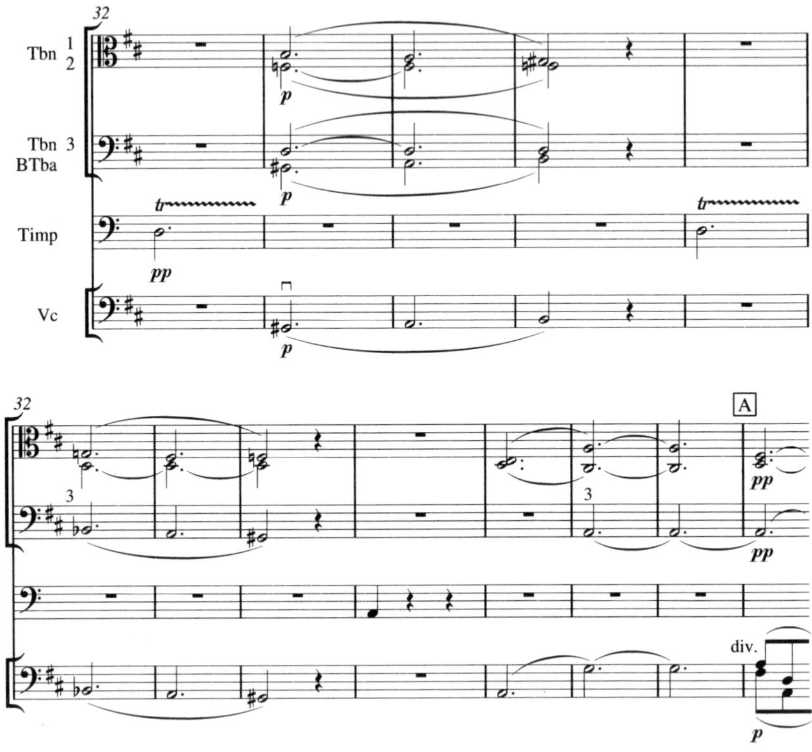

EX. 10.22

The reason for choice, therefore, stems from a largely esoteric combination of psychological and technical approaches to various aspects of a work's character and demands.

For student orchestras, practical considerations, even beyond those already discussed, need to be borne in mind. It will not generally prove beneficial to the progressive experience of the orchestra as a whole to withhold a work purely because an ideal alternative instrument is unavailable to one section. Equally, due regard must be given to the player involved. For trombones, it is possible that a player may attempt very high parts on the wide-bore instrument with limited success, or may want to use the alto when not fully capable. Either situation can cause unnecessary anxiety together with a mistaken impression of the demands of the passage. All aspects need to be thought through and the final decision must be made according to the prevailing circumstances.

TRUMPETS

When considering the trumpets as an independent section, it would be helpful to look at the requirements for three or more instrumentalists in isolation from the quite distinct tasks that confront just two.

The Triple Section

In purely musical terms the difficulties of balance and intonation faced by a section of three trumpets (nowadays the most common combination) will not differ greatly from those already outlined for trombones. The vertical distribution of notes for any three identical instruments playing together will always appear very similar, and in the case of an instrument capable of such penetrating and vital articulation, the disposition of three trumpets in close triadic movement remains prevalent.

Most frequently the preferred layout of parts will be with 1st taking the upper note and 3rd the lower. Immediately following the previously quoted passage from Kodály *'Peacock Variations'* (*Ex. 10.13*), three trumpets take over the theme from trombones, in identical layout and articulation (*Ex. 10.23*).

EX. 10.23

Once again co-ordinated breathing becomes the initial problem and, for this slightly longer passage, a division of three bars, two bars, three bars and two plus two (to allow room for the *sostenuto*) is preferable. It will be noticed that this takes the breath *over* the climax of the phrase – a different solution from that suggested for trombones – but the phrase is longer in this version, the *crescendo* extended by a bar (two bars in the parts) and the woodwind entry points the climax of the variation, not just the phrase.

Individual differences in articulation will not be so troublesome for trumpets as trombones, because the valve-mechanism ensures that, in this context, the production of an interval and the reiteration of the same note remain more similar. Intonation, however, becomes equally demanding, this time for 3rd as much as 2nd, especially the wide intervals of the fourth and fifth bars, which require considerable aural concentration and skill.

The intonation of the sustained chords in this variation is made more problematic because of the short notes preceding them. For inexperienced players the ability to return to an identical chord in each of the first three bars (D minor for trombones or F♯ major for trumpets) can prove particularly elusive. This type of chordal instrumentation relies heavily on the players' understanding of the idiosyncrasies of particular chord layouts (as discussed in Chapter 8) and on their total confidence in each other, which can be achieved only through the familiarity of regular performance together.

Examples of this same close, chordal instrumentation can be found where the responsibilities of 2nd and 3rd trumpets are reversed. With the exception of just two isolated chords, all the writing for three trumpets in Boris Blacher *Orchestral Variations on a Theme of Paganini* pitches 3rd between the other two, and keeps 1st and 2nd at least a fourth apart at all times. *Ex. 10.24* from the end of the work is typical.

EX. 10.24

This layout shows a conspicuous link to the Classical association of just two trumpets, with the 3rd instrument being used to provide the 'added' notes between the other two, rather than redistributing the chord – harmonically interlocking the extra players in much the same way as evolved for the two pairs of horns. The first chord in the bar of the pause shows one of the two lone departures in this work from an otherwise general practice. This can only be to retain the parallel upward scale, commenced by 1st and 2nd in the previous bar. Neither this arrangement nor that described in relation to *Ex. 10.23* causes particular difficulty, although most 2nd players would prefer to keep the more immediate aural association with 1st that is provided by the most usual distribution of 1st, 2nd, 3rd in descending order of notes.

Once again it may be seen that many of the most sensitive decisions of balance fall to the 2nd player, as the axis of any triple section and the foundation of a double. For student players the difficulty of this position is so often aggravated by the awkward range of the part and the frequently demanded 'presence' of the trumpet sound. As has been remarked elsewhere, it takes a very technically complete player to fill this position adequately and provide not only enough sound but also exact parity in quality.

Although the section of three trumpets is frequently orchestrated in this manner of concerted triads, opportunity will also be taken to divide passage-work across the section. A quite complex example of this from Britten *Four Sea Interludes* was included in Chapter 4 (*Ex. 4. 11*) to illustrate the range often expected of 3rd. For specific consideration of the techniques involved, a more serviceable passage might be *Ex. 10.25* from the *Scherzo* in the second movement of Rachmaninov *Symphony no. 3*.

EX. 10.25

As with so many passages of this type, imperfections in performance can most often be attributed to late breathing and the overwhelming desire on the part of each player to hear the completion of the immediately previous passage *before* starting their own. Both errors are equally fatal, and a combination of the two – the most likely initial response from student players – will undoubtedly cause the passage to collapse.

As far as breathing is concerned it is well worthwhile impressing on a non-professional section that there is *no* opportunity for breath within the scope of this passage, and insisting on at least one continuous run of the phrase (a six-bar breath span at this tempo is no great feat of endurance). While it remains true that almost all professional players will be seen to take a very shallow top-up of air in the rests, the situation is not at all comparable. Firstly, as is obvious, their technique will be so complete that the intake of breath will be integral and will certainly not adversely affect the production or position of any sound. Secondly, whatever they might appear to do in relation to the actual intake of air, they most certainly *will not* have relaxed their muscular support of the diaphragm. This, beyond anything, is the key to the immediacy of production.

With regard to any aurally based difficulties that might be experienced with this, or comparable examples, the concentration of each player must be on the rhythmic position of personal entry alone and take no account of what might come before or after. If the direction is clear, a passage like this will benefit from the simple dictum 'Play with what you *see* not what you *hear*!'

As with trombones, the separation of three trumpet parts into a definite division of 'two plus one' is quite common, indeed it is often enforced, as in *Ex. 10.25*, by the demand for a different instrument. However, the situation will frequently arise even when three identical instruments are to be employed, the only difference being that 2nd is equally as likely to be in direct association with 3rd as with 1st. In *Ex. 10.26*, from *Sirènes*, the third of Debussy *Trois Nocturnes*, such division is accentuated by the addition of mutes to the two secondary parts.

EX. 10.26

A passage of this sort, no matter how small and subordinate it might appear in the overall context of a work, places 2nd trumpet in a Principal position as far as all aspects of ensemble are concerned. The articulation, intonation and balance of these two voices, the latter with regard to both the combined level and its relevance to 1st, all rely on the ability of this player to judge the requirement precisely and successfully.

The Enlarged Section

The augmentation of the trumpet section to four players or more causes few new difficulties of balance or ensemble, but it might well exaggerate some of those already discussed. Much of the time the section will be found to be divided two plus two – trumpets 3 and 4 interlocked with 1 and 2 – as in *Ex. 10. 27* from Roussel *Bacchus et Ariane* (suite no. 1).

EX. 10.27

This layout corresponds to the standard arrangement for four horns, but it is nowhere near so universal for trumpets, as may be seen from *Ex. 10.28* taken from the same work. (Note how the associated horn writing still maintains the customary division.)

EX. 10.28

However, in a section of four, it will still be 3rd trumpet who is most regularly called on to play any solo passage work not assigned to 1st. In *Ex. 10. 29*, also from *Bacchus et Ariane*, the almost automatic division of the melodic line between 1st and 3rd causes 2nd to be placed right at the top of the instrument.

EX. 10.29

Division of this sort would hardly be considered for horns, where 2nd or 4th would complete the thematic line (simply by reason of its range) and 3rd would be assigned the high, rising figure.

Such ever-changing responsibility within the section will be found more frequently in trumpet writing than for any other orchestral instrument, and places considerable demands of flexibility on each of the players involved. Unless some unjustified and complicated redistribution of the parts is to be considered, it is essential to have a 2nd trumpet who can equal 1st in both range and control. The very marked specialization of the 'low' and 'high' ranges of the instrument, so often applied to horns and trombones, is rarely apparent in the scoring of trumpets once the section comprises more than two players.

The last three examples have been taken from the same work in order to underline the lack of any established practice and, therefore, the frequency with which the individual roles may change – it should not be taken to infer that Roussel's treatment of the larger section differs in essentials from that of any other composer.

Directly contrary to what might be expected, the distribution of passage-work tends to be *less* complicated when four players are called for, since the main purpose in augmenting the section is to increase its harmonic potential. Octave support is very noticeable however, both in separated passages for each pair, and for the section as a whole. In the latter case the 'horn layout' (1st = 3rd, 2nd = 4th) is almost universal and 3rd will only rarely be required to double the lower octave. This most difficult combination figures so prominently in the technique of two players alone that it is best dealt with under that heading.

The Double Section

For the inexperienced player the Classical section of two trumpets proves by far the most daunting. Mostly because they have to combine with a restricted orchestral sonority, the accuracy, control and concentration demanded of this small section is generally formidable, since the sound they produce is so instantly recognizable and penetrating, and the range of their melodic lines frequently limited. This style of writing, in which the two trumpets are required to undertake a fundamentally harmonic role, highlights the very considerable difficulties that always exist for any two instruments in direct combination.

Mention has already been made of the dangers that face inexperienced players in this repertoire when they perform orchestral parts that *look* undemanding. It is necessary to consider this in a little more detail in order to place it in its correct perspective, as a *technical* problem. Instrumental technique cannot be taken just to relate to the physical movements associated with the production of sound; equally important are the control of immediate preparation and the players' regulation of the primary motor force – that is, those parts of their anatomy directly responsible for the production of sound – for it is always in deceptively easy circumstances that this overall control is most liable to break down, whether through lack of concentration, misplaced self-confidence or simple ignorance.

Any orchestral score in Classical style will display trumpet parts consisting of isolated notes in unison, fifth or octave – the most difficult intervals in terms of balance and intonation. This in itself has to be an accepted part of the trumpet player's lot and, were it to be confined to the simple limitation of notes and intervals, it would demand only passing concern here. But further examination quickly reveals the empty bars between the entries, the periods of non-involvement that regularly account for more than three-quarters of the work. In *Ex. 10.30*, for instance, 54 bars into the second movement of Beethoven *Symphony no. 1*, the totally exposed *pianissimo* concert Gs are the trumpets' first contribution to the movement.

Even had the instruments been playing continuously up to this point these bars would remain difficult, especially for 2nd, where intonation and positive

EX. 10. 30

response at so low a pitch and subdued dynamic are decidedly awkward. However, when they have not played for more than a quarter of the movement, the situation becomes positively dangerous, particularly if the instruments have thoughtlessly been allowed to go cold or the mouth and lips to dry.

Ex. 10.30 also illustrates a particularly difficult instance of the octave distribution referred to above, so often found in the writing for any two similar instruments together. The responsibility that falls on 2nd trumpet to judge instantly the exact supporting level, absolutely in tune, is total. All that can possibly help here is a quality timpanist, one who is capable of providing a 'linear' rhythm with the resonance and harmonic stability necessary for the trumpets to combine. Perhaps the one advantage in this example is the strong rhythmic delineation of both the approach to the entry and the moment of production itself. On an instrument that tends to speak so distinctly, it does not help to introduce any flexibility at the moment of production.

The first entry of the solo piano in Brahms *Piano Concerto no. 1* is accompanied by trumpets and timpani alone, once more *pianissimo* and low on the instrument. *Ex 10. 31* is not as difficult as *Ex. 10. 30* from the point of view of intonation and production, as it is approached, without pause, from the end of the *tutti*. However, the inevitable rhythmic flexibility of the solo line, albeit minimal, makes exact placing of the notes no easy task.

In both these examples, and almost throughout the repertoire involving two trumpets alone, considerable help may be obtained by the physical placing of the two instrumentalists within the orchestra. Especially in the case of student orchestras, lone trumpets should not be left on the high, exposed levels above the woodwind but rather, wherever possible, should be brought right down to the stage floor, so that they play virtually into the back of the string players. This allows them to play at a slightly higher and more natural dynamic level and also reduces the risk of tentative production caused by feelings of musical isolation. It will not affect their regular association with timpani. Such a solution cannot be considered when trombones are included

EX. 10.31

in the orchestration (unless the orchestra is arranged on one level anyway) because of the need to combine and balance the brass as a whole. The quasi-Classical trumpet writing of composers such as Dvořák, and even Tchaikovsky in his earlier style, can rarely be helped by any physical repositioning.

Both *Exx. 10.30* and *10.31* refer to totally exposed *pianissimo* passages, but the situation is only slightly less acute at all dynamic levels and unless the techniques of preparation are taught and those of producing single, isolated notes accurately first time are practised, this style of repertoire will prove to be the undoing of many inexperienced players.

Trumpets and Cornets

The addition of cornets to the trumpet section will only occur when the rest of the brass section is in evidence, and direct harmonic association with trumpets will only take place with duplication of one or other instrument (2 cornets with 1 trumpet, 2 trumpets with 1 cornet, 2 of each, etc.). As such, general problems of ensemble will be similar to those considered above for three or four trumpets alone, and, perhaps surprisingly, no new issues of integration or balance will need to be resolved within this combination, the 'rounder' sound of the cornet tending to unify the combined sonority.

THE BRASS SECTION AS A WHOLE

The combination of trumpets, trombones and tuba – the standard brass section of the orchestra – does not pose the multiple problems of ensemble that beset the woodwind, as brass instruments, although technically very different, are much more closely interrelated. Nonetheless, as with woodwind and horns, specific difficulties arise for which the whole section needs to evolve a co-ordination based on familiarity and confidence in one another.

In student orchestras, sectional rehearsal provides the basis for this knowledge of each other's sound, musicality, strengths and weaknesses, and the primary function of these rehearsals should always be to promote this understanding and the integration of the section as a whole. The internal balance of the entire brass section, particularly with regard to the dynamic levels and support effected by 2nd trumpet (and 3rd if there is one) and 2nd trombone, is vital, and not helped by the physical width of the section apparent in its most usual layout. In fact, neither the continuous line nor the more confined layout (trumpets in front of trombones) provides a similar clarity to that enjoyed by the 'block' of woodwind, by reason of the position of the sound emanating from the horizontal bell of both trumpet and trombone.

Except in the four-trumpet section mentioned above, harmonic interlocking of parts is rare in the brass group as a whole, and chords will tend to be spread evenly across the section in ascending order from tuba, to trombones, to trumpets, as is the case in *Ex. 10.32*, which shows two short 'solo' passages from the slow movement of Glazunov *Symphony no. 5*.

The familiar spacing of tuba and 3rd trombone at the octave is apparent, and 3rd trumpet is used to 'bind' the root position chord at each cadence. This very close instrumentation of the chord can quite easily be balanced from within the section but exposes a problem evoked by the lack of interlocked voices – each trio of instruments will tend to balance to itself, rather than to the brass group as a whole. To some extent this is unavoidable, especially given the physical limitations outlined above, but a totally unified sound must be projected and the support of each lower note to the octave must be as evident as that of the root to its third and fifth. Herein lies the interdependence of responsibility that separates the accomplished section from the merely

EX. 10.32

adequate – in this case the support of tuba to 3rd trombone *and* 3rd trumpet, 2nd trombone to 2nd trumpet, and 1st trombone to 1st trumpet. For this passage to work correctly, a perfectly balanced trumpet section must be 'laying' its sound on an equally well balanced, but firmly apparent, chord of trombones and tuba. This is *very* different from simply doubling the chord at the octave, a subtlety which is made even more obvious by a wonderful passage from Dukas *La Péri*, which combines three each of trumpets and trombones, all muted, in identical layout.

EX. 10.33

However, support of this nature is not always so immediately recognizable, especially to the players, and will rarely be so uniform throughout a single phrase. In the final movement of the same Glazunov symphony, there appears another passage, where, on the third note of each phrase, the first two trombones drop to support 1st and 2nd trumpet respectively.

EX. 10.34

This is not quite the same as the two previous examples, as here it is more the responsibility of trombones to balance to trumpets, who alone have the complete phrase. The first note (concert B♭) is interesting (and somewhat dangerous) on both occasions in that its two octave span is doubled in all but the lowest note, making adherence to the marking *mezzo forte* of supreme necessity.

Support of the octave, such has been briefly encountered in these two examples, can be said to be the most important and fundamental ensemble technique of the brass group because it unifies the projected sound and widens the aural concentration of the individual players. Perfected, it would ensure that no passage was ever performed without total awareness of the inter-dependent responsibilities and, therefore, that every passage was balanced, in tune and perfectly delivered.

In passing, it is of interest to note that only five bars on from the passage quoted as *Ex. 10.34* there occurs a rare example of interlocking harmony within the trombone section (the tied notes), which arises out of the musical need to maintain the harmonic bass line in 3rd and tuba.

EX. 10.35

Even more unusual, at the first notes of bars 1 and 4, both 1st and 2nd trombones are pitched lower than 3rd.

Once more, rehearsal of intonation should be undertaken in the manner set out in Chapter 8, that is by breaking down the chords into their dependent intervals, but here there is one very important condition. It is much more likely that inexperienced trumpets and trombones will inadvertently change the technique of production – especially control of the air-flow – when concentrating solely on matters of intonation. In the case of loud passages, the level will automatically be considerably reduced, to induce a more controlled production of the individual notes. If this control is lost when the passage is approached *in situ,* then intonation and balance will be similarly affected. For this section it is important that, when the need arises to reconstruct a chord or passage requiring a dynamic of *forte* or above, it should finally be played at full level before continuing the rehearsal, taking extreme care that no change of production is apparent and that the section is totally aware of the musical consequences of any change.

Here again, it is essential that all players should realize the effect that the timbre of the different instruments might have on the appraisal of intonation from within the section. Apart from some of the problems mentioned in the above paragraphs, trumpets sometimes find it very difficult to assess the exact centre of the lower notes of tuba. In passages of full brass orchestration it very often becomes the responsibility of trombones to provide the fundamental centre of intonation, from which all else may be determined.

Specific consideration of the more advanced aspects of interdependent responsibility and sound control are best undertaken in Part III.

Specific Techniques

BREATHING

Any major differences in the breathing requirements for the brass group over and above those already discussed in respect of horns and woodwind refer essentially to tuba, where a great deal of breath is demanded by the size of the instrument, and opportunities for constant replenishment have to be found. Even in a passage such as *Ex. 10.36*, the first bars of Wagner overture to *Die Meistersinger von Nürnberg*, breath spans of more than one-bar length are unlikely to be contemplated.

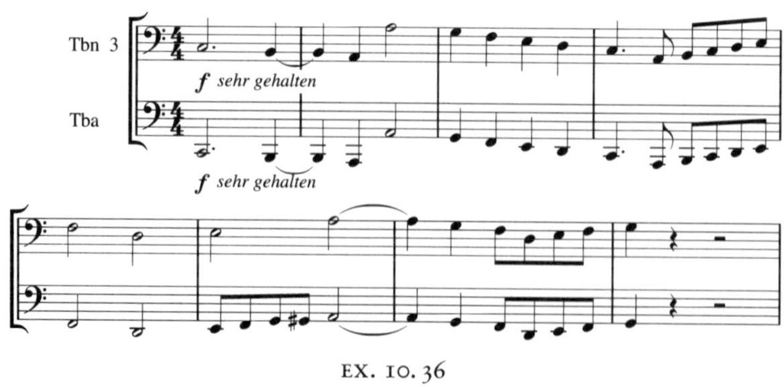

EX. 10.36

This is, in fact, one of the shorter passages required of tuba in this work which remains, in terms of breath control, one of the most arduous 12 minutes in the tuba player's life. However, as was remarked earlier, this unavoidable limitation of the long phrase is part of the tuba player's technique and, provided that reasonable fluency on the instrument has been achieved, it will not be an undue problem for the player. Indeed, in orchestral circumstances, the instrumentalist most affected will be 3rd trombone who will at least have to articulate the tuba breathing if not emulate it. Many bass trombone players will automatically consider passages of such direct collaboration in terms of tuba breath-spans, regularly taking breaths at places dictated by the needs of the larger instrument rather than their own. This swapping of allegiance between tuba and trombones according to the musical demands of the passage requires bass trombone to command two quite separate aspects of breath control and, often, two equally distinct appraisals of articulation.

When compared to trumpets, horns or woodwind, all the lower brass demand an increased air supply. For the trombones, requirements of pitch and dynamic level dictate this need to a greater extent, particularly when it comes to sustaining a phrase. Thus, in the long phrase from the fourth movement of Elgar *Symphony no. 2* (quoted above as *Ex. 10.17*) the first four bars can be taken in one breath because of the very soft dynamic and the fact that the second and third bars lie in the fluent middle range of the instrument. The following three bars, however, are likely to need the careful (and unnoticeable) separation of two plus one, the breath-span at this pitch being nowhere near so easy.

Breathing for trumpets has much more in common with that already considered for horns and woodwind, the smaller bore of the instrument allowing comparably long phrases to be taken in one breath. Extra allowance will be needed only in the extremes of the range, or in exceptional passages at the top, where the back pressure caused by the resistance of the instrument to the reservoir of air in the lungs can make it feel as though the player's head is close to bursting.

As with all wind instruments it is the note *before* the breath that is most at risk, especially in the lower brass, where the desire to snatch the breath too soon can be very potent. This is a problem of attitude – the assumption that a large amount of breath requires an equally large amount of time to replenish it is almost totally untrue. A good player can replenish a great deal of air in a very short time, and will never distort the previous note in order to do it.

A further consideration for trombones arises because they are the only wind instruments to involve physical movement of the arm, sometimes to a considerable degree. The temptation for the player of intermediate standard to relate a return to the shorter positions of the instrument, especially first position, with the opportunity to breathe can often be overwhelming, however much they might have been taught otherwise. Ideally, of course, the action of the arm should be quite independent of the diaphragm and control of the air-flow – much as the bowing arm in relation to fingering of the strings – but, in practical terms, this is no more true for one instrument than the other. Strings will use more bow in passages that are difficult for the left hand and trombones will expend more air in relation to the speed and distance travelled by the slide arm.

NON-*LEGATO* PHRASES

The complications inherent in the performance of non-*legato* phrases are no less dangerous for brass than other wind instruments, and have been dealt with in detail in the two previous chapters. No further specific examples should be necessary because previously discussed principles apply.

Perhaps the only additional point that needs making relates to the regularly propounded fact that the trombone is incapable of playing a *legato* phrase because of the necessary movement of the slide. While this is undeniably true in theory, in practice all that needs to be apparent is a slightly increased enunciation of the note changes, much as is the case for a singer delivering words. Indeed many *legato* phrases need this type of delineation and other wind instruments will produce it by techniques of soft-tonguing. For all practical purposes the trombone is as capable of delivering the smooth phrase as any other instrument.

ARTICULATION

Control of the air passing into the instrument by co-ordinated use of the diaphragm, throat and tongue is the essential technique of all wind players and is always at its most critical in soft playing, where even the slightest fault in any part of the technique will show. Especially in respect of use of the tongue at this dynamic, many players will adopt an action which is far too emphatic, causing the air-stream to burst into the instrument with consequent lack of control. The technique of soft-tonguing, a movement closer to the enunciation 'daw' rather than 'te', *has* to be applied to smooth production at subdued dynamic levels, especially at entries, but also necessary in a large amount of loud playing as well. *Fortissimo* production articulated by soft-tonguing is a regular requirement.

As important as the actual movement of the tongue is the vital co-ordination of the whole process. The change in direction of air, from breathing in to breathing out, must be continuous, and the tongue must not be used as a barrier to withhold an ever-increasing pressure of air, but simply as a release of that which sets the lips in motion. The technique may be practised (but *not* performed) by producing a note without any use of the tongue at all, a recourse that will usually result in a somewhat unsuccessful production, so that the relationship of the diaphragm, air-stream and embouchure are controlled in themselves. The tongue may then be added fractionally before the note starts.

This use of the tongue to articulate a note which is *already controlled* in the other aspects of its production is essential at all dynamic levels, but its application to accompanying *piano* or *pianissimo* chordal entries is probably most significant. The trombone chords quoted as *Ex. 10.15* (from Bruckner *Symphony no. 7*) must be approached with this technique in order to ensure both the quality and substance of the entry – one similar to that produced by the strings' approach with a moving bow.

But as far as the young orchestral player is concerned, the most overlooked aspect of *legato* articulation is the finishing of notes. This must not be accomplished with the tongue but simply by closing the air-flow from the throat in a perfectly natural way (as one would end a sung vowel with the mouth still open). Even short notes should be ended in this way and most circumstances will dictate that a very small phrasing *diminuendo* is also added – a more gradual control of the air-stream. All good wind instrumentalists will have practised the technique and those who have not cannot seriously approach performance of the orchestral repertoire until at least some degree of ability and understanding is apparent.

For the less experienced player, above and beyond even these musical considerations, is the unavoidable dependence of this technique on complete control, for it cannot be accomplished with anything but correct breathing and total support.

TONGUING

All forms of tonguing considered in relation to woodwind and horns are available to the brass group, but it is in the trumpet that faster forms of articulation will most usually be found. The trumpet, above all wind instruments of the orchestra, is capable of the most clearly articulated tonguing at almost any speed, and this capability is regularly used. The bright, stringent sound of single-tongued, fast repeated notes have a tightness that no other instrument can match. Once again Roussel *Bacchus et Ariane* illustrates this.

EX. 10. 37

For the trombones such fast movement tends to be limited to shorter passages of chromatic movement such as in *Ex. 10. 38*, for 1st, 3rd and tuba, from the end of Dvořák *Symphony no. 8*.

EX. 10. 38

There should be no doubt as to tuba's ability to equal and even surpass the agility of trombones (especially in *pianissimo legato*) and any apparent reluctance on the part of composers to exploit this side of the instrument is due only to the instrument's restricted breath-span.

DOUBLE-TONGUING

Double-tonguing sounds very clear on the trumpet and there are many examples of its use. As with all wind players, trumpeters of any standard will have developed the speed of their single-tonguing to a point where double-tonguing becomes an option rather than a necessity in many situations but *Ex. 10. 39* from *The Wild Bears* in the 2nd Suite of Elgar *The Wand of Youth* will regularly be double-tongued.

EX. 10. 39

Its frequent appearance for all wind instruments (but most especially trumpets) in small patterns following notes of longer duration can be very hazardous, as in *Ex. 10. 40* from the slow movement of Dvořák *Violin Concerto*.

EX. 10. 40

EX. 10.40 (continued)

From the fourth bar onwards these short figures must be related to the *following* notes, and not those that precede them, so that a clearly defined articulation is apparent. Inexperienced players will regularly attach such figures to the initial note of the group, thereby losing clarity of articulation. This miscalculation can also serve to lose the overall rhythm, especially in passages of this length, by causing arrival on the long note to be progressively earlier.

For tuba and trombone, some limitation in speed of articulation is imposed by the amount of air needed to produce the sound and the consequent slower response of the instrument. While both double- and triple-tonguing are perfectly possible, they remain a rarely considered option within the orchestra, as fast single-tonguing will cover most requirements and generally produce a clearer sound. A passage such as that quoted as *Ex. 10. 20* above (from Elgar *Falstaff*) may well be double-tongued, but even here, single-tonguing can still be considered by some players. On the whole, fast passages of repeated notes – where clarity of articulation can receive no assistance from melodic movement – are rarely employed. Tchaikovsky even goes so far as to avoid them altogether for these instruments in the last movement of the *Manfred Symphony*, electing to leave this aspect of the theme to lower strings, bassoons and bass clarinet.

EX. 10.41

TRIPLE-TONGUING

For trumpets, triple-tonguing proves clear and facile both in short melodic passage-work and the repetition of single notes. In the last movement of Rimsky-Korsakov *Scheherazade* examples of both may be found at the triplet figures of the bars marked [a] and [b] in *Ex. 10. 42.*

EX. 10.42

FLUTTER-TONGUING

Flutter-tonguing as described in Chapter 8 remains identical for the brass, where it can be required of all instruments. *Ex. 10. 43* illustrates it from the same context as previously (Britten *Sinfonia da Requiem*).

EX. 10.43

Its production, however, involves a great deal of air in the case of the lower instruments, and its most frequent use will be confined to trumpets, where the added advantages of higher pitch and 'tighter' sound make it clearly audible in almost all circumstances. Also, the speed of response in the middle and upper registers of the trumpet means that the technique requires very little extra breath and can be taken within the expanse of a single phrase, as here in Gershwin *Rhapsody in Blue.*

EX. 10.44

Noticeable here is the use of a descriptive term in addition to the three *tremolo* strokes in all parts. As has already been mentioned, some confusion can result in the use of tail strokes alone, since it is sometimes possible to play rhythmic figures at the indicated speed. However – as with strings – at a moderate or fast tempo, more than two tails to a single note may generally be taken as denoting *tremolo*. A real flutter-tongue will produce a very cutting and grotesque effect, unsuited to many contexts, and good brass players will, on the whole, avoid its use, preferring to tongue wherever possible. Once again, the use of various descriptions may be found. Beyond those already mentioned comes Rimsky-Korsakov's occasional use of the term *vibrando* when demanding flutter-tongue of trumpets (as in *Skazka op. 29*).

The replacement of flutter-tongue by the 'valve *tremolo*' is possible for certain notes on the trumpet and can be very effectively used, especially in powerfully orchestrated passages. The availability of many notes between the third and sixth harmonic in two separate valve combinations allows for a

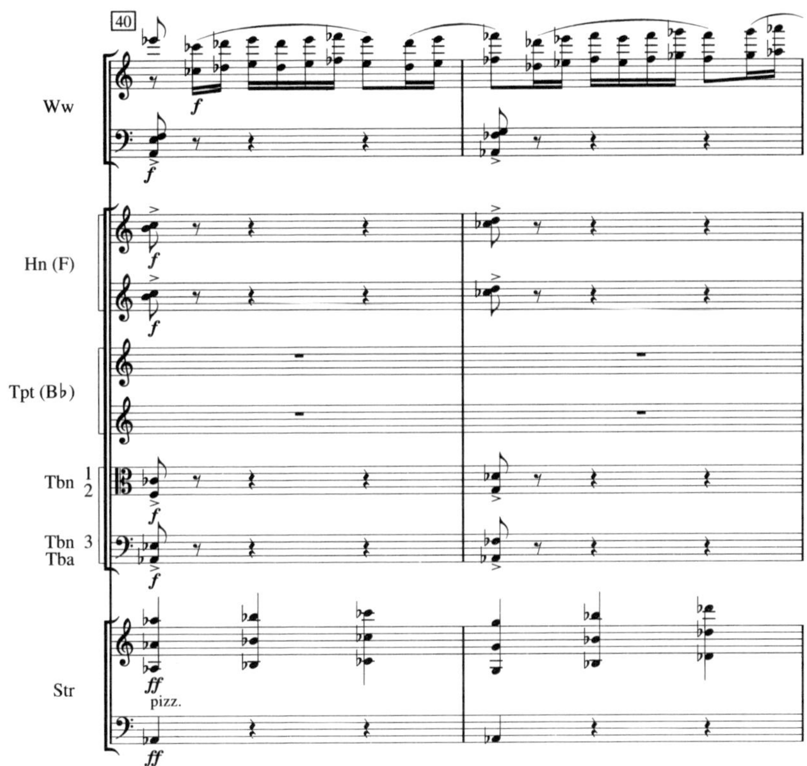

EX. 10.45

EX. 10.45 (continued)

rapid alternation of fingering to produce the same note. While not as vital as the flutter-tongue it can sometimes prove beneficial in attaining a sustained *tremolando crescendo*. Some players will choose to use it in passages such as *Ex. 10.45* from Shostakovich *Symphony no. 10*, where three trumpets must emerge from within a full orchestral *fortissimo*.

Most professionals, however, will prefer to use rapid tonguing, as it is easier to create the effect of a steady, and finally shattering, *crescendo*.

MUTING

For the trumpets, muting is probably more effective (and certainly more variable in tone and insinuation) than for any other brass instrument, and thus there are more types of trumpet mute available. Quite apart from the examples gleaned from the jazz idiom (the 'wha-wha' and 'Harmon' mutes being the most common), mutes vary in the material of their construction (cardboard, metal or fibre), their shape (straight or cupped at the bell), and even in their original conception (practice mutes, designed to dull the edge of the sound and restrict its carrying powers).

Generally, fibre mutes have more character in soft, melodic passages, while metal mutes provide the *cuivré* sound so beloved of composers writing within an expressionist idiom. A medium, all-purpose mute is that of black plastic. Inexperienced players can tend to over-use the 'cup' mute in soft passages, a sound which should truly be reserved for special effect, where particularly designated.

When playing a solo passage, a trumpeter will often automatically select the most appropriate mute, but in combination a considerable amount of trial and error may be required before the most suitable mute is decided on. In the second movement of Prokofiev *Violin Concerto no. 2* the most effective mute for the passage will not necessarily be chosen immediately, nor, when found, will it be the correct one for every acoustic.

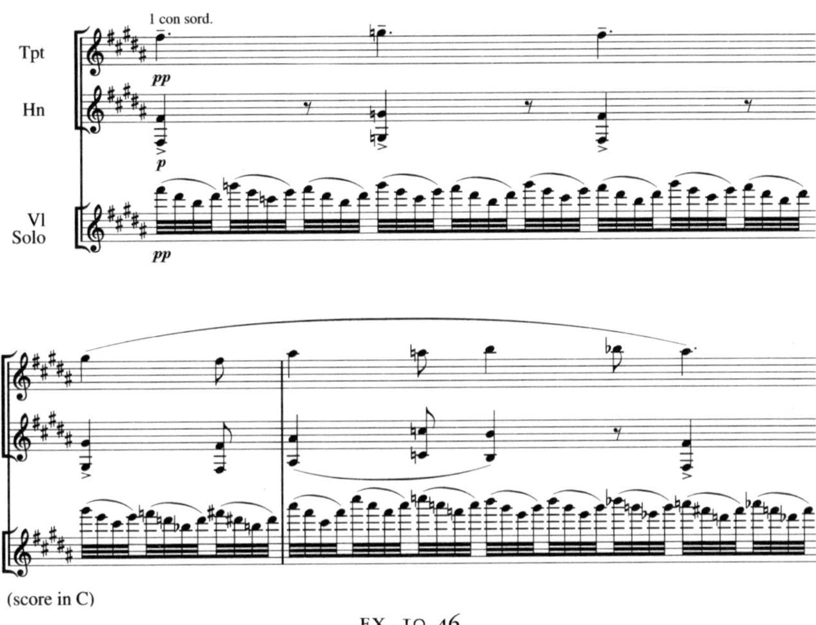

EX. 10.46

Not only must it allow a *pianissimo* quality without being inaudible but even more importantly, it must not cause the player any exaggerated difficulty in performing the passage, especially across the first half of the second quoted bar.

A more famous passage, which has caused much scratching of heads over the years (and some quite bizarre solutions) is shown in *Ex. 10. 47* from *Fêtes*, the second of Debussy *Trois Nocturnes*.

EX. 10. 47

The marking *un peu rapproché* (a little nearer) is really more problematic than the selection of an ideal mute, but the two get inexorably bound together. I well remember one of the great Russian conductors attempting, unsuccessfully, to convince a trumpet section to play the first part of this with their half-open cases on their laps and the bells of the instruments completely enveloped. While one can understand their natural reluctance to comply – the thin metal of the instrument can easily be damaged – I have always remained curious as to the live result. However, a cloth hung over the bell and mute, to be removed at the second phrase, works very well.

Deciding upon the 'felt crown' that adds the wonderful feeling of indolence to Gershwin's superb trumpet solo in *An American in Paris* requires a similar procedure.

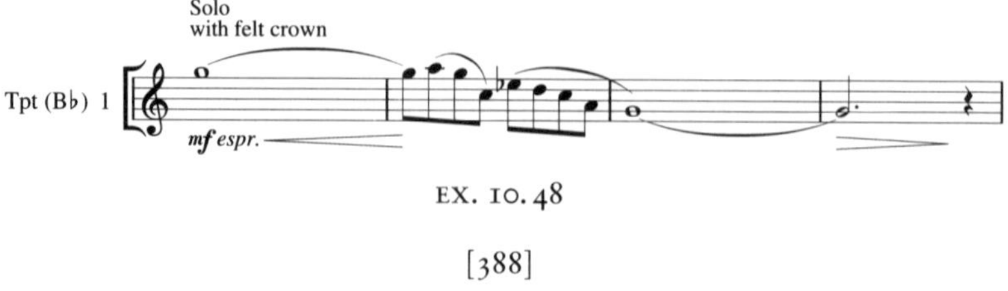

EX. 10. 48

A felt beret hung loosely over the bell will usually provide the sound.

For trombones the standard mute is the 'straight' mute, somewhat pear-shaped in form, which can be made of fibre, metal or wood. The cup-shaped variety, extending across almost the entire diameter of the bell should, once again, be used sparingly. Few young players will have access to the diversity of mutes employed by their trumpet-playing colleagues as the tonal demands made on the muted trombone have not, so far, generally been as various or specific. However, many different timbres can be elicited, even between individual examples of the same basic design, and similar experiments to that considered above will often prove beneficial. Generally, the trombone mute will provide a nasal quality, restricting the natural mellow complexion of the sound. This can sometimes cause chords in muted trombones to separate, making balance and intonation even more critical.

Perhaps the most notorious aspect of trombone muting is the speed with which many composers, Stravinsky and Bartók in particular, demand its insertion. *Ex. 10. 49* from Stravinsky *Violin Concerto* has often been considered impractical.

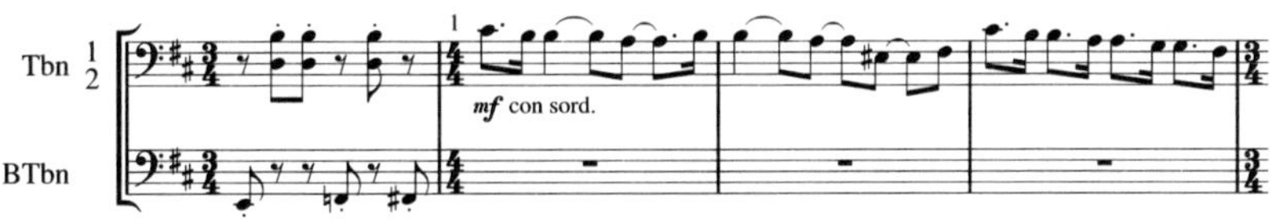

EX. 10.49

It is in fact possible, although it is extremely difficult for a number of reasons and likely to be beyond the ability of all but the most accomplished professional. Unless playing in the extreme ranges of the instrument it is feasible, for short periods, to support the trombone with the heel of the left hand against the rim, thereby allowing the mute to be held, clear of the bell, in the fingers. (This in itself is no simple accomplishment, since the trombone mute is never small and can be quite awkward to support in the air.) Insertion into the bell from this position can be made very quickly. However, there is a further complication. Many trumpet and trombone mutes require a very small twist of the hand so that they grip the inside of the tube and are not propelled forward by the force of the air around them. In circumstances such as that required above, this action has to be forfeited and the fingers have to be used to hold the mute in place, which adds yet another difficulty to the performance of the passage. Exigent techniques of this sort are the prerogative of highly competent players and should not be attempted by anyone who has not totally mastered the fundamentals of their instrument. Such skills cannot be learned quickly and need considerable practice and careful consideration of the unavoidable complementary adjustments that accompany them.

The use of an extra player to insert the mute is not to be recommended. However, the division of the passage between two 1st trombones (a solution too expensive to be considered by professional orchestras) is, of course, perfectly possible.

The only mute for the tuba is of the standard conical design, usually made of cardboard or similar material, although one constructed in metal is now available. Owing to the immense size of the instrument for which it is designed the mute is large and cumbersome, which makes very quick changes impractical. Its effect is to reduce the volume of sound while also diffusing such cutting edge as the instrument possesses. Except in the hands of a very able player it will also cause the tuba to 'speak' even later than normal. In passages where a sharply defined accented entry is required, such as the single bar in the 1919 version of Stravinsky *The Firebird*, it will always cause a problem, since the player will have to produce the note virtually 'on' the beat if it is to be heard in the right place.

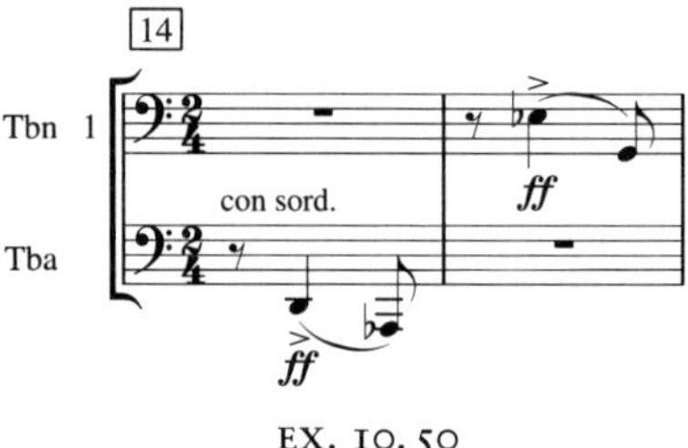

EX. 10.50

This accent is very difficult to produce clearly and a very rapid bulge is commonly heard as the player tries to contrive it with air rather than initial attack. A far more successful scoring of the bar occurs in the 1945 edition of the same work, where 3rd trombone takes on much of the responsibility for decisive attack.

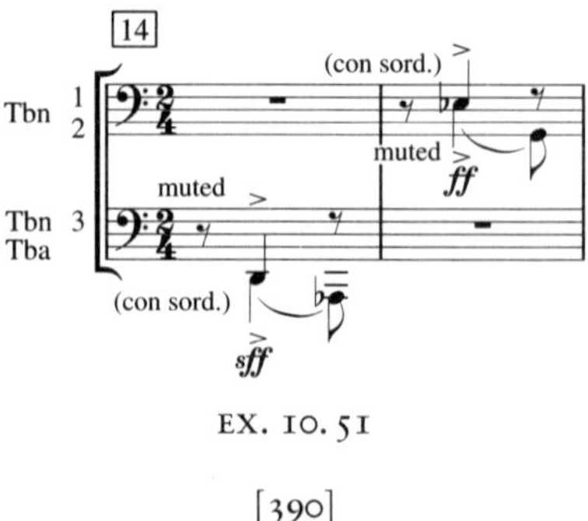

EX. 10.51

TRILLS

On the modern trumpet, trills are available throughout the range by virtue of the valves but orchestrally they tend to be limited to the upper register at fairly strong dynamic levels. With the exception of one or two awkward fingerings, affecting those lower down in the range, they are not difficult to execute and suffer only from a propensity to brashness in their approach by some inexperienced players. Lip-trills are possible in the high register but are generally not used in orchestral playing.

Trombone trills can only be made with the lips and are consequently limited to the upper register. Their orchestral appearance is rare, but one frequently encountered example is illustrated in *Ex. 10.52*, for 1st trombone, from Stravinsky *The Firebird*. This should be produced very strongly with the bell of the instrument up – apart from anything else, it is very good embouchure practice!

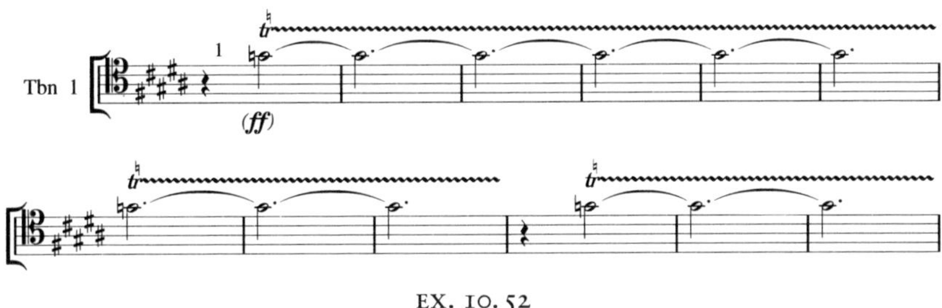

EX. 10.52

Tuba trills are effective but, once again, infrequently demanded in the orchestral repertoire, although *Ex. 10.53* from the overture to Wagner *Die Meistersinger von Nürnberg* demands inclusion in the context of this discussion.

EX. 10.53

Although quite heavily doubled by cellos and two bassoons with basses at the octave below, this whole-tone trill remains surprisingly dominant.

GLISSANDI

A lip *glissando* across adjacent harmonics is very effective on the trumpet but, as with horns, its orchestral use is usually confined to the upward direction, as in Panufnik *Sinfonia Sacra.*

EX. 10. 54

A *glissando* downwards is, of course, equally possible but is usually only encountered in idiomatic solos of an extemporized nature (the so-called 'Jazz fall').

Apart from stringed instruments and pedal timpani, the trombone is alone in its ability to play true *glissandi* by virtue of the slide. Within the span of the slide the device is effective across the range of the instrument. It will most often appear in solo writing, as in Arnold *Tam O'Shanter* (*Ex. 4. 12*), where its effect is that of an exaggerated *portamento* to the upper note. Bartók uses the true *glissando* to great effect in the fourth movement of the *Concerto for Orchestra*, where the full range (7th to 1st position) is used.

EX. 10. 55

It will be noted that the *glissando* of 3rd trombone (low B to F) is actually only available to the *original* bass trombone in F, the modern instrument being unable to produce a B natural in seventh position unless fitted with a second valve (*see* Chapter 4) so a certain amount of 'sleight of hand' is nowadays often required. Nonetheless, the interval of an augmented fourth, as used in *Ex. 10.-55*, remains the maximum possible range.

Instances do occur where a larger interval is demanded, such as the famous *glissez fantastico* of Elgar overture *Cockaigne* (*Ex. 10.56*); these are not possible across the range indicated, and require a degree of cross-harmonic 'cheating'.

EX. 10.56

The *glissandi* must be accepted as relating to the upper note, whereupon the lower note will be played and then the next higher harmonic selected with the lips and the *glissando* produced with the slide, as far from the note as time will allow. This display of gymnastics is by no means easy and the passage will tend to look as unbelievable as it sounds.

A lip *glissando* over the series of one harmonic is as equally effective on the trombone as it is on horns. Bartók once again provides an example, requiring it of all three trombones in the rarely performed 'second ending' of the *Violin Concerto no. 2*.

EX. 10.57

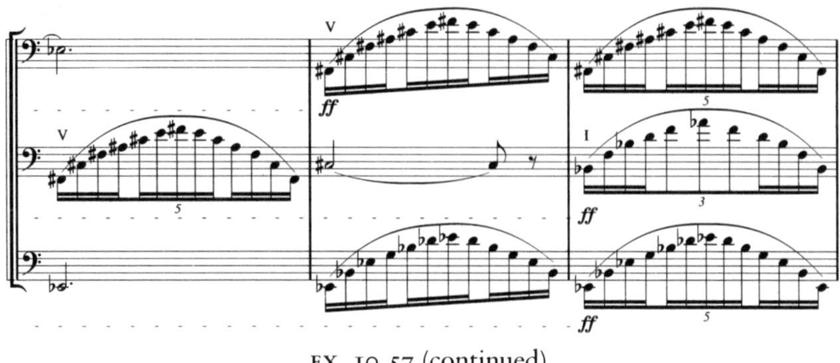

EX. 10. 57 (continued)

BELLS IN THE AIR

Most particularly in the Mahler symphonies, the demand is made of both trumpets and trombones to raise the bell of the instrument in a way that exaggerates the already near-horizontal playing position. In the case of these instruments, while the sound – if timed precisely – will command a very thrilling effect, the exhortation may be taken more as an intention of dominance of sound required, for it does not in itself automatically affect the tone and in neither case has it the same visual impact as when demanded of horns.

For trumpets it will most often relate to a much more *legato* phrase than is likely to be the case when the marking occurs for other instruments, and it is often applied to just one instrument in a solo passage of heavy orchestration. A prime example of this may be found towards the end of the 1st movement in Mahler *Symphony no. 9* (ten bars after rehearsal figure 16).

For trombones the association of this marking is with far more blatant and dramatic passages. From the same Mahler symphony comes *Ex. 10. 58* for all three trombones in octaves and additionally marked 'with great power'.

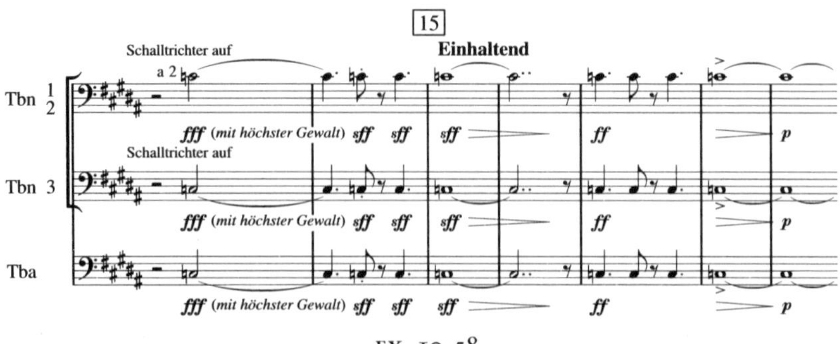

EX. 10. 58

Most especially in the case of trombones, the wide-bore instruments in general use today make it imperative for the marking to be obeyed with considerable care. In Richard Strauss *Tod und Verklärung* there appears a very similar passage.

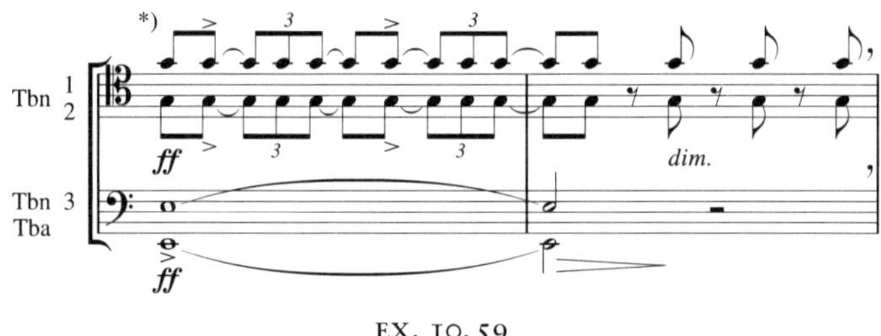

EX. 10.59

In this case the composer adds a footnote, insisting that the two bars be presented in a 'horrifying manner' and suggesting that 1st and 2nd trombone might lift the instruments and point the bells directly at the public. In either example, over-enthusiastic allegiance to the instruction when using modern instruments could well cause the death agony depicted by the latter passage to become suddenly very real!

With regard to all instruments, the marking *Schalltrichter auf, Pavillon en l'air,* or *bells up* is almost never cancelled and must be taken to apply only to the immediate text and not to any following entry or musically dissimilar passage. So particular is its use that there is generally little doubt as to where it might end.

PITCH VARIATIONS

The discussion under this heading in the previous chapter applies equally here. The problem of condensation is not so acute for trumpets, trombones and tuba, as these instruments are equipped with a water key which allows them to be cleared in general playing circumstances without the need for dismantling.

Related Techniques

More often than other orchestral instruments the trumpet – because of its penetration and the historical associations already considered – will be required to play 'off stage', at a distance from the main body of the orchestra.

Although this is by no means a frequent occurrence it is demanded often enough to warrant consideration.

Firstly, let it be said that under no circumstances should the direction be ignored or any attempt be made to secure a similar result from within the orchestra. No matter what the circumstances, 'off stage' means what it says and it cannot be reproduced in any other way. Nowadays the availability of video equipment means that the difficulties associated with visual contact or the need for a second conductor can be largely discounted, and only the musical problem of balance need remain.

In the most famous example, for one solo trumpet in Beethoven overture *Leonora no. 3*, visual contact is not necessary – the player only needs to be able to hear. Any problem experienced in this solo is confined to the player (who, according to countless experiences, risks physical abuse, criminal proceedings, getting lost or suddenly being transported to the basement by lift). In all other aspects the passage proves to be quite straightforward.

Far more difficult to synchronize is the off-stage flugelhorn solo that appears in Mahler *Symphony no. 3*, where some visual contact with the conductor must be maintained. (In later editions this solo, rather inexplicably, is changed to posthorn, but it is always played on the flugelhorn.)

The three off-stage trumpets at the opening of the first movement of Mahler *Symphony no. 1* can also prove problematic, although only 1st needs direct visual contact, since it is quite possible for this player to direct the other two. Unlike the previous example, which needs an extra player over and above those in the orchestra, this passage should be played by the three orchestral trumpets, who should return quickly to their place in the orchestra after the last fanfare.

A similar situation applies to the opening of the 'battle scene' in Richard Strauss *Ein Heldenleben* but, in this case, the players have both to leave and return to the main body of the orchestra. It is debatable which of the two manoeuvres provokes the more misunderstanding from an unwary audience, and consequent embarrassment to the players. In all these cases some variation in pitch will be noticeable, and it is essential that the off-stage instrumentalists tune a little sharp to compensate.

The four off-stage trumpets that are scored in Verdi *Requiem* are, once more, extra players. This is probably one of the most awkward instances, because ensemble must be maintained between these players and the trumpets within the orchestra. The most advantageous position is with the two trumpets either side of the orchestra, one pair to the right and one to the left, in order to maximize the drama of the 'last trumpet' effect, but balance is always critical – especially when they are integrated into the full orchestral sound.

EMBOUCHURE

Once again, the reader must be referred to this section in the previous chapter where, with the addition of one further consideration, similar principles apply.

In student orchestras it is very possible that the brass instruments will be touching areas of the range, both upper and lower, that have yet to become a familiar part of their technique. The embouchure is likely to be neither sufficiently mature nor strong enough to survive sustained playing in these areas, and great care must be taken not to cause damage, both in terms of the level of sound produced and in the desperately important area of choice of repertoire.

With regard to the latter more will be said presently (*see* Chapter 23) but, in relation to the brass instruments, it should be mentioned now that care in selection of repertoire is crucial. It is all too easy to judge the suitability of a work by the technical difficulty of the string parts, without properly considering the 'lie' of the writing for horns and trumpets. It is by no means impossible that lasting damage may be done by inducing immature players into an area of their instrument for which they are not yet totally equipped. Advice should always be sought from an experienced professional, preferably one who has had considerable first-hand knowledge of performance and will therefore know the 'feel' of the parts, since such difficulties are not always immediately obvious from the printed page, even to someone familiar with the instrument.

VIBRATO

Again, there are very noticeable variations in the use of *vibrato* associated with different schools of playing throughout the world, especially with regard to the trombone, but these will tend to be uniform within orchestral sections, rather than confined to individual players. The accommodation of the resulting sound thus becomes only a matter of adjustment for the conductor, and does not create problems for the section as a whole.

The use of 'slide *vibrato*' by trombones should be approached very carefully with regard to symphonic playing. In all circumstances *vibrato* should be considered as a warming rather than an undulation of the sound.

11 TIMPANI AND PERCUSSION

Consideration of a section of the orchestra which comprises single and (except for their general method of sound production) unrelated instruments will raise issues not relevant to other sections. Pitch is mostly fixed, harmonic collaboration is virtually non-existent and melodic line is limited to tuned instruments. The techniques of the percussion section are unique, as are the demands made on them, and their integration into the full symphonic sound needs to be approached from a radically different viewpoint. Although, to reinforce concepts of orchestral unity, this chapter will utilize the same broad subheadings as elsewhere, their direct relevance will sometimes involve considerable latitude.

Character and Influence

PERCUSSION

The character of the percussion section and its direct influence on the orchestra have changed out of all recognition in the last thirty years. So fast has been this development that there is no longer any textbook which can be said to be up to date, or any professional player capable of mastering all the varied techniques and available instruments.

The reasons for this are manifold, but certainly the increased contact of composers and instrumentalists with more diverse (particularly Eastern) cultures, and the generally more vertical sense of musical expression apparent in the last two-thirds of this century, may be taken as two of the most accountable. The percussion section has found itself expanding at a truly alarming rate, and the same symphonic players who, not so long ago, learnt to await their often ignored contribution with stoic patience are now ever more frequently to be found consulting journals, rearranging parts and adjusting unfamiliar instruments.

In the main this is a highly satisfactory state of affairs, because the greater involvement has brought a parallel increase in awareness, which has demanded a more structured teaching process and a more thorough appraisal of all aspects of performance.

Sound made by striking one object against another is as old as mankind, and its evolution to intentional and recognizable primitive rhythmic patterns probably almost as ancient. The manufacture and design of percussion 'instruments' – objects intended solely for the production of sound – is, in its most basic form, only a little more recent. Examples still in existence today can be traced back to biblical civilizations but, as far as this discussion is concerned, the character and influence of percussion instruments must be limited to the last few centuries of their history and confined to their direct association with the symphonic orchestra.

Like the trumpet, drums are often associated with their historic role. The repetition of simple rhythmic figures from an instrument that provides no harmonic direction tends to be associated with human movement and will very quickly influence the aural perception of any musical statement. *Ex. 11.1* is from Richard Strauss *Ein Heldenleben.*

EX. 11.1

The actual theme, while unquestionably confident both in its stark use of wide intervals and its instrumentation, would not, in itself, suggest the physical conflict that is so apparent. A similar, even more blatant example, may be found in Shostakovich *Symphony no. 7*.

EX. 11.2

This extraordinary line (repeated more than a dozen times and openly caricatured by more than one other composer) in itself contains absolutely none of the inexorable menace that is imbued, solely, by its uncompromising rhythmic accompaniment.

This ability to insinuate both style and dramatic content in an immediate and extremely concise way, typifies a particular use of percussion throughout much of the symphonic repertoire, which even extends to those instruments which have no direct association with human activities. More recently comes their employment in an imitative fashion to describe (and sometimes directly reproduce) specific sounds or actions. This aspect of their character, particularly in the field of opera, has spawned many imaginative and exploratory uses of existing instruments and led to the invention and discovery of so many others.

On the whole the evocative use of percussion in either of these two categories is self-explanatory and will cause no difficulties beyond those of fundamental rendition. In most cases balance is carefully predetermined by the orchestration and, especially in the first instance, the very nature of the role will often dictate rhythmic security and ensemble.

In this respect, it differs from the third and most subtle aspect of the percussion section's contribution – that of providing pure colour. Here, the immense variety of sound and infinite variation of nuance will often require the sounding-together of a large number of instruments, with no inflection predominant, and it is here that the true art of percussion playing begins to show. The individual *tour de force*, epitomized by Ravel *Boléro* or the 350-bar passage partly quoted above *(Ex. 11. 2)*, might well receive deserved recognition but the almost unnoticed modification of the complexion or pointing of a phrase remains more difficult to achieve.

For the tuned percussion, although isolated notes may be occasionally required as a direct representation of 'real' sounds, the influence is almost entirely one of colour in a melodic sense. As such, its character is usually predetermined by the choice of instrument to a far greater degree than is true of strings or wind. The highly individual qualities of glockenspiel, xylophone, marimba or vibraphone, for example, are unlikely to be scored at random or in a spirit of compromise. While some variation might be possible in the choice of hardness of the mallet head, this will have more effect on the instrument's dynamic and projection than on its character. Even with regard to the vibraphone and its choice of production with motor 'on' or 'off', this can truthfully be said to amount to the provision of two distinct instruments, and the two will never be interchanged within the same phrase.

With such an ever-enlarging armoury of available sounds, it is hardly surprising that, for many composers, the emphasis began to change and a situation has arisen in recent years where the percussion sometimes takes an equal, and even primary, role in symphonic musical expression.

TIMPANI

Much of the character of timpani writing is closely allied to its orchestral history and technical development and has, therefore, already been dealt with within the general considerations of Chapter 5.

The influence of the instruments, however, both within the orchestra and in a wider musical sense, is far-reaching and requires some broad analysis at this point.

Unlike any other percussive instrument, the timpani undertake a fundamentally harmonic role in the orchestra by virtue of their ability to produce notes of definite pitch, and thus their contribution must often be considered in terms of collaborative support, even though this will rarely prove to be the primary purpose of their instrumentation.

The early collaboration of two or three drums of fixed pitch with trumpets cemented the instruments' harmonic affinity with the bass notes of the primary chords and, as will be discussed later (*see* Appendix), probably allowed the instruments to be used as a means of emphasizing the architectural scope of a work or movement by underlining the harmonic progress. Some examples of this tradition may still be discerned in the works of composers writing for chromatic instruments. Be that as it may, this type of harmonic use, whether limited or universal, may be broadly referred to as instrumental colouring and covers the greater proportion of the instruments' symphonic orchestral involvement.

The timpani are rarely used directly to imply human action (as might be the case with snare drum, or instruments associated with particular dances) but they can very quickly engender an emotional reaction which will convey a similar dramatic sense, as in *Ex. 11.3* towards the end of Tchaikovsky *Romeo and Juliet*

EX. 11.3

or in *Ex. 11.4* from the opening of the *March to the Scaffold* from Berlioz *Symphonie Fantastique.*

EX. 11.4

A comparison between these passages and those quoted above for snare drum (*Exx. 11. 1* and *11. 2*) highlights the immense variety and subtlety of sound that have enabled the timpani to maintain their dominant position – the ability to produce notes of definite pitch is not their only advantage.

The timpani will less often be required to undertake the role of uncompromising descriptive imitation, but the rolling thunder clouds in the third movement of the *Symphonie Fantastique* (*Ex. 5. 6*) provide an example, and another, in very different vein, can be seen in *Ex. 11. 5* from Variation XIII of Elgar *'Enigma' Variations.*

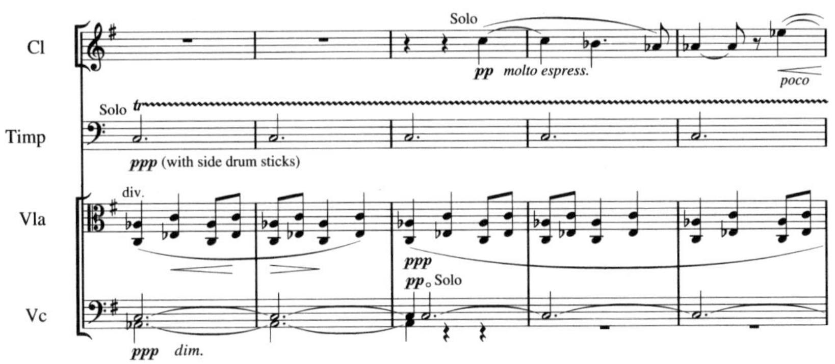

EX. 11.5

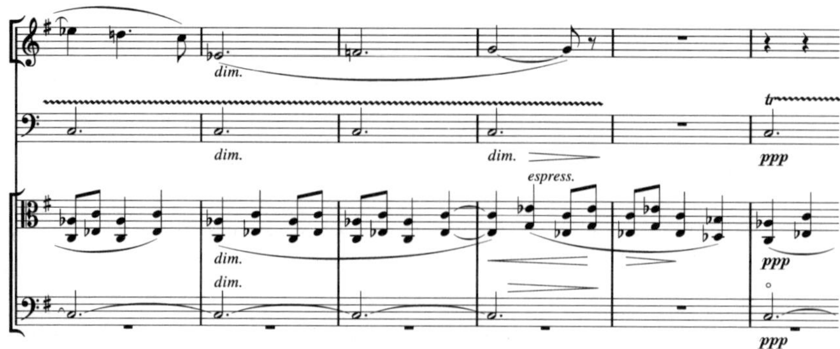

(score in concert pitch)

EX. 11.5 (continued)

This passage, representing the engines of an ocean liner, should always be performed with two coins, one held between the finger and thumb of each hand, rather than the side-drum sticks requested. This method, demonstrated by a famous player of the day, was much preferred by the composer.

Intonation

In this context 'intonation' refers to the instantaneous adjustment in pitch necessary for one instrument to sound notes which are in tune in relation to one another and, more particularly, with notes sounded by other instruments in combination. Thus this heading is not of concern to instruments of the percussion section except in the sense of 'high', 'medium' and 'low' that may sometimes be required of tam-tam, cymbal, drums etc., a differential best dealt with later. As was mentioned in Chapter 5, in view of their specialized orchestration, a similar limitation will be applied to rototoms. In the case of tuned percussion the notes are open to no immediate adjustment and any variation will either have to be accommodated by instruments outside the section or painfully ignored. Balance, however, is most definitely of concern.

TIMPANI

In student orchestras, although considerable interchanging of instrumental responsibility is generally accepted within the percussion section, it is nonetheless preferable to maintain a single timpanist throughout a programme. Unless two players of a *very* high standard are available, sharing of this position is not ideal. Many timpani and percussion tutors would disagree, arguing that the general standard of youth orchestra timpani playing is so elementary that the opportunity to give experience to more than one player will be of little detriment to the orchestra as a whole and of great benefit to the individuals concerned.

There is undeniable merit in this opinion, and I must admit to having gone along with it on far more occasions than I have resisted it. However, in my experience it has almost always been true that players spending the longest orchestral time with the instruments have shown a marked improvement over their colleagues in terms of tuning, balance, anticipation and touch, even in extreme cases where they began rehearsals as totally raw material.

The use of timpani in the symphony orchestra is unique in its almost continual support and responsibility towards other instruments, and a highly developed awareness of orchestral texture from the player concerned is of paramount importance. From a position behind and, usually, above the orchestra, the perceived sound is at best distorted, and a great deal of experience is needed to know the effect that is being produced. Projected intonation is often very different from that immediately apparent to the player and balance has to be 'felt' at all times, for there is little else to act as guide. Participation for the length of an overture or short concert piece is simply not enough time to come to grips with the problem.

With a good student the tutor will undoubtedly have begun to explore some of the subtleties of the instrument, such as lengths of stroke, gradations of damping, quality of sound and support. (Indeed this is probably the priority with any standard of player, since even mistaken entries benefit from the right sound!) However, except in the most obvious passages, the tutor is unable to predetermine the exact places where certain subtleties are required, the reaction of a good professional being instinctive in this respect and likely to change even over performances of the same passage, depending on the balance and level of other players. In student orchestras it becomes essential that the conductor gives clear guidance on both the balance and the 'insinuation' of the timpanist's sound, thus increasing the player's awareness not only of what is necessary but also *why* it should be so.

This is yet another reason why the tutor should be available for as many full rehearsals as possible and, in this particular case, spend many of them close to the player, who will benefit from the tutor's more experienced reaction to sounds. The technical ability to emulate the professional may or may not be there, but the prime concern is that the player begins to think in the right way. Once this is apparent, technical capability will begin to follow close on its heels. Within the orchestra, all instruments are played 'with the ears', and nowhere is this more true than in respect of timpani and percussion, the lack of melodic involvement requiring greater and more subtle control of the degree of influence intended in any single bar or passage.

When specifically considering intonation, all the above applies because, as with all instruments, the apparent intonation is inescapably fused to the method of production and its relevance to that with which it is combined. However, certain difficulties apply to these instruments, the often apparent difference in 'projected' intonation being one of the most formidable.

Unlike the majority of orchestral instruments, the timpani's problem with projected intonation is at its most acute in solo passages, especially those involving harmonically related intervals. No other instrument is so frequently blessed with the dubious privilege of providing a tonic/dominant accompaniment – as in *Ex. 11.6* from the very opening of the second movement of Tchaikovsky *Symphony no. 2*.

(score in concert pitch)

EX. 11.6

Because of the obvious harmonic relationship of the two notes, the B♭ will need to be slightly sharper than would be the case were it to be the fundamental, and a very different note from what would be sounded were the passage to be inverted. (This is because of intervallic tensions and harmonic relationships, the essential qualities of which were outlined with regard to woodwind intonation in Chapter 8.)

The fact that this example appears *pianissimo* and its pitch allows it to be played in the upper ranges of the drums, retaining considerable tension of the head, makes performance slightly easier. Nonetheless, both notes are liable to project an intonation noticeably different from that apparent to the player. At this dynamic they are likely to appear 'sharp', whereas in *fortissimo* the opposite will be true.

With some relevance to this it is worth mentioning one further aspect of intonation that applies most often to the inexperienced player and is, orchestrally, unique to timpani: notes can alter in pitch after they have been struck. This phenomenon is common to all sounds produced by a vibrating membrane when induced by violent action and, as such, applies to many percussion instruments, but only in timpani will it be perceived as a change in pitch. A timpani note struck loudly will rise in pitch as the vibration equalizes across the diameter. The process will be very quick and is due to the distortion effected by the initial impact, but it can sometimes be very noticeable, especially if the note has been produced without due care or technical proficiency. Should it cause a real problem, the most effective solution is to reduce the level, although, as always, a fine player can make it almost unnoticeable.

With really inexperienced players a further source of distortion becomes apparent when the hand-damping of individual notes (used to regulate their length) is not stringently performed. However, in such circumstances, this is likely to be the least of the problems!

Clearly the tuning gauge, fitted to most pedal timpani, can only be regarded as a useful guide and it provides no sort of guarantee before any aural distortions and acoustic vagaries have been allowed for. Fine tuning can *only* be effected by the ear and, to some extent, experience.

Pedal timpani, of course, have the great advantage of being able to make immediate adjustment to intonation, a situation which is quite impossible on hand-tuned instruments. However, noticeable adjustment within a passage such as that quoted above is probably almost as bad as one note's being slightly out of tune, and it is here that the whole question of perceived intonation, combined intonation and intervallic relationship needs to be thoroughly understood by the player. Familiarity with the instruments used also takes on a much more important role at this level so that what has been gleaned from rehearsal can be successfully reproduced in concert.

PEDAL (CHROMATIC) TIMPANI

The somewhat virtuosic chromatic capabilities of pedal timpani are often exploited, either intentionally or accidentally, in scores of the last forty to fifty years and provide problems of intonation all their own. The selection of specific notes, which often takes place while playing another drum, is an extremely difficult technique, and nowadays many timpani parts are far beyond the ability of young players apart from highly competent specialist students. Intonation is therefore totally bound to the ability of the player and cannot be influenced by anything other than practice.

The intricacies of parts that involve frequent changes of pitch are too numerous and idiosyncratic to be discussed here, but some consideration of the general principles and difficulties involved can be undertaken. Quite apart from specific problems of pedalling there comes the individual choice of the range and number of drums to be used. This most famous passage, from the fourth movement of Bartók *Concerto for Orchestra*, can be performed on two, three or four drums, entirely at the discretion of the performer.

EX. 11.7

In the way that it alters the tension of the head and retains a set position, the mechanics of the pedal can be variable, but the principle will remain constant. As the pedal is depressed so the tension of the head will be increased and a higher note obtained. The opposite action will provide the opposite result. In continuous movement the action of the pedal is smooth and it will not preselect any particular interval or give any physical indication of a note being reached. Added to this, the distance travelled by the pedal will alter, depending on where the notes are in the overall range of the drum. The raising of the lowest note of the drum by a semitone will require a relatively small movement while similar adjustment at the top of the range will be considerably larger. Thus, an apparently straightforward passage such as *Ex. 11-8*, which shows two bars of solo timpani from Panufnik *Sinfonia Sacra*, proves to be quite difficult to control.

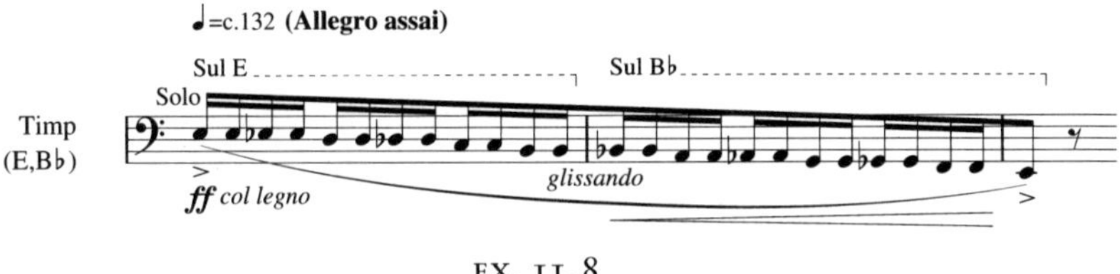

EX. 11.8

The *glissando* marking is rather misleading, for this must be performed as a clear chromatic run and not as an arbitrary movement between two fixed notes. As this passage has to be performed across two drums the downward movement makes it very tricky, since it is easy to misjudge the pedalling and arrive at a note considerably lower than the starting note of the next drum. The later inversion of the same passage, starting at the low octave and rising, is slightly easier.

There remains one further influence in relation to timpani intonation that must be mentioned. Variations in temperature and humidity will have an effect on the playing head of timpani, and extreme conditions, such as close television lights or outdoor performance, can prove disastrous. While this is somewhat less of a liability for 'modern' plastic heads than their calfskin counterparts, such changes will always have an effect on the note produced, because the head will contract or expand to some degree. No noticeable variation is likely to occur during one period of playing but some considerable change is likely between two sessions – rehearsal and concert, for example, or two different days, rehearsal spaces or concert halls. It is of the utmost importance that the timpanist be allowed sufficient time with the instruments, before they are needed for orchestral use, in order both to acclimatize them and to make any necessary adjustments.

Balance

PERCUSSION

This section of a young orchestra experiences more difficulty than most, not only from the point of view of how best to occupy themselves on the frequent occasions that they are not engaged in playing (a significant consideration), but also because of the often limited experience and expertise of those involved. It is rare for a section to be composed entirely of competent players, and many subtleties of percussion playing have to be forsaken until sufficient instruction and practice have been undertaken and familiarity with individual instruments has been achieved.

It is the misfortune of many young percussion players to have had little or no opportunity of handling many of the instruments outside of the orchestral or sectional rehearsal, a situation far removed from that of most other instrumentalists. Even a section of potentially specialist players will not necessarily be familiar with the individual examples of the instruments to be played, nor will they have evolved a defined or truly flexible technique. Thus it is only within a more mature section that one can realize the true potential of the percussion instruments.

Such limitations have to be accepted, but they cannot be taken as a reason for neglect, and a great deal of work with this section has to be taken on board as part of the conductor's normal rehearsal. As already mentioned, the most important aspect of orchestral percussion playing is for all players to be *aware of the texture surrounding their contributions and to understand thoroughly the sounds that they are colouring*. It is certainly not just a case of striking an instrument loudly or softly depending on the marking in the part. In even the most naive scores, the blend and balance of these instruments is extremely important and has a considerable effect on the playing of the rest of the orchestra. This much the conductor can, indeed must, influence, for the tutor will never have the same access to the full orchestra.

The balance of percussion instruments in their most illustrative use – for instance, dance and marching rhythms, or representation of specific sounds – need not be of great concern, as their employment will necessarily be dominant and, usually, pervasive rhythmically. Balance will only involve the comparatively simple relationship of the one instrument to the orchestra as a whole and will not cause especial difficulty. Percussion balance with regard to *colour*, however, is a very different and far-reaching problem and, as in previous chapters of Part II, consideration will be confined to balance within the one section.

When providing orchestral colour, the use of percussion will often be limited, and frequently confined to just one stroke. There is no personal melodic line, no harmonic involvement, just a momentary insinuation of colour, added to a continuous and passing instrumental sound. Even in its most simple manifestation – one instrument alone (most usually cymbals) placed at the summit of an obvious climax – the execution requires considerable musical judgement and technical facility. Perhaps only because it is so common is its difficulty so regularly underestimated. As soon as more than one instrument is involved, problems of balance emerge within the section itself.

The combining of two or more instruments, such as bass drum and cymbals, to provide an integrated sound is common. But varying methods of production and diverse characteristics of resonance make even this combination more complex than it may first seem. The bass drum will not 'ring' for as long as a pair of clashed cymbals; neither will it provide its sound with the same immediacy, tending to project its high point fractionally after it has been struck. Further, without considerable distortion, only a superb example could approach the same level of *fortissimo*. Some adjustment, caused entirely by the rigours of collaboration, will therefore have to be made by one or other instrument, depending on the circumstance.

This leads on to a particular ambiguity that needs to be addressed before the question of individual balance can be examined, and it pervades all aspects of percussion playing. Uniquely, much percussion writing gives no clear guidance as to where the sound should *end* and, where some indication of duration does appear, it often proves to be an arbitrary decision, which makes little or no allowance for the amount of sound that may have been maintained or lost by the instrument concerned.

This is a quite extraordinary situation; in combination, are the sounds of all the percussion instruments involved to be allowed their natural time of decay? Or does the most predominant instrument dictate the duration? Or the most short-lived? Or some instrument elsewhere in the orchestra? There are a hundred such questions and a thousand answers. The result, as so often has to be the case, is usually a matter of habit and always one of compromise. This is no slur on performance integrity, since it is hardly possible to consider, let alone experiment with, all the legitimate possibilities of percussion balance.

The situation is at its worst with regard to those instruments which ring freely after being struck and some short discussion of this problem appears later in this chapter.

The liaison of cymbals and bass drum, mentioned above, is probably the most frequent combination of any two instruments of the percussion section and it will often appear as short notes in a fairly fast tempo. The combination will generally be used to emphasize a rhythmic structure and is especially potent in any type of cross-rhythm or strong syncopation as in the last movement of Glazunov *Symphony no. 5* (*Ex. 11.9*).

Notice that the percussion is marked *mezzo forte* as against *forte* in the rest of the orchestra, and this level is all that should be necessary. The bass drum should control the balance, the clashed cymbals adding sound to it, and not the other way round. The equality of note lengths required of the two instruments is here dictated by tempo and their rhythmic significance, and will not truly correspond to the printed 'crotchet' of the parts. They must not interfere with the clarity of the second quaver in brass and timpani. In this passage *both* instruments will need to be damped after each stroke.

EX. 11.9

The combination of bass drum and clashed cymbals is capable of performance at all dynamic levels and, if necessary, repetition at great speed. This famous, but somewhat extreme, example is from Tchaikovsky overture *Romeo and Juliet*.

EX. 11.10

Once again both instruments will need to be quickly damped, but the linear character of this passage will require an opposite balance, the weight provided by bass drum dominance being, in this instance, too vertical and thus likely to stop the momentum. In this work these two instruments are the only percussion involved and their effect at this point is considerably heightened by its being the only time they are scored as one.

Similar orchestration is prevalent with suspended cymbal rather than clashed, whereupon the single plate will be struck with some designated stick (most usually a side-drum or timpani stick). Obviously this produces a quite different effect, and the two methods of production should not be considered as interchangeable; in passages such as those quoted above the use of suspended cymbal is not an option. For all interpretative purposes the two are best considered as different instruments.

A further variation is the appearance of cymbal and bass drum as an integral instrument performed by one player. This is specifically demanded by both Mahler (in *Symphonies nos 1* and *5*) and Berg (in the *Violin Concerto*), and is sometimes referred to as the 'Mahler Machine'. It involves a medium-sized, double-headed bass drum with one small-diameter cymbal plate attached to the top of the rim; the player uses a fairly hard bass-drum stick with one hand and holds an additional cymbal plate in the other. A greater degree of control over the cymbals can be maintained if the hand-held plate is slightly smaller than the mounted one. The drum is played in normal fashion but the cymbal is clashed downwards on to the fixed plate using a slightly glancing blow, providing a hollow, short-lived sound. When playing a succession of notes in unison, the player will need to make the cymbal stroke smaller, with little movement from the fixed plate. It is a sound most easily associated with amateur marching bands and is, orchestrally, at its most evocative if fairly poor quality instruments are used.

There are occasions where a more complex and individual use of the hands is required, such as in *Ex. 11.11* from the revised (1947) version of Stravinsky *Petrouchka*, where the rhythmic intricacies of the passage demand a high level of dexterity and co-ordination.

EX. 11.11

The much more delicate texture of cymbals combined with snare drum is found less frequently, although it is put to wonderful effect in a passage from *Fêtes* (from *Trois Nocturnes*) by Debussy. Balance here is critical, the snare drum just sharpening the edge of a suspended cymbal struck with a timpani stick.

CA,Cl,Bn,Hn
17
Fl(col8va),Ob
Ww/ Hn
Bn,Hn
Hn
Harp
Timp
Cym
Tamb
Strings
(pizz.)
CA, Cl, Bn, Hn
Bn, Hn

EX. 11.12

The 'immediacy' provided by snare drum will often cause it to be incorporated in the orchestration of cymbal and bass drum, particularly by composers of the middle and late twentieth century, as in Martinů *Fantaisies Symphoniques* (*Ex. 11.13*).

The instrumentation is used here both to punctuate (a) and distort (b) this fragment of theme. But when the line is extended, the darker orchestration, without snare drum, provides the necessary increased weight. In all cases the cymbal is suspended and struck with a side-drum stick and the snare drum

EX. 11.13

EX. 11.13 (continued)

balance needs to be literally between the other two instruments, giving a very sharp articulation to the sound.

Extension of this timbre may be introduced by the addition of aurally related instruments to the roles of both cymbal and snare drum, but bass drum will always be found sufficient to support the weight of the 'chord' alone. Triangle 'added' to cymbal, and tambourine 'added' to snare drum, can be seen in *Ex. 11.14* from Rimsky-Korsakov *Scheherazade*.

Suspended cymbal and snare drum are frequently combined in a sustained

EX. 11.14

roll, most usually with *crescendo*. This, a typical technique of both instruments, is capable of a quite shattering dynamic that should be only exploited rarely. Balance is best achieved with cymbal maintaining a level fractionally subordinate to snare drum, as in *Ex. 11.15*, from the fourth movement of Vaughan Williams *A London Symphony*.

EX. 11.15

Note the subtle absence of graphic *crescendo*, in the last bar of the cymbal part. The entry itself is demanding because there should be no sign of accent.

Once again, various additions can be found to either instrument. The triangle is often used to negate some of the tension projected by cymbal alone and the snare drum is often supported by tambourine, especially in condensed and violent *crescendi*. The tambourine roll, performed with the thumb, can be very clear and incisive in capable hands, and may actually be found replacing snare drum in orchestrations where a slightly brighter sound is required. *Ex. 11-16* from Dukas *La Péri* shows the instrumentation combined with cymbal and bass drum.

EX. 11.16

In the full score this passage is very fully orchestrated and great care must be taken by cymbal and bass drum to ensure that tambourine remains on top of the percussion line. They must not be tempted into balancing with the orchestra but must rather maintain the control within their own section. Again it is worth noting the different dynamics supplied by the composer.

Tuned percussion are far less often involved in such instrumentation, and are mainly reserved for more soloistic statements of thematic material, although isolated instances do occur, whereupon the individual role is usually more clearly defined. *Ex. 11.17* shows a number of bars of the percussion part in the last movement of John Adams *Harmonielehre*, where vibraphone, xylophone and two marimbas combine in a passage of harmonic repetition.

EX. 11.17

Equal balance must be maintained overall, but the changes of rhythm for 2nd and 1st marimba and harmony for xylophone must be made clear without any violent change in dynamic level or disproportionate accent – the full passage is over two hundred bars in length. It is essential that the instrumentalists are acutely aware of one another, for more will be achieved by surreptitious subordination of the repeated lines than by extreme assertion of those that change.

Combination of tuned with untuned percussion is surprisingly rare and will nearly always display a dual reponsibility. In *Ex. 11.18*, for instance, from the fifth and final movement of Bernstein *Serenade after Plato's 'Symposium'*, glockenspiel and xylophone are scored together with three drums and cymbal.

EX. 11.18

However, the glockenspiel doubles the upper string line and the xylophone the lower (at an octave above). The three drums (of different pitch in relation to one another, but untuned) clarify the rhythmic movement while the cymbal delineates the climactic nature of the passage. Balance is still of vital concern but over a wider spectrum.

Similar separation of responsibility can be found for this section in many other guises. In *Ex. 11.1*, a large and low-pitched tenor drum, cymbal and bass drum 'accompany' the vibrant side-drum part already discussed. Four different dynamic markings are in evidence and the three instruments have to balance between themselves before the combined sound can be related to the dominant line.

In a less obvious and more linear example, this wonderful use of percussion, from the second suite of Ravel *Daphnis et Chloé*, is analogous.

The snare drum has the pervasive rhythm, while the other instruments,

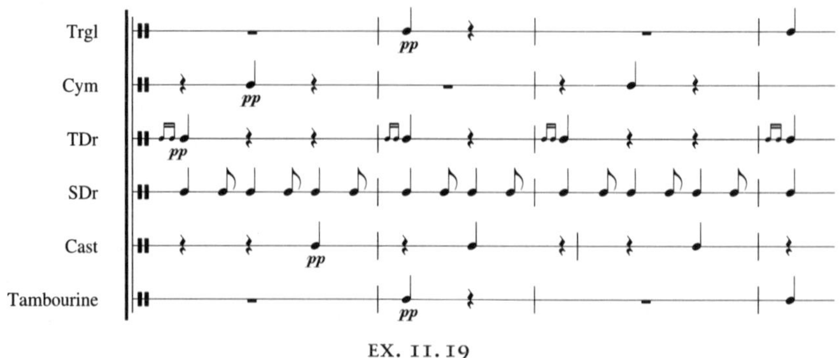

EX. 11.19

either singly or combined, provide a shape to each bar with a subtlety that is unsurpassed in percussion literature. Nowhere else in the orchestra is the difficulty of balancing immediately related but separately produced sounds ever likely to be so acute.

Quotation of the most famous of all examples, the last five bars of the percussion variation in Britten *The Young Person's Guide to the Orchestra*, must be forgiven, for it remains one of the most awkward passages for balance to be found anywhere.

EX. 11.20

Leaving aside any additional difficulties caused by the layout of the printed orchestral parts, this passage shows an alarming propensity for highlighting a different instrument every time it is performed. The delicacy and sureness of touch required of the players in these few seconds' music only comes with a lifetime's experience.

In *Ex. 11.20* balance cannot conveniently be divorced from rhythm. The relationship of beats in compound time is both subtle and critical to the momentum of the bar and nowhere is this more apparent than in 6/8, where the main beats of each bar are just close enough to maintain a clearly defined pulse but far enough away to require specific direction from the other five. Attempts to reproduce this 'natural' flow from individual players, each of whom is responsible for less than half a bar, can result in unintended distortion and a plethora of false accents. It is better, certainly with young players, to leave this aspect of the phrase to the strings (each of whose parts contains the vital crossing of a bar-line) and concentrate on the even balance of dynamic. But even here, the widely different characteristics of each instrument and their varying response make it exceptionally difficult, and finally, all success can be totally defeated by the acoustic qualities of the concert hall.

Less awkward but still very demanding is a similar passage from the *Turandot Scherzo* in Hindemith *Symphonic Metamorphosis.*

EX. 11.21

Balancing so many unrelated instruments is not simple, especially across the *diminuendo*, but the line is much easier to achieve and its projection likely to prove less of a distraction because each instrument is given a more rhythmically stable fragment of the bar.

Most orchestral percussion writing will generally comprise variations or amalgamations of the above combinations and the aural principles involved apply regardless of the number or type of instruments embraced; true balance will only be obtained by a general understanding of each player's role.

Timpani, where they appear in the above examples, have been intentionally ignored for the moment. Although orchestrations exist where their balance is directly allied to the percussion section, in all the cases cited above their primary relationship is to the harmonic movement of the orchestra as a whole.

Perhaps, before we leave this particular aspect of percussion playing, one final word of warning might be in order. The recording of percussion instruments is notorious. In defence of the recording industry it has to be said that many of the instruments are extremely difficult to reproduce in recorded sound, as the extraordinary overtones and sometimes violent disintegration cause immense distortion. But balance in recordings may also be achieved through technical adjustment and physical displacement. It remains imperative that any decisions of balance related to public performance are based upon live experience and are not influenced, in any way, by recorded or artificially reproduced illustrations.

Specific Techniques

TIMPANI

The ultimate goal of the timpanist is the perfection of the individual sound, and all aspects of playing will be geared towards this pinnacle of musical achievement. The prerequisite, however, is talent, and although any hard-working, determined student might approach tantalizingly close, the final objective will always remain just beyond most players' grasp. It is unfortunate that the appreciation of timpani playing, particularly with regard to tone, is generally more limited than that afforded to other orchestral instruments (although not altogether surprising given the fact that general recognition of most instruments is exactly proportionate to the size of their concerto repertoire). Obviously, the quality and condition of the instruments will affect the tone produced, some poor and neglected examples being beyond the redemption of even a great player, but this need not be directly proportionate – I have heard many experts demonstrate the most wonderful sounds on the most unlikely instruments.

Such artistry has all to do with 'touch' and the ability to coax a sound from the instrument, rather than demand it. It will not be evident from a younger player but the potential will sometimes be there and a very high standard can be achieved.

Number, size and range

The majority of programmes performed by student orchestras will, nowadays, require the timpanist to use four or five drums, sometimes more for specific works. The sizes of drum head diameter will vary slightly according to make, but all timpani are designed in sets to cover approximately the same overall range. The usable range of each drum is often a contentious matter, and many players, unhappy with the tone at extremes of tension or slackness, will consider the interval of a fifth to be the maximum. This will, of course, be determined in relation to the quality of each head. As most young orchestral players will usually receive specialist tuition during the preparation of a concert programme, this aspect of the technique must be left to the tutor concerned. For the sake of completeness *Ex. 11.22* shows the measurements of the five most common timpani, together with their generally accepted range and (indicated by black notes) the slightly more extreme reaches.

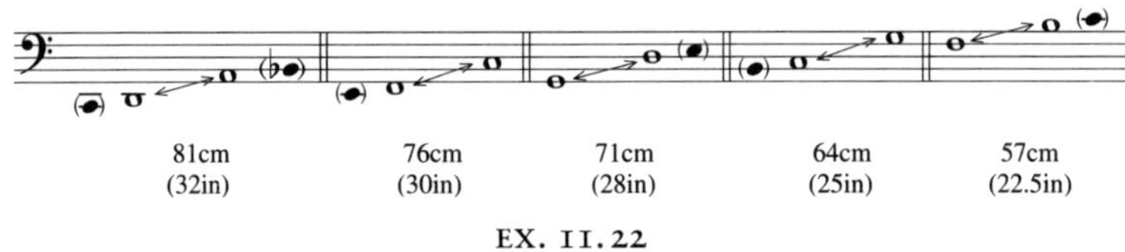

EX. 11.22

As can be seen, all the instruments overlap in range, which allows not only for a choice of drum for individual notes but also the opportunity to duplicate notes should an awkward passage in limited range so demand. Wherever possible, selection will generally be made in the middle or upper range of the drum, where the tension is fairly tight, but great advances have been made in the manufacture of the plastic head even in just the last few years, and the response and tone of the lower notes of the range have improved.

Production

The optimum position at which the stick head should strike the drum is about three and a half to four inches from the edge, and variation on this is only made for colouristic effect. Lessening the distance can be advantageous in extreme *pianissimo* but movement towards the centre will increasingly lose the quality of the note. Any movement in this direction needs to be minimal and very carefully considered. The 'heart beats' at the end of Tchaikovsky *Romeo and Juliet* (*Ex. 11.3*), where the tonality is also supplied by tuba, can be an example if an overtly 'throbbing despair' is required.

Such movement may occasionally be specifically requested by a composer, as in *Ex. 11.23* from Kodály *Dances of Galanta*, where a great variation in sound is achieved by alternating production at the middle and close to the rim of the timpani head.

EX. 11.23

Most extreme examples of this type will be clarified by the addition of a footnote, as here.

The technique of striking the drum must *always* be performed with the stick head moving away, leaving the vibrating membrane as quickly as possible, and it must never damp the sound by applied pressure. This is a most common fault with inexperienced players, especially at the commencement of a *fortissimo* roll, where a considerable temptation to lean into the instrument can be apparent.

Sticks

The number of pairs of different sticks available to the timpanist is legion. The head of the stick varies in shape, size and material of both the core and its covering, producing a wide variety of colouring to the sound. For the young orchestral player, apart from whatever might be the favourite 'standard' pair, two further pairs, one of softer and one of harder heads, are an essential minimum together with a carefully chosen wooden pair.

These last are the most dangerous with regard to the damage they can do to the drum head if not very carefully used, especially if they are of very small diameter, but they are so regularly called for that no youth orchestra timpanist will be able to survive for long without recourse to them. It is not sufficient to rely on the occasional loan of side-drum sticks, although these might be specifically requested in some passages, the marking *col legno* usually requiring something much bigger, as in *Ex. 11.24* at the very end of Walton *Symphony no. 2*.

Such a passage (for *one player*, not two) is very dangerous for the inexperienced player, most especially the penultimate bar. The timpani support full *fortissimo* orchestration of the rhythm and over-enthusiasm or lack of control

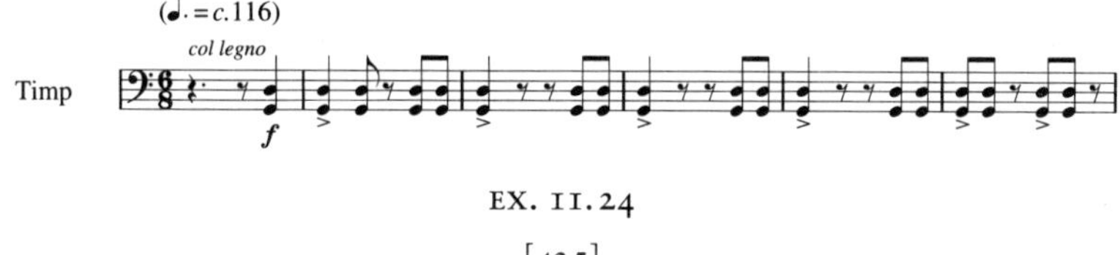

EX. 11.24

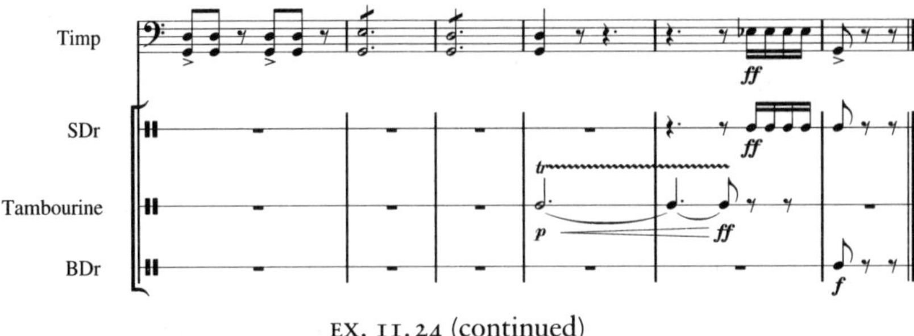

EX. 11.24 (continued)

will unquestionably damage the drum heads, probably beyond repair. Once more, the careful marking of *forte* in the timpani part alone for all but the final flourish should be strictly observed.

Usually the two sticks are used alternately to strike the drum but, especially in the case of complicated rhythms involving a number of drums, many variations can be necessary, and the timpanist will mark the order in the part in much the same way as a string player will mark bowings, only indicating deviation from normal alternation, or at the start of a passage where needed. This last can be very important, for disaster can ensue if the player starts with the wrong hand. A very simple example, and one which no timpanist would actually need to mark, can be taken from the penultimate bar of *Ex. 11.24*. With the lower drum to the left of the player, the left hand must strike the drum first in order to maintain alternate striking without needing to cross the hands. If, however, the lower drum were to be to the right then the passage would need to be started with the right hand for the same reasons.

The similarity of this entry technique to that of string bowing should be noted. The direction or, in this case, the order of the hands, is fundamentally determined by demands of the following passage and need not be influenced by any accent or dynamic that may apply to the entry note itself.

Careful perusal of continuous passage-work from just this one aspect will begin to reveal the complications that can ensue. It will also become apparent that simple alternation of the hands will often not suffice, particularly in fast passages where certain notes are immediately repeated or patterns occur involving more than two drums. In these and similar cases either two consecutive notes will have to be played with one hand or the sticks will have to cross, and the decision will depend on tempo, dynamic, distance to be travelled and – where feasible – personal preference.

Subtleties of this technique may be gleaned from the many textbooks at present available, and are not within the scope of this discussion. For anyone dealing with timpani performance, however, some basic knowledge is desirable.

Very occasionally alternation of the hands will be discarded altogether and a short passage played with one stick alone. This will always be confined to repetition of the same note on the same drum and many players will choose to use it for the four notes which open Beethoven *Violin Concerto*, considering it, in this one instance, to give greater control of equal tone and line. It will sometimes be specifically requested by composers, as at the opening of the *March to the Scaffold* from Berlioz *Symphonie Fantastique*, for example (*Ex. 11-4*).

The use of harder or softer sticks will not actually affect the length of the note but only the potency of its onset. Thus it is not always pertinent to request harder sticks for a passage of short notes, any more than it is to request very soft sticks for *pianissimo* passages of long notes. The implied character of the note is the essential consideration in choice of sticks.

Composers will occasionally demand the use of two contrasting sticks at the same time. *Ex. 11.25*, which illustrates alternation of a felt stick with one of wood, comes from the *Dance of Spirits of Fire* from Holst ballet music *The Perfect Fool*.

The demand for the wooden stick on the 'off' beats, coupled with later careful variations in dynamic, especially *subito piano*, makes the passage quite difficult to keep exactly even.

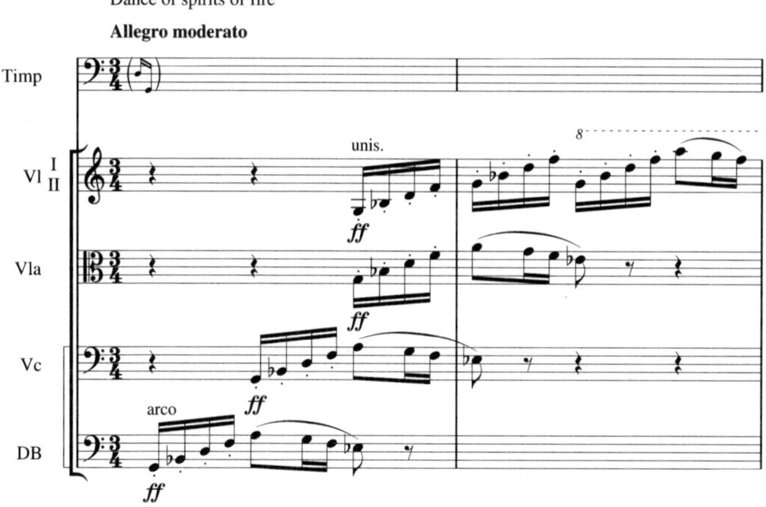

EX. 11.25

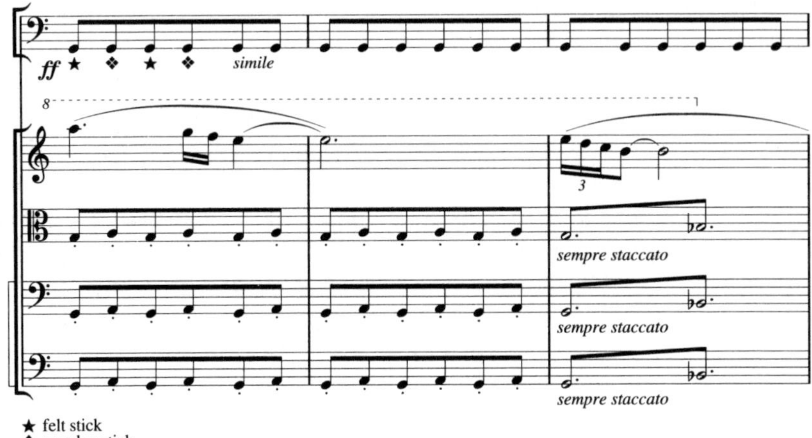

EX. 11.25 (continued)

Damping

The only method of control over the length of sound produced is damping – achieved by pressure of the fingertips or heel of the hand against the vibrating head in order to stop the sound. This technique is necessary not only to conform to written note values but also to stop the vibration of one drum as another is being played (the ubiquitous tonic/dominant passages, as shown in *Ex. 11.6*, are examples). It can be performed very quickly, the stick held between first finger and thumb and the other three fingers used for damping. The action must always be firm, otherwise distortion of pitch or sound will be all that results.

In *Ex. 11.24* (from Walton *Symphony no. 2*) damping is necessary at every rest, especially in the sixth and seventh bars. After the final note both drums will need to be damped very firmly with the heel of the hand. So often the inexperienced player will frantically damp the drum last played and forget about the one still ringing from the penultimate note.

With the drums arranged so closely around the timpanist the damping of heads not actually played but ringing in sympathy can be of real concern. If certain drums are not in use at the vital moment it is sometimes possible to damp them previously with a pad, but such opportunity doesn't often arise, and usually they will have to be damped as quickly as possible after those that have just been played.

Timpani rolls

A timpani roll is produced by fast alternation of the two sticks, the actual speed being subject to the size of drum and the tension of the head. A note where the tension of the head is very tight will need a very fast roll to cover the very short-lived resonance of each note, whereas low on the same drum something a good deal slower will be necessary, or the longer resonance will be muffled. Similarly, the size of drum will involve some adjustment of approach, as will the volume of sound required. In all cases, the speed will be dictated to some extent by the condition and quality of the head.

Notation of the roll is either by the addition of 'tr' over the note concerned (identical with the method of designating a trill in strings or wind but in this case not implying two different notes) or a number of strokes through the tail of the note (as in string *tremolo*). Both systems have their drawbacks. The latter raises the old problem that applied elsewhere of whether a measured or unmeasured number of notes is intended. Once again decisions have to be made on the basis of tempo, character and style, with the added awareness that measured notes for timpani will have a tendency to be even more pronounced than strings or wind.

Certainly in the case of the scores of Mozart, Beethoven and Brahms, strokes through the tail of a note indicate measured rhythm, all three composers marking the roll exclusively with 'tr', a clarity illustrated by *Ex. 11.26* from the 2nd movement of Beethoven *Symphony no. 4*.

EX. 11.26

Other composers of the same period, such as Schubert, tend to reserve two strokes for measured notes and three or more for rolls (*see* Appendix).

The practice of using the '*tremolo* shorthand' for designating rolls becomes more common in the middle to late nineteenth century, and this is where the majority of ambiguity appears. (Berlioz seemed to cement this practice, indicating rolls by four strokes even when discussing them in his *Treatise on Instrumentation*. However, the implication of two strokes always meaning measured can prove a little impractical in some of the faster movements.) Some composers are a little more specific in designating measured notes, often by recourse to writing out the first group of notes before succumbing to any shorthand – as in *Ex. 11.27* from the first movement of Tchaikovsky *Symphony no. 6*.

EX. 11.27

As far as the roll itself is concerned the prime uncertainties, apparent in either form of notation, are where exactly it should end and whether it should be continuous or reiterated (the use of the vital slur regularly being absent).

Extended rolls will often be notated thus

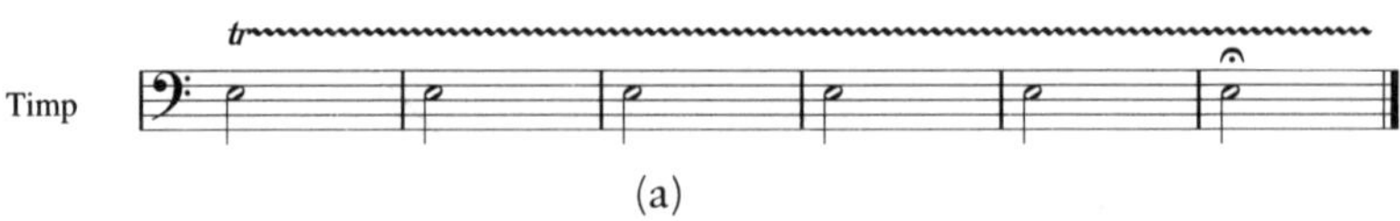

(a)

or thus

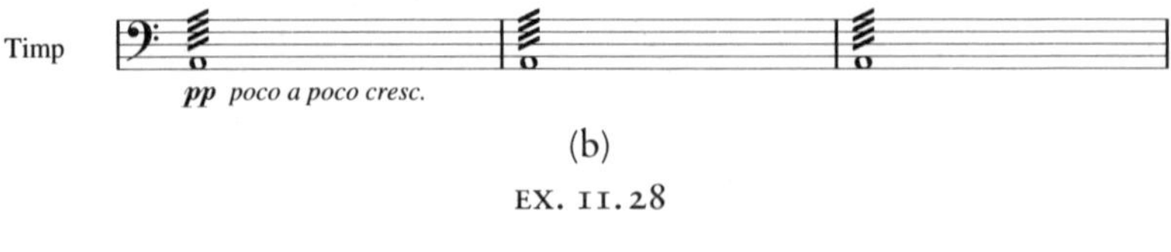

(b)

EX. 11.28

Such a succession of complete bars is generally clear in intention if not entirely so in exact notation. They are always supplied with individual dynamic, including *crescendo, diminuendo* or accent (where applicable) and, in the absence of any mark to the contrary, they should be taken as a continuous roll. In neither of the above examples could any noticeable reiteration have been intended.

The method of notation used in the second example of *Ex. 11.28* is in direct association with that used for string *tremolo* or measured repetition (and, as such, is more accurate than 'tr' would be as far as technical execution is concerned). For strings, no possible marking of phrasing exists in these circumstances, either by slur or any other means, and it is doubtless from this enforced practice that the timpani writing evolved. The use of 'tr', while generally clearer in its inherent meaning of 'unmeasured', will often bring its own problems, which will raise pertinent questions of interpretation.

What, for example, did Dvořák mean at the end of the introduction in his *Symphony no. 9 'From the New World'* (*Ex. 11.29*)?

EX. 11.29

or in the first movement of his *Symphony no. 7* (*Ex. 11.30*)?

Both readings – clear reiteration and continuous roll – have been heard in performance and, especially in the case of *Ex. 11.29*, where the timpani are solo, strong arguments can be made for either interpretation.

Considering the two examples separately, in *Ex. 11.29* the second 'trill' and its following graphic extension are clearly indicated above the semiquaver, and the *diminuendo* hairpin (in all editions) begins *before* the printed crotchet. Thus, for a roll to be indicated, only the joining slurs are missing. For the

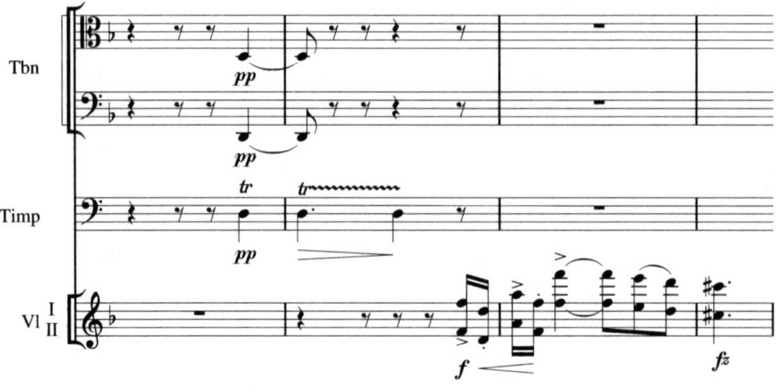

EX. 11.30

first note to be separate the 'tr' would have to be regarded as misplaced, as would the start of *diminuendo*, one implied slur would still be missing (across the bar-line) and, I strongly suspect, some mark of dynamic would be needed at the start of the crotchet. From the purely musical point of view a stronger case for separation is apparent. The alternation of similar rhythm between orchestra and timpani is obvious, but the less obvious relationship that this reading gives both to the extended perfect cadence (timpani roll exactly half violin *tremolo*) and the link passage itself (3 bars overall, now divided equally 1½/1½) must be considered. There would also seem to be considerable historic precedence.

In the second example, *Ex. 11.30*, a continuous roll is most likely in view of the tie in the trombone parts and the fact that any individual accent is undesirable on the last bar of this four-bar phrase. Separation of the first two notes, and the re-marking of 'tr', may be taken to indicate the placement of the *diminuendo*, as in a less ambiguous example, from Mahler *Symphony no. 7*.

EX. 11.31

The question of whether the final note of a trill should be marked or not is equally problematic and even more frequent. *Ex. 11.32*, from Mendelssohn overture *Ruy Blas* highlights both the problem itself and the difficulty in reaching any clear decision.

In the first four bars no slur occurs for the timpani roll but it is clearly marked in the wind and brass, whereas in the last four bars careful slurs are added for this instrument as well. Both are analogous with the writing for lower strings and so a simple decision with regard to relevance might seem all that is necessary. But as has already been mentioned, with the strings playing separate repetitions of the same note there is no way of marking a phrasing similar to that shown in the wind, so is a tie – in the sense of no noticeable accent – implied? Here, this is most likely, since the 'separate' crotchet appears on weak bars of the phrase and both timpani and strings have responsibility towards support of the sustained chord.

A further consideration highlighted by bars 9-12 of this example is the actual technique used to start the roll. Very often, when a roll is preceded by notes which conform to the general rhythmic movement of the orchestra it will be found preferable to underline the corresponding movement by delineating the start of the roll with a very short single stroke – the technique of *forte*/

EX. 11.32

EX. 11. 32 (continued)

piano without the *piano* probably describes it most simply. There are many occasions where an expert timpanist will judge this technique to be appropriate and, in doing so, will clearly define the rhythmic movement of the whole orchestra.

Such details are always difficult to interpret, and they have been discussed at some length here because they are of such vital importance when dealing with inexperienced players. Professional players will always resolve these questions having given due consideration to the idiosyncrasies of their own instruments, but this is not the case with student orchestras, and attention to these sort of details is the basis of a combined and unified performance.

The performance of the timpani roll will not only need adjustment of speed in relation to pitch but also of intonation in relation to dynamic. The ear of the timpanist must be most acute in these circumstances, and concentration unwavering. In an extended roll that includes a strong *crescendo* the pitch will tend to flatten as the head is struck harder, especially if the note involved is towards the lower range of the drum, and careful adjustment will have to be made to compensate for this. The same will apply in extreme *diminuendo*, although here adjustment would actually have to be made first, soft striking producing the more accurate intonation. Of course, on hand-tuned instruments, no such adjustment is possible.

The roll is equally possible across two drums, as demanded in *Ex. 11.33*, from the third movement of Debussy *La Mer.*

EX. 11.33

Double notes

The simultaneous production of two notes by one player has already been seen in *Ex. 11.24* and it is frequently found at a dynamic of *fortissimo*. It is, however, equally effective at the other end of the dynamic spectrum, as in *Ex. 11-34* from the second movement of the same Walton symphony.

EX. 11.34

Three drums are required for this passage, as the use of one pedal drum to produce the alternating A and B♭ cannot be contemplated. Apart from its immense difficulty, the retuning would cause an audible *glissando* on each occasion.

The alternation of double notes with single is required less often but can be very successful. In *Fêtes* from Debussy *Trois Nocturnes* it is combined with two harps and lower strings.

EX. 11.35

These create a very different effect from that which would be obtained if two players were involved, and not only because of the enforced 'single sticking'.

The provision of two players gives a clear individuality to the lines (in much the same way as division by two string players sounds different from the same notes 'double-stopped' by one), and is not contemplated merely to provide extra notes or variation in rhythm.

The octave rolls, for example, from the last movement of Mahler *Symphony no. 1* (*Ex. 11.36*), provide a very different sound from two players than if they were to be played by one, in the manner of *Ex. 11.32*.

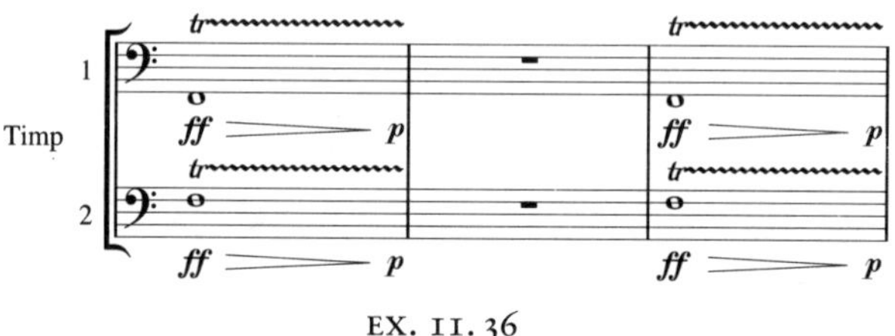

EX. 11.36

Much of this movement involves the most subtle alternation of two players on drums of identical pitch, as well as combinations of strikingly different rhythms.

Muting

The normal method of muting timpani is to place a piece of felt or a small folded cloth on the edge of the drum head (the exact position dependent on the result required). Immediately opposite the point of beating will give maximum damping of the resonance, while correspondingly nearer retains more of the pitch. The most usual direction is the same as for all other instruments (*con sord.*, *mit Dämpfer*, etc.) and will be cancelled in similar fashion (*senza sord.*, etc.) although, occasionally, the term 'muffled' will be found – a marking restricted to timpani and certain percussion drums.

A further variation, *coperto*, is interesting because it actually means 'covered', and there is considerable reason to believe that its use in many circumstances meant just that. Berlioz, in his *Treatise on Instrumentation*, states 'Particularly in the scores of old masters, the indication *muffled* or *covered* kettledrums is frequently found. This means that the skin of the instrument is to be covered with a piece of cloth, which damps the sound and lends it a mournful expression. Drumsticks with sponge ends are preferable in this case.'

He then continues, immediately and within the same paragraph, 'Sometimes it is advisable to indicate which notes the drummer should execute with two sticks and which with a single stick' at which point he quotes the opening two bars of *March to the Scaffold* from *Symphonie Fantastique*. The possibility that the example is included only in reference to the last sentence must be accepted, but the wider connotation must also be considered, especially as the relevant passage is printed in all editions with the additional marking *baguette d'éponge* (sponge-headed drum-sticks). (The marking of 'muting' however is far less general, although undoubtedly correct. In some editions – Donajowski, Eulenberg miniatures – it is missing altogether, in others – Breitkopf – it is marked throughout the movement. Others – Kalmus/Dover – mark it only by inference of *senza sordini* at bar 121.)

Whatever might have been the original intention of such markings, players nowadays will use a pad or cloth as previously described. Such damping procedures can also occasionally be used when not specifically requested by a composer, in order to obtain and control a particular quality or length, but this is entirely a matter for the experience and judgement of the player. This method, with the damper placed more towards the centre, will also be used to damp drums which are not in use.

Layout

For the percussion section the practical necessities of performance, so long taken for granted, can now be the cause of formidable problems. Performing spaces, designed to accommodate ever-increasing sections of strings and wind, are now often found to be too small for the requirements of the modern percussion section. Also, orchestral parts have generally proved unable to adapt to a large instrumentation performed by interdependent players, or even to be readable at the considerable distances so often necessitated by the layout of the required instruments. No other section of the orchestra is faced with so many practical considerations fundamental to performance.

Even with only one or two players, the instruments must be located in positions that are convenient for playing rather than simply those which can be most easily accommodated within the available space. As discussed above, considerations of balance will be severely jeopardized if the instruments are thoughtlessly arranged or widely separated from one another, since both aural and visual contact are of extreme importance.

Although the layout of a percussion section is very much the responsibility of the players themselves, initially overseen by a tutor in student orchestras, the principle behind the decisions involved should be understood by the conductor. The problems are, after all, a direct result of the score and thus, part and parcel of the eventual realization of the music.

At risk of stating the obvious, it must be said that the number of instruments listed at the beginning of a score has nothing to do with the number of players required. If no two instruments appear together and sufficient opportunity exists for an instrumentalist to get from one to another then one player can play any number of instruments. But the converse is also true and many scores that list one or two players will often turn out to need three or four. The essential problem here is that the requisite number of players cannot always be calculated simply on the basis of the maximum number of instruments playing at any one time. It must also take into consideration whether there is sufficient opportunity for players to get to those instruments. Half a bar of fast tempo is not enough time to move from xylophone to tubular bells, for example, or even to put down a tambourine and pick up snare-drum sticks.

Sometimes the difficulty may be resolved by a rearrangement of instrumental responsibility for one or two players. It might prove possible, for example, that certain bars of a tambourine part could be inserted by a different player, thus allowing time for the original player to make any necessary change of instrument or sticks. But this in itself is quite a complicated procedure and could only be contemplated by someone with considerable insight into the practicalities involved.

In the very specific percussion requirements of Lutosławski *Livre pour Orchestre* (Chapter 5) it was noted that timpani are listed in the score as part of the responsibility of 'Percussion 1'. Considering the severely limited involvement of the part, this would seem to be a very practical and thoughtful division. But closer inspection proves otherwise.

EX. II.37

At least four timpani are needed for this work so they can only be arranged surrounding the player, which makes it almost physically impossible to get to the xylophone in the time allowed, even if it were not necessary to change sticks for mallets. In this case a situation similar to that described above might prove possible. 'Percussion 2', who has a second xylophone, could feasibly play these few bars – coming from vibraphone it could even be arranged without change of mallets – but it would be far better, especially in view of timpanists' general specialization, to provide an extra player. In any event, any interchange is likely to be dependent on the design of the printed material.

Printed material

Especially in recent symphonic music, the number of percussion parts involved will sometimes cause practical problems as to how they might best be arranged in the players' copy. The restriction of one part to a copy may prove beneficial, particularly where any extended passage for tuned percussion would make a page turn impractical, but if any misjudgement has been made (and it very often has), a complete rearrangement will be necessary, usually involving the rewriting of more than just the one copy involved.

The provision of a short 'percussion score' for each player has the advantage of showing the complete percussion involvement but, again, it harbours problems. Unless an identical layout is maintained throughout, regardless of whether the full section is involved or not, such copies are very difficult to read. It is awkward enough continuously having to glance up at the fourth line of six, but quite impossible when, because other instruments are not playing, this suddenly becomes the second line of three or the third line of four. Unfortunately nearly all parts using this design are guilty of such compression at some point, not only in order to save paper but also as a means of avoiding page turns at inconvenient moments – a necessity which arises more frequently in this format.

Fundamentally, neither system will work unless the original division of parts, and a layout most suitable to their execution, has been undertaken by an experienced player – a concept, unfortunately, yet to be embraced by the majority of publishers.

Most orchestral parts of the standard repertoire that are currently in circulation will already have been adapted where necessary and, for student orchestras, the percussion tutor will always be at hand in the initial stages. Nonetheless, the fact that such complications exist for this section, before a note has been played, significantly adds to the pressures involved, especially in the case of inexperienced players.

Before we leave this brief appraisal of the 'non-musical' problems that beset the percussion section, two further pertinent questions need to be addressed. Firstly, the size and enforced position of many percussion layouts will frequently dictate that the music be placed at a greater distance from the player than is normally the case elsewhere in the orchestra. Thus, it must be clearly legible – a reproduction of the composer's handwritten manuscript, for example, will not suffice. Although little can be done about this at the time of rehearsal – apart from the regular chore of rewriting – it should be drawn to the attention of the publisher. A polite note enclosed with the parts upon their return after performance (or immediately on cancellation of the work) has been known to produce results.

Secondly, the part must be firmly supported on a music stand that remains steady at any height and does not prove to be unstable as the pages are turned or the copy transported from one instrument to another. Reaching forward across a tuned percussion instrument to turn the page of a copy balanced on a stand of the ubiquitous folding design, most probably teetering at its full extension, is potentially disastrous. Such stands are insufficiently stable and, even if they have to be used elsewhere in the orchestra, the percussion section *must* be provided with those of a more inflexible and rigid design.

Instrumentation

Although much orchestral percussion writing states clearly which instruments are required, areas of uncertainty can exist, especially in relation to the many types and sizes of small drum. The majority of instances will be found in works of the late Romantic composers where the greater descriptive influence began to demand a wider percussion range, but examples may be found both before and after this period. Fundamentally the problem is one of terminology and arises from the confusing similarity of the many names used to designate either the same or different instruments – for example, *Tamburin* (Ger. = tambourine), *Tambourin* (Ger. = Tabor or long drum). In the eighth of Beethoven's *12 Contra-Dances, tambourin* unquestionably requires a long drum or equivalent instrument rather than tambourine (despite the fact that at least one recording uses the latter and goes so far as to draw attention to the extraordinary nature of the part – one extended roll – in the sleeve note). The more general areas of confusion, however, are frequently exacerbated by the sporadic use of different names *for the same instrument* within a single work.

Considerable space is devoted to this problem by Norman Del Mar in his *Anatomy of the Orchestra* and it would be both unnecessary and somewhat discourteous to attempt any expansion or reproduction of so practical an appraisal here. Suffice it to say that I have been present at many rehearsals by eminent conductors (many of whom were either students or personal friends of the great Romantic and twentieth-century composers) who have differed one from another in their conclusions or changed their minds across a period of years, such can be the ambiguity and individuality of the problem. Equally, it is by no means unknown for the carefully chosen drum of yesterday to be changed for something completely different when the orchestra performs in a new and dissimilar acoustic.

For tuned percussion, the problem is more frequently concerned with range and, in some cases, intended pitch, since many composers write for some obscure local variation of an instrument which may prove to be unavailable. Bell parts are notorious in this respect, both in terms of single examples at very low pitch and racks of tubular bells. Lutosławski, once more in *Livre pour Orchestre*, writes for a rack of bells covering the standard octave and a half (C – F) but apparently pitched one octave below normal, with much of the part written in the bass clef. Such an extraordinary demand should always be questioned by the interpreter, even when it appears in a work of a composer so erudite and accomplished as Lutosławski.

In this particular case I feel the written octave to be dubious for a number of reasons. Much of the part involves fast repetition or alternation of pitch which, at the written octave, would be unlikely to sound very clear and would prove extremely difficult to accomplish on a rack of bells covering a width of some six to eight feet and upwards of twelve feet high (always providing such an instrument could be obtained). It also, and more importantly, proves itself open to question from a purely musical point of view in passages such as *Ex. 11-38*.

The octave is brought into question not only by the sound of such a passage, but also by the fact that each fragment must surely be at least partially

EX. 11.38

EX. 11.38 (continued)

damped. This situation effectively rules out the use of a number of individual bells, or of even more cumbersome bell plates, and insists on the overall damping mechanism incorporated in a rack. The possibility emerges that Lutosławski was, for some reason on this occasion, writing the bell part at *true* fundamental pitch (one octave *below* sounding). The lack of any cautionary footnote or emphasis of required pitch in the list of instrumentation – an unusual omission when a rare variation of an otherwise standard instrument is required – could be taken as adding weight to this view.

Whatever the final interpretative decision might be, the fact remains that questions of this sort arise with ever-increasing frequency and, especially in respect of the different character displayed by varying examples of the same instrument, the orchestral score will often prove less definitive for this section than any other. The ears of both conductor and players become the only true means of arbitration.

Notation

The above dictum also applies when decisions need to be made regarding the frequently encountered inexactitude of note-lengths within percussion parts. Many examples may be cited where the same note-values exist throughout a part, regardless of the multiple variations that might be apparent in the surrounding or immediately associated sounds. For all percussion – but especially clashed cymbal, bass drum, tam-tam and bells – the *forte* crotchet that appears with a fully orchestrated sustained chord looks exactly the same as that which appears with *staccato* brass. Although often no really successful alternative symbol exists, it does mean that percussion players must develop the ability to appraise and retain the character of each individual entry to a greater extent than might be the case elsewhere in the orchestra where the direction and emphasis are likely to be more apparent on the printed page.

For the conductor, while it is necessary to appreciate the fact that each case will require a particular interpretative decision, some general considerations, which add their own complications, need to be confronted.

Especially with regard to instruments whose natural period of decay is long (cymbals, bell, tam-tam), the control of their duration should not always be based entirely on their direct orchestral relationship. Idiosyncrasies of the individual instruments themselves will sometimes require that they be sustained longer or arrested earlier than the sounds with which they are associated.

A pair of cymbals, for example, damped immediately after they have been clashed produce a particular orchestral colour and provide a legitimate, and easily acceptable, *staccato* sound. Their sound is equally acceptable if they are allowed to ring and are only damped close to their ultimate point of decay. Damping at certain moments between these two extremes, however, especially after a strong initial dynamic, can prove inappropriate to a degree which will be noticeable and quite disturbing. In this case the quality of the instruments themselves (not to mention the player) will often become the determining factor, and some idealistic musical notions may well need to be adjusted. Nonetheless it is the musical reasoning that must remain fundamental to any individual judgement and, as such, it will usually be based either on the instrument's direct orchestral association or its dramatic influence.

While this complication is most frequently encountered with cymbals – the climactic *fortissimo* clash being one of the most troublesome of all orchestral

EX. II.39

techniques in inexperienced hands – it also holds true for all percussion instruments to some degree. (Elsewhere in the orchestra, only harp and, to a lesser extent, string *pizzicati* will ever confront a similar problem.) At the opening of Tchaikovsky *Francesca da Rimini*, for example (*Ex. 11.39*), the exact duration of the tam-tam note is not as important as its very considerable dramatic implication, but some degree of control is certainly necessary.

The stroke must be neither too loud nor too soft, and it must appear exactly with the lower note of cellos and basses – limitations that conspire to make this a deceptively difficult entry because of the tam-tam's tendency to reach its maximum projected level fractionally *after* it has been struck. This passage will benefit from a large, low-sounding, instrument, not only because of the dramatic implication but also, more importantly, because of the resulting affinity in pitch with the sustained low A♭. With a good instrument, control over duration can be very precise, as damping can be attained gradually with a circular motion of the free hand so that there is no abrupt deterioration or cessation of sound. While some patient experimentation will always be necessary for student instrumentalists, an added problem in *Ex. 11.39* will be finding a truly acceptable instrument.

It is not fundamentally possible to support or complement the sounds of orchestral percussion playing in quite the same way as in other areas of the orchestra, and results are more directly related to the quality of both players and instruments. Thus, as shown above, individual examples of an instrument, of which no two are exactly alike, will often play an unusually prominent part in the equation. It is also worth mentioning that neither dynamic nor duration need be directly related to the strength with which many instruments are struck. The actual position of impact is often much more important.

Rhythm and Phrasing

The general sparseness of orchestral percussion parts, together with the prevalent use of notes of relatively short time-value, can lead less experienced players into a very vertical way of thinking. Their rhythmic responsibility of playing 'on the beat' will very often be reduced to something more akin to 'at the beat', involving little awareness of the musical line elsewhere in the orchestra and virtually none of the inherent movement sparingly implied within their own part. Even the tam-tam stroke quoted above (*Ex. 11-39*) must be placed relative to the lowest note of lower strings and bassoons – itself decidedly 'gravity induced' – and any attempt simply to play by the beat, without giving thought to the required elements of ensemble, will produce all the problems of balance, sound and inflection outlined above. Even the most isolated sound is usually contained within a structure of overall movement and must be related to the motion in terms of phrasing and direction, whether its role be one of completion, co-existence or initiation.

While most percussion writing will fall into one of the first two categories just mentioned, a great deal falls into the last, and initiating a melodic phrase on a non-melodic instrument is no easy task. The need to provide flow and musical line to the adjoining phrase makes this the province of a highly skilled player. As this always involves responsibility to an instrument outside the percussion section, deeper discussion will be left until Part III.

In the case of timpani, despite their larger role and the fact that they generally have a more continuous line, orchestral timpani parts are almost never supplied with ligatures of phrasing. Thus, for example, in the *fortissimo* statement of the main theme in the second movement of Beethoven *Symphony no. 7*, the slurs, so vital to the players' visual appraisal of the phrase, are omitted for this instrument alone.

EX. II.40

The same is true of the *pianissimo* link passage a few bars further on.

(score in concert pitch)

EX. 11.41

This practice can make the part look deceptively vertical, especially to the inexperienced player, and it can take some time for the implied phrasing to be assimilated and reproduced. In all cases such linear misconceptions will prove disastrous to the movement of the phrase, the percussive production of the instruments highlighting any lack of shape that may be present.

This, again, is an area of performance where the experience and ability of professional players is most manifest and an almost unfathomable gulf appears between them and the talented student or amateur. However, so universal is the practice of 'isolated notation' that, on the very rare occasions where additional marking may be found, it can create its own misconceptions. Even a professional player might well question a marking such as this, from the opening of the third movement of Szymanowski *Symphony no. 4 (Symphonie Concertante)*.

EX. 11.42

The slurring of the up-beat notes is simply a reproduction of the phrasing as it applies to the later solo instrumental entries and most certainly *does not* imply performance of the two notes by use of a single stick or any sort of *glissando*.

Related Techniques

EDITING AND DISCRETIONARY ALTERATION

Timpani

The timpani parts of the Classical and Romantic composers were written before methods of fast retuning were developed, and are fascinating examples of enforced circumspection, imagination and downright frustration, even more so than instances of similar restrictions in the use of horns and trumpets.

Almost any score of the eighteenth and nineteenth centuries will contain passages where, because of the limitations in pitch, timpani are treated with considerable restraint. It is a practice worth considering in some detail for, apart from the incentive it provided to develop the instruments, it greatly affected the composer's choice of orchestration and taxes the mind of the present-day interpreter to no small extent.

Many conductors and instrumentalists will change isolated notes in the timpani part where obvious discordant harmony is produced, most usually to correspond with the note sounded by string basses. This must be recognized as a dangerous practice, inasmuch as once started it is very difficult to stop and can lead to quite ludicrous situations where timpani provide complete bass lines or are written in to passages where they were never originally scored. The real problem lies in the fact that it is very rare to be able to consider the timpani in isolation, without regard for the rest of the orchestration.

In general terms the situation is best demonstrated by reference to a familiar work where the instruments are never used soloistically but nonetheless maintain a vitally important role as far as dramatic emphasis and support are concerned. Schubert, whose natural melodic style and closely interdependent orchestrations did much to advance the demands of orchestral integration (however much the historians of orchestration might choose to ignore him), provides a most useful example in his use of timpani throughout the *Symphony no. 8* (*'Unfinished'*). Exploration of the timpani writing in the first movement of this symphony might provide a working principle on which to base consideration of other composers' intentions. A brief analysis and some discussion of the timpani part in this respect will be found in the Appendix.

For myself, I am fundamentally against changing the printed timpani part, but not to such a dogmatic extent that I won't consider isolated instances when suggested by an experienced player. But there can be no doubt that advances in engineering and design of the timpani, and the use of synthetic heads, have made the exact pitch clearer and more precise, especially in the lower register. The problem of 'dissonance' thus becomes more acute as time goes by.

Timpani writing of the Classical era deploys the instruments in two distinctly separate ways, both as instruments with an individual harmonic voice (as, for example, at the opening of the *Scherzo* of Beethoven *Symphony no. 9*) and as a rhythmic 'sound' of emphasis and colouration. Not until late into the Romantic era does the practice of consigning the latter role to other, related, percussion instruments become general. With the increases in size, number and importance of the percussion section the timpani are increasingly exploited in a melodic capacity. It is likely that modern perceptions have undergone a similar change, reinforced by the many advances in manufacture of the instruments, and thus, aural expectation differs widely from how they were originally perceived. Certainly, most musical analysts and commentators writing before the 1940s are prone to use the generic term 'drums' when making reference to any timpani entry, a descriptive practice that has been noticeably abandoned in more recent times.

Obviously, the foregoing applies to any design of modern timpani when pitched within its most effective range. Extreme slackening or tightening of the head (a very dangerous practice) will progressively lose the projection of actual pitch and enable the instrument to be used as a purely rhythmic drum, as is the case in *Ex. 11.43* from Walton suite *Henry V.*

EX. 11.43

Such use of timpani as percussion drums of no definable pitch is rare, but need not be confined to the smaller drums alone. In Gershwin *An American in Paris* larger timpani are used in much the same way (see *Ex. 11.44*).

When the timpani are struck at the centre of the head as requested (the point at which the tension is most relaxed), pitch is at its least definable and the instruments may be used as large drums of indeterminate pitch. In broad terms, differences in the diameter of the drum head will provide some differentiation between 'high' and 'low' so that different 'areas' of pitch, as demanded in *Ex. 11.44*, can be projected. The technique is at its best when used at strong dynamic levels. Soft playing, while never equalling the accuracy

EX. 11.44

of pitch attained nearer the rim, tends to make the pitch of the note more apparent.

Percussion

With the increased appearance of percussion have come the more specific and experimental demands from composers as to the method of sound production. These have now become so diverse as to be beyond any possibility of comprehensive discussion, and famous original examples are now accepted as standard: the use of the blade of a penknife on the edge of a suspended cymbal in Bartók *Violin Concerto no. 2*; the roll with side-drum sticks on the dome of the same instrument in the same work; the dropping of a tambourine at the end of Stravinsky *Petrouchka*; the scraping of a tam-tam in *The Rite of Spring*; bowing a suspended cymbal; tapping the frame of a side drum. None will nowadays cause so much as the raising of an eyebrow.

However, such exploration need not be the sole province of the composer, and the actual use of percussion instruments, even within the standard repertoire, remains open to much imaginative and creative experimentation, although this should never be simply for its own sake. The wide variety of instrumental examples and techniques that are available to the modern interpreter makes the refining and reappraisal of sound as relevant to this section as any other, the demand for 'a triangle' in present-day terms being almost as ambiguous as that for 'a woodwind instrument'!

Even within the confines of more clearly defined instrumentation there occur many instances where a single note or pattern can be played in many different ways, all of which basically conform to the printed demands of the composer. The regular substitution of a washboard for the guero in Stravinsky *The Rite of Spring* might well be placed in this context, as could the performance of the timpani roll, mentioned earlier, by use of two coins in Elgar '*Enigma*' *Variations*. Both these examples obtained support from the composer in question, but similar examples will be found, especially in works of the early Romantic composers, where specific sounds can be implied by the context but normal techniques of production have been retained. A famous illustration might be the isolated cymbal stroke from the fourth movement of Berlioz *Symphonie Fantastique* (*Ex. 11.45*).

Here, in the *March to the Scaffold* we are firmly in the territory of programme music and every note has association with visual imagery and dramatic insinuation. It is not unusual to find this note performed by the rapid scraping of a small piece of metal across the edge of the plate of a suspended cymbal and quickly damping the resultant sound ('the sharpening of the guillotine', as Maurice Handford described it).

Many such opportunities exist (although few so blatant as this) which in no way alter or detract from the composer's basic concept. Obviously a funda-

EX. 11.45

mental rule of musical integrity must prevail and it would be inappropriate to make every percussion entry a caricature of itself, but many passages will benefit from careful thought and a willingness to explore the available alternatives.

In Conclusion

For the percussion section as a whole there remains the ever–present hazard of accidental noise. No other orchestral section is required to move from one instrument to another and no other instruments are set in motion by striking. The dangers are obvious, and the sound of the instrument is intrusive and recognizable, regardless of whether the striking object be a stick, mallet or coat button. Free-standing instruments, such as gongs, tam-tam, bell plates and large bells, are most at risk but even drums and tuned percussion can be surprisingly vulnerable to any ill-considered movement.

Major accidents can, of course, happen in the best regulated circles, but the drastically increased opportunity for unintentional sound that beleaguers this section must be limited as far as is humanly possible. Little can be done about instances such as when a young player dropped a cymbal from a position high above the body of the orchestra, or when an exceedingly small and inexperienced percussionist who had little to occupy him at the time, decided helpfully to turn the page for a colleague. In stretching forward to the stand he lost his footing on a riser, grabbed for support at the nearest object and managed to deposit lethal sections of a xylophone throughout a very surprised horn section. Other instruments followed in a seemingly never-ending stream of sympathetic suicide! Fortunately neither of these disasters happened in concert, but I know that the fateful day creeps ever closer.

Perhaps examples such as these serve to underline how absolutely essential is the provision of sufficient space for percussion players to move freely from one instrument to another without danger of accidental contact. However, almost equal embarrassment can lurk for the percussion players in their routine compliance with a composer's demands. The ethereal ending to the slow movement of Malcolm Arnold *Symphony no. 2* was unceremoniously brought down to earth in one concert by over-enthusiastic removal of the side-drum snares, a consideration of which I had not thought to warn the player concerned.

Finally, may I end with a plea to those responsible for the performance and transportation of a young section, once the watchful eye of the tutor is no longer on them: it is *absolutely essential* that the same instruments are provided for *every* rehearsal and performance. As has been discussed throughout this chapter, instruments vary in design and, thereby, response. A young player cannot be expected to adapt quickly to the idiosyncrasies of any particular example. This is nowhere more true than with regard to tuned percussion where just the size of the keys can cause an octave to vary more than six inches in width from one example to another. Even under the rigorous financial restraints of touring, do not be tempted to break this inviolate rule. The sensibilities of too many young players are at stake.

12 HARP AND KEYBOARD

The highly individual character of all keyboard instruments confines their orchestral role to one of distinct additional colour. Such is the nature of these instruments that their involvement could rarely be conceived for any other instrument and, consequently, their appearance is both purposeful and severely limited.

A somewhat similar situation exists for harp, but this instrument's increased ability to blend and fulfil an integrated accompanying role has caused it to be a far more frequent visitor. In fact, in music written since around 1900, it has quickly established itself as an adopted member of the orchestral family. A similar union might well have applied to the piano had it not proved such an ideal foil in the concerto repertoire. The number of orchestral parts which lie halfway between the two roles can only be seen to substantiate this. In comparison, however familiar they might appear, the other keyboard instruments are far less often incorporated in orchestral scores. In all cases, techniques of orchestral production differ little from those used in other modes of performance, and the rigours of balance are confined largely to dynamic levels and are devoid of the added burden of blending into chordal textures spread across a number of related instruments, as would be the case with woodwind, brass or strings.

It therefore becomes apparent that, while their orchestral responsibility is in no way diminished, the role of harps and keyboard instruments maintains a distinctly soloistic quality even in the most subjugated circumstances.

Character and Influence

HARP

In the first chapter of his *Principles of Orchestration*, Rimsky-Korsakov remarks: 'Speaking generally, the harp . . . is more an instrument of colour than expression.'

Fundamentally this statement is probably as true today as when it was written in the first years of the twentieth century inasmuch as, orchestrally, the instrument is given relatively little melodic opportunity. However, the added 'expression' available to the orchestra by the careful addition of this 'colour' is almost boundless. In the hands of a sensitive orchestrator the harp is capable of conjuring attitudes of simplicity, reflection, stillness, restlessness, poignancy or vitality quicker than almost any other single instrument. It can both subdue and incite the most passionate outburst, personalize the most simple melody and focus the jagged processes of the most angular score. Colour perhaps it is, but few single colours possess such a range of suggestion.

PIANO

The character of the piano is well known and it shares with the organ the distinction of being the only instrument able to challenge the orchestra's powers of musical communication, and match the diversity and size of its repertoire. Perhaps for this very reason, its orchestral use most often displays only very limited facets of its immense emotional range and technical variety.

Within the orchestra, the more percussive side of its nature will often tend to be exploited, and it most frequently appears in the more rhythmically orientated scores of the twentieth century. *Legato* phrases are few and far between. That quoted as *Ex. 6. 15* from Debussy *Printemps* is among the most outstandingly beautiful of them. Even recognizably pianistic passage-work is generally confined to pieces where its role is more obviously soloistic. It will frequently be found as a doubling instrument, where it imparts a particular clarity to rhythmic passage-work and an almost malevolent resonance to low *pizzicato*.

CELESTA

The bell-like quality of the celesta ensures that in much of its isolated use it is firmly allied to the percussion section, as a softer-sounding relative of the glockenspiel. Its keyboard, however, provides an option for virtuosity that the standard glockenspiel would find hard to match.

The celesta is often partnered with harp or piano, alternating or imitating passages characteristic of either instrument and imbuing them with an aura of delicate charm. Fast passage-work is just as effective as progressions of chords, and solos abound – some, it has to be said, more felicitous than others. Although the celesta is easily overpowered by other orchestral sound, it remains popular with composers and is second only to the harp in frequency of appearance.

HARPSICHORD

Apart from its use as the most standard instrument of *continuo* playing (a discipline beyond the scope of this discussion), the harpsichord is an extremely rare visitor to the orchestra. It is occasionally included for purposes of 'antiquity', in modern arrangements of suites or collections of ancient dances, or when an aura of the Baroque needs to be pungently implied.

So powerful is this association that it is unusual to find the instrument scored purely for its own sake, without any motivation attached to its historic role. In this respect exploitation of its very individual sound has been slow, but there are definite signs of acceleration. The instrument is increasingly used in music of dramatic intent, such as film scores, where it proves capable of providing both a ghostly quality of tension and a delightfully impish caricature of melodic themes that might otherwise tend to sound banal.

An equally contributory factor in its omission, however, has always been the fear that the instrument would not penetrate modern orchestrations or project sufficiently well in large concert halls (a rather surprising reason for neglect, considering that such an attitude was never applied to celesta) and its reappearance is certainly connected both to the technical advances in recording and the availability of modern instruments possessed of greater carrying-power.

By far its most frequent appearance in modern orchestration, however, remains as a concerto partner as in Poulenc *Concert Champêtre* or the superb Frank Martin *Petite Symphonie Concertante* for harp, harpsichord, piano and double string orchestra.

HARMONIUM

While most examples of the harmonium are equipped to deal with a wide variety of intricate writing, orchestral exploitation is most frequently limited to the 'reedy' tone characteristic of the middle and upper register. It can be an instrument of very individual quality and need not be entirely reminiscent of religious services or sacred music, despite the fact that this is the role which accounts for most of its orchestral appearances, especially in the opera house.

As has already been mentioned, the harmonium is in no way equipped to substitute for the organ, especially in the more grandiose orchestrations, even though it might sometimes be asked to do so. Such a practice should be avoided and only considered in situations of some emergency (the lower octaves and pedals generally lack sufficient body of sound either to support or compete with the full orchestra).

ORGAN

The organ is probably the most self-sufficient of all instruments and it cannot truly be said to appear in the orchestra, but rather to act as a second, separate orchestra in itself. When used purely as an orchestral instrument it will most often be combined to express the most overpowering climax, or support the orchestra in full harmonic duplication. Elsewhere, it is almost inseparable from works of a religious nature involving chorus.

Both the harmonium and the organ possess one characteristic unavailable to any other instrument of the orchestra and that is the ability to sustain one or more notes for an indefinite time without need of breathing or changing bow, and with absolutely no change in quality or dynamic. No better example of this truly disturbing capability can be given than that already quoted as *Ex. 6. 5*.

ELECTRONIC INSTRUMENTS

The various tones and colours, combinations and distortions available to just the electric keyboard make any designation of particular 'character' impossible. The sound will always be recognizably different from that produced by human action. No 'instrument', with the possible exception of the Ondes Martenot, has to exhibit a particular tone or character, and their influence, therefore, pertains directly to their specific design as required for any one work.

Our consideration must now be widened to include general 'electronic involvement' rather than just reproduction of notes by electronic means. The 'influence' of electronic involvement, in terms of orchestral co-operation in live performance, has not yet been as great as might at first be thought. While a considerable number of comparatively recent works demand the involvement of some sort of electronic apparatus, these exist as an addition to the orchestral sound, and have not involved any major alteration in instrumental performance technique, orchestral design or even communicative intention – electronic intervention has remained recognizably, indeed essentially, an *orchestral* means of expression. (Compare this with the influence of electronics on performance outside the orchestra, particularly on reproduction, or in terms of complete substitution in other areas of music.)

Most especially with regard to student orchestras the addition of electronics (in whatever form) to the standard orchestra should *never* be taken as a reason for indiscriminate neglect in programming. Many works including electronics exist which are ideal for the continuous development of all levels of orchestra, and the various styles of writing no more or less difficult to perform than any other. To shy away from such examples, simply because they involve less familiar techniques and instrumentation, is to forfeit the opportunity of playing some very beautiful, and pertinent, music.

Intonation

With the exception of electronics, none of the instruments of this group has any means of altering or controlling the pitch of a note during performance. Intonation, in the sense of momentary adjustment, is therefore not within their capabilities. For the harp, however, tuning – in the sense of the overall set up of the instrument – is crucial.

HARP

The tuning of the strings of the harp takes time and it is not possible to accomplish anything but the most arbitrary adjustment of the pegs in the few moments available for orchestral tuning. The harpist must allow sufficient time – usually a minimum of twenty minutes – for the fundamental setting of the instrument before each and every rehearsal or concert in which it is involved. It should be undertaken in a degree of solitude, without any interference or distraction from other instruments or members of the orchestra, but it *must* be done *in situ*. The instrument should never be tuned in a different atmosphere, temperature or even position from that which it will occupy when being played.

In the student orchestra, it is important for the harpist to refer to 1st oboe when tuning, as a direct reference of orchestral pitch. (In professional circles this is not so necessary, although, without it, coincidence is by no means guaranteed.)

The situation is intensified when two harps are required and, although they can and probably will choose to tune the instruments together, extra time should be allowed.

Harps face the biggest problem of variable intonation in that they so often accompany other solo lines, and the slight change of pitch that will always occur after the orchestra has been playing for some time can be very disturbing for them. Especially when accompanying woodwind, many professional players will adjust the tuning of the harp to correspond with specific instrumental idiosyncrasies, even within the same piece if time allows, and this will also apply to any direct association with piano or celesta. But this is a very advanced technique and presupposes a great deal of experience and, especially in the case of adjustment to woodwind, familiarity with individual players.

Nonetheless, the adjustment of one or more individual strings will often prove necessary during the course of rehearsal or concert simply because the instrument itself will tend to go out of tune. Advanced players can perform this task quickly and accurately, without disturbing the concentration of the players around them or even the audience. The practice should be encouraged and the necessity, along with available opportunities for adjustment, pointed out to the player.

One further consideration is that the instrument should be tuned as far as possible with regard to the forthcoming programme. No matter how often it is overhauled and serviced, mechanical variations will often be in evidence which will affect individual notes when they are raised from the 'open' position. Checking the chords and sequences that appear in the piece will often disclose the need for very slight compensatory adjustment to the tuning of one or more strings.

KEYBOARD

Harpsichord (provided that it has not originally been set to a lower pitch) can generally be tuned and adjusted by a professional tuner in something over half an hour, and a well-maintained piano need only take a little longer. Most electronic keyboards will incorporate an 'instantaneous' overall pitch adjustment. For all practical purposes it is best to consider that the organ cannot be tuned. Although adjustment is possible within a matter of hours, it involves highly specialized technicians and such an opportunity will rarely coincide with orchestral performance. The celesta's tuning is established at the time of manufacture.

When keyboard instruments are in use, the orchestra should develop the habit of always tuning to them. The oboe should first take the keyboard A and then reproduce it for the rest of the orchestra.

Balance

In dealing with harp and keyboard instruments purely in relationship to one another, balance is far less of a concern than ensemble, and both (as previously discussed) will be influenced by physical position as much as performing techniques. Balance will largely be dictated, and often accomplished, by the very nature of the parts. With none of the instruments *needing* to combine in order to produce harmony or accompaniment, their combination will usually be confined to colouristic doubling or passages of such an idiosyncratic nature that their relationship with other instruments will be obvious. Very rarely, when two instruments are pitched in an area of their range that exhibits similar tonal characteristics – harp and piano very high, for example, or celesta and harp in the upper middle register – adjustment will have to be made, but such instrumentation is seldom encountered.

Combining the major keyboard instruments – piano and celesta, piano and harpsichord, or piano and harmonium – causes few problems of direct balance. The organ is never directly combined with any other keyboard instrument or harp.

Balance of each and all in relation to the rest of the orchestra will be dealt with in Part III.

Ensemble

The co-ordination of entries or any series of disconnected notes is difficult to achieve by any of these instruments in combination, owing to their slight differences in response. Once the instruments are totally familiar such idiosyncrasies as exist will be incorporated into the technique of the performer, but this presupposes considerable skill and experience, and is unlikely to be apparent in any but performers of the highest quality.

The actions of all the keyboard instruments respond differently to the pressure of a key, whether mechanical or electrical, and the gradation of sound available to the piano through weight of application alone is enjoyed by no other. Only the harp can equal the piano in this ability.

Specific Techniques

HARP

It is generally unwise to think of the harp as a totally chromatic instrument. Although all twelve notes of each octave of its range are available to it, only seven can be employed at any one time without recourse to 'retuning' via the pedals and, while this can be done during playing, it can only apply to strings not in use at the time. Some ingenious and highly complicated pedal changes do exist for the instrument (especially in the solo repertoire) but, for the most part, orchestral parts will allow a little more time and, usually, a complete pause when complicated re-setting is required. This highlights a matter of courtesy from the conductor which should be observed on all occasions in rehearsal when the harp is present. It is usually not possible for the harp to begin as quickly as other instruments when asked to start halfway through some passage twenty bars back. It is essential not only to give the player a moment to re-set but also to remember that the relative pedal placings may well not be marked anywhere near the bar in question. Nine times out of ten these will need to be worked out by visual appraisal of the bar itself.

Chords

The usual production of chords on the harp, whether they be in wide or close position, is with some degree of *arpeggiando* from the bottom note up, and this can vary from an almost unnoticeable spreading to something quite extreme. Although, in the absence of any marking to the contrary, an arpeggiated method of production is usually taken for granted, it is sometimes reinforced by the addition of a wavy line to the chord or chords in question. Fast waltz rhythms are regularly performed in this way (and very effectively, especially if not doubled elsewhere in the orchestra) as may be seen in *Ex. 12.1* from Suk *Scherzo Fantastique op. 25* (see page 462).

Speed is not a factor that should determine the spread or otherwise of chords, and is certainly not a reason for simultaneous production. Unlike the piano, fast chording on the harp is easier to play *arpeggiando*.

If a downward direction is required then arrows of direction will be apparent in the part, as in *Ex. 12.2* from Bartók *Violin Concerto no. 2*.

EX. 12.2

If no spread of the chord is required then the direction *non-arpeggiando* will normally be written. Playing chords on the harp by simultaneously producing the notes need not cause them to sound hard or brittle. The succession of

EX. 12.1

chords in *Ex. 12.3* from the very opening of the same work is often performed *non-arpeggiando* with no loss of quality or effect.

EX. 12.3

However, it is the naturally wider *arpeggiando* that is most usually associated with the harp and gives it greatest opportunity to display its uniquely resonant quality of sound.

Damping

The method of damping the vibrating strings of the harp has been described, but consideration of two further circumstances is required.

Firstly, it is one thing to damp the vibrating strings which lie within the compass of two hands and quite another to silence the whole instrument. *Ex. 12-4* from the very end of Walton *Symphony no. 2* can have harpists grabbing

EX. 12.4

at the instrument for all they are worth, even though the relevant strings cover less than two octaves.

The vital technique in these circumstances is that of damping the lower strings first, which will itself stop much of the ring of the upper ones.

Secondly, there are occasions, albeit rare, where the harp will vibrate sympathetically to sounds around it. Depending on where the instrument is situated, and the nature of the passage, this can prove very noticeable. Nothing surprises young harpists more, as they sit in rehearsal, *tacet* until the end of the movement, than to find the instrument playing itself. It is essential that tendencies of this sort are noted by the player, and the likelihood of sympathetic vibration marked in the part at the relevant place, even if it is in a movement where the harp is not required at all.

Harmonics

Again, actual methods of production have been previously dealt with but it should be added that the octave harmonic found at the halfway point on the string is the only harmonic possible on the harp.

As is often the case with strings, some confusion may also exist in the writing of harp harmonics as to whether they are designated at intended pitch or intended playing position (sounding one octave higher). The fact that there is no choice as to the required note makes the situation a little less fraught

EX. 12.5

than might otherwise be the case, but a decision based on the context will nearly always be needed.

Debussy, for example, in the first of the *Trois Nocturnes*, writes the passage shown as *Ex. 12.5* at pitch, intending that it should be played one octave lower, and thereby maintain a one octave relationship with the flute.

Possible confusion is compounded in the Eulenberg score. In the first two bars quoted above, and all the preceding passage, the harp part is printed in the wrong octave, and only corrected by the addition of a hand-written *8*_ _ _ ('*vo basso*' implied!).

Dukas, however, as has already been mentioned, writes the opening harmonics of *L'Apprenti-Sorcier* (quoted in full as *Ex. 6. 13*) as played, sounding one octave higher.

Glissandi

This, by far the most overworked effect of the harp, is the most easily accomplished, the player simply running the fingers over the strings in an upward or downward direction, covering all or a portion of the range.

With no pedals in use (i.e. all the pedals in the upper notch), all the strings will vibrate at full length and a diatonic scale of C♭ major will be produced. With all the pedals in the first notch the *glissando* will be in C major and in the second notch C♯. Various arrangements of the pedals will thus produce a diatonic scale in any key.

Diatonic *glissandi* will be written in one of two ways. Either the two extreme notes will be connected by a line, with the necessary pedalling written out (seen here, once more, in Bartók *Violin Concerto no. 2*, a work which also provides the following two examples)

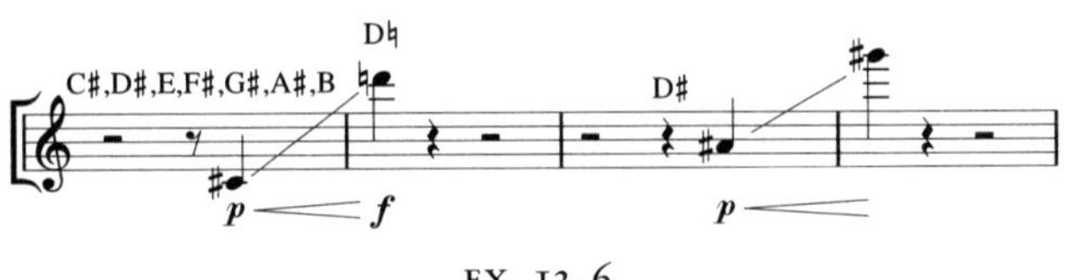

EX. 12.6

or with one octave written out in full.

EX. 12.7

Glissandi are perfectly playable by one hand or two, as a succession of repeated figures or overlapping. An example of each of the last two may be seen here.

EX. 12.8

Chords in *glissandi* are also perfectly possible, as in this example from Debussy *La Mer*.

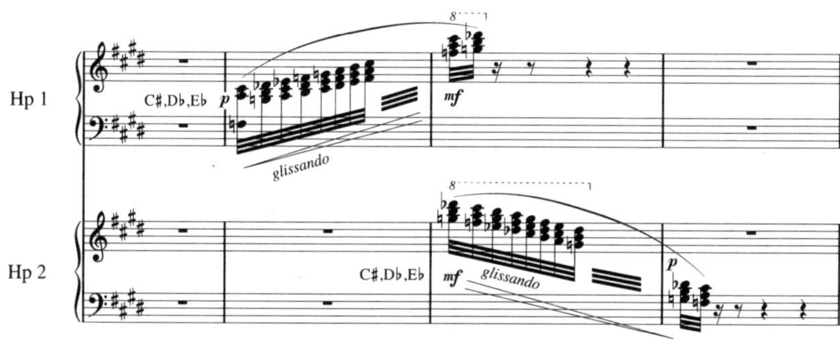

EX. 12.9

Glissandi may also be utilized in four-note chords. With all strings capable of individually producing the fundamental and the notes a semitone and a tone above, many notes are obtainable on two separate strings. In fact only three – D, G and A – are not, by virtue of the fact that the C♭, F♭ and G♭ strings cannot reach them. Thus, for example, a diminished seventh chord on C♯ (C♯, E, G and B♭ ascending) could quite easily be set as C♯ + D♭; E + F♭; G; A♯ + B♭ and played as a normal *glissando*. The only limitation for the key or harmony setting for *glissandi* is that no string may be omitted.

Once written out, as in *Ex. 12.10* from Debussy *Printemps*, it can look confusingly unlike a *glissando*!

Each pair of enharmonic unisons (homophones) has been written out as a repetition of the same note, as is the most usual practice.

The drawback that is experienced in the performance of *glissandi* chords (such as shown in *Ex. 12.9*) is that of the muffling effect produced as the following fingers pass over the strings that are already in motion. Given that

EX. 12.10

all strings must be played, once the pedalling is set the chording will be apparent whether produced by one finger or four, and many players will often only finger one or two notes of the chord in order to give the strings time to resonate before they are 'played' again. If two harps are available, it is sometimes possible to divide the passage, each starting the *glissando* from a different note of the chord – even *glissando* octaves will benefit from this.

Nonetheless, the biggest difficulty experienced in performing *glissandi* within the orchestra is determining the precise timing of their completion. An inexperienced player will frequently complete them too soon, especially if the end coincides with a major climax. In many such instances, both for this reason and in order to increase the sound, part of the last portion of the *gliss.* may be repeated before the final note is reached. This can only be considered in fairly blatant cadential circumstances and would not be possible, for example, in any of the previous four quotations. There it must be precisely timed, which generally involves starting more slowly than feels natural to the player.

Continuous *glissandi* – a succession of rising and falling figures without pause – may be performed by one hand or each alternately, depending on the musical requirement, the latter giving a smoother 'turn'.

Trills

Fast repeated use of a string is generally unsuccessful because it has to be set in motion by plucking, which limits the speed of production and can produce a rather ungainly result.

Trills are very rare and largely limited to the solo repertoire where quite extended examples can appear as decoration above a melodic line. Under these circumstances they must obviously be played by one hand alone, usually alternating thumb and first finger. Orchestrally, however, this technique, whether it be for a trill or fast repetition of a single note (both using two strings), proves generally unsatisfactory, and the two hands will be used alternately. Both methods work best at a soft dynamic and repetition will always be slow in direct comparison to its production on other instruments.

A similar situation exists with regard to *tremolo* alternation of chords, repetition of enharmonic triads or intervals, confined clusters and pairs of notes spaced wider than a major 2nd. While examples of all of these, but especially the first two, may be found marked *fortissimo*, and executed with varying degrees of success, their performance at a very soft dynamic level can be magical. For this the highly descriptive term *bisbigliando* will sometimes be used (It. *bisbiglio* – whisper, rumour).

Because of the wide vibration of the strings, fast repetition becomes less effective below the very upper range of the instrument and is rarely required of its lower strings.

Pedalling

The ability to change the notes of the instrument quickly and accurately by use of the pedals is a fundamental technique. It does, however, involve a great deal of skill, not only in terms of notational accuracy but also in not detracting from the more vital aspects of sound production.

Fluency is the product of time, but fast and continuous changing is always taxing and, especially in less experienced players, liable to cause varying degrees of rhythmic uncertainty. As with every other instrument, some awareness on the part of the conductor of the difficulties faced by individual players will always prove beneficial. For example, the single harp part of Walton *Johannesburg Festival Overture*, a work lasting some seven minutes, includes nearly 240 pedal changes.

On the whole, orchestral harp parts will allow sufficient time for pedal changes, however complicated they might be, and will rarely approach the exigencies of the solo repertoire. *Ex. 12.11*, however, for two harps in unison from Schoenberg *Pelleas und Melisande* is not unique in the extreme demands it places on techniques of pedalling.

In this example the composer adds a footnote in the score suggesting that

EX. 12.11

EX. 12.11 (continued)

the passage be divided between the two players, each taking alternate bars, should it prove not to be feasible as written.

PIANO

The orchestral piano part will usually require some adjustment in style from the player in that such writing tends to be altogether more sparse, rhythmical and percussive than is the case in the normal instrumental repertoire. Successions of short chords and *staccato* figures will occur more frequently, often calling for a much more positive finger action than some inexperienced players have yet developed. Otherwise, all aspects of advanced keyboard technique will be apparent.

The tendency of orchestral piano parts to be more widely dispersed, in terms of intervals and fast, disjointed phrases, may put additional emphasis on the player's facility over the keyboard. Some otherwise quite advanced young pianists can find such demands difficult, having learnt much of their technique practising pieces in more 'standard' pianistic styles, and a very careful appraisal of the part concerned needs to be made before a pianist is chosen.

At the risk of stating the obvious, an ever-present danger is to choose a pianist for, say, Prokofiev *Lieutenant Kijé* and then to add something pianistically incompatible, such as Copland *Appalachian Spring*, to a subsequent programme by virtue of the maxim 'we're already using piano anyway'.

Pedalling

One area of orchestral performance that often needs careful consideration is the use of the sustaining pedal. While some composers will be scrupulous in indicating their intentions, many examples may be found where the part offers no guidance whatsoever. By the very nature of much orchestral piano writing, use of the pedal will often be more circumspect than in the solo repertoire, but there are occasions where its use is relevant but not immediately obvious. Each example must be judged on merit, bearing in mind that the piano is here an integral part of the orchestral sound and decisions must therefore be relative to the overall requirement, not simply what most suits the instrument.

The soft pedal is rarely used and always directly requested (*una corda* or, sometimes, *mit Verschiebung*) when it is.

Sympathetic Vibration

The use of the technique of soundlessly depressing certain keys while playing others in the normal way can prove highly effective within the orchestra, where the instrument is prone to be affected by the sounds of other instruments as well as its own. *Ex. 12.12*, orchestrated with sustained strings, is from Lutosławski *Livre pour Orchestre* and includes the composer's footnote to the score.

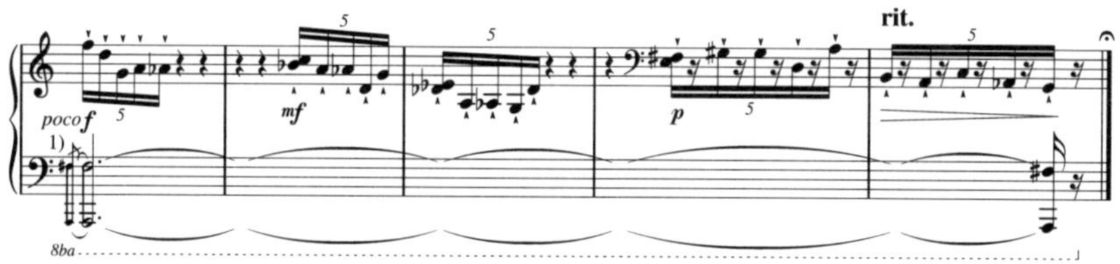

1) Prior to the commencement of this bar all keys lying between the indicated notes are to be depressed soundlessly.

EX. 12.12

The sympathetic vibration of the piano strings when *not* required can sometimes be a mildly annoying problem and there is nothing whatsoever that can be done about it. On occasions of abrupt cessation of *tutti fortissimo* the piano might sometimes be heard to continue ringing, especially the notes in the top octave and a half, a range which is not supplied with dampers. Such vibration is very short-lived and highly unlikely to out-live the general resonance of the sound except in very close proximity to the piano itself.

CELESTA

The celesta is fundamentally equipped to reproduce all keyboard techniques within a limited compass. It will not, however, respond as quickly as the piano, and therefore fast repetition is unsuccessful.

Production must be extremely firm and, for this reason, some piano-related fingerings have to be abandoned when approaching similar passages on many celestas. Because no gradation of dynamic is available to the instrument, the phrasing of solo passages is utterly dependent on the sense imparted in their line. In the wrong hands, the instrument can sound particularly 'square' in melodic solos, and melodies best suited to it retain some measure of verticality.

This aspect apart, orchestral parts will generally cause little technical difficulty for a competent keyboard player.

HARPSICHORD

Fundamentally, the harpsichord is the province of a specialized player. The touch is very different from that required of the piano keyboard, and some degree of accommodation will be called for in many areas of production.

The percussive nature of the instrument makes it traditional, indeed preferable, for chords to be spread in the manner of the harp, but it is perfectly possible (if a little 'explosive') to articulate them as one, and sometimes highly effective.

Considerable dynamic variation can be achieved on the harpsichord by the use of register stops, frequently operated via the pedals, and the coupler which combines the two manuals and it is in this area of technique that specialization is so vital. The majority of orchestral parts (including those of *continuo*) will contain little or no direction as to registration, and the musicianship of the performer will prove paramount in deciding what is most appropriate. Additionally, the range of available registration will vary from one instrument to another, as will the resultant sound, and it is thus important for the performer to be as familiar with the instrument being used as with the technical principles.

Modern instruments will generally exhibit greater power and vitality than older examples, which makes them more compatible in combination with a large orchestra, and the addition of subtle amplification is nowadays always available. The older examples, however, *always* prove superior in the *continuo* parts of the pre-Classical repertoire.

HARMONIUM

Keyboard technique for the harmonium is similar to that of the organ and, within the confines of this discussion, the player must be a specialist of the latter instrument. No pianist will have sufficient opportunity to become familiar with the available registration.

As has been stated, most orchestral uses of the instrument will be in imitation of the church organ and rarely for its own intrinsic sound. Wide variation in dynamic is available via the stops but, as was the case with harpsichord, little or no hint of required registration is likely to be apparent in either score or parts.

By the very fact of its orchestration, 'chorale' passages will predominate, but the harmonium is equally capable of more florid figuration, and possesses a clarity of production often superior to that of the organ by virtue of its less resonant sound. (It was originally a much-loved orchestral substitute, equally at home in the powerful Wagnerian *tutti* as in the delicate string writing of a Mendelssohn overture.)

Orchestrally, when given the opportunity it excels in *legato* production in the upper portion of the range, as in the solo example from Martinů *Field Mass*, shown in *Ex. 12.13*.

EX. 12.13

Note particularly the bare inference of registration implied by dynamic marks alone. Martinů's frequent use of successions of chords in close position is highly effective on this instrument.

ORGAN

There are no special techniques for the organ when combined with orchestra other than those already considered concerning the physical difficulties experienced by the player with regard to sight-lines.

The organ combines in glorious independence, and changes not one iota of its regal character by dint of either necessity or reverence. And neither should it!

ELECTRONICS

Orchestrally, electronic involvement may be divided into two broad categories:
1 Instruments that employ electronic means to generate sound.
2 Electronic treatments used to modify or regenerate the sound of acoustic instruments.

Into the first category fall the ubiquitous modern synthesizers of various design (the so-called electronic keyboards), older examples such as that designed by Robert Moog and the pioneering Ondes Martenot, as well as the electric piano and the electronic organ (as patented by Hammond).

The second category includes tape recorders, with their inherent abilities of speed change in play-back, delay and superimposition and the many forms of electronic modifiers – filters, reverberators and ring modulators, for example.

Synthesizers are fundamentally collections of individual modules, assembled in various configurations, which permit the direct creation of real sound. Depending on their component parts they can produce an immense variety of sounds, but in any collaboration with live orchestra, their role, in this respect, will most usually be severely limited. Some orchestral parts only require sound that is unavailable to the orchestra by any other means. Such 'orchestration' will cause no specific difficulty beyond that of balancing an unfamiliar timbre and this remains true regardless of the number or type of these instruments involved.

The electronic treatment of live orchestral performance is an altogether different and much more complicated device. Here, by use of recording and controlled play-back, chosen passages of orchestral score will be stored and variously modified during performance, and then superimposed, substituted or synchronized as an integral part of the work. This may or may not involve the additional use of electronic instruments and will often be extended to the modification of specific orchestral instruments by use of contact microphones.

It will be clear that such performances involve close co-operation between the conductor and the sound engineer who alone will be able to control the overall balance and many aspects of unification during performance. It follows that the sound engineer must always be a highly qualified professional, fluent not only in the techniques of electronic music but also in normal orchestral performance. A specimen arrangement of electronic equipment, from Edwin Roxburgh *Saturn* is shown as *Ex. 12.14*.

Saturn employs most of the techniques briefly outlined above, as well as many others. It is an especially beautiful work that could exist in no other medium and while, in common with all compositions of this type, it is

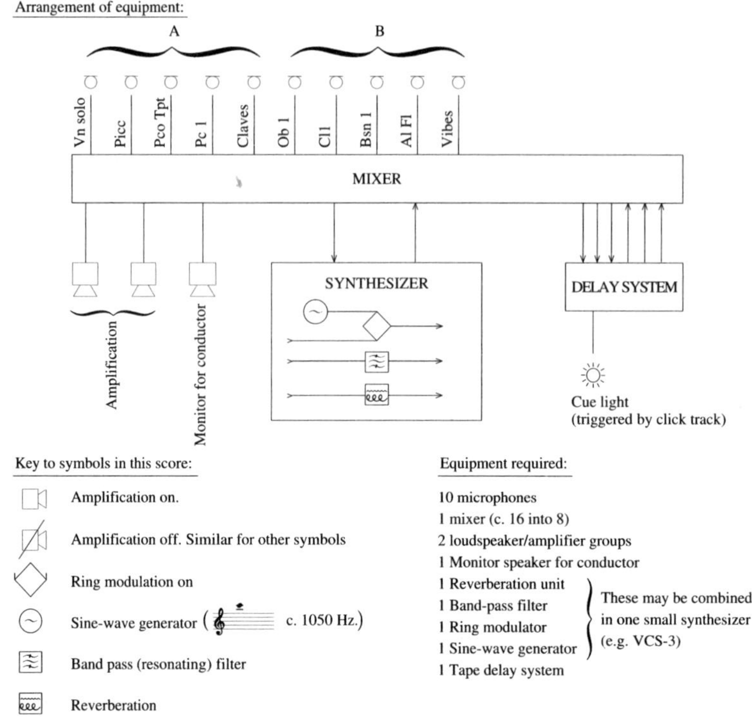

The complexity of this system will depend upon the available equipment. That used for the first performance was as follows:

A: Two four-channel tape-recorders used for the nine second delay (e.g. at letter Ⓒ). Track 1 = non-recirculating delay (Picc., Vn. solo, Picc. Tpt. and Glock). Track 2 = recirculating (feedback) delay (Claves). Track 4 carried a recorded click-track at mm. = 100 which triggered a cue-light to assist the precise synchronisation of this section. (A monitor speaker for the conductor is also needed here.)

B: A single-channel delay using tracks of two stereo machines, one having variable speed, which was used for the two and three seconds delays. One of these machines was also used to record the first part at letter Ⓒ and replay at two before Ⓗ.

EX. 12.14

unquestionably complicated to stage, it deserves to reach a far wider public than it has so far been afforded.

Despite the intricacy of such works, they require little more of the student orchestra and its conductor than a modicum of empiricism and a good deal of patience.

Related Techniques

ALTERNATIVE PRODUCTION

Very rarely is the harp required to be played in anything but its standard fashion. However, its use as a percussion instrument may sometimes be found, the sound-board being particularly well suited to light tapping with the fingers, as requested in Varèse *Amériques*.

*) Timpanic sounds – the right hand strikes the most sonorous part of the sounding board with the tip of the 3rd finger. The left hand plays normally.

EX. 12.15

By contrast, many methods of alternative sound production can be found demanded of the piano, especially in orchestral music of the *avant-garde*. Few are particularly innovative and even fewer make essential use of the instrument, being largely the province of the percussion group and capable of being reproduced in other ways. However, all are valid (if sometimes only visually) and will usually require no particular technique or training, the only proviso being that already discussed of possible damage to the instrument or case.

SUBSTITUTION

The substitution of one instrument for another is not an option to be considered lightly. It is always a re-orchestration and will never provide quite the same sound or aural inflection as the original. Basically, it should never be condoned.

In the area of student orchestral performance, however, the process might sometimes need to be considered in the light of other criteria. Should a work be withheld because an instrument is not available when the sound can be successfully imitated by another with little or no adjustment to the part?

As the premise can only be entertained with reference to a very small number of percussion instruments and some keyboard, it must occasionally be addressed. The following guidelines are for information only. They are intended neither to condone the practice nor condemn it, but simply state the only available alternatives should substitution become unavoidable.

For celesta parts that contain no essentially keyboard passages but only isolated notes – Liadov *The Enchanted Lake* for example – the glockenspiel can be considered as a replacement if necessary. The similar quality of this instrument can make for an extremely effective substitute, projecting only a slight 'presence' on the sound in comparison to the more delicate celesta. Many small parts can be transposed exactly (the glockenspiel sounds two octaves above written as against one octave on celesta) but the often deceptive nature of the sound in relation to its actual octave pitch will allow for even greater scope.

In other circumstances the celesta can be substituted by an electronic keyboard, a replacement that will generally resolve the awkward problems of balance in terms of audibility but will lose much of the essential quality of the original instrument. While this is possible even for works that involve isolated solo passages, it is not to be recommended for solos such as that in Tchaikovsky *Nutcracker*.

The substitution of electronic keyboard for piano is much less successful. Some examples might provide a vaguely acceptable imitation when judged in their immediate vicinity, but all prove to be quite unacceptable when combined with orchestra in any sort of concert hall.

Suitably-programmed electronic keyboards have been used as substitute for both harpsichord and harmonium. In the former case, while the actual sound can be quite close, the overall impression is altogether too refined, and imparts none of the inseparable 'action noise' or the characteristic 'settling' of the intonation as each string is plucked. The latter case is more successful, especially if the original part lies mainly in the harmonium's middle to upper register.

The organ may be substituted by harmonium only in the situations of dire emergency discussed earlier, and even this should not be considered in respect of the great doubling parts which exist for the instrument (in Elgar *Cockaigne* or *'Enigma' Variations* for example). These are omitted altogether when no instrument is available.

The harp allows no possibility of substitution.

Occasionally scores require members of the orchestra to make sound other than with their instruments. Although this practice is particularly infrequent, for the sake of completeness I shall consider it briefly here.

The most famous examples probably both occur in Bernstein symphonic dances *West Side Story* where members of the orchestra are required to click their fingers and also to shout. In the latter case, should there be any doubt (for it only appears in later printings of the orchestral score) the actual word is MAMBO, or perhaps it would be better to say *should be* Mambo – for very often it is something entirely different!

Such effects as rattling bunches of keys, tapping loose change in the pocket or providing a host of other everyday sounds may easily be performed. In melodic terms, whistling is the only non-instrumental effect to be demanded, and one instance of this occurs, for all the string players, in David Dorward *Golden City.*

EX. 12.16

The example is included because of the direction '2 octaves higher', which serves only to put the passage at normal whistling pitch. I, for one, had never before considered that whistling involved such extreme octave transposition.

PART III

The Infusion of Quality

13 STRINGS

Of the many attributes necessary to the orchestral string section the two most important are probably freedom of the bow arm and confidence. To project a string sound to the back of a concert hall, the string must be able to vibrate freely and the bow to move evenly and with judicious speed. A cramped, tight style with little bow movement will lock the sound into the instrument and although, in the case of the violin and viola, it may sound quite reasonable to the player, it will not travel more than a few feet from its source. Beyond this distance the quality of a combination of sounds produced in this way will progressively decline and increasingly tend to separate and distort. This is the sound most commonly associated with the inexperienced orchestra and, especially to the layman, most noticeably distinguishes it from its professional counterpart. The audience will be aware only of the difference in quality (not always so obvious to the conductor from a position close to the sound) which will continuously deflect their concentration and limit their acceptance of the communicative aspects of the performance. They will be quite unable (and probably unwilling) to analyse the reasons for it and consign themselves to an alternative appreciation based on charitable forgiveness. Those who have no personal reason for attendance will never return.

Outside the most elementary forays into ensemble playing such a situation should never be permitted. The sounds produced by any player or combination of players are their only means of transmitting content and intention. The hallmark of the great performer, in whatever field, is the ability to project meaning beyond the physical confines of the situation and achieve an equal strength of communication with all. This intensity of talent, so often lacking in the solo instrumentalist, is more easily achieved with the richer texture of orchestral sound and lies at the core of any concept of orchestral technique.

In order to examine the quality and delivery of sound in terms of orchestral strings, a wider theory needs to be understood and a basic premise embraced. In professional orchestras it becomes apparent that differing sounds are drawn from an orchestra, most especially the strings, by different conductors. This is not to be confused with a change in style, which is obviously also true, but refers to the much more subtle alteration in sound which is perceptible in rehearsal, on many occasions before a word has been spoken or any attention to detail has been attempted. It provides food for considerable thought that a group of experienced, excellent players, who are totally familiar with the repertoire and each other, should exhibit a unified change in sound almost before they are aware of it themselves. Most players accept this phenomenon as fact, but few with whom I have ever discussed it have been able to propound any legitimate reason beyond 'conductor personality'. This, without doubt, may be taken as a heavily contributory factor and is not without a large degree of factual basis but clearly, a more rational (or at least more workable) explanation needs to be explored. After all, however psychological the initiative, some definable process must be taking place, since it is translated into physical alteration.

If these changes are observed from within an orchestra, over a period of time, some pattern can be observed. As with so many complex problems the basis for discovery lies in simplicity; in this case, in two concurrent physical reactions, the second of which opens the door to an unparalleled exploration of orchestral sound.

In the first place 'conductor personality' is indeed a relevant factor, especially in the way it is immediately transmitted through gesture and physique. It must be understood that every attitude and movement of a conductor elicits a response, however minor, from somewhere in the orchestra. In purely non-musical terms the personality might engender feelings of relaxation or tension, concentration or abstraction, depending upon individual reaction. Musically the gestures may produce hard accent or rounded power, breathless agitation or spacious landscapes, by no more than the opening of the hand or the furrowing of a brow. All these things, and many more besides, are likely to have been determined within the first few seconds of collaboration.

This fact could be regarded as an alarming limitation on musical performance, were the conductor's influence to be limited to this facet of visual communication alone. Obviously this is not so as, at the very least, the conductor's technique and musicianship will broaden this initial response. Nevertheless, however this early appraisal may later be adjusted, its subconscious translation into sound is a proven aspect of corporate response.

An orchestral musician's personal contribution to the overall interpretation will vary between one repertoire and another, and for different conductors. An empathy can exist between the musician and a particular work, or between two musicians, that produces subtle alterations in sound production. When this occurs among string players a tenuous change in the section's sound begins to emerge. Clearly, were it to be confined to one or two players in random positions, all that would result would be a rather unfortunate imbalance within the section. Fortunately this does not happen because individual players influence those around them, and a prevailing attitude of identification with the musical personality of the direction ensues. Thus we begin to progress from any change in sound based on varying individual contribution, to the more satisfactory situation of combined alteration.

But if this alteration were totally based upon a 'chance' understanding of one musician by another it would remain a unique and personalized sound, capable of appearing only when certain personality vibrations became interactive. Such a limitation would preclude its use as an orchestral technique in any form. Fortunately there is another, considerably more tangible, reason for its existence.

For this second reaction one must examine the natural techniques of a large number of eminent conductors and then make a direct comparison with the sounds produced. The rather startling result can best be described as 'area of influence' and, in many cases, even conforms to the string sounds appropriate to an individual conductor's most successful repertoire.

There are those whose natural approach is to aim their direction and address their remarks to the front desks only, and who often display a slightly crouching style in performance as they seek to draw their sound from these most agile and soloistic players of the section. The result is a tight, 'front-orientated' sound, clear and dynamic, as might be identified with a brilliant overture or virtuoso orchestral show-piece. The dazzling bright sound often exploited by the more highly-charged American orchestras emanates largely from this (many having spent their formative years deeply influenced by such direction).

Other conductors' natural inclination is to concern themselves beyond the front desks, and to demand the attention of players towards the middle of the section above all others. A warm and powerful sound is produced, without edge or tightness. Rich and resplendent, it lends itself equally to deep harmonic integration and to colossal climax, the strength and projection that are a prerequisite for what are often termed the 'lush' sounds of the nineteenth- and twentieth-century Romantics.

Finally there are those whose contact encircles the back of the strings, whose smallest gestures seem to stroke the very perimeters of the sections, eliciting their support in width and distance. Bold shapes remain but a tranquillity envelops them, which enables the orchestra to display drama in more than sheer scale. This approach is well suited to the music of the French 'Impressionists', the edge of the sound imperceptibly blurred, focused but translucent as the light of early dawn.

Such definitive examples are intentionally somewhat oversimplified so that their cause and effect may be solidly understood and an aural perception of them conveyed. They encapsulate the broad outlines of a technique of positioning sound within the string group which has a most remarkable effect on clarity, integration, projection and ensemble. However the results must first be heard mentally before any attempt can be made to achieve them.

With student orchestras the variation and subtlety of sound produced is equalled by the benefits of involvement and individual importance that it demonstrates to the players, especially those behind the first two desks. Gradually they come to understand that string playing is not a matter of a large number of people doubling the same notes, but thirty, forty or fifty separate and distinct responsibilities. Once this monstrously ignored fact is truly comprehended by players and conductor alike, one of the main difficulties of orchestral string playing is more easily overcome. Listening to each other becomes a natural part of playing because the area of responsibility is not continually thrown to the front. In consequence a section will tend to synchronize their sound and movement, stay together and be able to accompany other sections and solos almost instinctively. Orchestral balance between wind and strings emerges and the all-important sensitivity towards transmitted sound begins to appear. This is the basis of orchestral technique, the production of the style of sound from which the content of the work will emerge. Notes without communication are nothing and will deceive only those who cannot aspire beyond the visual image of the printed page.

The Middle of the Sections

The most easily acquired and instantly recognizable sound is that procured by the weighting of a section towards the middle. Once the strength of the sound emanates from this point the tone becomes warm and round, mainly because its power is radiating from the place where most players are in immediate contact. It need not be loud but it is probably within a fairly full sonority that it can first be most directly perceived. Once again I turn without hesitation to Brahms for illustration since, notwithstanding my reservations regarding the suitability of the symphonies for performance by any but the most proficient youth orchestra, it is here that a clear aural perception of the sound is most readily available.

In straightforward terms, the string sound associated with this composer's style is one of size and substance. Once the sound is produced in such a way that the front desk can hear the full section (rather than just the second desk), then its quality begins to emerge. There are two reasons for this. Firstly (as is obvious) the middle of the section is taking more of the weight of sound; but more importantly, the first and second desks are thereby taking *less* responsibility for the output and ensemble of the section and *more* responsibility for colour and quality. Their own contribution will thus be one of enhancing a sound they can hear and effecting a subtle influence on it, rather than a futile attempt at projecting the main example. Much the same applies to the back of the sections, for it is not physical width that we are seeking but majestic splendour: a sound that can only come from the heart of the section. Never tight or hard, the sound of the instruments need not be forced but the players should simply be aware of the exact nature of their own contribution and where it lies in relation to the whole section. For the middle players in particular, a firm left hand and constant bow contact are essential, so that the sound can be enticed from the instrument with strength of purpose but freedom of movement.

During any consideration of the placing of sound, the term 'back desk' refers to those players, in all string sections, with no player of strings or woodwind *immediately* behind them. Thus it includes the last desk of the outside line on both sides as well as all the players on the perimeter of the seated string group as it curves to meet the extremities of the woodwind. In this one instance the physical presence of the basses, when placed directly behind the cellos, must be ignored, as must the similar positioning of any 'solo' instruments (for instance, harp, celesta or piano) behind the violins.

There can be no more effective learning process than experience. With respect to qualities as intangible as sound and timbre, the ability to produce them goes hand in hand with the aural perception and physical sensation of their successful achievement. It is therefore essential that such techniques be taught within a musical context, and only as and when the opportunity arises. With a full string section it is obviously advantageous to use a long *legato* phrase, where the contact of the bow on the string is uninterrupted and the span is of sufficient length to allow the sonority to build and become apparent. Brahms, probably the prime architect of the 'endless phrase', provides us with a perfect example that has the not altogether coincidental advantage of having been discussed earlier with regard to bowing. It is reproduced in *Ex. 13.-1* as it first appears at the opening of the *Allegro non troppo* in the fourth movement of the *Symphony no. 1*.

At first sight it might seem to fall short of our requirements because it does not involve the cello and bass in *arco* sonority, but actually this is an advantage because it insists on the warmth of sound from the upper strings alone. The natural size of sound from cello and bass cannot be used to disguise or falsely enhance the quality but their brilliantly orchestrated *pizzicato* fills the lower octave to produce an illusion of a fully orchestrated chordal sequence. It is difficult to find another passage so ideal for our purpose. The marking *poco f*

EX. 13.1

ensures that volume is not substituted for rich quality. All voices depart from a unison into close-knit harmony, making the aural centre clear, and the bowing is of the right length to set a perfect bow speed in the very first bar.

Many of the techniques necessary to the individuals' performance of this passage – the turning of the *legato* bow, the coaxing of the sound from the instrument, the quality of *pizzicato* – have been discussed in Chapter 7. To these must now be added the requisite care and control of the phrase structure, especially in so spacious an example as this.

It is a natural idiosyncrasy of nearly everyone's playing to perform a musical sentence very much as one would talk in everyday speech: a slight hurrying of the words linking the main objectives of the conversation. Translated into the musical context of *Ex. 13.1* this will show as a tendency to move towards the bar-line, not in a way that will enhance the flow of the passage, but one that will simply distort the phrase by ignoring the value of the shorter notes. In any line of this span it is these notes that require the time and room to sound and that project the expanse of the phrase. Encouraging every player to look after these notes will in itself do much to elicit the strength of sound and control of the bow needed to project the tone and sonority of the strings. If this passage is to be performed as on one large instrument, then all sections must be able to hear each other clearly and the lines move exactly together, the vertical harmonic movement as precise as the horizontal. For this reason alone the shorter notes should be given full value.

In rehearsal with a student orchestra the opportunity exists to allow the front and back desks to hear the sound they are playing to by working exclusively with the middle of the sections for a few minutes. This is possible even in quite small orchestras because the weight still has to come from the same place and it cannot be greater than these players can provide. Faced with a small section, the temptation to get the one or two stronger players at the front to power the sound through is sometimes very strong, but it will not carry, and the conductor, placed centrally among them, will only hear an illusion of strength that is not apparent from any other position.

When working with separate areas of the string sections in this way, two things are important. Firstly, that the total purpose is the production of the correct sound and *only* this aspect of the passage should be rehearsed. Secondly, that it should not be rehearsed for so long that the other members of the section lose concentration – the exercise is as much for their sake as for those actually playing. In a passage such as that quoted above, three or four times with the smaller group is the most that may be contemplated, and then only if the conductor can instil a noticeable improvement each time. As in all orchestral rehearsal, to repeat a passage without making a positive contribution to its improvement is both self-defeating and an unforgivable waste of players' time.

Such a depth of sound as can be produced by the middle of the section is unlikely to appear instantly, and sixteen-bar phrases, like the one above, will probably be about the longest practical opportunity for rehearsing it. However, constant reminders in other appropriate passages as to where the main area of sound needs to be, especially in places where a forced tone might be attempted, will suffice to build quickly on this foundation.

For the conductor, the most vital habit, especially in concert, is to make contact with these players above all others at the moment just prior to the sound's appearance. I once had occasion, with an orchestra who knew the technique quite well, to re-rehearse this sonority in order to allow some student conductors to 'feel' it; in this case in relation to the first movement of Brahms *Symphony no. 3*, probably one of the most difficult works that exist for any conductor. In the heat of the moment, one of them started to look at and contact the front of the sections, and the sound changed almost as if someone had turned off a tap. It was the most fortunate of accidents because it was noticed by all the conductors who, until that moment, had not realized that they had been having any real influence on the sound at all!

The Back of the Sections

The second significant area of the strings that may be used to great effect is the back of the sections (the perimeter, not just the last desks).

Apart from providing an easily attainable quality of ethereal imagery this area of the section is of paramount importance in the accompaniment of soft woodwind solos. An example wherein it may be used in both these ways is found in the first few bars of the third movement, *Romanza*, of Vaughan Williams *Symphony no. 5* (see *Ex. 13.2*).

The full string orchestra is used in a sequence of organ-like chords laid out in sixteen parts and, in some cases, spread over more than four octaves. Again, because of the complications of balance this scoring induces, it might not immediately appear an ideal model, especially as there exist many simpler passages where this same 'width' of performance may be employed. But it invokes such a clear aural perception of the sound and involves so many niceties of the technique within a mere eleven bars that I shall make no excuse for its inclusion. Besides, it is one of the most stunning examples of 'back desk' positioning.

It is important that the division of the strings is by player rather than by desk (*see* Chapter 1), as it is obvious that no attempt at distancing the sound can be contemplated if it takes three desks to play each chord in the violins. Three players, however, is a very different matter, since the chord at once becomes easier to hear from within and considerably easier for each player to balance.

Here the back desks take all the weight of the sound and responsibility for its projection, playing a little above the overall dynamic and using rather more

EX. 13.2

bow length than the rest of the section. As one moves progressively to the front of the section so the individual involvement in the level of sound produced becomes less, until the front desks are virtually making no sound at all. The most difficult facet of this technique is that it has to be the *same* sound in progressively diminishing dynamic. If any of the other players make reduction of sound by use of a very slow bow their tone will tighten and the effect is lost. It must be produced by similar means – almost the same speed of bow, the same left-hand pressure and *vibrato*, but less bow contact and further down the finger-board.

To create this sound within a student orchestra is relatively easy, since the effect is so quickly perceived by the players involved. In much the same way as in the previous example, it is possible to use only the perimeter strings at first, eliciting the required sound and the freedom needed to project it from them alone. Once this is set the rest of the strings should aim to hear it at all times as they play, and not to alter it in the slightest degree. Each desk forward will be forced to play less strongly than the desk behind them if this is to be accomplished.

Apart from the sheer beauty of sound, this technique provides many advantages to the players. As has been quoted many times, it is extremely difficult to play at the back of a string section, the distance from the conductor's beat and the centre of the orchestra often making it necessary to anticipate both movement and entries. Balance, especially that with another section, is hard to achieve and relies heavily on instinct and experience because of the aural screening effect of the sound in front. Once again, the full implications of these problems are not always apparent to the conductor, but the audience receives the sound of the entire width of the strings and the perfect balance that may be clear to someone standing among the front desks is often very distorted once the full spread of the orchestra is perceived. Most particularly this is true of a soft sequence of chords similar to that quoted above, the first six bars of which are bereft of even a melodic line to divert the attention.

The weighting of the sound to the back allows the players in this position better opportunity to hear the full chord and balance it sensitively, not only by virtue of the translucent quality produced but because of the relative lack of intervening sound. At the same time it will obviously have no detrimental effect on the ability to balance anywhere else in the body of strings. Further, it will be of benefit in eradicating the slight 'drag factor' so often experienced by even the best orchestras in a passage of this type where the front of the sections are allowed to take responsibility for the movement. When this responsibility is given to those for whom it is most critical the problem is considerably less acute.

The second, and most frequently used aspect of the technique may be illustrated by *Ex. 13.2* from the seventh bar – the entry of the cor anglais solo. For any woodwind soloist, the projection of sound from a position seated behind the body of strings is difficult. With student players the tone quality will often change and tighten in the effort to make the sound sufficiently clear against the accompaniment. The weighting of the accompanying string sound to the back of the sections (and, therefore, away from the immediate vicinity of the solo instrument) avoids any necessity or temptation to force. This is particularly important since it allows the quality of the accompaniment to be maintained, without the need for it to be minimalized in order to accommodate the wind soloist. A useful visual image that may serve to demonstrate the advantages more clearly can be gained by comparison of the graphic illustrations shown as *Figs. 13. 1* and *13. 2*, where the shaded area represents the string sound and (A) the source of the woodwind solo. The dynamic level of the accompaniment is translated into height and density as perceived from a position facing the orchestra.

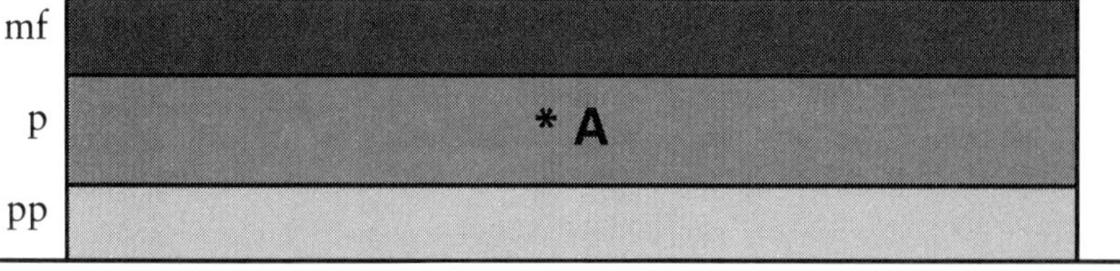

Fig. 13.1

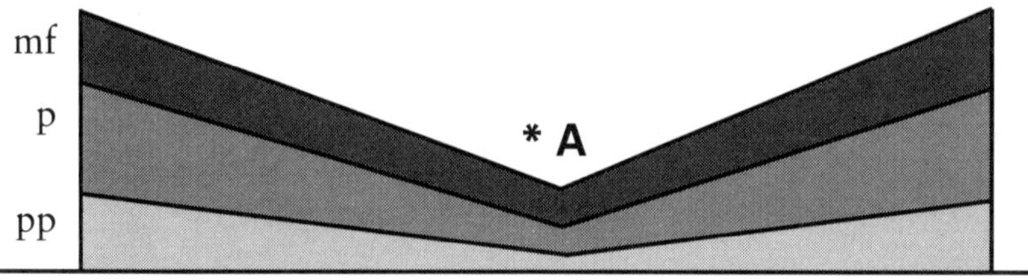

Fig. 13.2

In both these examples the solo instrument, as can be seen, would be playing at a dynamic level a little below *piano,* but no allowance has been made for the capability of some woodwind instruments, or players, to project more easily than others. However, *Fig. 13.1* does illustrate the 'blanket' effect that a uniform level of accompaniment can have and the level of sound that would have to be attained before the solo is clear. In *Fig. 13.2* not only is the solo free of sound in the area through which it needs to project but the level of accompaniment at a distance from the soloist can, if required, be increased considerably. Nonetheless, it is in very soft dynamic levels that the advantages are most obvious to the listener, where very extreme *pianissimi* can be obtained from the strings without loss of quality.

The conductor does not need to increase the size of the beat when the sound is so far spread. Provided it expresses musical logic and is high enough to be seen above the intervening players, the smallest movement is perfectly clear at the back of the orchestra. Eye contact and positive conveyance of the sound envisaged are the prerequisites.

A determination to avoid the problems inherent in *Fig. 13.1* is a contributory factor in both the traditional positioning of the concerto soloist at the front of the orchestra and the use of multiple dynamic markings in the scores of many composers from the late nineteenth century onwards. It has spawned many attempts at re-seating the orchestra, the most famous of which was probably Leopold Stokowski's lengthy flirtation with the seating of the woodwind immediately to the right of the conductor.

The Front of the Sections

As a deliberately considered performance technique the positioning and rehearsal of a sound centred on the front desks is used less often, mainly because such production is the natural tendency of most orchestras. However, the quality it imparts and the type of passage to which it is most suited must be thoroughly appreciated in this context.

The sound can best be illustrated at first by reference to the Classical repertoire, as this will help to limit any mistaken impression of thick orchestral texture. *Ex. 13.3* shows the first five bars of the overture from Mozart *Marriage of Figaro*.

EX. 13.3

The clarity of movement and effervescent sparkle of this whole work must be released by a tightly centred core of transmitted energy, the hallmark of the great chamber orchestras. Vivid articulation and arrow-like projection in the softest dynamic require the narrow beam of sound provided by a small, close-knit group of players. Once the production covers too great an area the sound is diffused and much of the essential quality lost. Most of the Classical repertoire is performed with this reduced size, not because the players are better but because the sound and style so often require these techniques of production.

In the symphonic repertoire the use of the smaller chamber ensemble, ever-present at the front of the symphony orchestra, must not be overlooked in this respect, neither must its natural resources be ignored. The vibrancy of all the orchestral virtuoso works, from Berlioz *Le Corsair* to Walton *Scapino*, and the brilliance they exhibit, is heavily dependent on keeping the string sound within this tightly compressed centre.

This technique of production demands that the main body of strings be aware that the performance is directed by the front of each section, and that the clarity of articulation secured by these few players must not be obscured. While maintaining dynamic level, bow contact and a quite deliberate panache, the section must have an overriding awareness of the sounds coming from the front, and make a conscious attempt to support them rather than compete.

It has to be said that the difficulty of this technique lies in understanding the exact moment to encourage its use. It is all too easy to lose the contribution of the majority of the section altogether. Any exaggeration of this type will tend towards an unnatural, soloistic sound which will totally defeat the musical objective. Primarily, such 'forward' bias is best regarded as a fundamental method of production to which specific reference need rarely be made. Should the focus of some virtuoso passage need sharpening then simply reminding the players of where the responsibility lies will probably be sufficient.

These three basic positions of sound source may be combined, exaggerated or subjected to variations of emphasis at all dynamic levels, but they should never be invoked for their own sake or taught out of context. However beneficial they may be both to the quality and technical range of the string orchestra, they remain essentially the means by which certain musical exigencies of performance might be fulfilled.

The Role of the Bass Section

The unique contribution of the basses in overall string texture is dictated by their physical arrangement and number. Because they are normally arranged in rows, rather than files, of players, any change in the area of sound from front to back is impossible, and the vague option of lateral movement is not worth considering. Thus their very important involvement in these techniques will be one of support, especially to the cellos. Their ability to darken or lighten the base of the harmony by total control of their sound, and their sensitivity to the varying textures of the orchestra are crucial. From a position generally on the edge of the orchestra this is no easy task, and the players' capabilities of listening will be stretched to the limit, as will their technical control of intonation and bow contact in order to produce a firmly centred sound at all dynamic levels.

Though it is very easy to overlook this apparently simple role and misjudge the effect it has on the strings' projection as a whole and that of the cellos in particular, a good bass section probably has more influence on the sound of the entire orchestra than any other single instrument or group. The sound of the instrument tends not to carry as far as its size would lead one to expect, yet it is still capable of supporting full orchestral climaxes and taking responsibility for many subtle changes in colour and weight. When working with a student orchestra it is essential that these facts are remembered, and that the bass section never feel ignored or forgotten. Their subsequent lack of involvement could prove costly.

The Perceived Sound

It is here that an ability to 'unlock' the corporate sound of the players, whether by means of gesture, technical knowledge or sheer personality, is so vital to the youth orchestra conductor. No sound, regardless of its beauty or intrinsic sensitivity, is of any use unless what it conveys to the very back of a hall corresponds exactly with its original conception. To the young orchestral player this represents the uncharted territory of the experienced professional and the student orchestra will tend only to perceive the quality of the sound at its source.

The entire responsibility of the conductor may be ultimately summed up as the need to obtain this single skill from the orchestra in terms of balance, sound and meaning. The foundations of projection will be laid by every aspect of rehearsal. Improvements in precision, intonation, phrasing and dynamic all serve to 'clean the edge' of the sound and define the texture. But finally the orchestra has to be aware of committing the sound to a point in the far distance, and this will not be acquired without practice.

There are many occasions for the youth orchestra where physical limitations of rehearsal facilities make this extremely difficult to achieve. Small rehearsal halls, where the orchestra is virtually touching all four sides of the room, put it almost beyond hope. Not only is there no space into which to project but a totally false impression is gained from the immediacy of the reflected sound. Under these circumstances it becomes immensely difficult to persuade string players that they are not making the sound they hear, and virtually impossible to provide them with an aural impression of what is actually required. Only when the orchestra arrives at the concert hall do the players become aware of their inability to fill it and the resultant inhibitions, which affect every feature of their performance, make all their hard work at rehearsal futile. A more detailed appraisal of this highly important aspect of youth orchestra performance appears in a later chapter, but let us assume for the moment that better circumstances prevail.

The instinctive approach of the student orchestra to production is to 'give' the sound to the conductor, as the focal point of their attention, and not to consider the need for it to travel beyond this point. When any distance in excess of about six metres is available in front of the orchestra it must be constantly used to entice the sound beyond the unnatural physical confinement of the performing area. This might at first be accomplished by actually leaving the rostrum and going some distance away, to draw the sound to a new focal point of attention. At a later stage, reminding the orchestra of this position, or entreating them to touch the very farthest wall with the sound, should enable them to reproduce a similar technique.

The fundamental awareness of the need to project will display two concurrent benefits, especially at the moment it is being rehearsed. Firstly, and quite obviously, it provides the desired result, in that it will cause the instrumentalists to release the sound from the instrument and consign it to a position some distance away. Secondly, it will encourage them, if only for short periods at a time, to submerge consideration of their own sound into that of the corporate whole, and thereby immediately enhance cohesion and blend.

The individual skills of every craft are totally interdependent, and the improvement of one will always open the way to a host of others. At every point along the way, however, there is one that will have the biggest cumulative effect on all the others so far mastered. For the orchestra, the ability to think of the sound beyond the confines of individual involvement is the basis of everything.

The Left Hand

With initial apologies to those very few 'left-handed' instrumentalists who use their right hand for the production of notes and will be forced therefore to read backwards from here on, it must be said that the strength and agility of the left hand is responsible for much of the clarity and tone of the string group.

Fingering, as related to specific passages, is often very personal, but the ultimate production of clearly centred notes is the province of the conductor. This is an area of instrumental performance in which no new techniques can truly be taught in orchestral circumstances. The limitations of ability are preset and can only be improved by time and practice. However, some passages that appear to be solely dependent on the dexterity of the left hand prove not to be so, and much can be done to improve them without the need for any increase in facility.

The implanting of positive finger action and firm rhythm in the movement of this hand at all times will serve to clarify many a passage that might have seemed technically beyond the section as a whole. Frequently it will be found that the left hand is skating over a passage, instead of firmly producing single notes at a time, with the result that the bow has no centred note to transmit, even though the fingers might be placing many of the right notes at the right time.

Certainly in the case of soft passages involving fast or awkward movement, the rhythm and ensemble of the line is often lost through the temptation to take the strength out of the left hand as well as the right. There are many passages of this type that could be quoted but *Ex. 13.4* from Elgar *Symphony no. 1*, involving all the strings, will always cause trouble.

EX. 13.4

Here the clarity of the four lines is dependent on vertical accuracy (not necessarily in rigid tempo) at the bar and half bar. If this passage is played with fairly small bow movement but at a full *forte* dynamic it always falls exactly right, partly because the right arm is a little more defined in movement but mainly because, at that dynamic, the left hand is automatically more firm and rhythmic. To perform it at the printed dynamic simply needs the weight to be taken off the bow without changing either the style of the right arm or the *forte* production of the left hand. In certain circumstances even the weight can remain, the bow being moved over the finger-board to attain *piano* or *pianissimo*. Many passages that seem untenable because of the difficulty of the notes or the intricate weaving of lines are actually unclear for this one reason alone.

A further example of the same deceptive difficulty may be seen in *Ex. 13.5*, this time for violas and cellos alone, at the very opening of Brahms *Symphony no. 4*.

EX. 13.5

The notes of these few bars can be rehearsed endlessly, with no discernible effect on their clarity in context, largely because they are not especially difficult. All that results when the passage is put back together is that a conscious drop in level is made to accommodate the violins, and the left-hand production loosens, effectively mirroring the right. Thus, after much careful work the passage is just as unclear as ever it was.

Most fast-moving passages in *legato* phrasing will exhibit the same fraudulent perversity, from the few *pianissimo* bars in Glinka *Russlan and Ludmilla* to the very different long *fugato* in Nielsen *'Inextinguishable'* (rehearsal figures 54–58). Apart from placing the notes under the hand, neither slow rehearsal nor repetition will do anything to clarify the line or help the ensemble in performance until the firm delivery of the left hand is understood and maintained.

The problems encountered in fast-moving passages that are to be bowed out, whether on or off the string, are very different. Here the left hand tends to retain much of its strength owing to the corresponding speed of movement of the bow arm. In this case slow rehearsal will tend not to alter any technical aspect of approach to the passage and therefore will be of benefit.

There is, however, another very important consideration that will often have much bearing on whether the passage is clear or not – that of phrasing, or more truthfully in this context, sub-phrasing. The example shown in *Ex. 13-6* (once again from Elgar *Symphony no. 1*) is a notoriously difficult statement of the main theme of the *Scherzo*, orchestrated, in this third and extended appearance, for full strings.

It is very obvious that the phrase extends over the full sixteen bars, but any attempt by the players to head for this point alone will spell disaster. The left hand must not only be given a frequent point of reference but also a moment, however infinitesimal, to reset. Thus the first placing is provided by the composer – bar 4 – and full advantage should be taken of it, with no player hurrying to start again at the E♯. The remainder of the bar is a link to the first of four two-bar sequences, each of which allows both a minute respite and a point of contact for the section. The last four bars may be viewed either as one whole, and played towards the final note, or as octave repetition of the first two bars followed by two bars of identical notes, the first bar being repeated in the second at the octave.

Although unavoidably complicated when explained like this, the passage does now become more logical and considerably shorter in apparent span. The eye now defines blocks of notes – something which the left-hand technique can handle far more easily than a long continuous line of seemingly unrelated difficulties. Presuming that the one or two awkward fingerings will have been looked at, once the passage is perceived in this way and the points of contact set, it will be found that most young string sections can play this passage successfully without the conductor, and arrive exactly together at the end of it.

The ability of an orchestra to perform difficult sections of music without 'the beat' should always be promoted. Not only does it encourage the orchestra to listen, but it will very often display the most natural and fluent tempo of the passage in question – not necessarily that insisted on by the conductor! Furthermore, it will always expose the places where a phrase needs to 'breathe', a vital aspect of all ensemble playing.

From the point of view of the conductor this will be discussed more fully in a later chapter but, having raised the subject, it is necessary to confront one aspect of it immediately. At least one professional player of my acquaintance, who has considerable experience in tutoring young string sections, views any exercise involving the orchestra playing 'alone' with some alarm, making the point that the orchestra never has to play in this way, and that much of the difficulty of orchestral playing is removed when the rigidity of the beat is taken away. While one has to agree with the underlying truth of the statement

(Allegro molto. 𝅗𝅥 = 69)
64
I
Vl
II
Vla
Vc
DB
ff con fuoco
ff con fuoco
con fuoco
con fuoco
sf

EX. 13.6

(although it might be argued that if a beat enforces rigidity it shouldn't be there!) it is nonetheless essential that an inexperienced orchestra be given some training in concentrated listening as well as a foundation of confidence in their own ensemble ability, for without this basic corporate technique they will be unable to concentrate on the more subtle problems of musical communication, and will be continually beset by the rigours of simply playing together.

Providing that such practice is not taken too far, and care is exercised in the passages chosen, I know of no method that instils the technique so quickly or with such lasting results. Besides, were it to come down to a matter of choice, I would rather an orchestra play together than with any conductor's beat!

The technique of mental sub-phrasing considered in the previous example will be found advantageous in many extremely difficult passages, and is not confined solely to those involving perpetual motion, although the benefits of increased rhythmic security will be most noticeable there. However, even this method of magnifying the moments of repose that are to be found in every phrase will not necessarily overcome the natural tendency, exhibited by all string players, to rush any figure involving downward movement. Thus, even when the passage incorporates an obvious degree of sub-division in the original structure, some of the available time for reasserting the rhythm can be lost because of the falling pattern of the preceding figure.

A prime example of such a passage is seen in *Ex. 13.7*, for 1st and 2nd violins, from the last movement of Tchaikovsky *Violin Concerto*, where the very apparent desire to rush the last group of every second bar is almost irresistible, and can only be defied by a very positive deliberation of these last four notes.

This is a tricky passage at the best of times (it was quoted by one eminent soloist as the most valid reason he could think of for not being an orchestral player!) but once it becomes rhythmically unstable it is quite impossible. That this should happen with such alarming regularity is due, almost entirely, to this descending figuration.

As so often happens, the fault becomes apparent at a point just after it has occurred, and frequently causes a perfectly innocent feature to be blamed. In *Ex. 13.7* no amount of rehearsal of the entry notes in relation to the quaver rest will help the passage in context, because the rhythm was lost in the bar before. In this instance the fault and its subsequent effect on performance are very closely related in time, being either side of a single bar-line, but, as was the case in *Ex. 13.6*, there are many occasions when a much more distant relationship has to be excavated.

A further problem of ensemble, which is regularly encountered in all orchestras, surfaces somewhat innocuously in this example: the commence-

EX. 13.7

ment of a passage before the main beat of the bar and after a rest. In bars eleven, thirteen and fifteen of *Ex. 13.7*, the two entry notes before the second beat can cause problems in two distinct ways. If they are bowed separately they can be over-accented, but slurring them across to the first note of the second group can make them rush – either way the ensemble will be affected. In entries of this type it is essential that the players head only for the nearest main beat of the bar (in this case the second), deliberately putting the passage together *on* the beat and not trying to synchronize the actual notes of entry. Approached in this way each short passage will always be together.

A far more extended example of the same technique may be shown in the exceptionally difficult second variation of Elgar '*Enigma*' *Variations.*

EX. 13.8

Here, the 'single beat' triple time is very difficult for an inexperienced section to pick up confidently, and the desire to be together on the first five notes causes panic and loss of control. It is impossible to synchronize the performance of these notes in relation only to themselves. A longer rhythmic span is needed and the second bar *must* become the point of collection. Only when the five entry notes are considered as an 'up-beat' to the following bar will they stand any chance of being together. The line of the phrase is the only possible point of reference.

It is very difficult to instil in a young section the combined control, relaxation and courage essential to the performance of this variation, especially as the notes themselves are so awkward and, for the most part, lie in a less easily projected part of the instrument. Personally I feel that the success of the entire work depends on playing of the highest order, and that this variation alone makes it the province of the virtuoso string section. The level of orchestral technique required, quite apart from individual instrumental facility, is very advanced and, even in professional ensembles, all may be ruined by just one unfortunate player who is unable to withdraw the sound and instantly get out of the way. As one highly experienced colleague taught me very early in my playing career: 'Orchestral playing, dear boy, is so much about what you *don't* do!'

The excerpts quoted in *Exx. 13. 6* and *13. 7* are obvious examples of the forward orientated sound considered earlier, and certainly work best if the sections allow much of the weight to be taken from here. But this does not mean that the players behind the second or third desks do not have to play the passages, rather that they should be aware of the area of the section which controls the line and direction.

The responsibility of the left hand for producing quality in the sound is at its most vital in *legato* phrasing, irrespective of whether it is slurred or separate, loud or soft. Finally the bow can only make audible a sound that the fingers of the left hand are producing and, although it may be capable of enhancing or destroying the tone, it cannot clarify something that is not there. There are almost no occasions where the strength and firm action of this hand can be slackened, least of all in places that require reduction in weight from the bow. The ability to keep the two hands working at totally independent power, with one relaxed and lifted and the other pressing into the string, is a long and slow lesson which, particularly in the upper strings, is often never completely learnt. In order to obtain a note the string must be stopped cleanly and solidly, irrespective of whether the dynamic is *pianissimo* or *forte*.

Equally, the relevance of this firmness to the moment of shift in left-hand position must be remembered. The slightest lifting of contact just before the shift is made, or lack of positive action in the movement itself, will involve a loss of tonal quality, especially when multiplied throughout a full section. Avoiding this requires a great deal of confidence from the players and a considerable amount of risk. It is one thing for the soloist to make a feature of the position change occasionally but quite another for it to be unintentionally apparent every time it occurs in the orchestra.

This is an added burden on the orchestral string player which limits the time available for the movement itself. The inevitable multiplication of numbers means that the shift often has to be accomplished with rather more clinical precision. The trust that has consequently to be placed in both the ability to hear the new note and the accuracy of the hand in placing it exactly is prodigious.

Cellists and bass players have to cope with this continually, the distance between notes being greater than anywhere else in the string sections. An apparently straightforward line (is there such a thing?) such as that shown in *Ex. 13.9* from Brahms *Symphony no. 4* demonstrates as early as the second bar the care that just this one aspect of technique requires from ten or twelve players together.

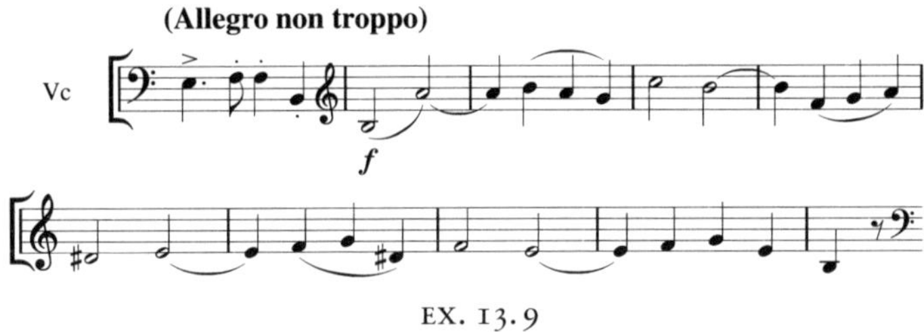

EX. 13.9

It is never so much the audibility of the shift itself that causes concern as the inequality of production afforded to the note immediately before it. The shift must occur almost at the instant the new note is required, with departure from the preceding note being left as late as possible. In solo performance considerably more emphasis of the moment of shift could be tolerated and, indeed, might well be desirable.

Such speed of movement is no less obligatory for the upper strings. In the coda of this same symphony the 1st violins are confronted by this demonic passage with little help, except harmonic emphasis, to be had from anywhere.

EX. 13.10

Such leaps can only be achieved by total belief that the hand knows exactly where to go, for there is absolutely no opportunity here to do anything but 'risk it'. If the players attempt any method of safety the loss of sound will be worse than if the note were missed completely. The all-important fact is that there is no safe method beyond complete confidence. In effect, the bow arm and the left hand must move exactly together.

The Control of Rhythm

For the orchestral strings, although the left hand is of prime importance in providing clarity and definition of rhythm, it is the bow arm from which much of the control of movement comes. It is all too easy to allow the left hand to dictate the movement of the bow, either waiting for it to finish a figure or hurrying the change because the fingers have rushed. In student orchestras, unrhythmic movement of the bow is the most frequent reason for passages both *being* unclear and, often, *sounding* more unclear than they really are. The bow arm must allow sufficient *time* for the fingers to get round the notes.

String players actually have a great advantage over wind players in this respect, in that they have recourse to physical rhythmic movement in a very positive way. Although articulation with the diaphragm or tongue will produce the same feeling, it is nowhere near as acute, nor so obviously unavoidable. All 'instrumental feeling' for string players comes through the bow arm, and the techniques of the left hand are, in truth, neither as demanding nor wide-ranging.

This ability to perceive rhythm physically must be seized on when dealing with any aspect of orchestral string playing, for it is so often the key to unified movement and definition of line. In order that it be achieved successfully it must be felt by the players, and this returns us to the all-pervading concept of 'contact' of the bow on the string – the secret of all string sound. It does not imply any accent in the bow change but it does mean that the bow cannot skate over the string as is so often apparent. Especially with the change from down-bow to up-bow, the contact of the bow must be *maintained* in *legato* and *reiterated* in *staccato* or any form of separated notes.

The importance of the bow arm in passages of fast-moving *legato* cannot be over-emphasized. Even in a fairly simple fragment of thematic movement, such as *Ex. 13.11* from Rossini *L'Italiana in Algeri* – a passage which regularly falls over itself – the importance of totally rhythmic bow changes can be easily seen.

EX. 13.11

Once in combined and heavy orchestration, as in *Ex. 13.12* from the last movement of Tchaikovsky *Symphony no. 4*

EX. 13.12

or in Elgar overture *Cockaigne*

EX. 13.13

this 'locking' of the rhythm via the movement of the bow arm becomes, quite literally, all that holds the string sections together, while the control it dictates over the left hand and the time it gives to each successive figure ensures that at least some of the notes will have an opportunity of being played.

When the going gets really tough, the ability to rely totally on the guaranteed rhythmic reliability of the bow arm is a vital bonus. There is simply no other way that this monstrous passage from Bartók *Concerto for Orchestra*, a mere fraction of which is quoted here, can even be contemplated!

EX. 13.14

EX. 13.14 (continued)

The notes are by no means easy, but their performance without taking advantage of the maximum time-span available is impossible.

Once any form of syncopated phrasing occurs, the need to control it via very deliberate movement of the bow becomes even more obvious. All forms of syncopation show a marked tendency to rush because the deflection of the rhythmic impetus creates an automatic desire to compress the figuration, regardless of the note lengths. The most successful means of counteracting this inclination is to emphasize whatever physical movement exists as a component part of the instrument's technique in relation to the phrase.

On many occasions the need for accented movement makes the process considerably easier, as in *Ex. 13.15* from the fifth movement of Britten *Matinées Musicales.*

Here one needs only to make certain that the bow direction changes in exact rhythm and that both directions begin with equal accent, not really a problem at the required *fortissimo* dynamic. *Piano* syncopation, however, can be a very different matter. It is a technique which is at its most difficult within

EX. 13.15

EX. 13.15 (continued)

a soft, *legato* phrase, a variation in rhythm of which Brahms was particularly fond and which may be seen in *Ex. 13.16*, the awkward ending to the eighth variation of his *Variations on a Theme of Haydn*.

The great difficulty in this example lies in the fact that, while a firm and contacted movement of the bow needs to be maintained, no alteration of either the dynamic level or the subdued quality of sound must be apparent. Provided that excessive bow lengths are avoided, this passage proves perfectly easy to accomplish at a *mezzo forte* or *forte* level, but becomes progressively harder as the dynamic is reduced. It is important to remember that, as with so many passages, the actual notes and their relative positions have not altered, and that the difficulty is, therefore, one of 'character' rather than hand or finger technique. Quite simply, it is vital that the clarity of movement, which is fairly easily obtained by a stronger approach to the passage, is preserved when performing it at the lower dynamic level.

No amount of rehearsal of the actual notes will help the passage in context because the notes themselves are not the problem. What needs to be addressed is accuracy of articulation, an issue which is complicated in this example by the totally *legato* nature of the approach (only really visible in bars 1–3 of the viola and cello line in the quoted excerpt, but extending to 1st violins in an earlier appearance). The figure must be played with considerable contact of the string at every bow change, but with very little length. Once the passage is clear, any necessary decrease in level may be obtained by using the same technique a little further from the bridge. Please don't attempt to rehearse the passage in terms of its dynamic level as the first priority. When asked to play softer, all that the inexperienced string player will do is to take the weight off

EX. 13.16

the bow – an irreversible disaster in this context! The required dynamic and sound can be achieved once the technique of performance is correct.

The deliberate movement of the bow arm while maintaining firm contact with the string can be extended to passages that include rests, widely punctuated examples making it technically very close to the *martelé* stroke (*see* Chapter 7). For accurate rhythmic movement and clear enunciation of the figure a production of this sort, positioned in the upper half of the bow, should be used in many passages similar to *Ex. 13.17* from the *Dorabella* variation from Elgar '*Enigma*' *Variations* (see page 510).

Although the figures appear in total separation, apparently giving more than adequate time to remove and replace the bow for each pair, it will be found in practice that this not only causes rhythmic instability but also loses

EX. 13.17

the initial definition of the up-bow figure by creating a quite unnecessary need for re-contact.

In much quicker tempo the same technique may be used to give firm control to a passage of continuously repeated figuration, such as *Ex. 13.18*, from the 1919 version of Stravinsky *The Firebird*.

EX. 13.18

Here, the almost inseparable relationship to *martelé* is more clearly apparent – a separated movement of the bow in alternate directions without ever losing firm contact with the string.

Initial contact of the bow might best be described as an infinitesimal gripping of the string with the bow hairs prior to movement, in order to ensure the string reaches its ultimate vibration immediately, rather than in the progressive manner more likely to be achieved by a smooth stroke. If precise and ultra-clear sounds are intended the technique must be repeated every time the bow returns to the string. Once two or more clearly separated notes are performed within one direction of the bow, some degree of re-contact must be achieved.

Individually this will often need to be of a quite powerful and calculated nature if real clarity is to be demonstrated by a complete section. The second portion of the first subject of Dvořák *Symphony no. 9*, where it is re-orchestrated for 1st violins and appears as a repeated figure, is a prime example (see *Ex. 13.19*). The two quavers in the second half of each bar necessitate the use of two up-bows, to comply with the composer's phrasing and to ensure equal accent on each *sforzando*.

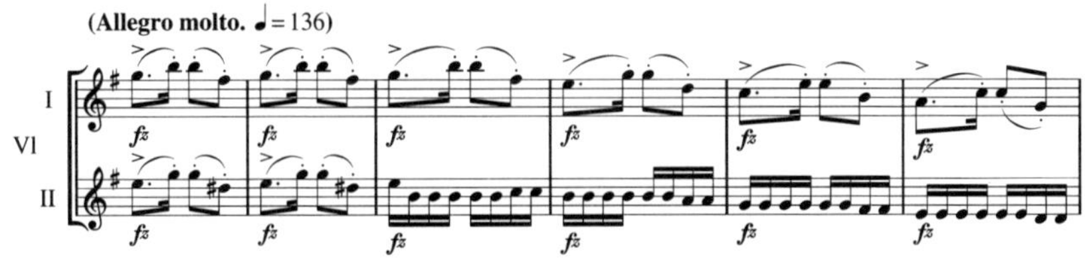

EX. 13.19

It will also be noticed that additional re-contact is required for the semi-quaver movement of each down-bow, this note being conspicuously separated from the first. However, it is *not* necessary, especially in the down-bow, for the bow really to leave the string. Although truly maintained contact will, in these circumstances, provide a sound with too little resonance, any attempt actually to lift the bow from the string will lose rhythmic control and make for a poorly articulated return on each quaver. The passage must be performed low in the bow and close to the string, the bow hairs never entirely leaving it but initial contact being reproduced on every note.

'Colouring' the Sound

All instruments of the string section are capable of producing the same note in a number of different places, the limitations being only the very lowest notes of the instrument (before the overlap of the second string) and the very highest. Throughout the range of instruments each string possesses a quite distinct sound quality, the topmost in all cases being the brightest and the middle two the most mellow or, in the case of the higher positions, mellifluous. The capacity of the lowest string to produce the most intense sound when strongly attacked and yet maintain considerable clarity and projection makes composers specify its use more often than they do other strings, especially on the violin.

For sheer audacity there are very few examples that can be found to approach *Ex. 13.20* from near the end of the third movement of Bartók *Concerto for Orchestra*.

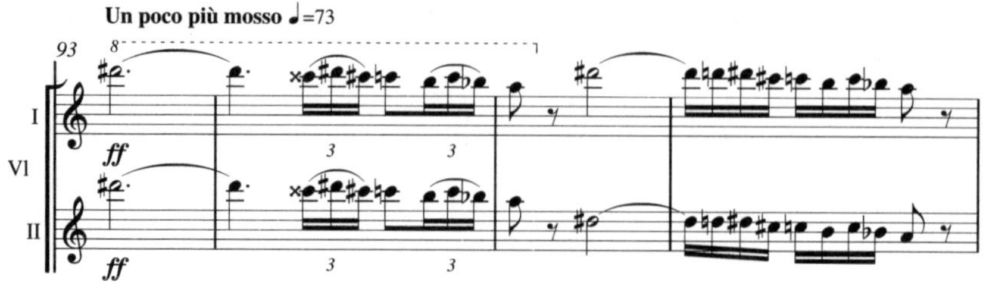

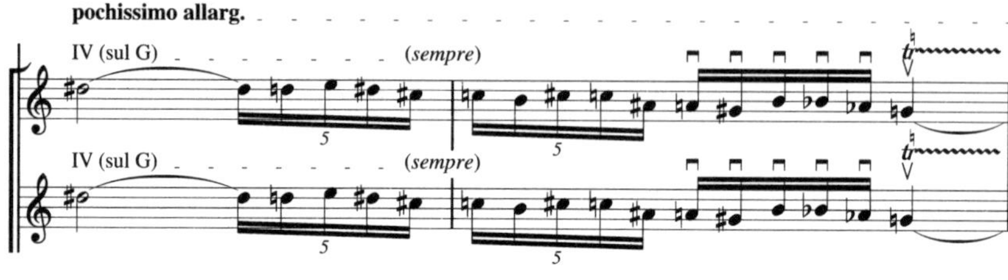

EX. 13.20

The combined effect of sudden change of timbre elicited from the G string, and one of the most blatantly exposed leaps known to the orchestral violinist, is of quite staggering intensity and an almost unparalleled example of a composer's understanding of the extreme demands that may successfully be placed on an unsupported string section.

However, contrary to the apparent belief of many young instrumentalists, such powerful dramatic effect is by no means the only sound available to the higher reaches of the lowest string. A very gentle and transparent quality can be produced when required. At the opposite end of the musical spectrum from the harsh drama of the Bartók example comes *Ex. 13.21* from very early in the third movement of Rimsky-Korsakov *Scheherazade*.

EX. 13.21

This wonderful second phrase of the main theme still retains the *piano* dynamic of the opening statement but radically alters the apparent texture, to the extent that an additional four bars may be grafted into the span of the phrase with consummate ease – an example of the sophistication of the composer's ear as much as of his highly accomplished manipulative skills.

For the young section such a subtle use of the G string is not at all easy, the power of the example shown as *Ex. 13.20*, for all its immense technical difficulty, proving much more natural to their approach.

An uncontrolled desire to increase the speed and potency of the *vibrato*, together with a tendency to press harder with the bow, is noticeable in all but the most accomplished violinists when playing in the higher positions on this string, and is due as much to the insecurity felt by the left hand when fingering so far over the instrument as to any wish to exploit the sonority for all it is worth. Avoiding the resultant pressurized and overtly dramatic timbre of the G string requires considerable technical ability and control from the whole section.

In truth, the quoted example is one of the less difficult in this respect because the desired sound is comparatively obvious. More difficult is a phrase where the melodic line enhances the natural depth of the instrument and the underlying harmonic texture increases the tendency to provide a large and sonorous tone. The fifth variation from Elgar '*Enigma*' *Variations* may be used as an example.

EX. 13.22

Here, the *mezzo forte* marking, the small *crescendo* at the beginning of the second bar, the addition of the direction *largamente* to the violin parts alone, and the octave grace notes approaching the main beats of the second and third bars all conspire to produce a totally erroneous impression of vibrant Romanticism, laying a trap for the unwary section that is avoided but rarely.

From a technical point of view there can be no question that the passage is far more difficult than may be immediately apparent to the non-string player – the intonation of any octave leap is extremely hazardous and the one in the third bar of *Ex. 13.22* is subject to all kinds of problems. The inherent weakness of the fourth finger, especially in less advanced players, is most noticeable in the higher positions of the lowest string but its use is, in this instance, virtually unavoidable, as is the tendency to over-stretch for the note and release the pivotal function of the first finger.

Even more alarming for younger players is that, with the exception of a few fortunate individuals, this area of their instrument is probably one of the weakest in terms of its ability to respond quickly and evenly. Only a very fine instrument will be of positive help in these heights, and the desire to over-compensate by applying additional bow pressure and 'forcing' the sound out can easily become irresistible.

The forcing of the tone on the violin G string will swiftly break the sound and produce an audible 'rattle', a situation which must always be avoided (it is *never* required, not even for effect). Even at *fortissimo*, when the full sonority is being drawn from the string, it is essential that each player plays only to the maximum capacity of their own instrument – a very variable standard in itself – and never allows the tone to break.

A similar, although by no means so critical, situation exists for the lowest string of the viola but, in this case, it is rare for this range to be exploited merely to elicit dramatic power. However, the noticeable increase in breadth and strength of the sound of the lowest string of all stringed instruments can propel the inexperienced player into the dangerous waters of trying to produce more sound than a particular instrument will provide.

The middle strings are less often specifically requested by composers but should be kept uppermost in the conductor's mind for the induction of subtle changes of sound and quality. The movement of the second half of the open-

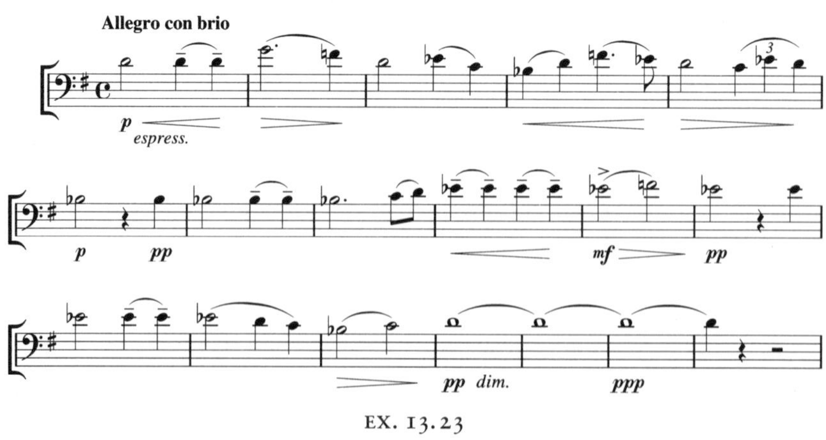

EX. 13.23

ing cello phrase of Dvořák *Symphony no. 8* (from the *pp* B♭) across to the D string creates the most wonderful effect (see *Ex. 13.23*).

Similarly, the performance of the main subject return in the *Andantino* of Tchaikovsky *Symphony no. 4* can be effective if the violins are limited entirely to their D string.

EX. 13.24

Here, the noticeable change of timbre if the A string is first used at the *mf* in the penultimate bar of the quoted section is sufficient reason in itself.

The careful control and imaginative use of the various tone-colours available to the string section as a whole, achieved by careful consideration of which string they might be playing on and whether performance across two strings is really necessary or just convenient, is a vital factor in the final transmission of interpretation. Although the notes might remain the same their communication will be radically different.

Integration of the Sections

Even beyond the techniques of production, projection, control and placement lie those of integration. The ability of a string section to exhibit sounds so unified in thought, style and phrasing that they might be taken as one player is the summit of string orchestral achievement. That it can be done at all is remarkable, but that many young orchestras manage to approach so close to it is little short of amazing. The requirements are many and exacting. Confidence, awareness, sensitivity, reaction and anticipation all play their part, but, above all, there is the slowly acquired craft of listening.

To refer to it as a craft is no exaggeration, for it is the one aspect of technique that sets the really high-class orchestral player apart, and it can only be achieved by the maximum concentration and dedication. In this context, the somewhat dualistic role required of all orchestral players, whether strings or wind, needs fully to be appreciated.

On the one hand, each player needs to produce a determinedly individual sound as a positive contribution to the output of one section or the orchestra as a whole, and to retain elements of the character of his or her personal approach, nuance and style as essential parts of the orchestra's corporate personality. On the other, he or she must be able to invoke a graded negation of all these, so that the sound may blend, the style particularize and the nuance become general. The situation, professed by many disenchanted players, of the complete submerging of the individual into the combined whole is neither necessary nor desirable – nor, for that matter, possible, if one thinks about it.

This craft requires considerable empirical knowledge of the boundaries of each situation as well as a sustained level of concentrated listening. These things are by no means intrinsic to the young musician, but the basic capability is there and the awakening of it incumbent on those who work with them.

Such is the reasoning behind encouraging a section to play some phrases in rehearsal without the conductor, or the entire orchestra to attempt lengthy passages in similar fashion, especially those they might find difficult to understand or put together. Quite apart from teaching the players to listen, this exercise demonstrates in the clearest way possible where a section or an individual needs to influence (or be influenced by) the dynamic level, the clarity, or the movement of the rest of the orchestra.

Many examples of this practice may be quoted that have successfully instilled sound, rhythm or accompanying level, but one instance comes immediately to mind. I was working with a student orchestra on Rachmaninov *Symphony no. 3*, and each time we covered the violin solo towards the end of the slow movement it was apparent that the Leader was experiencing difficulty in finding sufficient time in the phrase. During the two or three days of rehearsal, which obviously included other pieces, I worked on this passage in various ways but never managed to imbue it with the distance and tranquillity it needs. Finally I asked the strings to play it without me and *oblige* the Leader to play it at the right level and find the right amount of time. They did it so perfectly that I asked them to make him play it louder and without *rubato*; and then another way, and yet another. I have to admit to being surprised at the result, so amazing was the influence they had, simply by virtue of variation in sound and movement. Fortunately other professional players were present, so this remarkable demonstration of corporate thought did not pass unwitnessed! The quotation of the passage here will show just how little material they had at their disposal.

EX. 13.25

No aspect of technique can be singled out to account for their success, but probably the most significant in this passage is the ability of a large string group to provide so many differing levels of soft dynamic, from warm *piano* to almost inaudible. The fact that they first produced the right sound when playing undirected was because they were forced to concentrate their listening in order to move together at such a slow pulse and, in this section of the work, that fact alone is almost enough to secure the essential sonority.

The larger the string section, the greater becomes their ability to produce meaningful but extreme *pianissimi*, unequalled by any other instrument or group. When considering an orchestra of 465 instrumentalists in his *Treatise on Instrumentation*, Berlioz talks of the 'seraphic, ethereal expression in *pianissimo*' of 120 violins! But even beyond the infinite gradation of softness is the ability of the large string orchestra to imbue every level with a variety of timbre and expression ranging from magical stillness to awesome fear. It was certainly this ability that had the strongest effect on the solo violin in the Rachmaninov symphony cited above.

It is vital to provide such opportunities for the string sections to feel the influence of their own sounds. The early stages of understanding the movement within a section, and the dependency of one section on another, simply cannot be demonstrated in any other way. For an orchestra to be able to play together sympathetically, and react to changing sounds and motions, the ability must finally emanate from within, irrespective of how persuasive the helmsman may be.

Two very important points remain to be firmly restated. Firstly, all techniques of production, whether individual or collective, are simply a means to an end and never the end itself. Within the orchestra they can only be introduced as and when the opportunity arises in specific works, and cannot be considered in the abstract. Neither must they inherit any artificial importance in their own right beyond their necessity as tools of musical communication. Thus, a young string group who were concerned more with the direction of their bowing than the uniform positioning of it, occasioned one of the most perspicacious remarks ever to have scythed a string section, uttered, inevitably, by the great Nadia Boulanger: 'Strings – rid yourselves of the tyrannies of the bow!'

Secondly, and this cannot be repeated too often: all sounds must be heard and understood by the players involved if there is to be any hope of replicating them in concert performance. In the majority of cases the most successful approach will be to utilize some method of production in which the relevant aspect becomes unavoidable (as, for example, was suggested with reference to the passage from Vaughan Williams *Symphony no. 5* in *Ex. 13.2*). But this careful implanting of the important connection between specific techniques and their related sound, made within the context of normal rehearsal, is an ability that the youth orchestra conductor must acquire if any real quality is to be obtained in the final result.

The Accompaniment of Woodwind Soli

The clearing of the surrounding texture will provide solo woodwind instruments with an unchallenged path of communication while serving to direct the listener's concentration towards them. This need not, of course, be confined to such dramatically different tone-colours as strings and woodwind. However, it is certainly with regard to the string accompaniment of woodwind sounds that the young orchestra will first perceive the varied responsibilities of individual strands within a larger texture.

The musical connotations inherent in the techniques of exposing a solo line, whether by transposition of the sound source or tonal variation (considered earlier) or by any other means, necessitates some understanding of the nature and properties of accompaniment, irrespective of the number of players involved.

Firstly, in cases of essentially harmonic accompaniment only a skeletal outline is necessary and continuation can be just as effectively implied as prolonged. Thus the beautiful opening statement of the theme in the second movement of Tchaikovsky *Symphony no. 4* (*Ex. 13.26*) loses none of the composer's harmonic subtlety through not being supported by sustained chords.

The ability of the ear to retain harmonic background has much to do with

EX. 13.26

the implications of the melody line and the tonal tensions of notes and groups of notes related to one another. Especially in simple harmony, it requires no training on the part of the listener either to retain the progression during performance or to expect certain logical conclusions from it. Education will make it a conscious act, more appreciative of subtlety and with a heightened sense of anticipation, but it is only a prerequisite of understanding, not of acceptance.

Directly connected to this, and inseparable from the physical laws of sound pertaining to music, is the ability of a sustained note to outweigh adjacent notes of lesser duration. Difficulties of balance will always be caused by the relative strength of an immobile accompaniment and the considerable increase in level required to make any moving line clearly audible. (Clear aural perception of both these facets of accompaniment will probably be most easily achieved in relation to the piano – paradoxically, an instrument physically unable to sustain the level of any sound. The mechanics of its production determine that every note sounded must immediately decay, and yet apparently sustained lines and harmonies are produced all the time and the implication of equal *legato* continuation in all parts is the foremost technique.)

The principles responsible for such 'illusions' are interrelated, since they are simultaneously dependent on the tonal and rhythmic relationship of notes sounded together and separately, the aural perception of each fundamental and its overtones and the ensuing tensions that may be created or dissipated, as well as the degree of retention and expectancy thus produced in the listener. An awareness of the properties of lines of support or secondary importance is crucial to the performance of any concerted passage, from the point of view of both balance and inflection.

In orchestral playing, simple subjugation of the accompaniment is never the complete answer. The alteration in position of the sound source that becomes possible with a large body of instrumentalists allows for quite considerable strength and clarity of movement to be maintained if necessary, without obstructing the solo line. Similarly, the *tonal* variation available to individual accompanying instruments can produce the same effect. But it must be remembered that any accompaniment is still an integral part of the whole, and one of the main factors in determining the character of the passage.

Almost without exception, the accompaniment of a single woodwind instrument will take place at a relatively low dynamic level. Strong phrases will tend to be doubled in the melodic line, or to be of such short duration as to require no breaking of the phrase for breath or structural emphasis. Where the accompaniment is provided solely by strings, the projection of very soft sounds is liable to miscalculation, both in respect of its level and the ability to carry.

The type of spine-chilling *pianissimi* associated with dramatic effect and required by some late Romantic and twentieth-century orchestral works, and performed in the strings by using the minimum amount of bow and pressure, is of little general use in the accompaniment of a solo phrase. In the first place it most characteristically implies cessation of movement rather than the momentum essential to nearly every accompanying passage and most especially those of the *legato* wind solo. Secondly, it has virtually no projection, its purpose being to generate tension through its immobility and lack of definition in relation to its surroundings. The listener must strain to hear it. Such a sound – exclusive to a large string section – deteriorates rapidly unless composed of very fast notes; hence its frequent and highly successful use in *tremolo*. In *legato* it exhibits a 'dead' quality, its lack of depth or centre arising from the very small vibration of the string involved in its production. In anything but a totally static form of accompaniment such a sound in conjunction with a solo instrument will be utterly valueless and quite unable to impart any harmonic movement or support.

Simply to increase the *level* of sound, while retaining this same method of production, is not the answer. The 'tight' quality produced in stringed instruments by restrained bow movement will not match the liquid sonority of a sustained woodwind solo, and the excessive deterioration in projection cannot be overcome until an unacceptably high dynamic level is reached. Furthermore, until such a high level is achieved, above *pianissimo* this production displays a distressing ability to separate.

As has been mentioned, the most obvious aural variations to the sound of stringed instruments are effected by three techniques: the speed at which the bow is travelling; the strength or lightness of its contact with the string; and its position in relation to the bridge and finger-board. All three techniques are totally variable and, in combination, provide an almost limitless fund of subtle alteration. Harnessing this extraordinary resource, and channelling it into various parts of the section, is the basis of the techniques of sound distribution previously discussed.

The aural benefit of removing any accompanying sound from the path of a solo instrument is already apparent. The purely musical benefits of such unrestrained and flexible accompaniments must now be considered.

Except in the most simple chordal accompaniment, interlocking lines of melodic harmony and fragmented counter-melodies will always be found, of which many will be essential for the momentum of the phrase and the illusion of uninterrupted delivery. The ever-present problem of making these clear but unobtrusive is probably the ultimate goal of orchestral communication and the determining factor between the merely good and the meaningful performance.

With a widely dispersed string sound it must be remembered that there are no instrumentalists playing noticeably louder than the accompaniment requires, just an even spread of players providing progressively softer sounds, with the very back players taking most of the responsibility for projected quality, freedom and centre of the sound. The overall balance remains unchanged over a distance because these softer sounds, performed by the overwhelming majority of players, are the controlling influence.

The interweaving of lines, the provision and removal of solo support, and the colouration of cadences and sequential movement are now all achievable not by increase of sound, but by subtle change of focus – the movement of the sound across the section or the almost indefinable change of timbre within it. A very slight movement of the bow towards the bridge by only a few members of the section will be enough to provide the slightest edge on any particular sound, isolating the quality and making it clear without risk of false *crescendo* or uneven balance. The amount of variation within one single tone-colour and sustained dynamic is limited only by the imagination of the interpretation and the adroitness of the players involved.

Of equal importance to the wind soloist is the provision of direction. The line of the phrase must be as implicit in the accompaniment as it is apparent in the solo itself. It is not possible to project a continuous span unless the accompaniment, regardless of whether it be strings or anything else, displays an equal proportion of the movement and, indeed, anticipates and occasions much of it.

This is true not only of the 'concurrent' accompaniment but also of that which immediately precedes the solo entry – the passage which unveils the character, framework, and even the necessity of the solo line. From the point of view of the orchestral soloist this is often as crucial as a refined sensitivity to support the actual solo – after all, many players can project the substance of their line across an unsympathetic accompaniment, but few can recreate an atmosphere that has been lost, or fail to be influenced by a meaningless approach to their sound.

With reference to a very well-known example, the solo horn at the opening of the second movement of Tchaikovsky *Symphony no. 5* (see *Ex. 13.27*), some illustration may be attempted.

In this case the eight anticipatory bars are utterly inseparable from the following solo. They encapsulate the sound, the mood and the phrasing. They even determine the scope, and thereby the structure, of the entire movement. Without them the solo, for all its inherent character, could express something entirely different, and its inclination is, therefore, determined before ever a note is played. Few introductory bars are as potent as these, but all will display

EX. 13.27

some of the features apparent here. Musical control of this passage, in all its aspects, is vital because it is impossible for the solo line to redefine the mood, subjugate the indulgence or retrieve the momentum once it has been misjudged. In such a situation, nothing remains for the soloist but personal objectives of technique and musicality.

It would be foolish to take leave of these wonderful bars without even the most perfunctory further exploration. The striking similarity between this progression and that which opens *Romeo and Juliet* (written 19 years earlier) will have been noticed, but the implied structure is not necessarily so apparent. The fourth bar must surely be the last of a four-bar phrase and not the first of a five (or – worse – two plus three), otherwise the distribution of the inner parts would be appalling, and the effect of contriving the cadence half a bar early (the *pianissimo*) would be almost entirely dissipated. Even graphically, the reiteration of the *piano* dynamic in the continuous parts, would either be one bar late or totally unnecessary. Only by taking the upper line in isolation can any illusion of three bars plus five be truthfully maintained.

All discussion of string support has so far involved only solo accompaniment, soft production and *legato* phrasing – the most intelligible situations as well as the most technically difficult. Consideration might now be expected of other areas in which their support is equally necessary – in relation to particular instrumental timbre, small and large combinations of instruments or *staccato* passage-work, for example. But however many instances were cited, each would differ only in degree and all would comprise but a fraction of the total. Of overriding importance is that the premise should be thoroughly understood by its application in one area, such that it can be adapted and applied to whatever circumstances might arise.

My hope is that, as far as strings are concerned, many of the technical and instrumental opportunities have now been sufficiently exposed for this to be possible.

14 WOODWIND

The projected sound of the wind section is dependent on many things, from the acoustic qualities of the hall in which they are playing to the transparency of the sound around them. But, unlike the strings, each player contributes an individual line, and thus there are no 'corporate techniques' that might be applied to strengthen, diffuse or alter their sound. Apart from developing techniques crucial to the projection of their personal sound, woodwind players are largely dependent for clarity on the response they receive from other instruments. It will always be necessary, therefore, to place a greater degree of emphasis on refinements of woodwind phrasing, and proportionately less on combined techniques of orchestral production which might suddenly bring forth new and exhilarating sounds. As has been remarked, the individuality and diversity of woodwind make it impossible to aspire to the same level of homogeneity that can be elicited from a large body of strings. The soloistic nature of the majority of their orchestral involvement is unique, and they will generally only be required to provide backing for another section in the nature of structured harmonic movement. Their use as the catalyst of an underlying texture of sensation or pervasive effect is severely limited, if only because of their inability to produce broad enough areas of similar timbre. Even with each contributing section enlarged to three or more instruments, their role in this respect is considerably smaller than that of any other section of the orchestra.

In student orchestras much of the work of this section may be wasted, owing to the inexperience of the players in projecting every aspect of their line and articulation over and beyond the strings. The sheer energy involved in such concentrated sound production is frequently underestimated and only really understood by those few fine sections that experience it. For the sensitive young woodwind player, used to the private performance of Classical sonatas or delicately wrought short concert pieces, such levels of mental and physical exertion are likely to be quite beyond their comprehension.

Obviously it takes time before the ability to transmit different qualities and intensities of sound develops, and even then such talents are not often encountered, especially in respect of soft and subdued timbres. Nevertheless, some methods of enhancing the basic sound produced and freeing the entire section from the dangers of being obscured or obstructed must be considered.

No orchestral sound is so easily hindered or distorted by the insensitivity of accompanying instruments, and no other orchestral sound can do so little about it.

In *pianissimo* or *piano* production it must be remembered that the section as a whole is having to employ widely differing techniques in order to produce sounds which are in tune with one another, balanced and together. Each individual wind instrument, whether woodwind or brass, will vary in its response time according to the method of production, and there are further variations within any given area of a single instrument's range. In the performance of soft chords in particular, the problems of making the instrument speak at the required time and holding intonation are different for each member of the woodwind family, whereas for the strings the same basic technique of production applies across the entire section and, more important, will produce similar timbres.

As has been seen, although general collaboration within the woodwind section – combining instruments to produce chords or multiple lines – is comparable to that required of strings or brass, nowhere else are the individual techniques quite so varied. While such individualities are fundamental to each instrument and therefore come as no surprise to the players, the demands of ensemble are considerable, and each player must take into account whatever problems are experienced by other members of the section, especially with regard to the minimum safe levels of sound. Here, *illusions* of extreme softness (a trick at which the greatest orchestras are so adept) are critical, and the responsibility of the individual players to enhance and 'protect' the sound of other instruments absolutely vital. This is as true of players outside the section (strings and brass) as it is of those within, since much of the woodwind section's work will be consolidated or undermined by the degree of sensitivity and support shown by these two sections.

The fundamental principles of orchestral solo and ensemble playing, considered generally with regard to the woodwind in Chapter 8, must now be taken a stage further and combined with refinements of phrasing and care of instrumental support in accompaniment. Awareness of the responsibility that all players must have towards this section and, consequently, the responsibility of its players one to another will always be the key to the release of musicianship and clarity of performance. Orchestral playing is not only about the quality of individual contribution but it is also, and much more crucially, about the effect of that contribution on the sound of others.

It must be accepted that, whereas the playing of the strings can make an immense difference to the performance and clarity of both the woodwind and brass, and that the brass are often of positive help to the woodwind, the woodwind themselves are limited in their ability to return the compliment. While they may adjust their dynamic level and balance when in an accompanying role, they can do little to enhance the actual quality or sound of another section. They can, however, be of great help to the *articulation* of other sections, especially in circumstances where they are scored in unison with a soft *legato* line.

In *Ex. 14.1* (the opening of the fourth movement of Brahms *Symphony no. 3*) the influence of two bassoons on the full string group extends further than Brahms' obvious intention of darkening the line by increased emphasis of the low octaves.

EX. 14.1

The clarity of articulation is enhanced by virtue of the slightly more centred sound endemic to the two wind instruments and their unavoidably positive enunciation of the note changes – always presuming the players can get their fingers round the notes in the first place! This allows the strings to withhold some of the weight of the bow and concentrate a little more on controlled sound without the added burden of being entirely responsible for the projected clarity, although this is not to imply that, without the woodwind inclusion, the line from the strings alone would be anything but clear.

Similar scoring will be found throughout the orchestral repertoire and may be extended to passages far less obvious than that quoted above. *Ex. 14.2* from the 2nd movement of Walton *Symphony no. 1* places great responsibility on the full woodwind section to 'centre' the production of a large string section playing *fortissimo*.

Notwithstanding the undoubted benefit of the woodwind in these and similar circumstances, the section's first priority must be to balance within itself and the rest of the orchestra must be sensitive to it and aware of its needs at all times. Obviously, this does not mean that the section becomes a law unto itself – far from it – but the essential confines of its ability to be of help elsewhere in the orchestra must be recognized. Only from this initial standpoint can the full capabilities of these instrumentalists be released and encouraged.

EX. 14.2

EX. 14.2 (continued)

The responsibility of the members of the woodwind section to each other is of paramount importance and the contribution of the 2nd players becomes one of the most vital factors. With an experienced section of accomplished young players it is possible to use the balance of instruments, as considered in Chapter 8, to vary both the relationship and the substance of the sound conveyed. In the case of all woodwind instruments, but most noticeably oboes and clarinets, the degree and the type of sound projected by the 2nd player will influence the nature of the section's combined delivery. In much the same way as a composer might utilize the timbre of a subsidiary instrument in order to highlight the more obvious character of a passage – a piccolo to enhance brightness, for example, or a contrabassoon for added weight and darkness – so the mood of two similar instruments (when not in unison) may be affected by subtle alteration of the supporting sound. Obviously, as neither intonation nor projection may be disturbed, such variation must be rigidly controlled and can only be subtly applied, but the principle at least must be embraced when working with a student section, even if the ultimate goal is far beyond them.

As is true of so many musical inflections and gradations of sound, the end product is as much the result of increased care and reasoning in approaching the passage as of any actual technical processes. Nonetheless, in order to do justice to the power and tenacity of Beethoven's woodwind writing – or, for that matter, the total homogeneity of Brahms', the stark expanse of Sibelius' and the agile luxury of Richard Strauss' – the required sound must complement the genius of their scoring, and the pervading influence will often be found in the richness or severity of tone of the 2nd players when in direct collaboration.

A very similar technique is central to the ability of professional sections to make a solo line immediately apparent. This accomplishment has already been discussed in relation to the clarinet solo which opens the 2nd movement of Dvořák *Symphony no. 7* (*Ex.* 2. 4). In this example, as in countless others, the essence of the sound of the three accompanying instruments is almost more important than the level. Although a solo line can achieve some clarity simply by dint of its being pitched higher and performed more loudly than those around it, such arbitrary balance is hardly satisfactory and it becomes progressively less successful the closer the solo line is pitched to its accompaniment. Some degree of sound balance must be achieved by the wind section alongside the balance of harmonic structure and dynamic level.

In Chapter 13 reference was made to the technique of physically moving the sound source of the string section away from the area of trajectory of wind soloists, by transferring the weight of production to the back of the sections and minimizing the production of sound directly in front of them.

Quite obviously this is only possible when a number of similar instruments are duplicating a line and cannot be considered in terms of accompanying lines allotted to individual wind players. Nonetheless, the principle holds good for woodwind balance insofar as what one perceives as a consequence, from outside the orchestra, is not a displacement of sound but rather, a change of focus.

This technique, applied to any instrumental grouping, will allow a sound to preside over its accompaniment more successfully and, at the same time, extend the available margins of gradation in both timbre and dynamic level. Thus, similar (although by no means so totally variable) modifications of tone-colour can be used by woodwind players themselves in solo accompaniment, and by the horns and brass, where quite large variations are possible. This does not mean, of course, that an uncentred or ill-produced tone will suddenly take on qualities of projection (although it will certainly increase its chances of being heard), but simply that once the accompanying instruments are fully sensitive to their role, the solo can concentrate on techniques of quality and musical insinuation, rather than winning a contest of audibility.

For the woodwind instrumentalist, release from such responsibility is vital, since breath control is common to both circumstances. If it is being used to force a sound through the texture then it is simply not available for subtle inflections of tone. The concentration of effort on the quality and centre of the sound produced is at the very heart of attaining woodwind projection and, musically speaking, only the complete and perfectly formed sound will travel any distance from its source.

From the conductor's point of view, accompanying a woodwind section is very similar to accompanying singers. Room has to be found for the breath and time must be allowed for the width of the phrase and the expanse of the sound within it, and yet no outward sign of unseemly distortion may be permitted nor any *rubato* observed that may be traced directly to technical necessity or convenience. Indeed, the priority is one of extending the line and disguising such gaps as the unavoidable replenishment of air demand.

Phrasing

In long, sustained orchestral solos, all aspects of the player's technique and musicianship are intrinsically combined. That for 1st oboe, which opens the 2nd movement of Tchaikovsky *Symphony no. 4* has already been quoted with direct reference to the accompaniment, but it is worthwhile reconsidering in terms of the solo line alone.

EX. 14.3

Here, there should be no difficulties of balance (only the quality, texture and placing of the *pizzicato* accompaniment require care) so the solo is much less inhibited in terms of dynamic level than might otherwise be the case. Furthermore, the player alone may determine the actual moment of entry. Only, perhaps, in preliminary rehearsal will this involve the conductor, whose responsibility here lies in focusing the attention of the accompanying strings and the audience.

For the student instrumentalist, as in all solos, the control of an even sound across the required range of the instrument presents the most obvious challenge, especially the highest and lowest notes of the phrase where an unwanted *crescendo* or clumsy accent might well occur. It is counter-productive, for example, to begin the phrase at the most distant, ethereal *piano* if the low F in bar 5 is unreliable at the same dynamic or softer, otherwise any magic that might have been created will surely be lost beyond reclaim. Similar (although not usually so critical) consideration applies to the upper octave in the second bar. Some determination of the level and shape of the phrase must, therefore, depend on the player's overall technical ability, although this must not be taken as a licence for thoughtless distortion or alteration of character.

In most situations the student will consider the technical difficulties associated with the performance of the notes before those of phrasing and style, neglecting to appreciate that the one is the parent of the other and that many technical problems disappear once the style and phrasing are correct. Of all the assets that combine to make a solo clear, it is the time that is apparent in well-shaped and unhurried delivery that has the most effect. Subtlety of phrasing, expanse of line and shape of the musical sentence are disclosed as the sound immediately displays a new degree of substance and projection.

The appearance of a simultaneous improvement in more than one facet of performance is typical, instrumental techniques being so interrelated, but that which comes with increased musical understanding will always be the most conspicuous and lasting. As has been mentioned many times, this is by far the most persuasive means of nurturing orchestral technique and the route through which all guidance should be approached.

Unfortunately it is by no means easy to effect and, from the conductor's point of view, probably nowhere more difficult than in relation to the phrasing of an exposed solo line. It must never be forgotten that, for the solo player, considerable self-conscious appraisal is constantly taking place – often quite irrational and of little benefit to the final outcome – but care must be taken that this is never allowed to reach the point of obstructing any ability to perform. The pace at which musical shaping may be implanted is therefore crucial. Considerations of personality and attitude become as important as those of technical development and ability because certain aspects of performance must emerge before others may be attempted. The patient appraisal of the moment when a further inflection may be suggested involves the most delicate of all decisions for the conductor of the inexperienced orchestra.

The phrasing of a comparatively straightforward melody may often be achieved quite successfully by the student alone, with little help from tutor or conductor, although the simplicity inherent in the above example requires a great deal of artistry to project. However, many more complicated lines may prove to be altogether beyond the understanding of a young player. Indeed, the subtleties of 'misplaced' accentuation with which Rachmaninov forges the colossal span of the clarinet solo in the *Adagio* of his *Second Symphony* are

EX. 14.4

unlikely to be immediately apparent to the student instrumentalist, even one advanced enough to meet the technical demands of the passage.

Even as quoted, shorn of its intricate accompaniment, the difficulties of delivering this phrase are evident. At first sight the short expanses of slur seem to imply the possibility of many sub-phrases, but this is contradicted by the implication of the dynamic markings, particularly *diminuendi*, which clearly govern this theme and demand a far broader conception. Any false impression of short sentence structure is further eradicated if the reducing effect of the bar-lines is removed.

EX. 14.5

Now the full range of the phrase becomes clear and the ingenious use of anticipation and suspension to sustain an unbroken *legato* line is laid bare. It is highly unlikely that anyone, without prior knowledge of the passage, would automatically replace the barring as in the original.

When considered in this minimal context all the sustained notes appear to lead towards the following figure and to lose any feeling of repose that may be attained by being immediately preceded by a bar-line. The feeling of the inevitable movement of a phrase, irrespective of the varying length of notes within it, is vital to the sense. Surprisingly perhaps, this has less to do with tempi than might be imagined – although a judicious choice of speed is always essential – but it cannot, and will not, disguise uneven accentuation or disjointed performance. The linear quality of any phrase must first and foremost be conveyed by the sound and, even when a player has sufficient technical fluency, this will come only with perfect mental understanding of the tensions and relaxations of the notes in relation to each other.

In performance, such an understanding of line will have an immediate effect on the clarity for a number of reasons, not least because, since the structure is more universally apparent, the ear is drawn to the phrase. Equally important, however, is the fact that, in attempting to reproduce the phrase, and thus to preserve the relative values of every single note, the player will become more aware of the sound and centre of each note and not rush the breathing.

Finding time for the breath, however, is still only half the battle, for it is the disguise of the resulting gap, by careful phrasing of the notes either side, that is so difficult. A colleague relates a story of when, as a young professional, he came across a phrase which just would not go right, no matter how he tried. The conductor at the time was Sir Adrian Boult, a man of imposing musicianship (and stature) but never one to waste words. Realizing the difficulty he repeated the phrase, and then offered the sensitive advice: 'Just play through the breath, young man'. At the next attempt the phrase was clear and meaningful. It was typical of that rare artist that he could provide the most succinct description of exactly what a wind player needs to experience in order to produce an even and undisturbed phrase. Even for the non-wind player, a sensation of line and continuity is conjured by these few words and they may be applied to any phrase – it will quickly become apparent that the breath cannot be snatched and that the following note must be related in sound and dynamic to the last. In effect, it is the care and mental control of the note immediately prior to the breath, at the point at which the new breath is taken. Of all the skills a wind player might attain, the ability successfully to employ this technique will be the most noticeable.

Every phrase, whether for a solo player or a combination of instruments, will present a unique combination of technical and interpretative difficulties, and each will need individual consideration. Achieving the high B (written D) in *Ex. 14.4*, for instance, within *pianissimo diminuendo* is no easy task and will require considerable sensitivity and flexibility in the accompaniment. On the other hand, the clarinet's natural facility for soft production should reduce the risk of over-accented attack or playing too loudly. Were the phrase to be scored for oboe or flute, although the shape and meaning of the line might remain the same, a completely different set of technical problems would have to be addressed which, in turn, might result in a radically altered appraisal in terms of latitude of accompaniment.

When considering the shaping and accompaniment of woodwind solos, it is useful to re-score the phrase mentally for another instrument and carefully to note any changes in articulation, breathing or accompanying texture that might naturally be inserted. Quite apart from keeping the contrasting timbres and idiosyncrasies of various instruments in the forefront of the conductor's mind, this exercise will intensify the automatic response necessary when dealing with individual instrumental sounds.

Fragmented Phrases

It is not uncommon for a long phrase to be orchestrated across a range of changing instrumentation. It will most usually be found with some degree of overlap, although more blatant instances do exist, such as *Ex. 14.6* from Prokofiev *Symphony no. 7*:

EX. 14.6

In such situations, the care with which the players start and finish each individual fragment and, as far as possible, match their sound, is vital to the flow of the passage. Many of the finer skills of orchestral woodwind playing – tone and dynamic control, phrasing and projection – as well as a clear understanding of each other's instrumental colour and position in the continuous line will need to be apparent in a phrase such as this.

It is, however, more usual for one or more instruments to overlap the line, thus evoking a more even timbre but not necessarily making life any easier. The wonderful long phrase of the second subject in the *Andante* of Schubert *'Great' C major Symphony* is quite magically distributed around the woodwind section on its return (see *Ex. 14.7*).

The finesse of balance and ensemble required from all the players as they weave in and out of the texture is remarkable. This passage is a superb example of woodwind scoring and will repay close scrutiny in respect of the

EX. 14.7

ease with which every line approaches and quits its place in the phrase. The writing for the 2nd players is masterly. However, the performance criteria are no less demanding than those described in *Ex. 14.6*. The phrase must be continuous and even, with the changes of instrumentation being perceived only as subtle alterations of colour and texture. The necessary sensitivity and control to do justice to this phrase will not be readily forthcoming from young woodwind players and demands a great deal of patient work. In my opinion, this symphony, most especially its first three movements, extended the boundaries of orchestral *ensemble* technique further in one stride than almost any other single work from Beethoven's time to the present day.

Another manifestation of the fragmented phrase is where an instrument answers or reiterates a passage, using identical phrasing, emphasis and clarity (a frequently encountered occurrence in the woodwind section). This can be clearly demonstrated in *Ex. 14.8* from Kodály *'Peacock Variations'*.

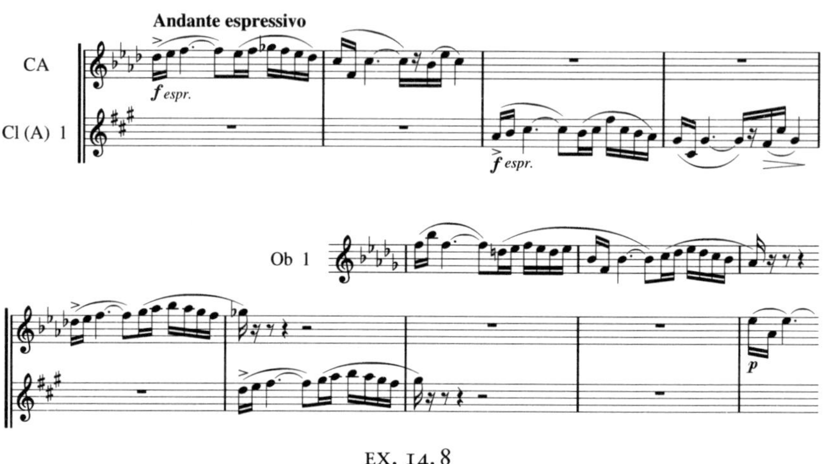

EX. 14.8

This is not an especially awkward instance, the style is both idiosyncratic and obviously soloistic. Even the young clarinettist should be sufficiently aware of responsibilities to the section to appreciate that any interpretative decisions must be based upon the phrase as it has just been played, and likewise, the oboe has little choice in the matter. However, such passages often reveal the limitations of aural concentration of some student instrumentalists, who will play the passage as they see it rather than as they just heard it!

For the orchestral wind player especially, concentrated listening cannot be relaxed simply because an individual is not playing, and a really good woodwind or brass section will automatically play an answering phrase with identical articulation to that first heard, even if it was wrong!

Nonetheless, unity can sometimes be very difficult to achieve across a range of instruments that display strikingly different qualities of production. Most saxophone players find it almost impossible to perform *Ex. 14.9* from *Montagues and Capulets* in Prokofiev *Romeo and Juliet*, with anything like the terse articulation employed by strings or upper woodwind.

EX. 14.9

The quotation is taken from the score and therefore appears at concert pitch in the bass clef – a regular paractice of Prokofiev which can be quite disturbing at times, apart from the confusion it can cause when conductors address the player who has a part for B♭ tenor saxophone written in the treble clef. The saxophone family show an aspect of the illogicality of taking transposition to extremes. All are written as transposing instruments in the *treble clef*, making this:

for E♭ baritone sound as:

(b)

(an octave and a major sixth lower) or – if anyone felt strong enough to wield the almost mythical E♭ contrabass – this:

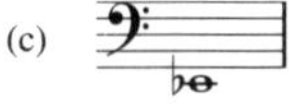

EX. 14.10

Projection

It cannot be stated too often that projection has no direct relationship with dynamic. It *does not* refer to playing louder, more stridently or with exaggerated articulation (all of which involve difficult techniques of compensation in relation both to tone and intonation). It refers only to the requirement of any sound to remain constant at considerable distance from the source.

In this respect, asking a woodwind player to 'play the centre of the note' or 'search for the core of the sound' will, when used at the right moment, usually result in the sound gaining substance and projection. As far as the actual centre or core of the note is concerned, this is probably no more than a mental attitude, but it invokes a concentration of all techniques into the note itself.

Accompaniments that involve complex movement or equally important counter-melodies can create balance problems which are neither so obvious nor so easy to resolve as the majority of those considered up to now. Often, this situation will cause a wind player to rely heavily on the ability to project sound through the instrumentation that threatens to engulf it.

Of all the woodwind instruments, only the oboe and clarinet have recourse to any positional help in this respect in that, in extreme circumstances, they alone are able to raise the bells of their instrument and go some way towards physically piercing the surrounding texture. The design and playing position of the flutes and bassoons make such movement impossible but, certainly for student orchestras, many of the difficulties facing these two instruments stem from another source.

For the bassoon the problem of projection is common, since the character of the instrument has so often beguiled Romantic composers to use it in orchestrations of dense instrumentation, or in conjunction with instruments of similar pitch.

For the flute, however, the problem is far more noticeable in student players where a production that may well sound satisfactory in isolation proves to be facile and poorly supported and no match for even the smallest orchestration around it. Many young players find it very hard to appreciate the fact that this one deficiency opens up a chasm between them and the successful professional. For every hundred young flautists who can rattle off the notes in Chaminade *Concertino* there is, perhaps, one with the control of production sufficient to carve a place in the profession.

Thus, the opening bars of Stravinsky *Petrouchka* (already quoted in this

EX. 14.11

context, but so worthy of re-emphasis) often prove to be a stumbling block to a student orchestra with a sufficiently advanced orchestral technique as to be able to cope with the rest of it (*Fig. 14.11*).

This is undoubtedly the most difficult of Stravinsky's works for large orchestra, in many ways far harder to bring off than *The Rite of Spring*, and these opening bars can only be successfully delivered by a truly outstanding young player. Indeed, were it not for the fact that many individual instruments are equally cruelly highlighted, the work could be regarded as something of a flute concerto throughout!

The ability to project a size of sound whose substance is actually greater than that of which the instrument is capable in terms of decibels demands extreme control of the air-flow and considerable energy in articulation. Performed at its best, the sound bears no trace of distortion or forcing. In fact very little of the physical exertion necessary to its production should be perceived in any way, but the result is riveting. This ability is the bedrock of technique for every great player and may be observed throughout the dynamic range.

Its use is by no means limited to the defining of a solo line through dense orchestration. A passage of intensely dramatic character will be achieved by no other means, even if it is unencumbered by surrounding texture. The very opening bars of Tchaikovsky *Manfred Symphony* (*Ex. 14.12*), scored for three bassoons and bass clarinet in unison, must presage the impassioned torment from which the outside movements of the work are forged.

EX. 14.12

A truly high-class trio of bassoon players will induce a breathtaking confrontation with the world of Byron's hero, not by dynamic level alone but through sheer potency of delivery. Originally the bass clarinet would probably have been included as support for the high-pitched bassoons across the first three bars and to modify any stridency of tone (two clarinets perform the same task a few bars further on where the whole passage is repeated, pitched a fifth higher). Modern instruments are somewhat stronger in this area of their range, but the original orchestration is still valid and, nowadays, it is more a matter of ensuring that the bassoons are aware of the implications, particularly with regard to bass clarinet, and that they do not simply unite for purposes of gleeful obliteration!

The writing for bassoons in this movement is exceptionally demanding, especially where modern instruments are used, since the bassoon, for all its sophistication in comparison with its nineteenth-century predecessor, still lags far behind many other instruments in terms of sheer volume of sound. The upper levels of the brass, middle woodwind and strings must be kept under very firm control if this movement is to be prevented from lurching towards misplaced and ill-conceived climaxes.

This rare use of three bassoons by Tchaikovsky both increases the dynamic level and provides complete chording within the dark timbre of the lowest woodwind instrument – indeed, this is the all-pervading texture of the movement. Although these are by far the most general uses of the triple-wind section, some composers, most notably Martinů, explore the different sound quality provided by three similar instruments in unison as much as the available harmonic expansion or dynamic level. The texture of this simple passage from *Fantaisies Symphoniques* is remarkable.

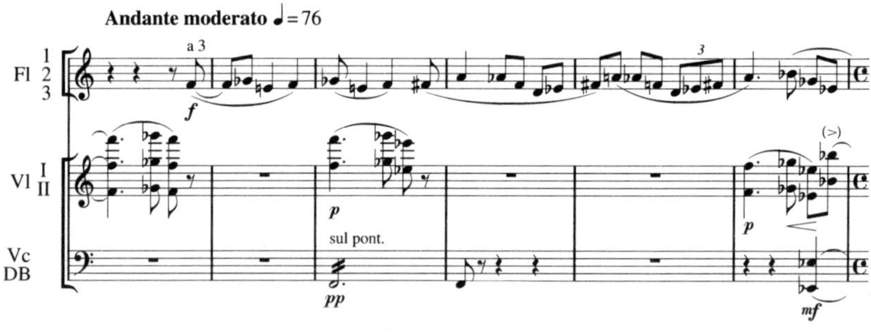

EX. 14.13

As may be deduced from the surrounding markings, it is vital that the three flutes provide a *combined* level of *forte*, rather than that three instrumentalists should each play *forte,* as the individual orchestral parts might have us believe. At this more moderate individual level a sound is attained very different from that of one player. (As an example of the skeletal nature of any written page of music this should be carefully considered. Various alternative methods of marking exist in this case but all are equally open to misinterpretation.)

Rhythm and Note Lengths

While a basic rhythmic understanding and proficiency may perhaps be assumed in all players who have reached a moderate technical standard on their instrument, the necessary concentration required for rhythmic accuracy, especially in any form of ensemble playing, can often be another matter altogether. Regardless of the quality of sound, projection, nuance and instrumental technique, no concerted passage will be clear and meaningful unless this aspect is correct.

Rhythm, in relation to scope (the implied structure) and line (its inherent movement) has, in basic terms, already been discussed in the context of phrasing and production. Clarity of rhythmic movement in a more vertical sense – the precisely timed appearance of notes – constitutes the foundation on which any musical language is built. An intelligible structure may be imparted without recourse to notes of definite pitch, but no two sounds, or even single repetition of one sound, can be delivered without some arbitrary rhythm being displayed.

Throughout the orchestra, precision of movement is fundamental as a means of imparting sense and character, transparency and definition. The wider orchestral ramifications will be considered in Chapter 21, but its particular relevance to the cohesion of the woodwind section must be mentioned.

Many techniques contribute to the expression of accurate rhythmic motion, but the overriding importance of concentration on note-lengths, especially short ones, is inseparable from all other facets. The different methods of production employed by the four main families of woodwind instruments will frequently result in mismatched articulation which, in turn, will blur the lines of movement.

In a fairly straightforward context such as *Ex. 14.14* from Tchaikovsky *Symphony no. 4* no great difficulties of balance or projection are experienced, but the movement of *staccato* quavers is rarely sufficiently positive and often inaccurate (see page 544).

Two miscalculations are primarily to blame. Firstly, the natural difference in enunciation between flutes and clarinets on the one hand and the double-reed oboes and bassoons on the other (a situation which must be overcome by technical proficiency); and secondly, insufficient distance between the notes themselves. It is extraordinary how difficult all musicians find the production of silence, especially when one considers that, in a passage such as *Ex. 14.14*, written or implied rests probably account for as much as half of every player's involvement. The temptation to play the next note becomes almost irresistible,

EX. 14.14

and yet, especially in this case, there must be considerable distance between the notes.

There is also an overwhelming temptation for the unison flutes to rush. It is very likely that all their concentration will centre on the performance of the fast figure and no attention will be paid to the 'easy' notes – the two quavers. This fault, as in a multitude of similar passages, can be rectified by mental reappraisal of each short phrase. If, in this case, the completion of the figure is considered as the third quaver of the bar, each repetition must therefore commence with the up-beat. The distance that this automatically places between the two notes in question is quite sufficient and the tendency to rush the beginning of each bar will be far less pronounced.

This particular passage (and the oboe solo that precedes it) can benefit from a very solid and 'earthy' articulation in any event, especially if the interpretation conceives it as a strongly characterized 'peasant dance'.

The general problem of rhythmic articulation, however, is by no means confined to notes in slow or moderate tempo; fast passage-work will exhibit it just as often and the same weakness can easily appear in *legato*.

One of the most profound pieces of advice I ever heard given, directed by a renowned quartet player to a professional 1st violin section experiencing some difficulty in the performance of a Mozart symphony was: 'Gentlemen, simply don't play any note until you have finished the one before!' The result was staggering in its instant improvement of almost every bar.

Without total control of the positioning of every single note as a separate entity, the performance of woodwind writing such as occurs in Stravinsky *The Rite of Spring* becomes impossible even to contemplate.

EX. 14.15

Internal Ensemble

The performance of any part, whether accompaniment or solo, in combination with other instrumentalists creates problems of synchronization which can only be overcome by sensitivity to the qualities and interaction of the various lines. Perhaps it is in this respect that the benefits of a woodwind section working together regularly are most noticeable, in that such reaction becomes almost second nature (but no less difficult). Basically, successful ensemble will only be achieved when every member of the section becomes aware of the demands and limitations placed on each individual by the overall performance, and this in itself will require careful and sustained listening.

In student orchestras, while the concept might be well understood, there is often a lack of understanding in what to listen *for*, coupled with a dangerously slow speed of reaction and anticipation. Only increased opportunity for practice and the experience gained from a large number of performances can help, for if it were possible to prepare for every eventuality, both reaction and anticipation would become unnecessary. However, the development of one specific technique can make life considerably easier and, for the woodwind player, this is the use of peripheral vision.

Every concerted entry, phrase and cadence displays a leading voice or predominant timbre influential in determining its shape or moment of resolution, and the focal player will usually divulge as much to the watchful eye as to the attentive ear. The natural movements of breathing, production, tonguing and phrasing are clearly discernible in every wind player, especially from within the section, and increased confidence of ensemble is guaranteed when each player is sensitively attuned to the others' presence and to their physical attitudes towards performance. The heightened awareness that the eye will give to the ear is of immeasurable advantage, and the ability to judge an entry or *rubato* by feel will begin to show itself remarkably quickly, as will an automatic improvement in balance and support.

But it is in relation to the ending of notes – that most difficult of all ensemble techniques – that visual communication within the section becomes so vital. In many instances the culmination of a phrase or the shaping of a chord cannot be achieved by any other means, and the perfection of this technique becomes the lifeline for the section's articulation and control. Taken to its extreme, the senses of musical collaboration can become so acute that the front row of woodwind will react to direction from behind them as precisely as if they could actually see it.

If there is any one technique that will hone the corporate production of the woodwind it is this initial use of the eye to focus concentration on the articulation and inflection of the section from within.

Outside performance, any moderately advanced woodwind section should also develop the habit of occasional short rehearsals alone. Beneficial use of the few minutes at the end of a general rehearsal in order to tune a specific chord or balance a short phrase is an acquired art, and the opportunity to develop it at times when there is no immediate pressure is important. From inside, the 'undirected' section sounds very different and it will expose many small details of dependent phrasing and production that can pass unnoticed in other circumstances. Apart from teaching players to listen and react to sounds independently, the chance it affords to discuss aspects of production in direct relation to personal technique and individual limitations is vital to this section.

Initially such rehearsal may be overseen by an experienced tutor (but not in any way directed) in order to guide the players' attitudes towards the methods of confined rehearsal and to identify the seminal features, but once the concept is understood the players should be left to pursue it alone. Such rehearsal need only be of a few minutes' duration – in fact longer may well prove counter-productive with anything but the most experienced section – and the players may remain in their normal orchestral positions or, for more intensive appraisal, arrange themselves in a circle.

Influences of Combination

Whatever difficulties might be encountered by the woodwind section in isolation, additional problems arise once they are combined with other sections of the orchestra. Chief among these is always balance, particularly in respect of some instrumental limitations imposed when attempting to play very softly.

Whilst it is true to say that no student woodwind group will even be able to think as softly, let alone play as softly, as a really first-class ensemble, the very nature of the instruments will always determine that this is louder than most other groups. The *pianissimo* ability of strings in particular, but also horns and trombones, is considerably superior, and allows for much easier control of both projection and intonation.

Such relative restrictions can have quite profound implications for the combined performance of *diminuendi*, especially those which appear as final cadences.

In the most commonly found instrumentation – a sustained cadential chord held by wind and strings together – the only major additional consideration becomes that of duration. The deceptive string foundation easily causes the chord to be too long for the woodwind to hold. A watchful eye on 1st oboe or 1st bassoon will resolve the difficulty.

But sometimes a much sharper divergence of capability will be noticeable. *Ex. 14.16* shows the last seven bars of Smetana *Vyšehrad*, the first of the six tone poems comprising *Má Vlast*.

EX. 14.16

Here, the string support can become so soft that the wind are quite unable to match it and find themselves left high and dry to finish the piece alone. With every chord needing to be separately articulated and much of the writing placed so low, it is vital that the minimum dynamic level is gauged correctly. The strings cannot afford to tail off to nothing, as so often happens, but must maintain a degree of careful support. Smetana allows for this by determining the string level three bars from the end and adding no further *diminuendo*, but in practice this is very difficult to achieve, the natural instinct of corporate string production being to continue *diminuendo* to the end.

Perhaps the most treacherous aspect of this particular example is that, because the last three chords are widely separated in time, the woodwind will automatically try to match the string dynamic, playing each one softer than the last and thereby compounding the problem by causing a similar reaction in the strings, which will consequently supply less support than ever. It is sometimes difficult to disentangle cause from reaction! Be that as it may, fundamentally the responsibility for support lies with the strings, and their sound will make it possible for the woodwind to negotiate these bars successfully. (One sees here an example of Czech composers' predilection for placing oboes at low pitch in a soft chord. The dynamic level of the above passage is virtually determined by the 2nd oboe's ability in this difficult area of the instrument.)

This is but one isolated example of woodwind in combination and, yet again, we see the major adjustments in balance and support directed towards the other instruments involved, a situation presaged by the opening paragraph of this chapter. It is not possible to consider combined woodwind orchestration from quite the same vantage point as can be applied to the other complete sections and, therefore, any further investigation of their orchestral role will have to be undertaken in relation to the techniques required of other sections.

15 HORNS

Influences on the projected sound of the horn section are similar to those pertaining to all three wind sections, except that the backward-facing bell renders horn players more susceptible to unhelpful positioning.

Although it is very rare that anything can be done about it, horns will be the instruments most affected by orchestral performance on a theatre stage or by significant limitation of lateral space. In the first instance, theirs will be the greatest loss of sound upward into the 'flies' and sideways into the wings. In the second, any solid upright surface in close proximity to horns will distort the sound. Thus the positioning of solid panels to minimize loss of sound into the wings of a theatre stage is usually of little help to this section, the necessary distance causing the panels themselves to be placed beyond the restricted width afforded by the proscenium arch. A specifically designed acoustic shell is the only true answer to orchestral performance on a theatre stage and even this has been known to cause almost as many problems as it solves.

Additionally, the playing position of the horn, and the section's inevitable location towards the back of the orchestra, mean that most ensemble playing will involve some degree of deliberate anticipation, which can often be quite considerable – when playing in combination with lower strings, for example. Many inexperienced sections will not fully appreciate by how much they need to anticipate and, even when they do, might find the technique very hard to accomplish, since the overwhelming influence will always be the sound immediately around them.

In order for the sound to arrive on time the desired moment *must* be anticipated, especially if it is to synchronize with other wind instruments possessed of forward-facing bells. Experience is the only answer to this, the players' production eventually being naturally timed to coincide with the required appearance of the sound; but it is difficult, and the student section will need to be regularly reminded of the danger whenever it threatens.

This need for anticipation makes for added difficulty whenever horns are involved in passages combining two or more interdependent moving lines, where co-ordination can only truly be achieved by listening. An extreme example occurs at the *cadenza* section from the 1st movement of Mahler *Symphony no. 9*.

[Plötzlich bedeutend langsamer (Lento) und leise]
[Misterioso]
Fl
Hn (F)
Vc/DB
pp sempre
open
p
Vc (3 desks) / DB (2 desks)
pp
cresc.
morendo
f cresc.
p subito
ff
Tutti
f
pp subito

EX. 15.1

This is a particularly difficult solo in any case, but it does illustrate many related aspects of the problem within one passage, for instance, the combination of two individual instruments across the first few bars, to which is added a third strand comprising lower strings.

Concentrated listening, while also determining all aspects of the projected line, is a very advanced technique, especially for wind players, where the actual hearing process will tend to be impaired by the necessary pressure of air. In the above example, the horn's association with flute might be close enough to hear, especially as the only vital point is the placing of the first note of the triplet in the third bar, where the flute is pitched high enough to be clear. The co-ordination with cellos and basses is a very different matter. At this dynamic level there is no hope of the horn hearing their rhythm, and any degree of adjustment can only be regulated by watching the movement of the bows, a technique which applies to both 'soloists' in this case, particularly with regard to the duplets and tied notes of the last three bars.

(Here is an instance where the seating discussed in Chapter 1, with 1st and 2nd violins opposite each other, causes a major problem. Either placing of cellos and basses – next to 2nds or next to 1sts – will impede the visual contact of 1st horn. In the first position the cellos will be masked by the woodwind and in the second only the backs of the players will be visible.)

Beyond these purely physical considerations, all the general techniques of enhancement of phrasing, projection and rhythm discussed up to this point apply equally to horns, with the one proviso that the section is greatly advantaged by comprising identical instruments. Every aspect of each player's performance will be exactly reproduced and no account need be taken of peculiarities of response, balance or blend caused by different mechanics of production within the section. Nonetheless, balance is not as easy a prospect as it might at first seem. Even without the specific difficulties arising from particular passages, influences of individual tone, projection and range have to be taken into consideration.

No true balance can be achieved unless the four players are equal in all aspects of their required production. Thus, in professional orchestras, players specializing in high or low playing will be found in the relevant positions so that the areas of range most common to them are best produced. Such an opportunity is, however, unlikely even in the best student orchestras because few players will have amassed the experience necessary for real specialization, especially with regard to low playing.

These 'limitations' on the sound production of the inexperienced horn section as a whole must be fully appreciated. Nowhere else in the orchestra is it likely to be so noticeable or so crucial, because no other section faces a comparable amount of 'internal' collaboration to be sustained in the upper or lower reaches of their instrument. For both woodwind and brass, the majority of their involvement will be confined to the most familiar, middle range. This is *not* the case with horns; there is no horn equivalent to the coupling of flute and bassoons, or trombone and tuba, and widely spaced chords must therefore be produced on examples of the one instrument alone. This section will consequently face passages of sustained high or low playing in almost every orchestral piece they encounter. Added to this, the horns' proportion of playing within a work will most often be greater than any other section except strings.

The writing for horns in much of the music of the twentieth century only serves to compound the problem. Much of the separation of responsibility in terms of high or low parts has progressively been disregarded, and an immense, comprehensive range required of all players. Without the availability of real instrumental fluency, a passage such as *Ex. 15.2* (taken from *Romeo at the Grave of Juliet* from Prokofiev *Romeo and Juliet*) is likely to cause 1st and 3rd horns to strain as much as 2nd and 4th.

EX. 15.2

In this case it is not only the pitch that is the problem but the enormous dramatic conception of the phrase, which induces an almost overwhelming desire to 'crown it' with a powerful (and frequently accented) top note. This passage is totally unsupported by the rest of the orchestration and begins at a pitch much lower than the most potent sounds around it. The temptation to force already arises as the players attempt to get the first note through the surrounding texture. Once a player is committed to such an approach there is little that can be done to stop the delivery getting tighter and tighter as the short phrase proceeds.

It is absolutely essential to maintain *mezzo forte* in *all* instruments (the main climax is yet to come), specifically with regard to the preceding woodwind and string *crescendo*, and for the horns to approach the phrase as a *legato* statement (which it is), especially in relation to the note immediately prior to each bar-line. It is usually necessary for the conductor to point out that there is no *crescendo*, and to be very careful not to induce one in performance.

This concentration on phrasing in terms of production, rather than of the outward appearance of dramatic influence, is vitally important to the horn section, and may be applied to all aspects of their involvement. There are few instruments more inclined by nature to force, and none given such regular opportunity. Controlled sound will *always* outweigh brute force, and nothing will sound louder or more dramatic than perfectly centred resonance. It is very rare that the specific quality of outright violence needs to be conveyed.

EX. 15.3

EX. 15.3 (continued)

For the horn section, nurturing the *quality* of the sound will have a significant effect on intonation where, as with all wind instruments to some extent, perfect production will cause the note to 'sing' and manifest a clarity of sound that will be profoundly centred. This is particularly relevant to individual melodic lines, although equally applicable to large areas of combined chording. This is a further reason for some specialization in particular ranges of the instrument, since few student players are able to find real quality of sound in the depths so often inhabited by 4th.

Whilst real quality is the product of outstanding ability, much can be done towards attaining it by placing increased emphasis on the section's responsibility towards the total orchestral sound in every aspect. Much of this is inextricably bound to the promotion of an attitude whereby players mentally 'play' every strand of a work. The changing responsibilities of colour, co-ordination and co-operation demanded of this section make knowledge of the tone and temperament of both the instrumentation and character of any given orchestration absolutely vital.

Even in a comparatively obvious thematic line, such as that shown in *Ex. 15.3* from Brahms *Symphony no.* 4, 1st and 2nd must be fully aware of the cello line which they colour *and* of the moment they diverge from it. Similarly, 3rd and 4th horn must phrase the three separated crotchets in conjunction with the upper wind, conscious of the natural phrasing of the whole line as it appears in bassoons and basses. This applies to all four players once the violins take over the theme. None of these nuances appears in the part, and can only be achieved by constant attention to the sounds as a whole.

Here is a place where the bumper horn can take the five notes before letter C so that 1st, at least, has time to be perfectly 'set' for the theme and can even (if so desired) add the low F♯ (concert) to enhance the commencement of the line. The 'addition' of notes not actually in the part to help some aspect of the phrase is fairly common practice among horn players but is generally limited, as here, to notes that are scored elsewhere in the section. The 'thinking' of notes, or even their 'silent' production, is even more widespread, however, and is highly to be recommended for many exposed entries. It will always promote the 'release' of a note rather than its 'attack', a technique vital to controlled production.

In this respect the horns enjoy another marginal advantage over most other instruments in being able to reproduce much of the normal playing technique at a virtually (or even totally) inaudible level, by firmly hand-stopping the instrument. A player, faced with an extended rest before a difficult solo will often judiciously 'play' some of the middle harmony line in order to keep the instrument warm and to prepare the approach. With many high entries this practice may be extended even to 'producing' a harmony note immediately prior to the opened sound, most usually the octave below if harmonically applicable.

While it might not be pertinent positively to suggest such techniques to student players (although most experienced tutors would do so, should the need arise), their availability should be borne in mind, especially with regard to playing mentally a preparatory phrase. The process will often overcome difficulties of secure pitching and intonation.

Such aids to performance should be seized on (there are few enough of them). However, within the horn section there are some helpful techniques not solely confined to the individual.

So far, all examples from the orchestral horn repertoire have been discussed in terms of the player in whose part the line appears. Thus any consideration of the frequently occurring solo phrases for 2nd or 4th (or even further down the line) has implied performance by these players alone. To some extent this is true, in that parts cannot be reassigned without very good reason, but certainly in professional orchestras, should a player wish to transfer a phrase (or part of it) to an available colleague more used to the rigours of exposed solos, or more adept within the required range, the situation becomes altogether different. Although it might surprise a conductor to find the famous opening of *Till Eulenspiegel* emanating from the 4th chair, should this ever be the case it would make no difference to the work itself. The *only* relevant musical criterion is that it be played in the most fluent and natural style available.

Of all sections, only the horns can consider such an interchange of responsibility, yet strangely enough, the youth orchestra – where the need might be most evident – is one of the last places where it tends to happen. In this situation the problem is undeniably awkward, primarily because two basic principles are suddenly in conflict: the orchestral development of the individual and the performing development of the orchestra. It is unwise to remove a passage from even the most inexperienced member of the section until some attempt has been made at it, by which time it is probably too late, since the true reasons for transfer will have been obscured by feelings of personal failure. Nevertheless, one occasionally comes across a student section sufficiently experienced and unified for an interchange to be possible, or a tutor so trusted by the section as to suggest it.

There is, however, no *musical* reason why 3rd should not play the infamous 4th solo in Beethoven *Symphony no. 9*, any more than there is against 2nd taking over the last three notes of the solo in *Till Eulenspiegel*.

Responsibility and Integration

The horn section is unique in that it is scored with and directly affiliated to both the woodwind and brass sections. There are many instances where its role cannot be considered as support or even colour, but only as an inseparable part of either section.

There can be few passages more intrinsically woodwind than *Ex. 15.4* for instance, from Wagner overture *Die Meistersinger von Nürnberg* (see page 558).

sehr kurz gesto en
Fl
1
2
immer stacc.
Ob
1
2
Cl (B♭)
1
2
a 2
Bn
Hn (F)
1
2
p
stacc.
tr
cresc.

EX. 15.4

nor is there anything (probably anywhere) more essentially brass than *Ex. 15.-5* from the opening of Korngold *The Sea Hawk*.

EX. 15.5

Horns appear in both examples and are indivisible from either texture.

The ability to collaborate in such an immediate way arises from many facets of the instrument: its sound, range, tonal variation and technical virtuosity. Perhaps surprisingly, it is unconnected to its wide dynamic range as such, since it is no less adept at joining the brass in soft playing (*Ex. 15.6* from Dukas *Fanfare* preceding *La Péri*)

EX. 15.6

as it is the woodwind in *fortissimo* (*Ex. 15.7* from the fourth movement of Mahler *Symphony no. 1*).

EX. 15.7

In both examples the horns simply provide increased width to the prevailing texture: the salient sound remains dominant. It is useful to compare the instrumental emphasis in *Ex. 15.7* with other orchestrations of the same figure which precede and follow it, from the eighth bar to rehearsal figure 5 of the same movement. In passing it might be noted that this same example illustrates a model piece of octave symmetry: 22 instruments divided as 10 on the bottom octave, 4 on the octave above, 6 above that and 2 at the top, followed by 7, 4, 9, 2.

Even though the majority of their direct association will be with these two sections, the horns sometimes display yet another side of their nature by artfully providing the middle harmony for strings. *Ex. 15.8* (at last quoted in its full orchestration) is from Brahms *Symphony no. 1*

EX. 15.8

and demonstrates the compatibility of horns if carefully orchestrated in this combination.

While all these aspects of horn duplicity stem from its intrinsic character, the instrument's connection with woodwind exposes a further ambivalence and will therefore be considered first.

WOODWIND

Among the many different tone qualities within the woodwind section, some are capable of providing one or two limited instances of instrumental 'impersonation'. Chief among these, the bassoons can provide an extraordinary similarity in sound to that of the horns when they are scored in combination.

It is a frequently used device where three-part harmony is required in scores including only two horns. Indeed, the bassoon sometimes replaces 2nd horn altogether, as in *Ex. 15.9*, the opening of the famous *Nocturne* from Mendelssohn incidental music to *A Midsummer Night's Dream*.

EX. 15.9

Here the scoring is dictated by the nature of the horn solo, the distribution of two horns plus one bassoon turning the line into a horn duet and changing its character quite dramatically. The 2nd horn is reserved for the second stanza, where both the dynamic level and the width of harmony are increased.

The exact opposite may also be found, where two bassoons require the addition of one horn if similar timbre is to be preserved. The very opening

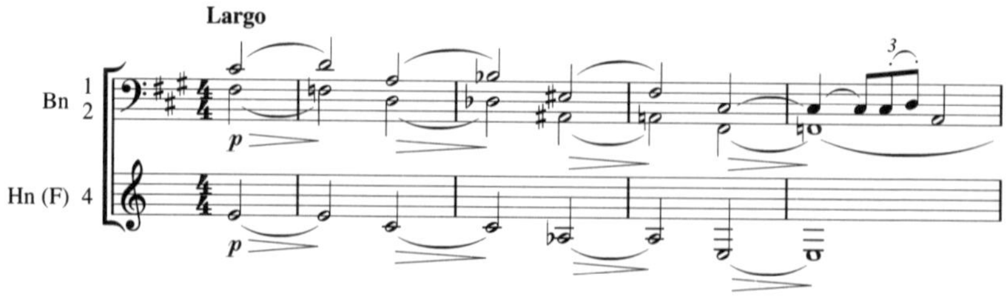

EX. 15.10

of Rimsky-Korsakov *Antar* (*Symphony no. 2*) (*Ex. 15.10*) unveils a highly atmospheric progression of minor chords orchestrated in this way.

Here, 4th horn provides the middle harmony (the sustained third to fifth) in each case. The second appearance of this progression, using identical orchestration but transposed up a major third (commencing with B♭ [A♯] minor) is much more awkward for intonation.

It must be mentioned that the solo in the Mendelssohn *Nocturne*, quoted as *Ex. 15.9*, is something of a *tour de force* for 1st horn. It may look easy, but its performance should not be contemplated except by a mature and assured player with considerable experience.

Most usually the combination of horns and bassoons alone will involve two of each, the bassoons pitched either within the two horns or interlocked as the lower parts. The opening two bars of the 2nd movement of Schubert *Symphony no. 8* are typical.

EX. 15.11

Both designs are in evidence here, 2nd bassoon and not 2nd horn taking the lowest note of the last chord in order to maintain contrary motion, and thereby adding considerable fluency to the line (such niceties of Classical harmony make life so much easier for players).

Bassoons are also quite capable of becoming the '5th and 6th horns' for a section of four, as in *Ex. 15.12* from the second of Debussy *Trois Nocturnes*.

EX. 15.12

The very subtle addition of clarinet to the orchestration in *Ex. 15.9* will have been noted, and this instrument will often be added more blatantly when extra strength or extreme articulation is required, as in the two *fortissimo* outbursts just before the coda in Beethoven *Egmont* overture.

EX. 15.13

The layout of the horn parts in this example also bears some scrutiny.

As they stand, doubling of the same note combines horn 1 with 2 and horn 3 with 4, an enforced orchestration because the natural horns are differently pitched. But it can cause balance problems, in that the unisons will tend to be more clearly audible to the players than the blend of notes within the chords. Certainly for many less experienced sections these passages may prove more successful in a combination of horn 1 with 3 and horn 2 with 4, as shown in *Ex. 15.14*.

EX. 15.14

Nothing has changed beyond the distribution of the notes among the section. (This redistribution can be extended to the first, second, fourth and sixth chords in the previous six bars. The addition of 3rd and 4th to the *fortissimo*, 12 bars before the *Allegro*, is fairly standard.)

If, as may be the case with *very* inexperienced orchestras, clarinets and bassoons are unable to provide sufficient weight, power and articulation (a situation which raises virtually insurmountable problems of balance) then additional orchestration of the full chords in the horns might be considered, along the lines of *Ex. 15.15*.

EX. 15.15

This should really only be contemplated in extreme circumstances as it does alter our conception of the two passages to a considerable degree.

Beethoven *Egmont* is one example of a Classical work that is eminently playable by various levels of student orchestra largely because of its powerful dramatic content, but also because it is stylistically built around fundamental and approachable techniques of production and collaboration.

The tonal association between bassoons and horns is an important ingredient in the suffusion of the latter instruments with woodwind, and largely responsible for 'letting them in' to the texture. Orchestration of horns with woodwind that does not include bassoons will always remain a more distinct combination of individual sound qualities, however closely associated these might be.

The majority of examples of full woodwind orchestration will find horns placed in the lower middle region of the harmony, fusing the sounds of the woodwind section whilst allowing the higher pitched instruments freedom to project the essential woodwind quality of the passage. *Ex. 15.16*, a superb passage from Wagner overture *The Flying Dutchman*, includes almost every detail pertinent to ideal collaboration.

(Note the placing of horns in this score, firmly allied to the woodwind section and positioned in order of pitch, between clarinets and bassoons.) In *Ex. 15.16*, 2nd bassoon retains responsibility for the lowest part, doubled at the octave initially by 1st bassoon together with 2nd horn, but later by 2nd horn alone (bars 4–7) and then 4th for the last two. Throughout the passage

EX. 15.16

EX. 15.16 (continued)

no instrument intrudes within the span of this bottom octave, but the deliberately close association of the two bassoons while flute and oboe are at the top makes for a very wide and open sound while still allowing for full instrumentation of the chromatic harmony. Once clarinet takes responsibility for the theme (bar 4), the release of 1st bassoon higher into the harmony and the resultant interlock of one horn part 'close' the perspective of the span (the *actual* span is wider than before). The 1st horn adds to the illusion, subduing the texture by doubling the clarinet at an octave below and providing the most wonderful link between the two colours (bar 3), but the retention of both 1st oboe and 2nd clarinet within this octave maintains the 'woodwind' dominance.

It must be said that it is not necessary for players to be aware of the sort of analysis sketched out here. Passages such as the above will generally be played perfectly well by sections with a modicum of musical intelligence and a feeling for the line. Examples used in the course of this discussion are cited solely to highlight cause and effect, so that the influences at work might be better understood and their results more easily detected. Any attempt to explain the varying responsibilities of 2nd horn during the course of a rehearsal will be met with a stare of incredulity – at the very least!

In general terms, the cohesive nature of horns when combined with woodwind will ease problems of intonation, both by moderating distinctive tone qualities and by providing a 'thicker' orchestration of the chord. But their sound in these circumstances must always be the most controlled and centred of all they produce. Especially as far as combination with the varying techniques of woodwind production is concerned, intonation and balance can only be achieved with near perfect production.

This is particularly true of balance in passages of *forte* unison or octaves. In *Ex. 15.17* from the *Scherzo* of Dvořák *Symphony no. 4*, over-zealous production by the two horns can almost outweigh the entire woodwind, especially if the latter's technique is in the least suspect.

The tendency towards such an undesirable balance is increased by the

EX. 15.17

rather square nature of the theme and (as can be seen by reference to the full score) the accentuation of each second beat in the other two horns and brass, and an ebullient upward *arpeggio* figuration in the strings. Nonetheless, such temptation requires even more control and the two horns must put quality of sound above all else. If the horns breathe at four-bar intervals there is a danger that the imbalance will first manifest itself in concert performance, simply because they will be tempted to play louder. This long phrase *must* be taken eight bars at a breath in order to maintain control in all instruments.

The proportioning of the breath is vital to all wind instruments but of paramount importance to horns in their performance with woodwind, where, because the main voice is elsewhere, it can easily be overlooked. If the opportunities for breathing are considered to be even more rare than would normally be the case, many of the necessary facets of this collaboration will begin to fall into place.

BRASS

The link with brass instruments is rooted in more immediately obvious aspects of the horn – similarities in design, manufacture and techniques of sound production. The actual sound produced, however, is still very different from any of the members of the trumpet or trombone family, and combined scoring will often be found where horns are required to undertake the same roles of cohesion and 'moderation' within the brass section as have been discussed in relation to woodwind. This is illustrated in an earlier quotation, *Ex. 15.6* from Dukas *La Péri.*

Although the purpose is most obvious in soft, *legato* phrases it is no less applicable to clauses in much more strident tone. Two powerful chordal passages from the last movement of Bruckner *Symphony no. 5* disclose a surprisingly similar design (see page 570) as does a very familiar passage of totally different character from the *Scherzo* of Tchaikovsky *Symphony no. 4* (see page 571).

In both examples, horns consistently take the middle harmony with at least half the section pitched below 1st trombone. Trumpets and trombones carry full responsibility for the line – most obviously in the Tchaikovsky example, where they alone have the shape of the phrase – and horns combine the sounds, interlinked throughout with trombones and often with trumpets as well. Trumpets and trombones are more than capable of producing a rounded sound without them, but the opportunity for 'thicker' orchestration of the chords, plus discreet doubling of the octave or unison, allows for a certain diffusion in the potency of each individual line – akin, perhaps, to similar

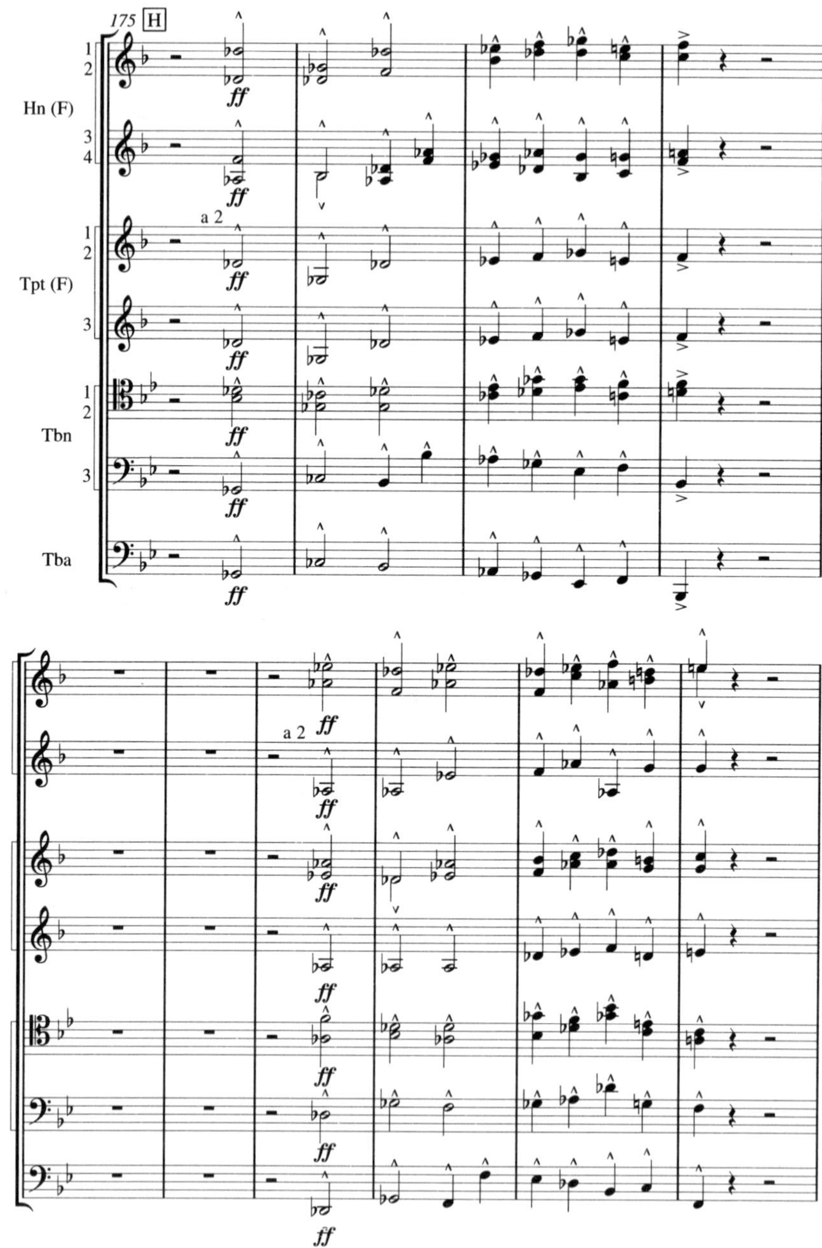

EX. 15.18

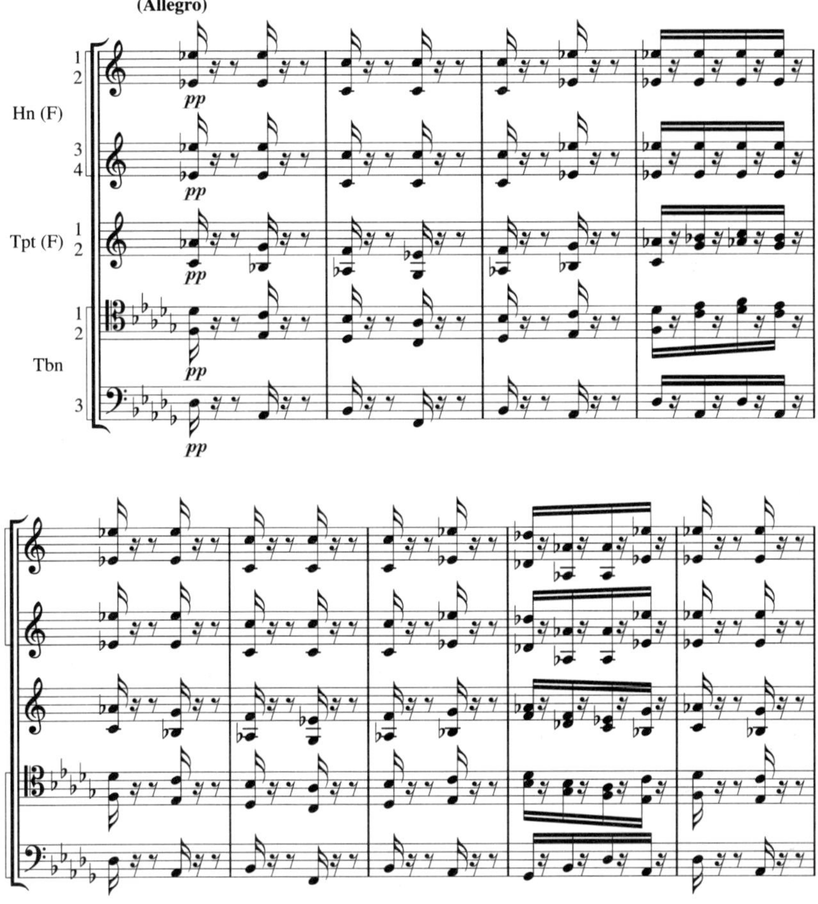

EX. 15.19

scoring evenly distributed across the full string body as opposed to solo strings.

Obviously, the horn *sound* is no less essential in these circumstances, but balance will only be achieved with understanding of this somewhat pivotal role.

The great majority of direct collaboration with full brass retains this basic design. As the sections become more isolated from one another in pitch, so the individual complexion of each group of similar instruments becomes increasingly manifest, and a much more terse colouring ensues. In *Ex. 15.20* from the *coda* of Walton *Violin Concerto*, the horn sound is integrated in a completely different way, and assumes total responsibility for the middle lines. The combination of separated blocks of sound thus provides a startling brilliance through the undiffused clarity of each individual section and note.

EX. 15.20

This is equally true (and probably even more obvious) in octave movement. *Ex. 15.21* from near the end of Vaughan Williams *Sinfonia Antartica* displays a much more insular sound than *Ex. 15.22* from the last movement of Shostakovitch *Symphony no. 7* (*Leningrad*), where the character of the passage and surrounding orchestration dictates that the potency of the individual instruments remains dominant.

EX. 15.21

As far as technique is concerned, the difference between the two layouts is minimal, but balance can prove critical. Especially for the student orchestra, it will often be necessary to balance trumpets and trombones towards the horn sound (rather than vice versa) in orchestrations of the latter type, not because of any limitation in the *amount* of sound the horns may be able to produce but rather because of deficiencies in its *strength* and solidity. Most student horn players will not yet have developed the requisite physical support of the sound, and any attempt to match the brass will be made by blowing harder,

EX. 15.22

EX. 15.22 (continued)

which will instantly lose the centre of the sound and its substance (as well as all control of articulation, intonation and rhythm). While a similar restriction in technique is likely also to be true of student trumpet and trombone players, the forward-facing bell of their instruments makes a considerable difference to the projected sound.

STRINGS

The link between horns and strings is somewhat more tenuous but occurs with comparable frequency. The intrinsic quality of the sound produced by the horn, particularly in the middle register, allows it to be effortlessly grafted to the sound of violas and cellos, in support of 'soli' or full string harmony. However, horns will not be used in quite the same way with strings as with woodwind and brass. They will not be found interlocked with one group of instruments to provide chording, for example, nor will they be used to *combine* the sounds of the strings. Sometimes their use diffuses the most dominant sound in string scoring but this is unlikely to be their primary purpose.

However, this distinction is very fine and, while the presence of one or two horns with solo lines for cellos might have more to do with combination than support, both sections need to be equally aware of one another. In a passage such as *Ex. 15.23* from Shostakovich *Festive Overture op. 96*, neither sound should predominate and it should be hard to determine whether the cellos point the *legato* movement of the horn, or the horn phrases the separated notes of the cellos.

EX. 15.23

In fact the *legato* implied by the horn phrasing also applies to cellos and is only omitted because any ligatures here would automatically be taken as bowing. (If only there was some way of differentiating between bowing and phrasing. The marking of bow changes within the lines of phrasing really does not work, and if it applies to more than two notes, players will put in ligatures to connect the bowing anyway.)

On many similar occasions the sheer size of the string sections will beg the question: 'Who is actually supporting whom?' In the third movement of Walton *Symphony no. 1* three horns double portions of the *divisi* line in cellos and one voice of violas (see pages 576 and 577). In such an immense *tutti*, where all melodic lines are doubled, only the relative dominance of the strings causes these horn lines to be designated as support. As far as production is concerned, neither section will increase or subdue their projection by reason of the other's involvement. Nonetheless, horns are once again to be seen in conjunction with middle and lower strings, the most expedient area of alliance with the string section since it does not risk undue separation of the two sounds.

Where the horns' collaboration is purely supportive, their use will often be confined to a single aspect of the line, most usually that of rhythmic emphasis (although a rare harmonic example is shown in *Ex. 15.8*).

a 2
poco allarg.
Fl 1 2
Ob 1 2
Cl (A) 1 2
a 2
Bn 1 2
poco allarg. e declamato
Hn (F) 1 2 3 4
Tpt (C) 1-3
Tbn 1-3
Tuba
f
Timp
poco allarg. e declamato
Vl I II
Vla
Vc
DB
ff

EX. 15.24

EX. 15.24 (continued)

Ex. 15.25 from early in the fourth movement of Stravinsky *Symphony in C* is still very much within the sphere of 'combination' and the accepted dualistic responsibility that it entails.

EX. 15.25

The absence of sustained notes in both horns and cellos tends to define their role in terms of punctuation of movement, rather than of simple combination of sound.

The famous passage for 16 cellos from Debussy *La Mer* (*Ex. 15.26*, already quoted in part as *Ex. 1. 6*) restricts the involvement of the horns yet further, but not to the point where a combined sound is no longer required (see page 580).

Individual horns join from the third bar of the theme in support of the small pulsating *crescendi*, and the full section accentuates the *fortissimo* climax. While undoubtedly adding colour (if mere *support* were needed, violas could do it), this collaboration is still confined to fragments of the phrase, and requires a sonority and subtlety of nuance virtually unattainable by any other wind instrument.

In much simpler circumstances, horn support can be given to isolated string accents while remaining almost entirely within the texture, as in *Ex. 15.27* from the first of Rachmaninov *Symphonic Dances op. 45*.

EX. 15.27

All of these examples (with the possible exception of the last) serve to demonstrate the larger degree of autonomy retained by horns in direct association with strings than in similar collaboration with woodwind or brass, and many have been chosen with this aspect in mind. Whereas the sound will combine to a very large extent, it will not *merge* in quite the same way as it might with either of the other two sections.

For the student horn section such ambivalence can prove elusive, not only because the horns' association with strings is generally even less obvious than that involving other sections, but also because it needs to retain something of their soloistic production. The passage from Shostakovich *Festive Overture*

Un peu plus mouvementé (♩ = 69) 9 Trés rythmé (♩ = 104)
Hn (F)
Vc
DB
1, 2
3, 4
5, 6
7, 8
1, 2, 3, 4
5, 6, 7, 8
9.10.11.12.
13, 14, 15, 16
pizz.
1°
4°
dim.

EX. 15.26

(*Ex. 15.23*), for example, will show an alarming propensity to lose balance even after it has been rehearsed, because of the *bravura* nature of the theme. Similar difficulties can be experienced in all the above examples, as well as many more besides.

The need for the horns to listen at all times is crucial, and extends far beyond the confines of the section itself. No instrument has the same ability for blend and varied association as this, and no instrument will be required to change the area of its responsibility so drastically or so often.

ACCOMPANIMENT

When called on to provide accompaniment, the horn section will find itself responsible to anything from one instrument to a whole section of strings, and both the level and the substance of its sound will need to be adjusted accordingly. With solo woodwind in particular, it will not be enough to adjust the level alone. The potency of the sound might still harbour qualities which make it difficult to penetrate or which provide the wrong mood.

A large proportion of accompanying sound from this section will be in the form of sustained harmony, which requires very good breath control to maintain balance, especially in very soft playing, but also means that the players must be acutely aware of the overall texture. In purely *physical* terms, four horns cannot match the width of sound provided by combined strings or even one section alone, but when they are accompanying a single woodwind instrument, it is all too easy to project a 'blanket' of sound which the soloist will find difficult to penetrate.

Any number of examples may be found throughout the repertoire, but Sibelius (who used this type of instrumentation as much as anyone) provides two particular instances within his symphonies. Outwardly the design is similar, but the scoring of the melodic line is radically different. In the first, from the opening of the second movement of *Symphony no. 1*, four horns hold the harmony alone, the E♭ pedal held by 4th in conjunction with harp and basses (*Ex. 15.28*, see page 582). Here, the theme is presented by two full sections of muted strings.

The second instance (*Ex. 15.29*) comes from the third movement of *Symphony no. 2*. Again four horns hold the harmony line, this time in conjunction with two bassoons, but the theme is presented by a single oboe (see page 582).

The difference between the two situations is considerable and extends beyond that immediately obvious from the text. Consider the first example. The width of sound projected by two sections of strings is extensive, and this coupling, in modern standard seating position, expands to the entire width of

EX. 15.28

EX. 15.29

the orchestra. But, even further, the character of the *pianissimo* will be found to vary from one interpretation to the next. Some will require a subdued full tone, others an ethereal quality of almost complete stillness; some will accentuate the two-bar phrasing, others the inevitable long extension of the line. Each of these, and all the possible variations in between, will require a subtly different approach from the horn section and bring specific difficulties of balance, movement and projected sound.

In the second extract all the width has gone. The horn chord is 'bound' by the addition of two bassoons, and the first three horns have a root position G♭ major triad. Already the inflection of a more contained production is apparent. The theme appears on soli woodwind, never more than two together and always in the lower, more plaintive, register. Both themes commence with the third of the chord, pitched a major sixth above the highest horn, but the scoring of the second example brings the note much closer to the chord than when it is assigned to full strings, and balance difficulties here become acute. The weight of the first chord, even produced at a soft dynamic, can easily compel 1st oboe to project something much closer to *mezzo forte* than *mezzo piano*. Balance of the upper three horns is the vital ingredient. The two bassoons and 4th provide the basic *pianissimo* level and the other three settle a *softer* triad based on these lower octaves.

Nonetheless, the misapprehension that the chord change in the first bar is an opportunity to breathe will sabotage even this approach to the passage. Two-bar breathing from the accompanying players is essential, with the breath in the second bar corresponding exactly to the articulation of the chord at the end of the first.

In *Ex. 15.28* the breathing is very difficult but vital to the projection of the phrase as a whole. What needs to be avoided is the gap at the end of the fourth bar so often evident in student performance. If 4th horn holds this through, even if the other three breathe, the small 'lift' will be less noticeable and an illusion of line projected. If possible, 4th should hold as far as the sixth bar (there is just a possibility at the end of the fifth if necessary), 1st, 2nd and 3rd not breathing again until halfway through the eighth. But this in itself can give an exaggerated accent to the cadence and it requires great control. This is a 'professional' passage if ever there was one!

Moving figures in accompaniment, often with short rests either printed or implied, constitute some of the horn section's most frequently encountered

EX. 15.30

EX. 15.30 (continued)

orchestral demands. The standard waltz rhythm occurs more often in this section than any other (however difficult 2nd violinists might find it to believe) and *Ex. 15.30* from Tchaikovsky *Swan Lake* is both famous and typical.

Again breathing should not be considered at every rest but, rather, taken in the longer span of the phrase. This is just another example of the fragmented phrases considered earlier, but here within the context of accompaniment. It is very easy to underestimate the degree of stamina and concentration demanded by this type of accompaniment. Similar passages in varying rhythm are legion (every one of Dvořák *16 Slavonic Dances* contains extended passages of this nature). Where rests are implied by the syncopated nature of the passage (rather than written) the situation is no easier, since articulation becomes an even more vital element of performance. In *Ex. 15.31* from the very opening of Dvořák *Symphony no. 6* continuous movement must be provided alongside the clear assimilation of rhythm.

EX. 15.31

While discussing sustained figuration, one might finish this brief résumé of horn accompaniment with one of the many passages in which they are also required to provide dramatic rhythmic movement. *Ex. 15.32* from Tchaikovsky *Manfred Symphony* is one of the most powerful.

EX. 15.32

In an already demanding work this passage occurs towards the end of both the first and last movements and, on each occasion, extends for seventeen bars without pause.

16 BRASS

Discussion of the brass group in relation to the whole orchestra must begin by addressing the difficulties which arise as a direct result of the section's physical position.

Some concert halls, especially those of older design, will incorporate fixed risers of considerable height, such that the brass group are placed high above the main body of the orchestra. From this position their sound will carry more forcefully, and there are many occasions when a dynamic level that has been perfectly acceptable in a rehearsal hall will suddenly appear far too strong. A new acoustic is never an easy situation to deal with and two aspects have to be borne in mind, both of which apply to preparation.

It is vital that balance in all venues is achieved in relation to the *actual* sound produced and not just that which might be *apparent*. Thus, in the single level layout of many rehearsal halls, allowance must be made for any sound absorbed by the body of the orchestra and the brass section not encouraged to play too loudly. If this important consideration has been misjudged, or even overlooked, there is little that can be done to rectify matters when faced with the problem of a new acoustic because the section has never been playing to *real* balance in the first place. While it is never easy to determine the true level at which people are playing, it is essential that as little false balance as possible is allowed to escape detection and that the vagaries of a rehearsal hall, both in terms of acoustic and layout, are always considered during preparation for performance elsewhere.

The second aspect that must be considered is the effect on the players that any extreme adjustment of sound level might have. For the brass, any excessive reduction is likely to bring with it a change of quality, particularly from a non-professional section. This type of attempt to reinstate balance can therefore easily cause a parallel loss of dramatic or musical effect. Any adjustment, only possible from a section reasonably fluent in the demands of orchestral technique, should be made with the minimum disturbance of actual sound and the maximum alteration in position, through deflecting the apparent result by lowering the angle of the bell of the instruments, or intentionally playing directly into the stands. Only the most minimal drop in actual level of sound should ever be considered – caring for the sound should be enough in these circumstances. Sudden and severe change in levels of production can cause untold problems of ensemble, internal balance and accuracy.

It follows, therefore, that no help can be forthcoming from elsewhere in the orchestra. Fundamentally the problem can only be forestalled. The orchestra must know its orchestral technique and be sufficiently capable in its use for the conductor to draw upon it in order to resolve such acoustic problems as might arise. However, many situations will have to be accepted as they are. Some halls simply refuse to be beaten!

In student orchestras a further problem may exist in this situation: the brass might appear to be too loud simply because they are playing across the weakest part of the string sections. This is not always noticeable from the rostrum but can be very apparent from within the body of the hall. Once again, prevention is the only answer. The back of the strings must *not* be the weakest part and this must be ensured both by initial careful positioning of the players and by continually encouraging their contribution as among the most important sounds of the section.

These difficulties essentially relate to performance on an open concert hall platform and, however awkward their resolution might be, they are but nothing compared to the problems experienced on a theatre stage, where the brass suddenly find themselves at the back of a narrow-set, deep orchestra. Here it will rarely be just balance or ensemble that is affected but audibility itself, as whatever sound has not been absorbed by the mass of bodies in front of them disappears up into the flies. Any attempt to resolve this by increasing the level of output is futile, the only resolution is to use small or medium height risers (6″–9″). But one must be careful – it is by no means guaranteed to help, and anything too high can insulate one or more players from the sound around them.

As was described in relation to the horn section, the unavoidable positioning of the brass group towards the back of the orchestra entails a large degree of anticipation from the players in respect of the moment of production. It is important that late production is never accepted by the conductor since it is not something that will improve by itself as, from the players' position, the sound will appear to be together. To a small degree the situation can vary from one hall to the next, so it does the brass no favours to presume they can automatically assess any time-lag for themselves.

For all the brass, anticipation will eventually become an automatic response, but trombones and tuba face the additional problem of being on the periphery of the orchestra, and having to contend with all the tricks of acoustic that such a position entails. Especially for 3rd trombone and tuba, the ability of some halls to aurally isolate players on the edge of the orchestra can be very disconcerting. Sometimes, such an acoustic illusion is sufficiently random that the players concerned can simply adjust their position and move a little nearer to the centre of the orchestra in order to resolve it. But movement is not always possible and the remedy might well have to be something more akin to 'damage limitation'.

The most acute problem, particularly in slower passages, will be that of ensemble across the section and, if the movement of other parts cannot be clearly heard, this will have to be judged by eye. Here, a 1st trombone capable of leading the section, and controlling their movement while playing, is of inestimable value. Obviously the conductor must help by being clear and precise, but the artificial feeling of playing alone within a large group will usually also require the closer, more intimate, support of the section Principal.

If the orchestra is relatively confident and musically sensitive, a large degree of balance can be maintained by each player's own familiarity with the response of the instrument in relation to individual passages. There are many occasions when tuba, for example, will have to rely on this form of 'instinctive production' because of the vertical position and resonance of the instrument, and it will often be the case when the instrument is scored with a quartet of Wagner tubas.

In this situation the distance between these two 'sections' can be considerable. Indeed, in orchestral layouts that place Wagner tubas behind the horns and orchestral tuba next to the trombones, it can only be described as vast. In this position the two 'sections' will stand no chance of hearing one another while they are playing, and a passage such as *Ex. 16.1* from Bruckner *Symphony no. 7* will have to be performed by the isolated orchestral tuba with reference only to judgement based on experience.

EX. 16.1

EX. 16.1 (continued)

(In student orchestras, if this seating cannot be avoided and a second accomplished tuba player is available, it might be worth considering a division of the part in this symphony, leaving one tuba with the trombones and placing the other with the quartet. With certain exceptions, this will involve one player in the first and third movements and the other in the second and fourth. The amount of playing, although considerably reduced, is still worthwhile for each of them, and quite enough in terms of the demand. In conservatoire orchestras, however, where the priority is to prepare students for a professional career, the part is probably best kept to one player.)

In addition to all these problems relating to position and distance, the brass section faces greater periods of inactivity during performance than many of its orchestral colleagues, and this will generally be found to increase the lower the pitch of the instrument: trumpets are involved more than trombones, and trombones more than tuba. Long rests will inevitably cause instruments to go cold and players' mouths to dry, and both situations will cause changes of intonation, quality and control.

For trumpets and tuba, because the pitch and tone of these instruments will not generally allow any true note to be played without the timbre becoming very apparent, all that can be done is occasionally to blow a gentle stream of air through the instrument, keeping the tubes warm and the embouchure flexible. Trombones, especially 1st and 2nd, can, however, actually allow the instrument to sound very softly, if the orchestration permits it. In many symphonies trombone involvement is limited to just one or two movements and yet their appearance, when it arrives, is very exposed. In this situation neither the player nor the instrument can be allowed to remain totally inactive, for they must both be in perfect condition for the entry that follows. Sometimes, as when approaching the chorale in the final movement of Brahms *Symphony no. 1*, it is quite possible to mute the instrument and very softly play certain sections of the middle harmony, but in all cases, much can be done to maintain the embouchure with the mouthpiece alone.

While perfectly possible, the substitution of particular notes or passages by other players of identical instruments (as already considered with regard to horns) is unlikely to be so relevant to the brass group except in one or two specific instances similar to those already mentioned (trumpets in Britten *Four Sea Interludes*, trombones in Stravinsky *The Firebird*).

Phrasing and Projection

The section on wind phrasing that appears in Chapter 14 applies equally to all instruments of the brass section and need not be reproduced here simply for the sake of an exchange of instrument or example. Musically, all the points made may be directly transferred to these instruments, as well as the technical requirements of breathing and support. Apart from obvious variations in embouchure and instrumental response (fundamental techniques peculiar to each and every instrument), the only practical difference that might be of concern here lies in a single aspect of phrasing.

For trombones and tuba especially, short disconnected fragments of phrases occur more frequently than for other instruments. It is much easier to recognize and appreciate the need for phrasing and nuance in the context of a long solo or a complete line than in a few isolated notes surrounded by rests, however logical and integrated these might appear from the score. Nonetheless, such inflections will be essential to the overall performance of the phrase and probably vital to the aural acceptance of its shape.

The ability to join and reinforce a continuous line with the introduction of a few notes is a very advanced ensemble technique, and requires a rare aural sensitivity. It demands a total involvement in orchestral sound and performance that is not just limited to the moments of playing but relates these to the sounds preceding and following, integrating harmony, colours and timbres within a passing overall structure. This, as much as ensemble, precision and balance, is what rehearsal is all about – the increased understanding of the relevance of sounds by those who have to make them. And this is finally what separates the good orchestral player from one who would be better off in some other field of performance.

The need to project sound and control its constancy over a considerable distance has been dealt with thoroughly in various earlier chapters but, with regard to brass instruments, I may be forgiven for repeating a warning with regard to the danger of misinterpreting this aspect of performance. 'Projection' has nothing whatever to do with dynamic. A sound will not necessarily travel because it is played louder and, in any case, it is the softer sounds that require it more. Projection is simply the directing of a sound from its source to the furthest necessary distance in such a way that its qualities remain constant at all points along its path.

Internal Ensemble

It now becomes necessary to re-admit a group of instruments whose total separation has so far been essential to this discussion. Orchestration of the *full* brass section must be deemed to include horns. This in no way alters the horns' allegiance to woodwind or their unique orchestral individuality but simply allies them more directly with a section which, in terms of orchestral instrumentation, is somewhat incomplete without them. Thus, if you like, trumpets, trombones and tuba might be considered the 'solo' brass section and the addition of horns the '*tutti*'. Nonetheless, it remains pertinent to consider many aspects of the section without them and terminology will always exclude them. If a conductor asks for a passage to be played by brass alone the horns will never expect to play.

Some examples of varying orchestration of the full brass group were shown and discussed in the previous chapter, but it is now important to consider aspects of actual performance. With the two sections so often placed on opposite sides of the orchestra, balance becomes crucial and is often very difficult to accomplish. This may be cited as yet another reason why the dynamic levels of trumpets, trombones and tuba often need to be balanced towards that of the horns, rather than vice versa. However, we are now not only concerned with balance in terms of relative instrumental dominance but also in terms of *sound* and musical intent.

In a passage such as *Ex. 16.2*, the second phrase from the opening of Sibelius *Finlandia*, balance with regard to harmonic relevance is notably easier to achieve than that to sonority (see page 592).

The trumpet sound proves not only the most awkward to balance but also the quickest guide as to whether the sound is right elsewhere. Played on B♭ instruments this part does not lie in the most flattering area of the range and can easily sound hard and somewhat nasal, especially if the players have to force because trombones and horns are too bright and loud. Controlled *fortissimo* is acceptable from horns, but trombones need only a firm *forte*, ensuring

(Andante sostenuto)
Hn (F)
Tpt (F)
Tbn
Tba
Timp
DB
a 2
ff
fz
sempre ff
dim.
p
A

EX. 16.2

a roundness and depth to the sound at all times. At these levels the trumpets can match the sound without losing real quality and the passage takes on a weight and solidity that becomes truly impressive.

Other aspects of the phrase are also worthy of discussion. Harmonic balance is always very difficult to maintain in *crescendi* and the first four bars of this example are no exception. Once again it will be trumpets who first succumb to the need to force and this, coupled with the octave doubling by all four horns, will tend gradually to overpower the upper two trombones who, alone, hold the central harmony. The control of these two separate *crescendi* really comes from the intended length and accent of the crotchet. If this is too short or brutal then control in the previous bar will not be maintained, the *crescendo* will lose balance and the sound will change, becoming hard and rasping as the chord gets louder. The crotchet must be given its full length and the accent given weight, articulated with a soft but fast tongue movement. There is also a danger that the third chord (bar three) will begin louder than the first, both because of the fact that its rhythmic position is more predictable and because of the dynamic level already reached. Thus, this *crescendo* might be unbalanced even if the first was not.

From bar five on, the sound should be dictated by a *quasi legato* production, each note articulated but not noticeably separated or accented until the penultimate bar, and even here the power of the accents will be lost if the gaps become too large. String basses will help by supporting the lowest line (it is their inclusion that makes the *legato* line obvious – they are not needed for strength). Breathing is certainly possible in two spans, four bars and six bars (bars 5–8 and 9–14 of the printed example), except for 3rd trombone and tuba, where an extra breath is best *after* the E♭ three bars from the end. This, of course, can apply to all instruments if desired but it is perfectly possible for horns, trumpets and upper trombones to articulate a separation rather than actually breathing. Owing to the doubling of the line in the last three bars, 2nd trombone should breathe with 3rd and tuba. The final chord must be phrased and finished exactly together with no sharp cut-off and no loss of control. (Personally, I have always asked the string basses to finish *with* the brass, extending their printed crotchet to a minim.)

As for balance, the blend and sound will best be maintained if horns start the fifth bar at a very slightly reduced level, thus allowing trumpets to lead and effecting an even approach to the fourth bar of the progression (bar eight) where the unison and octave doubling is quite suddenly removed. This will also go some way to ensuring a totally controlled and even sound across the section, so that 3rd trumpet will not have to force the lone third of the chord through the texture at the two cadences.

For all brass instruments, but most particularly for trumpets, the control of sound through *crescendo* is a difficult technique, since notes are so prone to a change of timbre as the dynamic level increases. Most often what starts as an even *crescendo* will undergo a total change of sound and quality as it passes through an approximate level of *mezzo forte* and continues to build. In terms of sustained *soli crescendi* such as those in the example above, two musical factors are responsible: first, that the players fail to predetermine the level at which they are aiming or the quality required once they have arrived; and second, that control of the *crescendo* is started too late. This last need have no effect on the ultimate level attained (it could be *fortissimo sforzando* or *mezzo piano* depending on the context), but it does affect the quality of sound produced, simply because of the control required in the early stages. It is not possible to produce an absolutely even *crescendo* without exercising immense control of this initial blossoming of the sound, and once accomplished it is less likely to be suddenly abandoned.

Technically, the *crescendo* should simply involve the reverse procedure from *diminuendo*, a gradual opening of the throat to allow a greater intensity of air through the instrument while maintaining diaphragm support. It is easier to appreciate the musical and technical functions involved in *crescendo* when applied to this type of even and continuous increase but, quite obviously, identical requirements of control will apply in all circumstances, regardless of speed and final level.

A clear understanding of the ultimate level, sound quality and dramatic reasoning of any *crescendo* before it begins is, however, the single most important ingredient in maintaining balance, and this will always make the point of arrival the most vital aspect. It is often possible to regulate this by rehearsing it quite separately from the approach, thus ensuring both the starting and finishing levels, but those that arrive at silence, or where the climax is supplied by other instruments, are more troublesome. *Ex. 16.3*, an ever-awkward little passage from the slow movement of Sibelius *Symphony no. 2*, illustrates this.

Here, not only are the *crescendi* difficult but the fast *diminuendi* that immediately precede them in the second and third bars prove equally troublesome. The temptation to play an accented *forte* and *piano subito* is hard to resist but, even on the first occasion, there is actually time for both dynamic inflections to be properly negotiated. In these bars it is the level of commencement that is so important. Anything above *forte* will dictate that the drop has to be made too quickly for it to be controlled, and will thereby automatically affect the balance of the subsequent *crescendo*. It is not possible for players to regain control in such a short space of time. Fundamentally, once

EX. 16.3

control is lost, it will always need a new entry before it can be re-established.

In examples of this type, the level to which the *crescendi* rise must be taken as that of the note following the rest, which must simply be inserted within the mental appraisal of a continuous *crescendo*. An identical situation exists when it is other instruments that complete the phrase: *their* level must be considered as the directing influence. The difficulties associated with the true *forte/piano/crescendo* are now apparent. If an arbitrary increase in the sound of separate instruments is to be avoided, two essential criteria must be fulfilled: first, the *softest* level must be taken as the basic strength and the *forte* (or whatever it might be) treated as an accent rather than a dynamic; second, a moment must be found to maintain the *piano* level and 'reset' the control before any *crescendo* begins.

For horns and brass no less than for any other section, all techniques of production are totally interrelated. Thus, in *Ex. 16.3*, beyond techniques of balance and dynamic variation, breathing becomes of vital importance. In this case the action must be incredibly fast and air absorbed into the lungs in a very short time. If just one player is unable to do this then balance will be lost, a deficit most apparent to the players within the section where it is very disturbing to find a supporting note suddenly withdrawn. If such a limitation in breathing technique is in evidence then it is best in instances such as the fourth bar of *Ex. 16.3* to adjust the length of the chord so that it intentionally finishes slightly earlier (in this case, *on* the second and fourth beats, rather than after).

Once the responsibilities and integration of the full brass section are appreciated within the context of immediately associated playing, similar functions can be considered in passages of a more linear nature. Now, perhaps, is the time to face the opening bars of Tchaikovsky *Symphony no. 4* (see *Ex. 16.4*).

This incredible passage is all the more remarkable for the ease with which we take it for granted. The entire work is encompassed here: the dramatic context, restless energy, compassion, scope and span. (This is the shortest of the 'big' four symphonies – 4, 5, 6 and *Manfred* – and the shortest of all apart from *no. 2*.) These few electrifying bars herald one of the most concise examples of all Romantic narrative.

Techniques of performance can never be totally dissociated from the more personal, interpretative, appraisal of their context and these bars are no exception. While my own view might reveal a 'darkness' of character not embraced by everyone, the difference will lie in the sound and implication of the passage and will not conflict with any technicalities discussed.

The importance of octave support (already discussed in detail) is as relevant to this phrase as to any in the entire repertoire. Nonetheless, the initial problem arises with the first note – there is no accent. No explosion should be apparent at the release of the sound, but a full and controlled *fortissimo*, as if in answer to some distant call. It is a very difficult sound to produce with no musical preparation and it frequently happens that the second bar is incomparably better than the first in every respect. There is a dangerous tendency to hold the breath and attack the note, with no possibility of influencing either intonation or sound. The final intake of air and the release of the note must be done as one continuous and smooth movement. It really does help if the conductor shows a very slight preparatory movement on the second beat before the actual upbeat, from which the whole process can be timed exactly.

The length of the two quavers should be determined by the second one, which approaches the bar-line and provides much of the momentum to cross it. If required to be particularly short, their length must be controlled by the

EX. 16.4

EX. 16.4 (continued)

2nd players who are slightly more constrained by articulation of the lower octave, but it should be noted that there is no real reason to play this phrase other than as a well marked *legato*. The same applies to the triplets, especially the lengthened second note which, whatever the preferred articulation, should never be performed as if notated with rests.

Breathing will depend on the ability of the section, but the last quaver of both bars three and four is a prime example of a note relative to both that which precedes *and* follows it (a quality discussed in a later chapter) and this ambivalent character should not be diffused. Nonetheless, a breath after the dotted crotchet is best (in the third *or* fourth bar, not both) but the articulation of each of these bars – with and without breath – must remain identical.

Bar five provides the first accent and it need not be over-emphasized, since it coincides with an extreme change in pitch. It also begins the two-bar link to the second statement and it is here, at the addition of trombones and tuba, that the balance is at its most critical. These bars must be regarded only as a widening of the sound spectrum, which culminates in a three-and-a-half-octave statement of the theme with its accompaniment, and not as a dramatic statement in themselves. Only horns and bassoons have the complete line, and the entry of each additional instrument takes place after a main beat and without accent, as part of a cumulative process, until the restatement becomes not only harmonically essential but also expansively inevitable. In this one particular circumstance it always proves difficult to convince trombones and tuba that they need only employ the standard up-beat techniques, aiming for the note *after* the entry and playing the first note fractionally softer than they mean to continue.

In student orchestras the entry of the trumpets at bar seven will generally be too hard, too loud, sharp and out of tune with each other, a situation underlined by the woodwind, who are unlikely to succumb to similar miscalculations, especially the last. (I wonder how many young trumpet players are even aware that the woodwind play with them at this point?)

This is a rather harsh appraisal, and it is fair to say that not all these faults will necessarily be apparent at one and the same time – but most of them will.

The problem is the same as that already described for horns, with the addition of an overwhelming desire to 'crown' the phrase at this point and provide the most stunning example of trumpet *fortissimo* ever heard. Relax . . . control . . . and just play it. Nothing you can do will ever beat Tchaikovsky at his own game.

Once again, support of the octaves of the main theme falls to the all-important 2nd players, but there now arrives a terrifying octave leap in the secondary line, and one that comes so close in pitch to the trumpets and woodwind that they will frequently feel the need to force their second bar even more than the first. For the lower instruments (horns, bassoons, trombones and tuba) the necessary breath between the lower and upper octave lies at the heart of the trouble. The lowest note will be hurried and shortened if the proportioning of the previous breath proves to have been ill-conceived and not designed to make this note both the culmination of the first statement and the impetus for that which follows. If the players approach the second note of this bar as if it were to be continuing downwards, any false accent or miscalculation of level will be eliminated and the first note will almost certainly be of correct length, ensuring that the momentum of the introduction as a whole is undisturbed.

The crotchet chords that appear for these instruments in bars nine and ten should be phrased very slightly in pairs, so that the quaver above them needs no accent to remain clear. The bare fifths of the following two bars must be balanced on the bottom E – especially by cellos and basses. No bulge should be apparent in the syncopation of trumpets and woodwind, since the beginning of each note should be the loudest point, and, although clearly articulated, they should not need the addition of accents.

The sudden, unexpected chord and cut-off is wonderful when not pre-empted by any suggestion of its appearance or result. Strings can carry almost the entire weight of this, with horns, brass and woodwind approaching the bar as if they were about to continue with a third statement of the theme and thus performing the chord without additional weight or accent. The following two bars should be treated identically.

We are fifteen bars into a forty-minute work and the level of concentration and performing ability needed to overcome the impending dangers should now be obvious.

For techniques directly associated with brass and horns this passage need be pursued no further but a vital point of interpretation should also briefly be considered.

At bar sixteen there arrives a moment of real decision, for a pivotal point in this introduction has been reached and the interpretative path pursued over the next few bars will determine the entire approach to the work.

Should the horns immediately moderate the drama by exposing a change of sound in conjunction with the lower dynamic? Or is the change as unexpected as the violent chords which precede it, determined by the strings' insistent repetition of sustained chords? Without straying from Tchaikovsky's vague programme (outlined in a letter of March 1878), is this the initial subjugation of the will to the destructive force of 'fate'? Or is it the opposite, the first hint that something so powerful and malevolent can be dissipated – at least to the point of survival?

The decision is musically crucial, for on it alone will depend the relative level of the horn statement, the strength of the supporting octave, all aspects of production of the entry and the technical approach to the string chords which follow. All these (and more) will need to be regulated and adjusted by the players to clarify any one interpretation, and it is worth remembering that, as with any work, interpretative aspects that have not been thoroughly considered can cause immense difficulty to the musicians trying to perform it.

The techniques considered in this and preceding chapters comprise the fundamental craft of the brass group and these will be endlessly pursued by instrumentalists in the quest for fluency and improvement. Attention may now be turned to the individual and collective adjustments and responsibilities that ensue when the section is combined with other instruments.

Responsibility and Integration

Because the section comprises different instruments, it must first be 'dismantled' before consideration of its combined orchestration can be attempted.

In this context, horns have already been discussed. Trumpets, the highest and most soloistic of the brass group, are most often to be found with the woodwind either as a combined colour or as a means of adding clarity to particular instances of rhythmic movement. Rarely will they be found supplying basic accompaniment or support, although this example, from the second movement of Rachmaninov *Symphony no. 3*, shows them in exactly that role.

EX. 16.5

2 Fl
2 Ob
Cl (B♭) 1 2
CA
Bn 1
Hn (F) 1,3 2,4
Tpt (B♭) 1 2
Tbn 1 2
Tbn 3
Tba
marcato
a 2
con sord.
cantabile
dim.

EX. 16.6

This is a highly unusual and very effective piece of scoring and the full instrumentation of the five bars is shown in the example. It proves eminently playable. The use of such a distinctive timbre as bass clarinet and the layout of the muted trumpet chords allow *pianissimo* to be obtained by a very pure style of production, without unnatural restraint.

More often, however, the combining of trumpets with woodwind will display a clearly dualistic responsibility, with neither actually supporting the other but both maintaining an element of individuality. *Ex. 16.6* occurs a little later in the same movement (see previous page).

The muting of the trumpets does not limit their audibility, in fact a muted sound will often penetrate the orchestral texture even more clearly than an open one, and in this example woodwind and trumpets will be equally prominent. Were the woodwind to be an octave lower or, more especially, the trumpets an octave higher, this would certainly not be the case and, irrespective of how many woodwind were used, the trumpet sound would be utterly dominant.

The scoring seen in *Ex. 16.6* is not at all uncommon but, interestingly enough, whatever combination of woodwind might be used, it will nearly always include oboes. This is another instance where a woodwind sound is sufficiently similar in certain characteristics to a brass instrument for it to be seconded into the section as an almost natural ally. Although the link is not so frequently exploited as that described between horns and bassoons, the oboe's keen articulation and acute projection in all registers mean that it is often scored in direct association with trumpets, as in *Ex. 16.7*, the very opening bars of Rimsky-Korsakov suite from *Le Coq d'or*.

EX. 16.7

Again the two solo trumpets are muted, but the *fortissimo* marking serves to emphasize that, as with all instruments, muting has nothing to do with dynamic – it only affects the sound. In performance of this passage, the sound of the two instruments in combination is almost inseparable, but the oboes' doubling is particularly relevant in the final two bars, where it is their sound which fuses this vibrant opening to the ensuing *pianissimo*.

There are a number of full brass orchestrations where oboes are included as the only woodwind addition, never for reasons of volume but because of the very tight focus of projected sound. *Ex. 16.8* from *Fêtes*, the second of Debussy *Trois Nocturnes*, illustrates this point.

EX. 16.8

As is often the case, here the pertinence of the orchestration only really becomes apparent by default. If the passage is played without oboes, the importance of their contribution will immediately be understood.

Because of the character of the trumpet sound, many combined instrumentations might be said to have effect on it rather than the other way round. Even in cases like those already discussed, the trumpet sound itself will not need adjustment, but the subtle combination of other instruments will alter the aural acceptance of its projection. This holds true in many circumstances, even with instruments much more closely related than woodwind. The two little 'fanfares' in the Rimsky-Korsakov orchestration of Mussorgsky *Night on the Bare Mountain* project a very different feeling in the first combination of trumpets with horns (bars 156–163) from that of the second with trombones (bars 256–260), and this is only heightened by the variation in dynamic and pitch.

Similarly, it is the range and sound of the trumpet which dictates that most of its direct association with strings will be of a soloistic nature in combination with the upper instruments. Very rarely will the trumpets find themselves in conjunction with cellos or basses but the opening *Allegro molto* from Kurt Weill *Symphony no. 2* is an exception.

EX. 16.9

(♩= 108)
Tpt (C)
1
2
Tbn 1
Vl
I
II
div.
restez
Vla
Vc
DB

32
poco sf p
sf
unis.
div.

EX. 16.10

This is a very unusual passage, all the more so because the solo trumpet has presented the entire theme, with very scant accompaniment, for the second half of the *sostenuto* introduction.

Elsewhere, the scoring of trumpet to reinforce violas is an intriguing combination, especially, as is so often the case, when trumpets are seated immediately behind them. Considering its effectiveness it occurs suprisingly rarely. Prokofiev is probably its most prolific exponent, and frequently doubles the viola line with muted trumpets in the middle register.

It is much more usual to find violins and trumpets supporting each other in identical line, or trumpets providing rhythmic emphasis to some aspect of it. *Ex. 16.10* from the first part of Stravinsky *Jeu de cartes* illustrates both instances (see previous page).

Here, trumpets duplicate the 1st violin passage two octaves below, but the reinforcement of the up-beat semiquavers in the fourth to seventh bars is equally typical, and will be found sometimes as single, isolated notes. These are always difficult, since all aspects of accuracy are dependent on instantaneous and perfect production. In this example similar demands are made of other brass instruments, trombone adding its own accentuation of the violins' line.

The close family relationship of cornets with trumpets might foster the assumption that all the above would also apply to that instrument, but this is not generally the case. Orchestrally, the sound of the cornet is most often reserved for its specific solo colour, and any combined instrumentation will tend to remain within the brass section, providing a distinctive sonority to chording and chorale passages, as in *Ex. 16.11*, a famous passage from the last movement of Franck *Symphony in D minor*.

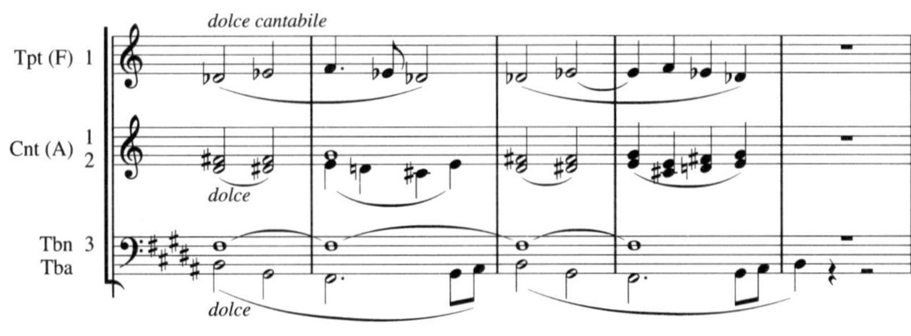

EX. 16.11

For trombones, it is also within what may loosely be described as the 'chorale' character that their most frequent direct collaboration will occur, although this is as likely to be with instruments of other sections as with the rest of the brass – the lower pitched, 'darker' woodwind instruments combine so perfectly with trombones. There is probably no passage (outside the Wagner operas) that demonstrates this so well as the intentionally Wagnerian theme on which the second movement of Dvořák *Symphony no.* 4 is based, shown in its first statement, at the opening of the movement.

EX. 16.12

This extract shows not only the combination at its most blatant but also the effortless and totally natural induction of horns into the same texture, a blending made easier by the absence of tuba. Dvořák uses no tuba throughout this work (a scoring he employed on many occasions), and the subtle differences between the 3rd trombone and 2nd bassoon line, so vital to each instrument's tonal character and approach to the phrase, are worth noting.

The phrase-marking is itself a rare instance of what needs to be in each individual copy in order to produce the same result, and makes articulation of this passage relatively easy to achieve. In the first bar, for example, lines above the clarinet notes will provide exactly the same articulation as trombone with a slur (slide action as against key action). A slur for clarinet, while looking more consistent in the score, would be performed very differently, with the immediate result that one or other would need to be adjusted. Unfortunately, comparatively few composers relate the musical necessities of their marking to the individual players' technical appraisal of it, and few interpreters distinguish the difference, so often accepting one or other marking as being 'correct', thereby causing other instruments to embrace an identical marking, without having considered the full instrumental connotations. Many editors and commentators seem to fall headlong into this trap at every opportunity (although, in the former case, it is extremely difficult to avoid).

As with horns, the timbre of bassoons, especially in the low register, combines superbly with trombones. *Ex. 16.13* shows part of the wonderfully sonorous fourteenth variation from the final movement of Brahms *Symphony no. 4*.

EX. 16.13

EX. 16.13 (continued)

Horns are again exposed with absolutely no change in the texture, although this passage is musically much more difficult to accomplish than the previous example. The 'life' imparted to the rests, especially those of the second and fourth bars, can only be achieved through sheer quality of sound, and an even and totally controlled *pianissimo* is required from all instruments, with great care exercised with regard to the balance in bar five. The *piano* marking for 1st horn occurs only because the instrument takes over the upper line at that point and it does not indicate a sudden increase of the general dynamic level. The projection of the trombone sound can be enhanced or diminished by altering of the position of the bells of the instruments relative to the stands, a technique that will also overcome many of the difficulties experienced with this passage in venues of differing acoustic response.

Although it is not immediately obvious, and it occurs in very different musical circumstances, there is an analogy between both the above scorings and that of the beginning of Dvořák *Symphony no. 8*. Only the doubling of the theme itself obscures the fact that bassoon and trombones once more combine to provide the harmonic substance. (There is, however, one major difference: 1st bassoon is unavailable and there is no 3rd trombone.) *Ex. 16.14* shows the opening few bars in full orchestration.

The bass of the chording is taken by 2nd bassoon alone, reinforced by string bass *pizzicato*, and all the harmonic responsibility is virtually focussed on this instrument plus the two trombones – hence the inherent lightness and space that this statement provides. As was evident in *Ex. 16.12*, there is clear

Allegro con brio ♩= 138
a 2
Cl (A) 1 2
Bn 1 2
a 2
Hn (F) 1 2
Tbn 1 2
pp legato
pizz.
Vla
Vc
espress.
pizz.
DB
p
pp
3

EX. 16.14

differentiation in the phrasing for all instruments, although in the second phrase this is likely to be less intentional than in the first. Nonetheless, the ligatures in the cello line unquestionably suggest a bowing and would prove very disjointed if transferred to clarinet, horn or 1st bassoon in this instance. In common with both the previous examples, this scoring achieves a totally unified sound when well performed, even the viola and bass *pizzicati* moulding into the texture.

None of these orchestrations is far removed from that of the famous chorale in the final movement of Brahms *Symphony no. 1* or many that occur in Schubert '*Great*' *C major*, but the latter work develops the woodwind connection a good deal further, even causing trombones to replace clarinet and bassoon altogether in passages such as *Ex. 16.15* from the 2nd movement.

EX. 16.15

EX. 16.15 (continued)

This association of trombones with upper woodwind alone is highly original and rarely to be found elsewhere, but in this context it is completely successful. Almost every example of trombone scoring lies innocently somewhere within these four movements, always determined by sound and never constrained by notions of dramatic inflection. For the orchestrations under discussion it is almost possible to refer exclusively to this score, so great is the detail and so wide the scope.

Orchestration of trombones with strings will obviously once more be fashioned by range and timbre, and their association will tend to be with lower strings rather than upper. The *legato* statement of the theme in the last movement of Elgar *Symphony no. 2* has already been quoted in this context

(*Ex. 10.17*) and remains a superb example, but a little higher in register comes this link with violas from the full orchestration of Copland *Appalachian Spring*.

EX. 16.16

Once again there is a deliberate discrepancy in 'phrasing' between the two instruments that is continued in the coupling of violins and horns. Even within the large accompanying orchestration, this passage can prove difficult to balance, the linking of the smaller viola section and the trombones with their forward-facing bells often causing this statement to be rather more 'brass-orientated' than that of violins plus horns which complements it. Even if the trombones cannot actually hear the violas (a most likely situation that adds to

EX. 16.17

EX. 16.17 (continued)

the difficulties experienced by both sections), it is important that the violas' relevance and responsibility should be thoroughly understood by the players.

Support or doubling of the violin line will usually only occur where trombones are divided in support of the entire strings. This use is found throughout the repertoire, especially in the works of the Classical style where a positive consideration of the section as alto, tenor and bass makes the instrumentation quite natural. Although such doubling is most frequently used in *tutti* passages that also include woodwind and other brass, it is by no means limited to these and can be found in much closer attachment as in *Ex. 16.17* from Weber overture to *Der Freischütz.*

This type of passage presents no major difficulties in performance except that an inexperienced 1st trombone may be tempted to produce an unwanted *crescendo* in the upward *arpeggio*.

The use of trombones to accentuate particular notes of a string phrase is as widespread as that of trumpets and, often, just as isolated. Just two notes across the bar-lines is all that is required in the very effective, extract from Liszt *Piano Concerto no. 2* (*Ex. 16.18*, see page 616).

The association of 3rd trombone with string basses is also apparent here, a role soon to be shared with tuba.

Apart from its partnership with the trombones, the tuba is most often combined with the lowest strings. In the introduction of the first movement of Rachmaninov *Symphony no. 2*, tuba alone joins double basses in the long approach to the climax (*Ex. 16.19*, see page 617).

This entry is very difficult to produce without exaggerated accent or violent change in orchestral timbre. The basses must support the previous bar, without further *diminuendo* beyond what is requested, and the cellos merge

EX. 16.18

their sound into them across the last three notes, thereby already preparing the low octave pitch and support for the tuba entry.

With a non-professional section of double basses, co-operation with tuba will sometimes highlight problems of balance, because of a lack of real weight and projection in the bass sound, especially on long notes like those in *Ex. 16.19*. Few young tuba players will have the control to play back to the bass sound and, in most circumstances, it is not right that they should, but few alternatives exist. String basses can divide their bowing on long notes in order to

EX. 16.19

achieve as much fluency of projection as possible, but this will rarely produce any additional centre to the sound.

The association with lower strings most often places tuba in the 'doubling' role, although this situation can sometimes be reversed, as in *Ex. 16.20* on page 619 from Franck *Symphony in D minor*, where each tuba statement is reinforced by a further section of strings.

This is such a wonderfully effective use of the instrument, so low against chromatic chording, that one wonders at the subsequent appearance of one or two of the ungainly leaps and the high passage-work that confront the instrument towards the end of the movement.

Thematic combination of tuba with cellos and basses is frequently encountered and, at its best, set quite low on the instrument, as in *Ex. 16.21* from Prokofiev *Violin Concerto no. 1*, a work in which it appears without trombones.

EX. 16.19 (continued)

EX. 16.21

EX. 16.20

Prokofiev's writing for tuba is generally very individual in its conception. He uses it soloistically even in accompaniment and always highlights its sound, as in *Ex. 16.22*, an aurally striking passage from the second movement of the *Symphony no. 7* (see page 612).

The tuba's direct association with the woodwind section (except as a doubling instrument with bassoons, contrabassoon, bass clarinet or baritone and

EX. 16.20 (continued)

bass saxophone) is very limited, a rare instance occurring in Stravinsky *Jeu de cartes* (*Ex. 16.23*, see page 622).

Otherwise, apart from solo use and the natural affinity to Wagner tubas

EX. 16.22

considered earlier, the bass tuba remains (somewhat unfortunately) firmly allied to the lower brass.

For the brass section as a whole, direct involvement with the other sections cannot occur in quite the same way as has been generally considered up to this point. Their sound is harmonically complete and the range and number

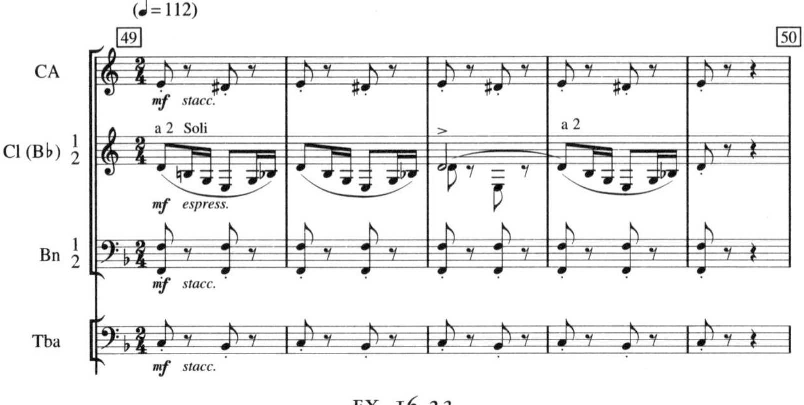

EX. 16.23

within each constituent section allows full chording to be obtained in a great variety of similar colours. The full section will thus rarely be used for accompaniment in the accepted sense but will mostly be reserved for full orchestral *tutti*, where it can provide almost anything from massive sustained chording to tight, biting rhythm, and can be relied on to support or cut through any size of instrumentation as required.

Chords orchestrated across the full section can be staggering in their intensity, simply because they are produced on closely related instruments. Uncontrolled levels of *fortissimo*, uncentred sound or deficiencies in production

EX. 16.24

will lose this quality and result in just a painfully loud noise. For this section, control of every aspect of the instrument at all times is critical and nowhere more so than in a passage such as *Ex. 16.24*, the climactic statement of the theme in the last movement of Bartók *Concerto for Orchestra.*

Immediate control of sound, balance and intonation is absolutely crucial to the projection of this blaze of instrumental sonority, and dynamic level alone has little to do with it. This is true of all vivid brass chords in similar scoring regardless of their length, and *Ex. 16.25* from earlier in the same movement makes identical demands.

EX. 16.25

The balance of any one section within the full orchestra cannot be taken for granted and is most relevant to the brass, where there can be a tendency to force in loud *tutti* passage-work. Often this may simply result from a false appraisal of the actual sound, assessed visually from the energy of those around them. At other times forcing might occur as a consequence of the way the parts 'lie' or the effort needed to project the sound. Only with a very inexperienced and orchestrally naive section will it stem from a desire to overwhelm every other sound. It is quite unjustified to regard the brass as potential musical vandals. (This might seem a quite unnecessary and inappropriate statement and I sincerely hope it appears so, for I have too often heard the opposite view endorsed by those who should know far better.)

Obviously there are similar problems of balance at the other end of the dynamic spectrum. A passage such as *Ex. 16.26*, the final few bars from Richard Strauss *Tod und Verklärung*, will present difficulties for any orchestra.

It is never easy to achieve the balance of the bass notes of a chord combined with high strings, and in this case only double basses provide any link to the texture at this pitch. Tuba and contrabassoon must take entire responsibility for the support of the brass and woodwind respectively, but both must judge their dynamic in the context of string basses for it is certain that neither instrument will be able to hear them, or each other, while playing. Trumpets must also judge their first entry very carefully, as well as the small descending phrase which follows, and all upper instruments will need to be aware of their continuing intonation in such a prolonged chord. The placing of the final chord requires concentration but is here made slightly easier by the orchestration of harps, whose natural spread of the chord will impart some aural appraisal of its position.

One brief reminder to conductors: before the penultimate chord and after the long, sustained note, the woodwind and horns will need to breathe. This will be accomplished with the up-beat and the consequent placing must be carefully judged. However, having done this, *please* remember to bring off the trumpets and trombones with a clear second beat. All control will be lost if they don't have the opportunity to finish this chord confidently and together.

Rhythm and Note Lengths

The necessity for rhythmic accuracy in performance by this, or any other section, is self-evident, but something of an extra responsibility often falls on the horns and brass. When the full section is entrusted with continuous rhythmic movement, as so often happens in full orchestration, it is their sound which will direct the entire orchestra by virtue of its aural dominance. The production qualities of trumpet and trombone in particular will ensure that all rhythmic synchronization will be in direct and unavoidable reference both to their placing of the beat and their intimation of the line.

Fl 1 2 3
Ob 1 2
CA
Cl (B♭) 1 2
BCl (B♭)
Bn 1 2
Dbn
Hn 1,2 (F) 3,4
(C) 1 2 Tpt
(F) 3
Tbn 1 3 Tuba
Timp.
Hp 1/2
Vl I II
Vla
Vc
Db
pp
p
tr
espr.
div.
8

EX. 16.26

EX. 16.26 (continued)

While there are many passages where their rhythmic influence is obvious, there are as many where it appears only as integrated accompaniment. In many ways these are the most dangerous. A long passage such as *Ex. 16.27* from Shostakovich *Festive Overture* might seem to be directed by the theme, yet it continuously re-locks to the brass rhythm.

Were this rhythm only to appear in other instruments – lower strings or lower wind, for example – any tendency to rush, slow down or otherwise distort the pulse would be likely to affect *them* alone, causing them to be late or early in relation to the other orchestral voices. But this is less often the case with brass, where the penetration apparent at all dynamic levels will influence the entire rhythmic stability. It is an important distinction because no other section will so dramatically affect the orchestra's rhythm, however set and stable this seems.

In this example, even the first eight bars are vital. Syncopation of this sort can only be played in a span of two-bar phrases and cannot be related to every

EX. 16.27

EX. 16.27 (continued)

beat. The composer's accent at the first and third bars helps immeasurably here because these are the first two points of rhythmic collection. The notes must be short and evenly produced, each given a dynamic subtlety that would be apparent if the progression were to be a *legato* phrase. An identical situation exists from bar 17 to the end of the printed example. Furthermore, the sustained notes of 3rd trombone and tuba (bar nine onwards) must not be late, since the rest of the brass will take their bar-line from these very proximate sounds.

It can only be re-emphasized that this passage, in common with many throughout the repertoire, will not sustain its rhythm through the more obviously continuous aspects of the theme, even though this is given to two sections of violins and, from the 17th bar, to all the upper wind. These instruments, overwhelming in numbers as they may be, *will* attempt to synchronize with the accompaniment, an instinctive reaction as unavoidable as it is disastrous!

Brief mention has been made of note-lengths in respect of this and earlier passages. For the whole brass group this area needs extreme care, not only in the overall adherence to any individual composer's wish, but also in the more subtle technique of differing production with regard to particular instrumental response. It mostly affects the production of short notes and, in normal circumstances, will require the lower instruments to play shorter than those above. Further discrepancies might be found in especially resonant areas of some instruments or singularly prominent notes of a chord, but these last will be less common.

The responsibilities and difficulties experienced by these players should, by now, be clear. Because of the demands made on them the need for motivation is critical (and usually very apparent), but it must be fully understood, for it is only from the point of equal care and involvement that this section's immense contribution to orchestral quality can be fully realized.

17 TIMPANI AND PERCUSSION

The exposed and distant position of timpani and percussion in relation to the main body of the orchestra dictates that any discussion regarding their collaboration with other sections must be prefaced by some consideration of the 'non-musical' difficulties which beset the section.

As with horns and brass, a degree of anticipation is required from all players, but this is not quite so straightforward as for other sections. For percussion, although the moment of sounding will be similar for a large range of instruments, some (as has already been discussed) will speak very late. Because the players move from one instrument to another, even the most accurate player may suddenly produce a sound late or early through momentarily neglecting to compensate for a different instrumental response.

The tam-tam is undoubtedly the most notorious instrument in this respect, although a similar delay in sounding can be experienced with any instrument producing low-pitched sounds by vibration of a large surface area – large bells, bell plates and bass drum (especially sizeable examples). For many instruments this will also vary from one example to the next, making it imperative for inexperienced players to use the same instrument throughout rehearsals and concert. Some instruments will also vary in their moment of perceived response in relation to dynamic level and/or requested method of production, and this causes even greater difficulties of anticipation and timing.

More than for other instruments, the apparent moment of perception of percussion can be affected by the surrounding orchestration, or even the musical context in which it appears. It is, for instance, much easier to 'time' a bass-drum note to sound with a bowed entry of double basses than it is to synchronize it with a short chord of brass, and this is true regardless of dynamic or tempo. This has nothing to do with any musical disparity between the two instrumentations, but rather, arises from the relative similarity in response of one combination and the variance of the other. Thus, a single note on snare drum would be affected in exactly the opposite way.

Such complexities of production, whether alone or in combination, will affect the synchronization of many percussion instruments, sometimes quite unexpectedly. Certain cymbal techniques will alter the response of the instrument and, among the tuned percussion, vibraphone with the motor on will prove more difficult to synchronize with isolated chords or notes than the same instrument without resonation. (All of this, of course, is before any idiosyncrasies of platform acoustic have been taken into account.)

The unavoidable placing of percussion at the back of the symphonic orchestra is, to say the least, unhelpful. Although the position has been determined as much through historical tradition as for any other reason (all instruments that arrived after the formation of the small pre-Classical orchestra have found themselves physically on the periphery of it), there is no successful alternative. Any change can only be accomplished by exchange and, for most other instruments, the *sound* would be adversely affected (consideration of the players has to come second in this one respect). Furthermore, because the section is never uniform either in instrumentation or number of executants, a flexible area will always be required.

For the vast majority of percussion instruments, however, the perceived sound is not defeated by the position, and often balance is more easily achieved than would be the case elsewhere. Nevertheless, in the varying acoustic qualities of some concert venues, the sound and resonance of timpani will always be affected. These instruments' method of transmitting notes of distinct pitch is always at the mercy of the surrounding fabric and any distortions of acoustic it might conceal. While much can be done to adjust discrepancies in the perceived pitch, the actual resonance of the note (though not necessarily its longevity) may be compromised beyond recourse.

Once again, theatrical stages with a proscenium arch cause the most problem, the vast areas of wings and flies frequently preventing the true sound from reaching the front of the orchestra, never mind the paying public. No improvised system of reflective surfaces or baffles will improve matters and, short of performing within a (good) purpose-built acoustic shell, little can be done. Depending on the stage, an improvement can sometimes be effected by opening (or closing) the final 'back-drop' curtains, but this will depend on the size of the orchestra and how near to the back wall it reaches. In any event it is a notoriously variable option and relatively minimal in its assistance. (Some stage-managers are also averse to exposing the bare wall at the back of the stage to public view.)

Rostra can help projection, especially those with a hard surface that stand on metal legs, but the wooden 'box' type, above 9″–12″ in height, can produce horrific resonances when used for timpani. It must also be accepted that, for percussion, no portable rostra will provide the ideal configuration desired, and a work requiring a large number of percussion instruments, or including any that need considerable lateral space, will rarely be successfully accommodated. The most practical solution will often be to use two levels of very small risers (3″–4″ and 6″–8″) for woodwind, horns and, possibly lower brass, with percussion set behind at stage level. Provided the maximum height does not exceed 8″, players will be able to see over the intervening bodies.

Because the player is seated on a stool, it is normally necessary to raise timpani, and rostra of some sort will be required, though their height should be kept to a minimum and the risers themselves should provide as little added resonance as possible.

Timpani are usually worst affected by the loss of sound so typical of this type of performing area, since many other percussion instruments have a more immediate and short-lived production.

The majority of concert venues, especially those unfamiliar to the orchestra, will require some small adjustment in balance or production from this section, but some designs are as notorious as the theatre stage. Those that provide fixed risers of considerable height (and, usually, very little depth) that ascend almost to the level of the balcony create difficulties far beyond the predictable restriction of space. These have already been outlined in relation to brass instruments and, in general terms, the same limitations of musical adjustment must also apply to timpani and percussion. It is not always possible to scale down the volume of an instrumental contribution while retaining its musical or dramatic influence. There comes a level where it is either unplayable or has no musical relevance, and this is as true of percussion and timpani as of any melodic section of instruments. There is a point, admittedly sometimes hard to recognize, where the quest for balance in an over-resonant acoustic becomes both futile and – very important with regard to student orchestras – detrimental to the playing technique of the instrumentalists. The well-meaning appraisals of rehearsal balance that may come from outside the orchestra will sometimes have to be politely ignored (even though they might be correct). Sports halls and those of multi-purpose design have an acoustic all their own and, if they cannot be avoided, they certainly cannot be challenged!

For timpani, a complete technical reappraisal becomes necessary in an epecially resonant acoustic. Churches and cathedrals will often supply a reverberation time of incredible length, particularly noticeable in notes of lower pitch and sounds produced by collision. Timpani, distorted by both criteria, will thus require additional damping between notes, especially in soloistic passage-work, and this places considerable extra demands on the players' technique and agility.

In such circumstances damping the instruments themselves with a cloth or sponge is not always the answer, as it does change the sound of the instrument and is fundamentally akin to muting. While it might work at softer dynamic levels it can rarely be applied to the more virtuosic uses of the instrument where hand-damping, after the notes have been struck, is the only possible control of duration.

Similar limitations apply to the substitution of sticks of varying hardness. Once again these will change the sound to some extent but, far more important, they will not affect the duration of the note, only its clarity of inception.

Phrasing and Projection

TIMPANI

While the supporting role of the timpani (doubling an existing bass line or providing one of equal importance) is that most frequently required within the orchestra, it is here that the subtlety and musicianship of the player are often at their most critical. Even in an apparently technically simple passage, the projection of the line and the consequent nuances of dynamic and timbre present a formidable challenge.

As an initial working example it would help to use a phrase whose other aspects have already been much-discussed: the first subject from the last movement of Brahms *Symphony no. 1*. The composer adds timpani as well as trumpets and woodwind to the recapitulation of the theme (shown in full score as *Ex. 17.1*) later in the movement (see page 634).

The passage only requires two drums, tuned to C and the G below, but the intonation, especially of the lower one, needs to be carefully set (this is another example of the vagaries of tonic/dominant tuning discussed in Chapter 11).

The part itself is a second (and largely independent) bass line, answering the movement of the string basses while acting as harmonic foundation for the chords in clarinets and flutes. With an early use of multiple dynamic markings more typical of composers of a later period and style, Brahms marks his theme, its bass line and its secondary accompaniment with three distinct indications: *poco forte*, *mezzo piano* and *piano* respectively. The only exception to this is the trumpets, firmly allied to the string basses but marked down to timpani dynamic, possibly for reasons of timbre but, more probably, habit (the Classical notion of trumpet allied to timpani being, for Brahms, almost automatic).

The balance of the timpani line is fairly straightforward. Apparent but not in any way dominant, it will probably be just above the level needed to balance with woodwind alone. The notes are of short duration but here timpani do

EX. 17.1

not require the addition of the *staccato* dots so essential to the other instruments' understanding of their production. At anything approaching a flowing tempo it is unlikely that the notes would require individual damping, but this will also depend on the acoustic of the hall, the size of the orchestra and, therefore, the actual level needed to obtain balance, as well as on the properties of the instrument used. In most circumstances however, only the end of each bar will need it, along with such fragments of the phrase as require the two drums in alternation.

The projection of the line is the most important aspect and this requires a

EX. 17.1 (continued)

very sensitive technique. Each bar begins with a crotchet rest and must be phrased away from the entry, but the first note cannot be given the same emphasis as if it were on a main beat. This subtle difference can cause the inexperienced timpanist to underplay the first note and, consequently, hardly touch the other two. The whole passage begins to feel like walking on glass as the player 'plays off' every stroke. It is fundamentally the last note of each group that determines the level, the first being played firmly but without rhythmic accent.

The repeated appearance of a crotchet rest at the beginning of a sequence of quadruple-time bars can cause problems for percussion and timpani alike, for it is the second note (the third 'beat') that will require a slight emphasis in order to project a sense of direction. In such cases, if the entry note is considered as an up-beat, rhythmically related to the next note and *not* to the previous bar-line, the necessary phrasing will be accomplished.

The technical aspect of this phrasing, as it appears in *Ex. 17.1* for timpani, is not particularly easy. Only two pairs of bars repeat the same configuration of drums (the first and fifth; and the seventh and eighth) and the passage fluctuates between repetition on a single drum and non-sequential alternation. Controlled and even production, although the most basic technique of the timpanist, will still require considerable skill.

Simple alternate sticking may be used throughout the passage, and is essential to bars where alternation of drums is required. The bars using one drum, however, especially as they appear as the weaker bars of the phrase (the second and fourth), might well benefit from single sticking of the last two notes (right-left-left, for instance), to regulate the phrasing more easily. This could also apply to bars seven and eight (but here, with the drums in the most common arrangement, with lowest to the left of the player, the sticking would be reversed to l-r-r), but it would not be ideal in the ninth bar for reasons of rhythmic emphasis already discussed.

The withdrawal of timpani in the two bars before the climax is certainly due to the original unavailability of the chromatic sequence but, personally, I feel that it should not be reinstated. The alteration of the trumpet line, the previous removal of the woodwind and the different rhythm of the timpani's final bar can all be related to this enforced re-orchestration.

The *sforzando* of the roll, and that marked for horns and bassoons (its absence from the trumpet part is almost certainly intentional), is related to the rounded accent natural to the strings' production of this climax and requires a feeling of leaning into the instrument rather than a hard, sudden emphasis. The following two bars, which include timpani's first appearance on a main, first beat, need to be phrased as a single entity.

Few of these performing subtleties are immediately apparent from the timpanist's single line part, and a thorough aural assimilation of the surrounding context is necessary. While this is true for every instrumentalist in the orchestra, no parts will appear quite as barren of phrasing and thematic intimation as those for timpani and percussion. For the conductor, who will have learnt the piece from the score, and will always be able to refer to it, this becomes an easily overlooked aspect of individual performance.

In many cases there is a much more direct association with lower strings, with timpani doubling the line exactly. *Ex. 17.2*, the final nine bars of a 41-bar rhythmic *ostinato* that pervades the last section of the *Scherzo* in Vaughan Williams *Symphony no. 4*, is both typical and extremely difficult.

EX. 17.2

This is, in fact, an inspired piece of instrumentation. The immediate aural necessity would seem to demand only the addition of timpani on the accented beats, but the inclusion of the whole figure promotes a better understanding of the total line and accomplishes automatic balance. The rare addition of phrasing slurs is, in this case, essential to the performance of such fast patterns of alternating rhythmic emphasis.

The association of timpani with the orchestral bass line, and especially the momentum thus implied, pervades much of the writing for these instruments, even through sustained rolls and *crescendi* that at first sight may seem primarily to be only of dramatic incentive. *Ex. 17.3* is a passage from the sixth movement (*Uranus*) of Holst *The Planets*.

This example culminates in a passage where two timpanists each state separate bass lines. 2nd takes the harmonic bass and 1st a somewhat dualistic *ostinato* based on the main theme. Although the whole passage is in a much more soloistic vein, neither part is far removed from that discussed in *Ex. 17.1*.

But more interesting here is the eight-bar roll that precedes it. This begins as a simple doubling of the sustained B pedal with horns, bassoons and bass oboe. Gradually, the timpani sound becomes more prominent, as first the horns are withdrawn and then the two woodwind. For the final four bars timpani alone are left to support the entire orchestra's approach to the climax, taking all the weight of the final *crescendo*.

EX. 17.3

EX. 17.3 (continued)

The bass note is harmonically necessary. All bass instruments make regular reference to it, but none except timpani actually sustains it. This is an important consideration for, in performance, these last four bars project a clarity of movement that belies their ponderous harmonic repetition and heavy orchestration. Were this note to be sustained at such a pitch by any wind or string instrument it would possess a greatly increased aural dominance, clearly pervading and binding the texture of even this colossal instrumentation. The ability of the timpani roll, by the nature of its production, to provide a continuous note without these additional qualities makes it unique, and illuminates many examples of its use as well as much of the reason for its having proved indispensable to the orchestra for so long.

'Phrasing' is as important to the extended timpani roll as to its more obvious application to themes and rhythmic lines. In *Ex. 17.3*, for instance, the phrasing of the final *crescendo* will set both the level and position of the climax, and this holds true for almost every example of its use. In these cases, phrasing of the bar and timing of the *crescendo* in performance are inextricably linked, each being totally reliant upon the other. But it is the understanding of the phrase, and therefore the structure, that is fundamental to the placing of any climax. Even when the timpanist plays in a purely solo capacity, such as the one-bar roll that opens Grieg *Piano Concerto*, the *tutti* chord will not be together unless a clear intimation of the position of the bar-line has been obvious. A really great player can make the position of this second bar so evident that soloist and orchestra can virtually enter by means of aural reference alone.

PERCUSSION

For percussion instruments, similar requirements of phrasing and projection of the musical line become most readily apparent in the more extended passages. Excluding tuned percussion for the moment, such examples will most usually appear for one of the many types of drum and, of these, snare drum will certainly receive the major portion.

As previously mentioned, really good young snare drum players are few and far between, and their ability will often be judged on their capabilities with regard to the more technically demanding aspects of the instrument. Such technical ability is unquestionably essential but, as with all instruments, the *musical* demands of the simple line will often be far greater, and will highlight the player's genuine ability.

The introductory figure to the second movement of Bartók *Concerto for Orchestra* is scored for snare drum alone and needs to be phrased so that the following entry of bassoons is both inevitable and rhythmically logical.

EX. 17.4

The difficulty of projecting this line is to some extent increased by the required disengagement of the snares, which causes the instrument to lose the little added resonance these would produce and the sound of each stroke to decay almost instantaneously. Thus there will be no actual difference between any of the printed note lengths and the phrase will consist of silence as much as sound. Without great care the aural effect will be one of unrelated, vertical rhythms, projecting no sense of line or expanse – a predicament which will have to be rectified by bassoons on their entry. (The use of two sticks rather than one will often help this aspect of the phrase.) The clear eight-bar rhythm should be apparent from the outset, and the accents only those of rhythmic emphasis, and never (especially the first two) any kind of musical 'full stop' within the overall structure. In many respects the most technically demanding portion of the phrase comes in the control of an even *diminuendo* across the last two bars. This apparently simple request can easily cause unequal stress and a consequent rhythmic instability that adversely affects the interlaced woodwind entry.

The ability that some players possess to transmit a real feeling of line to this and similar rhythmic phrases, while being both the most highly prized and easily disregarded gift, also exposes one of music's more enigmatic illusions. As I have seen demonstrated, if a player of such quality performed the above phrase and then asked a number of students to write down what they heard, most would produce a very similar notation to that shown above, and yet none would have heard anything but a succession of short sounds.

For snare drum, the mastery of intricate rhythms must eventually become secondary to this ability to impart musical sense to the extended phrase, for few other instruments will ever be supplied with such continuous and soloistic repetition of small rhythmic segments. In Rachmaninov *Symphonic Dances*, for instance, *Ex. 17.5* occurs towards the end of the last movement.

EX. 17.5

In the wrong hands this can sound hideously vertical, stopping the momentum of the theme and breaking the span of the line. With a talented player, not only will the cross-rhythms within the phrases become apparent but the melodic instruments will also suddenly find the passage easy to play and totally logical in its conception. The rhythmic impetus given by the snare drum will even control the length and emphasis of the tied notes and ensure that this aspect of the phrase is as stable as its own. A similar situation *cannot* apply the other way round.

In circumstances identical to those which applied to timpani, the snare-drum roll can be imbued with a rhythmic clarity unimagined by the average player. This same quality of phrasing and projection of the musical line is no less necessary for all percussion instruments, but the isolated nature of their involvement and the frequent brevity of their contribution will often obscure this fact. It is much easier to appreciate simple dynamic variation, control of duration and alternative methods of production than that the projection of one isolated sound within a musical structure still needs to be phrased. The sound must be relevant both to the dynamic level and orchestration of the passage and the position of its appearance within the musical line. Once again, no intimation of phrasing will be apparent in the printed material and, until the work has been played and some aural assessment of the passages has been absorbed, the notation will appear separated and meaningless.

Once the eye can perceive any sort of rhythmic pattern a natural phrasing will (or should) be performed. *Ex. 17.6* from Ravel *Alborada del gracioso* may be easily phrased by virtue of all parts having a complete and discernible rhythmic line.

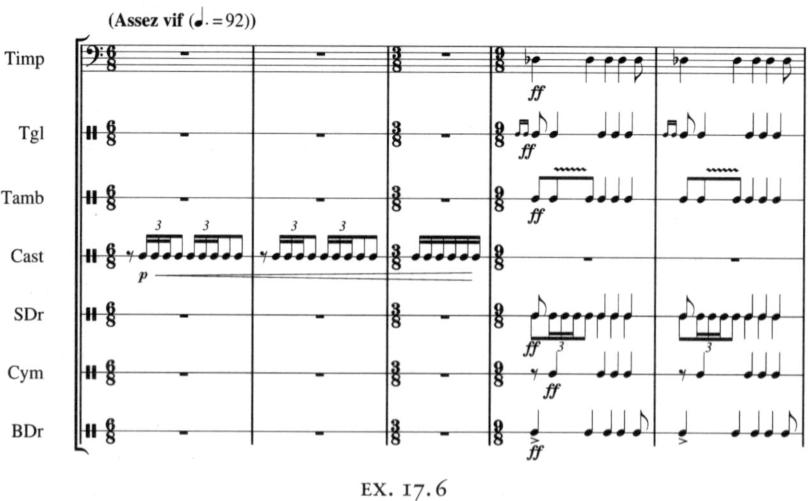

EX. 17.6

Even the shifting emphasis of the last two bars, with its evocative 'Spanish' syncopation, is quite obvious to each member of the full section. But later in the same work comes *Ex. 17.7* for bass drum alone.

EX. 17.7

The passage has an equally potent scan of two-bar rhythm, but the line is only apparent in the string parts. The *piano* marking for bass drum is no more than a general dynamic, relative to that of the main instrumental line, and the implication of the note itself is to emphasize the accent of the triplet rhythm in the strings – perfectly clear from the score but not even vaguely apparent in the percussion part. Because of its relative position in the phrase, the accent itself will not be performed with the same emphasis as if it were to be placed elsewhere in the bars, and the bass drum must adhere to this phrasing.

This is one of the most difficult aspects of performance for orchestral percussion because the concept is not easy to grasp and its necessity will only be disclosed by constant listening. Essentially, the two bass-drum notes above can only be played in complete association with the strings and *not* simply by counting three empty beats and striking the instrument.

Even in terms of the more obvious and continuous phrase, technical difficulties can be experienced when a composer requires the use of more than one instrument in alternation, especially when only one player is involved. The extreme variations in resonance between many percussion instruments will mean that a passage such as *Ex. 17.8* from Britten *Matinées Musicales* will need very careful control of relative balance if any idea of rhythmic movement is to be presented.

EX. 17.8

Here, it is very likely that the composer intended a small bass drum of about 28″ in diameter to be used, an instrument he frequently specified elsewhere (often referred to by percussion players as a 'gig drum' since its size makes it easily transportable to freelance shows and musicals). It could be supported clear of the floor with the playing surface horizontal, which would make the quoted passage a little easier to manage. However, this should never be adopted for larger symphonic examples of the bass drum, such proximity to the floor causing considerable deterioration of the sound.

For tuned percussion the situation is somewhat easier. Phrasing will be far clearer because of the melodic line and any isolated notes will occur within a more soloistic context. Nonetheless, phrasing is equally essential, some xylophone parts in particular often sounding extraordinarily unmusical as an energetic young player scatters notes around the orchestra in a seemingly random but rather fortunate order. It is possible to make a lot of musical sense on this instrument.

Balance

Balance of timpani and rhythmic percussion in relation to other orchestral instruments is inexorably bound to the purveyance of the elements of structure, phrasing and projection discussed above. For this section, unlike other instruments, balance will always relate to the degree of their rhythmic influence rather than to harmonic homogeneity, and its achievement is thus even more variable and ambiguous than elsewhere in the orchestra. There is no musical situation where the balance of this section can truly be any more separated from the linear aspects of performance than for any melodic instrument, and herein lies much of the difficulty experienced when working with the non-professional section.

The temptation for the players to think vertically in order to synchronize their contribution is actually aggravated by the amount of time spent counting empty bars, and the less the section is involved, the more noticeably difficult it becomes to obtain successful balance, particularly in terms of phrasing and movement. Added to this, the section has very little to guide it beyond the most general dynamic markings in conjunction with the most arbitrary note-lengths. Thus the Classical addition of bass drum and cymbals, sparsely orchestrated, proves to be one of the trickiest areas for the inexperienced section to negotiate, even though the entry might be in the right place at the right time.

Nonetheless, successful balance is achievable due, in no small part, to the sensitivity and enthusiasm apparent in even the most inexperienced player.

TIMPANI

For timpani alone, the close association with the bass instruments of the orchestra makes balance less difficult for the player to determine, and much that pertains to it has already been discussed with regard to phrasing. However, since the projected sound is as least as important as straightforward dynamic level, choice of sticks, as well as the player's touch, will prove vital. These factors are to some extent interdependent, and will affect the substance of the note in terms of its initial impact and sonority, although the touch will finally determine the projected quality. Especially in the passages by Brahms and Vaughan Williams considered earlier (*Exx. 17. 1* and *17. 2*), the sonority of the sound is crucial in terms of its blend with string basses in the second example and its relationship to them in the first. In neither case should the sound be noticeably different in musical implication, only in its generic origins.

In the non-professional orchestra much will depend upon both the quality and overall condition of the instruments. Those in poor condition will never produce a satisfactory sound nor be of any real use to the development of the player. With poor instruments balance can virtually be forgotten. Most youth orchestras, however, are aware of the need to maintain their instruments and many will possess very good examples, on which all subtleties of phrasing and balance are possible. These aspects of the timpanist's role should be fostered orchestrally almost above all others.

Mention should be made here of the distinctly different timbres produced by those instruments with playing heads of synthetic (so-called plastic) manufacture and those of vellum, even though as far as student orchestras are concerned the timpanist is unlikely to have any choice in the matter. The plastic head is now almost universal and has much to recommend it in terms of its durability and resistance to atmospheric change. The quality of modern plastic heads is far superior to those produced only a few years ago and so, as older heads are gradually replaced, more and more instruments are far better equipped in this all-important area of sound production. Apart from those which may be the personal choice of professional players, most vellum heads tend to be found on older instruments, where the head has never been changed, and can rarely be considered as a true alternative sound because the head is usually worn to a point far beyond its optimum quality. Other than this a number of perfectly good vellum snare drums will still be encountered, as well as some smaller bass drums.

In an ideal situation, with absolute availability of choice, the preference will prove to be very personal. There are no technical distinctions between good examples of the two manufactures and, apart from resilience and cost, selection can be made on sound alone. However, a mixture of vellum and plastic within the same set must not be considered.

In some areas of the range the difference between the two sounds is quite marked, the plastic heads providing a 'bloom' to the sound which is not always forthcoming from vellum, and many players express dissatisfaction with this aspect in some repertoire, notably that of the pre-Romantics. Certainly the 'dryness' of sound associated with the great Classical composers, particularly in extended rolls, is less easily attained from the plastic head, which will often produce something nearer a sustained note.

PERCUSSION

Orchestral balance of rhythmic percussion can be very difficult to achieve. The method of sound production is so different from that of the other main sections of the orchestra that the softest sound will often be clearly audible through quite dense orchestration. In the case of many percussion instruments, however, the dynamic level will have a direct influence on the character conveyed, and a distinction has to be drawn between the amount of sound required for balance and that which projects the required timbre or effect. Therefore the balance of percussion in relation to the rest of the orchestra will very often depend on the specific example of the instruments used and individual interpretation of their importance or degree of pervasiveness. This will not affect the direct balance between the percussion instruments themselves but only their relationship to the orchestra as a whole. Thus, balance within the section (as discussed in Chapter 11), will need to be considered *as a complete unit*.

On the whole, examples of multiple percussion orchestration will not cause too many problems because the overall balance will be predetermined, to some extent, by the very fact of their use. It is rare for a number of percussion instruments to be scored together with no specific regard for their effect, or where their appearance is not intrinsic to the style of the work or the orchestration with which they combine. With single instruments, the situation can be very different.

Snare drum, for example, will most often be used as a pervasive and continuous rhythm. The more soloistic examples (as in Shostakovich *Symphonies nos. 5* and *7*) are less relevant at this stage of this discussion than the subtler instances, such as *Ex. 17.9* from the last movement of Rachmaninov *Piano Concerto no. 3*.

With quite wonderful restraint, the snare drum points a different rhythmic perception in each of these four-bar progressions of solo piano and strings, from F minor, through D minor, to A minor. Coupled with timpani, trumpets and *col legno* strings, the instrument needs to impart hardly more than a suspicion of its sound, insidiously disturbing the acceptance of simple four-bar phrases.

It is not easy, however often a professional player might make it appear so. In the first place it requires expert control of very subtle touch. Then, it is the

EX. 17.9

EX. 17.9 (continued)

only entry in the work, and it is no less challenging to approach a demanding percussion instrument after a long rest than it is any other. Many young players can rehearse this passage successfully in isolation, but very few can instantly make it work after 37 minutes' enforced inactivity. Musically, a small (c. 4″ deep) instrument will often be preferable, as larger examples are usually not light enough and tend to merge with the string *col legno* to the extent that they require a little too much 'presence' in order to be heard. This smaller size can also help the player in this passage because it allows a modicum of dynamic leeway without imposing a strong sound. In any event, some experimentation with available snare drums will prove worthwhile.

It can be extremely beneficial to have the opportunity of using alternative examples and sizes of the same basic design when balancing the more commonly encountered rhythmic percussion instruments. Both snare drum and triangle can differ greatly in sound from one instrument to the next, and this is also true of cymbals, tambourine, tam-tam and bass drum (although choice of beater will often give as great a variation as a different instrument in this last case). Idiosyncrasies of sound in relation to design and manufacture are also found among most other percussion instruments but these will most often be used in more characteristic vein, where the orchestration will have been adjusted accordingly. Thus, variation of sounds (not just pitch) arising from different constructions of castanet, wood block and tom-toms, for instance, will not usually have any great effect on balance.

The triangle is a particular example of an instrument subject to wide variation because it is available in numerous sizes and thicknesses, and more time has probably been spent experimenting with different examples and beaters than on any other instrument. Especially in solos, such as the *tremolo* in the *Scherzo* of Dvořák *Symphony nos 5* and *9* (*From the New World*), an acceptable sound that does not have the freelance orchestra grabbing for their mobile phones can prove very elusive. Balance is actually the key to both these passages, as well as to many other examples. In this case a small triangle with a light metal beater, carefully balanced within the orchestral texture, will be most effective.

The connotations of this instrument, especially in the extended roll, are nowadays not what they were, and this has to be accepted. Many composers might well have rethought their orchestration had they lived to be more familiar with very similar mechanical sounds of summons. Be that as it may, the beautiful and very famous use of solo triangle from the opening of the second movement of Liszt *Piano Concerto no. 1* (see *Ex. 17.10*) is difficult for the inexperienced player to balance successfully.

As with so much percussion performance, the fact that rhythm is the prime means of expression can lead to over-emphasis of this aspect alone, losing both the simplicity of the passage and the technical control of dynamic. Balance in this example is vital if the triangle is to place the bar-line for the

EX. 17.10

EX. 17.10 (continued)

strings and imbue the movement with the necessary *scherzando* quality. Once again, a fairly small, high-sounding instrument is preferable and a delicate touch essential.

Similar opportunity for instrumental variation is available elsewhere within the section. In fast passages for clashed cymbals, slightly smaller examples will prove technically easier to manage and also often provide a 'tighter' sound, whereas the single clash of the great climax will always require plates of larger size and superb quality. Both cymbals and snare drum are the province of specialist instrumentalists, and an experienced and highly proficient player will always be required for true balance to be achieved in the subtler instances of their use, although this is not necessarily beyond the ability of the serious and talented student.

The bass drum must be able to offer an even greater variation in style and approach, although this will not prove as technically demanding as for some other instruments. Much of the writing for this instrument, while at first glance appearing rather uniform, will actually call for considerable alteration in the projected sound and, in many examples of combination, this instrument will control the basis of the section's balance.

As already mentioned, for most of the post-Classical repertoire, a large, double-sided instrument is preferable. The most important factor, however, is that there should be a wide variety of available beaters, ranging from one with a large, soft head of wool through to very hard. If there is a priority in the accumulation of percussion equipment for the non-professional orchestra, then in my opinion, a range of bass-drum beaters comes very high on the list. Outside professional sections, this instrument seems often to suffer from a perfunctory approach that somehow disregards its diverse musical implications and simply allows it to be played loudly or softly according to the marking in the part. While this is doubtless unintentional, it is regrettable and, in my experience, usually arises because the player has only one stick available and does not, therefore, have to consider either the options of sound or the possible range of inferences. With a number of different sticks some choice, however miscalculated, would have to be made, and this would result in an automatic assessment of the sound in relation to the overall musical texture.

As well as using beaters of varying size and density, it is possible to adjust the sound and resonance of all bass drums by striking at the centre of the head (instead of the optimum point, roughly half-way between the centre and rim), to produce a hard and dry sound, and by hand-damping in much the same way as timpani. In the case of double-headed bass drums, a degree of further control can be implemented by placing palm or fingers of the free hand on the opposite head.

Such a combination of positional adjustment and hand control may be used to balance and clarify a passage such as *Ex. 17.11*, the final section of Rimsky-Korsakov *Scheherazade* (see page 652).

The passage supports trombones but the final crotchet is also the basis for the full orchestral cadence. The softer stick required for this last note will not usually provide the necessary clarity in the preceding quavers, but initial use of the 'drier' sound obtained near the centre, together with some control of the opposite head, can accomplish dynamic, phrasing, articulation and any level of balance that is required.

In isolation, bass-drum support of the full orchestra as on the last crotchet of *Ex. 17.11* will usually require a weight of sound rather than a fierce impact, and the large, soft stick will most often be desirable. Faster, more soloistic movement, as in the quaver rhythm of the preceding bar, will usually require something a good deal harder. Direct association with other percussion instruments (discussed in Chapter 11), may well be best achieved with beaters offering something between the two. For this instrument, probably more than any other, sound and balance are totally interrelated, and one cannot be contemplated without the other.

The one area of percussion balance that seems to cause the most fear is the ease with which the section can dominate orchestral sound, especially those instruments of deep resonance and long decay (tam-tam, for example). It should not be necessary to counter this in detail, for all relevant aspects have appeared in the previous paragraphs and elsewhere. Fundamentally, if the *sound* of each instrument has musical integrity, the balance will be right.

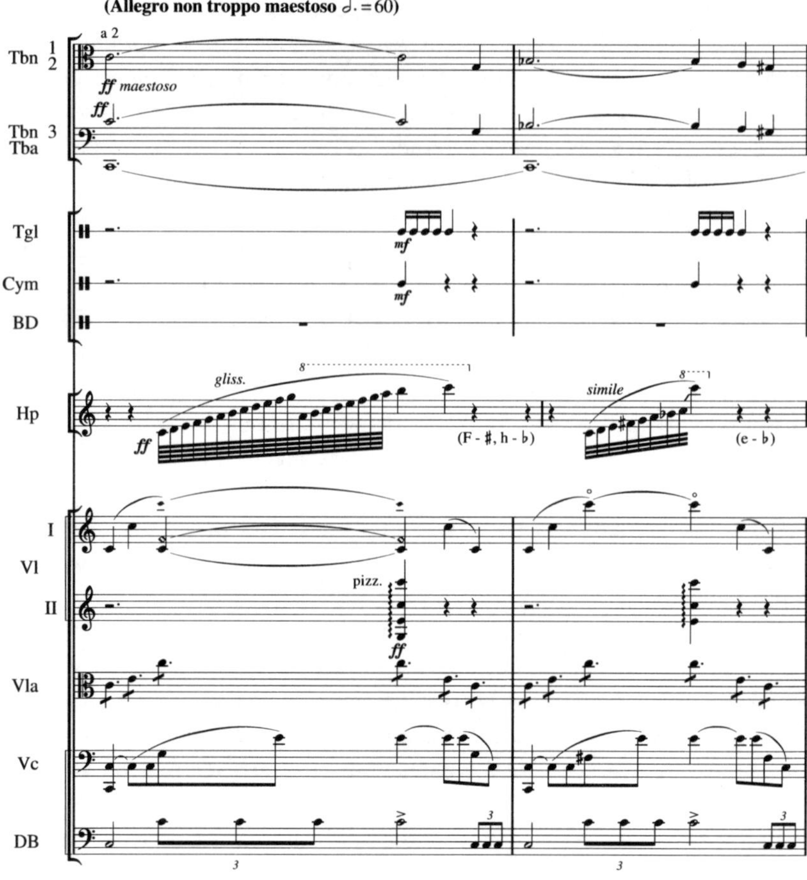

EX. 17.11

TUNED PERCUSSION

Balance for tuned percussion is not usually subject to the type of orchestral association found elsewhere. The writing is generally much more soloistic, even with regard to isolated notes, and any necessary adjustment of balance will more often apply to associated instruments elsewhere in the orchestra. The hard resonating instruments, such as xylophone or glockenspiel, will cut through almost any orchestral combination, but those of more sonorous quality (vibraphone and marimba for example) will sometimes need more care.

EX. 17.11 (continued)

Internal Ensemble

Occasionally the rhythm of combined percussion instruments will have to be guided from within the section by the single most dominant and continuous instrument, and the players will take their entries or associated rhythms from this one pervasive sound rather than directly from the conductor's beat. This can arise under otherwise normal playing conditions, when distance or a perverse acoustic prevents the section from having aural contact with the rest of the orchestra, and it becomes the responsibility of this player to maintain and direct the section's overall ensemble through the accuracy and momentum of the individual part. Such a technique becomes absolutely vital, however, when the section is positively divided in its rhythmic movement from that of the main body of the orchestra, as in *Ex. 17.12* at the end of the *Turandot Scherzo* from Hindemith *Symphonic Metamorphosis*.

EX. 17.12

This passage, for bells, triangle, tom-tom, wood block, cymbals and gong, is punctuated by chordal repetitions of the two crotchets which end the first timpani phrase, and the timpani are therefore firmly allied to the main movement of the orchestra. Thus it is these bar-lengths that need to be indicated rather than the equal bars of percussion. (Showing both rhythms is not really a viable option in this case, since it is not a simple 2 against 3 but a clearly defined syncopation. Beating two such closely related rhythms, where each movement is directly applicable to some aspect of each line, tends to become visually confusing and of little help.)

The rhythm of the bells relates exactly to the beat in the first two bars and maintains identical movement from there on. It therefore functions as the rhythmic 'lock' for the rest of the percussion and they must take their entries from it. For the bell player, 'independent' movement actually only extends for four bars (two phrases) from rehearsal letter Z. After this, the start of the fourth phrase corresponds with the second beat of Z + 5, and the following three notes to each beat of the next bar; thereafter the whole orchestra reunites.

Each percussion player must know the bell part and be fully aware of their own relationship to it, but this is always more awkward for the gong than anyone else, and this part will usually use cymbal as the main point of reference, a ploy that will sometimes cause it to be unrhythmic by playing 'off' the cymbal too soon. The tom-tom player must close the ears to everything except the bell. (One word to the conductor: the 2/2 bars are obviously beaten in 2, and each 3/4 *beaten out* – one beat in a bar here can be calamitous!) While this passage is undeniably difficult, it tends to look more confusing than it actually is, and even quite inexperienced sections can cope with it very well.

Not actually as difficult, but considerably more disturbing rhythmically, is a second, and more famous, example, this time from *The Procession of the Sage*, towards the end of the first part of Stravinsky *The Rite of Spring*. (*Ex. 17.13*, overleaf, excludes the woodwind but includes all elements of movement.)

The pervading pulse is minims, pertaining to the theme in tenor and bass tubas, and the 6/4 is thus divided into three groups of two and cannot be contemplated as two groups of three. It is, of course, possible to beat all six crotchets but this is not really of any help to anyone except, perhaps, the conductor.

For the three percussion instruments, bass drum is the pivotal player, having always the first beat and the half bar, and tam-tam and guero will relate to this very strong rhythmic indicator. Timpani will easily continue identical quavers, simply changing the rhythmic emphasis to groups of three, and the only potential problem in this very vociferous passage is likely to arise from overplaying the tam-tam, thereby losing the aural help that bass drum can provide. In fact, no percussion part is marked above the *mezzo forte* of its initial entry, although the general level of *fortissimo* is usually regarded as implicit for timpani and all percussion at this point.

EX. 17.13

For tam-tam especially, the passage immediately prior to *Ex. 17.13* is far more difficult. Over the preceding twenty-four bars, bass drum has injected a rhythm of three crotchets against the prevailing four which, for the last eight bars, tam-tam has evenly divided into two, a rhythm that is continued by the duplets in the 6/4. The notation of rests and tied notes of this previous passage, however, means that tam-tam naturally relates to the predominant rhythm and not that imposed by the bass drum, which is thus of little initial help in the performance of the duplets and the point of reference will usually need to be relocated.

EX. 17.13 (continued)

In music of aleatoric design, such internal reference, while often necessary, will obviously not hold any responsibility for rhythm or ensemble but will, if required at all, simply mark the entry or cessation of a free rhythm or the commencement of a dynamic or tonal change.

In Conclusion

More than for any other group of instruments, the orchestral integration of percussion sounds hinges on decisions of their specific responsibility within a given work or passage. The musical alliance and application of the aspects discussed so far will only be accomplished by understanding their role in relation to any individual composition.

The use of percussion instruments in symphonic orchestral writing may be said to fall into four broad categories:

1 Rhythmic figuration, in either a pervasive or supporting role, such as the continuous snare drum rhythm of Ravel *Boléro*, or the few bars for the same instrument in Rachmaninov *Piano Concerto no. 3*, quoted above.

2 The underlining of a harmonic or melodic climax or structure such as the cymbal clash at the last appearance of the C major theme in Wagner *Prelude* to *Die Meistersinger von Nürnberg*, or the same instrument's lone appearance in the slow movement of Bruckner *Symphony no. 7*.

3 The expression or heightening of a dramatic or sensual effect such as the tam-tam stroke at the beginning of Tchaikovsky *Francesca da Rimini*.

4 The representation of some actual non-musical sound, in more recent repertoire, most often performed by an 'invented' instrument such as the wind machine of Vaughan Williams *Sinfonia Antartica* and Ravel *Daphnis et Chloé* or the anvil of Walton *Belshazzar's Feast*, but also described by inventive use of more standard instruments such as the timpani 'thunder clouds' of Berlioz *Symphonie Fantastique*.

In addition, and something of a combination of all of them, is the general colouring of orchestration as found throughout the French repertoire and exposed in perhaps its most peerless form by Debussy and Ravel.

This use of percussion instruments as orchestral colour has been intentionally separated from the other categories, mainly because the notion of percussion as 'colouring' permeates much of the thinking on the role of this section. While this characteristic is doubtless inherent, it is actually no more typical of this section than of any other. Every orchestral instrument, or combination of instruments, will 'colour' the statement they are making. Indeed, it is often the use of a particular sound (or amalgamation of sounds) rather than any melodic, harmonic or rhythmic aspect of the line, that will express a particular sensibility. The immediate inference of colour in relation to percussion stems from their melodic limitation (and, therefore, the enforced circumspection with which they are used), but as a general concept it seems extremely dangerous. As an attitude, it relegates the role, overlooks its harmonic (and melodic) implications and diminishes awareness of the orchestra as a complete instrument.

In recent years there has been a growing interest in, and understanding of, the percussion section, largely as a result of the increased repertoire that has become available. But this interest is in danger of being limited to these examples alone and, especially with regard to rhythmic percussion, results in no greater consideration of their symmetry within the more standard repertoire than was previously the case.

I do not see that it is possible to work orchestrally with this section in any way other than one would approach the contribution of melodic instruments – through phrasing, balance, intonation, sonority, dynamic and significance as each applies. It is not the number of players, nor the variety of instruments, nor the complication of the part that is the criterion, but simply the *fact* of the sound. This alone is the starting and finishing point of every musical communication.

18 HARP AND KEYBOARD

The discussion of combined orchestral technique in relation to harp and all keyboard instruments requires a rather different emphasis from that previously applied. In each case one is here dealing with an individual player and an instrument that not only retains considerable soloistic production but also its own characteristic sound. None will be used in the type of combination found in other sections and, indeed, none is capable of a similar involvement of single sustained notes, or of complete integration of sound.

It is not possible to enhance or modify the sound of these instruments by combination or other means, nor is it ever their role to influence other instruments or sections in this way. Examples of ensemble which include all or any of these instruments will always maintain a degree of aural partnership rather than combination in the more orchestral sense, and orchestral integration will be much more based on simple relative dynamic than happens with other sections.

Thus, many of the necessary skills have already been outlined, either in direct relation to this section or in terms of other instruments. Nonetheless, because there are further subtleties that should be mentioned, the same format will be pursued in this chapter as elsewhere, although similar depth of discussion will not always be applicable.

The section will also be considered in more general terms, and examples will only be given for individual instruments where a fundamental difference in approach or technique is occasioned. Thus, an aspect of orchestral combination considered specifically in relation to the harp may be taken as applying also to any keyboard instrument in similar circumstances, and vice versa.

Each of the last three chapters began by considering the adjustments and anticipation required from players to overcome problems caused by distance or idiosyncrasies of acoustic. These factors can also affect harp and keyboard players, although the effect of various performing spaces on the sound of these instruments will not generally be quite as critical.

Theatrical stages again prove to be the most awkward. These are frequently too narrow to accommodate a full-size symphony orchestra comfortably, as the arrangement has to be set deeper than would ideally be the case. Once large instruments such as harp or piano are included within the main body of this configuration, difficulties of playing space and visual contact are aggravated.

For this reason harp and piano must be kept on the periphery of the strings, even though this will often mean that they are placed almost (never completely) in the wings and beyond the view of the majority of the audience. In neither case will the perceived sound be adversely affected, because of the percussive nature of its production, although it will sometimes require an adjustment in balance with other sections of the orchestra.

For harp alone, this limitation of lateral space sometimes makes it difficult to keep the pillar of the instrument out of direct line with the conductor and, if this is the case, it is better to place the instrument on the other side of the stage. If it is positioned behind the violas and cellos but in front of the double basses, it will have the advantage of being slightly nearer the woodwind and the centre of the strings. Nonetheless, this can still cause problems of sight-line, not only to the string basses themselves but also (in cases of extreme restriction of width) any one of tuba, trombones, trumpets, oboes and bassoons.

The celesta should not normally perform from outside the line and, except when it appears as a doubling instrument with piano, must be brought further in to the body of strings. Its width corresponds almost exactly to that of a desk of string players so it can always be placed within the edge of the strings, forming, as it were, the last desk of 1st violins and dividing the two sections at the back. Just this amount of infiltration within the string body will make a considerable difference to its audibility. If space permits, the celesta can be placed on the other side of the orchestra, but any attempt to angle the instrument can make things difficult for the player and will have absolutely no effect on the perceived sound which, with most examples of the instrument, emanates from all positions around the case.

Halls with purpose-built high, narrow risers will cause most difficulty in the positioning of these instruments. A piano, even a small upright, cannot normally be considered in any position other than on the basic stage area and the same is generally true of celesta, although its slightly smaller size will sometimes allow it to be placed on a riser, leaving just enough room to play it. Sometimes the problems of accommodation caused by the addition of piano (or, especially, piano and celesta) at such venues can prove almost insurmountable. With use of every available square inch and careful adjustment of desks to allow absolute minimum playing space, I have not yet been faced with the necessity to reduce the number of string players within any orchestra, but it has sometimes been very close.

From the purely musical standpoint, these halls will not cause intrinsic problems of keyboard balance. However, the harp, if raised, can sometimes acquire an undesirable extra resonance, for which a capable player will have to make continuous adjustment (a weak or inexperienced player should, if at all possible, be moved).

In churches, cathedrals, sports halls and the like, available space does not generally prove to be a problem. Acoustic, of course, can be an altogether different matter, but only insofar as it affects the sound of the entire orchestra. It will not usually be a specific problem for these instruments.

For organ and harmonium, as already discussed, there is little available opportunity for rearrangement. In any event, separate organ consoles will generally be placed at some distance from the orchestra.

However, there are some halls where the organ console comes up into the centre of the stage area within a pit of some considerable size. The entire area is lost to the orchestra, not only for the work in question but also for the whole concert, and it sometimes becomes impossible to set any functional layout. On one occasion, after some hours of experimentation the night before the concert, I declined to use the organ on the grounds that it was quite impossible for the woodwind to be placed either together or indeed anywhere where they could hear or be heard. Fortunately the organ part was not absolutely essential. Had it been so I have absolutely no idea what could have been done beyond a complete rearrangement of the orchestra, something I was not prepared to risk in the rest of the programme.

Electronic involvement will generally be easily accommodated, the more complex designs being controlled from outside the orchestra and little equipment needing to be placed where it might take critical space from the orchestra's normal layout. Electronic keyboards, where appropriate, occupy a very small space.

Internal Ensemble

Techniques pertaining to the direct association of instruments within this section have largely been covered during the discussion of relative seating (Chapter 6) and little need be added except in relation to the often encountered scoring of two harps.

In a number of works, this will be found to be a simple doubling of one part, usually for reasons of balance but also to obtain the distinctive sound of two instruments, a fact that should be carefully borne in mind whenever a reduction is contemplated where two players are not available. Such works do not tend to cause problems of ensemble or balance between the two harps beyond those that arise in combination with other sounds.

Separate parts scored for the two instruments, generally to increase the harmonic range, can, however, require especial care. On the whole there is likely to be little difference between the two parts, and certainly nothing that would make 2nd subordinate to 1st. Thus, no experienced harpist would be surprised to find *Ex. 18.1*, a completely unaccompanied passage for two harps as the very opening sounds of Smetana *Vyšehrad*, the first of the cycle *Má Vlast*, commencing with 2nd.

By far the most eccentric thing about this is that the whole passage is perfectly playable by one instrumentalist alone, although the musical benefit of using two players is undeniable. It remains probably the ultimate example of 'fair distribution' (even the later *cadenzas* are divided) and only the traditional seniority of the 1st player dictates that this part contains the initial flourishes.

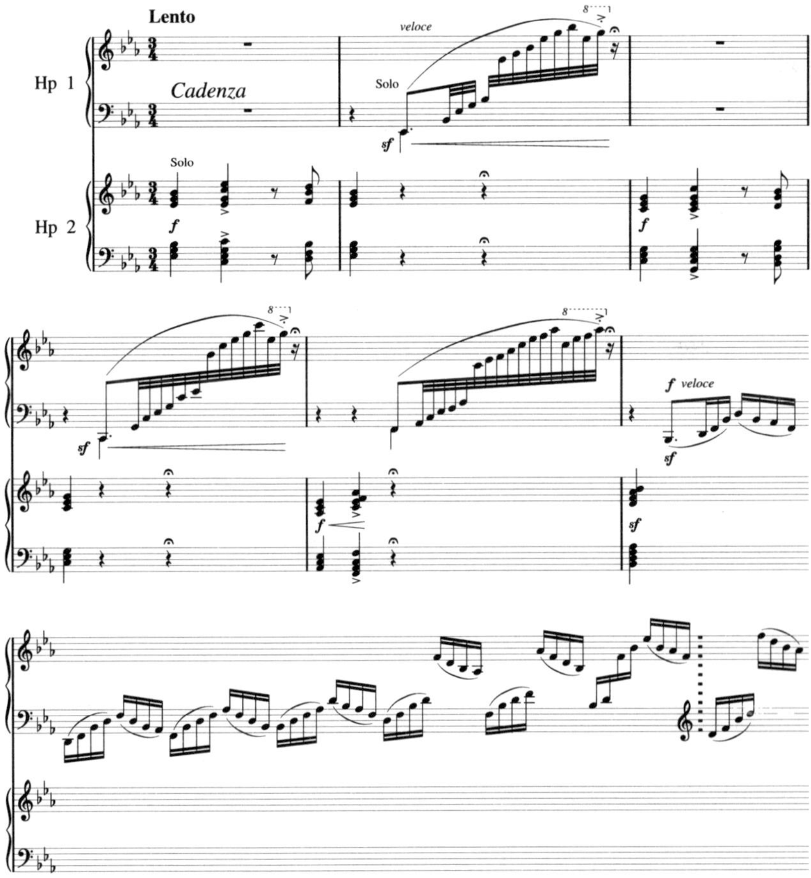

EX. 18.1

EX. 18.1 (continued)

The work itself is not of the virtuosic design that might be associated with instrumental display of this sort and is dominated by this opening chorale. The *cadenzas* are more thematic extension than technical ostentation, analogous to the pianistic embellishments of Chopin rather than the more *bravura* displays of Liszt. For 2nd harp, the statements need to remain unpretentious in style and sound, straightforward assertions to which 1st appends ornamentation.

Such musical dissimilarity, most apparent in sound and approach, will be found in much of the writing for combined harps, and only when the instruments are used to provide chromatic or octave extension will the two parts be identical in production. Elsewhere each voice, while retaining an undoubted degree of interdependence, will need to project sound qualities specifically relevant to the individual part, as in *Ex. 18.2* from the 2nd suite of Ravel *Daphnis et Chloé*.

EX. 18.2

In orchestrations including just one harp and piano, the two instruments will frequently be found in direct combination, the latter often presenting motifs and figurations more typical of a second harp. While this scoring can never be said to be strictly in lieu of 2nd harp (nowhere is the availability of harps so restricted as to impose this limitation on a composer), some similarities to harp production will need to be considered, as in *Ex. 18.3* from the third movement of Prokofiev *Symphony no. 7*.

EX. 18.3

Here, the piano part will need to suggest something of the harp's natural production in order to combine successfully, and this must not be confined to use of the sustaining pedal. The harp at this pitch is very clear, and individual notes do not ring for as long as pianists might believe. While very discreet use of the pedal might be necessary, touch and articulation will be most important.

External Ensemble

The direct combination of harps or keyboard instruments with the totally different production techniques of wind and string instruments exposes the one most difficult aspect of orchestral collaboration for the players of this section. The placing of entries and, in many cases, the movement of continuous lines, can prove extremely difficult to synchronize, especially for inexperienced players.

For piano especially, this will extend beyond the obvious problems of vertical alignment, to the projected sound itself. The musicianship of this player, discussed in Chapter 6 with regard to the very simple opening of Debussy *Printemps* (see *Ex. 18.4*), may now be seen to be doubly important, for the passage, in context, actually occurs with solo flute.

Ensemble will depend on awareness from both players, and flute can assist greatly by reacting slightly earlier than if playing alone, but synchronization will be of little relevance if the quality is wrong. The piano must produce an

EX. 18.4

even sound, with perfect control of weight, and so carefully balanced as to complement the woodwind instrument without distracting from its natural, seamless production. Although professional players can make this appear easy, with considerable concentration and sensitivity two less exalted players will be able to perform this phrase successfully.

It is, however, with strings that the real perplexities of ensemble lie, especially in the production of soft harmony. Apparently simple cadences, as in *Ex. 18.5* from Martinů *Sinfonietta la Jolla* are extremely difficult for piano to place exactly, especially in performance, where the string sound will tend to appear even later than in rehearsal.

EX. 18.5

String production of low chords at this dynamic will display no immediacy, but will sound as if they have been sighed from the instruments. It is a means of production that piano cannot emulate, and it can only produce an approximation by extreme control of touch. The extra care that such pianistic technique entails will help but, especially if the chord should be arranged to be played up-bow (quite possible here), the strings can present such an indefinite start to the note as would confound the most experienced pianist. They must therefore be aware of their responsibility to the piano and, without pointing the entry, must perform it exactly together within a clear and logical time-span.

Numerous similar examples exist for this combination, and also for harp and strings (although, in this case, the percussive production need not be so restricting, as most occasions will demand a discreet spreading of the chord). Nonetheless, in the frequent association of single notes with lower strings, harp can encounter situations of equal suspense.

Responsibility and Integration

Orchestral responsibility for the various instruments of this 'section' is idiosyncratic, and will relate entirely to their specific involvement within specific works. It will always cover the complete range, from solo to accompaniment, and often both aspects will be required within the same piece.

In accompaniment, reasoning must always extend further than basic dynamic, and considerable sensitivity in terms of sound will be necessary, especially in support of just one solo instrument.

In the famous *Sicilienne* from Fauré *Pelléas et Mélisande* (*Ex. 18.6*), harp, in combination with *pizzicato* strings, accompanies one solo flute (later to be joined by muted solo violin).

In this example the harp sound must be very fluid and gentle, with no sign of accent or over-emphasis of the half bar, and should impart a sense of movement to the phrase. This is a very different sound from what is likely to be required in most orchestral circumstances, and can be quite difficult for the player to achieve. Although the instrument is unlikely to be too far removed from the solo, the player will still have to judge balance rather than truly hear it, and few harpists will believe how softly this passage can be played. The string *pizzicati* should be soft but resonant – as similar to the harp quality as possible.

Use of the harp in accompaniment of this sort is frequent, since it exploits one of the most characteristic qualities of the instrument, but the subtle

EX. 18.6

modifications in sound required in so many ostensibly similar examples are not always obvious. A further, and basically very similar, illustration is shown in *Ex. 18.7* from the opening of the second movement of Rachmaninov *Symphony no. 3*.

EX. 18.7

Here the harp accompanies solo horn but in a very different guise from that of the previous example. The single chords call for a more full tone even within the subdued dynamic of the opening bars (they are normally slightly spread) and most of the responsibility for movement lies with the solo. The mood of the whole passage is much more ruminative than in the Fauré example, and the sound of the harp needs to be within the same tonal sphere as that of the horn: rounded and warm.

It is also a much less autonomous accompaniment than the previous example, relying entirely on the movement of the horn rather than the other way around. Thus the third bar (the second chord) will be placed early enough for the horn suspension to be fluent and not in any way unnatural, and the time allowed for solo breathing, previously dictated by the harp movement, will here need to be accompanied.

Orchestral piano will rarely find itself in situations similar to these last two examples, since it is most often used either in the performance of soloistic rhythmic and melodic lines or the reinforcement of instrumental sections by doubling. In these more general circumstances, the necessary control of sound will often be determined by style or register, as in *Ex. 18.8*, from the original version of Stravinsky *Petrouchka* (and identical, as far as piano is concerned, in the revised, 1947, version).

This is hardly 'accompaniment' in the true sense, but more of a decoration of the solo flute phrase. It thereby serves to illustrate both roles and is probably as close to this type of partnership as orchestral piano will ever come.

EX. 18.8

EX. 18.8 (continued)

It is in supporting more rhythmic aspects of a phrase that piano finds its most idiosyncratic orchestral niche, and its responsibility in such situations will be primarily to enhance clarity. However, it will also frequently enable a composer to double at the octave without adding weight to the line. The famous unison *staccato* doubling of string basses from Shostakovich *Symphony no. 5* has already been quoted (*Ex. 6. 6*), but the octave doubling of flute and oboe, from Martinů *Symphony no. 3* (*Ex. 18.9*), is even more vital, because of the added width that piano supplies and its precise articulation, especially of the lower notes within the phrase.

EX. 18.9

This passage demonstrates the adjustment in style, rather than production, that is required of piano in much of its orchestral use. It is not entirely natural for the instrument to perform syncopated phrases of this sort with clear but very short rests, whereas good wind players will almost certainly do so. In *Ex. 18-9* little difference would probably be discernible, but in many similar passages of such direct rhythmic associations the piano should emulate the method of articulation employed by the orchestral section.

Phrasing and Projection

Phrasing of melodic lines and isolated passages within the context of orchestral playing will be achieved by the instruments of this section through the same techniques of refinement as apply to their solo performance. There are no circumstances where phrasing (as distinct from articulation) will need to be adjusted in collaboration, although these instruments will often carry the responsibility for its revelation.

Especially for harp and piano, *legato* phrasing is very important, sometimes even more so than in solo performance, since any melodic phrase is certain to be repeated by instruments capable of absolutely smooth production. This situation of direct comparison can prove invidious to any but the most proficient keyboard or harp players, whose performance of true *legato* is an illusion rather than fact. Even in circumstances of accompaniment or interpolated decoration, this aspect of performance must be a priority, for it is all too easy, especially in student orchestras, for players to obscure or deflect from *legato* qualities elsewhere in the texture, by thoughtless assertion of detached production.

For the harp, phrasing and its consequent interdependent articulation become vitally relevant to the ubiquitous rising cadential *arpeggio*. This is again an orchestral responsibility that can sometimes evoke a perfunctory rendering from the inexperienced player, mainly because nothing so ostensibly simple is likely to have been encountered in the solo repertoire. In *Ex. 18.10*, the conclusion of the second movement of Franck *Symphony in D minor*, the final note can easily be over-emphasized, both by reason of its pitch in relation to the sustained chord and because the player has so little tangible involvement on which to base it.

In such circumstances of isolation the phrasing, as well as the balance, of a fragment like this is not easy.

Balance

Chordal balance, in terms of direct and sustained tonal relationship, is not relevant to this section in the way that it applies to woodwind and brass. However, a relationship between the instruments themselves, similar to that discussed in relation to percussion (and elsewhere), will be required from the section in isolation and also when combined with others, and this aspect of balance should be of most concern.

Because harp and keyboard are strikingly individual, and they are always additions to the orchestra, balance with instruments of similar production is limited to the few occasions when a number of them appear together (for example, harp with piano, two harps, harp and celesta). However much they might be considered part of a section for purposes of discussion, more often than not they each appear alone, and the number of examples that have included more than one instrument in the course of this appraisal is rather misleading, since the proportion of repertoire in which this occurs is relatively small.

The opportunity to balance with instruments that are in any way physically close is also severely limited (unless it be full sections of strings) and problems of balance are heightened by this fact. The examples quoted above of harp accompanying woodwind or horns, and piano with flute, are never likely to be performed with the players close enough together really to hear each other, nor will they be able to inflect subtleties of phrasing or ensemble in a way that would be possible in recital or chamber music. The players learn to cope with

236
poco rall.
a 2
1
Fl 1 2
pp
molto cresc.
f
pp
Ob 1 2
mf
molto cresc.
f
CA
pp
mf molto cresc.
f
Cl 1 2
mf molto cresc.
f
pp
BCl
mf
molto cresc.
f
pp
Bn
mf molto cresc.
f
pp
Hn 1 2
pp
mf
molto cresc.
f
pp
3 4
mf
molto cresc.
f
pp
Tpt 1 2
a 2
mf cresc.
f
f
Timp
p
molto cresc.
f dim.
pp
poco rall.
Hp
pp
molto sosten.
Vl I
mf
f
pp
div.
II
mf
molto cresc.
f
p
Vla
div.
mf
molto cresc.
f
pp
Vc
mf
molto cresc.
f
pp
DB
mf
molto cresc.
f
poco rall.
(score in C)

EX. 18.10

this, and the ability to know instinctively the level at which balance will be found with any single instrument or group of instruments is really down to experience. It is an exceedingly elusive aspect of performance for less seasoned players in this section, as improvement can only be regulated by outside opinion. They will not necessarily be able to hear it themselves.

Much variation in sound is available to most instruments in this group, both by technical alteration and variation in touch. The harpist, for example, can alter the position at which the string is set in motion, plucking nearer the soundboard to produce a somewhat harder, metallic sound. But the sensitivity of the production will also provide differences in quality, and this is probably the prime weapon of a proficient player. Similarly, use of the piano pedals will only provide a foundation on which to build gradations of sonority. While such subtleties might be beyond the average player, it is very important that the potential is understood and emphasized in orchestral performance.

For harpsichord, harmonium and organ, most change will be effected through registration. Only for the celesta is there no possibility of tonal adjustment, but its scoring will generally have taken this into account and be in a totally characteristic vein.

Wth regard to the piano, the abilities mentioned above underline the necessity of involving a *pianist* rather than just someone who can play the notes, for sensitivity to balance is an essential quality for this instrument. Perhaps more than for any other instrumentalist in this section, much of the pianist's initial difficulty in achieving balance can ensue from the wrong attitude – misconstruing the role as that of a featured instrument rather than a component part. This can affect all aspects of orchestral piano performance but balance, particularly for a specialist player who has learnt no other instrument and has little chamber music experience, will be one of the last to be mastered. The ease with which this instrument pervades orchestral sound has always been one of the prime reasons for its being so superlative a concerto partner, but the same quality can make it something of a liability within the orchestra if it becomes undesirably dominant, especially when the player's appraisal of the instrument's role is also at fault.

A composer who really understands the instrument will, however, capitalize on this characteristic potency. Few instruments could state a countermelody against four full sections of *molto espressivo* strings with such facility as demonstrated in *Ex. 18.11* from the first movement of Rachmaninov *Symphonic Dances.*

The apparent ease this passage displays in terms of balance should highlight the dangers of performing on the instrument in an inappropriately soloistic manner.

EX. 18.11

For organ and harmonium, balance may be determined quite easily, and the necessary adjustments made. It is worth remembering, however, that most cathedral organs, as well as those in large churches, will generally project their greatest sound at some distance from the orchestra, owing to the design and structure of the building and the frequent high position of the pipes. The worst place from which to judge balance thus becomes a point fairly close to, and below the level of, the pipes – the position most frequently occupied by orchestra and conductor. Especially in low areas of the range (underpinning basic harmony and collaborative movement with low strings and wind), the organ might well be found to be over-balanced from a position some distance from the orchestra, and this is always worth checking.

Rhythm

The emphasis of rhythmic movement and the clarification of that implied elsewhere in the orchestra are regular prime responsibilities of the harp and keyboard players. Whether by simple repetition of a rhythmic figure or intervention of a more elaborate nature, the percussive qualities of all the instruments within this group will frequently be utilized. In the upper register especially, the sharp articulation of which piano, harp and harpsichord are capable in *staccato* production may be compared to the 'dryness' apparent in tighter forms of string *pizzicato*. Both piano and harp will often be directly

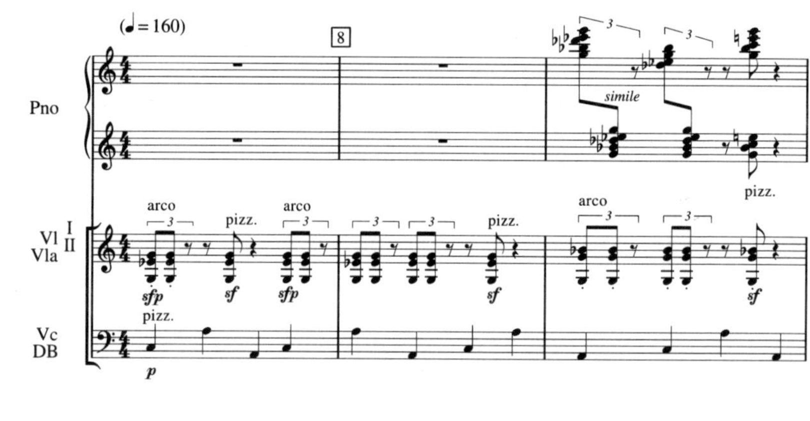

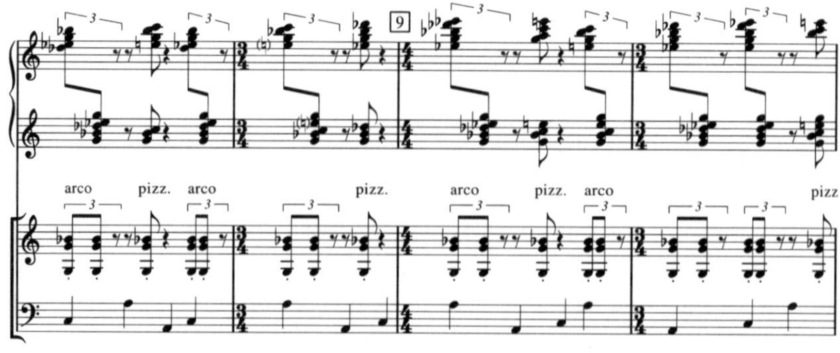

EX. 18.12

combined with this in passages of rhythmic character, as in *Ex. 18.12* for piano and strings from the first movement of Stravinsky *Symphony in Three Movements*.

Even in so restless and vertical a passage, a sense of underlying horizontal movement must be felt – here clearly transmitted by the movement of the lower strings – and the dependence and relationship of the triplet figures clearly defined. The melodic implication of the upper notes of the piano part is vital to this, and the tonal relationship must be projected as clearly as any rhythmic element. Although the piano cannot be of direct rhythmic help to the strings (the passage is too hazardous for them to rely on such scant aural insinuation), a considerable degree of logic and inevitability will be injected by this line.

The control of complex rhythms of this sort is made easier for the instruments of this group through the necessary physical movement involved in their production (a situation that elsewhere only applies to strings and percussion). The disciplined use of the arms and body in the performance of rhythmic patterns, especially in the placing and physical feeling of rests, can be of tremendous help. This does not, of course, refer to any extraneous movement, but only to that demanded by the production of sound, and the movement preparatory to it. For piano, even though the hands remain very close to the keys, the necessary movement can suffice to underline the rhythm and control its motion.

A high proportion of orchestral collaboration for harp or piano will depend on the ability to provide harmonic insinuation to passages of essentially rhythmic character, and either instrument (particularly in the lower register) will combine easily with percussion or lower string *pizzicato* for this purpose. *Ex. 18-13* shows the full orchestration of a passage previously quoted for its use of timpani, and is the opening of the middle section from the second of Debussy *Trois Nocturnes*. While far removed in all aspects of musical character, the harmonic function of the harps is surprisingly similar to that of the piano in *Ex. 18.12*. (This is also the eight-bar introduction and supporting texture to the trumpet phrases discussed and quoted in Chapter 10 as *Ex. 10. 47*.)

This needs quite careful production from 2nd harp, since the lower strings of the instrument will provide excessive resonance if plucked too firmly. In student orchestras it is also a moment where the player is horribly prone to double the tempo – not only because the previous orchestral rhythm has been more than twice as fast, but also through the powerful impulse to place the upper octave with that of timpani and (later) 1st cellos.

Even though timpani and lower strings play more notes, the fundamental rhythm of this passage will be perceived from the harps, especially following

EX. 18.13

the entry of 1st, because of the increased harmonic emphasis they bring, albeit discreetly.

Such rhythmic influence can be far more blatant, however. *Ex. 18.14* is taken from the original version of Stravinsky *Petrouchka*, where two harps provide tremendous impetus to the theme by fast repetition of single notes.

This is extremely awkward for 1st harp to produce at this tempo, since the G is enharmonically available on no other string. (This is no easier in the revised version where, effectively, one harp takes both parts, doubling the low C at every quaver.)

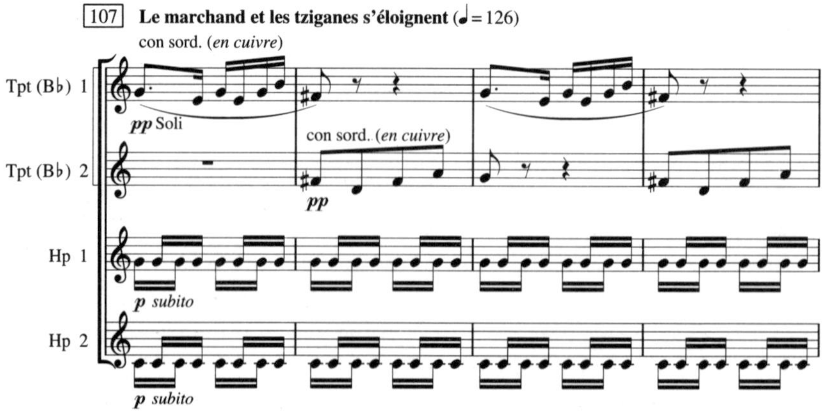

EX. 18.14

In less soloistic passages, the direct combination of either harp or piano with other instruments will always provide increased articulation to the line, especially in the fast production of slurred notes by woodwind or strings. In *Ex. 18.15* from Tchaikovsky *Capriccio Italien* the clarity given to the second

EX. 18.15

quaver of each group by the harp's necessary re-articulation gives the phrase a distinct edge.

In Conclusion

It remains only to reiterate the importance of the role of each of the instruments that comprise this somewhat independent section. Electronic involvement has not been considered in any detail because it mostly involves specific alteration, distortion or repetition of sounds otherwise normally produced. Where melodic keyboard is directly involved, techniques outlined above will apply.

As has been remarked, while all instruments of this group retain a greater independence of involvement than elsewhere, their approach must always remain firmly entrenched in the attitudes of ensemble. The biggest concerns of the young harpist will be those of trying to remember the pedalling and playing 'on the beat', while that of all keyboard players will be counting bars' rest. As important as these might be, the overriding factor is ensemble in its broadest sense – the integrated projection of sound, rhythm and phrasing.

Perhaps the final statement of Part III, equally applicable to all of the chapters so far (but not to be taken too literally) should read:

'The notes are only a guide.'

PART IV

The Orchestra as a Whole

19 LAYOUT

The seating and positioning of each section has been thoroughly dealt with in Part I, and all that follows must be taken in conjunction with this and whatever modifications have subsequently been considered. In the following discussion of the placing of the whole orchestra these section layouts will be treated as entities, for no adjustment within them is possible. However, the position of each relative to another may be varied to some slight degree; indeed it often has to be in order to resolve the jigsaw presented by many playing areas. Specific cases will be considered as they arise.

The standard layout for strings will always be that of 1st violins opposite cellos. If a different arrangement of the string group is contemplated it will not affect the fundamental premises discussed below, although it might well affect the available space. Individual and contentious layouts of the full orchestra have been discussed in their relevant context and will not be considered further.

Rehearsal Spaces

Most rehearsals, other than those at the concert venue, will be undertaken with the orchestra set out on one level, utilizing a proportion of the floor space in an otherwise empty hall. This may be a school assembly hall, a sports hall, a community hall or any other large, enclosed space, but it should possess fundamentally acceptable acoustic qualities, and be neither too resonant nor too dry. It should also be large enough to accept the orchestra in its normal layout with space to spare. Most usually the hall will be rectangular in shape and the orchestra will be set with front and back parallel to the longer walls.

The first consideration of any layout must be the position of the woodwind, which should not be too far distant from the conductor: a depth of three string desks is the absolute maximum. The width of the section will vary according to the number of players, but the centre is determined by 1st oboe, who should be seated just to the left of the centre line (to the right as viewed from the front of the orchestra).

The 1st bassoon should then be placed in the row behind, slightly nearer centre, with a clear view over the right shoulder of 1st oboe. The other wind Principals will then be set as close as is practical, a consideration which extends to the remaining woodwind players. There should be no attempt to 'square off' the ends of the lines, irrespective of the number of players of any one instrument, and the two lines should be straight, parallel with the front of the orchestra.

The first desks of the string sections should now be set in a rough semi-circle, the centre line passing between 2nd violins and violas. The first desk of violins and of cellos must not be set too close: there should be at least one metre on either side between the conductor and the music stands of these players. This is important because the front players must be able to gain some indication of ensemble from the conductor while viewing the music, and this is impossible from a position too close, especially if a podium is used. The placing of first desk 2nd violins and violas will now automatically be correct and this should result in a layout corresponding to that in *Fig. 19.1*.

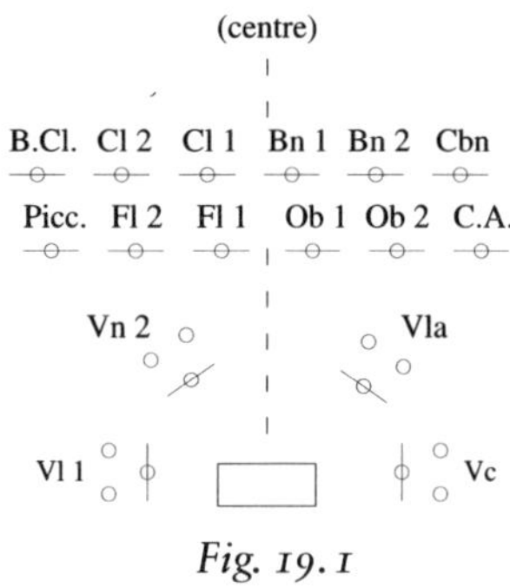

Fig. 19.1

With a small to medium size orchestra (10–14 1st violins) the remaining string desks can now be set. With larger numbers, however, it is better to set horns and brass before this, in order to *restrict* the available space and avoid the temptation to push these sections too far back.

Horns should be placed either immediately next to clarinets (if that section does not exceed four) or with bumper horn just behind the last of these players. 1st horn should have no woodwind player immediately in front, and the line of horns is then continued to the right of this player and at a slight angle.

Brass will be set at the opposite side, in one of two possible positions: either 1st trumpet will be placed next to the last bassoon and the section continued to the left, with trombones and tuba set separately behind them; or, without altering this position of trombones, trumpets will be placed next to them, behind the woodwind, whereupon 1st trumpet will be next to 1st trombone and the section will extend to the player's right. In either configuration the position will be determined by trumpets. Once again the lines will be slightly angled towards the centre of the orchestra, except for the single line placing, where this will apply only to trombones and tuba. A layout similar to the following would then have been obtained.

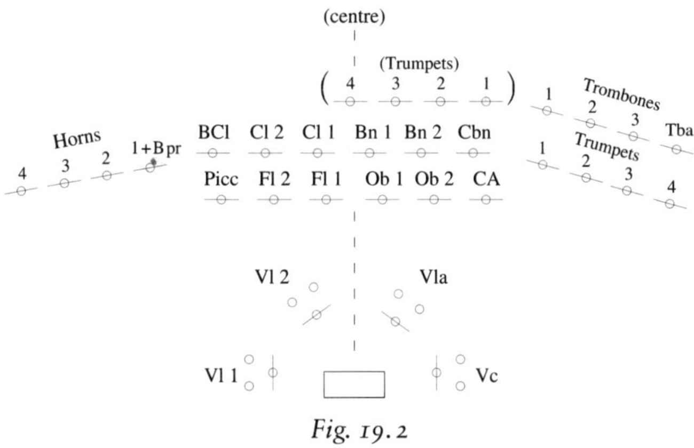

Fig. 19.2

Timpani and percussion may now be set with a clear, empty row between them and the woodwind, as if the brass line had been extended right across. Timpani are best set slightly to the left of centre (trombone side) but not so far that they overlap the trumpets of the single brass line. Percussion should be set to the right of timpani in an order practical for their accessibility during any specific programme, though ideally, untuned percussion should be nearest to timpani, and tuned furthest away.

The outside line of strings should be extended to a maximum of five desks either side of the conductor (no concert platform will take more than this) and kept close together. Where sections comprise an odd number of players, the lone player should sit at a single desk in the heart of the section and never isolated at the back; for 1st violins or cellos this can be situated at the front of the second line; for 2nd violins and violas it is best accommodated in a position towards the centre of the orchestra, either beside or in front of the woodwind.

Four basses may be set in a line behind the cellos, but preferably slightly further in – the outside player placed at about the centre of the cello desk in front. With more than four players two lines will become necessary, in which case the line of cellos should be shortened by one desk if possible. Once again, if the section comprises an odd number, the lone player should not be separated – if five, then 3 + 2 or 2 + 3 will be required unless space exists for five in one line.

The layout for an orchestra of 16.14.12.10.8; triple woodwind, 4 horns + bumper, 4 trumpets, 3 trombones, tuba, timpani and percussion is shown below.

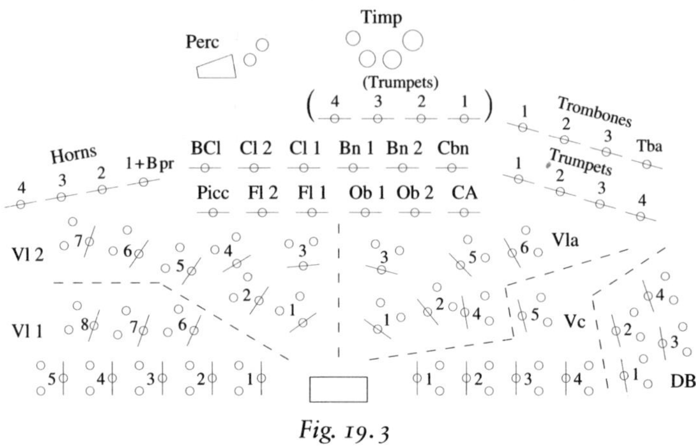

Fig. 19.3

Additional instruments, such as harp, piano or Wagner tubas, will be set as discussed in the relevant chapters.

Behind and to the sides of this layout there should be at least sufficient space to move freely. The worst possible conditions in which to work are those where the orchestra touches all or any of the walls, and this should be avoided at all costs. Especially with regard to strings, a hall of insufficient size, which forces the front of the orchestra too close to a wall, is extremely dangerous. The strings will be working to a reflected sound, thinking they are providing a sonority which is not truly apparent, and no amount of explanation or inducement will convince them otherwise. Only when the orchestra is in concert, and must project sound to the back of the auditorium, will the strings realize their deficiency and be quite unable to do anything about it. The situation is not only musically detrimental, but it is also fundamentally unjust.

To correct this, a distance of approximately three metres in front of the orchestra is all that is required, but where this is impractical the orchestra should be set in a narrow and deep configuration, with the back parallel to one of the shorter walls, for at least the last part of the rehearsal period. In many smaller halls, this is by no means ideal and will doubtless provide additional problems of ensemble for woodwind, horns and brass, but overall more will be gained than is lost. However, such a situation should be averted through the simple provision of a hall that is big enough to rehearse in.

Many larger halls will be sufficiently wide for the orchestra to be set at one end without disturbing its natural width (a positioning which is ideal for the projection of string sound mentioned above) and these will often include a stage. It is possible to place timpani and percussion on the apron area (in front of the proscenium arch) with the main body of the orchestra on the floor of the hall, directly in front. But under these conditions, it is preferable that rostra should be provided for woodwind, horns and brass, so that the orchestra may be stepped. Timpani and percussion placed high above an orchestra that is otherwise on one level will cause considerable problems of balance. This is the only section that may be set in isolation at such height – a lengthways setting with horns or brass separated on the apron stage must *never* be contemplated.

One further essential for an orchestra in rehearsal is the provision of somewhere to store instrument cases. The cases of the more portable instruments, such as violins, violas, woodwind, horns and brass, should never be brought into the orchestral space itself. Placed on the floor between chairs and stands, they will force the orchestra to be widely spaced and cause the players to sit too far apart.

Concert Venues

The basic layout of the orchestra in concert will, of course, remain unchanged from that of rehearsal, but small adjustments, mostly with regard to the addition of risers, may often be necessary.

In my own case, when working with non-professional orchestras I will always set the orchestra out myself, including the placing of all rostra and chairs. The only exceptions to this rule will be with conservatoire and national youth orchestras who employ their own *professional* staff, and even then I make a point of being there.

SCHOOL HALLS

For concerts at these venues it is generally not advisable (or possible) to place the entire orchestra on the stage, and a layout with at least the main body of the orchestra on the floor will be most successful. Such a layout was briefly mentioned above and will work as well for concerts as rehearsal unless the floor area in front of the stage is limited by audience seating.

This type of venue, where the audience seating is flexible and on the same level as the strings of the orchestra, is something of a mixed blessing. There is always the temptation to squeeze in 'just one more row of seats' and this is invariably at the front, nearest to the orchestra. On numerous occasions I have seen an orchestra cramped and uncomfortable, with acres of barren space available behind the back row of audience. The audience seating must be set in relation to the *front* of the orchestra, leaving at least 3 metres of clear space before the first row, and then continued back from this fixed and immovable point.

I am well aware that this is idealistic and not always possible (although it is surprising just how much orchestral space can be found through polite but determined persistence), and sometimes, in smaller halls, more of the stage area will need to be used. The only limiting factor for this entire layout is the height of the stage and the difficulty of raising the orchestra evenly towards it. Unless the stage is very low – 2′6″ or less – a simple 'two level' layout is out of the question: the result will be two separate ensembles, incapable of hearing each other or balancing in any way. Some form of rostra must be used but, unless the heights are carefully regulated, performance problems will not be resolved.

The ideal height for the front row of woodwind to be set above the strings is no more than 6″, and even less than this will often be most successful; a similar limitation applies to the second row in its relationship to the first. Anything greater will require some adjustment of balance and projection, but this does not mean that it cannot be used; simply that individual reappraisals will be necessitated by even the most minimal disturbances of instrumental position, and many inexperienced orchestras will be unable to cope. Thus, in most circumstances, a sudden and undesirable rise to stage level of something more than 18″ will be apparent immediately behind clarinets and bassoons. Placing any melodic instruments so far above the body of the orchestra will cause untold problems of balance and ensemble and the front of the orchestra should therefore be far enough forward to accommodate horns and brass at the same level as the second row of woodwind. It should not become necessary to place more than timpani and percussion on the stage area itself.

Additional instruments, such as harp, piano and celesta, can only be set on the floor area within the bounds of their previously discussed positioning.

As will have become evident, this is one of the most difficult orchestral arrangements to decide on, not only because of the permanent obstacles but also because the available space is *not* predetermined or inflexible. Pressures of a non-musical nature will always be forthcoming, and these, as far as is humanly possible, should be resisted.

THEATRICAL STAGES

Many of the individual difficulties encountered in these venues have been discussed in relation to the instruments most affected, but it remains to consider the performing area in a more general sense.

Once again, the position of the orchestra must be determined by that of the front row of woodwind (*not* by the back wall of the stage), which should be set as close to the line of the proscenium arch as possible, after which the procedures of layout described above should be followed. Two levels of rostra will be adequate but a third may be considered for timpani and, if possible, percussion. Essentially, the lowest level is for the front row of woodwind, and the next for the second row plus horns and brass. Unless trumpets and trombones are set in a continuous line, the horns and lower brass may be placed at the lower level, whereupon trumpets will similarly be lowered to the platform floor. Both sections should be set at a slight angle towards the centre of the orchestra, as previously demonstrated. Incidentally, stands for players on risers should always be placed on the level in front of them, lower than that of the players' chairs.

It is this design of concert venue that most frequently makes it necessary, because of its restricted width, to have three desks of strings between woodwind and the front of the orchestra. With very large string sections this can still be quite a tight squeeze but the distance should not be increased beyond this other than in the most exceptional circumstances (I have never had to employ it).

A number of theatres will have extra staging available that will extend the platform level beyond the proscenium arch, either in the form of portable rostra or as a more substantial addition that can be raised electronically to the required level. In either case it will involve the removal of some proportion of audience seating and should therefore be arranged with the theatre well in advance of performance. If available, it should always be used because it will bring the woodwind forward and minimize the danger that their sound will be lost in the flies.

Such venues will always exhibit a dry acoustic (something that is not beneficial to any orchestra) and they must be dealt with carefully. The individual players will feel isolated in sound and be aware of an appreciable difficulty in producing a combined and resonant quality. They should not be encouraged to force in any way but only to produce the rehearsed qualities in the knowledge that, except in the very worst circumstances, the sound will combine at a distance from them.

SPORTS HALLS

From the point of view of layout, these venues provide more than adequate space for the orchestra to be set in its most comfortable and ideal configuration. Rostra should be used in an identical way to that considered for theatres, whether the main body of the orchestra is placed at ground level or on specially constructed staging (in which case the staging itself will be set to the various levels required).

With so much space available, the only dilemma lies in deciding in which area of the hall the orchestra should be. Except in halls that provide rigid, tiered seating for the audience, any one of the four possible permutations will suffice, and decisions will probably be made with regard to the relative position of exit points as much as anything else.

Acoustic qualities are never good and often appalling, the sound exhibiting the sort of transparent echo associated with swimming baths. There is generally little, if anything, that can be done about this, but the effect will usually be lessened by leaving some distance between the orchestra and the back wall (contrary to one's instincts of trying to utilize a reflective surface).

For the orchestra, such venues are usually musically depressing in that, because of the acoustic, the players receive none of the emotional sensation associated with immediate orchestral production.

CATHEDRALS AND CHURCHES

The precise position of performance in these venues will vary according to space, tradition and design. In most churches, the orchestra will be situated in the chancel, in front of the altar rail, but in those of cruciform design it will most often be west of the transept. However, some will use the opposite end of the building, setting the orchestra against the west door or wall, and others (although rarely) will utilize the north or south wall or even either transept. The only constant will be stone pillars, around which the strings of the orchestra will have to be set as successfully as possible.

Except when the orchestra is set against the west wall, the use of rostra in the terms considered above will not be possible. Some cathedrals and larger churches which promote regular concerts have staging available or specially built for the purpose, but, on the whole, these are exceptions. Normally, the only opportunity of raising sections of the orchestra is by use of the chancel steps and the sanctuary, a situation which is more often obligatory than elected.

The frequently narrow area afforded by the chancel will usually only provide sufficient room for strings, and even then, the outside players will find themselves bowing into the first row of pews. The chancel steps are often just wide enough to take the first row of woodwind, with the second row, horns and brass placed within the sanctuary itself. But many churches in Britain have choir stalls at each side of the sanctuary, severely restricting the width, so the woodwind, horn and brass sections will have no option but to sit behind one another, with timpani and percussion even further removed, in an ever-diminishing line of bodies that can neither see nor hear.

As regrettable as this is, it can sometimes be quite unavoidable. However, in such circumstances the time spent setting an orchestra at other venues (and learning precisely what will work and what cannot) becomes worth every second. In most locations, there are ways to help the projection of performance and allow players to be in the best possible positions. Horns may be placed at floor level, next to the woodwind and behind the violins; brass may take up a similar position; percussion could be moved to one side of the strings. All these are sometimes possible, and one has then to ensure that players are not isolated, and that they, and the entire orchestra, benefit from the change in position.

The acoustic qualities of churches and cathedrals are well known and will often be diametrically opposed to those pertaining to theatres. Dynamic levels will need to be generally reduced, short notes played even shorter, articulation made crystal clear, and the weight of sound taken out of the bass, particularly on sustained notes.

CONCERT HALLS

After the rigours of the foregoing, arranging orchestras within specialist concert halls can seem like a rest cure. Platforms will have been designed with orchestras in mind and so will the acoustic qualities (although not always so successfully). No matter what the cost, no student orchestra should be denied the benefit of performing in one of these at least once a season. Audience numbers are secondary in this consideration. An orchestra can only discover what playing is really about by experiencing the sound and feeling of a purpose-built hall.

The layout will not vary from that so far discussed, and the risers will be incorporated, either in fixed or pneumatically variable positions. In older halls, or those not originally designed exclusively for the purpose, fixed risers might sometimes be found of considerable height or depth, either of which would involve some adjustment of balance, but specific problems associated with these have already been considered.

It cannot be over-emphasized how much such playing areas influence and mould the performing capabilities of any orchestra.

OUTDOOR VENUES

This is truly a step from the sublime to the ridiculous. Except for specially designed acoustic shells, incorporating the most sophisticated electronic amplification, there is no circumstance where an orchestra can be heard successfully outside the confines of a building. Stringed instruments *will not* project in the open air and there is no arrangement, layout or repertoire that can alter this fact. With this borne firmly in mind, I will endeavour to set out some of the criteria that might help to provide an illusion of orchestral sound.

Fundamentally the orchestral layout will remain the same, but the horns and brass (the instruments best equipped for outdoor performance) cannot be raised to the same level as would otherwise be the case and are, in fact, best left at ground level. The woodwind, however, should be raised as normal. As has been said, it is the strings who will suffer most and there is absolutely nothing that can be done about it. No adjustment of other sections will help in any way. For the string players themselves, it will help both the individual and collective ensemble of the sections if they sit very tight together, each player occupying the minimum possible space required to play the instrument and see the music.

In place of the usual acoustic considerations come those of climatic conditions, and the challenge that these present offers a far more futile contest. Wind, rain and fading light all play a greater part in these concerts than the orchestra could ever hope to combat, and they have scant respect for art or endeavour. The efforts to stop pages of music turning over, or the whole copy being blown away, are enough to occupy most players for the duration of the programme. Clothes pegs, paper clips and large weights of angled iron are all in evidence as the players engage in a hopeless attempt to hold on to the basic material of their task. The whole thing is fraught with problems and, for the symphony orchestra, is better avoided. There are other instrumental ensembles which can do the job far better.

Lighting

With an abrupt, but thankful, return to indoor concerts, some brief consideration of lighting is in order.

The symphony orchestra *must* be lit from above. There is no other way to provide sufficient light to read the copies or cater for the various sizes and configurations of ensemble that might arise within a single concert. Lighting from the front is impossible, not only because it will shine directly in the eyes of many players but also because it is of no help when reading music. Additional lighting from the side is possible, but the source must be very high so that it, too, does not blind players sitting directly opposite. Increased lighting from the back needs also to be at this level, to avoid projecting the shadow of back players on to the music of those nearer the front.

Lighting is fundamentally for the benefit of the players. In circumstances where it is sufficient and successful it will be enough to focus audience attention on the performers, especially if the house lights are dimmed.

Chairs and Stands

Ideally, the seat of the chairs used by an orchestra should be flat, without the raised sides apparent in so many of the pre-formed 'plastic', stacking designs, and this must certainly be the case for cellos even if the latter type are used for the rest of the orchestra.

For upper strings there exists a misconception which needs to be removed: they are *not* seated for their comfort, and there is more than a hint of truth in the phrase: 'the only reason that the strings are sitting down is so that the rest of the orchestra can see'! From the waist up, the position of violin and viola players should be identical to that of standing, which means that the back of the chair is never used as support. This one fact can save more space in the upper string sections than anything else, for it means that chairs may be set almost straight to the stands and any necessary positional adjustment effected by the player alone. But its significance is even more momentous, because as well as affecting space and attitude, it also alters the projected sound, producing a much more vital and centred communication.

As for music stands, few non-professional orchestras possess their own other than those of folding type, which are not ideal for either performance or rehearsal, however often they may be used. Certainly, as has already been mentioned, those players who need the music placed at an extended height should be provided with stands of a more solid design. There are many varieties available, and most regular concert venues will provide them for the whole orchestra.

There is, however, one design that proves troublesome: where the desk is constructed of thin, vertical bars and the supporting pillar of tubular steel is welded to a large, L-shaped foot, the angle of which projects inward. Not only is it impossible to write on music supported by this type of desk without some solid surface behind it, but the whole thing takes up too much room. When placed in front of a woodwind riser the pillar will stand more than 12″ away from the edge and, on some occasions, it has proved unusable on any of the higher risers, because of the lack of space, so that stands of folding design have had to be substituted. (The conductor's stand which accompanies these models must have been designed for theatrical directors. It is of the same basic design but of immense width, and most orchestral scores quietly fold up and fall through the bars.)

One final word with regard to judging the acoustic properties of a hall. The frequently used method of standing at the front of the stage area and clapping the hands together will divulge nothing except how that particular hall reacts to the sound of clapped hands from the front of the stage. From it may be deduced, to some degree, how generously or otherwise the hall will transmit the sound of applause. It will tell nothing whatever about the properties of continuous instrumental sound spread over a seven octave range or – far more important – how it will feel to the musicians attempting to transmit it.

20 REHEARSAL

The techniques used for the preparation of a programme during a period of intensive or prolonged rehearsal will vary considerably from one conductor to another, but certain basic principles will always apply, the most obvious being the process of musical development from sight-reading to performance. This development may be achieved in a number of ways, ranging from continuous repetition to detailed explanation and painstaking interlocking of carefully rehearsed individual fragments. Somewhere between these two extremes lies a strategy that allows the orchestra to play and develop its own personality while at the same time improving its ability to deal with the challenges provided by any individual work or programme.

Fundamental Concepts

It is very important that rehearsal of any ensemble, whether amateur or professional, orchestra or chamber group, should not be approached from the point of view of instilling an interpretation, but rather from that of moulding one. While interpretation will remain the prime factor in any musical statement, it must be viewed from a far larger perspective than mere choice of tempi and rigid, predetermined design. Rehearsal, especially with student orchestras, is not so much to determine *how* something goes as *where* it goes. If the essential framework of familiarity, technical ability, style, dynamic variation and sound is successfully instilled, then tempi, *rubato*, accompanying levels and dramatic influence can all be subtly adjusted within the context of performance.

This can be something of a contentious statement in the company of some conductors, who will pronounce that interpretation, in its preconceived and very personal context, is the sole element of the conductor's art and the complete reason for its existence. In essence I might not disagree, but would perhaps suggest that such an edict might foster both a disregard for the many obstacles that must be overcome before any interpretation can be forthcoming, and the danger of overlooking the fact that the conductor is not the only musician present.

Undoubtedly the conductor above all performing musicians faces something of a dilemma in that, because the structure of interpretation must so often be formed through a purely mental concept, it is all too easy to ignore the influence of the sound and technique of the actual 'instrument'. For the conductor, divorced from the rigours of individual instrumental technique, the concept of interpretation can become obsessive to the point of near blindness, and the decoding and understanding of the printed page may frequently be reduced to structure and analysis alone.

The relationship of sound to decisions of tempi, dynamic range and even style may very easily be overlooked. This would be impossible for any solo performer, for whom the total concept is always inseparable from the sound and only a conscious decision to study the printed page away from the instrument would provide a similar situation. But even then, sound, technique and musicianship would all be inextricably linked.

For the conductor, only the formula of a particular interpretation can exist, since it is up to the orchestra to reproduce it, and success rests entirely on their individual and collective ability. The genius of the great performer is not only the ability to produce a wonderful sound but also to integrate the mechanics of production with the projection of intelligible communication in such a way that the two become indistinguishable. The great virtuoso performers such as Rachmaninov, Casals and Heifetz each developed a magnificent technique and an individual sound, but their real genius lay in the *use* of those attributes and the total relevance of them in their concept of performance. Therein lies the hallmark of interpretation.

The conductor assumes responsibility for moulding a concept of every work around the strengths and idiosyncrasies of each orchestra. He or she must influence the sound but also use what is available. Trust is more important than almost any other single facet of a conductor's technique.

The conductor must also seek to foster a positive attitude within the orchestra, in relation both to its approach to work and its appraisal of itself as a corporate unit. The sort of pride that fuels the ability to perform superbly can only really result from taking part in a number of high-quality and successful concerts, but the appropriate attitude towards other players and the interdependent responsibility vital for this level of performance must be subtly implanted very early on. Even with an orchestra who have no real understanding of rehearsal discipline, a naturally attentive silence from other sections while one section is working should be apparent, without continuous reminders, within the first few hours of full rehearsal. It must be emphasized that this cannot be achieved by iron-fisted dictatorship, but only through an implicit and mutual understanding that every part of a rehearsal affects everyone and that the orchestra will play better as a result.

To play better is all that an orchestra – of any age – wishes to accomplish, and they will endure the most punishing rehearsal schedule if they think they are achieving this objective. As a conductor, all one is doing in these circumstances is tapping the natural desire of the orchestra.

However, the initial phase is not always so simple, and the conductor has to make a very quick and accurate appraisal of the direction required in each particular case. There exists now, for example, at least one orchestra of very young players (an average age of around 13) who are capable of playing extraordinarily well and need no major interpretative adjustment for either their instrumental capability or age-range. They will, however, require a radically different rehearsal technique from that employed with orchestras containing more mature instrumentalists. I normally rehearse quite fast and intensively, but nowhere else have I worked at quite the pace necessary to harness the short concentration span of these young players, especially during the early rehearsals of my first meeting with them. Apart from anything else, I found myself keeping a mental log of exactly how long it was since each person had played or been specifically contacted, as any extended period of inactivity would have lost them altogether.

Basically, the conductor must ensure that the maximum time is spent playing and the orchestra is not overwhelmed by too much emphasis on technical variation and musical subtlety at too early a stage. A broad approach should be employed, where everything rehearsed has a very noticeable effect on the orchestra's sound. Here again, preconceived concepts of interpretation might well have to be adjusted, and some details abandoned altogether, at least for the time being.

The one thing that is categorically useless and totally counter productive, is *any* attempt by the conductor to impress the orchestra, whether by knowledge of the score, strength of control, technical prowess or anything else. The *only* thing that will impress an orchestra is its own playing!

Intonation and Tuning

The rehearsal of woodwind and brass intonation, and the frequently encountered vagaries therein, have already been considered. Intonation as applicable to string sections, however, needs to be examined further, for, however wide the capacity for adjustment might be, it is subject to numerous inconsistencies, aural misconceptions, whims and fancies.

In orchestral playing, one of the fundamental difficulties of playing 'in tune' is the unwitting difference in perception of intonation that often occurs between wind and strings. It is by no means impossible to encounter these two sections performing together in two basically different keys, the strings having sharpened in pitch to a point that the woodwind can no longer match (or no longer care to!). Thus, I have quite intentionally approached this topic with the initial emphasis on intonation and its dangers for the performing string player *before* considering the tuning of the orchestra, since it is very important to have some understanding of the origins of such a divergence of opinion.

Many erudite people, conversant with the theories and laws governing sound, relative acoustic properties and the perception of hearing, have sought to explain this phenomenon with recourse to various scientific equations and analyses, all of which have considerable bearing on it. Nonetheless, speaking now as a string player, the fundamental problem is one of human error, and one that can be avoided by some understanding of the results of the forces at work.

In the first place, much as with woodwind and brass, it must always be remembered that the string section contains four substantially dissimilar instruments, albeit built to related 'family' specifications. The techniques of sound production differ in many subtle ways, and the radically different playing positions of the horizontal violin and viola compared with the vertical cello and bass make for a totally altered perception of sound and intonation, both from the instruments themselves and in relation to other instruments playing with them.

All the stringed instruments are deeply influenced by the tuning of their open strings, not only because, obviously, the lowest string is the base of the range, but also in a much more general sense. The free-ringing open string, with its clearly apparent overtones, is an instantly recognizable sound. It is, in fact, not only one of the most beautiful sounds on a stringed instrument but also, without question, the most dominant. Its influence, whether by unadulterated use, sympathetic vibration or harmonic implication, is all-pervasive for, in normal playing circumstances, up to three strings will remain 'open' and unstopped at any one time.

On the violin, for example, two keys have their tonic, dominant and subdominant fundamentals available as open strings: D (dominant A, subdominant G) and A (dominant E, subdominant D). It is no coincidence that a large proportion of concerti for the instrument are in these two keys: those in D major include the Beethoven, Brahms, Tchaikovsky, Stravinsky, Paganini no. 1, Prokofiev no. 1, Mozart K211 and K218 concerti, while the Sibelius, Khachaturian, Schumann, Wieniawski no. 2, Paganini no. 4, Bruch no. 2 and Bach (for 2 violins) are all in D minor. In A major there is Mozart K219, while the Bach BWV 1041, Dvořák, Glazunov, Goldmark and Shostakovich no. 1 are all in A minor. (This formidable list is by no means complete.)

The two outer strings, G (with dominant D) and E (with subdominant A), prove to be almost as magnetic: in G major, Mozart K216; in G minor, Bruch no. 1 and Prokofiev no. 2; in E major, Bach BWV 1042, Bruch no. 3 and Paganini no. 3; and in E minor, Mendelssohn.

It becomes apparent that few important concerti lie outside this list, and of those that do, four – Elgar, Walton, Paganini no. 2 and Saint-Saëns no. 3 – are in B minor (the relative minor of D major) and one – Britten – is in F (the relative major of D minor). Even the lone example of C♯ minor – Shostakovich no. 2 – has a relative major of E.

Even cursory exploration of other composers, such as Bartók, Barber, Szymanowski, Delius, Schoenberg and Berg, who wrote concerto repertoire for the instrument in a more exploratory or personal harmonic style, will show frequent examples of similarly related tonal centres (from the B major/minor opening of Bartók no. 2 to the blatant exploration of the four open strings in Berg).

Examination of the viola and cello concerto repertoire will show a similar ratio of keys to open strings, slightly more orientated towards the top strings of the instruments (D, A and their immediate relations). For the double bass, as might be expected, keys tend to relate to the lower strings (even if much of the actual writing is way up in cello pitch): E, E♭ and to a lesser extent C are predominant here.

The above lists are simply intended to show that when a solo stringed instrument is highlighted against a large orchestration, composers are most likely to use a tonality that employs its aural advantages to the maximum. It most certainly does *not* imply that they cannot play totally successfully in any other key or harmonic system, or that they are not frequently used in such tonalities.

However, the dominance of the tonalities closely allied to the open strings favours the 'brighter' side of the instruments – there are few 'flat' keys in the string concerto repertoire – with the individual strings set at their maximum ideal tension in relation to the build of the instrument and their own width and playing length. Slackening, even to a very small extent, loses much of the natural 'bite' and cutting edge of the sound, *especially as perceived by the player*. This loss will also be very apparent on notes which invoke no sympathetic vibration of an open string (most particularly on the middle strings of all bowed instruments), and keys which predominantly fail to elicit this response will be noticeably dark in quality.

Having demonstrated the *relative* dominance of certain tonalities it becomes possible to consider the proportional influence on the players' perception of intonation and general feeling for the instrument. The influence of the open strings and their consequent pull towards the 'brighter' keys of the instrument can certainly be felt by the player, and the immediate contact of the facial bone structure with both violin and viola enhances the perception of the overtones and increases the vivid quality of the 'fundamental' keys in both their major and minor mode. Only the cello and bass escape this deceptive contact, but even here the proximity of the ear to the production of the sound makes truly analytical hearing extremely difficult.

Once in combination with four or more similar instruments, individual string sounds blend together and take on a corporate intonation, which is why many players and teachers consider orchestral string playing to be detrimental to personal intonation – an argument that will be considered more fully in a moment. This ability to combine has an obvious tendency to submerge the individual sound, progressively lessening the dominance of each single contribution as the section increases in number, and making any individual control of intonation increasingly difficult. The section will be drawn towards the perceived intonation of the corporate sound, and inexperienced players, not fully conversant with the techniques of section playing, will also be prey to the danger of separating their own sound in an almost unconscious effort to hear individual intonation more clearly.

There is one guaranteed way of contriving this separation and that is by utilizing the 'brighter', and more dominant, side of the instrument, either by 'tightening' the sound with the bow a little closer to the bridge or, considerably more dangerous but much more of a temptation, by 'pushing' a fraction sharp. In all circumstances, this 'adjustment' will be most noticeable towards the extremities of the instrumental range (high on the violin and low on the cello and bass), the areas outside the 'easiest' range of hearing, where assimilation of intonation and pitch are at their most critical. On the cello and, to a slightly lesser extent, the bass, notes started low on the instrument, particularly if they are sustained, are prone to this slight sharpening in any event, through the process of adding quality and projection. On the violin, even ignoring the technical difficulties of fingering in such an exacting area of the instrument, any rising passage on the E string will be subject to similar sharp intonation, both in an effort to release the full qualities of this thin and taut string and for the individual player to hear the notes. Separation between strings and wind, where many instruments tend to flatten at the top anyway, is thus inevitable.

But the connotations go even further than this. The aural dominance of the open strings extends to the initial set-up of the instrument, where it is these notes, and these alone, that are tuned. Already the temptation to tune every instrument to its apparent optimum playing quality – its 'brighter', more soloistic side – can be overwhelming. In private practice every instrument will be set to its most generous playing qualities, and to lose even a fraction of this, for whatever reason, demands considerable self-control and discipline.

This seductive organization of a stringed instrument becomes part of the overall feeling a performer has for the instrument, an ultra-sensitive combination of touch, ear and eye that is sufficient to outweigh any scientific logic that might interfere. Thus the strings of the orchestra will most naturally tune a fraction sharp to the oboe A before a note has been played or a problem of performance intonation confronted.

It must be patently clear by now that my consideration of this problem centres around the frailties of human perception and not on the cold facts of science. Fundamentally it is a human problem, albeit probably induced (and certainly abetted) by laws of acoustic science, and it remains, as do almost all things orchestral, outside the scope of measurable action and reaction – which is why no amount of electronic gadgetry can solve it. Thus, it can often become a more difficult problem to deal with than if dogmatic principles of unquestionable rule could be applied, an A that satisfies the strings regularly being fiercely contested by the wind and vice versa. However, particularly in student orchestras, the opportunity arises to instil some basic understanding of the problem and achieve a genuinely successful outcome based on mutual respect and consent. The given A must, however, be generally constant and reliable.

THE OBOE A

Nowadays, apart from the familiar tuning fork, there are two main electronic ways of determining an unfluctuating A: the first is a small, portable machine that can accurately measure the number of vibrations of the given note and produce a read-out on a calibrated scale; and the second is a device that itself emits an electronically induced and unwavering 'note' audible to the whole orchestra.

The first is of use only to the 1st oboe as a means of checking the given A and ensuring that it does not alter at various times during the rehearsal or, indeed, over a number of consecutive repetitions. As such, it can be of great use to inexperienced players who have not yet learned to be confident of their own intuitive feel for the instrument. In many circumstances it is of no less support to the beleaguered professional, who then at least has some tangible evidence with which to repel accusations and disagreements. Beyond this, however, it has no practical use, and certainly does not guarantee similar intonation from the rest of the orchestra.

Use of the second type is pointless for many reasons. In every case, whether it be taken as substitute for the 1st oboe or as a guide for all players, all the previously mentioned variations of personal perception still apply. I can assure you that they are no less likely because the sound is supposedly electronically 'pure'. Coupled with this, it is an 'instrument' of the recording studio (if anywhere!) and cannot be used in concert without offending the sensibility of the orchestra to an unwarranted extent.

I am not partial to the use of any outside guide, except as a reference for the 1st oboe in the original set-up of the instrument, as nothing can ever allow for the vagaries of individual perception. In this respect I will often prime an inexperienced oboist to reserve the perfect A for the wind and make that for the strings almost imperceptibly flat – or perhaps, to put it a less devious way, never err towards sharp. It is also worth reminding the strings, in every circumstance, to tune a shade flat in order to negate the natural tendency discussed above.

It would be worth mentioning at this point that there are many orchestral Leaders and oboe Principals who would firmly argue that, in professional circumstances, there is no real case for an orchestra to tune in the accepted collective sense at all, and certainly not until it has been playing for some fifteen minutes or more. To quote probably the most experienced of all British orchestral leaders: 'Why should we need an A? It's the fingers that do the damage!'

While it may not be wise to transfer similar attitudes into the student orchestra without some allowance for their overall inexperience, the argument provides considerable food for thought.

INDIVIDUAL INTONATION OF STRING PLAYERS

The vexed question of the possible detrimental effect of regular performance within a large ensemble on an individual string player's awareness of personal intonation has been touched on above and is often the subject of heated debate. There can be no doubt that many players (and teachers) unfortunately lay the blame firmly on the ensemble situation without the least consideration of how, or even if, it can be avoided. One is frequently forced to the conclusion that various technical inabilities would probably remain even if the player concerned were to spend an entire performing life in totally isolated conditions of most perfect acoustic.

Nevertheless, the problem certainly exists, and confronts every orchestral player. It is therefore necessary to examine it, however briefly, and try to untangle some of the truth from the myth.

It has been already explained that the combination of more than a small number of similar string instruments results in a corporate, rather than an individual, sound and intonation, and makes it increasingly difficult for the individual player to assess his or her own intonation. In sections comprising between four and ten players, this problem increases in fairly direct proportion to the number of players employed. After that, the difference between twelve players and twenty-two will prove minimal in this regard.

The following are, however, equally contributory factors. Only the most arbitrary decisions of personal intonation can be made from within a section (a) which is so diverse in standard as to include players incapable of producing a clear sound; or (b) where, for whatever reason, a clear sound is not *apparent*; or (c) which, as a whole, is unable to articulate notes and rhythms in a unified manner. These three factors in combination comprise the basic and only tangible reason for the problem. Therein ends the truth.

The myth begins at the point where the word 'difficulty' is confused with 'impossibility'. The difficulty is very largely caused by transferring the same aural perception of the instrument from one medium to another. The assimilation of individual intonation under circumstances of solo playing involves a great deal of concentrated listening and a concurrent narrowing of the hearing process into this one aspect. Slow, individual practice will involve a very close co-ordination of ear, eye and hand and often the temporary removal of production qualities such as *vibrato* and tonal variation. Within the orchestra such a confined method of listening and personal concentration is obviously not possible – equal awareness of balance, integration, ensemble and dynamic level must be maintained at all times – and a more subjective approach is necessary, which places greater emphasis upon trust in the hand's technical accuracy attained (and maintained!) through careful practice. This is directly analogous with solo concert performance, where it is the training and practice that will guarantee any successful intonation, not the mere fact of playing alone.

Thus the hand must be trained to take on a larger proportion of the work often done, in other circumstances, by the ear. It requires no new technique, only the extension of one that is continually employed.

With considerable concentration and perseverance, of course, it is perfectly possible to train the ear to distinguish and define any single sound within almost any combination – especially when all aspects of its production and source are known, as with a player's own sound – in the same way as must already have been accomplished to perceive and relate basic pitch. Gradually, the two techniques in combination come closer together, so that, eventually, the ear can be relied on to maintain almost as powerful and clear an appraisal of intonation in combined playing as it does in individual practice.

As often reiterated, intonation within a large ensemble requires specific appraisal of the sounds relevant to any individual note as well as an understanding of the effect that varying timbres may have on the perceived pitch. It is altogether different from the perception of one instrument in relation to itself or, indeed, in relation to an accompanying ensemble of whatever size. However, the difference lies *only* in appraisals. It causes no alteration to the actual technique of note production. It is therefore vital that a conscious mental adjustment be made to the perception of intonation, as well as training the hand and ear to alter their working relationship slightly in terms of their relative interdependence.

THE TUNING OF THE FULL ORCHESTRA

There are some basic concepts of orchestral tuning that must be considered and, in some cases, clarified. A is used as the note of reference for two, equally important, reasons: firstly, because the note appears as an open string on every stringed instrument; and, secondly, because an example of it occurs close to the middle of the range on all instruments. The A above middle C is used because it fulfils this last requirement for the majority of instruments, including the oboe.

The use of the oboe for reference is not because it is more reliable than any other instrument but rather, because it provides the most clearly perceptible sound to which adjustment can be made. In orchestrations that do not include oboe the responsibility will usually be undertaken by another woodwind instrument or, where no woodwind are included, by a solo violin. The use of any brass instrument to provide the initial A is not recommended (and, in any event, all instruments prove inferior to the oboe for this purpose).

Some understanding of the fundamental purpose of ensemble tuning is essential. It is very important for it to be perceived less as the tuning of individual instruments than of the *orchestra*: the adjustment of basic intonation of the one combined and complete instrument. Although this might appear to be a very subtle distinction it is, in fact, of vital significance to the orchestra, in that it presupposes the initial set-up of the instruments themselves.

Any attempt to fine-tune an instrument that is cold or has not been played for a few minutes prior to adjustment is pointless. It may be possible to attain some general consensus for a short time but, especially in the case of woodwind and brass, as the instrument warms, so its relative intonation will change, and any adjustment that has been made will progressively become redundant.

This is why, in professional orchestras, the general tuning of individual instruments to the oboe A may often appear a more casual process than it actually is, the primary arrangement of each instrument having been carefully accomplished some time before. Neither is the ritual so necessary to the professional in terms of its secondary function: that of gathering concentration and focusing the ear.

The groupings in which corporate tuning is undertaken will vary from one orchestra to the next – anything from the smallest individual sections at a time to the whole orchestra together – but especially in the early stages it is best to separate woodwind, brass and strings, the latter often being subdivided into double basses, followed by cellos plus violas and then violins alone. The main advantage of this further separation is that it allows the lower instruments, especially the basses, the opportunity to hear the A more clearly, without the blanket effect of the upper octave provided by violins and violas. String basses will also take a little longer to tune than the other strings and, because they use natural harmonics to check the A at a more reliable pitch, require as little intervening sound as possible.

For the woodwind and brass it is, of course, essential that the *instrument* be adjusted and *not* simply the individual note. (The whole process is very different from adjusting the intonation of individual notes in performance.) For instruments of the clarinet and flute families this means adjustment of the head joint, fractionally lengthening or shortening the tube length in order to raise or lower the *overall* pitch of the instrument. Double-reed instruments will adjust the reed at the point at which it enters the instrument, pushing in or pulling out the reed tube on the oboe or, similarly, the base of the crook in other cases. The possibilities of adjustment by these methods, while severely limited (hence the importance of strings not pushing sharp) are sufficient to make quite an appreciable difference. In all cases, tuning in this situation by using the embouchure, diaphragm, reed pressure or any means other than some adjustment of the instrument as a whole is totally pointless.

A similar situation exists for the brass, where it is the tube length that must be adjusted via the slides. Here, however, because the natural fundamental of B♭ exists for so many of these instruments, some orchestras use this note as the basis for the brass, thereby requiring the oboe to sound a different note for them than for the rest of the orchestra. While this may be helpful to brass instruments appearing entirely alone, once they are part of an orchestra (or any other mixed ensemble) it is neither entirely necessary nor particularly beneficial, since the overall tuning tends to suffer when the orchestra refers to two different notes.

One cannot argue with the reasoning behind choosing B♭, since in all cases A requires the introduction of a valve into the basic tube-length of the instrument or, in the case of trombones, extreme accuracy in positioning the slide. Even so I have yet to find any improvement in intonation from sections that use it, nor have I encountered any substantial number of experienced orchestral brass players who recommend its use. If B♭ is to be used then it is perhaps best for it to be sounded first, *before* any A has been heard, so that the dominance of the main tuning note is retained by the strings.

The dynamic level at which tuning of the orchestra takes place is also important: it should never be loud. Loud playing will distort the intonation of any note on every instrument, and technical adjustment has always to be made to compensate. In most cases extremely soft playing will require similar alteration. The tuning of the orchestra should be accomplished at the softest level at which the A can be clearly produced without any adjustment of basic production technique, so that the instruments are producing a sound of optimum quality and the oboe A – to which reference should be made continuously – is never obscured.

The dynamic level of tuning is especially important in concert, particularly when tuning between movements of a single work, where the concentration of the audience needs to be maintained. The tuning of all instruments in these circumstances should be quiet and controlled. There should be no sounds made other than those directly necessary for the *checking* of each instrument's tonal organization, and it is very helpful to the continuity of performance if the strings finish on the lower notes of the instrument, and the oboe, after all other sound has ceased, carefully phrases off the sustained A.

One further, easily overlooked requirement remains. It is essential that the wind players of the orchestra, especially the clarinets, know which work is to be rehearsed first, so that they may tune the right instruments. It is counterproductive, to say the least, for a player to spend five minutes patiently tuning the B♭ clarinet only to find that the work to be played requires the A! Similar consideration should be extended to all players of alternative or doubling instruments.

'Artificial' Balance

An intentional augmentation of the number of players used for a work, over and above the number specified by the composer, may occasionally be seen in professional orchestras and is even advocated by some musicians. Such doubling is limited to the woodwind section and occurs most frequently in the symphonic works of Beethoven and Brahms, where the sheer intensity (*not* loudness!) of the required sound is extremely taxing and may occasionally be felt insufficient to balance with a large string section. The practice of doubling in such cases, utilized by some undeniably great conductors, raises a few interesting points which must be fully resolved before any attempt is made to emulate the practice with anything less than world-class players.

Firstly, except in fairly extreme registers, two instruments will not necessarily provide more sound than one, and certainly nothing even approaching a 100 per cent increase. Thus, a string section can obliterate sixteen woodwind instruments just as easily as eight if the passage allows it and if the players feel so inclined. Secondly, players simply doubling a single part will tend to cause a reduction in intensity from each of the instrumentalists involved, rather than the intended increase of projected sound. This is not only because of a psychological impression of divided responsibility. It is also because, for woodwind players, it is far more difficult to hear and control the centre of the sound when the line is doubled by a similar instrument. Thirdly, even a slight variation in intonation will cause the edge of the sound to blur and, consequently, decrease its ability to cut through a dense texture. This last is the most noticeable difference when performed by less capable players as opposed to a first-rate professional section.

Overall the situation will lose more than it gains in almost direct proportion to the standard of players used. The less able the instrumentalists, the greater the loss of clarity, projection and centre in comparison to playing the same passage with single players.

What *might* be apparent is an increase in width of the sound source, which, especially in close proximity to the orchestra, can seem to give a louder dynamic level because of the greater spread of sound. This is a somewhat dangerous illusion, and unlikely to persist at any distance from the orchestra unless the production is superb.

In addition, the provision of extra wind players will not help to project a sound through undisciplined string playing. In fact it will probably only create further confusion by encouraging the strings to place even less emphasis on articulation and rhythmic clarity. Once the vital control of balance, articulation and clarity has been successfully achieved by the strings, then a single wind section will pierce it as easily as a multiple one, probably more easily in most cases. Certainly in student orchestras, the benefits of doubling that may sometimes be made apparent by professional players are most unlikely to be reproduced.

Preliminary Rehearsal

The preliminary rehearsals of any orchestral programme will determine the approach and flexibility of the orchestra with regard to its final performance. It seems to be a frequently ignored fact that it is as important for the orchestra to have some overall view of the work to be performed as it is for the conductor, and there is little worse, for players of any standard, than to be working at some area or passage of a work without any idea of where it lies in relation to the piece as a whole. Rehearsal under these conditions is rarely of benefit.

For this reason it is essential that the orchestra should have *seen* all the notes before real work commences, and that they should have played the work through, however sketchily, with the minimum interruption or comment. It is always instructive for a conductor to see just how much will have put itself right when it is eventually repeated, and how much easier and more logical the process of rehearsal becomes.

For student orchestras the first rehearsal, whether of a short intensive course or one spread over a longer period, should *always* comprise a read-through of one work, usually the major item in the programme, and any remaining time should be used to begin work on it. In the case of a symphony or a work of similar expanse, such early detailed rehearsal need not necessarily be from the very opening. The main consideration should be to use any movement or major section that will show the most benefit in the shortest time span. It should *never*, at this point, concentrate on an isolated instrumental passage.

I would stress that this applies to the very first rehearsal of a programme, before any sectional rehearsals have been undertaken and irrespective of whether the orchestra have previously seen the music. Sectional rehearsals are of little use before the tutors have heard the orchestra, assimilated the strengths and weaknesses of their section in the context of the whole and made some appraisal of the conductor's approach to the work concerned. Even for an experienced professional the individual page looks very different from its sound in performance, and the slightest variation in interpretation, tempo or style can often cause the priorities of each section to be rethought.

With sufficient technique, knowledge and visual persuasion, it is possible for the conductor to guide the orchestra successfully through a reading of any work in standard notation, with minimum interruption. Only when works employ a radically different technical language – unfamiliar signs and symbols, rare methods of sound production or eccentric designs of visual representation – do players need to approach the work in isolation before a collective appraisal can be attempted.

Once the first rehearsal has been completed then, in the case of a residential or intensive course, sectional rehearsals may take priority for about the first third of the total rehearsal period, but it is important to make sure that the orchestra continues to play regularly together as a group. In this way every note of a programme should have been covered in the first three or four full rehearsals, while some detailed work will also have commenced. The exact amount of time this requires will obviously depend on the number and length of the works to be performed as well as the duration of each rehearsal.

Sectional Rehearsal

While it is worth considering the relevance and beneficial effect of sectional rehearsals on the overall result, specific techniques (either in terms of method or results) are the province of the individual specialist tutor and, as such, require no elucidation here.

Despite their enormous benefit to the players, sectional rehearsals can be something of a double-edged sword if not handled very carefully. The unavoidable focusing of attention on isolated passages and awkward fragments can, especially in the strings, cause weaker players to lose confidence rather than gain it. Everything depends on the attitude of the tutor. The section that shows improvement will be the one whose tutor has fostered the confidence of the less experienced players, in conjunction with a feeling of responsibility from the others. There will be few variations in the amount of work individual tutors get through or the choice of passages to which they devote most time, but their attitude, and the way the section responds to them, will prove to be of vital significance. All too few have the ability to impart technical information, musicianship, balance and quality side by side with the essential courage and self-reliance needed to implement them.

For the strings, it is extremely important to rehearse within the confines of the individual sections. Most string parts are very demanding and all contain an enormous amount of sustained playing which can only be unravelled in circumstances where the needs of the full orchestra are not being concurrently addressed. Quite apart from mastering the actual notes, the players are given the opportunity to refine the style and subtlety of their orchestral bowing and to gain some understanding of the need for corporate musical responsibility and support.

For woodwind it is less crucial to work in small groups of individual instruments, and much can be accomplished in full sectionals. If sufficient time is available, some work with specialist tutors of each instrument should be considered, but the priority for these players is that of working together as a group to confront the difficulties of combined intonation and balance. Nonetheless, it is invaluable to have four specialist tutors to hand, so that specific difficulties relating to each woodwind instrument can be dealt with.

As already mentioned, horns are a separate case and they require a tutor to themselves, irrespective of whether only one has been allocated to the woodwind, and one to brass. The demands on the horn section are usually quite distinct from those confronting the other groups, and the tutor's initial priority is to mould the players into a successful and combined section. Once some work has been done in glorious isolation then the section can very usefully join up with either woodwind or brass. Ideally, they should divide their time between the two, but if only one combined rehearsal may be contemplated then, in most repertoire, a coupling with the woodwind will probably prove most useful.

As with the woodwind, the brass will certainly be rehearsed as a group (along with any subsidiary brass instruments that may be required). For the majority of repertoire, the brass will not need to spend a great deal of time in sectionals for each instrument separately. Intonation, balance and interdependence need to be rehearsed across the entire section.

It is rare (and undesirable) for timpani to be separated from percussion. Because the players interchange roles (most often including timpani) for various pieces in the programme, each will need to learn the techniques pertinent to the other. This is the section that most often finds itself with too much sectional time, but the whole process should be viewed as much as a percussion class as a rehearsal of particular repertoire.

For all sections, responsibility extends beyond the confines of the notes contained in the programme, and a good tutor will direct them in matters of preparation, approach, pacing, conservation of energy and similar indirect aspects of performance. These less-considered essentials are of particular relevance to instrumentalists faced with extended periods of inactivity, where the actual notes to be played are neither numerous nor, in themselves, demanding. As an example I should, perhaps, quote the case of two young trumpeters faced with the restricted (but by no means easy) parts of Dvořák *Symphony no. 8*. The somewhat inexperienced tutor working with them at the time took the very familiar parts at face value, as if they were to be played by a professional section, and failed to consider the associated pitfalls of playing these isolated and exposed entries in concert. A false confidence was engendered, along with a somewhat dismissive attitude to the notes, which no amount of warning in full rehearsal could temper – the brass group will emulate the attitude of a professional player more quickly than any other section. At the performance, bereft of even the slightest idea of how to approach and set themselves for the part, hardly a single entry worked.

For individual woodwind, horn and brass players, knowing how to prepare for a passage so that it stands the greatest possible chance of success is as important as practising the notes.

As the work achieved in sectional rehearsal progresses, it becomes increasingly important that it is not nullified by demands placed on the orchestra in full rehearsal. This is a further argument (if any were needed) for the interspersing of sectional and full rehearsals and the retaining of tutors over as long a period as possible. It is essential that the tutors have a clear idea of the demands placed on their section, not only in relation to the music, but also in the attitude, consideration and style of the conductor, for it is this that will determine the boundaries of the performing standard and, therefore, the relevance and degree of subtlety of the players' work. If this aspect of the conductor's art is ignored, then sectional rehearsals might as well be dispensed with altogether for all the constructive use they will be.

Given the limitations on the total time available for rehearsal, the number of sectional rehearsals will be broadly determined by the needs of the strings, a criterion that often allows more time than is strictly necessary for other orchestral sections. Some thought must be given as to how the wind and percussion sections should best use this extra time, since simply to repeat work on the programme will certainly prove counter-productive. Often tutors will provide other ensemble material which may be used to reaffirm the same playing principles while providing a welcome change of notes. Or they might choose to explore other technical aspects of the instrument, or even to give individual help to players. Whatever option is chosen, it should never be forgotten that it *is* possible to let the players have one session free. Many wind players will never have played for such sustained periods before, and might actually *need* the time to recuperate. Decisions must be made based on what is best for the orchestra, rather than whether some players have put in more time than others.

It is necessary to have at least one rehearsal for the full string group, even when rehearsal time is undesirably restricted. It will be of enormous benefit to the whole orchestra, as the section's techniques of balance, support and musical co-operation can only truly be refined in these circumstances. The priority of such a session, however, *must* be to concentrate on every aspect of the sound, rather than to engage in further discussion of bowings and fingerings.

Intermediate Rehearsal

The full rehearsals between the first reading of a concert programme and the day of the first performance must be carefully handled, so that the orchestra can be brought to a level of playing and self-assurance that is close to its peak – close enough for adrenalin, concert atmosphere and total concentration to do the rest. For a conductor, this involves a multitude of intuitive skills, considerable risk and apparent limitless confidence in the orchestra's progress and ability (a confidence that may well not be so unshakeable in the privacy of one's hotel room). Be that as it may, there are certain guidelines around which the instant decisions, common experience, flashes of inspiration and personal anguish may be fashioned.

The prime objective of rehearsal should always be the gradual approach to a fully integrated orchestral technique, where each player is both a support and a driving force for the rest, and each sound has meaning and relevance. This is what orchestral performance is all about, but only the world's greatest orchestras are able to achieve this ideal with no more rehearsal than is needed to rediscover familiarity with the works to be played. However, the criteria of rehearsal remain the same, and nothing should be rehearsed just for the sake of it, or outside the overriding framework of orchestral understanding.

There is a need for the orchestra to discover the broad limits of its own performing ability (and again, we are not speaking in terms of notes or difficult passage-work, but of sound, combination and dynamic levels). All rehearsal must guide the orchestra towards a corporate technique that will be pertinent in performance of a given programme, initially by implanting notions of style and technique that will form the basis of the whole orchestral sound, rather than dissecting individual passages in specific works. As the relevance of the sound is understood and applied, the general craft will gradually be absorbed into the fundamental style of the orchestra. This is why a programme exhibiting some stylistic similarities is often so successful, and why an inexperienced orchestra finds it so difficult to handle one which calls for very diverse stylistic techniques.

Emphasis must be given to the production, control and shaping of sound, because techniques of articulation, intonation and combination depend on them. To attempt to structure a performance from the initial standpoint of notational accuracy will result only in an insubstantial framework, unsupported by the substance of sound that makes it intelligible.

It is not my intention to dictate any rehearsal format or give the impression that similar results will not be forthcoming without similar rehearsal techniques. However, it does seem only common sense that the majority of any rehearsal should be spent playing, rather than talking about it. Obviously certain things will need to be explained, sometimes in detail, but however clear the verbal explanation, only by reproducing it musically will any result be obtained. This is analogous to the teaching precept: 'What you hear, you learn; what you do, you understand'. Essentially, a single sentence should suffice in most situations, and a word in more than half of the remainder.

Verbal explanation not only interrupts the flow of music but also the sensibility and vitality that it generates. The continuity of musical expression should not be sacrificed by unavoidable interruption, and the verbal communication should, to some extent, reflect the mood of that to which it refers. Thus, in a very broad sense, one would speak faster, and with more animation, when making a point relevant to a fast movement than to a slow one. Whatever is said, however, should be clearly audible to *all* the orchestra, even if it only directly applies to one section or even one player. It is not possible to expect an orchestra to play as a unit unless they are treated as a unit, and nothing is more frustrating than the feeling of being excluded from a rehearsal because you are unable to hear what is being rehearsed or why. Besides which, something said to the 1st violins might well be of relevance to the third percussion player – if only in determining what stage in the piece the rehearsal has reached (most percussion parts are notoriously poorly cued). It is also important to enunciate rehearsal numbers clearly, and to avoid confusion over the relative number of bars before or after them that rehearsal is intended to start. It is so much quicker to say the reference letter first and then to count aloud before or after it – 'Before A; two, four, six, *seven* bars'. The players will by then have found the place and immediately be ready to recommence. Nine seconds of silence with the head in the score, followed by an abrupt '27 before W' is to court total confusion. The neglect of such apparently minor irrelevancies can waste a great deal of valuable time as well as putting the concentration of the orchestra at risk.

There are two aspects of rehearsal, broadly related to the best use of time, that all orchestras find difficult to develop. Firstly, what has been rehearsed in one context will invariably apply exactly to any repetition later in the work. Thus, from a conductor's point of view, it is nothing short of infuriating to have rehearsed (for example) the exposition of a symphony only to have to rehearse it again in the recapitulation. This exposes, unfortunately, the amount of rehearsal that is accepted in relation to the page and the particular signs appearing on it, rather than to the sound. Secondly, something that has *not* been rehearsed is probably right as it is. It is no less frustrating to be asked, after three days of rehearsals, whether the articulation or phrasing that has been apparent since day one is actually what is wanted!

But there is also an aspect that applies the other way round. The conductor must take responsibility for the edition that is used. Especially in the Classical repertoire, if particular phrasing, bowing, or articulation is required beyond the normal adjustments, then either a marked set of parts must be supplied or those that exist accepted. It is not reasonable to spend orchestral rehearsal time getting the players to re-mark an entire copy. It is also counter-productive because the players will be totally bored by the exercise and this will show in performance.

Time must always be given for new concepts of performance to sink in, and no passage should be 'worked to death'. It is better by far to initiate the process and then refine it a little at a later rehearsal, allowing the players time to digest the technique and then reproduce it in context, a contingency which will often prove to be of considerable benefit to the surrounding music as well.

This process of repetition and refinement requires a conductor to be able to proportion the rehearsal time, mindful of the minimum time that should be devoted to each piece and, therefore, the speed at which work must be achieved. Frequent adjustments to this mental schedule need to be made, as musical opportunities arise where it might be beneficial to spend a little longer on one part, or possible to economize in relation to another. Increasingly subtle and detailed work may be undertaken as the orchestra progresses, but not before the aspects of sound and communication fundamental to the performance of each work are attained.

Orchestral Flexibility

It has already been stated that rehearsal should essentially be a matter of showing *where* something goes rather than *how* it goes. The approach should always encourage ensemble, balance, sound and response within a basic framework of an interpretation, but the final element can only be added when all other necessary components – the work, the performers *and* the audience – are assembled. Under these conditions every piece will exhibit what might best be termed a 'concert life': a totality of substance and meaning brought about by the interaction of performers and audience, and displayed through the multiple tiny variations of phrasing, sound, energy and drive that this engenders. The purpose of all rehearsal is to formulate a condition where the performers are capable of the flexibility and sensitivity necessary to acheive this.

For student orchestras this is a peripheral concept and one that cannot be directly rehearsed, because it involves the fusion of all the techniques discussed in these pages (and many others), along with the confidence and ability to react to each other immediately and unselfconsciously. Nonetheless, something of this awareness and malleable cohesion can (indeed, must) become a part of the performance technique of every orchestra.

Initially, this can most easily be achieved through the discipline of accompanying concerti. The immediacy of the solo line and the realization that it must be accompanied in terms of balance and *rubato* (both rehearsed and instantaneous) serve to wrench the players' attention from their own individual lines towards wider appreciation of the whole. Once the players have achieved some flexibility in supporting such an obvious solo line, this can be diverted to the more subtle and ever-changing responsibilities of the orchestra alone. Of course, it is possible to develop this essential facet of performance without the aid of a soloist, and very often has to be, but it is distinctly more difficult and will take considerably longer.

Obviously the essential ingredient is concentrated listening on the part of every member of the orchestra, and for this, two things are absolutely vital: the players must be sufficiently familiar with the printed page to concentrate on the total, rather than the individual sound; and they must be able to perform each section as a whole, and not be constrained by having to find the notes. Any passage not conceived as an entity will prove impossible to shape naturally, because any flexibility within the phrase will be unexpected and, therefore, illogical. A similar problem will arise with passages in which players do not display some degree of technical fluency. These limitations always cause problems, regardless of whether the passage is for a solo instrument alone, clearly defined theme and accompaniment, or totally integrated orchestral movement.

Above all else, the conductor must therefore clarify the shape of the phrase and the direction of each passage. The importance of the initial read-through of a piece before any detailed work is even considered becomes doubly clear. In order to achieve fluency, it is essential to have an understanding of the direction and momentum of the phrase or passage. Notes do not come simply by constant practice of the fingering that provides them, but by an acceptance of their relative status within the structure.

Technically this is a tricky period for the conductor because it is a thin line that divides the point at which attention must be momentarily deflected from the shape of a passage in order to refine its component parts. A misjudgement here might well take some time to rectify and there is no hard and fast rule. Certainly to err on the side of later rather than sooner will achieve most success in the majority of cases.

The Final (Pre-Concert or Dress) Rehearsal

The final rehearsal on the day of a concert is very often of critical importance to the orchestra's confidence and musical self-esteem. It is crucial that this rehearsal be dedicated to the needs of the orchestra and soloist (if there is one), rather than those of the conductor, administration, hall porter or anyone else. On this occasion, the well-being of the orchestra comes above *everything* else.

When there is a soloist, the choice of starting time for rehearsal of the concerto is up to him or her. Some soloists prefer to rehearse early and go away to rest, while others prefer as little time as possible between rehearsal and concert: the choice is theirs, and theirs alone. If the luxury of specifying a time is offered to the conductor, then, generally, the latter portion of the rehearsal will tend to be most convenient. The time allowed for rehearsal of the concerto should never be less than an hour and always at least half-an-hour longer than the concerto takes to play through, regardless of how much pressure this puts on the conductor (and *only* the conductor – it must never be transmitted to the orchestra at this stage) to complete the rest of the programme. I believe this to be an inviolate rule. The occasional five minutes one way or the other is not going to cause great distress, but that is all. Basically, one times a pre-concert, three-hour rehearsal to correspond with this formula and one makes it work. If this is beyond the powers of the conductor, whatever the programme, then he or she has no business being there.

The order of the final rehearsal should be arranged before the penultimate rehearsal, and fairly accurate timings for the start of each piece decided upon. The schedule must then be adhered to (a situation that makes the whole rehearsal much easier for the conductor to time) and the orchestra informed, even if it is known that they will all arrive together on the same bus. There is certain to be someone who is not involved in one or more pieces, and there is nothing worse than to unpack an instrument, warm it up and sit down, only to find that you are not required for two hours. It really does affect subsequent performance.

If the final rehearsal is the only one in the concert venue, as so often happens, then it is best to start with a work the orchestra knows well and with which they are fairly confident. Ideally, they should be allowed to play all of it, or (in the case of a symphony) at least one movement, without interruption, and this time can be used to gauge the acoustic and to determine what idiosyncrasies of balance, timing and clarity the players might be experiencing. An orchestra will always respond most quickly to adjustments that they think are the fault of the hall rather than their own, and such an opportunity should be seized. The salient points with regard to the acoustic can be made first – shorter, more clear and precise playing in a resonant ambience; concentration on quality above all else in a dry one – but the attributes of the hall can then be used as a justification for rehearsal almost throughout.

A very resonant acoustic will usually cause an orchestra to drag in slow-moving music, especially where the main movement is controlled by strings, because of the aural delay experienced by players at some distance from the centre. In fast passages the opposite is true; the tendency will be to rush, but the reason for it remains the same. Apart from the fact that short notes will need to be *very* short and phrasing somewhat exaggerated, the orchestra may have to consider a much more vertically orientated rhythm than in other halls, playing very much with what they see, rather than what they hear. As far as balance is concerned, bass notes will show a propensity to cover other sounds, especially when sustained. This will remain true at all dynamic levels and proves to be one of the most trying idiosyncrasies for the players to overcome.

The less resonant the acoustic, the more emphasis must be placed on the quality of sound leaving the instrument, since sounds become proportionately more reliant on the projection of the source as the reverberation provided by the hall diminishes. Balance again becomes critical, although more because of apparent instrumental separation than undue emphasis of certain ranges. The unaccustomed gaps in the sound will again tempt the orchestra to rush, curtailing rests and closing the distance between any notes that are short. Depending on the degree of dryness in the response, the ends of notes will appear to lose much of their natural phrasing, sounding clipped as the acoustic adds less 'bloom' to the basic production. In the worst circumstances, *all* qualities of projection, centre, phrasing and clarity will have to be instilled in every note by every player.

A hall with a very dry acoustic is, from everyone's point of view, best pulled down and rebuilt. It is the most depressing and pointless exercise that any musician can experience and only a professional orchestra can deal with it at all successfully. The sound feels as if it is drawn away from the instrument at all times and, no matter how hard the player might work, no tangible result is forthcoming. The only way to cope is to relax, produce what is known by experience to be an even and controlled sound, and look forward to a better hall tomorrow! An inexperienced orchestra will attempt to match this feeling of inadequacy with the production of a harder, more concentrated sound, chasing the qualities of warmth and sonority which elude them – a solution as musically divisive as it is fruitless. Fundamentally, the whole situation should simply be avoided.

21 PERFORMANCE

It is not truly possible to separate orchestral techniques into those pertaining to rehearsal and those to performance. All are *playing* techniques and, as such, must relate to performance, regardless of whether this constitutes the public presentation of the finished article or various stages in its preparation. In any case, only the necessity of working to a prearranged date and time separate the two, since no performance is, strictly speaking, a finished article. The distinction implied by the heading of this chapter is therefore a fine one, in that its purpose will be to consider some aspects of using and adjusting the natural sound, rather than methods of invoking various techniques of production.

The sound produced by an orchestra, a section or even a single individual will alter depending on the circumstances surrounding its production. Some examples of the immediate effect a conductor's gesture may have on the sound have already been discussed, but mainly in the context of initial reaction and not in the more subtle and nebulous terms of either continuous or intermittent influence. To understand these, one needs to explore some of the options available and consider the reasons for their existence.

Influencing the Sound

Musical sound may be influenced by a wide variety of direct and indirect factors. Quite apart from techniques employed by the instrumentalist to elicit particular qualities of tone and colour from an instrument, there are subtle changes brought about by more subconscious reaction to various superficial causes.

As a very obvious example, one might cite the automatic increase in output occasioned by a passage of technical fluency and confidence, or the similar decrease in one that is more ill at ease. There will be a noticeable contrast, not only in dynamic level but also in sound and tone quality, between the two.

Although not always so pronounced, a similar effect can be perceived in the reaction of players to tempo and structure. A musically confident phrase will tend to exhibit a full sonority, whereas one where the shaping is less secure will sound more tentative in its delivery. Both these phenomena arise from an identical source – a subliminal change in the technique of production caused by an alteration in the players' mental approach to the passage.

These indirect modifications will be most apparent when sections of instruments play together. Confidence in the direction of the phrase will release a freedom of performance born out of a corresponding reduction in the concentration needed simply to stay together. This situation can very often be perceived from the opposite angle with inexperienced orchestras – having rehearsed an awkward passage in order to improve ensemble, one might well then have to reinstate the sound.

Many passages, however, present no great problems of ensemble, and this is where the 'cause and effect' will come into its own, and much may be deduced from the changes in tone quality that appear when a group of players perform them unencumbered by the 'restrictions' of a beat. This can be illustrated by *Ex. 21.1*, the opening of Dvořák *Symphony no. 8*.

Most cello sections of average ability will intuitively play this phrase much as the composer intended. It is musically intelligible and, once heard, memor-

EX. 21.1

EX. 21.1 (continued)

able and highly expressive. It will, however, exhibit a clearly audible change in quality when played at slightly different tempi. With the whole orchestra left to themselves (just a first beat to help them start together and a fluid 'accompanying' second beat, followed by complete withdrawal), the passage will exhibit a warm, free tone, frequently well balanced across the cello section, and the tempo will settle into one allowing very natural length and speed of bow. In this situation time will always be found within the phrase for the natural placing of the structure. At a slightly slower speed the tone will 'centre' and tighten fractionally as the bow speed is reduced and the corners are initially 'turned' rather than felt. At a faster tempo the sound becomes a little more diffused as the production is ever so slightly hurried. Any extreme choice of tempo will exhibit a proportional increase of these same results.

It is in this aspect of performance that professional orchestras excel. Within reasonable limits, the required sound will be produced in all circumstances. Even here, however, it would be hard to disguise the freedom of sound that appears at a tempo most naturally suited to the production qualities of the instrument.

At this point it must be very firmly stated that these are merely resulting alterations in the basic sound, and do *not* imply that there is anything wrong with variations in tempi chosen by different interpreters. It should also, perhaps, be added that the described clear differences are not just a matter of opinion but an oft-proven fact. I have used this phrase many times, along with some from other works, with a variety of orchestras simply to demonstrate to student conductors this one facet of sound production. In every case the same clearly audible result has been achieved without ever priming the orchestra, or intimating the desired effect beforehand.

The situation arises to a greater or lesser degree in every phrase, whether for full orchestra or solo instrument, and it needs careful consideration, especially when dealing with student orchestras. If an easy, flowing, warm sound is required, the conductor must be prepared to 'ride' the orchestra to some extent, fully aware of what any adjustment in movement will bring forth in terms of sound. Quite obviously, vastly different qualities of sound production may be rehearsed into the orchestra and, indeed, maintained through a wide range of tempi, but it is important for the conductor to be aware of the extent to which the players' technique is having to compensate for the difference in sound that a chosen speed of performance might instinctively produce. This is particularly true for wind players where some choices of tempo could well necessitate a complete reappraisal of the points at which breath may be taken. Many examples which make this danger abundantly clear have already been given in the chapters on woodwind and brass.

Influencing the Movement

There are few *accelerandi* and *rallentandi* that do not utilize some inbuilt momentum of the phrase. Although the inexperienced conductor may often find movement of this kind difficult to control, it is in fact not so if the natural movement of the phrase is used at the right moment. This applies to variation in either direction. After all, one spends a large proportion of rehearsal time imploring an inexperienced orchestra either not to rush or not to drag, so the invocation of whichever natural tendency might be required should not be too difficult. In practice, of course, it is never quite that easy, some perverse law dictating that such movement is only successfully avoided at the one point it is needed. However, the principle remains true and must be exploited.

Both rhythm and harmony play their part. A dropping phrase or figuration comprising short note-lengths will always demonstrate a propensity to rush, as will most phrases that are heading towards obvious tonic harmony, especially if they involve repeated chords. Short, insistent rhythmic movement, where the last note is longer than those preceding it, is prone to the same fault, along with almost any passage of sequential movement. Repeated notes of long duration, however, display an opposite tendency and, similarly, passages that involve movement immediately after a bar-line or main beat. Sustained *legato* movement in minor tonality can also usually be relied on to slow down.

Although none of the foregoing can be said to constitute hard and fast rules, they are some of the more basic examples of musical structure that may generally be guaranteed to cause distortion.

MOVEMENT FORWARD

In the 13-bar *accelerando* from early in the first movement of Bartók *Concerto for Orchestra* (*Ex. 21.2*), some of the above-mentioned facets may be seen in characteristic light.

The repeated figure in the lower strings will show a natural inclination to be rushed slightly because of the dropping interval of the last two notes. A

EX. 21.2

EX. 21.2 (continued)

similar tendency is noticeable in the rising wind figuration, where, in the attempt to restart each figure (again a falling interval), the last note will be subject to shortening. The slightest inducement on the part of the conductor to place the bar-line a fraction early will be enough to make both figures push forward. Indeed, were it not for the irregular and well-defined trumpet line, any attempt at holding this passage in a controlled tempo would prove quite difficult. The trumpets themselves must go with the prevailing movement, in this case helped by the shortening of the rests and obvious forward drive of the note-lengths. The reiterated octaves of the horns are most likely to drag behind here, since long, repeated notes are subject to late movement and lack of initial clarity.

EX. 21.3

The conductor needs to keep the beat small and confined, just pushing the first few bar-lines. After that it would be very unlikely that anyone could stop the passage gathering pace. Obviously the last six bars or so (the exact point depending on the conductor's technique and fluency) need to be shown as one beat per bar.

Many passages of increasing speed contain similar structural or harmonic patterns that require no more than an exaggeration of their natural flow to make them work. However, some have an equal propensity for movement in both directions, and it is these that can cause problems for many conductors.

The famous *accelerando* into the *coda* of the last movement of Beethoven *Symphony no. 5* is a case in point (*Ex. 21.3*).

Taking the woodwind and horn phrase first, the opportunity for late playing, even at a steady tempo, can clearly be seen. Syncopated figures are notorious, and an inexperienced section will almost certainly breathe (or at least relax) at every rest, making movement even more slovenly than it might naturally be. However, the strings, later to be joined by contrabassoon, trumpets and drums, have the dominant rhythm. (NB the scores that print the trumpet entry note on the last beat of the bar are unquestionably wrong. It must be identical in rhythm to that of the timpani.) It is the string line that will take

EX. 21.3 (continued)

EX. 21.3 (continued)

the *accelerando* forward, using the last two natural four-bar divisions of a twelve-bar phrase, and the successful outcome will be found to depend as much on control of balance as of movement. Again, 'one in a bar' four, five or six bars before the *Presto* is essential.

These last two examples (*Exx. 21.2* and *21.3*), while not easy, occur close enough to the new tempo for a clear knowledge of the ultimate speed and the necessary increase to be retained. In *accelerandi* of greater length the problem is exacerbated. Probably the most famous example of this occurs at the end of the first section and virtually *throughout* the second section of Sibelius *Symphony no. 5*, a passage that requires an even and progressive increase in speed over some 402 bars from *molto moderato* to *presto*.

Unlike the technique discussed above, where a gentle push from the conductor is virtually enough to start the orchestra moving, here absolute control must be maintained. A complete grasp of the span of the passage is essential, to the point where almost any bar could be started at exactly the right relative tempo. Beyond this, it requires from the conductor a rhythmic technique that can only be born of practice (even conductors must practise some things). Given the complexity of the writing, the passage will only work if the technique can be relied upon to take the orchestra evenly from one speed to another almost automatically, so that the conductor's total concentration can focus on ensemble, balance, phrasing and dynamic level. Over a passage of this length it is no easy task, but it is definitely possible and quite essential.

MOVEMENT BACK

In the case of slowing down, the process involved is similar, although it can sometimes prove more awkward because of the ease with which it can happen suddenly, if only slightly misplaced, or spasmodically, if the wrong notes of the phrase are extended.

Almost always, any reduction in speed should be effected through cherishing the naturally weaker notes of the passage, especially the extension of notes of smaller value within the beat. In *Ex. 21.4*, an awkward *rallentando* over two bars from Elgar concert overture *Cockaigne*, deliberate care of the short notes is really all that is needed to begin control of the momentum of the phrase and ease the passage back naturally.

It is all too easy here to extend only the notes between the figuration (the F naturals) and thereby provide a series of ever-extending short pauses. Although the feeling of repose on each of these notes is essential, the passage must broaden evenly, each note providing its neighbour with a clear example of the relative speed required of the following note.

Such logic in the relationship of one note to another is vital to the performance of any slackening in speed and, once understood, not only guarantees the natural line of a *rallentando* but also prohibits its accidental use in passages where a composer has inserted one by use of extended note-values. Any additional *rallentando* in these circumstances would obviously go against the composer's intentions.

In general, the use of protracted movement is more often employed in the *rubato* sense of expanding a passage in order to delay, and thereby heighten, the effect of new harmony or tone colour, whereas the *accelerando* will much more often be solely related to speed. Even when *rallentando* is simply used in

poco rall. al
Fl 1 2
Ob 1 2
Cl 1 2
Bn 1 2
DBn 3
Hn 1 2
Hn 3 4
Cnt 1 2
Tbn 1 2
Tbn 3 Tba
a 2
Timp
Vl I II
Vla
Vc DB
(DB unison)
(DB octaves)
dim.
ff
p
tr
(score in C)

EX. 21.4

EX. 21.4 (continued)

a passage for reasons of cadential approach, as in Variation I from Elgar *'Enigma' Variations* (*Ex. 21.5*), great care must be taken to maintain the natural flow (see page 730).

The line of the phrase must be continued across the second and third bars, both for reasons of musical purity and also to maintain the rhythmic pulse without which the composer's delicate use of syncopation would pass unnoticed.

EX. 21.5

It is in expansion of this type that, so often, *two* distinct *rallentandi* are noticeable, each undermining the effect of the other. Thus one must approach bars similar to *Ex. 21.6*, from Dukas *La Péri*, with considerable forethought, since the addition of written instructions alongside altered note values can very easily destroy the musical purpose.

Within such a phrase, it is important to find the *true* line of expansion – that of the thematic continuation, which in this case can easily be submerged by the rising chromatic decoration. Without the 1st violin line, the continuity of the phrase played by cor anglais, 1st bassoon and 2nd violins would become

EX. 21.6

far more obvious, and it is this which holds the key to this corner. A natural relaxation of tempo based on this line alone will provide the logic for the direction of the phrase and, therefore, the framework on which the *rubato* can be built. Some exaggeration of the last two beats may then be contemplated in direct relationship to the entire structural movement rather than the demands of one isolated line.

There are many similar examples where the real controlling force of tempo variation is not always as obvious as it may at first seem, but the ear will usually be subconsciously aware of it and, if it is mishandled, be disturbed by a feeling of disorientation.

The measured *rallentando*, taking the tempo from one speed to another in exact ratio, is just as difficult to handle as that considered earlier in terms of *accelerando*. For a clear example of it we must, once again, turn to Sibelius, this time a section in the *Symphony no. 7* (*Ex. 21.7*, see pages 732–3)

Here again, this passage requires a complete understanding of the span of the entire work and a clear knowledge of the two tempi relative to one another. Once more, it is the conductor's technique that must be relied on to provide the framework for a totally even and controlled slackening of tempo which arrives at exactly the desired speed. As in previous examples, it is the expansion of the notes *between* the main beats (the second and third notes of each triplet figure) that will ensure success but, as with all *rallentandi*, it requires extreme aural concentration and an awareness of ensemble from every player – it cannot be forced. Subdivision into triplet beats will be found necessary at the point where crotchet equals quaver, (𝅗𝅥=♩.), widening into minim beats on, or around, rehearsal letter L.

(Vivacissimo)
Timp
Vl I
Vl II
Vla
Vc
DB
tr
ppp
p
mf
f
pp
mp
rallentando al
pppp

EX. 21.7

EX. 21.7 (continued)

From the conductor's point of view, this passage calls for maximum control of the notes around each beat (the most essential and elusive of all techniques of gesture) and cannot be effected by use of the 'band-master beat', which will only show the rough position of every third note in retrospect, and will be devoid of any direction as to how much variation is needed to arrive there.

TEXTUAL INSTRUCTIONS

It would, perhaps, be unwise to leave this section without some brief reference to the numerous and varied written instructions that may be found attached to passages of tempo alteration, many of which can be seen in the above examples.

Of Italian words used to indicate a slackening in speed *rallentando*, *ritardando*, *ritenuto* and their respective abbreviations – *rall.*, *ritard.* and *rit.* or *riten.* – are most frequently encountered. The first two are interchangeable and mean effectively the same (gradually slowing down/getting slower and slower). *Ritenuto* however, has a proper meaning similar to that of *meno mosso* (held back/in slower tempo), and although often used incorrectly (especially, one suspects, in its abbreviated form), it can well mean just that. It is interesting, for example, that Tchaikovsky uses this word throughout the heavily marked slow movement of the *Symphony no. 5* but *rallentando* in what might at first be considered similar places in the *Symphony no. 6* where indeed both terms are in evidence. Although interpretative conclusions might well be reached that treat both directions alike, the possibility that some positive distinction between the two is intended cannot summarily be ignored.

Within the same general meaning of slackening speed, *slargando* and *slentando* (growing slower) appear infrequently enough to be generally unambiguous, while the terms *allargando* and *largando* (growing broader) usually imply a somewhat more marked and expansive approach to the passage itself, and are rarely used to indicate a gradual slowing of a passage as an approach to either a cadence or a new section.

Similar inconsistencies may be found in the use of Italian terms associated with forward movement, only *accelerando* (accelerating) strictly meaning a gradual increase in speed. *Stringendo* (squeezing/pressing), *affrettando* (hurrying) and *incalzando* (pursuing hotly/warming up) truthfully imply a more sudden acceleration. Once again, interpretation of a composer's intention requires careful thought, not only in terms of any specific passage but also how a particular word is used most frequently by that composer.

The addition of some qualification such as *poco a poco* (little by little) to any of the above removes any possibility of doubt, and will often give a much clearer illustration of the musical feeling implied, especially when used in such glorious opposition as, for example, *poco a poco meno lento*.

It is largely in the more expansive musical expression of the second half of the nineteenth century that such ambiguities began to arise in the interpretation of Italian terms. These were as much a by-product of the desire to induce a more flexible approach to the rhythmic structure as the result of accidental misuse. It was during this period that many of the more Romantically inclined composers began to mark scores in their native language, so that subtleties of movement could be more fluently expressed. Thus while Brahms predominantly maintained the use of traditional Italian in his orchestral works, Mahler continued the practice of later Wagner, and turned to his native German for instructions of pace in all his compositions. Similarly,

French was used by Debussy, Dukas and Ravel (see *Ex. 21.6* above, where especially *cédez* [yield] is highly evocative), and English and Russian composers also invoked their natural tongues.

The Illusion of Tempo

Apparent speed, whether pertaining to one short passage or an entire work, depends on many interrelated criteria but, certainly initially, its aural perception comes through the relative time-span of note movement, most usually in association with some form of harmonic structure. Thus, moderately rapid repetition of a single note, devoid of all rhythmic emphasis, will take time to be correlated aurally into some arbitrary repeated rhythmic pattern, whereas similar performance of a basic five-finger exercise will establish a rhythm almost immediately, through its harmonic relationship with tonic and dominant notes of the scale. This natural assimilation of closely related notes into rhythmic patterns will provide a very obvious 'pulse' which, in turn, will determine the projected tempo of the music. Neither of these need have any direct relationship to the 'beat' as far as the written structure of note-lengths and bar-lines is concerned.

In *Ex. 21.8* the opening of the third movement of Tchaikovsky *Symphony no. 4*, the aural collation of notes in groups of four will always be clear, largely because of the obvious change in direction of the notes at the first bar-line, which accentuates the strong melodic structure.

EX. 21.8

Were this passage to be composed of random, harmonically unrelated notes, then the pulse would take a little longer to assert itself. Nevertheless, however clear the pulse of this example, the overall rhythm from the listener's point of view might well be taken as four groups of semiquavers (hearing the quoted eight bars as two of 4/4), or two groups of quavers (four bars of 2/2), or any of a number of other possible combinations. The conductor's decision to show the passage in one or two 'beats' per bar will make no difference to this aural appraisal of the fundamental pulse. It is relevant only to the technical aspects of performance. However, this particular passage will always sound 'fast'. In music based on a slower pulse the situation can be most disconcerting.

In many works, no positive aural indication of tempo emerges for some considerable period, even though the time-span is meticulously notated in terms of bar-lengths and speed of pulse. The listener has little guidance as to pace until some movement occurs with which to make comparison.

The long, sustained pedal C which opens Richard Strauss *Also sprach Zarathustra* (*Ex. 21.9*) is timeless as far as the audience is concerned until the appearance of the trumpets, which give it something of a retrospective time-scale.

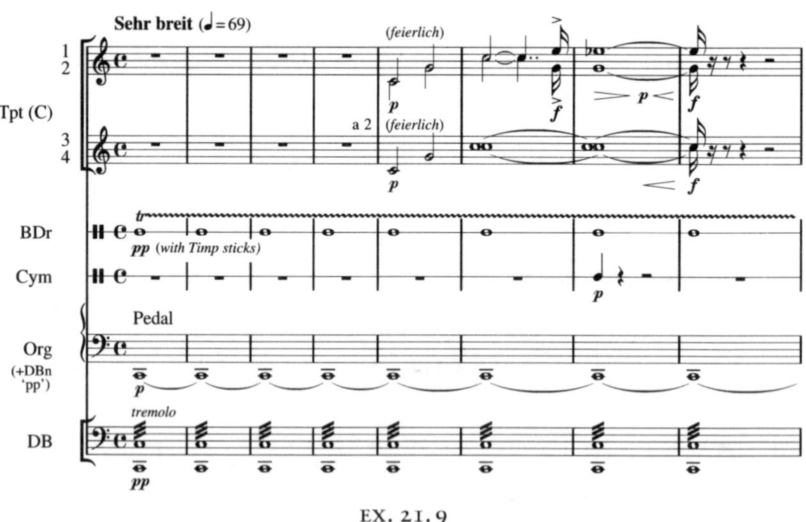

EX. 21.9

The composer defines these first bars at crotchet = 69, but such information is there simply as a guide for determining the overall tempo and, therefore, the duration of this pedal note in relation to the following entry. Theoretically, even were it to be known that the piece was conceived in 4/4 time, until the movement of the trumpets in bars five and six this note could be four bars at crotchet = 69, sixteen bars at crotchet = 276, or (to be pedantic) one bar at crotchet = 17.25. In fact, even an accurate relative time-scale will not be adhered to strictly in most performances, since the C will tend to be slightly extended or shortened according to the influence of many outside criteria, not least the contrabassoon player's ability to sustain the note *pianissimo* without change of balance or intonation. However, once the note has exceeded two bars' duration at around the demanded tempo it is, from the listener's point of view, exceptionally long and the further extension serves to heighten a feeling of anticipation, itself born of insecurity of form – the very *absence* of definable pulse and the consequent lack of shape, architecture and direction.

Such an example highlights not only the factors responsible for rhythmic comprehension but also the aural ramifications of their removal. As such the situation can apply equally to performers and listeners, a passage of slow-moving note-lengths often giving an erroneous impression of actual tempo. *Ex. 21.10*, the well-known opening to the slow movement of Dvořák *Symphony no. 9*, illustrates this (see page 738).

Here, the wonderfully elongated resolution of the opening brass chorale, together with the sense of repose imparted by the strings in the following bars, may often result in an inexperienced cor anglais player's attempting to perform the phrase far too slowly, simply because the underlying rhythm has been submerged by an actual movement of slow-moving notes. The cor anglais solo, when it eventually appears, is built around notes which are, for the most part, twice as fast as anything that has come before and the sense of tranquillity must be established by the shape and quality of the phrase and not by slow tempo alone.

Such a miscalculation might well be noticeable for the first time only in performance, where the introductory bars will have taken on both a substance of sound and a level of dynamic not apparent in rehearsal, a situation which can also cause the player to attempt the phrase too softly.

There is a very real sense of timelessness about these opening bars that suspends any real feeling of rhythmic movement. Initially this arises from the sombre nature of the orchestration combined with the low pitch of the whole progression – a fact immediately emphasized by the initial downward movement of every instrument except those of the upper line (both trumpets) and 2nd horn. Harmonically we are disorientated, not only by the remoteness of the chord relations themselves (E-B♭-E-D♭ in the first two bars) but by the deceptively ingenious layout and orchestration which allows the upper line to be reassuringly predominant but hover tantalizingly between two notes, E and F. When a chord of D♭ major finally appears from a plagal cadence it

EX. 21.10

is with a sense of some relief, although tinged with no little uncertainty regarding how exactly we arrived! Were the cor anglais solo to appear now (at the fifth bar) there would be no problem, the powerful tonic chord having established such harmonic control that *any* continuation in terms of tempo is possible. But its effect is dissipated by two extra bars of *pianissimo* strings, forged in a new rhythm which settles on the weakest beat of the bar. It is this, a stroke of pure genius, which finally destroys all sense of rhythmic orientation.

In passages that require slow tempi (especially those involving minimal obvious melodic movement) the conductor, isolated from the purely technical reminders that lack of breath or bow-length will instantly provide, is more likely than any other performer to miscalculate. A conductor can often make insufficient allowance for his or her own movement and the consequent feeling of rhythmic flow which it engenders – a false impression of speed can be obtained by virtue of a *physical* awareness of motion that is not necessarily transmitted to the listener. This can only be rectified by a sufficiently fluent technique that allows concentration to be solely on the true sound of the orchestra, undeflected by digressions of movements necessary to ensemble or dynamic variation. Considerable experience in handling orchestral sound is of course the prerequisite, but a conscious effort to limit drastically the size of the gesture in these circumstances will always help. The less air being covered, the less likely one is to expand the distance between the beats.

The two most important facets to be considered of any work or movement (but most especially one of slow pulse) are line and direction. Without a clear idea of the direction and purpose of travel there can be neither precise understanding of any position along the way nor any true reasoning of its relevance to the whole. It is not enough to have worked out the structure and musical meaning of a work without having also considered the means of imparting them to the listener. This can often involve a quite radical change of emphasis.

To a very large extent this analysis will involve much that was considered in the earlier part of this chapter – the total effect of sound upon the perception of tempo and its unavoidable relevance in the projection of shape and reason. Although interpretative decisions of pace are unlikely to be substantially altered, the sound of the orchestra performing must be an allowable factor in their presentation. As already remarked, while a professional orchestra or section might be able to maintain a slow tempo and still imbue it with continuity and direction, a less able orchestra may well require something fractionally faster to realize the same effect.

Once the pervading pulse has been established, the actual number of notes that appear can do little to change the prevailing impression of tempo. Thus there is nothing 'fast' about *Ex. 21.11* from the second movement of Elgar *Symphony no. 2* even though it contains a large number of notes.

Nor is there anything 'slow' about *Ex. 21.12* from the final movement of Berlioz *Symphonie Fantastique*.

EX. 21.11

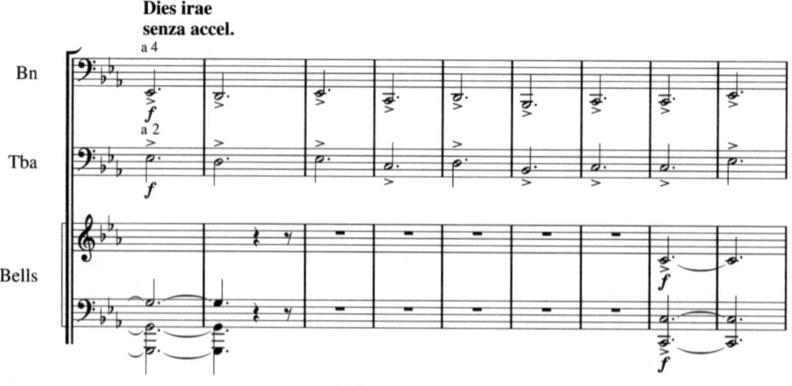

EX. 21.12

EX. 21.11 (continued)

EX. 21.12 (continued)

These examples expose the fundamental contradiction that exists when speed is measured only by the relative expedition of the fastest notes – the predominant notes of Berlioz' *allegro* (dotted crotchet = 108) moving more than eight times slower than those of Elgar's *larghetto* (crotchet = 60). The illusory nature of tempo can thus be seen to depend also on harmony, underlying structure and, above all, rhythmic impetus.

It is from this last that the sense of pace of 'fast' movements is derived, the mere performance of notes as quickly as possible rarely giving any impression of true speed. Once again, it is the relative proximity of the pulse which provides the feeling of tempo, and not necessarily the number of notes. Only positive control of the basic rhythm will provide tangible rapidity. Breathlessness is not an essential ingredient of speed, and speed, in itself, will not necessarily project tension or excitement – except, perhaps, in terms of impending disaster! This fact has long been understood by every stage and film director who ever manipulated an audience. It is a pity that it has been increasingly overlooked by so many performing musicians. In musical terms, clarity will always give a more vibrant design. Time must be found for a passage at least to be assimilated even if it is not intended to be heard note by note.

This contradiction between 'pulse' and 'tempo' is best exemplified by works that include sections of clearly opposing character built on an identical speed of pulse. The third movement of Brahms *Symphony no. 2 – Allegretto*

EX. 21.13

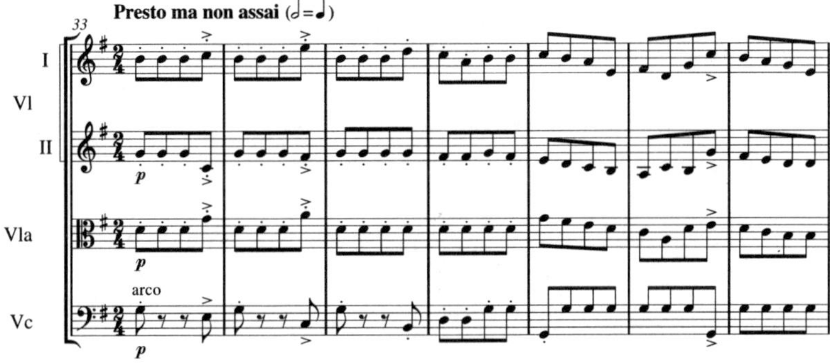

EX. 21.13 (continued)

Grazioso (*Quasi Andantino*) – contains two sharply contrasting, although thematically closely allied, sections (see *Ex. 21.13*). While both maintain a close affinity to the overall rhythmic movement, the first (*Presto ma non assai*) also maintains a direct relationship in pulse, one crotchet of the *allegretto* 3/4 being exactly equal to one bar of *presto* 2/4.

Quite apart from the length of the *staccato* notes, much of the change of feeling of this new section derives from a much more subtle change of rhythmic scan, the lilting three-crotchet pulse of the *allegretto* now becoming a clear rhythm of four bars. However, if the two sections are considered independently, the tempo of the first is quite definitely that of a gentle *andantino* while the second can be nothing but a *scherzo*. The dexterity of the composer and the familiarity of this movement will often cause us to overlook the fact that our ears have been subjected to masterful trickery – the fundamental pulse of the movement has undergone no change whatsoever.

To illustrate similar change in the opposite direction, from fast to slow, there is probably no better example in the whole repertoire than the return of this same passage to the original *allegretto*, an even more deceptive manipulation of rhythmic perception than that quoted above (*Ex. 21.14*).

The whole passage is masterly, but the subtle introduction of the woodwind chords, the outline of the cello accompaniment and the nonchalant introduction of a three-bar phrase length over the last six bars before the return provide us with just enough insight into the technique of deception to appreciate its implausibility.

Another method in which a composer may accomplish a similar (although not so precipitous) change of character is by superimposing the new section on top of the original structure. A passage of this type (but too long to be quoted here) can be found mid-way through the *Rondo* of Elgar *Symphony no. 2*. In this case, however, the change of feeling is neither so abrupt nor quite

EX. 21.14

so extreme because the rhythmic grouping within the pulse remains constant and a four-bar scan of 3/8 has been apparent for some time. Nonetheless, a distinct change of mood and impulse is engendered by the use of longer note-lengths that extend through the original bar-lines, at first disturbing their hold

EX. 21.14 (continued)

on the rhythm and then (rehearsal figure 119) forcing their withdrawal to a position of less determined influence. Only because the passage has been totally integrated within the movement as a whole is its effect any less startling than that of Brahms'. Again, by separating this section from the main material of the *Rondo*, Elgar gives a substantial change of character and rhythmic line, even though the pulse is the same.

Of particular interest in this case is the retention of the 3/8 figuration in the accompanying instruments by use of dotted bar-lines, rather than a total change to 4/4 with the quavers marked as triplets and a demand for dotted crotchet = crotchet. Unlike the passage from Brahms, this is a *combination* of movement, the substance of the *Rondo* having been subdued, rather than supplanted.

The ability of the pulse, once established, to maintain its dominance regardless of the note-lengths or rhythmic syncopations to which it might be subjected is, of course, the basis of all movement, phrasing, direction and *rubato*. It can, however, sometimes prove awkward to handle when in immediate proximity to an unrelated change of speed. Thus, in another Elgar *Scherzo*, the link between the second and third movements of the *First Symphony* (see *Ex. 21.15*) can be quite difficult to accomplish.

Regardless of the fact that the melodic pattern becomes increasingly fragmented, the pulse of the *Scherzo* remains abundantly clear. Were this movement to be complete within itself then one more bar, with cellos and basses

EX. 21.15

completing the implied cadential progression on to the short D alone (V-VI-I), would suffice. In this case the passage could be performed in exact tempo, the pulse disintegrating in the silence following the last note. The fact that the first chord of the *Adagio* forms both the beginning of a new movement and the long-awaited resolution of the previous, raises the problem of where exactly the pulse can be dispersed.

Approaching the chord 'in tempo' (easy to imagine but extremely difficult to achieve in practice), enforces an elongation of the first note of the *Adagio* in order to allow the pulse to settle, thereby causing the 'cadential' significance of the chord to dominate. This can hardly have been intended, since the continuity of this passage (a rhythmic variation of the first twenty-four notes of the *Scherzo*) is so vital. Besides, an almost total predominance of F♯ is hardly the scoring for a D major cadence. But to ease the tempo back over the last few bars of the *Scherzo* seems to fly in the face of the composer's explicit demands.

Suffice it to say that I have never heard, or been involved in any performance where some adjustment to the pulse was not apparent in order to prepare the sound, if not the movement, of the *Adagio*. (As a player, I did have the good fortune to perform this work many times and to record it on four separate occasions, with four different conductors and three different orchestras.) While it is quite understandable why the composer did not indicate any form of *rallentando*, a deliberate 'placing' of the first chord of the *Adagio*, by elongation of the connecting F♯ at the very least, is almost unavoidable.

As has been seen from the above examples, pulse will only establish itself when some grouping of rhythmic movement, regardless of note-lengths, occurs within a constant time-scale. As such, it can be either clearly obvious or deceptively insinuated. It is, however, immediately destroyed by any change in rhythmic impetus, even when some component part remains constant, as in the ever-changing and highly disturbing nature of *Ex. 21.16*, the opening passage from John Adams *Harmonielehre*.

EX. 21.16

EX. 21.16 (continued)

Precision of Movement

Precision of movement becomes the essential technique to impart not only pulse and speed of movement but also sense, character, transparency and definition. This is not simply the control of rhythm but encompasses the much larger concept of coincidence of movement, most generally referred to by the all-embracing and deceptively simplistic title 'ensemble'.

Passages of soft, supportive texture are most at risk, simply because concentration on the techniques required for the production of sound quality and dynamic level will so often override the equally important consideration of uniform movement, especially when a large number of executants are involved. Even a passage as rhythmically obvious as *Ex. 21.17* from Delius *The Walk to the Paradise Garden* will suffer if the performing technique is not capable of projecting definition and flexibility as *well* as subtlety of sound quality.

All the mobility of this passage, as well as much of the initial mood, is implied by this line of gentle muted syncopation. Control and clarity of movement is essential, not only for the passage itself but also to accompany

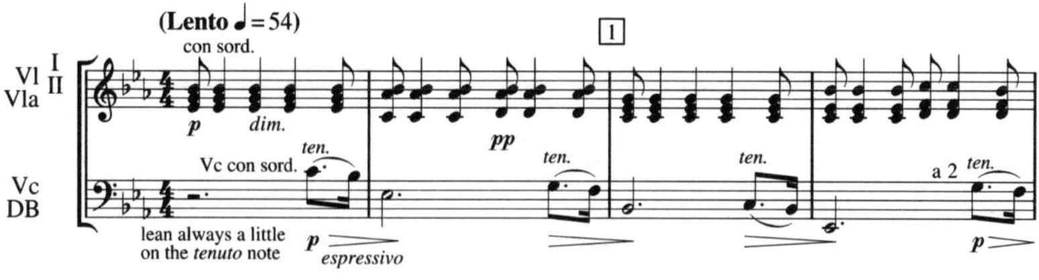

EX. 21.17

the moment taken by the *tenuto* up-beats of the cellos. The orchestra must 'feel' this passage together so that they move together.

Primarily, such uniformity of movement requires concentrated listening from every player, so that every line, regardless of how soloistic it might appear, is approached from the point of view of its association with and relevance to all other concurrent sounds. This in itself will quite quickly lead to a situation where a degree of anticipation is also apparent, which allows rhythmic flexibility to be natural and largely inconspicuous in its effect on the pulse and flow of the music.

In *Ex. 21.17* the mood, dynamic level and quality of the desired sound are fairly self-evident and, once achieved, require only sensitivity of rhythmic nuance to effect ensemble. But not all soft string passages are so accommodating, and many will demand an actual method of production that is far removed from the musical perception of the projected sound. In these circumstances flexibility in accurate ensemble becomes that much more difficult. The opening of Wagner Prelude to Act I of *Lohengrin* (see *Ex. 21.18*) provides an illustration.

(For all the musicological problems that exist in matching the score with the printed parts, as mentioned in Chapter 1, this still remains one of the clearest examples to use.) Clarity in such a passage demands a firm left hand, a definition of fingering and a verticality of movement that feels very much at odds with the smoothness of the projected line. Some flexibility is unavoidable, and the degree to which it affects the movement is only really apparent from within the violin sections. Neither the necessary tranquillity nor the enormity of the unbroken line can be attained within a metronomically rigid pulse (it extends for a further 40-odd bars in the violin lines alone). Even the

EX. 21.18

apparently simple figures of the third and fourth parts are ambivalent, sometimes initiating the movement, sometimes accompanying it.

Exactly the same applies when woodwind and horns join the statement a little further on. Their naturally more focused sound in comparison with that of combined strings makes life no easier for them. In fact it can be harder because the movement of notes will tend to be absolute, without even that infinitesimal shading of the edge typical of a string section. From this point of view the movement of demisemiquavers in the first bar of the quoted string passage, while requiring a great degree of accuracy, will not prove as difficult for the lower woodwind and horns as the resolving crotchet on the third beat of the second bar.

There are many similar examples, particularly for the body of strings, where the techniques necessary for projection can feel very much at odds with both the sound and sensibility of the passage to be performed. The disturbing semiquaver triplet rhythms that pervade much of the first movement of

EX. 21.18 (continued)

Sibelius *Symphony no. 5* pose insurmountable problems of ensemble until the techniques of production have been thoroughly mastered. *Ex. 21.19* is but one of many similar passages.

For the passage to be performed successfully, the bow arm must control the

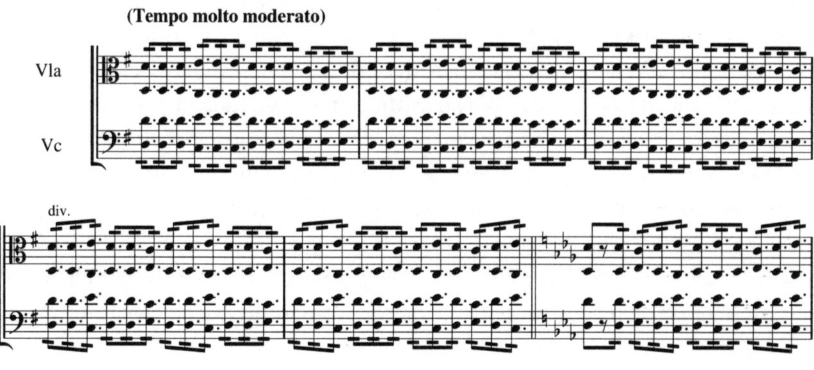

EX. 21.19

rhythmic movement (and in a somewhat over-deliberate fashion). Firm contact of the bow with the string must be maintained to control the rhythmic movement and preserve clarity of articulation, after which the necessary dynamic – however soft it might be – can be achieved by using very little bow, and moving it away from the bridge to a position where minimum sound will result. Eventually, some of the weight of contact will obviously be taken off the bow, but this should *never* be the main performance technique in such a passage, and should never even be suggested to inexperienced orchestras. Once the passage is 'bow-arm' controlled (and thus capable of reliable ensemble within the larger span of the beats) the musical insinuation of dynamic level can be implanted gradually and lighter contact will be employed automatically.

This is a prime example of one of the most fundamental differences between solo and orchestral technique for string players. Were this passage to appear in the solo repertoire, the clarity of movement endemic to one individual instrument would allow for a physical production more in keeping with the artistic demands of the passage. The weight could be taken off the bow and a quite 'loosely contacted' technique employed. With a large number of other players, however, especially in the preparatory stages, primary reliance on this technique is likely to prove fatal to both rhythmic movement and articulation. In essence, solo string playing utilizes variation in bow weight while broadly maintaining contact at the optimum point of sound production. Performance within large string sections has much more to do with varying the *position* of the bow in relation to its point of contact with the string.

The variation of technique needed for performance in different media is one of the hardest lessons for any instrumentalist especially when, as is so often the case in ensemble playing, it calls for some aspect of production which feels alien to the musicality of the phrase. In many ways this whole concept lies at the very core of the art of performing music and separates those who can play from those who can communicate. How many times has one encountered that frail and delicate student who plays so carefully and aspires to be a chamber music player without the least idea of how much sheer power and controlled energy it takes to project that gentle Mozartian line?

These are qualities also essential to a conductor, and the basic understanding of two almost opposing concepts is vital to the projection of logical movement. Firstly, no tempo can be maintained as a totally inflexible *rule* of movement, since the shape of every phrase needs at least an infinitesimal variation in pace, and frequently demands something rather more obvious. Secondly, even in circumstances where the pulse is rigorously maintained, there is likely to be a certain amount of flexibility within it. (Perhaps this last is nowhere more obvious than from within the orchestra during the performance of a passage similar to that quoted as *Ex. 21.19*.)

It is once again all too easy to find that the conductor's obsession with tempo and its associated movement, divorced from the actual production of sound, can negate the very essence of the motion needed to project it. Even in the rare cases of a quite rigidly enforced equality of pulse (as in Ravel's orchestral exercise *Boléro*), subtle movement within the phrase will be evident. For the most part this is true illusion, for it is almost totally projected by control of sound and dynamic variation, but it is nonetheless essential to the communication of the work, and most noticeable when absent. While in no way detracting from Ravel's virtuosity of orchestration, the subtle variation in the approach of each instrumentalist, both in solo and small combination, is what gives the work its ultimate charm. This also ensures that, while this work can be played by a good student orchestra, its musical character is such that it can only be *performed* by highly experienced professionals.

However, in pieces less rigid in their rhythmic construction some actual flexibility of tempo will be apparent, and here, judgement of the overall span will be at its most critical, for the ultimate object is to project line and instil forward motion within the phrase. Thus the fundamental tempo of a slow movement should be regularly touched on but rarely exceeded, so that the speed of motion forms the basis of the structure but not necessarily its totality.

As the relative time-span of the discernible pulse becomes shorter, so the structure of the musical phrase appears faster and the focus of the inherent technical problems of ensemble and projection changes. Some of the impulse for projecting forward motion will now come from the relative speed of the notes themselves and, more important, from the energy and drive induced by a faster melodic process. Technical fluency and potential limitations that affect clear articulation now become ever more critical.

It does not always happen, however, that the fastest notes take full or even the major responsibility for the impetus of fast passage-work.While passages such as occur in the *Scherzo* of Elgar *Symphony no. 1* derive all their projected energy from the articulation of the single line, many others, such as *Ex. 21.20* from Shostakovich *Festive Overture*, rely no less on the positive energy derived from the accompaniment.

Although the 1st violin line in this example is undoubtedly important, its clarity will have little effect without precise and determined articulation of the chords from the rest of the strings, and the same holds good for trombones and tuba in their support of the trumpets. As in much of this overture, especially in the string writing, these supporting rhythms need far more work than the melodic passages above them.

EX. 21.20

This principle can be applied to a large proportion of works or movements in 'fast' tempo. It becomes extremely important to appreciate where the real impetus of a musical structure lies. A great deal of time can be wasted on passages of obvious difficulty without any appreciable difference to the projected result, while a few words directed at the secondary line and a little time spent sharpening its rhythmic precision and tightness will often prove far more effective. Once the accompaniment is able to assume full responsibility for projecting the musical character and the harmonic direction of the phrase, a wider choice of tempi becomes available, any one of which will probably sound faster than the original. Not only has room been found for the primary passage to be played more accurately but also, and more important, time has been allowed for it to be *heard*.

Projecting the Line

The projection of overall movement depends on the direction given to each small component part, and also the handling of that *bête noir* of all performers, the bar-line. An example of the heightened understanding of the expanse of a phrase which results from the total removal of bar-lines was considered in Chapter 14 (*Exx. 14. 4* and *14. 5*) in respect of a solo phrase. A somewhat wider appraisal needs now to be undertaken.

Bar-lines serve to clarify the synchronization of different instrumental and vocal lines. They were, originally, intended simply to aid the eye in assimilating necessary vertical coincidence, and their placement when they were first introduced was quite arbitrary. As demarcations of equal time value, they were not widely used before the sixteenth and seventeenth centuries. Essential as they are to the ease of comprehension of the written page, their purely musical value is minimal to say the least, corresponding, perhaps, to the grid reference of a map. Any effect that they may be thought to have on the underlying rhythm of movement is illusory. In this respect they are simply a graphic illustration of something that is already there.

However, in performance, bar-lines visually fragment the horizontal span of a phrase into smaller vertical segments, an effect which, especially in orchestral performance, can be communicated in the projected line. The bar-line may very easily be exaggerated both because of the sheer number of players using it for rhythmic reference and its significant correspondence to the conductor's down-beat.

In any passage composed of short sub-phrases this, coupled with the natural emphasis that most players will put on the note immediately following the bar-line, can prove damaging to the overall phrase. *Ex. 21.21*, the beautiful 12-bar subject that opens the second movement of Brahms *Symphony no.2*, illustrates this.

Adagio non troppo
Fl 1 2
Ob 1 2
Bn 1 2
Hn (B) 1 2
Tbn 1 2
Tbn 3 Tba
Vla
Vc
DB
a 2
poco f
p
pp
Tba p
div.
espress.
Hn 1 2
1

EX. 21.21

EX. 21.21 (continued)

Especially in the first three and last four bars of this extract, both the structure and melodic line of the phrase retain close association with the confines of the bar-line. Almost any additional emphasis (especially that bestowed by accident) will certainly break the continuity of the statement and impart a metrical compass far too short for the overall span. Only when the 12 bars are projected as a complete sentence can the rest of the dialogue be supported. In order to achieve this it is vital that a sense of movement is conveyed by every note of the phrase and that their relationship to one another as part of a continuing discourse is clear. It is hard to think of a thread more difficult to project than this one. As Tovey remarked: 'It is never the complexity of Brahms that makes him difficult for us – it is simply his originality.'

However, it may sometimes be that, while some elements of the primary theme appear somewhat restricted by the barring, much of the impetus for continuous movement has been subtly implanted in the supporting structure, as in *Ex. 21.22*, the opening bars of Variation IX *(Nimrod)*, from Elgar *'Enigma' Variations*.

The confinement of the melodic line is largely diffused by the suspensions in the harmony, which tend to pull the phrase inexorably towards its own resolution, and thereby supply (almost!) unavoidable momentum to the complete line.

The *rhythmic* structure of the accompaniment may achieve this same end, as in the first eight bars of another *Adagio*, from Schumann *Symphony no. 2 in* C (*Ex. 21.23*, page 759).

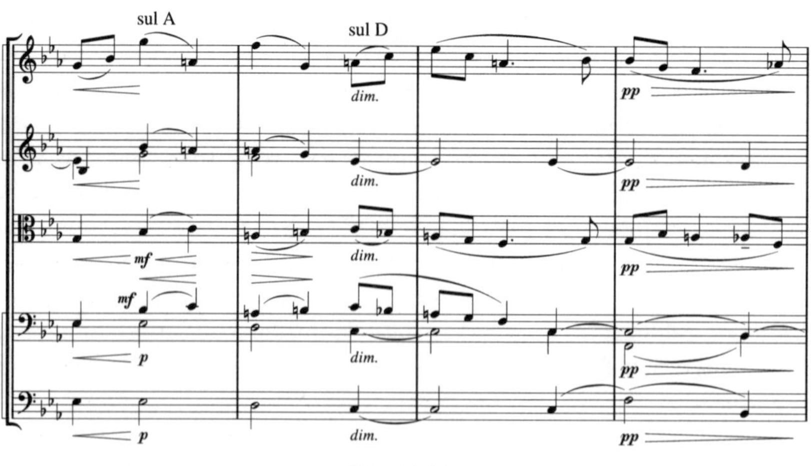

EX. 21.22

Forward motion is here helped by the syncopated figures of divided violas.

EX. 21.23

However, no amount of rhythmic or harmonic influence will rescue the phrase if undue emphasis has been placed on any part of it or the individual notes have lost relationship to one another in terms of the dependent tensions that might have been set up or resolved. In this respect the sound previous to each note is important, and projecting the significance of where a note has come from becomes as essential as that of where it is going. If these two aspects of the note are projected concurrently, the content of almost any long phrase, derived from however stark and vertical a form, will prove more achievable in its design. Rests, far from obstructing the line, will punctuate it, heightening rather than relaxing anticipation.

Ex. 21.24 from the opening of the second movement of Beethoven *Symphony no. 3* displays a formidable instance of concise and restricted structure, but it proves to be another long phrase, this time even more cryptically shrouded by small fragments than *Ex. 21.21*.

The written silences can easily make each two-bar figure appear as a dramatic statement in its own right. While they each have their own undeniable importance, it is the sense of the whole paragraph that must be transmitted in performance, by relating every note to what has gone before, as well as to what follows. (In terms of musical lucidity this must also apply to the very first note of a phrase.)

EX. 21.24

If this extreme concentration on the relationship of each note (or rest) to its immediate surroundings is applied to any of the phrases quoted above, it will be found that, quite apart from an increased accuracy of note-lengths, the sound will be even and continuous, with no false dynamic changes and no undue emphasis on the bar-line. Furthermore, the passage will begin to develop naturally its most musically coherent tempo. Far from restricting the movement of the phrase, such appraisal will highlight the interdependence of every aspect of the structure and actually free the overall line in a way that a more general consideration cannot accomplish.

From the listener's point of view it is vital both that the sense of each musical sentence is transmitted and that the underlying pulse of the discourse is thoroughly established. Especially in works of 'slow' tempo, opening phrases such as those considered above almost always provide the key to the entire mood and reasoning behind the text. Although a later passage may well have considerable influence on both direction and pace, it is not enough to rely on the more expansive appearances of the material to make retrospective sense of the whole notion. In any communication, the very first statement made is the foundation on which all development proceeds. *Rubato*, and all its attendant inflections of emphasis and direction, is of no useful musical purpose without a clear understanding of the fundamental concept of tempo.

Unnecessary emphasis of the bar-line is at its most destructive in fast-moving music of short measure. All the 'one-in-a-bar' orchestral *scherzi* can lose much of their essential momentum from the weight allotted to closely spaced down-beats. The principal subject of the *Scherzo* from Mendelssohn incidental music to *A Midsummer Night's Dream* (*Ex. 21.25*) is a case in point.

This work demands a lightness of touch that allows it to skip forward without ever touching the ground, and the slightest unintentional exaggeration of bar-lines will stop it dead in its tracks. The conductor must not only

EX. 21.25

EX. 21.25 (continued)

provide a beat that is very contained, but also one that encourages the forward momentum of the line – not the easiest result to obtain from a succession of down-beats.

Like most 'one-in-a-bar' movements, this *scherzo* has an underlying scan of sub-phrases, in this case based on four-bar groups. If at least the beat on the last bar of each group is conducted as an 'up-beat', much of the necessary momentum will be implied and, even more important, the beat will be far less obstructive. For obvious musical and visual reasons, passages of this type should not be conducted in any recognizable pattern, whether four, three or anything else. However, consciousness of the phrase groupings might well ensure a slightly less deliberate beat on the weaker bars of the line, and further assist the horizontal movement. This technique may, of course, be extended to sub-phrases of any division, three-, five-, six- or seven-bar structures working equally well.

In *scherzi* of faster pulse (as in Beethoven *Symphonies nos 3, 7* and *9* for example), this technique will always help the fluency of performance, but the basic understanding of the required phrase structure is its most essential attribute. (The conductor's effect on the projection of line is potentially far more dangerous and damaging than that of any other performing musician, since the physical delineation of rhythm disassociated from the *actual* production of sound is one of the most easily attainable lunacies known to modern man!)

A comparison of the *scherzi* of Beethoven and Mendelssohn exposes a fundamental difference in notation which extends beyond the printed page. The only Beethoven *scherzo* to employ a similar tempo to that of Mendelssohn *A Midsummer Night's Dream* is that of the *Symphony no. 5* which, in common with all his other symphonic *scherzi*, employs note-values of twice the length (3/4 as against 3/8). This is almost certainly because of their historical association with the 3/4 Minuet and Trio, but nonetheless highlights a critical balance of interpretation. On the one hand, the choice of note-value has no direct relationship to speed; the *scherzi* of the other symphonies are considerably faster than that of the *Fifth*. But, on the other hand, it will, to some degree, affect the attitude of interpretation and the *substance* of the sound.

The listener's judgement will be based solely on an aural perception but, as has already been seen, such a divergence between the written and aural concept of movement can have far-reaching results.

Scope

The scope of a work or movement may be considered both in architectural and aural terms. In a perfect structure, scope will be apparent from the outset. To quote two contrasting examples, the opening bars of Beethoven *Symphony no. 9* make it abundantly clear that the process of the work will take considerable time, while those of Mozart *Symphony no. 40* divulge equal knowledge of a tight and closely wrought statement. It would be as inconceivable for the former work to last thirty minutes as it would for the latter to take twice that time.

There are probably no finer examples of perfect scope in the entire repertoire than these two works, but every composition must have tackled this problem of structure to some degree. It is only the span of a work that can make musical sense of the sounds, whether the actual duration is fifteen seconds or three or four hours.

For the performer this architectural scope is translated into pacing. Movement and climax must be gauged so that the listener is drawn inevitably to the crux of the argument, and no false emphasis is given to the discourse. The pacing of a work is inseparable from the individual performer's concept of it as a total communication (and, therefore, of the expanse needed to express it).

With this understanding of scope comes true understanding of sound and its relevance to the projection of musical intelligence. Here one finally lays to rest any idea that it will suffice to play the notes and hope that their rhythmic, tonal and harmonic relationship to one another will project a sensible and coherent whole. The interpreter is now forced to address a number of difficulties which might otherwise conveniently have been ignored. Firstly, the performer must be thoroughly conversant with the work in question, not only with all structural aspects but also the requisite sound, and the effect on the whole that even small changes of timbre might bring. Beyond this comes the question of emphasis, which may or may not correspond to that of the compositional structure – on many occasions the disposition and 'aura' of a work may be responsible for the development of line, rather than simple progress.

This is particularly true of symphonic works comprising three or four movements, where both aspects of pacing (of individual movements and of the whole structure) are apparent simultaneously. Too often, one hears a symphony performed as a suite – a series of unconnected movements separated by coughing, and only distinguished from four entirely separate pieces by the fact that the conductor fails to leave the stage. This is to lose the essence of symphonic performance, and although it is an impression fostered by broadcasting stations that allow separated movements to be played in isolation it is nevertheless essential that the power and continuity of the whole discourse be maintained.

Undoubtedly there are works where the scope has been misjudged at the compositional stage (or where, for whatever reason, the performer *feels* that it has been misjudged) and these will always be difficult to pace. This weakness is most prone to emerge in works of some length, especially within large areas of thematic repetition, and there is little that can be done beyond encouraging as much flow as possible and allowing the work to run its course. Cuts should be avoided. It is no exaggeration to say that musical surgery never solves the problem of scope and usually serves only to unbalance some other aspect of the performance. It is less a matter of blind dedication to the composer's original manuscript than of plain practicality. Because the work is complete and published, any cuts contemplated have to be made to and from places of related harmony or dramatic inflection, which never correspond either to the most beneficial areas to be lost or to the ideal length. If a piece needs shortening it needs re-writing and, as this is usually quite impossible, it must be performed as it is, or refused.

ADJUSTING THE PERFORMANCE

For the perfomer, the projection of scope cannot always be accomplished within a totally predetermined span. This is especially true of orchestral music due to the large number of individual performers involved. Many new and changing circumstances will influence every musical performance, and some allowance for these will have to be made at the time. The ability to do this successfully is probably the most instinctive area of the conductor's art and accounts for much of the '10 per cent inspiration' in the famous cliché. However, certain ground rules (or, at least, warnings of probable danger areas) can be put forward.

In performance with inexperienced or technically limited orchestras, reassessments of pace and emphasis are likely to arise accidentally, or through forgivable negligence. A young orchestra is prone, for example, to pre-empt a known *rallentando*, thereby increasing (or sometimes lessening) the intended emphasis of a section. This will affect the design of the work in question, and some reappraisal will be necessary to make sense of both what has been said and what remains to be said. In verbal communication this tends to be an automatic process, where a speaker will change tack altogether because of some accidental emphasis or choice of words. In music, such an extreme luxury as total change of direction is unavailable (much as one might often pray for the opportunity) and, therefore, it is only possible to adjust the perceived scan. This is *not* tampering with the ultimate architectural design, but simply realigning its focus.

The exaggeration of rehearsed *rubati* is probably the major cause of this type of performance adjustment, although sound, dynamic range and inflection also play their part. Musical timidity as well as over-enthusiasm can cause a performance to project a variation in substance of communication, as will slight variations in tempi and articulation. All these will, in turn, have a bearing upon the overall shape of the work.

There is no way of explaining this somewhat complicated process of adjustment in more detail. Without such essential sensitivity and musical sincerity, the symmetry of discourse is lost. This cannot be taught in the accepted sense, but it can be learned, and it is there for all who wish to recognize it.

Once the implications of structure in relation to communication are accepted, the difference between rehearsal and performance becomes even more marked. It becomes essential to understand the purpose of the former, as well as its inevitable limitations: to show *where* things go and not altogether *how* they go.

The 'ifs' and 'buts' that abound in the areas of interpretative performance briefly covered in this chapter are the life blood of musical communication. They can, quite probably, be cited as the most fundamental distinction between the imparting of any sort of intelligence through so-called 'art', and its communication by any other means.

22 CONCERTO ACCOMPANIMENT

The accompanying of concerti and other solo pieces is probably the most beneficial discipline for any orchestra. Nothing else so quickly promotes flexibility, awareness of balance and total concentrated listening. For student orchestras it generates an understanding of individual and collective musical responsibility in a uniquely effective manner, and, as such, becomes the most vital of all ensemble playing opportunities as well as the most demanding.

Unfortunately, because it is largely regarded as a secondary role, insufficient rehearsal time (and consequently, too little exploration of its highly individual techniques) is often allowed. First-class orchestral playing is all about the substance, quality and flexibility of the secondary lines. An orchestra that can accompany a soloist can accompany itself, which means, ultimately, that every line will have reason and meaning in relation to the whole, and every player will perceive the ever-changing responsibility of the individual contribution.

There are surprisingly varied concepts of accompanying, but I personally believe that, while the orchestra and conductor have an unquestionable responsibility towards the work concerned, it must be directed through the needs and desires of the soloist, and that every effort must be made to help soloists realize their musical goals and feel unrestricted in the opportunity to give of their best.

Decisions of tempi and phrasing are largely a matter for the soloist. They are very personal and will have been conceived via a combination of musical, interpretative and technical considerations which, in the case of a high-class player, will be at one with the sound produced. In addition, a soloist's interpretation will have evolved through long and arduous preparation and experience, and there is little likelihood that any major changes (even were they to be accepted) would be successfully incorporated within hours of the performance.

If this does not deflect the determined conductor, there is also the rather less esoteric consideration that, come the concert, the direction will have to go with the soloist regardless of personal preferences. Any musical argument between conductor and soloist during performance is always won by the latter in the eyes of both audience and orchestra (and, come to that, of *any* good musician). However, it is not a totally one-way process and some injection of musical personality is incumbent on, and indeed, expected of, the conductor and orchestra.

Before considering the specific difficulties and techniques of accompanying, some general considerations must be addressed, chief among which will be what size of orchestra to use. For student orchestras this is an important decision, since it is not always possible to use the entire string group, and never feasible to use more than the required wind and brass. The exact number will depend on the concerto to be performed as well as the quality and experience of the orchestra, but as far as the woodwind is concerned, this constraint is a very good reason for not having an unnecessarily enlarged section in the first place.

String Numbers

It must be stressed that there should not necessarily be an automatic reduction in the number of string players for the performance of concerti, and such a decision should only ever be taken to achieve an appropriate texture and *never* as a means of reducing the dynamic level. (A large string group can play far more softly than a small one in any case, because the sounds can be more diffused and there is less temptation for players to project in a soloistic manner.) It is more the weight and sheer density of sound produced by the large string group when in direct accompaniment, at whatever dynamic level, that can sometimes be at odds with the timbre of a solo instrument or the style of the concerto. This should be the only reasoning behind any reduction of numbers.

For an inexperienced orchestra, clarity and flexibility might also benefit by the centring of the orchestral sound that smaller forces will produce, although this is by no means guaranteed. In the more Classically orientated concerti, however, the multiplicity of movement inherent within a number of interdependent and equally important lines will always demand a lightening of the string texture.

Most usually, string numbers will be reduced by desk (two players at a time from each section), a convenient system which precludes an odd number of players in any one section. But for student orchestras it is more important to consider the strengths and weaknesses of each section individually (especially with regard to 2nd violins and basses) rather than slavishly adhere to custom.

(In the following consideration of string section size, reference to *even* numbers of players will be maintained throughout, as the overall concept is under discussion rather than its relevance to any one orchestra. Individual modification according to circumstances should always be considered.)

If an orchestra's technique is sufficiently flexible, it is quite possible to undertake preliminary rehearsals of the concerto with a larger section than required for actual performance but – and this is absolutely vital – the intention to reduce and the exact personnel expected to play must have been made clear to the orchestra from the very beginning. To make the decision only on the day of the concert is thoughtless and unforgivable.

PIANO CONCERTI

Most nineteenth- and twentieth-century piano concerti will be able to cope with a full complement of strings. In fact many were conceived for larger forces than are likely to be available. The concerti of Mozart will generally need reduction but, unless the strings are of exceptional standard, not usually below 10.8.6.6.4. (or however many basses there are) and *never*, except for the most superb professional ensemble, below 8.6.4.4.2. Less than this strength can cause extreme difficulty, in terms of the sound produced: six 1st violins find it very hard to blend and will in any case tend to play louder and more soloistically than a larger section. Attempts to produce a combined 'symphonic' sound can virtually be abandoned, especially if the lower line is reduced to two cellos. Two similar instruments playing the same line is the worst possible combination for intonation, balance, projection and sound. Really fine bass players can manage it in works of a Classical nature but, even here, many will prefer to use just one, even in support of four cellos. Elsewhere in the strings two solitary players should never be contemplated.

The first three Beethoven concerti can be performed with a similar reduction (10.8.6.6.4.) although the Third, in particular, will benefit from the more powerful-sounding *tutti* attainable by the addition of an extra desk of both violins and violas. This size (12.10.8.6.4.) is probably ideal for the Fourth Beethoven concerto and (especially with less experienced orchestras) for both Chopin concerti (in E minor and F minor). These last two might be more flexible with the further reduction to Classical proportions – 10.8.6.6.4. – but this will certainly be to the detriment of the expansive first movement *tutti* in both cases. In extreme circumstances, use of the smaller orchestra during the 'solos' alone may be contemplated; this was certainly practised for performances in the nineteenth century, Liszt even going so far as to warn against it in relation to his own works in a footnote appended to the First Concerto. For student orchestras, however, certainly with regard to the Chopin concerti, it proves to be very unrewarding for the excluded players.

Mendelssohn's solo piano concerti are best performed with 12.10.8.6.4. in order to balance the wind writing, but his concerti for two pianos need a larger string group in student orchestra performances, especially in the lower strings, to support the solo instruments. Apart from these, only the small-scale concerted works, such as the Fauré *Fantasie op. 111*, or *Ballade op. 19*, Saint-Saëns *Caprice op. 76* (piano and strings only), Litolff *Scherzo* from *Concerto Symphonique op. 102* and Chopin *Andante Spianato and Grande Polonaise op. 22* will usually require a reduced string group, as of course will works where the composer specifically requests a limited size, for example Ravel *Piano Concerto in G* (8.8.6.6.4.).

STRING CONCERTI

The Mozart violin concerti possibly will require even fewer strings than his piano concerti – as few as 8.6.4.4.2. can be considered (even with less experienced orchestras), with 8.8.6.4.2. probably proving marginally preferable. There is certainly no need to contemplate a number in excess of 10.8.6.4.2. and only where extra players are gaining experience should the maximum forces obtained by the use of one further desk all round be called on.

The major nineteenth-century concerti (Beethoven, Brahms, Bruch, Tchaikovsky) should all be performed with a full complement of strings but Mendelssohn (in E minor) might prove an exception if the string group are unable to maintain a tightly focused *piano* sound.

Again, some of the smaller-scale works – Dvořák *Romance*, Saint-Saëns *Introduction and Rondo Capriccioso* and *Havanaise*, Vaughan Williams *The Lark Ascending* and similar pieces – may need reduction (although, if carefully handled, this last work actually benefits from a large string group). The two Prokofiev concerti also need to be treated with care. They are both very transparent in texture and are at their best when accompanied by strings of smaller than symphonic numbers. However, this is not automatically true of all concerti of similar conception and orchestration. The Bartók *First Concerto* (*op. posth.*) and the Samuel Barber, to name but two, require a large string group, to attain an expanse of sound when the orchestra plays alone.

The nineteenth-century '*virtuosi*' concerti, particularly those of Paganini, work extremely well with *tutti* strings, reduced to Classical proportions for much of the time when the solo instrument is playing (much more successful here than in the Chopin piano concerti). This 'best of both worlds' approach gives just that: full sounding orchestral statements and clearly dominant solos.

This method of instrumental balance is actually written into the scoring of the Walton *Viola Concerto*. The viola is an instrument that will usually benefit from some slight reduction in orchestral forces throughout most of its concerto repertoire and certainly in the works of the Baroque and early Classical period (for instance, by Telemann and Stamitz). One cannot generalize to the same extent about the cello. Though the two Haydn concerti and the Boccherini should be performed with relatively small string groups, some reduction should also be contemplated for accompanying Schumann, Saint-Saëns, Lalo and Tchaikovsky *Rococo Variations*. Other concerti might need a reduction in the lower line of strings only, to avoid duplication or over-emphatic use of a similar range. Works of the stature of the Elgar, Dvořák, Prokofiev and Shostakovich concerti must have full numbers, since these are among some of the most symphonically conceived in the repertoire.

WOODWIND CONCERTI

In my experience there are very few woodwind concerti that will not require some reduction in string numbers. Almost the lone exception is the *Concerto for Clarinet* by Thea Musgrave which, apart from being scored for very large orchestra in other departments, requires the soloist to move from site to site within the orchestra. Other clarinet concerti, as well as those for flute, oboe and bassoon, tend to need no more than 10.8.6.6.4. and considerably fewer for Classical examples (8.6.4.4.2. would be possible here). Much of the twentieth-century repertoire – Chaminade, Ibert, Seiber and Nielsen for the flute; Françaix, Martinů and Richard Strauss for oboe; Busoni, Copland and Debussy for clarinet – is specifically designed for chamber orchestra. Other concerti of this period often require an accompaniment of strings alone and here it is possible to use a slightly larger group. The clarinet concerto by Finzi as well as that for alto saxophone by Glazunov come to mind in this context, the first of which is a superb string piece in its own right and one for which an upper string size of 12.10. or even 14.12. can be contemplated, provided that control of a wide dynamic spectrum is technically available and exercised.

HORN AND BRASS CONCERTI

It is unlikely that any concerto in this repertoire will require a full-scale string group, although a slight weighting of cellos in some of the more recent examples for trumpet and trombone can prove beneficial. Thus, where 12.10.8. may be an ample number of upper strings for works similar in conception to Arutyunyan *Trumpet Concerto* and Grondahl *Trombone Concerto*, 8.4. rather than 6.4. may well prove preferable for cellos and bass.

Concerti of the Classical period – those by Haydn and Hummel for trumpet and the four by Mozart for horn being the most well-known examples – need no greater forces than their woodwind and string counterparts. This small symphonic group will also prove best able to deal with the intricacies of both Richard Strauss concerti for horn. Even the great Schumann *Konzertstück* for four horns never needs a string strength exceeding 12.10.8.6.4.

For the orchestral bass tuba, still something of a rarity as a solo instrument, the concerto by Vaughan Williams and (in the UK at least) the orchestral version of the one by Edward Gregson are the most familiar. Neither is without its problems of balance, particularly in the slow movements, and a string complement of 10.8.6.6.4. tends to be quite sufficient. In this context it is worth issuing a word of warning with regard to the Vaughan Williams. The orchestral writing of the first two movements is relatively straightforward, but the last movement gleefully hides a most horrendous and exposed string passage, accompanied by some very awkward wind writing. Any conductor who may harbour hopes of putting this piece together in a short time will be knee-deep in incalculable disaster when it comes to the concert!

PERCUSSION CONCERTI

The increase in composers' interest in percussion instruments, together with the rise of percussion virtuosi, has brought forth an ever-increasing number of concerti and concerted works for various combinations of percussion instruments and orchestra. So varied are they in orchestral requirement (not to mention musical style) that any attempt to generalize in terms of optimum string numbers is hopeless. Suffice it to say that many composers are most specific about the number of strings they envisage, and very few will contemplate anything approaching a full symphonic section.

Of those now considered part of the standard repertoire for student orchestras, the Milhaud *Concertino for percussion and small orchestra* specifies only 6.6.4.4.2., while Panufnik *Concertino for timpani, percussion and strings* needs no more than 10.8.6.6.4. Bizet/Schedrin *The Carmen Ballet*, for percussion and strings alone, is the single exception where a full symphonic section should be contemplated.

CONCERTI FOR OTHER INSTRUMENTS

A string strength of 10.8.6.6.4. is most suitable for the majority of the concerto repertoire for organ, harpsichord, accordion, harmonica, harp, guitar, saxophone and the subsidiary woodwind instruments. Concerti of the Classical period will again require some reduction. At the two extremes, a somewhat larger section may be considered for Poulenc *Concerto for organ, strings and timpani*, while a smaller section is demanded by the same composer for the *Concert Champêtre* for harpsichord and orchestra (8.8.4.4.4.).

VOICE

Here a more varied application is necessary. Apart from concert and operatic arias of the Classical era (where reduction corresponding to the above guidelines applies) much of the rest of the concert repertoire was conceived for large orchestral forces, and works of the nature of Richard Strauss *Four Last Songs*, Berlioz *Nuits d'Été* and Ravel *Scheherazade* are at their most radiant when played by surprisingly large string forces (the ability of the large string group to perform the softest *pianissimo* has already been mentioned).

The more dramatic examples of the operatic repertoire may well require some adjustment in concert performance for, certainly with operatic giants such as Verdi, Puccini and Wagner, the subduing effect of the opera house pit was by no means overlooked in their original conception or decisions of orchestration. Even so, in the opera house there are many examples where only the most mature and powerful voice can hold its own in many passages, and once transferred to the 'open' concert hall the balance can become extremely critical. Allowance *must* be made for the maturity, experience, and carrying power of the particular voice to be accompanied. No hard and fast rules can apply and decisions should be taken within the framework of these criteria.

In all the above, adjustment must be contemplated in relation to the strengths and weaknesses of orchestra, soloist and (indeed) composer. Sometimes, for all sorts of reasons, a different string strength from those discussed here will prove better for a particular collaboration. However, the above guidelines will prove to be generally successful.

Position of Soloist

It is easier for an orchestra to accompany a sound that is within its perimeter than one outside it. Placing a solo instrumentalist at the front of a large orchestra causes difficulties of ensemble and balance which increase the further away the players are, and are especially acute for those directly behind the sound. Many solo instruments are highly directional in their projected sound, and it is not unusual for the orchestral woodwind and brass to be able to hear very little of the soloist, particularly when they themselves are also playing.

Unfortunately, this situation cannot be avoided altogether in concert performance, since there is no successful alternative position for the concerto soloist. Such small help as might be possible, however, should be given.

There is an immense difference in the orchestra's aural perception of the solo sound when it emanates from totally outside the front line of strings compared with even fractionally within its compass. Although it directly affects only comparatively few players, this closer position brings the focus of the sound back into the orchestra to some extent, and guarantees that at least the front desks of strings can hear it more clearly. Even more significantly, it unites the soloist with the orchestra, engendering a visual rapport and collaboration difficult to achieve when the soloist is physically separate from the body of the orchestra.

In front of the orchestra, with the 1st violins maintaining their normal situation close to the rostrum, the soloist is backed by a solidity of 1st violin sound that, for the majority of accompanying passages, is simply too close. Contact with the orchestra as a whole is lost, and there is no opportunity for the personal musical influence that is the hallmark of any really high-class soloist to mould the performance. The situation will be immeasurably improved if the soloist is placed just a metre further back, encroaching on the physical confines of the orchestra, and this will also enhance the soloist's aural perception of the centre of the orchestral sound.

Except for a piano or other keyboard instrument, room may easily be made for the single instrumentalist or singer by moving the 1st violins back a little over one complete desk's distance (about two metres). In the case of a solo cellist this may well have to be increased a little, as indeed it might in a number of other cases should the soloist feel in any way crowded or cramped for space. The soloist is now free to take up a position in line with the very edge of the orchestra, utilizing maximum aural separation while maintaining aural contact with the players and visual contact with the conductor. It is generally not necessary to provide a separate rostrum except for a solo cellist where, because of the relatively low position of the instrument, most players will prefer to be raised a few inches above the platform level.

Most soloists usually take up position on the violin side, by the conductor's left hand, but this is really more so that the most frequently encountered soloists (pianists and violinists) are able to see the conductor than for any profound musical reason. Left-handed violin and viola soloists *have* to stand on the other side and many singers (especially male) prefer to. I am sure that I, along with many other conductors, have accompanied Britten *Les Illuminations* or Mahler *Lieder eines fahrenden Gesellen* as many times with the soloist on my right as on my left.

The positioning of the soloist in line with the edge of the orchestra holds good for keyboard instruments as well, but the physical placing of an instrument as large as a concert grand piano causes considerably more upheaval. Both the 1st violins and cellos will need to move back a full desk's distance and the conductor's rostrum must be removed and replaced by one that has no back railing. The piano may then be placed within the orchestra to a distance of half its width so that, once again, the player is in line with the edge of the orchestra, as shown in the following diagram.

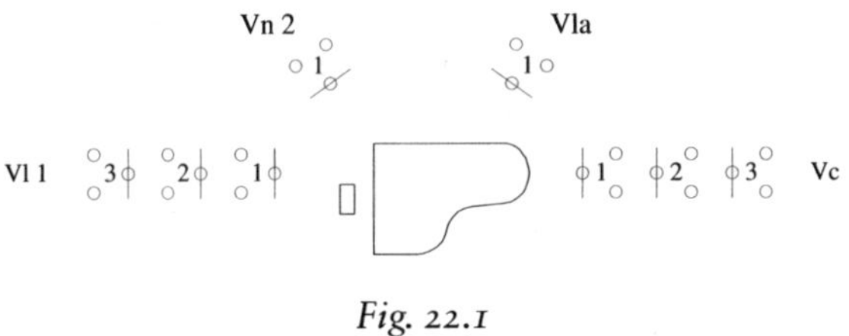

Fig. 22.1

The following adjustments will then need to be made.

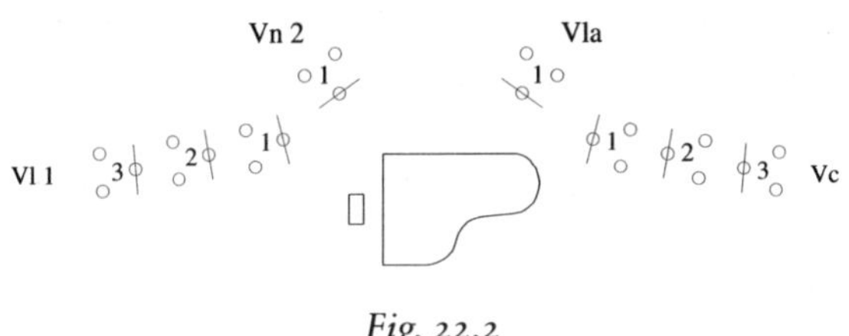

Fig. 22.2

The conductor will obviously be placed further into the orchestra than usual and will also need to stand to the left of centre, half turned towards the violins, in order to maintain close visual contact with the soloist and (far more importantly) the *hands* of the soloist. The first desk of 1st violins and of cellos will need to move slightly inwards and turn towards the centre of the orchestra, so that contact with the conductor is maintained in a direct line with the music stand; second desks of these sections will also need to turn, but to a lesser extent. It will be noticed that, in this position, the conductor has turned his back on the cellos – a situation they are quite used to, and for which they are mostly very grateful! However, clear contact can still be achieved whenever necessary by a small movement of the body in their direction. Close contact with the soloist *must* be maintained.

MULTIPLE SOLOISTS

The positioning of more than one soloist can often cause considerable difficulty, not only in the direct relationship of one to another but also in preserving contact and sight-lines between the conductor and the first desk of 1st violins. This can never be absolutely guaranteed unless the soloists are placed in front of the orchestra, a position – as implied above – that is disadvantageous to ensemble and balance, and not to be recommended.

In works that do not include piano or vocalists, the positioning of just two soloists together is unlikely to cause great concern, especially when one of them is a forward-facing instrument: combining oboe, clarinet, bassoon, trumpet, trombone, tuba, cello, bass or harp with any other single instrument usually means that one instrument can be in the normal position with the other slightly forward and beyond, angled just enough to maintain contact. This is further simplified if the second instrument is of the 'side-on' variety. Oboe plus violin, cello plus violin, clarinet plus viola, and harp plus flute are the most common examples of this combination and can be staged quite easily.

Two violins, violin plus viola, violin plus flute, or two flutes prove slightly more difficult. Here, the two instrumentalists will need to stand in echelon, almost overlapping as viewed from the audience in order that their own visual contact may be ensured and, often, with the lower pitched instrument on the outside. Two flutes will tend to be placed with one or both of them much more face-on to the body of the hall than if playing alone.

Once three or more instrumental soloists appear together, the problems really begin. The most common combination of this size not including a keyboard instrument is the wind quartet – oboe, clarinet, bassoon and horn – as in Mozart *Sinfonia Concertante K297b*. In this instance, as in all *concertante* concerti apart from those involving a string quartet, certain further criteria need to be applied. The ensemble might choose to perform the work seated rather than standing (a bassoon player who uses a spike rather than a sling to support the instrument will make this unavoidable), and either position may be adopted with or without the use of music stands. A frequent choice of relative position for each soloist is (from left to right, facing the group) oboe, horn, bassoon and clarinet, but almost any combination is possible, and the quartet's preference might well influence the available options for the group as a whole.

If the solo quartet is to be seated then, with or without music stands, the players are best accommodated in a semicircle around (and in front of) the conductor. Although this position will always disturb the sight-lines of some members of the audience, there is no practical alternative. With the smallish string group necessary for performance of such a work, it is quite possible for the conductor to dispense with the rostrum, thereby removing the main obstacle to vision, but any attempt to place the group at one side, having created space by moving one or other string section far enough back to accommodate all four players, or pairing the quartet, two either side, is fraught with intense musical danger.

Hazards associated with positioning soloists outside the orchestra have already been highlighted, but some further clarification might be in order. The position is treated with caution because of the musical difficulties it can cause to the orchestra and the soloists, *not* because of the awkwardness of sight contact between the conductor and soloists, although this is an additional consideration. Therefore the problem cannot be resolved by moving the whole orchestra back and effectively replacing the outside line of 1st violins with the solo instrumentalists, leaving the conductor in the original position. The soloists would still be outside the orchestra and the same performance problems will arise.

Should the wind quartet prefer to stand, we slip deeper into the realms of compromise, for there is no possibility of their being arranged in the same way as the seated group, and any straight line will bring its own limitations of contact (the group are certain to have rehearsed in some sort of quartet formation, the outer two facing each other and the others angled towards the centre). With the 1st violins moved back a little further than normal, some sort of shallow curve must be formed by the soloists starting from a point next to, and slightly in front of, the conductor.

Similar restrictions apply to the string quartet. Although the great majority of ensembles perform seated there are those whose normal arrangement is for the violins and viola to stand. For most concerti (such as those by Spohr, Martinů and Schoenberg) placing can be similar to that of the woodwind group discussed above, but later examples may well need some adjustment. At the première of the concerto by Derek Bourgeois, for instance, we found it necessary to place the quartet in front of the orchestra to achieve a successful balance, in spite of the problems of contact that such a position entailed.

To all rules, of course, exceptions must exist. Thus the four horns of the Schumann *Konzertstück*, whose lines are almost entirely chordally integrated, will stand in an almost straight line in front of the violins of the orchestra.

Larger numbers of solo instrumentalists are very rare and require only an extension of these principles. Frank Martin *Concerto for Seven Wind Instruments* is accompanied by strings and percussion, with the solo players (flute, oboe, clarinet, bassoon, horn, trumpet and trombone) seated, forming a semicircle in front of the conductor, with the percussion behind the strings. The Baroque *concerti grossi* are not within the scope of this book, and are rarely performed in concerts that also include large symphonic forces.

The inclusion of piano in concerti for more than one soloist is less problematic than might at first be thought, owing to the drastically limited options for its positioning. The piano and the orchestra must be placed as described in *Fig. 22.2* with further space allowed for the additional soloists. Thus in triple concerti for violin, cello and piano (Beethoven *op. 56*, Martinů *Concertino*) the two string soloists will have to be set, rather awkwardly, at the pianist's back, since few stages provide sufficient depth to accommodate a normal piano trio positioning *plus* orchestra. Were adequate depth available such a placing might be attempted but the piano lid would have to be removed completely so that the orchestra and conductor could hear the solo cellist, and its removal could prove counter-productive to the balance of the soloists.

Two pianos may be interlocked, end to end with keyboards directly opposite. For these few, but impressive concerti (Mozart, Mendelssohn (2), Bruch, Poulenc, Vaughan Williams and Bartók – his own arrangement of the *Sonata for two pianos and percussion* – are the most familiar) the 2nd piano, with the keyboard to the cello side of the orchestra, must obviously have the lid removed. Whether the first piano should retain the lid on full stick or remove it also depends largely on the acoustic of the concert hall. (Examples of the square-cased double piano with a single lid do exist, but I have never been fortunate enough to hear one used in concerto performance. It would certainly be a wonderful experience.)

Vocal soloists tend, by habit, to stand somewhat further forward than instrumentalists, perhaps because of the long tradition of oratorio performance where the trio, quartet or quintet of soloists is often placed in line in front of the orchestra, frequently (but by no means essentially) divided either side of the conductor. However, it is quite possible (and usually advantageous) to accommodate up to four vocalists nearer the orchestra by moving both outside lines of desks of strings back and positioning two singers either side. Although chairs must be provided for use in the periods when individual singers are not involved, sufficient space can be comfortably found in most concert halls.

There remain only the *concertante* works that require a complete reseating of the orchestra – Frank Martin *Petite Symphonie Concertante* for piano, harp, harpsichord and double string orchestra, for example. Works of this nature must be considered individually, but decisions as to placement must be based on criteria of balance and ensemble, rather than on what looks good.

Orchestral Responsibility

It is the orchestra's responsibility to make the soloist sound wonderful. In fulfilling this task it will have accomplished all others.

For the conductor and orchestra, there is no such thing as an easy concerto. Some might, perhaps, be easier than others in their technical demands, but no concerto, however simple the accompaniment might appear to be, is without problems that can only be overcome by a very fluent and mature orchestral technique. Furthermore, the most obvious difficulties – balance, ensemble, support and interaction – are totally interrelated and cannot easily be taught or induced in isolation. For the purposes of this discussion, however, it would be most useful to consider them under individual headings.

BALANCE

Balance – the subordination of one or more voices to one or more others (most commonly translated in the context of concerti as making sure the orchestra is not 'too loud') – has, in fact, only a limited relationship to the dynamic level of sound. Balance is as dependent on substance, articulation and sensitivity as on simple volume. It is very easy to destroy the solo line of a Classical string concerto with *soft* playing if the combined movement is not clear, the phrase endings undisciplined and the general relationship with the soloist unsympathetic. As with all orchestral performance, articulation and sensitivity become the prime disciplines of accompaniment, but here they are subject to even greater pressures of interaction and support.

It is of no musical benefit simply to reduce the level of sound in relation to a solo line if the character of the sound is lost. Balance must, therefore, be continuously related to the required character of the sound as well as its direct relationship of sonority and substance. In order to attain a measure of this duality from a student orchestra it is essential for the orchestra to be allowed to find and determine the required sound first, and then to reduce its level and potency as and where necessary. This process need not take long, and many other aspects of the work may be rehearsed concurrently, but it is a very important consideration, and might be best clarified by illustration of an occasion where I neglected to do it.

The work was Brahms *Violin Concerto*, the orchestra was that of one of the major conservatoires and the soloist was a post-graduate student of considerable ability and some experience. The rehearsal schedule was normal for a work of this nature: an initial rehearsal of between an hour and an hour and a quarter in which to play through the piece and do some preliminary work, a second session of two hours in which to rehearse in more detail, and a final rehearsal on the day of the concert. (This, by the way, is fairly minimal, and certainly less than any youth orchestra should set aside for such a piece.) The soloist's instrumental professor, a friend and colleague with whom I had played many times, was present at the initial rehearsal and suggested very early on that the orchestra was generally too loud in accompaniment, an observation which, out of misguided deference to him, I acted on throughout that first rehearsal and subsequently, keeping the orchestral sound subdued in all the solo passages. Because the substance of the accompanying sound had never been grasped, the orchestra complied in the only way they knew, taking the weight off the sound and dropping the level by changing the production to something much lighter and softer in texture. In the performance the orchestra played Brahms' notes in the style of Mozart.

What was actually required in this case was the same weight and purpose as had been apparent in the orchestra's over-energetic reading of the accompaniment, reduced to a lower level by a very different set of technical criteria. It would not have been difficult. The orchestra only had to be given time to recognize the sound that needed to be reduced.

The technicalities involved in the projection of an unchanged sonority at a softer dynamic have been previously discussed, but (perhaps surprisingly) in the specific circumstance of accompaniment, such adjustment can often prove easier to induce. Once the relevant substance of sound has been attained, and the concept of maintaining it understood, few orchestras will allow it to escape, largely on account of the direct and continuous example supplied by the solo sound.

Obviously, some orchestrations will call for more modification from the orchestra than others, as will the individual sound of some soloists. The particular instrument involved will have considerably less effect, however, since the composer should have engineered the original concept of the sonority towards its particular strengths and weaknesses. Thus, the circumstance mentioned above with regard to the Brahms *Violin Concerto* could equally have applied to either piano concerto or that for violin and cello. The chosen instrument was not of consequence, only the sound.

Balance, in terms of orchestral sonority against a solo sound, is at its most critical in the late and post-Romantic repertoire where, very often, large orchestral forces are employed. Large string sections, while capable of playing incredibly softly in any style, may not always do so when required, or have the technical capability to maintain such a level. Sustained notes constitute most of the problem and, even in a work of such instrumental complexity as

Richard Strauss *Four Last Songs*, where every bar presents a labyrinth of potential pitfalls, a passage such as *Ex. 22.1*, from the end of the second song (*September*), will prove as troublesome as any other.

In full score these few bars contain minimal wind doubling – single woodwind for the first four bars and a lone clarinet for the others. The strings, with the exception of 1st violins, maintain simple, *piano* chordal support, and the bars look comparatively tame and docile. But if the movement of the lower and middle strings is not absolutely vertically accurate, or there is any sign of false *crescendo*, change in bow speed or projected solidity within them, the solo voice will be smothered. This is a place where the right sound can be projected by movement of its source, as discussed in Chapter 13. If the sound is moved from the direct proximity of the solo it can provide the necessary harmonic support without fear of discomforting the solo line, and it will also move much more accurately as a result. Precision of movement is fundamental to the balance and flexibility of any accompanying line. No matter how softly such a line is performed, a lack of precise movement will counteract its effectiveness, as well as losing the sense of the phrase.

ENSEMBLE

The unavoidable link between ensemble and balance, demonstrated in the preceding paragraph, destroys any illusion that the former may be confined to simple coincidence of movement between soloist and orchestra. Its significance is far greater than that but, at the same time, totally dependent on many other aspects of association.

Within the confines of an overall structure, the prevailing influence on any concerto will be that of the soloist. Both spontaneous and predetermined inflection will need to be reflected in the accompaniment if the combined statement is to be delivered as a comprehensible discourse. Ensemble, in the mere sense of being together, will be of purely decorative benefit if soloist and orchestra are saying different things.Thus it is the soloist's overall concept of a work that has to be accompanied, rather than just individual variations of tempi.

It is this personal inflection – the 'soul' of the interpretation if you like – that becomes difficult to tamper with, because it is a product not only of personality and musical preference but also of technique and sound. Any instrumentalist's interpretation will contain as much that has been derived from their approach to the instrument as from their approach to the particular work.

It is important that this aspect of accompaniment is emphasized because I

F
Voice
Lang - sam tut ___ er die müd - - ge - word - nen
Vl I
Vl II
I
Vla
II
I
Vc
II
DB
Au - - - - - - - - gen zu.
pp

EX. 22. 1

believe it to be the essence of the association between soloist and orchestra, regardless of age or experience. Thus the point of development reached by any soloist in terms of maturity becomes irrelevant as a measure of the extent of this relationship; indeed, many younger soloists will need an even greater degree of musical support for a number of reasons, not least of which may be confidence and sheer courage.

In this respect I must reiterate and briefly expand on a point made at the beginning of this chapter. Any attempt by the conductor to alter or determine a soloist's performance, whether by restricting the musical framework, verbal persuasion or any other means, is doomed to failure. Apart from very slight adjustments for instrumental accommodation or structural emphasis, an alteration of approach is not possible in the time-scale applicable to rehearsal and performance, and, in cases of extreme disagreement, the only tangible result will be to cause the soloist to focus even more attention on matters of personal technique, for reasons of sheer self-preservation. This is fact, and extends from the most inexperienced player to the world-class soloist.

This is not to say that suggestions cannot be made or musical differences discussed, but it must be accepted that these may have little effect on the end result in concert and that a greater service will be done to the composer by absorbing the intentions of the soloist than by staging an outright contest.

SUPPORT

The complete interdependence of support with all other aspects of accompaniment has already been exposed and its relationship to all facets of music-making touched upon. Its component parts may at different times (and with differing emphasis) embrace the musical conditions of sonority, harmony, rhythm or melody, as well as those of alignment, dynamic, interpretative freedom and sound projection.

This is at once the most vital and difficult area of concerto accompaniment as far as the student orchestra is concerned, because its realization involves a great deal of experience in the production of sound and assessment of balance.

The difficulties of balancing and articulating passages of subdued harmonic support were mentioned in reference to *Ex. 22.1*, as was the critical point at which dynamic subjugation of the line will cause support to be lost. This was in relation to a phrase predominantly projected by strings, with all their inherent abilities of combination and diffusion; a similar situation for woodwind can expose even greater demands of instrumental control and judgement, as in *Ex. 22.2*, a few apparently simple bars from Mendelssohn *Violin Concerto*.

EX. 22.2

Both intonation and internal balance are essential, together with the provision of a dynamic level neither too dominant nor too ineffectual to support the solo line. It takes considerable experience and ability to judge the appropriate level from a position that is rarely beneficial to any aural appraisal of the soloist. It is, however, rather easier when the accompanying line is sustained than when it comprises more isolated notes, even though these might well amount to only the separation of a basically *legato* phrase. *Ex. 22.3* from the second movement of Beethoven *Piano Concerto no. 5*, illustrates this type of accompaniment.

EX. 22.3

The line of the phrase must obviously be extended through the rests, though this is made much easier by its proximity to a *legato* statement (the preceding bar has been included in the example to demonstrate this point). Nonetheless, woodwind balance in this example can only be successfully accomplished by extreme concentration on the continuity of the phrase, as is the case with the answering chords of the strings. The musical emphasis might well be considered to rest with the piano in this phrase, but this harmonic decoration stems from an ornamental variation of the theme. The beautiful restatement of this theme by the same three wind instruments was set within clear margins of associated responsibility, which is what makes the balance, substance and projection of each separated note of the quoted phrase so difficult.

It is worth mentioning, in reference to earlier chapters, that the clarinet part (written for A clarinet) might well be transposed on to the B♭ instrument. Both outer movements demand the latter, and few clarinettists will risk the extreme demands of this movement on a cold instrument.

Direct Association

Notwithstanding all that has gone before, straightforward co-ordination of movement between orchestra and soloist is very difficult, and must be given some separate consideration.

For student orchestras, rhythmic flexibility and aural dexterity will be required to a degree probably never before experienced, and considerable patience will be needed until the processes of listening, assimilating and re-acting become instantaneous. It is not at all easy to retain flexibility while maintaining a clearly produced sound and even the most proficient student orchestra will always take time to relocate the necessary techniques. With an inexperienced orchestra, the required agility might sometimes appear to be beyond them, but this is certainly not the case and, once the concept has been embraced, the group will become as responsive as any other.

For the orchestra, the fundamental 'technique' of accompaniment relates to attitude. As far as rhythmic movement is concerned, *nothing* may be taken for granted, whether in rehearsal or performance. Not a bar may be turned, nor even a single note played without direct reference to the soloist. The orchestra must listen and watch *all* the time. Basically, this is no different from the attitude required for solo orchestral playing, except that the main point of influence comes from outside the orchestra rather than from within, and that the concept of the work will be more focused towards extreme tonal and technical demands made upon a single instrument. It is this last aspect, common to all concerted works, that distinguishes the structure from any other, and, consequently, causes the *feel* of the individual orchestral parts to be entirely different.

This distinction stems from the necessary fragmentation of so much of the writing and may be cited as the only technical variation relevant to orchestral accompaniment. Instrumentally, there are no new techniques as such, but the agility with which various corporate and individual orchestral skills must be employed constitutes a technique in itself. This, almost beyond anything else, lies at the root of difficulties experienced in ensemble, balance, support or any other aspect of concerted accompaniment.

For the strings of the orchestra especially, the rapid changes from rhythmic to sustained accompaniment, fragments of melodic line to harmonic insinuation, *tutti* interjection to solo support, are technically formidable if only from the one aspect of being in the right place in the bow to accomplish them. Such dexterity of bowing technique as has already been discussed will be extended to the ultimate level by the demands of solo accompaniment. The concerto, beyond any work in the programme, requires the addition of *specialist* bowing in the parts to have any hope of being successfully performed.

Once some degree of flexibility is evident it is the conductor's responsibility to use it efficiently, and this demands an extensive and fluent technique. Only two of the more basic requirements vital to the accompanying of any solo line will be highlighted here.

Firstly, the control of sound *within* the beat; that is, the ability to control the speed and placing of notes without recourse to subdivision of the beat. In its most simple form this can be practised with the help of one instrumentalist performing an ascending scale in 4/4 time, such as the following.

EX. 22.4

While showing only the four main beats, the conductor, by gesture alone, must provide a *rallentando* across the last two or three notes that the instrumentalist *cannot* ignore, vary or pre-empt in any way. When this is sufficiently fluent as to be technically reliable, it may be extended to this:

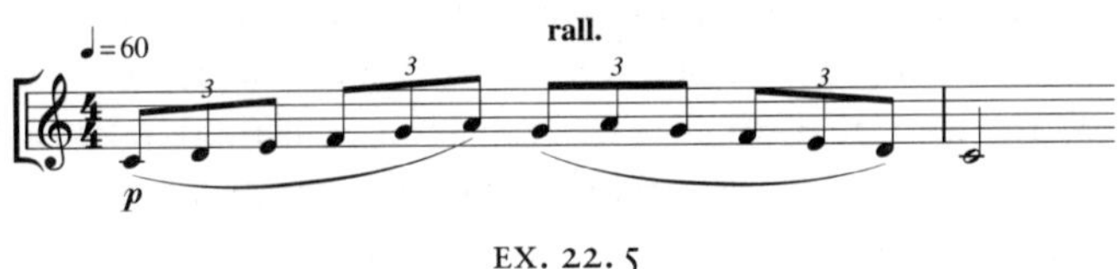

EX. 22.5

Thereafter the position of the *rallentando* may be varied at will, returning either to the original speed or to any variation of it.

The second essential technique, linked to similar origins of control, is that the conductor's hand must not be committed too soon. It must not travel towards the subsequent beat as an automatic reaction. The movement must be totally controlled, so that it may be protracted or abbreviated at will, and the arm is not suddenly 'found' in a position where no adjustment is possible.

In a passage such as *Ex. 22.6*, from the second movement of Chopin *Piano Concerto no. 1*, any lack of awareness in the movement of the conducting arm can have disastrous results.

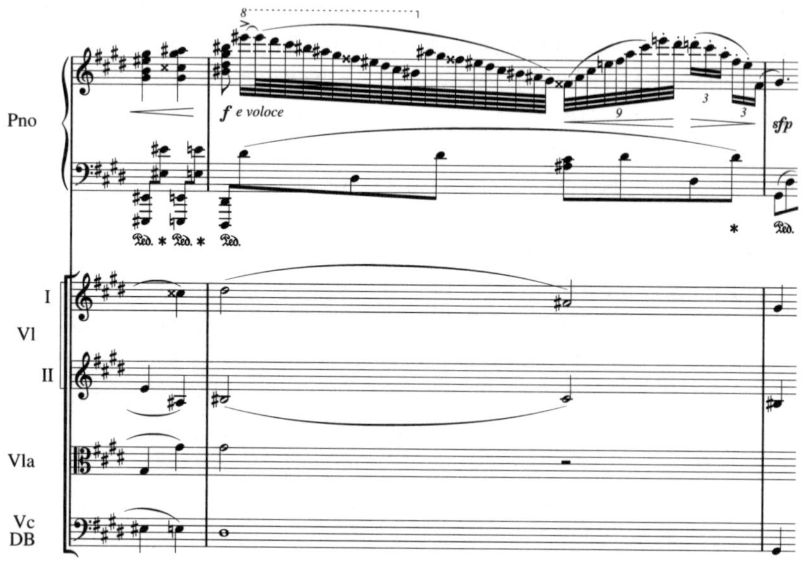

EX. 22.6

To be able to anticipate and control the accompaniment of overtly decorative piano passages of this nature, it is always important to concentrate the ear on the left-hand movement of the soloist and not try to 'follow' the embellishments of the upper line. The passage will usually be found to contain far less *rubato* than might be imagined, and any that *is* apparent will usually be better judged from listening to the accompanying hand than from the figure itself.

As far as the general concept of accompaniment directly relating to the conductor is concerned, one misapprehension (or perhaps just a misnomer) needs to be put to rest. The conductor never follows a soloist: the conductor *anticipates* a soloist. This is directly analogous to the whole technique of conducting which is not to show where something *is*, but where it *will be*. In practical terms, this requires extreme concentration and the ability to react instantly to nuances, and to sense what might be implied by any phrasing or musical approach on the soloist's part. With renowned solo artists, any slight alteration or *rubato* they might introduce for the first time in concert will usually be very logical, both in reasoning and accomplishment. Only with less experienced performers does the likelihood of real surprise forever lurk in the background.

Appraisal need not, however, rely entirely on the ear for, in most cases, some visual clue will be equally apparent. Thus, with string soloists, the speed, movement and position of the bow will often be much more informative than mere aural perception of the line. The *only* way of exactly determining the position of the soloist's second note in *Ex. 22.7*, for example, from the slow movement of Sibelius *Violin Concerto*, is by watching the movement of the bow and anticipating the change.

EX. 22.7

Most soloists will use a separate bow at the start of the second note (not entirely in order to free the sound of the first but to facilitate the phrasing lift before the following accent), and the first note will accordingly never be quite 'in tempo'. Throughout this opening passage, careful attention to the soloist's bow movement is the only way to anticipate the slight forward impetus that is often implied. Similar attention should be paid to the hands of a pianist and the breathing (both in terms of intake and span) of wind or vocal soloists.

It must be stressed that these are an additional guide, and should not be used to supplant the concentration of the ear, but, especially in the case of string, wind and vocal soloists, where the rigours of concert performance will often lead to slight reappraisals of tempi, they become very important.

In Conclusion

Little need be said that directly relates to soloists except with regard to student performers. Personally, I have no strong feelings one way or the other as to whether a concerto is performed by memory or with music. It is entirely *how* it is performed that matters. Nonetheless, many professors will insist that their students perform from memory, and this undoubtedly helps concentration in many circumstances. It should not, however, be insisted on in situations where it might prove detrimental to the final performance, both for aesthetic reasons and those more closely associated with the personal sensibilities of the player in question. Some concerti are notoriously dangerous to perform by memory (the final movement of Prokofiev *Violin Concerto no. 2* is a notable example) and should not be undertaken in this way if anything more than a calculated element of risk is involved.

When actually learning a piece for performance with orchestra, the soloist should refer frequently to the full score and not just the piano reduction or arrangement, in order gradually to assimilate those areas of the orchestration that may impose limitations on the solo line. There are also many cases where the two sources differ widely: the final movement of Lalo *Symphonie Espagnole* for violin and orchestra, for example, contains a 20-bar introduction in the arrangement for piano and violin, whereas this is extended to 30 in the orchestral version.

The soloist, whether international virtuoso or the most junior member of the orchestra itself, should always be extended the courtesy of a welcome at the first rehearsal and be treated with consideration. Any *cadenza* or extended solo passage must be treated to *total* silence and *absolute* stillness in both rehearsal and concert.

The subtle and far-reaching demands made on the orchestra in any musical association with a solo instrument or voice expose the furthest reaches of its corporate technique. As such, it is probably the most beneficial learning process for any orchestra, while the attitude shown towards concerto playing becomes the most shrewd and precise calibration on which to judge an orchestra's standard.

PART V

General Considerations

23 REPERTOIRE

In many respects, this chapter brings together all that has gone before, since it is not possible to discuss available, suitable or feasible repertoire in isolation from the musical and technical demands it imposes on those who perform it. Nor can it be divorced from the ability and knowledge of those entrusted to direct it. Thus, the discussion that follows assumes an understanding of the extent to which technical and musical considerations might apply in some circumstances, and the extent to which opportunities are made available – or limitations imposed – depending on the competence of the direction.

Fundamental Principles

The repertoire performed by student orchestras will be chosen subject to varying criteria. Age-range, ability, and availability of players (and instruments) will all play their part, together with the preferences of the conductor and the orchestra themselves.

Although I have suggested several times within these pages that certain repertoire may not be *ideal* material for student orchestras, this does not imply that any work mentioned is necessarily out of range – otherwise its discussion would have been irrelevant, and, on a broader level, all exploration and development would be undermined by an implied limit, and this is certainly not so.

It is relevant, however, to consider certain criteria, both in relation to a work's suitability for ensembles of varying standard, and to any stylistic difficulties that might not immediately emerge from the score. Obviously no orchestra should be totally limited to the repertoire that encourages only its inherent strengths, but it is important to have some awareness of why certain things work and others may not.

TECHNICAL CONSIDERATIONS

The initial decision as to whether a piece is suitable for a particular orchestra will largely be made with regard to the string parts and whatever technical demands (in terms of exposure and agility) are made upon them. The amount of rehearsal time available and the size of the sections are also important considerations. Where there there are fewer than the optimum number of players, this will affect rehearsal time, in that the techniques that overcome such deficiencies need to be taught and practised.

Obviously, any attempt to play a Tchaikovsky symphony with six 1st violins is doomed to failure, not solely because of the appalling balance that would result, but also the technical dangers that would be faced by each of these players. Nevertheless, a similar insubstantiality with regard to violas or basses is very likely, and the dangers are no less pertinent.

Performing large orchestral repertoire with string sections of insufficient size can cause technical damage, both as a direct consequence of the part itself and the mental approach towards it. A small viola section, for example, will not be able to ignore the amount of sound around them or the demands of sonority dictated by the wind and brass. It is essential for them to be able to deal with it, and to know what levels they must maintain to protect their technique and where the projection of a particular sound will disguise their numerical shortcomings.

Above all, the players should never attempt to produce a bigger sound than the numbers can naturally support, and never be tempted to separate their sound, even if one or two players can produce a stronger sound than the others. To fall prey to this seductive illusion will actually mean that the section has been *reduced* in size, as any noticeable increase in output will have been localized. In strong, *legato* production, a slight centring of the sound, effected by using a little less bow with firmer contact, will increase its potency and, therefore, its *apparent* balance. This perception may be further increased by small adjustment of the contact area towards the bridge. Neither of these will provide the same sound as that of the larger sections but they will, in many situations, provide the same level of aural dominance, and this is the best that can be hoped for. Continuous use of this production can be tiring, both with regard to bow-arm control and the concentration needed to maintain it. But it is not in any way technically damaging and no work will require it in such extended periods as might cause distress.

For passages of more virtuosic nature, where the demands of the left hand outweigh those of sonority, the opposite approach is necessary, with the section in fact reducing their sound while preserving the bow-arm and left-hand emphasis necessary for rhythm and articulation. Clarity will be attained, as always, by accuracy and contact.

These techniques will be of help to the middle and lower sections of strings, but are far less likely to make an appreciable difference to 1st violins where the projection of the upper line cannot be effected without sufficient numbers. However, whenever one deals with comparatively small sections these techniques *must* be instilled.

For woodwind, horns and brass, the corporate sound cannot be altered in this way and the parts must be taken much more at face value. When selecting repertoire, the main criteria will include the incidence of sustained high playing, demanding solos (from the point of view of technique *and* exposure) and other technical requirements. With regard to horns and brass in particular, it is helpful to consult a specialist player as to the suitability of some of the larger orchestrations, since the demands of stamina are not always revealed by the parts alone.

Some consideration should also be given to the amount of playing involved, especially the limited involvement for certain instruments that some scorings provide. This is an important factor, but very easily overlooked, and is often of great relevance to the percussion section.

For the 'extra' instruments, such as harp and piano, availability of a player (or instrument) will probably be the first consideration, but the specific demands of each part must not be disregarded.

MUSICAL CONSIDERATIONS

These may be divided into those affecting (or determined by) a particular concert programme or series of programmes, of which more will be said later, and those which directly affect the orchestra themselves.

Decisions involving the major piece of any programme must take into consideration the players themselves. The work selected should be rewarding to perform, either in its content or the challenge it presents. Of direct relevance here, of course, is the standard of performance expected from them by the direction, the most substantial and exciting work becoming very unrewarding and tedious to play if insufficient demands are made on players' capabilities.

While all styles of composition will benefit the orchestra to an extent, and all need to be introduced within the orchestra's natural span of membership, some can be mastered more easily than others. Of these, the Romantic repertoire (in the broadest sense) provides the greatest number, and also the widest variety, of works performable by the non-professional orchestra. Exploration of other compositional styles and periods, however, reveals an equally inviting number of works that may be successfully performed by a wide range of orchestras.

Nonetheless, repertoire must be chosen that is known to be within the possible scope of the orchestra's corporate ability – regardless of whether they may ever previously have reached the required level. This entails the most difficult and least definable of selective judgements, which must obviously be flexible in relation to the general standard, experience and age-range of the orchestra involved.

There are unquestionably certain boundaries which, in any but the very highest circles of non-professional playing, prove very difficult to penetrate. Such limits extend across the accepted historical confines of compositional style and therefore, headings such as Classical or Romantic must, in this context, refer only to particular characteristics most readily associated with the techniques of performance. What follows is a very personal chain of reasoning, which might prove helpful to the eventual extension of such performing boundaries. The results are undeniable and oft-proven by experience.

Classical Style

Symphonic writing of the Classical period, as well as that in the Classical tradition, involves the most subtle and perfect techniques of performance and, in its ultimate communication, is simply beyond the technical scope of all but the greatest orchestras. Composers whose music provides a large proportion of works in this style include Haydn, Mozart, Beethoven, Schubert, Weber, Rossini, Berlioz, and Mendelssohn, but certain aspects of the music of both Schumann and Brahms may be added for the purposes of this discussion.

The basis of the style is one of formal architecture and harmonic structure, characterized by a clearly defined opposition of dynamic range. To be able to reproduce the necessary subtleties of just this last-mentioned aspect without change of balance, alteration in quality, misplacement of chordal structure or loss of vertical relationship, requires playing of an immensely high standard. The bars shown as *Ex. 23.1* come from the second movement (*Larghetto*) of Beethoven *Symphony no. 2*.

Even without detailed examination, the nature of the writing in this very typical passage can be seen to demand extreme clarity of texture, control of phrasing and purity of intonation. But perhaps the most formidable aspect is that dramatic tension stems entirely from the subtle influence of each individual line. There is no large orchestration or reserve of instrumentation to highlight a climax or provide obvious changes of colour. To communicate a work or movement which is cast in this restrained mould, with no recourse to corporate support and where every sound must be perfectly judged in relation to itself and the immediately surrounding texture, takes little short of total artistry.

Cl (A) 1 2
Bn 1 2
Hn (E) 1 2
Vl I
Vl II
Vla
Vc
Fl 1 2
Ob 1 2
Cl 1 2
Bn 1 2
Hn 1 2
p
sf
ff

EX. 23.1

EX 23.1 (continued)

It is this feature of the style that first begins to bring into focus the thin dividing line between those works that communicate through concepts of structure and harmonic relationship and those that employ more overt methods of dramatic influence. Obviously a number of orchestral works by the composers listed above lean heavily towards the latter category, displaying sufficient increase in their dramatic use of the orchestra that this aspect of their language may be successfully emphasized. Symphonies such as Beethoven *5*, *7* and *8* and Schubert *8 (Unfinished)* may (still with careful handling) be considered in this context. However, their two largest-scale symphonic works (Beethoven *Symphony no. 9* and Schubert '*Great*' *C major*), combine the two styles so perfectly that their very apparent dramatic power can sometimes mask the highly Classical concepts of orchestral technique that each demands.

This is the area where miscalculation arises most frequently and which often ensnares those of us entrusted with choice of repertoire. Those works which so deftly engineer power and weight of sonority, drama and Romantic perception entirely through an extension of Classical harmonic language are magnetic, but highly dangerous material for the inexperienced orchestra. All the orchestral works of Brahms, for example, require this most elusive aspect of orchestral technique.

But the distinction needs to be defined more clearly, for at the moment it has been proposed merely as the projection of quality as against colour, and it is surely more complex than that. *All* forms of music will benefit from enhanced quality of delivery, and this must always be the ultimate aim.

It is in the works of Berlioz that the beginnings of a clear demarcation of technique in terms of projected communication appear, and in one work in particular, the *Symphonie Fantastique*. The last two movements of this symphony (*The March to the Scaffold* and *The Witches Sabbath*), for all their technical difficulty, are much easier to perform than the other three, in that the communication is direct, the dramatic purpose undeflected, and the language extravagant and full of imagery. The movements project a direction and strength of purpose that are hard to avoid.

However, this is still only the effect of the language and not the essence of it. What is significant is not the *fact* of the music's being manifestly descriptive, but rather, the methods applied to make it so: the relationship of the notes themselves and the resultant effect on the harmonic and structural processes involved. This small change of emphasis imbues the notes with a dramatic influence which, from the point of view of performance, increases their linear relationship and makes their structural purpose both more recognizable and accessible. It is no longer the juxtaposition of harmonic and dynamic implication that provides the discourse, but the inflection of the sentence itself. And this becomes a far more tangible concept as far as the young performing musician is concerned.

Any actual change in performance technique, apart from a subtle change in instrumental demand and orchestration, remains very hard to define. The Romantic style entails no specific adjustment to either individual or corporate instrumental techniques. Nor does it make life noticeably any easier, as some of the most difficult and demanding passages for every instrument occur in this repertoire. It is simply that as the communication becomes more objective so it adds, especially for the student orchestra, a measure of momentum and support to its own delivery. It is no longer entirely dependent on the quality of every note but on the inflection of them.

As a result of this subtle alteration, it is possible to identify a whole range of works by the composers listed above, as well as others of the period, which lie at the very outermost limits of ability for the average student orchestra. It is a very frustrating situation, for such Classical techniques are at the heart of fine orchestral playing and every ensemble is in desperate need of them. But until an orchestra reaches a *very* high standard of technical performance, few of these works can be attempted. They possess, as every experienced interpreter knows, the infuriating ability to become more difficult as time goes by, as well as insisting that the performers are technically superior to their demands, if the music alone is to speak.

This is the essence of the problem as far as inexperienced orchestras are concerned. The more the players work at them and the closer they approach the style, the more they become aware that the piece is eluding them, and of their own deficiences. Such a situation is counter-productive.

For the sake of completeness there follows a general (rather disheartening) list, by composer, of the works of which I personally remain very wary. Their performance by student orchestras of anything other than excellent standard must be approached with great care, especially in view of the present-day familiarity of the works through recordings.

Haydn: All the orchestral works, with the possible exception of three of the last five symphonies (*nos 100, 101* and *104*).

Mozart: All the orchestral works (*especially* the last three symphonies), with the exception of some of the operatic overtures by virtue of their brevity and the consequent confinement of the style. These will, however, take necessarily longer to rehearse than other works of similar length.

Beethoven: All the orchestral works, with the possible exceptions of *Symphonies nos 5, 7* and *8*, the *Battle of Vittoria op. 91* and the overtures *Egmont, King Stephen* and *Leonora no. 3*.

Schubert: The symphonic output with the lone exception of *Symphony no. 8*. The two overtures '*In the Italian Style*' and some of the *Rosamunde* incidental music are more accessible.

Weber: The two symphonies and all overtures, with the exception of *Euryanthe*.

Rossini: Overtures with the exception of *William Tell*, *The Thieving Magpie*, *Cinderella* and *Signor Bruschino*.

Berlioz: While many works display pronounced aspects of Classical style, an equally pressing consideration must be the extreme technical demands made of so many instruments. Thus, most of the overtures will work with sections good enough to play the notes (a severe limitation in itself), but the *Symphonie Fantastique* is stylistically very difficult, especially the first three movements.

Mendelssohn: The symphonies with the exception of *no. 2* (*Hymn of Praise*) and *no. 5* (*Reformation*), and the overtures, with the exception of *The Hebrides* and (possibly) *Ruy Blas* and *The Fair Melusine*.

The above list makes no allowance for technical difficulty, and the exceptions quoted should not be considered as technically easier examples of the genre. Some contain passages as demanding as anything that may be found in the repertoire. Arrangements, or orchestrations by other composers, have not been considered.

Brahms: the orchestral works are more or less essential if the musical diet of an orchestra is not to be horribly restricted. However, quite apart from the clarity of much of his orchestration and the demands of intonation, it is the actual *sound* that is so elusive: the warmth and maturity necessary in every note. This is something that may be successfully instilled within the confines of the *First Symphony*, but is far more difficult to find in relation to the *Second* (although no less essential). Both the *Third* and *Fourth Symphonies* require a very high standard of orchestral unity, something that is equally true of the *Variations on a Theme by Haydn* (*St. Antoni Chorale*) and the two *Serenades* (the second of which, *op. 16 in A*, uses no violins). The *Academic Festival* and *Tragic* overtures are considered standard repertoire for the youth orchestra, and they are, to an extent, quite appropriate. Nonetheless, they should not be considered easy, and will usually require more time and work than is generally afforded to them.

The same general considerations apply to the orchestral works of **Schumann**, but it is the vital clarity that is difficult to achieve here and, unless the result is to sound like Brahms (as it so often does), they need very careful handling and superb playing. All contain exceptionally difficult passages of exposed string writing, epecially for violins (in the fourth movement of *no. 1*; the *scherzo* of *no. 2*; the *scherzo* of *no. 3*; the first movement of *no. 4*), although the last two are by far the most approachable. From the technical point of view the overtures *Genoveva* and *Manfred* are less demanding, but the *Overture, Scherzo and Finale* should be left firmly in the repertoire of the great chamber orchestras.

For reasons discussed elsewhere, the concerto repertoire of all the above composers allows considerable scope for performance, and it is in this area that initial forays into the style can successfully be made.

Romantic Style

Once again the definition is used loosely in this context and will not necessarily correspond to the accepted boundaries, but rather to the inflection discussed above, as it applies to the performing techniques of the orchestra. For student orchestras, the two most important distinguishing features of this style are the more immediate identification of musical content and the subtle changes apparent in the orchestration.

Unfortunately, from a technical point of view, the classification does not fall into easily discernible periods of musical language, or even encompass individual styles of composers, and many works that may at first sight appear to be forged from such dramatic uses of the orchestra prove not to be so. What is of significance to the student orchestra is not the fact of a more descriptive approach, but the method used to convey it. This very direct relationship between the fundamental scheme of communication to the manner in which it is fashioned is crucial, for it extends far beyond the confines of the notes or instrumentation.

It is important to understand and recognize the influences at work within a composition to be able to judge what the predominant demands on the orchestra are, and how players are likely to respond in performance. Many subtle differences will be found between works, even those of similar style, which will be far-reaching in their effect on the orchestra.

Certain salient features can be demonstrated by directly comparing *Exx.* 23.2 and 23.3 respectively from the *Fourth* and *Fifth Symphonies* of Tchaikovsky, where contrasting aspects of performing style appear within the creative output of one mind. The earlier example presents the opportunity for fatal miscalculation. The opening bars of the main section of each first movement (immediately after the introduction in both cases) are shown.

EX 23.2

EX. 23.2 (continued)

These examples reveal a great deal of superficial common ground. Both are formed within the confines of obvious triplet rhythms. Both opening themes are of eight-bar structure, doubled at the octave and accompanied by a string orchestration of skeletal rhythmic harmony, carefully weighted towards the

EX 23.3

(score in C)

EX. 23.3 (continued)

darker side of each instrument, but whereas in *Ex. 23.3* this clearly defines the rhythmic structure, in *Ex. 23.2* it contrives to dissipate it. Both phrases utilize dotted rhythms and both incorporate syncopation that disturbs the inner feeling to a degree that makes the direction *con anima* (common to both movements) almost superfluous. Furthermore, both phrases are firmly rooted in the tonic minor and both begin on the somewhat ambiguous sixth note of the minor scale, the *Fourth Symphony* using it in a downward semitone approach to the dominant (the note's most hauntingly reflective resolution), while the *Fifth* resolves it immediately upwards to the tonic.

This last apparently minor detail proves to be deeply significant, for it is no accident that the *Fifth Symphony* exposes the tonic note so soon or that the theme, which breaks down into the clearly defined four-bar sub-phrases first implied by the accompaniment, is so unwilling to escape it. Examination of the corresponding bars of the *Fourth Symphony* shows no such propensity for aural security but a disturbingly long and mysterious line that is never allowed to rest, a characteristic which not only affects the aura of the work, but also the style of the whole orchestration. Tchaikovsky demands the minimum of dynamic variation, a controlled *piano* that rises evenly in the second half of the phrase and reinforces the expectation of resolution, only to be brushed aside by repetition in dramatically changed instrumentation.

This is a far cry from multiple markings to be found in the corresponding bars of the *Fifth Symphony*, where the use of alternating *crescendi* and *diminuendi* actually serves to emphasize the confines of both the harmonic and architectural structure. From the very outset of this *Allegro con anima* it is abundantly clear that this movement will never escape the vice-like grip of its underlying rhythm, and nor does it – not even for a single moment. Tchaikovsky allows his listeners the extraordinary assurance of being able to predetermine the exact moment of every sentence, retaining only the masterly control of what will actually be said. It is a consummate display of charismatic oratory, the fundamental technique for which most politicians would gladly sell their soul!

In terms of orchestral playing technique, the strict adherence to short, structured phrase-lengths within the *Fifth Symphony* makes certain aspects of performance far easier, not only from the point of view of orchestral unity but also because the direction and span are easier to grasp. In addition, because the whole of the first movement is composed of tautly crafted answering phrases which either expound or negate those which precede them, it takes on a momentum and dramatic tension of its own, imbuing even the most artless and basic early attempts to perform the movement with a sense of direction and meaning far beyond what is actually projected by the individual players. For student orchestras, who need to build on successfully heard and understood concepts of sound, this presents a heaven-sent opportunity, and further rehearsal of the work may be approached with a clear understanding of what is required and an almost immediate aural conception of the result.

This is not true of the *Fourth Symphony*, even though it may appear outwardly similar, for the phrase-structure, musical content and implication are entirely different. The work provides no room for manoeuvre. The orchestration, for all its power, is sparse and economical, and every line has an individual and unsupported responsibility. To the inexperienced orchestra it can come as something of a shock to find that a symphony of such intensity and immediate appeal refuses to meet their endeavours until each player has met its every demand. This aspect of its character should come as no surprise, for it is only because it is frequently bracketed with the composer's later works that false expectations arise. In fact it belongs, very firmly, with the earlier symphonic works, all of which adhere to Classical concepts of style and structure.

Among the major symphonic output of the Romantic era there is only one other work which, in my opinion, displays a similar perversity, and that is Dvořák *Symphony no. 7*. All Dvořák is difficult. The high, exposed string writing and the tight, rhythmic character of so much of the material calls for a versatile and clean technique throughout the orchestra, but in none of the other symphonies is the demand of production so unremitting. Elsewhere in this repertoire, apart from a few exceptions that will be discussed in due course, the suitability of works may be more easily judged with regard only to the technical difficulty of the notes.

Within the boundaries of so large a repertoire it is obviously impractical to consider many works in any sort of detail, but a very brief résumé of the major output by the more frequently performed composers might be beneficial. In a number of cases, of course, a more detailed discussion of particular aspects of certain works has already appeared elsewhere in the text. Any glaring omissions that arise probably relate to works that I have not performed, either as a player or conductor, and where I therefore have no first-hand knowledge of the performing idiosyncrasies they might conceal.

Once again I must remind the reader that the composers listed are not necessarily related in compositional style but only with regard to the wider concepts of similar performing requirements.

Having already touched on two symphonies of Tchaikovsky, it would seem logical to begin with a broader consideration of his works, and continue with other Russian composers, some of whom wrote in a related style.

Tchaikovsky: All the orchestral works may be considered, but the first three symphonies display a pronounced Classicism in both the orchestration and structure, as discussed above in specific relation to the profoundly more mature *Fourth*. Both the *Sixth* (*Pathétique*) and the *Manfred Symphony* are difficult but entirely successful with good orchestras. Most of the ballet scores show the composer at his most Classically orientated and are very demanding, especially movements such as the overture *Nutcracker* (scored without cellos or basses). The majority of the later output is only playable because it is familiar, and were any of the works to be approached totally 'cold' they would be considered impossibly difficult, a point well worth remembering in relation to student orchestras, where performance so often hangs on this thin thread of gallant self-belief. However, the string parts of the overture *1812* will probably confound even this.

Balakirev: A similar technical approach is required as for the early Tchaikovsky symphonies, determined more by a charming naïvety of style than any Classical concepts. This is particularly true of the *Symphony no. 1 in C* (though it was written over a period of 32 years). But the composer's small output, especially the symphonic poems *Thamar* and *Russia*, is worthy of exploration by student orchestras.

Borodin: Much the same technical approach should be applied to each of the three symphonies (the *Third* remained unfinished, and comprises only a rather confined *Moderato* and a difficult 5/8 *Scherzo*). The very popular *Symphony no.* 2 is actually quite difficult, and *In the Steppes of Central Asia* is virtually an exercise in intonation. A very exuberant and extrovert style is required overall, especially for both the overture and *Polovtsian Dances* from *Prince Igor*, the latter including a really awkward clarinet solo.

Rimsky-Korsakov: The orchestral demands, which should not be underestimated despite the familiarity of *Scheherezade,* are considerable for all works. As has been mentioned, the famous violin solo of *Scheherazade* can only be approached by an outstanding instrumentalist, but this is also true of many solos for a range of instruments that appear in other works. The three symphonies are all worthy of exploration, especially that which is known as the *Second* (*Antar, symphonic suite*), but the popular *Capriccio Espagnol* and the suite from *Le Coq d'or* are extremely demanding for all concerned.

Mussorgsky: All works are possible but the two most popular are most often heard in arrangements by other composers. *Night on the Bare Mountain* was arranged, orchestrated and virtually re-written by Rimsky-Korsakov (I was involved in a recording of the original instrumental version, *St. John's Night on the Bare Mountain*, and was surprised to find much of the familiar music missing). *Pictures from an Exhibition*, originally for piano, appears most frequently in the superb Ravel orchestration, but smaller orchestrations exist (none of which are any easier). The four *Songs and Dances of Death* for low voice and orchestra, have each been orchestrated by a number of different composers, most successfully by Rimsky-Korsakov (no. 1: *Berceuse*), Lyapunov (no. 2: *Serenade*), Glazunov (no. 3: *Trepak*), and Borg (no. 4: *The Field Marshal*).

Glinka: A very forthright and exuberant style is required. Violinists must *learn* and *memorize* the famous *piano* passages in the ever-popular overture *Russlan and Ludmilla* before ever trying to put them together in concert. Both *Kamarinskaya* and the overture of *A Life for the Tsar* are rewarding miniatures.

Liadov: The three small symphonic poems *Baba-Yaga*, *The Enchanted Lake* and *Kikimora* are all wonderful pieces, and the second one is almost mandatory for enhancing techniques of subtlety, listening and orchestral unity. This is the work that requires *con sordini* of oboes and bassoons (*see* Chapter 8).

Glazunov: The style is immediately attractive and enjoyable without being particularly profound or dramatic. The works tend to be thickly orchestrated, but never become awkwardly heavy and provide considerable opportunity for improving orchestral technique. The *Symphony no. 5* and the *Violin Concerto* are notable in this respect, but the same applies to earlier works such as the *Suite Caracteristique op. 9*.

Rachmaninov: His works lie on the very outer limits of the Romantic period, but should be considered here because of the performing style. All the orchestral works prove magnetic to student orchestras, especially the gigantic *Symphony no. 2* (which should on no account be performed with cuts). All the orchestral compositions are extremely difficult, but once the style has been absorbed and the techniques mastered, the *Second* and *Third Symphonies* and the *Symphonic Dances* in particular may be numbered among the comparatively rare pieces that really repay the orchestra for every moment of its work. The piano concerti are among the most important in the repertoire for enhancing techniques of accompaniment, as is the *Rhapsody on a Theme of Paganini*, but they are all very challenging and require a flexible and relatively experienced orchestra.

Turning now to East European composers:

Dvořák: The dangers inherent in the *Seventh Symphony* have been discussed, and similar care needs to be extended to the rarely performed first three symphonies, although more for reasons of structural naïvety than straightforward orchestration. Of the later symphonies, *no. 8* and *no. 9 'From the New World'* receive frequent performance, even though the latter is not really ideal youth orchestra material – once more the apparent drama is built on very insubstantial pillars of orchestration. There is, however, considerable scope in the less often performed 'middle' symphonies, *nos 4, 5* and *6*.

Both the *Symphonic Variations* and the *Czech Suite* require a more Classical approach, but the 16 *Slavonic Dances* and the 10 *Legends* are superb, albeit technically difficult, miniatures. Of the *Nature, Life and Love* cycle of overtures (*Amid Nature*, *Carnival* and *Othello*) the second should only be attempted by the most advanced student orchestras, and this is also true of each of the four symphonic poems – *The Watersprite*, *The Noonday Witch*, *The Wood Dove* and *The Golden Spinning-wheel*.

Smetana: All the Czech composers favour a clarity of orchestration that always causes difficulty both because of the instrumental demands and also its extraordinary propensity for exposing certain areas of the harmony. The fact that Smetana's orchestral output is comparatively small must not deflect from this aspect of his style, since all his works are equally challenging in this respect.

The most popular concert pieces are undoubtedly the overture to *The Bartered Bride* (always a problem with any orchestra) and the second and fourth of the six symphonic poems that comprise *Má Vlast* – *Vltava* and *From Bohemia's Woods and Fields*. There is good reason for looking at the other four although *Tábor* and *Blaník* (nos 5 and 6) should not really be separated. *Šárka* (no. 3), while very difficult, is an exciting work to open a concert, and *Vyšehrad* (no. 1), a beautiful piece in its own right, is as effective as *Vltava* in providing a substantial change of colour to a four- or five-piece programme. The other symphonic poems, *Richard III* and *Wallenstein's Camp*, might not offer quite so much to student orchestras.

Suk: The expansive *Symphony no. 2 'Asrael'* is in my opinion both underrated and neglected. It is long and unashamedly sentimental at times. The devastating loss of both his father-in-law (Dvořák) and his wife (Otilie Dvořák) during its composition caused him to dedicate the work to them – Asrael is the Angel of Death – and divide the five movements into two parts, but it is full of inventive orchestration and some wonderful writing.

The *Scherzo Fantastique op. 25* and the *Fantasy* for violin and orchestra remain particular personal favourites, but the erstwhile most famous orchestral work, *Ripening op. 34*, presents exceptional difficulties.

Before considering some composers of central and western European origin it is necessary to mention one remaining from the eastern side of the continent who must be singled out both because of his musical style and personality.

Liszt: There is in fact quite a lot of somewhat neglected orchestral music which will help the more Classical side of production, despite the fact that its musical content remains firmly descriptive. The two piano concerti provide significant opportunities to develop techniques of both accompaniment and sound, as do some of the other virtuoso works for piano and orchestra – *Totentanz, Wanderer Fantasia* and *Fantasia on Hungarian Folk Songs*, for example.

Of the works for orchestra alone, the 13 symphonic poems – 1. *Ce qu'on entend sur la montagne* (*Bergsymphonie*), 2. *Tasso*, 3. *Les Préludes*, 4. *Orpheus*, 5. *Prometheus*, 6. *Mazeppa*, 7. *Festklänge* 8. *Héroïde funèbre*, 9. *Hungaria*, 10. *Hamlet*, 11. *Hunnenschlacht*, 12. *Die Ideale*, 13. *From the Cradle to the Grave* – must be said to be variable in content, but by no means out of the range of the adventurous student orchestra. The *Faust Symphony* is long and taxing, but it contains a wide range of playing styles that are beneficial to the technically advanced orchestra.

Wagner: The operatic preludes and overtures are all successful but some, such as *The Flying Dutchman*, are very difficult. The *Prelude* and orchestral version of the *Liebestod* from *Tristan und Isolde* is essential repertoire for any orchestra, preferably *before* they accompany singers in similarly scored works. A vocal work for smaller orchestra (double woodwind, four horns but only one trumpet and no trombones or tuba) is the beautiful *Wesendonk-Lieder*, all except the last of which (*Träume*) were orchestrated by the composer's disciple Felix Mottl.

Richard Strauss: His works are the province of the very advanced student orchestra and, even then, the two most popular symphonic poems – *Till Eulenspiegel* and *Don Juan* – will generally be beyond them. Strauss had an understanding of the Romantic orchestra, and an instinct for orchestral 'habit' that was almost unequalled (only Mahler and Elgar approached it), and the individual parts can be as difficult as many that appear in the solo instrumental repertoire.

Apart from the violin solo, *Ein Heldenleben* is, rather surprisingly, the most playable of them all, but the solo can only be approached by an advanced student, with a great deal of preliminary notice and the *full* co-operation of the instrumental professor. *Tod und Verklärung* is also possible, but the beguiling opening bars of *Also sprach Zarathustra* entice the orchestra into a web of immensely difficult playing.

Elsewhere, the symphonic fantasy *Aus Italien* is worth consideration, especially as a first excursion into the style, but it is still not easy. The two horn concerti and the one for oboe all require smaller than full symphonic forces. They are ideally chamber orchestra works, but important repertoire. The *Horn Concerto no. 2*, however, requires superb technique from the orchestra, particularly in the last movement.

Mahler: A similarly high level of technique is essential as for Strauss, and a number of individual parts call for considerable courage as well as technical skill. All the symphonies require very large orchestra and *nos 2, 3, 4* and *8* require vocal soloist/s and/or chorus. *Nos 1* and *5* seem to be most attractive to non-professional orchestras, but the more standard scoring of *no. 9*, in many ways the most beneficial to the high-class student orchestra, is often overlooked. The suitability of the song cycles should also be remembered.

Bruckner: All the symphonies are within the scope of good student orchestras but the techniques of performance are very specific (see relevant instrumental chapters) and *nos 7, 8* and *9* require Wagner tubas. There are a number of different versions of all the symphonies, as well as some that are inauthentic. In this respect care, at least in matching the score to the parts, must be exercised when any of the works are first programmed. The *Overture in G minor* is the only smaller-scale orchestral work other than the posthumously published *Three Pieces for Orchestra.*

Saint-Saëns: The popularity of the *Symphony no. 3 in C minor* (*'Organ' symphony*)and *The Carnival of the Animals* may sometimes eclipse all else. The two small symphonic poems *Le Rouet d'Omphale* (the first example in the genre by a French composer) and *Danse Macabre* must not be completely overlooked by student orchestras. The major concerti (five for piano, three for violin and two for cello) are all rewarding to play, as are the smaller concerted works that exist both for violin and piano (*Introduction and Rondo Capriccioso, Havanaise, Caprice-Valse 'Wedding Cake'*).

Bizet: The suites and incidental music (*Jeux d'enfants, L'Arlésienne* and *Carmen*) are well known and very often performed. The *Symphony in C*, however, should be given a wide berth (the last movement is very difficult in performance) and left to the great chamber orchestras of the world as their own personal nightmare.

Chabrier: The orchestral rhapsody *España* and *Marche Joyeuse* are standard repertoire. Further afield there is the overture to *Gwendoline*, but this is far more demanding than either of the other works.

Chausson: Although this composer is most regularly represented by performances of the wonderful *Poème* for violin and orchestra, the *Symphony in B♭ op. 20* is a very good work for enhancing sound and orchestral collaboration broadly in the manner of Franck. The symphonic poem *Viviane op. 5*, while not quite in the same class, can also be recommended.

Roussel: In a much more forthright and demanding style, the orchestral works of this composer are very rewarding to perform. Both the suites of *Bacchus et Ariane* are vibrant and powerful in their design and orchestration, a feature that is equally true of the last two symphonies, particularly *no. 3*.

Franck: The *Symphony in D minor* is one of the few large-scale works that may actually be used as an orchestral exercise for the infusion of a wide range of orchestral techniques – not that this should ever be implied in rehearsal or apparent in performance. The opportunities available for the woodwind and brass in terms of sound, balance, intonation and ensemble within the context of readily accessible structure and orchestration are legion, and even further possibilities exist for the strings. From this point of view it is a work that no emerging youth orchestra should be denied.

In addition, there are the *Symphonic Variations* for piano and orchestra and the symphonic poem *Le Chasseur Maudit*, a work that makes an excellent, if challenging, opening piece for the right programme.

Delius: The large-scale orchestral works are difficult in that the style of communication is very individual and relies heavily on the control of sound and texture, but none are beyond the reach of a good student orchestra. Of the more familiar, smaller works the *Two Pieces for Small Orchestra* (*On Hearing the First Cuckoo in Spring* and *Summer Night on the River*) were originally written for the concert hall, but many of the others were arranged from the composer's operatic repertoire by Sir Thomas Beecham or the composer's former amanuensis Eric Fenby. These are authentic editions and the form in which the works in question are most usually played; they include *The Walk to the Paradise Garden* (from *A Village Romeo and Juliet*), the *Intermezzo* and *Serenade* (from *Hassan*), and *La Calinda* (from *Koanga*), as well as the larger *Irmelin* concert suite and the *Florida Suite*.

In the concerto repertoire, which includes the *Double Concerto* for cello and violin, and the *Cello Concerto*, the *Piano Concerto* is somewhat neglected and the *Violin Concerto* is superb.

Elgar: All the orchestral works are notable for the extreme (and sometimes unique) demands they place on almost every instrument. Of the two works most frequently performed by student orchestras, the overture *Cockaigne* presents many difficulties which are rarely successfully overcome, and the *Variations on an Original Theme* (*Enigma*) should be treated with great circumspection. The *Symphony no. 1*, despite its difficulties, may be considered one of the most approachable works, together with the concert overture *Froissart*. The *Symphony no. 2* is much more demanding than the *First*, as is the symphonic study *Falstaff* (especially one horrendously difficult passage for violins). The rather disarming title of the two *Wand of Youth* suites belies the fact that they contain some very difficult numbers. The *Cello Concerto* provides exacting techniques of accompaniment without being exceptionally difficult, but the *Violin Concerto* is a *tour de force* for both soloist and orchestra.

Holst: The popularity of *The Planets* as a choice for student orchestra performances never ceases to amaze me, as the work contains some of the most difficult orchestral writing in the repertoire (an opinion which has only been strengthened by some performances I have heard – and taken part in). I cannot envisage performing the work with a non-professional orchestra of anything but the very highest standard. Of the shorter works, the ballet music from *The Perfect Fool* is very effective, although by no means easy, and both the symphonic poem *Egdon Heath* and the Oriental Suite *Beni Mora* should not be forgotten.

Before progressing further, a word is in order with regard to the magical overtures, waltzes and polkas of the Strauss family, Lehár and others. While some examples may not be especially demanding, others most certainly are, and all require a finesse signally elusive to both the student orchestra and any musicians without a natural affinity to the lighter, 'Viennese' style. Some aspects of it might be imitated with varying degrees of success (the 'off-beat' crotchets of the waltzes, which have a lilting rhythm just out of tempo, rather than the grotesque syncopation so often substituted), but the true vivacity and joy inherent in these works is very difficult to project, and they should not be approached in any perfunctory fashion.

In conjunction with this there is a purely practical consideration. The parts are usually 'band parts' of small size, which involve numerous repeats, first- and second-time bars, *segues* and possible cuts. They are difficult to read and confusing to all except those orchestras to whom the repertoire is totally familiar. Student orchestras must carefully *rehearse* each of these indications as they occur, because the position of following bars is neither logical nor recurrent.

The French 'Impressionists'

I am aware that to use the term 'impressionist' to categorize any musical genre, tendency or aesthetic is to substantiate a misnomer that has little true application in sound and most certainly does not reflect the musical intentions of the composers to whom it is most frequently applied. Neither is it uniquely French. Nonetheless, in considering the necessary changes in orchestral performing technique, there is no better descriptive term with which to isolate those related works where the subtleties of light and shade and the merging of instrumental sounds are intrinsic to their communication.

It is probably the most difficult of all large-scale symphonic repertoire to perform successfully. Much of it requires a quite virtuosic instrumental technique, and the techniques of orchestral collaboration are unique and only find some points of contact with those of the avant garde. Furthermore, the transparency and fine textures typical of Debussy and much of Ravel require from the orchestra the most perfect judgement of balance and extreme control of sound.

Typically, the writing interweaves melodic and harmonic lines through a kaleidoscopic orchestration, creating a delicate web of totally homogeneous sound. It is the most difficult texture for any orchestra to recreate because it frequently provides players with only individual fragments of the melodic line and rarely allows any instrument or section the time to become familiar with the sound or assimilate the ever-changing techniques required.

Above all things, works that fall within this style require the musicians to be able to anticipate the very subtle character of their own contribution within the context of the orchestration, an immensely difficult technique to induce. In a programme that contains a major work in this style, some common ground, in terms of texture and responsibility, has to be found. Only a professional orchestra can gravitate towards it at a moment's notice and, from playing experience, I can vouch for how difficult such a change of gear can be.

The following brief consideration of works in this style will commence with two composers, Fauré and Dukas, whose orchestral output begins to lay the foundations of the necessary performing technique. In both cases, the number of orchestral works is tragically limited, but they are of inestimable importance to the student orchestra.

Fauré: The orchestral works involve only relatively small orchestra, but his very personal harmonic and melodic style, most apparent in the songs and chamber music, was to be of considerable influence on composers of a later generation. All the orchestral pieces require a delicacy of performing technique and the most acute awareness of balance and timbre from the orchestra. In particular the four movements of the suite *Pelléas et Mélisande* call for a rare transparency of texture and control of sound, and these aspects are also appropriate to the *Pavane*, the four orchestral movements of *Shylock* and the vivacious *Masques et Bergamasques*.

Dukas: The orchestration of the famous *Scherzo*: *L'Apprenti-Sorcier* is simply dazzling and displays a craftsmanship that remains virtually unsurpassed. The tight, Classical structures of both this very difficult work and the sadly misjudged *Symphony in C* reflect an early compositional leaning not so apparent in the more free form of the magnificent *Poème Dansé: La Péri*. Here, the combinations of orchestral colour and the total integration of orchestral responsibility, together with an increased rhythmic fluidity, foreshadow the demands of later performing styles.

La Péri is a difficult work, requiring considerable technical fluency from the woodwind in particular, but it is quite performable by good orchestras of limited experience. The individual parts are such that the subtleties of combination and the more linear aspects of phrases are unambiguous, and the predominant concern of every player can be the transparency of the sound.

Ravel: Perhaps it is in what was once described as the 'wistful pursuit of innocence' that this orchestral style most applies to Ravel, for it was certainly not his intention to blur the edges of either his harmonic invention or its orchestration. Nonetheless, the simplicity of the communication in works like *Pavane pour une infante défunte* and *Ma mère l'oye* requires delicate instrumental partnership and extreme control of the substance of the sound. This is equally true of the larger works, particularly the accompaniment of the three songs that comprise *Scheherazade*, the '*poème choréographique*' *La Valse* and both orchestral suites from *Daphnis et Chloé*. These last are the most substantial and difficult of the orchestral works, the more frequently performed second suite being no easier than the first. Both demand fluent and mature technique from the instrumentalists, together with a corporate ability to evoke colour and nuance of the highest order.

This is one of the works where the demands of technique and ensemble are so severe as to make those of sound and texture very difficult to develop within the context of the work alone. Some understanding, experience and ability in this direction must be apparent from the orchestra before such a work is programmed.

Debussy: Nowhere in the entire orchestral repertoire is the text of the last paragraph so vital as here, where the subtle inflections of harmony and colour can only be approached with a cohesion and orchestral fluency that is, to some degree, already part of the orchestra's experience. Examples from *La Mer*,

Printemps and each of the *Trois Nocturnes* have appeared throughout this book to illustrate the control of sound and phrasing necessary in respect of individual instrumentalists, but the combining of every element into a cogent whole is more difficult in the music of this composer than any other.

In terms of instrumental facility, only *La Mer* and the three works which comprise *Images* (*Gigues*, *Iberia* and *Rondes de Printemps*) are excessively difficult. In concerted works, where the orchestral style might be more easily accomplished, there is the *Fantasie* for piano and orchestra and the *Rhapsodie* for clarinet and orchestra as well as the group of songs *Trois Ballades de François Villon*.

Post-Romantic Style

Again the heading should be interpreted broadly, as a means of embracing those later composers (only a limited number of whom will be discussed individually) whose orchestral compositions all – or largely – lie outside the general concepts of the Romantic era. Those associated with more idiosyncratic styles of composition (such as atonal or aleatoric) will be considered separately.

In the main, the post-Romantic orchestral 'style' is even more virtuosic than that of Romantic composers, with an increased emphasis on rhythmic content and more sharply defined orchestration, although there are some similarities of performing style. The distinction, which is finely drawn, is as much for convenience as for implications of musical language.

We may begin as the last section finished, in France.

Messiaen: He is perhaps the most illustrative of this precarious heading, in that his work adheres to no school. *Turangalîla-symphonie* is probably the work towards which a student orchestra will gravitate, but it is extremely difficult and contains a truly virtuoso solo piano part. *Chronochromie* is really no easier and the best approach to the composer might be either through the earlier '*méditation symphonique*' *Les offrandes oubliées* or the song cycle *Poèmes pour Mi*.

Vaughan Williams: (A geographical, rather than a musical, progression from the last composer.) The orchestral music encompasses a variety of styles, from the tranquillity of much of *A Pastoral Symphony* (*no. 3*) and the romance for violin and orchestra *The Lark Ascending*, to the violent imagery of the *Fourth* and *Sixth Symphonies*. It is not easy to make categorical statements about relative difficulty, since the music fluctuates between extreme technical demands and equally difficult orchestral serenity. Within these opposing boundaries all the works are most suited to a more experienced orchestra, but all offer the most wonderful opportunities for string sound.

Walton: All the orchestral works demand extreme technical facility and rhythmic accuracy, none more so than the overtures *Scapino* and *Portsmouth Point*. The *Symphony no. 1*, a work of monumental stature, veritably challenges the orchestra to meet its formidable demands, a situation which is only slightly less apparent in the less often performed *Symphony no. 2* and the *Partita for Orchestra*. At the other end of the spectrum *Crown Imperial* and the suite from the film music *Henry V* are quite straightforward, while *Johannesburg Festival Overture* presents an opportunity to sample the complexities of the style.

In the concerto repertoire the orchestral parts remain very demanding, but all three works (for cello, violin and viola – the latter only to be played in the 1962 revised version) are quite magnificent, and feasible for a student orchestra of above average ability.

Britten: There are few large orchestral works, but among them the *Variations and Fugue on a Theme of Purcell* (*Young Person's Guide to the Orchestra* when performed with narrator) remains ever popular, closely followed by the difficult *Four Sea Interludes* from the opera *Peter Grimes*. While these can be made to work in the concert hall, they never project quite the same atmosphere as they conjure within the opera. Otherwise, apart from works that involve chorus and vocal soloists, only the *Sinfonia da Requiem* approaches the strength of musical purpose apparent in the composer's operatic and chamber orchestra output.

There are also two original overtures, *The Building of the House* and the *Occasional Overture* as well as some in authorized orchestrations by other hands (*Paul Bunyan* orch. Colin Matthews). Two larger works in lighter vein should also be mentioned – *Canadian Carnival* and the more difficult *Prelude and Dances* from the ballet *The Prince of the Pagodas*.

The *Piano Concerto, Violin Concerto* (revised 1950) and *Diversions on a Theme* for piano (left hand) and orchestra are all worthwhile for the student orchestra, but the late *Symphony* for cello and orchestra is extremely difficult and of a very complex style.

Sibelius: The first two symphonies, both of which present considerable problems of interpretation, tend to be standard repertoire, to which should be added the *Symphony no. 5* at least. *Finlandia* and the *Karelia* suite are also justifiably popular in youth orchestra circles but the less often performed *Karelia* overture should not be forgotten.

The symphonic poems, such as the *Four Legends from Kalevala (Lemminkainen and the Maidens of Saari*, *The Swan of Tuonela*, *Lemminkainen in Tuonela* and *The Return of Lemminkainen*), *The Oceanides* and *Tapiola* all present difficulties of a very idiosyncratic nature and can only be recommended for the experienced student orchestra. The benefits and demands of the *Violin Concerto* need no further advertisement.

Nielsen: All six of the symphonies work well in performance by student orchestras but each presents specific problems, especially in terms of isolated passage-work for the strings. They are very individual in concept and it often takes time for the orchestra to become familiar with both the harmonic style and structure, though this is not an indication of their long-term technical infeasibility. The overture *Helios* is very approachable, but the *Violin Concerto* is very demanding. The two other concerti (one for clarinet and one for flute) are scored for chamber orchestra.

Kodály: All the orchestral works are eminently possible for the good youth or student orchestra, most of whom are capable of looking further afield than the justly famous suite *Háry János* (which requires solo cimbalom) or the *Dances of Marosszék* and the *Dances of Galánta. The Variations on a Hungarian Folksong* (*Peacock Variations*) has been mentioned in previous chapters, but there is also the unjustly neglected *Symphony in C*, and the beautiful *Summer Evening* (for small orchestra).

Bartók: The Classical concepts of clarity and division demonstrated by most of the orchestrations mean that all the works are difficult, even on the rare occasions where extreme instrumental demands are relaxed. The *Concerto for Orchestra* is a virtuoso work and should only be approached by orchestras that are not only capable of meeting its demands but also of projecting its very powerful discourse. Much the same applies to the complexities of the *Dance Suite* and the extreme instrumental difficulties which are exposed in the suite from *The Miraculous Mandarin*. The *Four Pieces* are a little easier in this respect, but still require considerable technical fluency.

The orchestral parts of all the concerti are highly demanding, the most approachable being, perhaps, the *Piano Concerto no. 3* and the *Violin Concerto no. 1 op. posth.*

Stravinsky: This is one of the most important areas of repertoire for the student orchestra; the exacting rhythmic movement and imaginative orchestration requires the most precise articulation and concentration of sound. While the rhythmic complexities and instrumental demands of *The Rite of Spring* might still cause alarm it remains, as has already been remarked, eminently playable by the high calibre orchestra and *Petrouchka* (in either version) still has the edge in sheer difficulty of performance in my opinion. The symphonic poem *Le Chant du Rossignol* belongs with these works in its demands of orchestral virtuosity.

The Firebird, in all versions but particularly the shortened 1919 suite, is vital repertoire and might only be replaced by the more vertical demands of the *Symphony in C*, *Symphony in Three Movements* or *Jeu de cartes*. In smaller scope, but no less difficult, is the four-minute fantasy *Fireworks* and, in the vein of the early Russian symphonies, the *Symphony in E♭ op. 1*.

Apart from the *Violin Concerto*, the *Concerto for Piano and Wind Instruments* should not be overlooked as it uses a symphony orchestra wind section plus timpani and string basses.

Prokofiev: This is a very elusive style and apart from the few works of obvious descriptive design (*Lieutenant Kijé*, *Peter and the Wolf*) and the massively scored *Scythian Suite*, this intangible quality manifests itself to some degree in all the orchestral works, from the symphonies to the suites from *Romeo and Juliet*. The very Classical treatment of the orchestra creates problems, especially those of intonation and balance, but the greatest challenges lie in interpretation.

Within these confines, all the works are possible, with the outstanding exception of the *Symphony no. 1 'Classical'*, which should never be attempted by anything other than a professional group.

The concerti are very good material for the student orchestra. Only the *Sinfonia Concertante op. 125* for cello and the *First* and *Third Piano Concerti* are scored for full brass, the remaining three for piano (including *no. 4* for piano left hand) and two for violin all use various smaller configurations of the brass group.

Shostakovich: The symphonies, in particular *nos 5* and *10*, draw the eager eyes of youth orchestras the world over, but they are not easy, and each demands the most advanced solo qualities from various individual instruments. The majority are scored for large orchestra of standard design apart from *nos 2* (with chorus), *4* (with enlarged woodwind and eight horns) and *7* (with two sections of horns and brass). *No. 14* is for soprano and bass soli, percussion and small strings – with *five-stringed* basses – only. All are possible, but the Classical lines and scoring of the two 'smaller' symphonies (*nos 1* and *9*) render them least accessible.

A number of suites, many based on film music, are worthy of exploration, and there is always the *Festive Overture* to pin the audience to their seats.

None of the concerti (two for cello, two for violin, one for piano [*no. 2*] and one for piano and trumpet) involve orchestral trumpets or trombones and only the *Violin Concerto no. 1* involves tuba (alone).

Janáček: The famous *Sinfonietta* is not quite as difficult as it appears (although it does contain one of the highest passages in the symphonic repertoire for violins) and is within the range of any good student orchestra that can find the extra brass, as are both the *Lachian Dances* and the rhapsody *Taras Bulba* (which includes organ). The *Capriccio* for piano (left hand) and wind instruments is only scored for flute doubling piccolo, two trumpets, three trombones and tuba.

Martinů: The most prolific of all twentieth-century composers, he wrote a large number of works for orchestra of variable quality. The six symphonies, however, are all of high standard, but the extreme rhythmic flexibility that is a hallmark of this composer makes a number of them very difficult, especially *Symphonies nos 5* and *6 'Fantasies Symphoniques'*. This last of the numbered symphonies (although *Les Fresques de Piero della Francesca* is considered by many to be a seventh) is probably the greatest work, but all are extremely beneficial in developing the adaptability and ensemble of the orchestra and are highly seductive if well performed.

The concerto repertoire is equally wide, but the *Piano Concerti nos 3* and *4 'Incantations'*, the *Violin Concerto no. 2* and the *Oboe Concerto* (for chamber orchestra) can be particularly recommended.

Hindemith: Despite the originality of the harmonic style, there is a logicality and momentum in several of the larger works that allows some very difficult passage-work to be accomplished more easily than would seem possible. Sections of the *Symphonic Metamorphosis of Themes by Weber*, for example, are actually very difficult in isolation but can be successfully performed by many youth orchestras. Both the symphony *Mathis der Maler* and the *Concerto for Orchestra op. 38*, however, are rather more difficult and the first movement of the latter work contains *concertante* parts for oboe, bassoon and violin. (It is also one of the very few works to be scored for just three horns.)

There are many concerti for both individual instruments and instrumental combinations, the scorings of which are mostly small, and all are technically very challenging.

Ives: The complexities of the unique style are well known, especially in relation to the later works, but the true greatness of this composer lies in the originality and conviction that is apparent in the more conventionally structured works. The *Symphony no. 1* is sadly neglected and provides wonderful material for student orchestras (the beautiful slow movement requires the most subtle control of sound and ensemble), and much the same may be said of the more eccentric *Symphony no. 2*.

As the works progress chronologically, so they become more complicated, especially in the intricate rhythms used to reinforce aspects of polytonality. These may sometimes synchronize only fleetingly with the main rhythmic structure, and require a great deal of expertise for their ultimate co-ordination. In this respect, the published parts of nearly all the complex works are lamentably lacking in clarity – at least, all those that I have experienced. Bars are of arbitrary length and note spacings have no relationship to their rhythmic value; intricate patterns are squashed together and notes beyond the stave unevenly distributed. It is this, more than any other factor, that makes the works largely unmanageable for the student orchestra and limits the number of professional performances outside the USA. There are no concerti.

Copland: The precise rhythms and scrupulous orchestration call for a high standard of ensemble technique, balance and instrumental ability, but it is in the contrasting mood of the subdued sounds that the most severe demands are made on the orchestra's technique. This is probably nowhere more apparent than in the orchestral version of *Appalachian Spring*, where the opening and closing sections require the most subtle control of sound and colour. This aspect of the composer's style is present in all the works, and is as important an ingredient of the highly evocative pieces (*Billy the Kid*, *El Salón México*, *Danzón Cubano*) as the vibrant and often complex rhythms.

One of the great practical problems in programming Copland for the student orchestra is the amount of time the works take to rehearse, in inverse relation to their comparative brevity. Few are long enough to sustain half a concert by themselves and consequently involve a four- or five-piece programme – something which, ironically, their demands upon rehearsal time will very often not allow. Thus important works, such as the very difficult *Symphony no. 2* '*Short Symphony*' can rarely be considered.

The heavily scored and jazz-influenced *Piano Concerto* (*1926*) contains some demanding writing for horns and trumpets.

Problems of the Shorter Repertoire

Before considering the more esoteric styles of composition, mention of rehearsal time in relation to length of works leads naturally to an important digression which applies to two connected aspects of programming. Firstly, that it takes considerably longer to rehearse three 12-minute pieces, of whatever style, than it does to rehearse one work of greater total length. Secondly, that as soon as one considers works of between about 8 and 20 minutes, the 'virtuoso' orchestral repertoire looms large.

To take the second point first, even a cursory glance through any catalogue of orchestral works will reveal many compositions, in all styles and periods, of roughly this duration. What will also become obvious is that at least 75 per cent of them, whether by accident or design, are orchestral show pieces – the symphony concert equivalent of the Paganini *Caprice* or the Chopin *Etude* of the solo recital.

I once compiled my own list of orchestral works, catalogued by average time of performance rather than composer, as it was of vital significance to programming in the days of live studio broadcasts, when the threat of being 'faded' for the 9 o'clock news was ever present. I have the book in front of me as I write, the list being tabled in one-minute intervals from three to sixty-five minutes. A *random* selection gives:–

8 min: Arnold, *Tam O'Shanter*; Berlioz, *Beatrice and Benedict*, *Le Corsair*; Mendelssohn, *Ruy Blas*; Weber, *Euryanthe*, *Der Freischütz*, *Oberon* (all overtures, of course).

10 min: Copland, *El Salón México*; Dukas, *L'Apprenti-Sorcier*; Smetana, *Šárka*; Wagner, *The Flying Dutchman* (overture).

15 min: Ravel, *Boléro*, *Rhapsodie Espagnole*; Tchaikovsky, *Capriccio Italien*.

17 min: Bartók, *Dance Suite*; Britten, *Four Sea Interludes*; Richard Strauss, *Don Juan*.

Each page of these, and intervening, timings contains between 35 and 40 comparable works, not all necessarily so vibrant in design, but none that could be attempted with anything but a technically very capable group of players. This area of the repertoire will always include the most difficult pieces, and to look to it for reasons of avoiding the rigours of a symphony is very misguided (which leads to consideration of my first point).

In any longer work, however apparently dissimilar the movements may be, the playing *style* (the most difficult aspect of performance) will remain fundamentally the same. Thus, for example, three works, one by Beethoven, one by Dvořák and one by Sibelius, will each require a distinctive stylistic approach, and few aspects of any one will be applicable to either of the others. Beyond rehearsal of the notes, balance, ensemble and everything else to do with technical achievement, time will always be needed for the orchestra to assimilate and reproduce each fundamental style. This will probably take about the same amount of time for each, regardless of the relative length of the works involved.

These last few words are most important. The understanding and projection of any style is not dependent on the length of the work, only the difficulties inherent in the style itself. Thus the implications of the style will take approximately as long to be assimilated within a Beethoven overture as in a Beethoven symphony (we will not consider just *how* long this period can sometimes be). A programme consisting of a large number of works by contrasting composers takes much longer to rehearse and is much more demanding to play.

This application of similar styles may be taken one stage further. Given that there is no such thing as 'easy' repertoire (only that which may, at first sight, appear to be less complicated to put together), the technically advanced works which have come into the youth orchestra repertoire comparatively recently (such as Stravinsky *The Rite of Spring*, or Janáček *Sinfonietta*) will often be easier to accomplish in a programme where similar demands apply to other pieces as well. If aspects of technical continuity are carefully provided, what might seem an outrageously difficult programme will sometimes stand a greater chance of success than one which includes apparently less demanding pieces in widely differing styles.

The 'Second Viennese School'

Once the techniques of serialism are confronted, the orchestration becomes fragmented as far as each individual line is concerned, a situation that raises performance problems that are in some ways comparable to those already discussed with regard to composers of the twentieth-century French school. But there is an added complication, in that the relationship of notes is not apparent through tonal melodic or harmonic implication but only through the structural relationship of the scheme. To the orchestral performer, the relative importance of each note is not easily discernible, and balance must be achieved through less intuitive processes of musical understanding than would be the case elsewhere. This involves a great deal of time because it applies to every single bar of any particular work, and cannot be generally nurtured in the manner appropriate to any tonal style. Even beyond mastery of the formidable technical demands, these works depend on balance in order to transcend their purely structural functions and project a combined and sensible whole. It is this aspect of the discourse that makes them so difficult, and not the more basic craft of simply unravelling the apparent visual complications of the score.

The works of the three composers listed below are all exceptionally demanding and can only be contemplated by non-professional orchestras of very high standing. If one work is here implied to be slightly easier than any other it is only a matter of degree, and comparisons relate more to the few works themselves than to any music that has been considered previously.

Schoenberg: The early symphonic poem *Pelleas und Melisande* is a most beautiful work of the late Romantic period but sufficiently complex to need considerable time in preparation. It can be played by the advanced student orchestra but requires great attention to detail if it is not to sound indulgent and over-scale. The orchestration is very large (quadruple woodwind, eight horns, five trombones) and the individual demands unsparing.

The *Variations for Orchestra* are cast in the composer's typically structured serial technique, and are very demanding in all aspects of performance, not least the smooth interweaving of some individually difficult rhythms. The scoring includes a part for mandoline. Similar challenges occur within the earlier *Five Orchestral Pieces, op. 16*, although the instrumental lines are somewhat longer and provide a more logical individual musical responsibility.

The *Piano Concerto* and the *Violin Concerto* are no less difficult but this genre becomes a little more accessible through the presence and the influence of the solo instrument.

In a style quite distinct from Schoenberg's other works is his inventive orchestration of Brahms *Piano Quintet in G minor op. 25* and the transcription of Handel *Concerto Grosso op. 6 no. 7* as the *Concerto for String Quartet and Orchestra*, of which the former is within the capabilities of the good youth orchestra. (The concerto is rather more difficult and requires a professional solo string quartet.)

Berg: The *Three Orchestral Pieces op. 6* are very difficult. In addition to the demands previously discussed, the instrumental writing displays even less deference to the possible limitations of human agility. It is a great work, although only to be recommended to the most experienced and advanced non-professional orchestras, and then only if there is considerable time for preparation.

The wonderful *Violin Concerto* is more approachable, although still very demanding, and is an essential work for any orchestra whose technique is reaching a high level of refinement.

Webern: The terse and concise style of this most self-critical of composers is unique, and very perplexing to an orchestra rehearsing any of the works. The brevity to some extent obscures appraisal of the longer line, and the consequent compression induces a verticality of production which is hard to overcome. Nonetheless, the *Six Orchestral Pieces, op. 6*, are within range of the good student orchestra both in the original large orchestration or the 1928 reduced version, and remain important repertoire.

The *Five Pieces op. 10, Symphony op. 21* and *Variations op. 30*, are all for small orchestra with various configurations of mostly single wind and brass, although none of them, interestingly enough, involve bassoons.

The *Passacaglia op. 1* is in the more post-Romantic style of early Schoenberg and, while still extremely demanding, is more easily projected by the student orchestra both stylistically and because it is the longest continuous movement among any of the composer's works (*c.* 10 minutes).

Avant-Garde Performance

It now becomes less pertinent to group compositional/performing styles in terms of specific structure or personalities. Musical composition for the orchestra since the 1950s has covered a wide range of designs, among which has been the work of creative artists who have used innovative compositional and instrumental techniques.

As elsewhere, the compositional techniques only become of direct concern where some adjustment of orchestral technique is necessary to comply with the demands. Thus the total serialism in the works of Stockhausen, Boulez, Berio and others may in performing terms be considered to have been covered in discussion of the works of Schoenberg and related composers, for they involve only an extension of the same performing techniques.

One minor but very important consequence, however, is the frequent reconstitution of the orchestra, not so much in terms of numerical reduction or instrumental variation but in respect of a more exact division and specification of the body of strings. The string size of the symphony orchestra had always accepted numerical diversity, and any specification of minimum strength had been more to achieve necessary balance and sound than to dictate exact numbers. Thus the 16.16.12.10.8. of Richard Strauss *Ein Heldenleben* for example, does not preclude performance by 20.18.14.12.10. In fact, as a guide to balance, it virtually insists upon it in non-professional circumstances. This is by no means always the case with the apparently similar demands made by more recent composers. In a number of the works of Boulez and Stockhausen the specified size of each section of strings, frequently quite large, can neither be exceeded nor depleted, because of the individual lines accorded them. This very precise division, pertaining to many contemporary works, focuses on an important concept in the use of the instrumentalists. No longer are they the means of producing an infinitely variable but singular timbre. They become part of a concordance of individually perceived voices.

Such use of orchestral strings is most noticeable in aleatory composition, where each instrumentalist is allowed responsibility for the permutations of composed fragments, and only the overall structure of the passage, section or work is determined. This style of composition, prevalent in the works of Penderecki, Lutosławski and others, presents the orchestra with a novel and unique responsibility which can be very difficult to achieve.

The natural tendency of the human mind is to arrange things into familiar patterns, automatically finding points of reference. Faced with a number of random notes of indeterminate duration, the musician will divine an obscure harmonic relationship from which a rhythmic pattern may be evolved. This, in itself, is not dangerous until such rhythms become pervasive, supplying a spurious harmonic and rhythmic stability that destroys the very principles of the technique. Many compositions will counter this by supplying each player with a slightly different order, pitch or number of notes or by implying different rhythmic relationships through visual spacing or sporadic use of standard symbols of duration. But however helpful the composer might be in this or any other respect, the responsibility, as in all forms of musical projection, must finally lie with the players.

It is of course possible to develop a fluency and ease in production of these 'permutive' techniques merely by familiarity with the repertoire, but such opportunity is unlikely to be available to the student orchestra, and some deliberate readjustment will be necessary. A number of basic guidelines, applicable to all instruments, can be suggested:

1 The technique is not to be confused with any kind of improvisation. It is solely the permutation of predetermined notes, patterns or dynamics, nothing else.

2 No attempt should be made to impose melodic, harmonic or rhythmic correlations, or any soloistic appraisal of 'musical' line or meaning, unless specifically requested.

3 It is important not to be influenced by sounds or rhythms apparent elsewhere in the orchestra. Concentration should focus solely on the fragment to be played, its possible variations and, above all, the dynamic level applicable to it.

4 Particularly in the early stages it will help if certain qualitative aspects, such as *vibrato* or tonal variation, are removed from the production.

Beyond these, it is essential to believe that such techniques work and are positive and effective methods of musical communication. An identical mental attitude must be applied to abnormal techniques of sound production, many of which have been dealt with in the relevant instrumental chapters. New and experimental demands are appearing all the time and, if they are to work at all, the performer must approach them with sensible commitment.

In certain areas of more recent repertoire, particularly the 'minimalist' style of composition, some difficulties may be experienced as a direct result of the notation in orchestral parts, long sections of repetition often being notated as one bar with 'Repeat x times' written over it. Provided that this is limited to three or four times it is possible (although always dangerous), but some parts will extend this to 12 or more. As can be imagined, this may cause considerable confusion which can only be safely overcome by the addition of obvious 'cues' (not always apparent in such music), or by very careful attention by the conductor.

It must be accepted, unfortunately, that a great deal of the music written between the 1940s and the late 1980s suffers from inadequate printing methods similar to those described in relation to the works of Charles Ives. A marked improvement has been noticeable in recent years and one can only hope that some of these later techniques of printing are applied retrospectively.

The Orchestral Catalogue

At some point in the programming for any orchestra, one of the many orchestral catalogues must be consulted in order to ascertain the necessary instrumentation, approximate length and available sources and editions. With minor variations, orchestration will be set out in a standard fashion which is worth repeating here. The sections will always be listed in the order in which they most frequently appear in the score – woodwind, brass, percussion, harp/keyboard/unrelated extras, and strings. The instruments within each section will be listed in similar fashion.

For the woodwind the order is flutes, oboes, clarinets, bassoons. These basic instruments of the section will never be named but designated only by the number of players required. Thus a section comprising two of each instrument will read 2 2 2 2. Should any one of these fundamental instruments be omitted from the scoring, '0' will be inserted at the relevant position – the woodwind section without clarinets will appear 2 2 0 2.

For the most frequently employed related instrument (piccolo, cor anglais, bass clarinet, contrabassoon), two systems exist. One will designate them only by an additional numeral, the other by name; but both will use the sign + to designate the extra *player* required. A section of two flutes and one piccolo, two oboes and one cor anglais, two clarinets and bass clarinet, two bassoons and contra could therefore read:

2+1 2+1 2+1 2+1 *or* 2+picc 2+ca 2+bcl 2+cbsn

The less frequently encountered relatives will *always* be named. Thus, if alto flute and E♭ clarinet were to be added to the above orchestration it would read:

2+1+alto 2+1 2+1+E♭ 2+1 *or* 2+picc+alto 2+ca 2+bcl+E♭ 2+cbsn

If any instrument appears as a doubling instrument (that is, not requiring a separate player but being performed by one of the players already present) it will be designated in the first system by a stroke and in the second by parentheses. Two flutes with one doubling piccolo will be shown as 2/1 or 2(picc), and similarly for the other instruments. Once again, the less frequent relations will always be named, two clarinets with one doubling E♭ being shown as 2/E♭ or 2(E♭).

These symbols will always be used in the same way: '+' for an additional player and '/' or '()' for doubling.

In cases of doubling *and* additional players, the doubling instrument will appear nearest to the player concerned. Thus, two clarinets with one doubling E♭ plus an additional bass clarinet = 2/E♭+1, or 2(E♭)+bcl. Two clarinets plus additional bass clarinet who also doubles E♭ = 2+1/E♭ or 2+bcl(E♭). The system applies even if it were to be the same instrument that was both doubled and added – two clarinets, one doubling bass clarinet plus an additional bass clarinet = 2/1+1, or 2(bcl)+bcl.

An identical format will apply to the brass, in the order of horns, trumpets, trombones and tuba(s). The standard section will therefore be 4 3 3 1. For this section, only cornets will be considered sufficiently related to trumpets to require designation by number alone in the first system, otherwise *all* additions will be named. Six horns and two Wagner tubas, four trumpets and two cornets and one D trumpet, three trombones and one alto trombone, one tuba and euphonium will appear as:

6+2wt 4+2+D 4 1+euph, *or* 6+2wt 4+2cnt+D alto+3 1+euph.

The alteration to trombone listing should be noted and this can apply to both systems. Under normal circumstances the three trombones will never be specifically designated even if they appear so in the score. Thus, one will never see a listing of alto + ten + bs, since this has long been the accepted section. Sometimes, when alto is added over and above the section of three it will be named, but more often only the overall number of trombone players required will appear. When alto trombone is named it is most usual for it to be placed before the section – alto + 3 – but it may also appear after, as in 3 + alto.

Timpani will be designated by 'T' when only one player is required (regardless of the number of drums) and prefixed by the number of players required in other cases. Similarly, percussion will be designated by number of players alone (*very* unreliable) – 2P or 5P for example – and very rarely will any hint of instrumentation be given. All additional unrelated instruments will be named (hp, pno, org, for example).

Strings will only rarely be listed by number, and then only when a specific requirement is essential or a section missing completely. The list will be in order from the highest instrument to the lowest – 1st violins, 2nd violins, violas, cellos, basses – and a space will be left (usually underlined) if any instrument is omitted. Ten 1sts, eight 2nds, NO violas, six cellos, two basses will be shown as str (10 8 _ 6 2).

A colon will be used to separate the sections. A 'normal' Romantic-size orchestra with triple woodwind of only immediately related instruments will therefore appear as:

2+1 2+1 2+1 2+1 : 4 3 3 1 : T 2P hp : str

or

2+picc 2+ca 2+bcl 2+cbsn : 4 3 3 1 : T 2P hp : str

The catalogue is extremely useful as a work of reference, but final decisions can only be made by reference to the score. While every possible care is taken in the compilation of such a register there is a limit both to what information can be drawn on and what can be imparted. It is not possible for the compilers to peruse every score and discover which instruments have been overlooked, which doubling is impractical or (as is most often the case) where the percussion personnel have been grossly underestimated.

Neither can they give any musical information relating to the demands on particular instruments or the amount of playing involved. For example, Dvořák *Symphony no. 7* includes two important bars for piccolo in the third movement, but the instrument is not listed in any score until the moment it appears and consequently is not included in any catalogue of instrumentation that I have ever seen. Similarly, Gershwin *Rhapsody in Blue* lists four horns, both on the title-page of the score and in many catalogues, but there are only three parts (although it is quite beneficial in many places in the work for 4th to double the 3rd part).

It is, however, with regard to the amount of playing – an important consideration for student orchestras – that instrumental listing alone can be most misleading. The famous case of the tuba in Dvořák *Symphony no. 9* hardly needs repeating – just eight bars divided between the two entries which frame the slow movement – but many other works prove to be similarly unrewarding for some instruments. Janáček *Sinfonietta* provides very little for either bassoon or 3rd and 4th horn.

This is also true of the small or unusual scoring of one or more movements that might exist within a work of otherwise large orchestration. The second movement of Berlioz *Symphonie Fantastique*, for example, uses only 2/1 1 2 0 : 4 0(+1) 0 0 : 2hp : str. It is so easy to start a rehearsal with this movement, or continue into it after completing the first, forgetting that a large number of the orchestra will not be required. For rehearsal purposes it is worth marking the instrumentation of each movement at the front of the score.

The provision of an extra specialist player for the doubling parts of the woodwind, especially cor anglais and contrabassoon, is a regular and often very essential occurrence. For example the cor anglais, bass clarinet and contrabassoon doubling in Bartók *Dance Suite* are all rather impractical to attempt in the time allowed. But once again, reference to the score is essential: the provision of a separate cor anglais player in Dvořák *Symphony no. 8*, for example, would give the player precisely one bar in the entire work.

All these aspects are important and must be checked and considered before any work gets to the stage of rehearsal. When programming for student orchestras the orchestral catalogue can be a dangerous tool. On the one hand there is the important information it can provide; on the other, the vital knowledge it cannot.

24 RELATED ASPECTS

There are many important aspects of orchestral technique which, while not directly bearing on the production of instrumental sound, nonetheless have great influence on the way in which an orchestra performs. This discussion must now focus on a number of closely related but peripheral issues without which all previous considerations and conclusions would be incomplete, and will include attention to some non-musical aspects of performance as well as the crystallization of some interpretative concepts. Primary among these is the process of relating the technical and supportive elements necessary to the orchestra's performance to the more aesthetic considerations of musical communication itself. For this, one must return to the source material and examine what it actually contains.

The Orchestral Score

In considering the structure and nature of student orchestras, their performing techniques and capabilities, and their strengths and weaknesses, a wide range of musical styles and their associated demands have been reviewed and various interpretative nuances unearthed. Just as aspects of individual instrumental technique have proved in need of adjustment when players are faced with the rigours of orchestral collaboration, so too have a number of interpretative decisions and attitudes. It is not possible to transfer musical ideals directly from one medium to another without some allowance for the genre, and it is not always possible to transfer interpretation from one orchestra to another without similar adjustment.

The orchestral score, in common with any notated music, contains as much information as possible about the nature, substance, style and processes of the work it represents. It provides both the overall picture and the means by which to approach the detail, to extract and magnify facets of its construction and demands. Even beyond the musical boundaries, it provides a text from which conclusions may be drawn and meanings realigned by analysis and dismembering.

In itself it is lifeless and static. The moment it is given any sort of life, the moment it transcends the barrier from notional to realized sound, its demeanour alters and it becomes subject to the forces of movement and reaction. The vagaries of the printed page are many but none so difficult for the composer to judge or contend with as this transition to life, particularly with regard to marks of phrasing and dynamic.

AN UNDERSTANDING OF DYNAMICS

Dynamic variation as a means of expression, either as gradations of volume or clear distinction between contrasting levels, is totally natural to the performance of music. Even as late as the middle and end of the Classical era, actual markings of dynamic were relatively sparse, and the responsibility for inflection and contour was very largely left to the discretion and musicianship of the performer. Since that time the inclusion of dynamic interpretation has become more and more conspicuous, until it is now almost a compositional art in itself.

The proliferation of markings to be found in orchestral music since the turn of the twentieth century should not be taken as a gradual negation of the performers' individual interpretative responsibility but rather as a graphic illustration of the relationship and interdependence required of increasingly numerous and more complicated lines. In orchestral terms, dynamic markings have at least as great a relevance to the individual players' judgement of the isolated line as they do to the overall scheme. Thus there can be little doubt that composers such as Mahler, Elgar and Richard Strauss were as concerned with the players' understanding of the individual line as with the conductor's appraisal of the more general musical concept.

It can be argued that this approach is the only reason for the score to show variations in the dynamic marking of different instruments within the same phrase, for they relate only to the natural production qualities of each instrument as a means of maintaining balance. There is no *fundamental* reason why the conductor should need greater illustration of an aspect of interpretation that forms the very basis of the art. But given the added complications of ensemble and the wider field of colour, there *is* reason for each player to have a visual reinforcement of the relationship of his or her own involvement, and therefore a need for the conductor to be aware of what each player has in front of them.

It is interesting that the composers whose works are first to show advanced use of this technique (the three listed above and, to only a slightly lesser extent, Wagner) possessed unparalleled knowledge of instrumental technique and knew and understood the orchestra as a performing unit. All had worked with orchestras of varying standards on music other than their own, and

Mahler was a well-known conductor in his own right. But all must have faced at first hand the problems of balance and ensemble arising from orchestral scores of minimal marking, and all were certainly aware of the inherent difference in interpretation that the same request would elicit from different instrumentalists.

The influence of this knowledge on the marking within their own scores, both in terms of dynamic and instruction, is hard to doubt. *Ex. 24. 1* is an early instance from Wagner overture to *Die Meistersinger von Nürnberg*, where four instruments combine with the same theme.

The two bassoons are marked only with dynamic, 2nd horn has *immer sehr markiert* (always very clearly marked), tuba has *sehr gebunden* (very *legato*) and cellos the contrasting *nicht gebunden aber sehr gehalten* (not slurred but very sustained). Each instruction is entirely relevant to the qualities of the instrument, and the result is an identical realization of the phrase (were cellos to be slurred they also would need no instruction, as is the case for bassoons). Many similar markings exist in the works of other composers, a number of which have have been mentioned in the course of discussion.

The relevance of such marking, particularly with regard to the multiple markings of the later twentieth-century composers, must be understood if the interpreter is not to be weighed down by the apparent detail of the information and lost in its minutiae. The players are given the information in their parts and the score reproduces this; the interpreter will determine the *degree* to which it is applied.

This, in itself, is quite straightforward but there is another side to the coin, and one that seems to cause much more difficulty. Once a composer is committed to such detailed marking, inevitable as it may be, it becomes increasingly difficult to withdraw from it, because the *absence* of a marking then acquires significance in itself. It is common therefore to find a range of dynamic nuances carefully marked in the score, many (if not most) of which are inherent within the phrase, and one has to decide whether the markings are there for additional emphasis, or because a more dangerous inference might have been drawn from their omission. The only satisfactory approach to this sort of dilemma is to consider such markings from these two opposing directions. Often, the true dynamic inference can only be drawn if the marking is removed and the passage considered without it. The process involved is complicated, although not as time-consuming as one might think. The passage must be considered in terms of its particular orchestration, harmonic implication, melodic line and every other facet of direct influence, after which an attempt should be made to re-mark it in a way that could be largely guaranteed to obtain the musical result. This process involves giving as much

(score in C)

EX. 24. 1

attention to avoiding the wrong implication as to providing the correct one. Many times this exercise will result in identical marking to the original, but sometimes discrepancies will appear and the reasoning behind the original might well become evident.

This process will also highlight the parallel use of graphic or verbal indication to prevent misinterpretation of a phrase, hinted at above. It may seem a very subtle differentiation, but it is nonetheless important. Such 'negative' indications occur in works of much earlier style than those immediately under discussion. The *non troppo* addition to a general indication of tempo, or specific demands such as *senza rallentando* or *senza crescendo* all originate from reasons of prevention. (Both the last mentioned are dangerous orchestrally, the positive element of the instruction tending to register more strongly than the negative.) It is therefore only rarely that any mark or indication can be taken at face value, without some thought as to what caused it and what its most potent implications may be in relation to the particular phrase or fragment.

It is common to find a greater distribution of dynamic marking coupled with a greater *range*. A famous example of this tendency occurs in Tchaikovsky *Symphony no. 6*, where the dynamic range is taken from *ffff* to *ppppp*. In practical terms this cannot be judged to imply louder or softer production than the maximum markings to be found in many other works, but it does give the composer control over a greater gradation of dynamic, emphasizing the fact that dynamic marks are relative rather than definitive. Dynamic limitations are as much applicable to the orchestra as to any individual instrument, and there should be no attempt to force or minimize the sound beyond musical limits. For softer sounds, the level will always depend on the orchestration, for it is possible to project an almost inaudible sound from strings but not always from other instruments. But the opposite end of the dynamic spectrum must be approached with great care, as there very quickly comes a point for all instruments where the sound 'breaks' and loses all capacity for projection or combination (and a considerable amount of actual dynamic level as well).

One marking which is impossible to specify accurately within the confines of an individual part and can only be apparent from the full score is the relative association of *crescendo*. As a conductor one is often asked whether a *crescendo* exists at a particular point, or what dynamic it attains, but I have yet to hear any player question to whom the *crescendo* belongs, which voice is leading it and how much support or restraint should be apparent in the associated line.

In situations where there is a melodic line and accompaniment such a relationship can be obvious, but often it is not so, and the leading voice may be unclear or ambivalent from within the orchestra. It is fundamental to the understanding of all 'extraneous' marking that such musical relationships are addressed.

In all the scenarios described above, the collaboration of certain instrumental timbres or the sound of specific players or sections will have their role, and the score thus becomes something akin to a highly detailed map. Everything that relates to size, position, relationship and scale is defined but the final, and very vital, influences of sunlight and season are not. This ever-changing visualization is the province of interpretation and something that applies in all forms of music.

The Conductor

Little further need be said with regard to this, unquestionably the most influential section of the symphony orchestra. It is, as has always been obvious, the one position from which the success or failure of the orchestra's performance may be determined, and it is also the most commonly misunderstood.

The prevalent public misconceptions are not within the scope of this book to disperse. It is to be hoped that a number of the more dangerous generalizations might already have been assaulted, but one particularly persistent argument might benefit from brief discussion.

It is often remarked that 'the orchestra without conductor can produce music; the conductor without orchestra cannot'. Although apparently obvious, this statement contains a deeper significance. A good orchestra can feasibly perform without a conductor and even disguise mistakes. It can also ignore a poor technique and take from it only the relevant musicianship.

Two powerful lessons (which have indeed provided the basis for this entire discussion) can be learnt from this. Firstly, that only a *good* orchestra can transcend direction; and secondly, the implicit fact that conducting can be the one area of music-making where a lack of even the most basic technical prowess may not deter success.

The second point has been proved many times (although not as often as some might have us believe), but it is only in direct relation to the first point that it can be 'achieved'. No youth or student orchestra, of whatever standard, can actually override the direction in the way that a professional orchestra can, and sometimes has to. It is vital that this is understood.

It is not possible to undertake a discussion of conducting technique or even attitude beyond that which has already been included, but the physical technique should be as multi-faceted as those demanded of instrumentalists. A large number of disciplines must be practised and mastered, such as complete isolation of the two hands, very slow movement and ultra-smooth movement. But one thing is absolutely certain, no orchestra should, and a student orchestra can't, be waved at!

Only two very dangerous and easily overlooked areas allied to conducting technique will be mentioned, both with regard to *fermati*. The sustained chord or unison so often found at the end of a work or movement will usually have been organized to some degree in regard its length, and the strings will have decided whether to use one bow or two. In the case of just one bow (usually sufficient and certainly most powerful), the duration of the pause is obviously limited and cannot be exceeded, and the conductor must be aware of both the speed of movement and the consequent moment of cessation. Watching the Leader's bow is the only way to be sure of success.

All other *fermati* involve careful control of the arm at the point of arrival. Most 'accidents' arise when the conductor informs the orchestra that there will (or will not) be a following up-beat and then finds that the arm has arrived in the wrong place to comply. If the bar following the pause starts on the first beat and there is to be no up-beat then the hand *must* stop at the top of its movement. If there *is* to be one, then it is no less important for it to rest at the bottom of the movement. Ensuing entries on any beat of the bar follow this general rule: the required movement *after* the pause will always determine the hand's position. It is purely this accidental wrong positioning, arising from insufficient thought and practice, that can make such moments dangerous.

Beyond all such technical considerations, the conductor must have the ability to find and control the pervading movement (discussed elsewhere, but directly in Chapter 21) and know what the orchestra is actually doing at any given moment and what influence can or cannot be impressed on it. Finally, he or she must be able to communicate sound to the orchestra, evoke the quality of performance from them, and actually *make* things happen. Without these abilities, all the painstaking processes of rehearsal are wasted.

MARKING THE ORCHESTRAL SCORE

The preparation of a clearly marked score relevant to the conductor's particular interpretation is essential, but it often proves extremely difficult for the inexperienced conductor to accomplish. The process is by its nature very personal and will be geared to each individual's interpretation of the work.

Thus one can only provide guidelines to some of the more useful markings and some of the pitfalls that need to be avoided if possible.

Initially it must be remembered that all the necessary information is already there, and that additional marking will be inserted only to highlight or clarify particular aspects. With regard to the sudden appearance of 'short score', where many printings omit the instruments not playing and vary the accepted layout as a result, some form of instrumental marking is useful. A form of personal notation that is consistent and instantly recognizable should be decided on. Whether it is verbal, symbolic or a mixture of the two, it must be concise. Instrument names should be abbreviated and totally unambiguous (trmp. and trmb. for trumpet and trombone is dangerous). Such markings should always be against or on the relevant line as matter of course, and *never* in the top or bottom margins of the score – the eye must be concerned with the *whole* page and not what amounts to a separate 'cue sheet'.

Every inserted mark detracts to some extent from what is already there and will always remain the most prominent feature of the page, and for this reason alone some suggestions may be put forward (or, perhaps, long-suffering pleas made):

Do not mark in coloured pencil, especially any form of colour-coding, whether directly related to instruments, sections or anything else.

Do not mark anything through a line of music in a way that obliterates notes, dynamics or any other markings that originated from the composer.

Do not mark predetermined rehearsal suggestions (out of tune, use *vibrato*, for example); they are, as should be obvious, of no use whatsoever.

Other than these, mark only what is necessary to interpretation and helpful towards its realization. Intricate analysis is best undertaken elsewhere, written on a separate sheet of paper, to be kept with the score if desired, but there is rarely sufficient room to write this into the score except in its most abbreviated form. Notes pertaining to suspected misprints, instrumental impossibilities or other ambiguities can be marked with an asterisk and noted in the upper or lower margins. Actual misprints should be corrected.

One final remark – do not be tempted to 'hear' misprints during rehearsal in order to impress the orchestra. Many that appear in scores are not replicated in the corresponding parts, and those that do have often been corrected. It is a very dangerous game.

PERFORMANCE BY MEMORY

It is with great reluctance that I approach this emotive subject. My feelings about it are very firm and personal, and I cannot be certain whether they can be traced to experiences as a player or a more recent perversity. Be that as it may, I shall endeavour to be as unbiased as possible.

There can be no doubt that many conductors feel less inhibited when performing without the distractions of the score before them, and this (where it is genuine) is very understandable. However, it must be pointed out that it is a dangerous practice with the non-professional orchestra. While things are going smoothly it is perfectly acceptable; when things go wrong and players need to know the *next* entry (not the one that has just been missed), things get a little more difficult. Something rather more than 'how the piece goes' needs to be apparent under these circumstances. It also, to my mind, alters the balance of conductor and orchestra from an audience point of view, the wide open space placing the conductor in a position of virtuosic prominence unrelated to the basic commission.

If the conductor prefers not to use the score out of a desire for improved communication and enhanced freedom, there is still no reason why the desk and score should not remain. We have all conducted performances where the score has never been turned from page 1 throughout, and it can even remain shut if so preferred. This is *not* inhibiting to gesture – it might as well be said that the front desk of strings get in the way! But the presence of the desk and score does emphasize a feeling of unity between conductor and players, in relation to both the rigours of performance and the responsibility taken towards them.

Programming

As mentioned in Chapter 23, attitudes towards concert programming will always remain very personal, and nothing that has been, or will be, remarked should alter this.

The 'three-piece programme' of overture, concerto, symphony (or comparable works) has much to recommend it. It is possible to rehearse it within most reasonable schedules; it tends to avoid the dangers of detracting from works because of their immediate relationship to those that precede or follow; it provides a natural flow of content; and it usually avoids appalling miscalculations of length.

Against these may be set its relative inflexibility, its stylistic limitations and its general tendency to involve only permutations of a small number of frequently performed works. Nonetheless, its strength of communication is proven and it does form a firm basis on which variations might be envisaged.

Concerts including four pieces can work equally well, especially if, again, one of them is a concerto. But if such a piece is not included, then at least two of the works will need to be major orchestral pieces of 20 minutes or more, which can cause problems with rehearsal time and limit the choice of possible works (*see* Chapter 23). Five works present considerable problems and anything more begins seriously to affect the 'flow' of the programme, unless a number of the works are obviously connected – as in a 'Viennese' concert, for example.

It is not necessary always to begin with an overture, nor to end with a symphony. A concert may commence or end with a work of any type or length, provided that the rest of the programme is carefully arranged. The only criterion is that each work is in its best and most effective position in relation to the others. Only the placing of a concerto should be considered immovable and this (out of deference to the soloist) should come immediately before the interval or, in very rare cases, at the end of the concert. Except where two concerti are performed (where they will usually be placed either side of the interval), no work should be performed between a concerto or solo item and a break in the programme. Due prominence cannot otherwise be given to the soloist.

If a concerto is to be the last work in the programme it will most often take the entire second half of the concert and must therefore be a major work of great stature and considerable length. Very few concerti are suitable for this position, and, of those that are, most are for piano (for example, Brahms *Concerto no. 2*, Beethoven *Concerto no. 5*, Busoni *Concerto* and Rachmaninov *Concerto no. 3*). Elsewhere, only the violin concerti of Beethoven, Brahms and Elgar, and the cello concerto of Dvořák, can really fulfil all the requirements of this position.

As far as specific works are concerned, the opportunity must be taken to perform new and less familiar pieces. The student orchestra has the advantage of playing to 'captive' audiences more frequently than might be the case elsewhere, and the chance to provide a wider range of music should be seized. These days, for commercial reasons, few professional orchestras can really exploit the advantages of this type of mixed programme, and it thus becomes something of a responsibility that the youth orchestra should do so. However, as discussed in Chapter 23, the relationship of the stylistic demands of the programme must be carefully considered.

The Printed Programme

The standard of the printed programme will always reflect the expectations of the promoting body. While few non-professional orchestras will nowadays present only a badly designed piece of folded paper, many have not progressed a great deal further.

No audience is so loyal or so starved of music that they can be counted on to attend concerts given by orchestras who appear to care nothing for their own standards or for the needs of those who listen. The programme must reflect the orchestra's concern that the audience is provided for. This does not have to involve a glossy brochure, or pages of photographs and advertisements, but it must contain some useful and interesting information relevant to the orchestra and the music.

Programme notes should be concise, well written and designed towards enhancing enjoyment of the works. Constructional elements can be included, if relevant, but more general information about both composer and work will be of greatest interest. Works may also be considered in relationship to others presented in the concert (an aid to unity and progression so often overlooked) rather than in isolation.

The listing of the orchestra personnel will *always* be included, although it might vary in design. Personally I feel that, if the individuality of each position is to be understood and relished in an appropriate way, some specific placing should be apparent, and mere alphabetical order is unworthy. This is often a most noticeable omission where violins are concerned. A desire to avoid the use of '2nd violins' may often result in their being listed as one section, a practice that does little to promote the understanding of the equality or the specialization involved in these sections, and it would be better to use the headings 'Violins' followed by 'Section 1' and 'Section 2'.

Presentation

An orchestra's presentation in public performance is a very important factor that affects both their playing and the appreciation and acceptance of the audience. Pleasant as it would be to assume that the concert-going public will judge the standard of playing above everything else, this is simply not the case, and even if it were, certain courtesies remain obligatory. First impressions count, and continuing impressions even more.

It is important that the orchestra should make some contact with the audience and that acknowledgement of applause should take on a more personal acceptance than is sometimes apparent. If, each time the orchestra stand, those players not actually facing the audience turn towards them, and even allow themselves to smile, a greater degree of association is immediately consolidated.

Nothing need be said here specifically about entrances and exits, but it must be remembered that the orchestra is 'public' from the moment the first player walks on stage. Someone outside the orchestra must take charge of this vital aspect of performance for the sake of the orchestra's playing standards, its continued goodwill and self-respect. Players with instruments that are not easily portable but still require attention with regard to tuning, such as timpani and harp, will need to go on to the platform considerably before the rest of the orchestra.

As far as back-stage, pre-concert warming up is concerned, it should literally be that: the warming of the instruments and the technique alone, and not an informal concert of excerpts from the concerto repertoire and extemporized jazz groups. Horns and brass need only to play long, controlled notes, warming the instrument and the embouchure; woodwind, much the same with some specific attention to related intonation and a final check of the instruments themselves; strings, slow and careful scales with some small exercises for the left hand. Beyond these, little else is required.

Audition Techniques

Any form of audition, however informal, is the most nerve-wracking ordeal for any musician. It is no overstatement to say that they will all play at their worst. They will all be feeling more self-conscious than in any public performance and all will give the most wooden and stereotyped impression of their individual personality, irrespective of standard, experience or ability.

The procedures for auditions will vary from one orchestra to another, but the widespread professional system of keeping the auditioning player hidden from the panel is of no use to the youth and student orchestral. Very different criteria apply and personal contact is not only necessary for the panel but very important from the player's point of view.

Sight-reading may either be unprepared or sent out *shortly* in advance, but it should always be kept to a passage where the player is likely to have some aural conception of the whole, and all that needs to be determined is the player's flexibility and understanding, not his or her instrumental agility. The purpose of sight-reading tests is to discover natural musicianship and sensitivity, as apart from what might have been taught or carefully pre-rehearsed. Technical limitations or agility should have been unearthed in the player's performance of their chosen work.

For determining the Principal positions for the strings, the Leader in particular, a few minutes' playing with other people will show capabilities in this direction more quickly and genuinely than anything else. A few bars of a string quartet performed with three other experienced musicians is worth an hour's solo playing.

The Chamber Orchestra

The re-emergence of the chamber orchestra in the twentieth century was largely occasioned by the search for new sounds and methods of communication by composers wishing to relinquish the styles of the Romantic era. It is neither possible nor pertinent to undertake a detailed appraisal of the repertoire that might prove either useful or dangerous to less experienced ensembles because the specific techniques pertaining to it, although strongly related to those of the symphony orchestra, are beyond the scope of this discussion. However, there are times when student orchestras find it necessary to approach this repertoire, and so some brief and general consideration is desirable.

The small size of the chamber orchestra string sections and the limited number of woodwind and brass curtail the available colours of orchestration (the very reason that many twentieth-century composers embrace it), and place techniques of articulation and dynamic variation in a position of high priority. This change of emphasis is much the same as that required by the symphony orchestra between the Classical and Romantic repertoire (*see* Chapter 23), and similar inherent dangers apply for the student chamber orchestra.

However, two very important aspects slightly alter the perspective. Firstly, there is a psychological change in approach occasioned by regular playing within a small ensemble; and secondly, the nature of many of the works themselves allows Classical performance techniques to be employed without the additional constraints of providing the more powerful symphonic sound. These considerations by no means guarantee successful performance, but taken together they tend to allow the inexperienced chamber orchestra to approach successfully a greater number of works of Classical style than might be the case for the larger ensemble.

Nonetheless, the same *basic* criteria that have been discussed in reference to the symphony orchestra apply. The style of all works for chamber orchestra necessarily incorporates very exposed lines as well as advanced techniques of production, and there is often little to deflect in the slightest degree from the demanding standards of playing required. Performance can only be contemplated with a group of excellent players and, indeed, it will only be of benefit to students of such a standard. The players' technique has to be sufficiently advanced for them to reap their rewards from simply playing, rather than from the enhanced warmth of emotional experience so often provided from within the symphony orchestra.

This is where a great dilemma presents itself for the school orchestra, where (very often) the unavailability of instruments and large numbers of strings makes the chamber orchestra repertoire very seductive. But many of the works are out of their range, and many of those that are playable prove to be unrewarding for the individual instrumentalist struggling with the notes and surrounded by equally unsuccessful supporting sound. Repertoire for the 'enforced' chamber orchestra needs to be very carefully chosen, and arrangements of pieces originally written for a larger or altogether different ensemble will often prove preferable to eminent examples, however short, of the true chamber orchestra repertoire. Music is a language, and those playing it *must* be able to communicate something of their own understanding and experience. If this is confined to the production of sounds which cannot be attained then the orchestra will benefit as little as the audience.

Something of an old trap exists here. It is very easy to think that because people are not yet capable of achieving an ideal, they cannot comprehend what is wrong. This is just as untrue in terms of an ensemble as it is for an individual. It might not be translated in exact terms, particularly by an elementary orchestra (bad intonation might only be perceived as a rather nasty sound) but the fact that it is incorrect *will* have registered, as will the consequent inability to draw from the piece the rewards they desire. It is probably this aspect more than any other that makes the wrong choice of repertoire for any orchestra dangerous rather than just unfortunate.

Orchestral Responsibility

Much has been said about instrumental responsibility: of balance, ensemble and communication; of one section to another; and of the conductor towards the orchestra. But little has been mentioned about the individual player's responsibility towards the orchestra as a whole, and nothing is more important. In terms of rehearsal, performances commitment and ideals, the individual's responsibility towards every other member of the orchestra is total. There is no room for attitudes of superiority, conceit or jealousy, only those of unified determination and hard work.

In rehearsal, every player with notes to play must always be present. Orchestral rehearsal is rarely for the sake of any individual or section – it is for the sake of their influence on other sounds, the demands of balance and ensemble. However small or apparently significant the part, however adept the player, they *must* be present at every rehearsal which covers their contribution to the work, for the sake of other players' involvement. The whole *raison d'être* of combined rehearsal is the blending and adjustment of every musical influence on all instrumentalists; otherwise the piece could be practised in isolation and put together at the concert.

The orchestra is composed of individual players, unified and integrated in a way almost unknown in any other human activity. The commitment and response of those involved must be equal to the task.

25 A CONSIDERATION OF PERSPECTIVE

The previous chapters have attempted to promote an understanding of the orchestra as an entity, the forces that influence its performing technique at any given time, and the way that it is aurally perceived by the listener. These subjects are limitless and ever-changing and far beyond the scope of a single book but certain basic concepts, and a number of questions arising from them, have been addressed. However, it remains impossible to tamper with orchestral sound until a true understanding of its possibilities and restrictions in live performance has been achieved, and all other preconceptions and misunderstandings have been stripped away. The one remaining aspect to discuss, therefore, is our own ability to perceive the natural results of instrumental collaboration and the place of live musical communication in an age of 'sound saturation'.

In all probability there has never been a time where the influences on our acceptance of sound have been so potent. Recorded sound has changed our perspective and performing priorities to a very large extent, and the recording industry (by accident or design) exerts a strong influence not only on what people want to hear, but also on their judgement of what constitutes an acceptable final result. In order to present recorded music to the public at large for purposes of repeated reproduction, noticeable errors in the original performance are eradicated. Gradually this censorship has extended from notes, to ensemble, to balance and to sound. Alongside has come the opportunity of *direct* comparison, something unknown in music previously, based as it was on memory and impression and thus similar ideals have extended to interpretation and the fundamentals of communication.

The benefits of recordings are unquestionable (if somewhat more limited than is often appreciated), especially to the musician. There are few performers who have not at some time heard recorded reproduction of their own sound and adjusted aspects of it in consequence, or listened to other artists for reasons of historic and/or interpretative interest. But in all instances some factors are missing, the most powerful of which is the ambience of the audience with whom the performer should be communicating, and its direct effect on the music.

For a considerable period of musical history it was *impossible* to communicate without both performer and audience being present, and even the visual aspect must have played a not insignificant part. Furthermore, music could not be envisaged in any other way, by the composer, performer or anyone else. The concept of 'disembodied music' was totally unimaginable. Present-day familiarity with sound in isolation has led to an alteration in both the attitude and requirements of the listener, providing false expectations of concert performance.

The most dangerous aspect of this is without doubt that of the acceptance of certain sounds and combinations of sounds as being instantly achievable. The unquestioning trust in (and acceptance of) the recorded product as being a complete and realistic representation of the original is an easily formed misconception which has been affirmed and even promoted by many who should know better.

It is almost pointless to ask how many people recognize when the sound of a recording has been enhanced or 'separated', or how many can perceive the balance that is impossible to achieve without rearrangement, multiple microphones, sound screens and other technicalities of the recording studio, or how many can distinguish between performed sound and synthesized. It is not of real consequence until such manipulations are transferred to the expectations of both audience and interpreters in live performance. It is not possible to work with or listen to any orchestra with any such false impressions of sound still in place. Balance, ensemble and other technical aspects of performance all relate to communication, and the specialized techniques of recording and their effects must be recognized so that the unique qualities of live performance are appreciated. These qualities are completely at odds with the techniques necessary for the production of sounds designed for repeated listening, which are often influenced by commercial considerations. Recognition of this distinction is far more difficult than it might appear because of the amount of synthetic duplication of sound available by choice, accident and intrusion.

While the proliferation of recorded sound can no longer be contained, it has to be possible to overcome the resultant repression of direct musical communication. The disease is basically one of saturation producing credibility, and it is a perilous path that we are treading, not only in terms of interpretation but also because our ability to assess and understand the human capabilities of performed sound is being slowly eroded. If this is to be the nature of music, then there will be no place for the student orchestra except as an instrument of education for its members, for it can neither compete with nor reflect such surgical concepts of technical performance.

If, however, music is to continue to be the international language of the deeper emotional and philosophical experiences of humanity, then it is possible that the freshness and optimism of the student orchestra could provide a shining beacon for the future.

APPENDIX

Analysis of the Timpani Writing in the First Movement of Schubert *Symphony no. 8 in B minor*

The general use of pedal-operated 'chromatic' timpani has made possible the readjustment of all timpani parts written for their more limited forebears. However, the process is by no means as straightforward as one might suppose, and is often fraught with complex related considerations of balance, orchestration, harmonic implication and musical expression.

To illustrate some of the problems that must be addressed, there follows a brief analysis and discussion of the timpani writing to be found in the first movement of a work chosen both because it is familiar and because it is constructed within a broadly Classical scheme. If, for whatever reason, any change in the timpani part is to be considered in a work, regardless of style or period, a similar exercise will prove useful.

It is necessary initially to examine every timpani entry in turn – along with some glaring omissions – and then consider certain examples with specific reference to any change in the part that might be contemplated. Reference is made to bar numbers as they appear in the 1967 revision of the Eulenberg miniature score – that which most faithfully follows the original autograph.

Fundamentally the instruments are used solely to reinforce harmonic climax, with one major exception which will be referred to in due course. The player requires two instruments which are, in accordance with Classical tradition, confined to the tonic and dominant notes of the prevailing key (B and F♯), and appear only once entirely without trumpets.

(1) Bars 28–9

The first entry, coinciding with the first use of full orchestra, reinforces a powerful imperfect cadence on to the dominant minor ninth. As would be expected this early in a work, the timpani notes are those of the fundamentals of the chords.

The absence of *sforzando* marking is noticeable, and this could have been intentional, given the instrument and its natural method of production. Such a reading is, however, very unlikely, especially in scores of this period where markings of accent or dynamic were most regularly intended to be a general instruction. That the editors have chosen not to include it is likely to be an oversight, for there is no really good reason why it should be omitted from this one instrument alone and at least some guidance as to level is required in the performer's copy.

(2) Bars 35–8
The expected cadence to the tonic, turned aside in the previous example, appears with considerable force. Timpani are prominent in typical collaboration with trumpets, but pitched to underpin the bass of the chords.

(3) Bars 63–71
Here, there is a complete absence of both trumpets and timpani in a dramatic and powerful *tutti*, owing to the latter's inability to accompany a progression from C minor, through G minor and E♭ to a series of ascending seventh chords. The Classical linking of the two instruments is highlighted by this omission, trumpets being at least theoretically capable of participation throughout with repeated concert Gs. Their lone final note may be taken as a rare example of two trumpets taking over the timpani's role of harmonic emphasis in the enforced absence of their partner.

(4) Bars 85–93
This passage is interesting in where the timpani do *not* appear and the written note-lengths where they do. With only B and F♯ in his armoury, Schubert removes the timpani from the second bar of each sequence, not wishing to blur the movement of the orchestral bass line (trombone 3, bassoons 1 and 2, cellos and basses). For similar reasons the duration of each of the semiquaver entries (*not* unmeasured rolls or trills) had to be shortened in relation to the strings (see third paragraph of (6) below).

The timpani are also removed from the first cadence (bars 88–9), as are the trumpets on both occasions, but the second far more deliberate approach to G major includes the timpani, even though they are forced to finish on the third of the tonic chord.

(5) Bar 104
A single stroke, in direct collaboration with the string octaves that accent the appearance of a sustained B, most likely necessitated by the entry of trumpets and lower brass.

(6) Bars 110–11 (2nd-time bar)
A bar of semiquavers, once more allied to the entry of trumpets but here, for

the first time in the movement, also adding a quite independent colour of its own.

Even discounting the highly important considerations of scope, the arguments for retaining the exposition repeat in *every* symphony where it is demanded are furthered to a great extent by '2nd-time bars' as magical as these.

It is worth noting here the 'extra' timpani note (bar 111) which forms the end of the semiquaver 'roll' and first appeared in bar 85. This is general in all timpani writing until well into the twentieth century and always demands care in performance so that it does not sound either as the start of a new phrase or a distinct 'full stop'.

(7) Bars 142–4

Three *sforzando* first-beat entries point the octave rise in the string basses as the climax of a 12-bar F♯ pedal is approached. These bars are particularly interesting. Firstly, the timpani enter without trumpet support (the high F♯ was perfectly possible) and are withdrawn from the bar before the cadence is reached, since they cannot participate in the sudden turn to C♯ minor. Schubert therefore elects to take the height of the *crescendo* without timpani, so that their enforced removal at the climax is not so noticeable. Here again the trumpets take responsibility for the added weight that the timpani cannot supply, which explains their absence in the four previous bars.

(8) Bars 154–6

Essentially the same outburst as the final four bars of the previous passage, but this time a diminished seventh based on B allows the timpani to be used. The trumpets are retained in order to maintain the same unity between horns and trombones as before, and also to reinforce the potency of the diminished seventh, the same task that they fulfil in the following entry (bar 162), in which timpani can play no part.

(9) Bars 170–6

Timpani are demanded in this *fortissimo* statement of the first bars of the theme, even though they can supply only the fifth of the implied E minor. Again they resist supporting the bar before the first orchestral *sforzando* in order that the B should not become too dominant and, very important, retain the same note in the penultimate bar, both to avoid an obviously wrong perfect cadence (F♯-B) and equally to avoid movement of the thematic F♯ to anything other than E.

This is also the first time in the work where timpani support reiterates long notes of the trumpets with only a single stroke. The careful addition of rests in the part is a clue to the required substance of sound but it also reveals the obvious care apparent in all the writing – a fact which may be taken as confirmation (if any were needed) of the composer's intentional differentiation between semiquavers and 'rolls' where they occur.

(10) Bars 178–80
Simple cadential support. Once again, note the careful inclusion of rests.

(11) Bars [182]–93
Along with horns and trumpets the timpani are withdrawn from the approach to this, the second cadence, probably more because the other instruments were unable to provide C♯ than for their own necessary substitution of B (which on this occasion would sound a tone below string basses). The support of trumpets and horns in the two following rhythmic phrases is tailor-made, but a third appearance, at bars 192/3 (one of the most powerful moments in the work) has to be relinquished, neither B nor F♯ proving an acceptable substitute for the necessary E.

(12) Bars 242–3
The use of the timpani sound in the corresponding place in the exposition (bars 28/9) forbids their exclusion here, even though they must sound B against the fundamental C♯ as the cadence is once more turned aside. As was the case the first time, the dynamic markings are omitted for timpani although the editors have seen fit on this occasion to furnish the basic level. It is noticeable, too, that the overall marking differs from the exposition in that only the first beat of bar 243 has a *sforzando* – a much more logical and effective marking, although it is one that is rarely complied with.

The quite specific alterations in layout of the trumpet parts in these two instances highlight the care and consideration that had to be given to the orchestration as a whole when using instruments of limited range. This is perhaps the one place in the work where the timpani notes could be substituted (C♯ for the written B) without affecting the overall orchestration – the 1st of the two trumpets sounding the seventh here as they both do the first time.

(13) Bars 249–52
A clear example of how the dramatic intensity available from trumpets and timpani finally becomes the overriding factor in all Schubert's orchestration. In bar 250, when the trumpets have to withdraw from their reiteration of the string chords because they have to substitute for horns in the sustained chord,

removal of the timpani as well would obviously prove too much, and the composer uses his available resources even though it once more involves use of the seventh low in the chord.

(14) Bars 281–9
No longer unable to use the timpani, as was the case in the exposition appearance of this passage (see (3) above), Schubert allows the trumpets to add their weight as well. Although the addition of such powerful instruments makes the passage slightly more difficult to handle compared with the first time, the re-orchestration subtly underlines the feeling of climax and final resolution apparent in this portion of the movement.

(15) Bars 299–311
A direct comparison can be made with the similar passage as it appears in the exposition (bars 81–93). Not only is a dramatic increase in the use of the timpani evident in this second appearance, but also a totally different rhythmic involvement appears, in the approach to a key closely related to the home tonic. The crotchet-grouped semiquavers of the previous example have now been replaced by full minims, in direct collaboration with the overall orchestral movement and corresponding to the trumpets' availability to complete each progression. The timpani are only omitted for the accented appearance of the G♯7 chord since Schubert was unwilling, on this occasion, to double the seventh at the bass of the chord, as it would negate the use of the same note in the perfect cadence one bar later. But even here the F♯ appears at the beginning of the bar, to complete the instrument's cadential movement, and so that the necessary final note is applied to the semiquaver roll.

Also noticeable is the retention of B in the second inversion of the tonic chord (bar 303), where the basses of the orchestra have F♯, probably to maintain unity with the trumpets.

(16) Bar 322
A direct analogy with bar 104 [see (5)].

(17) Bars 340–8 and (18) Bars 356–60
Beyond their magical use at the approach to the development (exactly on the 2nd-time bar), there are two further examples of the timpani being used as a quite independent timbre in order to accentuate the darkness of the mood. These may be found in the first few bars of each of these final two entries, the first of which (17) begins unquestionably with measured semiquavers and then a roll at the fifth bar. This, the only timpani passage without trumpets, dem-

onstrates the instruments gaining the independence that was later to become their hallmark and being used solely as an agent of underlying disturbance and dramatic influence. Similarly the second entry (18), albeit in closer collaboration with the rest of the orchestra, accentuates the emotional power expressed by the rise and fall of this fragment of the main theme in a way that was to become second nature to the late Romantics.

In undertaking the above brief analysis we begin to perceive a skeletal outline of the close relationships between combining instruments and the effect that small details may have on other aspects of orchestration.

Now is the moment to examine certain sections of the work more closely, considering whether it might be possible to adjust some of the more blatant 'wrong' notes to be found in the timpani part, or even add the instruments in places where they were originally forced not to participate. For the purposes of this discussion just two of the most obvious examples will suffice:

(1) Bars 85–93 [(4) above]
Here we encounter the first clear problem with regard to the written notes of the timpani part. The final cadence, if nothing else, appears to be far from ideal. Merely to alter the notes of the cadence to correspond with those of the lower strings (D, D, G) is to make nonsense of the unsupported entry of the trumpets on an octave concert B. As these instruments have also progressed to attaining full chromatic range, should we now consider changing one or both of them also to G? Perhaps an immediate comparison with the cadence as it appears towards the end of the recapitulation (bars 310–11) is in order.

Conveniently ignoring the complete change in orchestration and involvement for these instruments that occurs throughout the preceding eleven bars, we now find the trumpets supporting the entire cadence (F♯, F♯ F♯/B). Transposed down a major third this would complement any alteration of the timpani notes in bars 92–3 very well. However, even cursory comparative examination of the two passages reveals a change in layout of the final chord in both wind and strings.

Immediately obvious is the removal of the widespread four- and three-note chords in the 1st and 2nd violins. This makes a far more noticeable difference to the comparative sound, approach and deliberation of the two cadences than even the addition or omission of timpani and trumpets. The chords could easily have been included at bar 311, 1st violins playing (from bottom to top) B-F♯-D♯-B and 2nds B-F♯-D♯. Why then are they missing? The only explanation is the necessary underpinning of the bass notes of the chord essential to the first appearance by virtue of trumpets and timpani being forced to sound the third.

It is likely, therefore, that had the composer the means at his disposal to use the dominant and tonic notes on both occasions, some adjustment would have been made to the scoring of this final chord in the violin parts at least. (The rearrangment of the woodwind scoring may well have remained, since it almost certainly has more to do with the rise in pitch of a major third than subtleties of support and integration.)

The situation now emerges where the simple alteration of three timpani notes has led to a reappraisal of string scoring which fundamentally affects the method of performance of these two cadences. The differences of approach and deliberation between arriving on a four-note chord and a straight octave are considerable, as Schubert well knew. Note carefully the three-note approach chord apparent in the first example!

With the timpani notes changed to match the lower strings these wide-spread chords now become either harmonically redundant the first time or musically essential the second, depending on the individual's point of view. All this without even considering changes that would be implied by the drastic orchestration differences of the previous bars.

(2) Bars 63–71 [(3) above]
An even more thorny problem follows. We are faced with the very awkward decision of whether to add timpani to a passage in order to comply with the orchestration as it appears in the recapitulation. This is one of those treasured moments when you find someone prepared to embrace every concept of reincarnation by glibly announcing: 'Obviously, Schubert would have used the timpani here had the notes been available.' Obviously? Well, let us start by trying to reconstruct the passage.

Firstly, there is the 'simple' decision of which notes to use. In the recapitulation the timpani are confined to a B, doubling the trumpets and thereby providing the fifth of the first chord, the tonic of the second chord and the third of the following sevenths. It would therefore seem that G is the most appropriate, but it certainly cannot be considered without addition of trumpets as well, in which case the printed notes of bar 71 must also be changed.

Having arrived at some decision regarding the note itself, it remains to decide in which octave it should be played. The low B present in the timpani part of the recapitulation leads us to consider using the G a third below this, but the bass line is different on this first occasion, in that the very noticeable octave drop in the sixth bar is missing. (This has nothing to do with the accepted range of the string basses. At the very opening of the work Schubert takes them down to a C, adopting the somewhat unusual course of writing cello and bass on separate staves in order to make his intention doubly clear.)

Were we to use this low note, it would sound awkwardly dominant and unsupported, pitched a sixth lower than cellos, bassoons and 3rd trombone. Similarly, an octave higher would contradict the weight and power achieved by the low register of the entire orchestra in the first five bars. An octave rise at the second crotchet of the sixth bar, corresponding with the basses' octave drop the second time, is equally unsatisfactory. It tangibly alters the feel of the passage and the dramatic rise would make the note dangerously predominant.

An identical difficulty applies to the trumpets. Octaves based on the concert G below the stave are horribly low for 2nd and quite uncharacteristic in a work of this type. Octaves based on the G above place 1st far above the rest of the orchestra and would certainly need adjustment of the bass line the second time in order to maintain the weight of the climax. Horns also would need to be rearranged into octaves, as they are in the recapitulation, in order not to lose support of the centre. This is also true if both trumpets were to play the G in the middle of the stave, the most likely solution. However, even ignoring the still outstanding problem of timpani pitch, we have yet only reached the point where the orchestration of the recapitulation has been approximated, not restored.

We are now forced to examine the possibility of re-scoring both passages and having the timpani follow the bass line, or at least the line of the 3rd trombone, for the octave drop is not to be recommended. Aurally, such a solution is as patently appalling as it is musically indefensible. It is doubtful, even if the passage could have been written one hundred years later, whether any composer would even have considered it.

It becomes very clear from the above discussion that many associated aspects of orchestration, harmonic emphasis, and even musical structure may well need to be considered when contemplating even the smallest changes of notation.

In the case of timpani, even beyond the limitation of the instruments themselves, we must also question to some extent whether the refusal to alter the tuning within a movement was inherent in the Classical composers' approach to the instruments – that they were quite specifically connected to passages of harmonic approach firmly associated with the home key and that their absence from otherwise identical passages in widely alien keys was not only enforced but also preferable, the absence of the instruments serving to underline the transitory nature of the modulation.

Thus we might consider the absence of timpani and trumpets in this extraordinarily dramatic passage to be a matter of choice rather than necessity. Their appearance in the identical passage of the recapitulation (bars 281–9) helps, as has already been implied, to underline the fact that we are returning to, rather than departing from, the home key.

Another consideration that should not be ignored is that there can be little doubt that the instruments used in the eighteenth and nineteenth centuries produced a less clearly defined note than those in use today, especially in the lower part of the range, where dissonances might not have been so clearly audible. In those circumstances a 'wrong', or perhaps 'less desirable', note on the timpani was more likely to have been aurally affected by the prevailing harmony and somewhat less likely to have been heard as a distinct pitch. Against this, of course, must be considered the increased harmonic awareness of the listener. At the time the accustomed ear had never been exposed to sustained dissonance, let alone advanced chromaticism, atonality or note clusters.

Nonetheless, the practice of supporting orchestral climax with timpani often at odds with the correct bass note of the chord was common, and just how much it jangled the nerve-ends of the listener can only be guessed at. I suspect little, for I cannot accept that any composer would have consciously employed a device that might be guaranteed to detract from the listeners' understanding of and involvement in the work as a whole.

Finally, since decisions of adjustment or alteration can only be made by each individual interpreter, the above paragraphs are not designed to guide the process in any particular direction, but rather, to highlight the associated problems and demonstrate the pitfalls of allowing the casting vote to rest with an inexperienced performer, or to be based on casual whim.

INDEX

Figures in bold denote music samples.